RULING CLASS, REGIME,
AND REFORMATION
AT STRASBOURG
1520–1555

STUDIES
IN MEDIEVAL AND
REFORMATION THOUGHT

EDITED BY

HEIKO A. OBERMAN, Tübingen

IN COOPERATION WITH

E. JANE DEMPSEY DOUGLASS, Claremont, California
LEIF GRANE, Copenhagen
GUILLAUME H. M. POSTHUMUS MEYJES, Leiden
ANTON G. WEILER, Nijmegen

VOLUME XXII

THOMAS A. BRADY, Jr.

RULING CLASS, REGIME,
AND REFORMATION
AT STRASBOURG

LEIDEN
E. J. BRILL
1978

RULING CLASS, REGIME AND REFORMATION AT STRASBOURG

1520–1555

BY

THOMAS A. BRADY, Jr.

LEIDEN
E. J. BRILL
1978

ISBN 90 04 05285 2

Copyright 1978 by E. J. Brill, Leiden, The Netherlands

PRINTED IN ENGLAND

T. A. Brady, Jr., *Ruling Class, Regime and Reformation at Strasbourg, 1520-1555*
(1978)

ERRATA

Page	Read	Instead of
v, line 6	*parentium*	*peretium*
xi, line 3	51	50
23 note 69, line 1	František	Frantisek
26, line 3	orders	order
26, line 17	interpretations	interpretation
43 note 139, line 4	Steven	Stephen
51, Table 1	Other merchants 19 (18.1)	Other merchants 18 (17.1)
	Artisans 15 (14.3)	Artisans 14 (13.3)
	Unknown 5 (4.8)	Unknown 7 (6.7)
51, line 5 from bottom	36.2%	35.2%
51, line 4 from bottom	14.3%	13.3%
51, line 2 from bottom	79.1%	78.1%
53 note 2, lines 1-2	sub-title should read: „Zu den Forschungsergebnissen über das Patriziat besonders der süddeutschen Städte"	
54 note 7, line 5	*einer schwäbischen*	*eiber schwänischen*
70, lines 3-4	well-to-do	well-to do
70 note 66, line 2	*des celtes,*	*desceltes,*
73, Table 5, line 12	1550 29	1550 229
136 note 62, line 2	steblerpfrünen	steblerpfrunen
154, line 22	By 1526,	By 1526.
166, line 15	identical with,	identical, with
177 note 42, line 4 from bottom	gesagt	gasagt
177 note 42, line 2 from bottom	muss	mass
183, line 7	rentier	tentier
186, Table 18, line 2	105	1905
235, line 3	invasion	invasions
235, line 10	their social cohesion and political	its social cohesion and its political
311, No. XXVI, line 1	b.	d.
311, No. XXVI, line 2	d.	b.
323, No. LXV, L, line 6	Christina	Christiana
336, No. LXVI, line 1	HILDEBRAND	HILDERBRAND
339, No. LXXI, M, line 4	109^v, 110^v; AMS,	109^v, 110^v, 110^v; AMS,
352, No. XCIV, J, line 1	Endingen (d. by 1516)	Endingen (d. 1516)
355, No. XCVIII M	Rentier;	Rentier:
360, I. A.	Hüffel 6.0	6. Hüffel 6.0
397, line 16	(1332-1499)	(1332-1449)
399, line 7 from bottom	1865-69.	1865-96.
403, lines 6-7	sub-title should read: „Zu den Forschungsergebnissen über das Patriziat besonders der süddeutschen Städte"	
404, line 2	28-58	47-52
405, lines 21-22	title should read: *Horizons européens de la Réforme en Alsace. Mélanges offerts à Jean Rott.*	
427, line 4	*Réforme*	*Reforme*
438, Joham v. Mundolsheim, Conrad	322-323 (No. XLV.)	323-324 (No. XLV.)

CONTENTS

PART TWO
REGIME AND REFORMATION

LIST OF TABLES

PREFACE

The ultimate objectivity proposed to us as an ideal by positivist historical thought remains as elusive as the unicorn. Whether the seeker of that ideal must bring to the task the same qualifications as the tamer of that fabulous beast is difficult to say. This book does not argue for the achievability of the ideal but only for the employment of modern canons of historical criticism in a field where their use is not yet self-understood. It appears very odd that the history of the German Reformation has proved so resistant to the application of the forms of analysis we use for other peoples and other times. It *appears* odd, until one realizes that this resistance is the fruit of two generations of striving to insulate the era and a few of its leading personalities from the norms of historical criticism and to do so by insisting on the subjects' unique metahistorical value. Given the domination of such principles on both sides of the ocean, it is hardly surprising that serious, non-clerical historians tend, at least west of the Elbe, to avoid the history of the German Reformation.

An English historian has written that most social history is the packing and repacking of bags for trips that are never taken. Rather than pack one more bag by relating in detail how I think historians ought to proceed in this field, I have decided to get underway by presenting an extensive example of what I believe "the employment of modern canons of historical criticism" to be. That this happens in a book about one of pre-modern Germany's liveliest and most interesting towns is partly coincidence, partly design.

One of the truest elements of the frequent comparison of books to children is the propensity of each for turning out quite differently than it began. More than ten years ago, in a quiet room in Chicago's The Newberry Library, I began to study the career of Jacob Sturm (1489–1553) of Strasbourg, whose career, one of my teachers, Hans Baron, suggested to me, was well worth investigation. I intended to write a study of Sturm as a politician, and I still do; but between the intention and the realization the present book gradually interposed itself. It began with a recognition that the role conventionally assigned to Sturm, that of heroic, omnipotent shaper of Strasbourg's reforms and foreign policy, rested on serious misconceptions about social and political institutions and power. More generally, it was the incompatibility of conventional pictures of the politics of the German Reformation with my own understanding of the social structures of the late feudal city in Europe that drove me to formulate the questions that lie at the basis of this book.

The most elementary of these questions inform the first, structural part of the book: Who ruled? Where did they come from? How did they rule? Then I came to the questions that govern the second, properly historical part: How did the Reformation movement challenge and change aristocratic rule? Why could Strasbourg's ruling class and regime weather so well the great crisis of 1524–25, only to be nearly ruined by the post-war crisis of 1547–48? This book is thus built upon a very deliberate logic: Part I defines the parameters and principal structures of the social and political systems; and Part II examines the responses of the systems to the two major crises of the reform generation. This involves a certain amount of repetition of data and a good many internal cross-references; and the finished work thus lacks the cleanness and economy of purely narrative history.

Some of the themes normally treated in a preface, such as point of view, method, and critique of the literature, are here the subjects of an introductory chapter (chapter I). Its length betrays a certain self-consciousness of invading a relatively isolated field of historical studies with approaches and a point of view which are there somewhat alien, though common coin in other fields.

To my students at the University of Oregon, past and present, I hope that this book may partly compensate them for the pleasure they have given me. To my colleagues at the same institution, I hope that they will find their critical objections well met. To my readers, I hope they will enjoy this book.

Besides effort, energy, and, one hopes, a bit of intelligence, works of historical scholarship represent accumulated debts, ranging from small piles to very large heaps. This book is no exception. The seven years' work that went into it piled up a mountain of debts to the generosity, kindness, and talents of others. As usual, the acknowledgements here are all the public recompense they will ever get.

First, there are the institutions that supported the research and writing of this book. The University of Oregon Graduate School financed a research trip in 1970 and several purchases of microfilms. In 1972–73, I was able to take a leave-of-absence from my teaching obligations because of grants-in-aid from the American Philosophical

Society, the American Council of Learned Societies, and the trustees of
The Newberry Library. During the same year, a grant from the William
Stamps Farish Foundation of Houston, Texas, enabled me to spend five
months in Strasbourg. Some of the book was written and all of it revised
and prepared for the press in Tübingen, where in 1975–76 I was a fellow
of the Alexander von Humboldt-Stiftung and a guest in Professor H. A.
Oberman's Institut für Spätmittelalter und Reformation. To the trustees,
directors, and staffs of these institutions I extend my thanks.

The directors and staffs of many archives and libraries helped me in
various ways to find and use the sources on which this book is based.
First of all come the director, M. F.-J. Fuchs, and his assistants, MM.
Georges Foessel and Edmond Ponsing, of the Archives de la Ville de
Strasbourg, quite possibly one of the most congenial places a scholar
could work. Next come the Archives Départementales du Bas-Rhin,
where special thanks are due M. Christian Wolff. Then, in no special
order, I thank the staffs of the Archives Municipales de Mulhouse, the
Bibliothèque Municipale de Strasbourg, the Bibliothèque Nationale et
Universitaire de Strasbourg, the Badisches Generallandesarchiv in
Karlsruhe, the Hessische Staatsarchive in Darmstadt and Marburg, the
Niedersächsische Staats- und Universitätsbibliothek in Göttingen, the
Herzog August Bibliothek in Wolfenbüttel, and the university libraries
at Tübingen and Freiburg im Breisgau. Finally, my special thanks go to
Lawrence W. Towner and the staff of The Newberry Library, Chicago,
where I have worked on this and other projects, and to the long-suffering
inter-library loan staff of the University of Oregon Library. To these
and to every other archivist and librarian who helped me, wittingly or
not, my heartfelt thanks.

Next come those to whom my debts are more subtle, because their aid
came in the forms of advice, criticism, and encouragement. Here I name
first my grand colleague and priceless friend, John W. Perrin, with the
wish that his struggle for justice may be crowned with success. Then
come those who read early versions of this study and whose criticisms
helped me to clarify my ideas at an early stage: Thomas P. Govan, Val R.
Lorwin, Robert M. Berdahl, and Gustave Alef of the University of
Oregon, and Natalie Z. Davis (Berkeley). I have had continuing,
interested support and help from two fellow members of the Société
américaine de l'histoire de Strasbourg, Miriam U. Chrisman (Amherst)
and James M. Kittelson (Columbus). Two other North Americans
gave me welcome assistance at Strasbourg, for which they deserve
special thanks: Steven Nelson initiated me into the mysteries of the

notarial archives; and Jane Abray gave me items from her own research, checked references, and sent me a number of texts.

At Strasbourg my work has been supported, enriched, extended, and strengthened again and again by the two masters of Strasbourg's history in the age of the Reformation, François-Joseph Fuchs and Jean Rott, without whose talents and generosity this book would, if it existed at all, be much poorer. Another Strasbourgeois, Charles Wittmer (1901–74), who died too soon to see this book, gave me, during my first visit to that lovely city, counsel and kindness I shall not forget.

My thanks, too, to the colleagues who allowed me to read their un-published dissertations, Jean-Pierre Kintz (Strasbourg), Jean-Daniel Pariset (Paris), and Erdmann Weyrauch (Tübingen).

To Heiko A. Oberman I owe a dual debt, for the hospitality of his Tübingen institute and for the acceptance of this book into the series in which it appears. My thanks go as well to others who helped to make my Tübingen year a profitable one, including Professor Hans Martin Decker-Hauff, who gave me the freedom of the house in his Institut für geschichtliche Landeskunde, and the many scholars who staff sections O and Z 2 of the Sonderforschungsbereich Spätmittelalter und Reforma-tion. My thanks also to Heinz Holeczek (Freiburg im Breisgau), who read the finished typescript.

An author's spouse conventionally receives the final thanks. It is due only to her express wish that Katherine Gingrich Brady's name appears here rather than where it should, on the title page as collaborator. She has seen this book through thick and thin, from its first form as a short paper to its present one. Important aspects of the book are largely her work, such as the checking of the place names (no mean task for a region where every village has at least two names) and much work in published genealogical literature. She also has shared every stage of the drudgery of typing and proofreading. Most of all, she has given the love and care without which this study would have remained merely an idea. If this book belongs to anyone, it is hers.

A book largely on Alsatian history written in English requires some explanation of the usage of place and personal names. In most cases, the French forms of place names are enough like the old and the modern German forms that no confusion is likely; and, for the principal towns, I have felt free to use the one form or the other, as it pleased me: Mul-house rather than Mühlhausen im Elsass, Hagenau rather than Hague-nau, Strasbourg rather than Strassburg, and Saverne rather than

Zabern. Occasionally, where the difference might confuse—as in Sélestat/Schlettstadt, Wasselonne/Wasselnheim, or Obernai/Oberehn-heim—I have given both names at the first mention; and, in any case, both forms can be found in the Index of Place Names. I have avoided the modern French forms of Alsatian village names altogether.

The places still exist, but the people do not, and I have therefore avoided the common practice of gallicizing Christian names. Where a French form is well established in the modern literature, such as "Jean Sturm" for the man who was not a native French-speaker, I have retained that usage. Normally, however, I have used the old German names, though sometimes in modern spellings. I have rarely put the *k* into Jacob, allowed several forms of "Katharina" and of "Margarethe" to compete, and used short forms ("Hans," "Claus," "Bastian") as freely as sixteenth-century Strasbourgeois did.[1] My rule has been to permit variety to hold sway until just short of the point at which it might produce confusion. Only in the plural forms of family names is my usage consistent and unorthodox. Instead of adding an "s" to the singular form, as English usage requires, I have followed German and French practice by adding the definite article to the singular form to indicate a plural form. Thus, the plural of the name "Mieg" is "the Mieg"; and, as the usage is consistent, it should not create any confusion.

Tübingen, St. Patrick's Day, 1976

---

[1] Jean-Pierre Kintz, "Anthroponymie en pays de langue germanique. Le cas de l'Alsace, XVIIe–XVIIIe siècles," *Annales de démographie historique*, 1972, pp. 311–317.

SIGLA

AAHA	*Archives alsaciennes d'histoire de l'art*
Adam, *EKET*	J. Adam, *Evangelische Kirchengeschichte der elsässichen Territorien*
Adam, *EKSS*	J. Adam, *Evangelische Kirchengeschichte der Stadt Strassburg*
ADBR	Archives Départementales du Bas-Rhin (Strasbourg)
AEA	*Archives de l'Eglise d'Alsace* (continuation of *AEKG*)
AEKG	*Archiv für elsässische Kirchengeschichte* (continued by *AEA*)
AESC	*Annales. Economies, Sociétés, Civilisations*
AGCS	Archives du Grand-Chapitre de Strasbourg (in AMS)
AHR	*The American Historical Review*
AJb	*Alemannisches Jahrbuch*
AMM	Archives Municipales de Mulhouse
AMS	Archives Municipales de Strasbourg
AMS, KS	AMS, Chambre des Contrats
AMS, AA	AMS, Affaires étrangères
AMS, XXI	AMS, Procès-verbaux du sénat et des Vingt-et-Un
AMS, H	AMS, Hôpital
AMS, R	AMS, Réglements (formerly: MO)
Ann. Brant	*Annales de Sébastien Brant*, ed. Léon Dacheux
ARG	*Archiv für Reformationsgeschichte/Archive for Reformation History*
ASAVS	*Annuaire de la Société des Amis de Vieux-Strasbourg*
AST	Archives du Chapitre de Saint-Thomas de Strasbourg (in AMS)
BCGA	*Bulletin du cercle généalogique d'Alsace*
BDS	Martin Bucer, *Deutsche Schriften*
BLBK	Badische Landesbibliothek Karlsruhe
BMS	Bibliothèque Municipale de Strasbourg
BNUS	Bibliothèque Nationale et Universitaire de Strasbourg
BSCMHA	*Bulletin de la Société pour la Conservation des Monuments historiques d'Alsace*
CAAAH	*Cahiers alsaciens d'art, d'archéologie et d'histoire*
CH	*Church History*
CR	*Corpus Reformatorum*
DFN	Deutsche Führungsschichten in der Neuzeit
DGB	*Deutsches Geschlechterbuch*
DHMN	Deutsche Handelsakten des Mittelalters und der Neuzeit
DRA, JR	*Deutsche Reichstagsakten, Jüngere Reihe*
ELJb	*Elsass-Lothringisches Jahrbuch*
FDA	*Freiburger Diözesan-Archiv*
FUB	*Fürstenbergisches Urkundenbuch*
GHDA	*Genealogisches Handbuch des Deutschen Adels*
GHDA, FH	*GHDA, Freiherrliche Häuser*
GHDA, GH	*GHDA, Gräfliche Häuser*
GLAK	Generallandesarchiv Karlsruhe
HABW	Herzog August Bibliothek Wolfenbüttel
HStAD	Hessisches Staatsarchiv Darmstadt
HStAM	Hessisches Staatsarchiv Marburg
HStAS	Hauptstaatsarchiv Stuttgart
JGOR	*Jahrbuch für die Geschichte der oberdeutschen Reichsstädte* (continued by *ZSSD*)
JGSLEL	*Jahrbuch für Geschichte, Sprache und Litteratur in Elsass-Lothringen*
JRG	*Jahrbuch für Regionalgeschichte*

KDBadens	*Die Kunstdenkmäler (des Grossherzogthums Baden)*
Kindler, *GBS*	J. Kindler von Knobloch, *Das goldene Buch von Strassburg*
Kindler, *OG*	J. Kindler von Knobloch, *Oberbadisches Geschlechterbuch*
MBHK	*Mitteilungen der Badischen Historischen Kommission* (appended to *ZGO*)
NSUG	Niedersächsische Staats- und Universitätsbibliothek Göttingen
PCSS	*Politische Correspondenz der Stadt Strassburg im Zeitalter der Reformation*
PSSARE	Publications de la Société Savante d'Alsace et des Régions de l'Est
QBLG	*Quellensammlung der badischen Landesgeschichte*
QFRG	Quellen und Forschungen zur Reformationsgeschichte
RA	*Revue d'Alsace*
RHMC	*Revue d'histoire moderne et contemporaine*
RHPR	*Revue d'histoire et de philosophie religieuses*
RUB	*Rappoltsteinisches Urkundenbuch*
SHCT	Studies in the History of Christian Thought
SKRG	Schriften zur Kirchen- und Rechtsgeschichte
SMRT	Studies in Medieval and Reformation Thought
SVRG	Schriften des Vereins für Reformationsgeschichte
SWIELR	Schriften des Wissenschaftlichen Instituts der Elsass-Lothringer im Reich (an der Universität Frankfurt am Main)
TQ Strassburg	*Quellen zur Geschichte der Täufer*, VII–VIII: *Stadt Strassburg*
UBB	*Urkundenbuch der Stadt Basel*
VIEGM	Veröffentlichungen des Instituts für europäische Geschichte Mainz
VKLBW	Veröffentlichungen der Kommission für geschichtliche Landeskunde in Baden-Württemberg
VSWG	*Vierteljahrschrift für Sozial- und Wirtschaftsgeschichte*
WABr	*D. Martin Luthers Werke. Briefwechsel*
WLBS	Württembergische Landesbibliothek Stuttgart
ZBLG	*Zeitschrift für bayerische Landesgeschichte*
ZC	*Zimmerische Chronik*
ZfG	*Zeitschrift für Geschichtswissenschaft*
ZGO	*Zeitschrift für die Geschichte des Oberrheins*
ZKiG	*Zeitschrift für Kirchengeschichte*
ZSSD	*Zeitschrift für Stadtgeschichte, Stadtsoziologie und Denkmalpflege* (continuation of *JGOR*)
ZSSR, GA	*Zeitschrift der Savigny-Stiftung für Rechtsgeschichte, Germanistische Abteilung*
ZSSR, KA	*Zeitschrift der Savigny-Stiftung für Rechtsgeschichte, Kanonistische Abteilung*
ZW	*Huldrych Zwinglis Sämtliche Werke*
ZWLG	*Zeitschrift für württembergische Landesgeschichte*

ABBREVIATIONS

The following abbreviations are used extensively in the appendices and less frequently in the notes:

b. = *	born
Bp.	Bishop (of Strasbourg)
d. = dec. = †	died

fam.	family
fl.	florin (Rhenish gulden) OR flourished
gen.=dit	called, named
H.R.E.	Holy Roman Empire
Jr.	Junior/der Jüngere
m.	married
N.S.	New Series/IIe série/Neue Folge
Sr.	Senior/der Ältere
v.	von
z.	zum

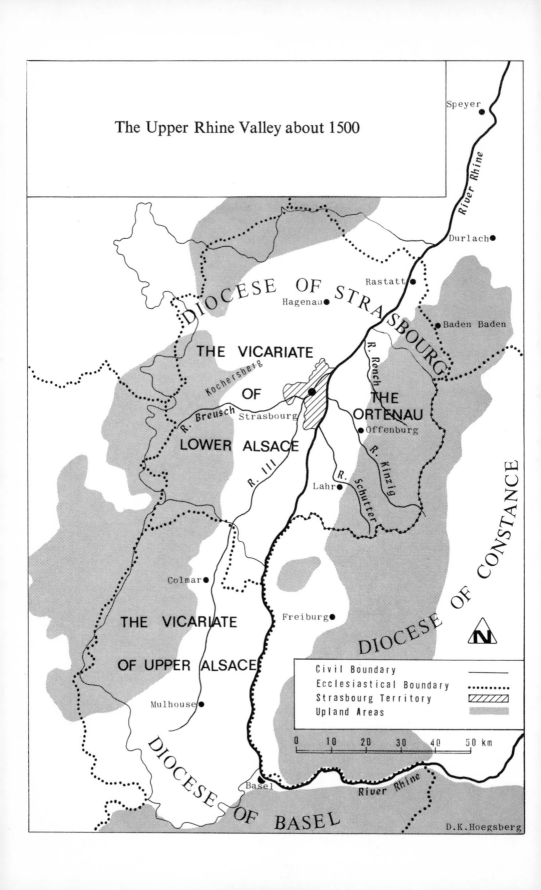

The Upper Rhine Valley about 1500

Speyer

River Rhine

Durlach

Rastatt

DIOCESE OF STRASBOURG

Hagenau

Baden Baden

THE VICARIATE

R. Rench

Kochersberg

OF

THE
ORTENAU

R. Breusch

Strasbourg

Offenburg

LOWER ALSACE

R. Kinzig

R. Ill

Lahr

R. Schutter

DIOCESE OF CONSTANCE

Colmar

Freiburg

THE VICARIATE

N

OF UPPER ALSACE

Civil Boundary
Ecclesiastical Boundary
Strasbourg Territory
Upland Areas

Mulhouse

0   10   20   30   40   50 km

DIOCESE

Basel

River Rhine

OF BASEL

D.K.Hoegsberg

CHAPTER ONE

PROLEGOMENA

Historical fields, like books, have their particular histories, besides reflecting the general movement of historical thought and changes in research methods. The historiography of the German Reformation is more peculiar than most, perhaps because of its origins in clerical polemics and apologetics and its continued nourishment by modern Christian confessionalism. One of the stranger chapters in its history is the retreat into the dimmer recesses of Luther's theology during the inter-war years. This "flight from history"[1] has largely exhausted itself, and the study of the German Reformation has moved back toward historical paths.

The recent study of the German Reformation as the object of historical interest shows three main lines of development. Pride of place belongs to the new flowering of the great tradition of socialist historiography, descending from Friedrich Engels (1820–1895) and Karl Kautsky (1854–1938), into an entire school of historical studies centered in the German Democratic Republic.[2] Secondly, there is an effort to re-

---

[1] Max Steinmetz, "Probleme der frühbürgerlichen Revolution in Deutschland in der ersten Hälfte des 16. Jahrhunderts," in *Die frühbürgerliche Revolution in Deutschland. Referat und Diskussion zum Thema Probleme der frühbürgerlichen Revolution in Deutschland 1476 bis 1535*, ed. Gerhard Brendler (Berlin, 1961), pp. 17–52, here at p. 32. See also Max Steinmetz, "Reformation und Bauernkrieg," in *Kritik der bürgerlichen Geschichtsschreibung. Handbuch*, eds. Werner Berthold, *et al.*, 3rd ed. (Cologne, 1970), pp. 140–141. Important but more cautious critiques of the Luther cult are by Bernd Moeller, "Probleme der Reformationsgeschichtsforschung," *ZKiG*, 75 (1965), 246–257, now trans. by H. C. Erik Midelfort and Mark U. Edwards, Jr., in *Imperial Cities and the Reformation. Three Essays* (Philadelphia, 1972), pp. 3–16; and Heiko A. Oberman, "Headwaters of the Reformation: *initia Lutheri—initia reformationis*," in *Luther and the Dawn of the Modern Era. Papers for the Fourth International Congress for Luther Research*, ed. Heiko A. Oberman, SHCT, 8 (Leiden, 1974), pp. 40–88.

[2] Max Steinmetz, "Reformation und Bauernkrieg in der Historiographie der DDR," in *Historische Forschungen in der DDR, Analysen und Berichte* (Berlin, 1960), pp. 142–162; *idem*, "Forschungen zur Geschichte der Reformation und des deutschen Bauernkrieges," in *Historische Forschungen in der DDR 1960–1970, Analysen und Berichte* (Berlin, 1970), pp. 338–350. These volumes were prepared for the historical congresses at Stockholm (1960) and Moscow (1970) and appeared as special supplements to *ZfG*, volumes 8 and 18 respectively. There is no satisfactory general history of socialist historiography on

establish the study of the Reformation in the broad context of cultural history and the history of ideas, drawing upon the strands (or the "tributaries," in the language of a leading exponent) of late medieval and Renaissance thought—especially nominalism, Augustinianism, and humanism—as conceptual tools for the analysis of Renaissance and Reformation thought.[3] Thirdly, there have been new efforts to resolve "the Reformation" into its various forms and find the social and political principles which seem to have determined the proliferation of forms of Reformation thought and religion.[4] As different as these lines are from

---

this theme. New material on the role of Ludwig Zimmermann appears in Abraham Friesen, *Reformation and Utopia. The Marxist Interpretation of the Reformation and Its Antecedents*, VIEGM, 71 (Wiesbaden, 1974), chapter V, a work which is otherwise vitiated by the author's hysterical characterization of Marxism as a modern version of Joachism. The profound impact of socialist scholarship in this field can be seen in the two volumes edited by Rainer Wohlfeil, *Reformation oder frühbürgerliche Revolution?* nymphenburger texte zur wissenschaft, 5(Munich, 1972), and *Der Bauernkrieg 1524–26. Bauernkrieg und Reformation*, nymphenburger texte zur wissenschaft, 21 (Munich, 1975); and in two commemorative volumes, *Deutscher Bauernkrieg 1525*, ed. Heiko A. Oberman, as *ZKiG*, 85/2 (1975), and *Bauernkrieg-Studien*, ed. Bernd Moeller, SVRG, No. 189 (Gütersloh, 1975).

[3] See *The Pursuit of Holiness in Late Medieval and Renaissance Religion. Papers from the University of Michigan Conference*, eds. Charles Trinkaus and Heiko A. Oberman, SMRT, 10 (Leiden, 1974), esp. the contributions by Heiko A. Oberman (pp. 3–25), William J. Courtenay (pp. 26–59), Steven Ozment (pp. 67–92), and Charles Trinkaus (pp. 339–366); and William J. Bouwsma, "Renaissance and Reformation: An Essay in their Affinities and Connections," in *Luther and the Dawn of the Modern Era*, pp. 127–149. This development is largely the work of scholars who write in English and has met significant resistance wherever the formula Reformation = Luther reigns. See the qualified resistance of Lewis W. Spitz, "Headwaters of the Reformation: Studia Humanitatis, Luther Senior, et Initia Reformationis," in *Luther and the Dawn of the Modern Era*, pp. 89–116, esp. pp. 112–115; the much stronger opposition of Bengt Hägglund, "Renaissance and Reformation," in the same volume, pp. 150–158; and the violently polemical work of Ernst-Wilhelm Kohls, *Luther oder Erasmus. Luthers Theologie in der Auseinandersetzung mit Erasmus*, vol. I, supplementary volume 3 of the *Theologische Zeitschrift* (Basel, 1972).

[4] The chief works are Bernd Moeller, *Reichsstadt und Reformation*, SVRG, No. 180 (Gütersloh, 1962), English trans. in *Imperial Cities and the Reformation*, pp. 39–115; and Ernst-Wilhelm Kohls, *Die Schule bei Martin Bucer in ihrem Verhältnis zu Kirche und Obrigkeit*, Pädagogische Forschungen, 22 (Heidelberg, 1963). That the older, sociologically oriented German school of ecclesiastical history grew out of studies on the varieties of Protestantism is convincingly argued by Manfred Wichelhaus, *Kirchengeschichtsschreibung und Soziologie im neunzehnten Jahrhundert und bei Ernst Troeltsch*, Heidelberger Forschungen, 9 (Heidelberg, 1965). In his zeal to give Troeltsch a scholarly genealogy, however, Wichelhaus neglects the profound impression made upon Troeltsch by the ideas of Karl Marx, a point stressed by Leo Kofler, *Zur Geschichte der bürgerlichen Gesellschaft. Versuch einer verstehenden Deutung der Neuzeit*, 5th ed., Soziologische Texte, 38 (Darmstadt-Neuwied, 1974), p. 13.

one another in methods, intentions, and commitments, they share the drive to re-historicize the German Reformation after a period in which Luther and his reform were placed above and beyond mortal time.

The third tendency, the search for the principles of variation within the Reformation, has in common with socialist historiography the drive towards a social understanding of the Reformation, although it employs historical sociologies far less adequate to the task than is historical materialism's class theory. One product of this tendency is the revival of interest in the "urban reform" in South Germany and Switzerland, where the civic milieu and its mentality are seen to have transformed Luther's gospel into a kind of proto-Calvinism. The most characteristic feature of the "urban reform," that which made it different and more (say some) or less (say others) effective than Luther's, was the synthesis of the new gospel with civic and humanist thought. The result was the doctrine of the sacral corporation, the identity of city and church as the collective child of God.

A. The "Sacral Corporation" and the Urban Reformation in Germany

1. The chief proponent of the doctrine of sacral corporatism as the best analytical key to the history of the Reformation in the German cities is undoubtedly Bernd Moeller, whose *Reichsstadt und Reformation* (1962) remains the single most influential work in this direction.[5] In his exploration of the roots of the peculiarities of the "urban reform" in the Holy Roman Empire, Moeller lays great weight on "the unique mentality of the German townspeople before the Reformation."[6] Each citizen understood "that he was part of the whole, sharing responsibility for his part in the welfare of the great organic community, the 'collective individual,' to which he was tightly bound by laws and duties."[7] The organic community, in Moeller's view, was symbolized by the oath each citizen took, which affirmed that the town "became for him the embodiment of the empire and the center of his world. It also set the absolute limits of his experience."[8] The importance of this mental world to the urban reform lay in the fact that the legal and psychological

---

[5] There is a French version, earlier than the English one, in *Villes d'Empire et réformation*, trans. Albert Chenou, Travaux d'histoire éthico-politique, 10 (Geneva, 1966).

[6] I quote from *Imperial Cities*, p. 43 (*Reichsstadt und Reformation*, p. 10).

[7] *Ibid.*, p. 44 (*Reichsstadt und Reformation*, pp. 11–12).

[8] *Ibid.*, p. 45 (*Reichsstadt und Reformation*, p. 12).

corporation thus formed rejected the sacral-temporal dualism of medieval society and saw the civic corporation as a holy community, a sacral corporation (*Sakralgemeinschaft*),[9] through which the citizens' welfare—religious and temporal—was seen to be mediated.[10] Although weakened during the period before 1520 by the growth of oligarchical and authoritarian tendencies in the towns, this sacral corporatist mentality was still very powerful on the eve of the Reformation.[11] This unitary, corporate, semi-egalitarian mentality formed the lens through which the urban reformers of the South—chiefly Ulrich Zwingli and Martin Bucer—adapted Luther's gospel into a new doctrine of collective religious responsibility which, having taken root in the citizenry through evangelical preaching, generated the popular pressure for reform that pushed the urban regimes into *a* Reformation. The urban reform in the South "*is finally explained by the encounter of the peculiarly*

---

[9] Bernd Moeller, "Kleriker als Bürger," in *Festschrift für Hermann Heimpel zum 70. Geburtstag zum 19. September 1971*, ed. by members of the Max Planck-Institut für Geschichte Göttingen, 3 vols. (Göttingen, 1971–72), II, 195–224, here at p. 222.

[10] Moeller, *Imperial Cities*, p. 46 (*Reichsstadt und Reformation*, p. 13): "Material welfare and eternal salvation were not differentiated and thus the borders between the secular and spiritual areas of life disappeared. We can grasp an essential trait of the late medieval urban community if we characterize it as a 'sacred society.'" It would be more correct to say that contemporary consciousness did not distinguish clearly "material welfare and eternal salvation" (approximately the public-private distinction of bourgeois thought), even though this is a tautology to all but the staunchest members of the "religion vs. politics" school of Reformation history. A sounder view is suggested by Eric J. Hobsbawm's remark: "However, insofar as religion is the language and framework of all general action in undeveloped societies . . . ideologies of revolt will also be religious." Hobsbawm, in "Labour Traditions," *Labouring Men: Studies in the History of Labour* (London, 1964), p. 375. See esp. Natalie Z. Davis, "Some Tasks and Themes in the Study of Popular Religion," in *The Pursuit of Holiness*, pp. 307–336; and her "Rites of Violence," which first appeared in *Past & Present*, No. 59 (May 1973), and is now revised in her *Society and Culture in Early Modern France. Eight Essays* (Stanford, 1975), pp. 152–187, here at p. 155.

[11] Moeller, *Imperial Cities*, pp. 49–53 (*Reichsstadt und Reformation*, pp. 15–18). The strength of urban corporatist traditions is stressed by Hans Morf, "Obrigkeit und Kirche in Zürich bis zu Beginn der Reformation," *Zwingliana*, 13 (1970), 164–203; and, in a highly romanticized version, by Gerhard Pfeiffer, "Das Verhältnis von politischer und kirchlicher Gemeinde in den deutschen Reichsstädten," in *Staat und Kirche im Wandel der Jahrhunderte*, ed. Walther Peter Fuchs (Stuttgart-Berlin-Köln-Mainz, 1966), pp. 79–99. Against all idealizations of the corporative character of urban political life at the end of the Middle Ages must be set the oligarchical transformations of the guild regimes well before the Reformation. See Eberhard Naujoks, *Obrigkeitsgedanke, Zunftverfassung und Reformation. Studien zur Verfassungsgeschichte von Ulm, Esslingen und Schwäb. Gmünd*, VKLBW, B 3 (Stuttgart, 1958), p. 14.

'urban' theology of Zwingli and Bucer with the particularly vital communal spirit in Upper Germany."[12]

Stressing the corporate unity of the urban populations, Moeller can lay little weight on their internal structures. True, he does recognize at least one important social distinction in the pre-Reformation towns, that between commune and clergy, which he calls sometimes "social bodies" (*Sozialkörper*) and sometimes "estates" (*Stände*);[13] and he maps the process whereby the urban clergy in South Germany were forced to become citizens—a process to which the reform movement gave a decisive impulse, although the theology of the urban reformers was not entirely comfortable with the notion that the clergy should become citizens like any others.[14] Moeller insists, however, that the principal agent of the urban reform was the entire corporation of townsfolk living in a condition of relative legal equality, and that it was the communal element that gave the urban reform its characteristic, largely medieval shape. He therefore rejects the idea of an *independent* reforming role of the urban regimes, distinct from their succumbing to pressure from the *populus*, and therefore also the possibility of the regimes acting as instruments of certain parts of the social order.[15] The unity of *populus* and *ecclesia* was complete, the hegemony of the popular will nearly so.

So far Moeller's original position: that, by adapting, "correcting," and "deepening" the gospel of Luther, the urban reformers revived, refurbished, and revitalized the old civic ideal of the sacral corporation and thereby made the gospel effective to a degree that Luther, perhaps, never achieved.[16] This transformation naturally had its consequences for the chief doctrines of the Evangelical movement. Justification by faith alone gave way to an emphasis on sanctification through an ethically formed faith operating in a social context—in a word, through love. This, like the theocratic moment with which Zwingli and Bucer altered Luther's dualistic ecclesiology, committed Protestant historians have always seen as a reversion to or a lapse back into medieval modes of

---

[12] Moeller, *Imperial Cities*, p. 103 (*Reichsstadt und Reformation*, p. 67), emphasis in the original.
[13] Moeller, "Kleriker als Bürger," pp. 203, 224.
[14] *Ibid.*, esp. p. 224.
[15] Moeller, *Imperial Cities*, pp. 60–63 (*Reichsstadt und Reformation*, pp. 25–28). His assertion (p. 60) that "the urban Protestant movement in the first half of the sixteenth century had its basis exclusively among the people," is hardly weakened by the later concession (p. 62) that "we must no doubt take social factors into account" in explaining the regimes' caution vis-à-vis the reform movements.
[16] *Ibid.*, p. 90 (*Reichsstadt und Reformation*, p. 54).

thought.[17] There is no doubt that this transformation did take place—or, to put it more accuràtely, that the urban reforming clergy did not regard Luther as the *norma normans* to the degree that many modern Reformation scholars do—nor that these differences are to be seen as the consequences of the social and political milieux in which these urban reformers worked. Moeller, at least in his early work, saw these changes as largely progressive, correcting the individualistic thrust of Luther's doctrine of justification and the authoritarian possibilities of his dualistic ecclesiology. In his more recent work, however, it is no longer clear that he believes that the urban reformers represent a distinct "reformed Reformation" (as opposed to, or at least as distinct from, the "Lutheran Reformation") which is to be regarded as a corrective to the weaknesses of Luther's doctrines and whose centerpiece is the transformed doctrine of the sacral corporation. In his study of the integration of the clergy into the citizenry of the Evangelical towns, Moeller writes of the Evangelical citizenry as the "citizen community before God, 'church community'," which is no longer a "sacral community."[18] This shift would have to mean that Moeller now regards the urban reformers as having been faithful to Luther in that they preserved his conception of the church which made true theocracy, or, more accurately, the total conflation of society and church, at least theoretically impossible. Bucer and his Strasbourg colleagues, to whom Moeller specifically refers, would have to be seen as having maintained the chief points of the Lutheran gospel and, therefore, as the gravediggers rather than the renovators of the (already decaying) sacral corporatist tradition.[19] Moeller's recent work, then, seems to return to the classic position of grading the other reformers according to their faithfulness to Luther. Consequently, where Moeller once saw the urban reform as a salutary transformation of Luther's gospel by the proto-democratic mentality and traditions of the free towns, he now tends to see the Lutheran gospel

---

[17] See in brief Wichelhaus, *Kirchengeschichtsschreibung*, pp. 178, 184. The latter is the so-called "problem of the corpus christianum" (Wichelhaus, p. 178), which was the chief point of attack by Troeltsch's conservative nationalist critics on his historical sociology of Christianity.

[18] Moeller, "Kleriker als Bürger," p. 217.

[19] Steven E. Ozment, *The Reformation in the Cities: The Appeal of Protestantism to Sixteenth-Century Germany and Switzerland* (New Haven-London, 1975), p. 170n26. James M. Kittelson, *Wolfgang Capito from Humanist to Reformer*, SMRT, 17 (Leiden, 1975), however, concludes that although theologically a reasonably faithful follower of Luther (pp. 222–237), Capito was politically a Zwinglian corporatist (pp. 200–206).

itself as more an agent for change, as the ethos which gave the coup
de grâce to the spiritual world of the medieval town.

2. The change in Moeller's perspective brings him somewhat closer
to the position of Ernst-Wilhelm Kohls—although not so close that
the two agree on anything except the fundamental irreducibility of
Luther's gospel. Kohls, too, believes that the cities of the Southwest
developed a peculiar "urban theology," whose chief characteristics were
its replacement of Luther's doctrine of justification by a strongly ethical
and rationalistic doctrine of sanctification, and of his ecclesiology by a
doctrine of collective sanctification rooted in the concept of "gemein
Nutz."[20] Where, for Kohls, the first alteration of Luther's gospel was
rooted in the rationalizing tendencies of urban, Erasmian humanism,[21]
the concept of "gemein Nutz" derived chiefly from communal
("bürgerlich") sources and was theologized by the urban reformers of
the first generation.[22]

Although Moeller and Kohls differ radically in their evaluations of
these alterations of Luther's gospel by the urban reformers, regarding
them as progressive and retrogressive respectively, they are very close
together in their judgments of *what* the alterations were. As to sources,
Kohls lays great weight on humanism—which he understands as a kind
of ethical rationalism, not so different, one suspects, from Liberal
Protestant theology—and correspondingly less on the political traditions
of the free cities.[23] The two scholars also agree in seeing the original

---

[20] This is the basic argument of Kohl's *Die Schule bei Martin Bucer*, and, indeed, of
nearly all of his many writings on Reformation thought. Kohls believes, against nearly
the entire world of Erasmus scholarship, that Erasmus's thought formed a systematic,
theological whole, a rationalistic (i.e., "humanistic") and therefore false alternative to
the true theology of Luther, which it tended to corrupt wherever the two came into
contact—as they did in the Upper German and Swiss towns. The groundwork for this
extraordinary view Kohls laid in *Die Theologie des Erasmus*, 2 vols. (Basel, 1966), and he
brings it to a climax in his *Luther oder Erasmus*, one of the most revealing documents of
the entire "Luther Renaissance." The work of Luther, Kohls writes (*Luther oder
Erasmus*, I, xiv), "ist jene Zeitenwende, in der Gott durch die Bibel und die Sakramente
selbst in die Geschichte eingreift, um alle Menschen wieder unmittelbar durch die hl.
Schrift auf jenen rettenden Weg der Busse und Neubesinnung zu rufen, den Gott von
uns begangen wissen will und den wir in unseren philosophischen, soziologischen
theologischen Landkarten gar nicht verzeichnet finden."

[21] Ernst-Wilhelm Kohls, *Die theologische Lebensaufgabe des Erasmus und die oberrheinischen
Reformatoren. Zur Durchdringung von Humanismus und Reformation*, Arbeiten zur Theologie,
1st series, 39 (Stuttgart, 1969), esp. pp. 36–40.

[22] Kohls, *Die Schule bei Martin Bucer*, p. 155.

[23] Ernst-Wilhelm Kohls, "Evangelische Bewegung und Kirchenordnung in oberdeutschen Reichsstädten," *ZSSR*, *KA*, 84 (1967), 110–134, here at p. 116.

bearers of the reform in the (socially undifferentiated) citizenry, although Kohls, in keeping with the religion-politics dichotomy peculiar to his tradition, maintains that the Reformation became "political" only when urban regimes intervened to employ the new religion for strengthening and rounding out the institutional structure of the corporate civic order.[24] The tendencies in this direction, Moeller and Kohls agree, were much older than the Reformation; but neither scholar moves much beyond the analysis of a single main feature of urban history—church-state relations for Moeller, humanism for Kohls— supposed to be chiefly responsible for the special character of urban reformed religion.[25]

3. The concept of a "naturalization" of the Reformation in the South German towns through the transforming power of the ideal of the city as a holy *respublica* is quite old. Its grandfather was surely Otto von Gierke (1841–1921), the magisterial jurist-historian, who developed the doctrine of organic, corporate consciousness of the medieval German urban commune, and to whom all recent employers of the doctrine pay tribute.[26] Gierke's *Genossenschaftslehre* was one form of a continuing effort in German public thought during the nineteenth century to find historical justification for the protection and reconstitution of com- munitarian institutions in a world hostile to all social forms except that of the self-aggrandizing individual. And while his romantic idealization of the medieval urban commune bears, on the one hand, similarities to the romantic, radical-liberal, communitarian sociology of his con- temporary, Ferdinand Tönnies (1855–1936), it also has some kinship with the mainstream of conservative *Ständelehre*. Which tendency be- comes dominant rather depends on whether emphasis is laid on the organic unity of the corporation or on the basic equality of its members. This ambiguous doctrine was then adapted to the pre-history and history of the Reformation in the German cities by another jurist, Alfred Schultze (1864–1946).[27] The completed doctrine of the shaping of the

---

[24] *Ibid.*, pp. 124–130.

[25] *Ibid.*, pp. 131–133; Bernd Moeller, "Die Kirche in den evangelischen freien Städten Oberdeutschlands im Zeitalter der Reformation," *ZGO*, 112 (1964), 147–162, here at pp. 161–162.

[26] Esp. volume III of Gierke's *Das deutsche Genossenschaftsrecht*, of which see the citations by Moeller, *Imperial Cities*, pp. 42–43 (*Reichsstadt und Reformation*, p. 10), and Kohls, "Evangelische Bewegung," pp. 124–125.

[27] Alfred Schultze, *Stadtgemeinde und Reformation*, Recht und Staat in Geschichte und Gegenwart, 11 (Tübingen, 1918); adapted to the Swiss towns by Leonhard von Muralt, "Stadtgemeinde und Reformation in der Schweiz," *Zeitschrift für Schweizerische Geschichte*, 10 (1930), 349–384.

urban reform by the civic, communal traditions of the medieval German town—whether or not mixed with humanism—has gained wide currency in certain tendencies of Reformation scholarship,[28] although it has not gone unchallenged.[29]

Moeller's most recent critic is the American and self-confessed "recent convert" to the study of the urban reform, Steven Ozment.[30] Despite his *apparent* interest in social history (Ozment spares only one line for socialist historiography, the longest continuous tradition of social study of the Reformation),[31] he wants to turn the study of the urban reform back to the old paths and lead it back under the sovereignty of Luther. Thus he attacks Moeller's attempt to explain historically the variations in early Protestant thought and practice, for Ozment believes that Moeller's interpretation of Zwingli's and Bucer's theologies as welcome, progressive reinforcements of communal values against the rising tide of oligarchy reduces the value and stature of these Protestant theologies by making them too "medieval."[32] Ozment complains that Moeller's interpretation would make "the Reformation most successful where it changed religious thought and practice least,"[33] which he can do only by ignoring the entire line running from the German urban reform into Calvinism. Ozment's own interpretation, that Protestant theology gained widespread assent because of the "swelling popular desire to be rid of the psychological and social burdens of late medieval religion itself,"[34] is far more psychological than social and is, in fact, little more than a universalization of Luther's account of his own conversion. As for the variations in Protestantism, the departures of the urban reformers from Luther in response to different social milieux, Ozment is forced to state

---

[28] Especially in the English-speaking world. See, for some examples, Robert C. Walton, *Zwingli's Theocracy* (Toronto, 1967), xxi–xxii, and pp. 16, 29, 55n; Miriam U. Chrisman, *Strasbourg and the Reform: A Study in the Process of Change* (New Haven-London, 1967), p. 27; Harold J. Grimm, "The Reformation and the Urban Social Classes in Germany," in *Luther, Erasmus and the Reformation. A Catholic-Protestant Reappraisal*, eds. John C. Olin, *et al.* (New York, 1969), pp. 75–86, here at pp. 76–81; Basil Hall, "The Reformation City," *Bulletin of the John Rylands Library*, 54 (1971), 103–148.

[29] R. W. Scribner, "Civic Unity and the Reformation in Erfurt," *Past & Present*, No. 66 (February 1975), 28–60, here at pp. 28–29; Heide Stratenwerth, *Die Reformation in der Stadt Osnabrück*, VIEGM, 61 (Wiesbaden, 1971), p. 123n81.

[30] Ozment, *Reformation in the Cities*, p. 1.

[31] *Ibid.*, p. 208n3.

[32] *Ibid.*, p. 6.

[33] *Ibid.*, pp. 7–8.

[34] *Ibid.*, p. 9.

his belief that they never existed,[35] although the contrary was maintained longly and loudly by most parties to the doctrinal controversies of the sixteenth century.

The strength of Moeller's view of the urban reform—a strength which none of his non-socialist critics has engaged—is his return to an historical interpretation of the theology of the Reformation era[36] according to social principles of determination. He thereby picks up once more a thread of interpretation which has been lying dormant in non-socialist scholarship since the death of Ernst Troeltsch (1865–1923).[37] Troeltsch's life-work closely paralleled what the South German urban reformers (by Moeller's account) were trying to achieve. "The victory of the 'Reformed' Reformation in the Upper German imperial cities," writes Moeller, "is finally explained by the encounter of the peculiarly 'urban' theology of Zwingli and Bucer with the particularly vital communal spirit in Upper Germany."[38] As for Troeltsch, his work on the sociology of religion "must be understood as a 'political ethic' of Protestant Christianity in the post-Bismarck era," striving to correct and shape the unavoidable democratization of modern life "through the Protestant forces of the West, recommending at the same time as a necessary corrective to this the German organic-corporative social ideal."[39]

---

[35] *Ibid.*, p. 215n71.

[36] See Steinmetz, in *Kritik der bürgerlichen Geschichtsschreibung*, 3rd ed., p. 141.

[37] Moeller, "Problems of Reformation Research," in *Imperial Cities*, pp. 4–5. "Dormant" is perhaps too strong a word, for Troeltsch's sociology of Christianity has been further developed and refined by Herbert Schöffler (see Wichelhaus, *Kirchengeschichtsschreibung*, pp. 189–192), who, however, has had little impact on the study of the German Reformation.

[38] Moeller, *Imperial Cities*, p. 103 (*Reichsstadt und Reformation*, p. 67).

[39] Eckehard Kühne, *Historisches Bewusstsein in der deutschen Soziologie. Untersuchungen zur Geschichte der Soziologie von der Zeit der Reichsgründung bis zum Ersten Weltkrieg auf wissenssoziologischer Grundlage*, dissertation, Marburg (Marburg/Lahn, 1970), pp. 166–167. Manfred Wichelhaus (see note 4 above) describes the emergence of the sociology of Christianity from the comparative study of Christian confessions, and its heyday coincides, naturally enough, with the decades before 1914–18, when permanent world hegemony seemed to belong to the North European powers and their predominantly Protestant ruling classes. A special American variant is the Protestantism-and-Democracy theme with its common affinity for English-speaking Calvinism. This theme, reversed into a Democracy-and-Protestantism form, has inspired an entire sociology of the Reformation era in Guy E. Swanson, *Religion and Regime: A Sociological Account of the Reformation* (Ann Arbor, 1968). Unlike the clerical scholars who would see in democracy the finest child of Protestantism (usually in its Calvinist form), Swanson reverses the causal relationship and sees in the major forms of Reformation and post-Reformation religion (ranked in the order: Catholicism, Lutheranism, Anglicanism, and Calvinism) the products of political regimes having progressively

In a passionate intellectual response to the Marxian critique of society and the advance of the German labor movement, Troeltsch framed the first comprehensive sociology of Christianity, his *Soziallehren der christlichen Kirchen und Gruppen*, one of the great synthetic attempts to understand the history of European Christianity in terms of its fate in the modern world. In the Protestant theological faculties in Germany, however, the future belonged not to men of the breadth and insight of Troeltsch but to Karl Holl (1866–1926) and his disciples, the creators of what came to be called "the Luther Renaissance."[40] What they could not forgive in Troeltsch was that he had been "the first to recognize dependence from economic and social-historical factors as the object of sociology of religion."[41] The new wave of the post-World War I years,

---

more widely distributed legislative powers. Just as the clerical version needs a primal event to serve as the source of the new, which it finds in the conversion of Luther, Swanson identifies a (purely mythical) primal event in a general political transformation which is supposed to have occurred in most of Europe during the century before the Reformation. This invention, and not the manifold errors of detail which are catalogued in the gleefully negative reviews by historians, makes the Swanson model next to useless as a theoretical construct for the guiding of historical research. Swanson's book is a particularly bald example of the myth-making power of idealist-functionalist sociology. The best recent research suggests, on the other hand, that it is difficult to correlate any significant social change in sixteenth-century Europe with the introduction of Protestant religion. See Davis, *Society and Culture in Early Modern France*, pp. 60–61, 94–95, 186.

[40] That there has not yet appeared a history of the "Luther Renaissance" is probably due to the movement's ambiguous political connections. The basic facts and the theological context, but no more, can be had from Horst Stephan, *Geschichte der evangelischen Theologie in Deutschland seit dem Idealismus*, 3rd ed. by Martin Schmidt (Berlin-New York, 1973), pp. 407–412, 427–431. For the men of the first generation, such as Karl Holl and Heinrich Boehmer, the chief inspiration was almost certainly the need to rescue Luther from the relativizing tendencies of both Roman Catholic and Liberal scholarship—the same motive which led to the founding of the Verein für Reformationsgeschichte (1901). For the next generation, the "Luther Renaissance" was a movement of struggle against Liberal Protestant theology, political Liberalism, and all forms of socialism. Its excision of Luther's thought from the historical context and elevation of his teachings into religious, political, and social norms (see, e.g., Werner Elert, *Morphologie des Luthertums*, rev. ed., 2 vols. [Munich, 1953; 1st ed., 1932]) was basically a special form of ideological warfare against the Weimar Republic, in the government of which the two chief enemies, Catholicism and Social Democracy, were allied. The hallmark of the movement was ever the doctrine of Luther as the spiritual father of the "modern world," by which was meant a rejection of nearly all foreign ideas and much of German culture (the non-Prussian, non-Protestant parts), plus the entire legacy of the French Revolution and British Liberalism. All of this, plus what came after, belongs to the history of the "Luther Renaissance."

[41] Kühne, *Historisches Bewusstsein*, p. 163, the force of which is somewhat weakened, but not destroyed, by Wichelhaus's demonstration of a long pedigree for certain aspects of Troeltsch's sociology (*Kirchengeschichtsschreibung*, chapter 1).

however, built a many-celled structure of glosses on and textual (one is tempted to write "exegetical") studies of Luther's writings. The historicization of Luther and his works, which had been advancing all through the nineteenth century, now gave way before the effort to keep Luther's ideas free from the social and other historical elements which relativize the thought of lesser men. What passed for "Reformation history" belonged to this tradition until well into the post-World War II period, since when the guardians of this meta-historical Luther and his highly theologized reformation have been increasingly hard pressed—by the three tendencies named at the beginning of this chapter—to explain how Luther escaped the historical contingentness which is the fate of other men. Few now would dare Emanuel Hirsch's (1888–1972) fantastic identification of Luther as the sole fountainhead of all true modernity; few, indeed, would go beyond Gerhard Ebeling's plea that Luther was "uniquely responsive to events."[42]

The work of Bernd Moeller on the urban reform, which in some important respects resumes that of Troeltsch and thus represents an advance over the remnants of the "Luther Renaissance" tradition, points the way—if quite cautiously—toward the reintegration of Luther and Reformation thought into the history of the German Reformation. If his work is open to a fundamental criticism, it is so on the point that, although it tries to interpret Reformation thought historically, it does so on the basis of a highly idealized, romantic conception of urban society, the ideal of the sacral corporation. This conception, as the following paragraphs argue, is inadequate to an analysis of the urban societies of the Reformation era.

4. Whether the German towns are believed to have exerted a transforming influence on early Protestantism (Moeller and Kohls) or not (Ozment), whether that influence is believed to have been positive (Moeller) or negative (Kohls), these writers on the urban reform share a

---

[42] Quoted by Moeller, "Problems of Reformation Research," in *Imperial Cities*, p. 13, from "Luther: II," *Die Religion in Geschichte und Gegenwart*, 3rd ed., IV (Tübingen, 1960), col. 496. Ebeling is perhaps even more cautious in "Luther and the Beginning of the Modern Age," in *Luther and the Dawn of the Modern Era*, pp. 11–37, esp. pp. 33–34, 36–37. To Ebeling's characterization of Troeltsch's view of Luther's relation to medieval culture should be added the notice by Bouwsma, "Renaissance and Reformation," p. 127n1. Ebeling's essay has also appeared as "Luther und der Anbruch der Neuzeit," *Zeitschrift für Theologie und Kirche*, 69 (1972), 185–213. Emanuel Hirsch's position may be studied in his *Der Reich-Gottes-Begriff des neueren europäischen Denkens* (Göttingen, 1921). That besides Ebeling's cautious meta-historicization of Luther an aggressive, total meta-historicization still exists, may be seen in the quotation from Kohl's *Luther oder Erasmus*, I, xiv, in note 20 above.

belief in the special nature of the towns. Ozment expresses this notion when he asks whether Wittenberg was so different from Zürich, implying that all Protestant theology—Luther's included—was city-born and therefore in some sense "urban," or perhaps in some sense "bourgeois."[43] At this point we can identify what is surely the most damaging weakness of the whole literature, namely, the assumption of the political, social, and cultural uniqueness of the cities.

The unique historical character of the medieval European town as a forward-looking enclave in a sea of primitive feudal society is one of the finest creations of Liberal historiography, developed and nourished in various forms by Sismondi, Villari, Gierke, and Pirenne. Whether as a vision of the urban community as an island of freedom in an ocean of servitude,[44] or as a glorification of the enterprising spirit of medieval merchants as the forerunners of modern capitalism (Pirenne, Fritz Rörig), this belief—hallowed in the textbook cliché of "the rise of the middle classes"—has never entirely lost its luster. The recent literature, strongly revisionist on this point, sees the towns as creations of, and recognizable if transformed versions of the social forms of, feudal Europe. Nowhere is this tendency clearer than in recent views of Europe's earliest urban upheaval, the Italian communal movement. As Marvin Becker has put it:

> It would be well to recall that the city did not subvert the feudal order, but instead sought to insert itself into it. Further, it would be a gross error to believe that the commune scotched feudalism. Many of the feudal institutions were included as a part of the commune, with the norms of feudal law encompassed in the communal statutes.[45]

An extreme form of the same view is expressed by Otto Brunner:

> The constitution of the European city can be understood only in the total context of the "feudal" world, with which it was connected through its lord, the lord of the city. . . . Lordship and association are the basic forms of the older constitution. Although struggle occurred over the delimitation of their spheres of competence, yet all associative forms came to the fore within the bounds of lordship and even created elements of domina-

---

[43] Ozment, *Reformation in the Cities*, pp. 7–8.

[44] A moderate version of this position is taken by Edith Ennen, "Die Stadt zwischen Mittelalter und Gegenwart," *Rheinische Vierteljahrsblätter*, 30 (1965), 118–131, reprinted in *Die Stadt des Mittelalters*, ed. Carl Haase, I (Darmstadt, 1969), pp. 416–435, here at p. 422.

[45] Marvin B. Becker, "Some Common Features of Italian Urban Experience (c. 1200–1500)," *Medievalia et Humanistica*, N.S. 1 (1970), 197n8.

tion within their own area. The two structural principles are conceivable only together. Just those typical characteristics which differentiate the European city from the city-states of older civilizations are explicable only from the construction of the "feudal" world.[46]

Brunner, in his zeal to seal off pre-industrial Europe as a social whole and to preserve its memory from any contamination by modern concepts of the state and modern class relations, certainly goes much too far in seeing a harmonious relationship between towns and the larger feudal order.

Whether called "feudal" or "aristocratic," the remarkable tenacity and even revival of traditional, land-based social and political power in Europe is nowadays thoroughly recognized in the literature. Henry Kamen writes of the century after 1550, "The peculiar importance of the aristocracy and the gentry . . . lay at this time in their almost complete monopoly of political power and social position."[47] This is not to deny the existence, from the beginning, of an urban social moment potentially hostile to the feudal order. The cities were never—at least not since the inception of the communal movement—totally feudal in their institutions, their class systems, and their culture. In the German towns, a triple wave of revolt against established patterns of domination attests to the creation, by the freer economic conditions within the towns, of social forces contradictory to the simple division of society into rulers and ruled.

---

[46] Otto Brunner, "Europäisches Bauerntum," in his *Neue Wege der Verfassungs- und Sozialgeschichte*, 2nd ed. (Göttingen, 1968), pp. 199–212, here at p. 208.

[47] Henry Kamen, *The Iron Century. Social Change in Europe 1550–1650* (London-New York, 1972), p. 129. Despite efforts to exorcise the concept of feudalism from the historical vocabulary altogether (see Elizabeth A. R. Brown, "The Tyranny of a Concept: Feudalism and Historians of Medieval Europe," *AHR*, 79 [1974], 1063–1088), the tendency in the newer literature is to affirm the survival of feudal institutions through the Renaissance era. For France, see J. Russell Major, "The Crown and the Aristocracy in Renaissance France, in *Lordship and Community in Medieval Europe*, ed. Frederic Cheyette (New York, 1968), pp. 242–251, reprinted from *AHR*, 69 (1964); and for England, see R. B. Smith, *Land and Politics in the Reign of Henry VIII* (Oxford, 1970), pp. 43–61, 254–258. These works concern, however, the continuation of "feudal" institutions in the juridical sense of the term rather than feudal social formations; and the latter concept, despite the work of Marc Bloch, has met with indifferent acceptance among non-socialist historians. This is the main reason why there is no systematic historical sociology of what is sometimes called "Late Medieval and Renaissance" Europe. The only serious, coherent discussion of the class structure of late feudal society and the place of the urban bourgeoisie therein has taken place in the *ZfG*, 20 (1972), 21 (1973), and 22 (1974), a running discussion in which a large number of younger scholars of the German Democratic Republic took part. The discussion is an enviable achievement and one that should be continued.

After the communal movement and the movement of the guild revolts (fourteenth–fifteenth centuries), the third and final such upheaval comprised the urban plebeian participation in the anti-feudal outbursts of the late fifteenth and the sixteenth centuries—the beginnings of the urban reformation.[48] Down to the early sixteenth century at least, this ever renewed rebellion against the built-in structures of domination in the German cities is firm evidence of the continuing existence of an antagonism between urban society and the surrounding feudal order.

Much has been written about the easy flow of urban commercial wealth into the land and the movement of urban aristocrats into the nobility—what, looking at its social and political side, Fernand Braudel labelled "la trahison de la bourgeoisie."[49] The guilds, too, once seen as associations of equals embodying the principles of urban freedom, are now usually regarded as privileged corporations of promoters of monopoly.[50] We have come a long distance from the naive equations of feudalism with the land and capitalism with the cities. It is thus well to be reminded of the social and economic roots of an enduring urban "foreignness" in the late feudal world. This strangeness is most apparent at the uppermost and nethermost ends of the urban class system: at the top, where the merchants strove for "freie Kaufmannschaft" and for new investment opportunities in the interstices and protected monopolies which appeared in the feudal order, and at the bottom, where the urban plebs, unprotected by—even exploited by—the guild system, was driven with increasing frequency into free wage labor. In France, already in the early sixteenth century, there began to emerge in literature an image of the *bourgeois* with modern features, the bourgeois as the grasping

---

[48] Karl Czok, "Zur Stellung der Stadt in der deutschen Geschichte," *JRG*, 3 (1968), 9–33, here at pp. 16–18, by far the best overview.

[49] Fernand Braudel, *La méditerranée et le monde méditerranéen à l'époque de Philippe II*, 2nd ed., 2 vols. (Paris, 1966), II, 68. On the entire complex of issues that lurks behind this phrase, see now Immanuel Wallerstein, *The Modern World System. Capitalist Agriculture and the Origins of the European World-Economy in the Sixteenth Century* (New York-London, 1974), pp. 273–297. So far has revision moved on the feudal origins of capitalist society, that Barrington Moore, Jr., has argued that all post-feudal social formations (capitalism, socialism, fascism) are determined by different systems of relations between lords and peasants. See his *Social Origins of Dictatorship and Democracy: Lord and Peasant in the Modern World* (London-New York, 1974; 1st ed., 1966), esp. chapter 1.

[50] Reinald Ennen, *Zünfte und Wettbewerb. Möglichkeiten und Grenzen zünftlerischer Wettbewerbsbeschränkungen im städtischen Handel und Gewerbe des Spätmittelalters*, Neue Wirtschaftsgeschichte, 3 (Cologne-Vienna, 1971).

money-maker, unheedful of established social lines, rather than the bourgeois simply as town-dweller.[51]

Here is no space for an extended analysis of the place of urban communities in the late feudal society. It suffices to indicate here that the state of research—beyond all disputed questions, many of them fundamentally important—will not support the notion of the late medieval town (in Germany or elsewhere, self-governing or not) as a distinct society, politically, socially, and culturally (not to speak of economically) separate from the greater, essentially aristocratic (or neo-feudal), land-based society around it. The idea of urban self-sufficiency (temporal and sacral), therefore, requires a quite different type of analysis than what it has received at the hands of recent writers on the German urban reform. As descriptions of ideas held and promoted by urban lay and clerical leaders, the works discussed above—especially those of Moeller—have given good value. But as to the social roots and functions of the corporate ideal in urban history, these writers are silent. Silent, perhaps, because they believe the ideal to have been an adequate portrait of the basic structures of urban life. But the ideal of the sacral corporation not only ignored many aspects of urban life, it actually obscured and even denied the manifold dependency of the urban societies on the world outside the town. Nowhere is this more graphic than in Caspar Hedio's idealization of the city as a great ascetic community of love—a morally self-sufficient cosmic monastery.[52] It can hardly be doubted that this and other versions of the sacral corporate ideal devised by the German urban reformers drew, as Moeller has insisted, upon political and religious conceptions reaching well back into the pre-Reformation era. But that they represented the fundamental social ideal of "the people" may well be doubted.

The corporate ideal, whether in its urban or in its national form, was a typical expression of aristocratic political consciousness in Europe at the end of the Middle Ages and all through the early modern era. The

---

[51] Jean V. Alter, *Les origines de la satire anti-bourgeoise en France. Moyen âge-XVIe siècle,* Travaux d'Humanisme et Renaissance, 83 (Geneva, 1966), pp. 20–23, 109–112, 214–217.

[52] See Hedio's preface to his German version (dedicated to the regime and commune of Strasbourg) of Juan Luis Vives's "De subventione pauperum" (Strasbourg, 1533), reproduced by Otto Winckelmann, *Das Fürsorgewesen der Stadt Strassburg vor und nach der Reformation. Ein Beitrag zur deutschen Kultur- und Wirtschaftsgeschichte,* 2 vols., QFRG, V (Leipzig, 1922), II, 170–171, No. 118. Entirely in the same vein is his *Schwörtag* sermon of 14 January 1534 (Strasbourg, Johann Albrecht, 1534), of which an extract is reprinted in *TQ Strassburg,* II, 262–263, No. 492. See also Ozment, *Reformation in the Cities,* pp. 153–154.

ideal of society as a *communitas perfecta*, "while it may have reached down, in some form, to the lower levels of society, . . . was essentially the pre-serve of the dominant social and vocational groups in the state—nobles and gentry, urban patriciates, the lawyers, the clergy, the educated."[53] The urban corporate ideal thus belongs to the age of the rise and flourish-ing of self-governing towns, just as the national corporate ideal belongs to a succeeding age. In northern and central Italy, where the humanists early on constructed a neo-classical *paideia* for the urban aristocracies, the corporate ideal came to be expressed in a classical, rather than a Christian, idiom.[54] At Florence, however, the original home of this "civic humanism," the refashioned ideal of classical republicanism co-existed with a popular, Guelfic form of corporate patriotism, whose millennialism grew out of Christian rather than classical sources.[55]

The cities of the Holy Roman Empire were less independent, politically weaker, and smaller in size than their Italian counterparts, and neo-classicism made few permanent inroads into German urban culture before the Reformation. The corporate ideology of the German cities understandably maintained a more traditional, Christian flavor. The ideal of civic Christianity, however, is nearly an exact analogue to the Italian ideal of civic humanism, although the concepts of virtues to be emulated, appropriated, and practiced are quite different.[56] The sacral corporatism of the Reformation era, like Italian civic humanism, was a

---

[53] J. H. Elliott, "Revolution and Continuity in Early Modern Europe," *Past & Present*, No. 42 (February 1969), 35–56, here at pp. 48–49.

[54] *Ibid.*, p. 50. See now J. G. A. Pocock, *The Machiavellian Moment: Florentine Political Thought and the Atlantic Republican Tradition* (Princeton, 1975), pp. 83–103, developing the line of study of "civic humanism" begun by Hans Baron in preliminary studies to and in his major work, *The Crisis of the Early Italian Renaissance* (1st ed., Princeton, 1955; 2nd ed., 1966).

[55] Donald Weinstein, *Savonarola and Florence: Prophecy and Patriotism in the Renaissance* (Princeton, 1970), pp. 35–66. It is easy to forget, given the elegant secular gleam of civic humanism, that an intensely patriotic civic Christianity flourished in the Italian city-states at the same time. See David Herlihy, *Medieval and Renaissance Pistoia. The Social History of an Italian Town, 1200–1430* (New Haven-London, 1967), pp. 257–258; Marvin B. Becker, "Aspects of Lay Piety in Early Renaissance Florence," in *The Pursuit of Holiness*, pp. 177–199, here at pp. 185–197.

[56] The entire literature on Florentine civic humanism has been subjected to a searching critique from the standpoint of historical-political realism by Peter Herde, "Politische Verhaltensweisen der Florentiner Oligarchie 1382–1402," in *Geschichte und Verfas-sungsgefüge. Frankfurter Festschrift für Walter Schlesinger*, Frankfurter Historische Abhandlungen, 5 (Wiesbaden, 1973), pp. 156–249, here at pp. 156–161, where Herde charges the (overwhelmingly American) literature with ignoring foreign (especially German) criticism and with mythologizing the Florentine republic in an idealist sense.

solution to the dualism of purpose (spiritual-temporal) and power (clerical-lay) which had so troubled the lay aristocracies of medieval Europe. Two solutions to this tension, each with its peculiar concept of freedom, permitted the urban society to be viewed as a morally independent actor in history: the Italian solution of secularizing public life (civic humanism); and the German one of sacralizing it (sacral corporatism). The former solution projects the unified urban society into a history ruled by *fortuna*, the latter into a history ruled by the Christian God; but both solutions make of the urban society a new kind of historical entity, an internally integrated, externally independent collective actor. The city becomes, in a word, a nation.

It is true enough that the "myth of civic spirituality"[57] served well the immediate political needs of Zwingli, Bucer, and the other urban reformers; but the ideal of the sacral commune also represents the theological counterpart of the alliance they made with the urban regimes during the great crisis of 1524–25.[58] It is quite true that the integration of Evangelical religion into urban corporate ideology was not total, both for theological reasons (Luther's doctrine of justification was incompatible with the notion of collective salvation) and political ones (the reformers' drive to reconstruct ecclesiastical authority). The integration was nonetheless complete enough in the early, crucial stages to leave the urban reformers helpless before a rising tide of practical Erastianism, a tide they themselves had done much to foster.[59]

This discussion has tried to show the discontinuity between the sacral corporate ideal and the situation of the pre-Reformation town, especially in South Germany, and to suggest the political and social conditions which made such an idealized compound of real social vision and political propaganda both useful and popular. The subject leads to two, much larger questions. In the first place, the study of the literary/theological sources and the analysis of the various forms of the corporate ideal are fundamental to any explanation of the urban reform in Germany —but they also lead far beyond the history of the German towns, into

---

[57] The apt phrase is from James M. Kittelson, "Wolfgang Capito, the Council and Reform Strasbourg," *ARG*, 63 (1972), 126–140, here at pp. 136–137.

[58] Sigrid Loosz, "Butzer und Capito in ihrem Verhältnis zu Bauernkrieg und Täufertum," in *Weltwirkung der Reformation*, eds. Max Steinmetz and Gerhard Brendler, 2 vols. (Berlin, 1969), I, 226–232; and Kittelson, *Wolfgang Capito*, pp. 120–122, who attacks (p. 122n20) but does not refute Loosz's argument. In point of fact, Mathis Zell would have made a better case study than either Bucer or Capito.

[59] A point recognized by Moeller, "Die Kirche in den evangelischen freien Städten Oberdeutschlands," pp. 159–161.

the beginnings of national consciousness in Europe.[60] Secondly, there arises the question of social structures, those social formations which were partly revealed, partly disguised by the sacral corporate ideal. The historical meaning of a social ideal cannot be judged if its relation to real social structures is unknown. In other words, the significance of the corporate ideal can be gauged only by an understanding of what the objective, unidealized city was, a question not of social theology but of historical sociology.

B.   Estates and Classes: Historical Sociology and the Age of the Reformation

1. Understanding late medieval urban society in both its structural and its dynamic aspects requires, above all, adequate conceptual tools, of which the categories of social stratification are doubtless the most important. On this ground has been renewed in the historical literature one of the deadliest struggles of the nineteenth century. When, in the post-Napoleonic era, the Liberal social theorists advanced a holistic social theory based on the doctrine of classes, the Conservatives (Le Maistre, Stahl, Adam Müller) counterattacked with the romantic concept of the *Ständestaat*, the society of patriarchal, hierarchial order, in which each social stratum had its place ordained by God or by Nature.[61] While in our own century the doctrine of classes has step-by-step invaded ever more regions of historical thought, including thought about the structure and meaning of pre-modern European history, there has arisen to meet this new challenge a renewed version of the doctrine of the *Ständestaat*, the *société des ordres*. The main battery in this counterattack is Roland Mousnier, who has advanced in a most aggressive form his historical sociology of pre-modern Europe in categories of estates (*ordres*).

---

[60] The sacral corporate ideal was translatable from the urban context to that of the territorial monarchy, just as the Italian ideal of civic activism was (see Pocock, *Machiavellian Moment*, pp. 335ff.). Martin Bucer, one of the creators of the Reformation version of the ideal of the urban sacral corporation, had surprisingly little difficulty in translating it (during his English exile, 1549–51) into the context of the English kingdom, the result being his *De regno Christi*. On this subject, see Helmut Kressner, *Schweizer Ursprünge des anglikanischen Staatskirchentums*, SVRG, No. 170 (Gütersloh, 1953).

[61] Robert M. Berdahl, "The *Stände* and the Origins of Conservatism in Prussia," *Eighteenth Century Studies*, 6 (1972–73), 298–321, here at pp. 311–315.

> In the stratification into orders or into "estates," the social groups form
> hierarchies not according to the wealth of their members and their
> capacity to consume, not according to their roles in the production of
> material goods, but according to the prestige, honor, and dignity
> attached by society to social functions which have no necessary con-
> nection with the production of goods, such as the profession of arms or
> the vocation of the educated man to the magistracies.[62]

Precisely the same conception flourishes on the other side of the Atlantic,
as witness this passage from a monograph on the Knights' Revolt of 1522:

> In fact, the very word "class" is suspect when used in this period, for it is
> a term peculiar to an "acquisitive society." The word "estate," . . . which
> was familiar to Luther's contemporaries, included more than the amassing
> of wealth. The "estate" was a "way of life," a complex of cultural factors
> emphasizing tradition and custom and hence far richer in content than
> the concept of "class." The way of life of an estate, including its privileges
> and duties and its social prestige, was not bound entirely to its fortune.
> The former was not gained solely through the latter nor entirely lost
> by its absence. It might be interesting to compare, in this respect, the
> flexibility of the older "estates" with the newer "classes."[63]

The principal theoretical defects of this conception are not direct
consequences of its political intent; for, as Robert Mandrou has pointed
out, the widespread notion that this position is politically neutral, while
the class-oriented historical sociology of Marxist and other historians
is politically committed, is patently false. The pseudo-positivism, writes
Mandrou, of those who try to banish the concepts of class and class

---

[62] Roland Mousnier, "Présentation," in *Problèmes de stratification sociale. Actes du
colloque international (1966)*, ed. Roland Mousnier, Publications de la Faculté des Lettres
et Sciences Humaines de Paris-Sorbonne, série "Recherches," 43 (Paris, 1968), p. 8.
In the discussion, Karl Bosl (Munich) objected (p. 27) that "la seule histoire des notions
ne nous conduirait pas à une interprétation entièrement satisfaisante de la réalité
historique." Bosl's own writings are, indeed, far less romantic and more realistic than
those of the Mousnier school. See, for example, Bosl's "Kasten, Stände, Klassen im
mittelalterlichen Deutschland," in his *Die Gesellschaft in der Geschichte des Mittelalters*,
2nd ed. rev., Kleine Vandenhoeck-Reihe, 231/231a (Göttingen, 1966; also in *ZBLG*,
52 [1969]). This is the German version of his contribution to Mousnier's colloquium
and may be read in French in *Problèmes de stratification sociale*, pp. 13–29.

[63] William R. Hitchcock, *The Background of the Knights' Revolt, 1522–1523*, University
of California Publications in History, 61 (Berkeley-Los Angeles, 1958), p. 82. Now
common in American scholarship, this dubious estates-classes contrast seems to be
gaining strength. Harold J. Grimm, for example, who wrote about urban "classes"
in 1962, by 1969 denied that classes had existed in the sixteenth century. See his "Social
Forces in the German Reformation," *CH*, 31 (1962), 3–12, here at p. 12; and "The
Reformation and the Urban Social Classes in Germany," pp. 76ff.

conflict from all periods before the nineteenth century, "reflects a solid political conservatism." It idealizes the image of the Old Regime

> as a refuge and a consolation in face of the ills of the contemporary world; it claims to define social relations within a double framework of entirely adequate juridical definitions—those of orders, and that of a paternalism which is pronounced perfectly legitimate in a hierarchical society: the lord protects his peasants, the king protects his fair cities and his good citizens, the master artisan his journeymen . . .[64]

The chief defects of this historical sociology lie, rather, in two fundamental assumptions, both demonstrably false: in the first place the assumption that "classes" and "estates" are two mutually exclusive types of social formation, the one purely economic and the other rooted in privilege, esteem, and honor—in a word, in juridical and largely subjective categories; and, secondly, that because the concept of social class—the division of society into two, at least potentially hostile, social groups—was unknown before the recent era, there were no social classes before the nineteenth century.

2. There are two major objections to the position of estates *rather than* classes, one theoretical and one empirical. The theoretical objection is based on the inadequacy of estate theory as a complete historical sociology. Its great defect is that, like every form of true structuralism, it has a fatal propensity for synchronism and a corresponding inability to explain major social (i.e., structural) change. This can be easily seen if a model of society of estates is made to function as a tool of historical analysis. Such a society, as C. B. Macpherson has pointed out in his picture of "customary or status society," allots (by custom or compulsion) the productive and regulative work within the society to discrete social groups (crudely, laborers and masters), neither of which can invade the province of the other in a regular way. This is another way of saying that there is a free market neither in land nor in labor, no arena of competition in which individuals and groups could win the material basis for wholesale changes in their social statuses. Politics, competition, in such a society can embrace only struggles among the masters for a greater share of the total social product extracted from the laborers, but the sum total (or at least the proportion) of the social product extracted cannot be significantly expanded without running the risk of

---

[64] Robert Mandrou, *Introduction à la France moderne. Essai de psychologie historique 1500–1640*, L'évolution de l'humanité, 52 (Paris, 1961), pp. 138–139.

massive resistance in the form of insurrections to protect and restore customary social relations.[65]

It is true enough that this model of a "status society" reproduces some features of medieval European social relations, but it is just as true that nothing like the stasis required by this model was ever achieved. From about the twelfth century onward, the development of market agriculture in Europe fuelled basic alterations in feudal obligations and thus in social relations. One result was the flourishing of the towns and all they represented. Here, where the lines of subordination and domination were more abstract (at least since the rise of the communes) than on the land, typical class relations appear in clearer, bolder relief, stripped of much of the disguising overlay of old-fashioned juridical categories. It is thus tempting to identify the towns with classes and the countryside with estates,[66] a temptation that ought to be resisted. For town and land formed a single society that was not fundamentally threatened by the growth of trade. As Wallerstein has written, "Feudalism as a system should not be thought of as something antithetical to trade. On the contrary, up to a certain point, feudalism and the expansion of trade go hand in hand."[67] By far the most impressive proof, however, of the inadequacy of an historical sociology constructed of estate categories to the history of late medieval Europe is the development—beginning around 1350 and lasting for nearly two hundred years—of a state of endemic social warfare between lords and their labor force, between seigneurs and peasants—but also, it should be noted, between dominators and dominated in the towns.[68] This social warfare was rooted in a

---

[65] C. B. Macpherson, *The Political Theory of Possessive Individualism; from Hobbes to Locke* (Oxford, 1962), pp. 49–50. See Wilhelm Schwer, *Stand und Ständeordnung im Weltbild des Mittelalters. Die geistes- und gesellschaftsgeschichtlichen Grundlagen der berufsständischen Idee*, Görres-Gesellschaft, Sektion für Wirtschafts- und Sozialwissenschaft, 7, 2nd ed. (Paderborn, 1952), p. 6, who contrasts the static character of estate structures with the dynamic character of class structures in an unusually clear manner.

[66] As Oliver C. Cox does in his otherwise admirable *Class, Caste and Race; a Study in Social Dynamics* (New York, 1959), here at p. 146. See the unusual schematic diagram of class and estate structures in feudal society by Johanna Maria van Winter, *Rittertum. Ideal und Wirklichkeit*, trans. from the Dutch by Axel Plantiko and Paul Schritt (Munich, 1969), pp. 80–88.

[67] Wallerstein, *Modern World System*, p. 20.

[68] See esp. Michel Mollat and Philippe Wolff, *Ongles bleus, Jacques et Ciompi. Les révolutions populaires en Europe aux XIVe et XVe siècles* (Paris, 1970), now in English as *The popular revolutions of the late Middle Ages* (London, 1973). See also the analysis of the Ciompi revolt by Achatz Freiherr von Müller, "Ständekampf oder Revolution? Die Ciompi Bewegung in Florenz," in *Ansichten einer künftigen Geschichtswissenschaft*, 2: *Revolution—ein historischer Langschnitt*, eds. Immanuel Geiss and Rainer Tamchina

general crisis of the feudal order,[69] in which the social relations typical of the second age of feudalism (eleventh-thirteenth centuries) underwent systemic disintegration. When, as during the fourteenth and most of the fifteenth century, change and not stability is the dominant condition of social relations, such an age is relatively impervious to the static historical sociology of estates. For, except for natural causes (climate, disease) and disruption from without (invasion, cross-cultural influence), estate theory has no tools to explain large-scale historical change.

Estates did exist as social groupings in feudal Europe, they developed especially from the twelfth century onward, and they were typical phenomena of the late feudal age. The clue to the meaning of estate schemes as they appear in the late medieval sources is that estates, properly taken, embraced only those groups that participated in the structures of domination. The estates which appeared all over Europe and which found their typical and unparalleled institutional expression in the assemblies of estates which form one of the hallmarks of late medieval history,[70] these estates were in the first instance groupings of lords, of those who shared in power over others. This fact has been sometimes obscured by modern writers who conceive estates in terms of contemporary functionalist social theory, a task made much easier by calling upon those late medieval writers who employed anatomical metaphors to explain the relationships of the various estates to one another and to the society as a whole.[71] In the German territories, the development of estates goes hand-in-hand with the construction and expansion of the power of the territorial princes. It was then, for example, and not during the High Middle Ages or even earlier, that the lesser nobility (the *Ritter und Edelknechte*) was forged from the most various elements into the readily identifiable estate it was to form all through the

---

(Munich, 1974), pp. 34–75, which is relevant to the entire question of class conflict in pre-modern Europe.

[69] Frantisek Graus, *Das Spätmittelalter als Krisenzeit*, Medievalia Bohemica, I, Supplementum 1 (Prague, 1969); and Ernst Werner, "Spätmittelalterlicher Struktur-wandel im Spiegel neuer Forschungen: Das italienische Beispiel," *Jahrbuch für Wirt-schaftsgeschichte*, 1969, pp. 223–240.

[70] Although in some regions—France, Spain, Sicily, and Flanders—the assemblies themselves antedate the division into estates, which tends to support the view that the estates represented not different parts of the population but different sectors of the "notables."

[71] Joachim Bumke, *Studien zum Ritterbegriff im 12. und 13. Jahrhundert*, "Euphorion," Beiheft 1 (Heidelberg, 1964), pp. 138–144.

early modern era.[72] In the same period, that is to say, after 1250, the typical urban social formations also appear, the commune and its division into the estates of patricians (*Honoratioren, Ehrbarkeiten*) and guildsmen (*Handwerker*). Among the aristocrats the principle of birth as the chief gateway into an estate undoubtedly always played some part—hence the development of the pseudo-biological theory of nobility of the blood in Castile and the mania for genealogy almost everywhere—but the normative principle in estate formation and maintenance of privilege was and remained the degree and form of participation in the system of lordship, of domination over other men. This was seen already by Thomas Aquinas, whose trifold scheme divides men into those who have power (the nobles), those who do not (the commons), and those in between (the *populus honorabilis*).[73] Medieval estates were not occupational status groups (*Berufsstände*),[74] a misconception which rests not least upon the tendency to view medieval societies in functionalist terms.

3. The citation of Thomas Aquinas leads from the topic of social structures to its complement, social consciousness. By "social consciousness" is meant here the variety of forms (more or less schematized) of awareness of social stratification. The importance of the topic here lies in the oft-repeated assertion that the concept of class formation—that is, the division of society into two (simple or complex), naturally antagonistic and at least potentially hostile social groups, based *ultimately* on the social division of labor—was quite unknown to Europeans before its fateful discovery by certain thinkers of the nineteenth century. Furthermore, class consciousness is sometimes said to be incompatible with the enduring characteristics—custom, privilege, the gradations of honor—of pre-modern social institutions. Theoretically, as Stanislas Ossowski has argued, there is no compelling reason why radically different forms of social consciousness cannot co-exist in one and the same society.[75]

---

[72] For which Otto von Gierke, with his stress on the organic theory of medieval society, may be largely responsible. *Das deutsche Genossenschaftsrecht*, III, 546–557.

[73] *Summa Theologiae*, I, qu. 108, art. 2. See Schwer, *Stand und Ständeordnung*, p. 35: "Völlig unbefangen erkennen Thomas von Aquin und mit ihm die anderen mittelalterlichen Theologen die Zweiteilung der Menschheit in Herrschende und Dienende auf Grund natürlicher Vorausbestimmung an. . . ."

[74] See Bumke, *Studien zum Ritterbegriff*, p. 138, but long ago (1st ed., 1934) anticipated by Schwer. On the literature of medieval estate theory, see also Ruth Mohls, *The Three Estates in Medieval and Renaissance Literature* (New York, 1933).

[75] Stanislaw Ossowski, *Class Structure in the Social Consciousness*, trans. Sheila Patterson (London-New York, 1963), pp. 65–66, by far the best theoretical work on the subject.

More specifically, two-, three- or multi-level estate schemes, arranged in a graduated hierarchy of privilege (and perhaps even cemented with the comforting functionalist notion of harmony), could and did co-exist in pre-modern Europe with dichotomous schemes built on a principle of antagonism and (at least potential) social warfare. The subdivisions of one scheme may very well overlap those of the other, so that the first term in the class-oriented pairs—rich and poor, rulers and ruled, honorable and dishonorable—might embrace groups on both sides of the estate line that divided nobles from commoners. In such a society, Ossowski believes, class consciousness will predominate at the top and at the bottom of the social order, while those in between will tend to think of themselves and others in terms of the estate hierarchy and will therefore also accept the harmonious, "everything in its proper place" mentality which goes with it.[76]

The schemes of estates themselves can be rather deceptive. The classic forms, such as the three-fold division of society into *oratores*, *bellatores*, and *laboratores*, probably never had much practical significance and certainly had little or none by the sixteenth century.[77] The literary tradition of social classification contains, in fact, a bewildering variety of *principles* of social distinction, such as divisions of society into the estates of men and women, clergy and laity, not only among different authors but in one and the same author.[78] When the sixteenth century is reached, estate schemes often become either extremely florid or very crude, without in either case attaining a consistency in norms of classi-fication. François de Corlieu, for example, in his *Briefe instruction pour tous estats* (Paris, 1558, pp. 66ff.), discerns no less than twenty-one "ordres," ranging from "les rois et princes," "les pasteurs et ministres," and "les médicins," through "le mari," "la femme" and "les enfants," down to "les malades" and "les laboreurs."[79] This scheme betrays not so much a complex social consciousness as a lack of any conceptual integrity. On the other side, there is the very simple but also inconsistent scheme advocated by Thomas Lindner (Tilianus), author of a catechism composed (1546) for use in the South German town of Ravensburg: "Nemlich das Predig-Amt, die weltliche Obrigkeit und der Ehestand.

---

[76] *Ibid.*, p. 67, already perceived by Botero and Bodin in the late sixteenth century (see below, notes 96–97).

[77] Mandrou, *Introduction à la France moderne*, p. 139.

[78] See Mohls, *The Three Estates*, pp. 8–9, who maintains nonetheless that estate theory appears only in a feudal context.

[79] Arlette Jouanna, "Recherches sur la notion d'honneur au XVIème siècle," *RHMC*, 15 (1968), 600.

Dann dise Staende haben Gottes Wort vor sich und alle andere Staende darein gefasset."[80] If, to Corlieu's scheme we may add Robert Mandrou's remark that "the order, from this time onward, no longer had the social importance attributed to them by the strictest of the jurists,"[81] then to Lindner's text we can only add Otto Brunner's comment that "the theoretical literature of the Middle Ages needs first to be related to the historical reality from which it derived."[82]

On the other side, there is the ancient and rich tradition of class consciousness, the literary expressions of which lie, since the High Middle Ages at least, at every hand. The dichotomous scheme of society —lords and subjects, rich and poor, gentlemen and commons—was by the fourteenth century as common as the better-known trichotomous harmonic conception of three (or more), functionally related, divinely ordained estates. The dichotomous model came in two versions, an aristocratic and an anti-aristocratic, popular one, each recognizing the same social fact but giving different explanations for the fact and different (and opposed) moral interpretation of it. The social fact is the fundamental division of society into two kinds of persons. In the popular view, subjects and lords are at the same time producers and parasites. An English preacher of the fourteenth century, for example, spoke on behalf of the poor, charging the rich before God's throne:

> Our labors and goods . . . they took away, to satiate their greed. They afflicted us with hunger and labors, that they might live delicately upon our labors and our goods. We have labored and lived so hard a life that scarce for half a year had we a good sufficiency, scarce nothing save bread and bran and water. Nay, rather, what is worse, we died of hunger. And they were served with three or four courses out of our goods, which they took from us . . .[83]

How this situation came about is explained by the ploughman in his polemic against the knight in the sixteenth-century English dialogue, "Of Gentleness and Nobility," probably written by the London lawyer, John Rastell (d. 1536).[84] The ploughman, in the sacred verse of the great

---

[80] Ernst-Wilhelm Kohls, ed., *Die Evangelischen Katechismen von Ravensburg 1546/1733 und Reichemweier 1547/1559*, VKLBW, A 10 (Stuttgart, 1963), p. 53.

[81] Mandrou, *Introduction à la France moderne*, p. 139.

[82] Otto Brunner, *Land und Herrschaft. Grundfragen der territorialen Verfassungsgeschichte Österreichs im Mittelalter*, 4th ed. rev. (Vienna-Wiesbaden, 1959), p. 399.

[83] Norman Cohn, *The Pursuit of the Millenium*, 2nd ed. (New York, 1961), pp. 213–214.

[84] The text is printed with *The Spider and the Fly*, ed. John S. Farmer (London, 1908). I quote from Mohls, *The Three Estates*, who discusses the problem of attribution on p. 17. Rastell married Elizabeth More, Thomas's sister.

tradition of social warfare against the lords, sings of the golden age of equality:

> For then Adam delved and Eve span,
> Who was then a gentleman?
> But then came the churl and gatherèd good,
> And there began first the gentle blood;
> And I think verily ye do believe
> That we came all of Adam and Eve.[85]

Then came the fall, as the parasites began to steal from their brethren, the producers:

> For when people first began to increase,
> Some gave themselves all to idleness,
> And would not labour, but take by violence
> That other men gat by labour and diligence.
> Then they that laboured were fain to give
> Them part of their gettings in peace to live,
> Or else for their lands, money a portion;
> So possession begun by extortion.[86]

Lordship is founded in property, property began by extortion and theft.

The lord's reply to Rastell's ploughman affirms the same social distinction—between lords and people—but explains the origin and purpose of the distinction in the manner typical of all aristocratic political theory. The development of lords out of the original equality was a measure taken by the people for their own good, establishing over themselves a group of peacemakers whose virtue they recognized and rewarded with lands and incomes:

> The people, perceiving then their goodness,
> Their great wit, discretion, and gentleness,
> Were content to give them part of the profit
> Coming of their lands, which they did get,
> As corn, cattle and such things as they won.
> But after, when that coin of money began,
> They changed those revenues, and were content
> To give them in money an annual rent.
> So for their good and virtuous conditions
> They came first to lands and possessions;
> So possessions began, and were first found
> Upon a good and reasonable ground.[87]

---

[85] Mohls, *The Three Estates*, p. 290.

[86] *Ibid.*

[87] *Ibid.*, p. 291.

Lordship is rooted in the common good; the rich have their wealth by common consent and for the good of the entire society; the dignity and honor of gentlemen has been well earned and not unjustly seized. Here, in one simple poem, far from the artful archaisms and subtly constructed social pyramids of the lawyers, the entire inner meaning of the late feudal order is laid bare.

It is important to remember that the aristocratic form of class consciousness was just as strong and just as well cultivated as the popular form. The debate between the two revolved about the most ancient of social questions, the origin and meaning of social inequality.[88] A particularly vicious poetic form of the aristocratic explanation circulated in Germany before and during the Reformation. Its literary source is the sixth eclogue of the bestselling Italian poet, Baptista Mantuanus (1448–1516), cast and recast by German poets and writers, notably Hans Sachs (1494–1576) and Erasmus Alber (ca. 1500–53). This is the story of the children of Adam and Eve, the beautiful and the ugly ones. The basic story is that Eve showed her beautiful children to God, who blessed them and ordained them to estates of high degree—kings, princes, knights, rich townsmen, merchants, and learned doctors. When Eve finally brought forward her dirty, ragged, ugly children, of whom she was ashamed (the dishonor and shame of poverty and subjection are therefore fixed in the *natural* social order), God laughed at them; but, out of pity, He also blessed them and ordained for them all the servile crafts, trades, and estates.[89] Here, in a story laced with the ugliest form of humor, derision, all who could read were taught—to their satisfaction or disappointment—that lordship and subjection, wealth and poverty, honor and dishonor, were part of God's law for human society. Especially satisfied must have been the German big bourgeoisie, for whom Hans Sachs cast into verse no less than four versions of this story.[90] In his *Meisterlied* of 1546, Sachs has God's reply to Eve's query

---

[88] *Ibid.*, pp. 91–95.

[89] *Ibid.*, discussing and quoting texts of Hans Sachs, who worked this theme three times in 1553 and once in 1558. This fable, which came to Germany in Baptista Mantuanus's "Eclogues" (ca. 1470), was especially popular in Philipp Melanchthon's version (1539) and especially beloved of Protestant poets and dramatists. Besides Sachs, at least seven other Protestant writers produced pieces based on this fable between 1539 and 1559. Helmut De Boor and Richard Newald, eds., *Geschichte der deutschen Literatur von den Anfängen bis zur Gegenwart*, IV, 2: *Das Zeitalter der Reformation 1520–1570*, by Hans Rupprich (Munich, 1973), pp. 350–351.

[90] Mohls, *The Three Estates*, pp. 92–93.

as to why children of the same parents—brothers and sisters in every sense—should be treated so differently:

> Got sprach: "es stet in meiner hant,
> das ich im lant
> mit leuten muss besetzen ein ieglichen stant,
> dazu ich dan leut auserwel
> und iedem stant seines geleichen leut zu stel,
> auf das niemant
> gebrech, was man sol han."
> Also durch dise fabel wirt bedeute,
> das man zu iedem stant noch findet leute;
> dabei man spuret heute,
> wie got so wunderbar regieret,
> mit weisheit ziert, er ordiniert
> zu iedem werk sein man.[91]

But, and here was the crucial point for Sach's audience, the rich and powerful, the lords of every kind, were the descendants of the beautiful children, the merchant as well as the king or the knight or the prince—a fundamental unity far beyond any such quarrels over status such as the knights might bring against the urban rich. Here is an estate scheme resting lightly on top of a basic class consciousness—a class system within an estate system. That such complex social schemes were fairly common among German writers of this period could be easily shown.[92]

Gradually this sort of social realism penetrated all levels of social and political theory. In France, as late as 1484, Philippe de Poitiers could repeat the traditional wisdom about the social order:

> Everyone knows how the commonwealth is divided into members and estates: the clergy to pray for the others, to counsel, to exhort; the nobility to protect the others by arms; and the people to nourish and sustain the nobles and clergy with payments and produce.[93]

And another French writer, Georges Chastellain (1405–75), maintained that the composition of such estates was fixed by divine decree. Some years later, however, Claude de Seyssel (d. 1520) thoughtfully allowed that the clergy were not a separate social group but were common to

---

[91] *Ibid.* On the social content of Sach's poetry, see J. Münch, *Die sozialen Anschauungen des Hans Sachs in seinen Fastnachtspielen* (Erlangen, 1936).

[92] See the complicated catalogue of "estates" in *Des Teufels Netz* (ca. 1415–18), discussed by Mohls, *The Three Estates*, pp. 88–89.

[93] This and the following French texts are quoted and discussed by P. S. Lewis, *Later Medieval France: The Polity* (London-New York, 1968), pp. 167–170, whose discussion of social consciousness is unusually good.

all levels of society, and that the possibility of social mobility—the ascent of individuals from the lower into the higher ranks of society— was the surest specific against rebellion and social warfare.[94]

The discarding of traditional categories began earliest and proceeded most rapidly in Italy, where the recovery of classical literature combined with indigenous culture to provide the North Italians with a rich and varied material for political thought; and the turbulent history of the peninsula gave them plenty of stimulus to think about social and political forms in new and critical ways. Most sophisticated is the political sociology of Niccolò Machiavelli (1469–1527), who not only used the dichotomous, conflict-immanent scheme exclusively but was able as well to differentiate the class systems of heavily feudal regions (where there were many "gentlemen," a "gentleman" being one who enjoys direct power over others) and the looser, more egalitarian social systems of the cities.[95] It was left to writers of the later sixteenth century, however, to discover the importance for political stability of those persons who belonged neither clearly to the rich and powerful nor clearly to the poor and weak—the middling element. Jean Bodin (d. 1590), a French apostle of order, launched a vigorous defense of class society, for, he argued against Plato and Sir Thomas More, "equality of possessions is subversive of the commonwealth," for the preservation of which it is necessary that "the poor, the weak, and the unprotected defer to and obey their betters, the rich and the powerful, most willingly, with a view to their assistance, and the advantages they hope will accrue."[96] The problem is that such a sharp division engenders social hatred and therefore instability, so that it is dangerous not to have an "intermediate position between the rich and the poor, the good and the bad, the wise and the foolish." Giovanni Botero, rather less of an apologist for order, argued a little later (1589) that society is divided among the rich, the poor, and those who lie between the extremes; the latter are "usually the quietest and easiest to govern."[97] The middling folk are thus seen to be

---

[94] Claude de Seyssel, *La monarchie de France*, ed. J. Poujol (Paris, 1961), p. 127.

[95] *Discorsi*, I, 55. See Alfredo Bonadeo, "The Role of the 'Grandi' in the Political World of Machiavelli," *Studies in the Renaissance*, 16 (1969), 9–30; *idem*, "The Role of the People in the Works and Times of Machiavelli," *Bibliothèque d'Humanisme et Renaissance*, 32 (1970), 351–378.

[96] Jean Bodin, *Six Books of the Commonwealth*, Book 5, chapter 2 (trans. M. J. Tooley [Oxford, n.d.], pp. 158–159).

[97] Giovanni Botero, *The Reason of State*, Book IV, chapter 2 (trans. P. J. Waley and D. P. Waley [New Haven-London, 1956], pp. 82–83), a text pointed out by William

the key to social peace and civil order, as they tend to check the greater propensities to violence of the rich and the poor.

It is clear, therefore, that, well before Thomas Hobbes thought out the first general social theory based on the principle of the free market that every person may freely compete with and challenge the power of every other, without the restraints of chartered privilege, customary law, or even of religion, the ability to conceive the social order in terms of classes and social tension and antagonism had already become a well-established feature even of formal political theory. Among the common people, it was probably as old as the feudal order itself. Certainly, conceptions of society in terms of hierarchies of estates continued to flourish, just as estates themselves continued to exist right down to the opening of the modern era and, in some places, well beyond. But the existence of such schemes does not prove that the society of the Old Regime was a "société des ordres" alone. Against the subtle classifications of the lawyer Loyseau, the darling of the "société des ordres" literature, one may place the clean, razor-edged rage of the parish priest of Estrepigny, Jean Méslier (ca. 1711):

> une si étrange et si odieuse disproportion entre les differen etats et conditions des hommes, qui met, comme on le voit manifestement, toute l'autorité, tous les biens, tous les plaisirs, tous les contentements, toutes les richesses et même l'oisivité du côté des grands, des riches et des nobles, et met du côté des pauvres peuples tout ce qu'il ya de pénible et de facheux, savoir la dépendance, les soins, la misère, les inquiétudes, toutes les peines et toutes les fatigues du travail; laquelle disproportion est d'autant plus injuste et odieuse, qu'elle les met dans une entière dépendance des nobles et des riches, et qu'elle les rend pour ainsi dire leur esclaves, jusques-là qu'ils sont obligé de souffrir non seulement toutes leurs rebufades, leurs mépris et leurs injures, mais aussi leurs véxations, leurs injustices et leurs mauvais traitement.[98]

4. Thus far, the tendency of the argument is that class analysis is the form of historical sociology best suited—both from the standpoint of social structure and from that of social consciousness—to the serious study of social formations and social relations in late medieval and Renaissance Europe, including the urban ones. Several traditional

---

J. Bowsky, "The Anatomy of Rebellion in Fourteenth Century Siena: from Commune to Signory?" in *Violence and Civil Disorder in Italian Cities, 1200–1500*, ed. Lauro Martines (Berkeley-Los Angeles, 1972), p. 270.

[98] *Le testament de Jean Méslier* (Amsterdam, 1864), II, 178, as quoted by Ossowski, *Class Structure*, p. 24n1.

objections to the employment of class analysis in studies of the pre-modern era may well require some replies. First, there is the objection that classes are "economic classes," and they reduce the rich multiplicity of social relationships to economic relationships only. To this it may be replied that social class is not a thing or even a characteristic but a relationship between two or more groups of persons which form a complete social formation; its parts, though analytically distinguishable and susceptible to separate study, exist in a state of tension which is part of the definition of each class. Thus, to speak of "economic classes" is highly misleading, for the class system, whose *ultimate ground* is the structure of the economy, will, except in times of full structural crisis, embrace every aspect of life, including politics and culture. Political power and cultural domination are not just "mirrors" of some more fundamental relationship but are constituent parts of the relations among social classes. The political structure forms the primary societal controls, the culture the primary context of self-understanding and self-definition. In "normal" times, despite the existence of standing antagonisms which point to potential conflict, the political system maintains its control and elicits patriotism, and the cultural system maintains its hegemonical effectiveness and elicits conventional piety.

A second objection, and one that has an apparent legitimacy, is to the tendency of "Marxising" historians to identify the classes of pre-industrial society with those of the age of industrial capitalism, finding the first bourgeois in every merchant and the first proletariat in every group of the urban poor.[99] Against this tendency must be said, once more it seems, that the class systems of feudal, or "late feudal" or "pre-capitalist" Europe were not those of the age of industrial capitalism, and that the confrontation and definition of classes was neither so conscious nor so precise as in the modern era. Here the structural approach, with its bias for the synchronic, the enduring, has much to contribute. The estate model of society, with its total innocence of the forces of change, is *one type* of such structural analysis that is particularly appropriate to pre-capitalist European societies, because the organization into estates was one of the features of those societies. On the negative side, feudal societies lacked the distinction between state and society— although the beginnings of such a theoretical distinction go back far

---

[99] I here use "Marxising" as an English rendering of the French "marxisant." Mandrou (*Introduction à la France moderne*, p. 139) employs the term "paramarxiste."

beyond Machiavelli and the Italians to the medieval civilians[100]—and between the public order (of equality) and the private order (of competition and classes). The political language of the late medieval and Renaissance era was overwhelmingly that of the world of estates, the language of divinely ordained social tasks, the common good, the lack of any distinction between private and public duties.

5. Several conclusions supplied by the foregoing analysis are important to this study. In the first place, in the study of social structures of late medieval and Renaissance societies, the historian must work with estate and class categories simultaneously, realizing that the predominance of class over estate solidarities (in, for example, the study of politics) will vary according to the issue and to the social strata involved, as well as to the solidity of the social order. In the well-integrated society, whose ruling class is not rent by internal rivalries and factions, even great turbulence may not seriously shake the effect of traditional political language as the carrier of traditional values and loyalties. Secondly, the study of social consciousness—which is not the direct subject of what follows—needs to be oriented to an accurate understanding of social structures. Finally, the basic lines of structure and consciousness in later medieval and Renaissance Europe were common to the urban and the seigneurial sectors of society; and, for the High Middle Ages onward, neither type of social formation may be regarded as a self-sufficient whole. For the ruling classes, this means that beyond the categories of "nobles," "seigneurs," and "gentlemen" for the lords in the land, and beyond the categories of "patricians," "popolo grasso," and "big bourgeoisie" for the urban rich, we may employ the term "aristocracy" as a comprehensive term for the lords of society in the towns and in the land.[101] This is how the term is used in the following study of the lords of Reformation Strasbourg.

---

[100] Gaines Post, *Studies in Medieval Legal Thought: Public Law and the State, 1100–1322* (Princeton, 1964), pp. 333–367.

[101] See Kamen, *The Iron Century*, p. 129. Machiavelli (*Discorsi*, I, 55) actually uses the term "gentlemen" to refer to aristocrats in the land or in town, defining them as those who live idly on the proceeds of their possessions and who shun agriculture or any other useful pursuit; they are most dangerous, he says, when they also own castles and command subjects in the countryside. On the Italian term "popolo grasso" and its counterpart, "popolo minuto," see Bowsky, "Anatomy of Rebellion in Fourteenth-Century Siena," p. 233; and, on the London equivalents, Sylvia L. Thrupp, *The Merchant Class of Medieval London* (Ann Arbor, 1948), pp. 14–15.

C. Historical Method and the Study of
Aristocratic Societies

1. There are few better solvents of romantic idealization than the
assembly of as much and as precise information as possible about
individuals and groups of individuals. Much of what flies under the
modish banner of "social history" is no more than this more or less
precise study of human groups.[102] A good example of what this type of
research can achieve may be seen in the revision of scholarly opinion
about the "guild revolts," those guild-based movements against
political oligarchy in the European towns of the thirteenth to fifteenth
centuries. Once the darling of Liberal medievalists, the proto-democratic
character of these movements has vanished, after three decades of
research, into thin air. What was broken in successful revolts, it turns
out, was the protected political monopoly of the old patriciates, not the
domination of urban regimes by rich aristocrats. As Erich Maschke has
written, the guild revolts produced "eine Erweiterung des Kreises . . .
der bisher die patrizische Ratsverfassung getragen hatte . . . . Auch
die Stadt der Zunftverfassung war in ihrer Führung eine Stadt der
Kaufleute."[103] The guild regime, conceived as a political supremacy of
artisans and other small producers, simply never existed.[104] Karl Czok,
one of the closest students of the guild revolts, sees them as having brought
some of the middling citizens into the inner circles of power, although
he warns against seeing the struggles chiefly in class terms and recom-
mends calling them "civic struggles" (Bürgerkämpfe).[105] The meaning
of this revision for our understanding of the later histories of the towns
has been summed up by Philippe Dollinger: "Car après comme avant
le régime des villes allemandes demeure oligarchique, aux mains des
plus riches."[106] Despite radical differences between their constitutions,

---

[102] Which has led Eric J. Hobsbawm to draw the distinction between social history
and the history of society. "From Social History to the History of Society," *Daedalus*,
100, No. 1 (1971), pp. 20–45.

[103] Erich Maschke, "Verfassung und soziale Kräfte in der deutschen Stadt des
späten Mittelalters, vornehmlich in Oberdeutschland," *VSWG*, 41 (1959), 289–349,
433–476, here at pp. 475–476.

[104] Czok, "Zur Stellung der Stadt," pp. 16–17.

[105] Karl Czok, "Zunftkämpfe, Zunftrevolution oder Bürgerkämpfe?" *Wissenschaftliche Zeitschrift der Karl-Marx-Universität Leipzig*, 8 (1958–59), 129–143; *idem*,
"Die Burgerkämpfe in Süd- und Westdeutschland im 14. Jahrhundert," *JGO*, 12/13
(1966–67), 40–72, here at p. 48.

[106] Philippe Dollinger, "Les villes allemandes au moyen âge: les groupements
sociaux," in *La ville*, vol. 2 (Recueils de la Société Jean Bodin, VII; Brussels, 1955),
pp. 371–372.

therefore, the social complexion of the ruling class was much the same in the guild towns (Strasbourg, Ulm, Constance) as it was in Nuremberg, where there were no guilds at all.[107]

The demythologization of the German guild revolts has its forerunners and counterparts in the literature on the towns of other regions of Europe;[108] and it is gradually revising the entire approach to the social and political dynamics of the late medieval town.[109] Years ago, before this current was very strong, Leo Kofler asserted the ambiguous social nature of European urban guilds:

> Despite the frequent victories of the guilds, what remained ultimately decisive—and not only in Germany—was that the victorious guildsmen sought to displace the patriciate politically but not economically. The social structure of the society of estates was untouched, so that the domination of the big bourgeoisie naturally reconstructed itself.[110]

Time has proved Kofler right.

2. The new history of the guild revolts is an example of what may be achieved by bringing social-structural questions and empirical methods of research to traditional subject matter. For German (as for other) towns of the late Middle Ages and the Reformation eras, relatively new techniques have enabled historians to study urban social structures with a precision formerly unknown. The quantification of levels of wealth, derived from urban tax registers, has given access to important sectors of the urban population.[111] Stratification by tax categories works

---

[107] Wolfgang von Stromer, *Oberdeutsche Hochfinanz 1350–1450*, 3 vols., Beihefte der *Vierteljahrschrift für Sozial- und Wirtschaftsgeschichte*, Nos. 55–57 (Wiesbaden, 1970), p. 341.

[108] Examples in Philippe Wolff, "Les luttes sociales dans les villes du Midi français, XIIIe–XIVe siècles," *AESC*, 2 (1947), 452–453; Hermann Van Werveke, "Les villes belges: histoire des institutions économiques et sociales," *La ville*, vol. 2, pp. 557–558.

[109] See the critique by Gerd Wunder, "Die Sozialstruktur der Reichsstadt Hall im späten Mittelalter," *Untersuchungen zur gesellschaftlichen Struktur der mittelalterlichen Städte in Europa. Reichenau-Vorträge 1963–64*, Vorträge und Forschungen, 11 (Constance-Stuttgart, 1966), p. 34.

[110] Kofler, *Zur Geschichte der bürgerlichen Gesellschaft*, p. 119, and see pp. 123–124.

[111] See esp. Friedrich Blendinger's remarkable "Versuch einer Bestimmung der Mittelschicht in der Reichsstadt Augsburg vom Ende des 14. bis zum Anfang des 18. Jahrhunderts," in *Städtische Mittelschichten in den südwestdeutschen Städten. Protokoll über die VIII. Arbeitstagung des Arbeitskreises für südwestdeutsche Stadtgeschichtsforschung*, eds. Erich Maschke and Jürgen Sydow, VKLBW, B 69 (Stuttgart, 1972), pp. 32–78. Both the state of the literature and that of research techniques may be studied in Erdmann Weyrauch's "Zur Auswertung von Steuerbüchern mit quantifizierenden Methoden," his contribution to the recent *Festgabe für Ernst-Walter Zeeden*. To the literature cited there should be added Ingrid Bátori's contribution to the same volume, "Besitz-

very well for social groups which, though wealthy enough to have been regular payers of property levies, are too large to be manageable by biographical reconstruction. The middling elements—small merchants, shopkeepers, artisans—lend themselves very well to such treatment, by the use of which some impressive results have been obtained.[112]

At the bottom and at the top of the urban class system, stratification by tax category is less, or not at all, satisfactory. At the bottom, because the poorest townsmen—servants, day-laborers, beggars, criminals—paid no taxes at all and, indeed, stood outside the effective system of class relations, as Friedrich Engels noted when he baptized them the "plebs."[113] The usual tax category of *habenits* reached, in fact, well up into the strata of non-paupers, and it therefore conceals persons of widely differing social positions.[114]

The top of the urban social hierarchy poses different problems. The structure of a society perpetuates itself in the documentary remains of the society—both qualitatively and quantitatively—and, for the societies of pre-industrial Europe, only among the upper classes can we reconstruct the biographies of relatively large numbers of persons. The centuries-long traditions of genealogy and heraldry, studies born of the waxing caste-like tendencies among the aristocracies of the late Middle Ages, contribute mightily to this ability. The lower classes, on the other hand, with occasional exceptions, remain faceless generalizations, interesting individual cases, or just statistics. Thus, in its reconstructability, as in so many other ways, a society may be said to have belonged to, to have been the property of, its ruling class.

---

strukturen in der Stadt Kitzingen zur Zeit der Reformation," and C. R. Friedrichs, "Capitalism, Mobility and Class Formation in the Early Modern German City," *Past & Present*, 69 (November 1975), 24–29, a study of Nördlingen. My thanks to Dr. Weyrauch and Dr. Bátori for letting me read their studies in typescript, both of which are concrete results of their participation in the research group Sonderforschungsbereich Spätmittelalter und Reformation (Tübingen), Unterprojekt Z 2.2: "Sozialschichtung in Städten Süddeutschlands in Spätmittelalter und Reformation," under the auspices of Prof. Zeeden and the direct leadership of Hans-Christoph Rublack.

[112] Hence the efforts at quantification in *Städtische Mittelschichten* are on the whole more successful than those in the earlier *Gesellschaftliche Unterschichten in den südwestdeutschen Städten*, eds. Erich Maschke and Jürgen Sydow, VKLBW, B 41 (Stuttgart, 1967).

[113] *Der deutsche Bauernkrieg*, in *Marx-Engels Werke*, VII (Berlin, 1960), 346. The term "plebs" tends to be avoided by non-socialist historians, including many who find nothing objectionable about the complementary term, "patriciate."

[114] Bernhard Kirchgässner, "Probleme quantitativer Erfassung städtischer Unterschichten im Spätmittelalter, besonders in Reichsstädten Konstanz und Esslingen," in *Gesellschaftliche Unterschichten*, pp. 75–81.

It has long been recognized that prosopography, or collective biography, is a useful and profitable method of studying aristocracies. Nor
is it any accident that the method's greatest successes have come in the
study of ancient, chiefly classical, societies; although since the work of
Lewis Namier it has been employed increasingly in the study of pre-
modern European aristocracies as well.[115] Some major successes have
been scored in the Renaissance towns. Lauro Martines, for example,
has conducted two major prosopographically based studies at Florence,
one of humanists and the other of notaries and lawyers.[116] The German
towns of the Reformation era have also yielded some secrets to this
method. Walter Jacob's analysis of the careers of sixty-five politicians
of Zürich during the decade 1519–28, although the time span is somewhat
brief and his stratification categories merit revision, is receiving deserved
recognition, imitation, and adaptation.[117] Just as suggestive in another
way is Hans-Christoph Rublack's treatment of the regime of Constance
and the introduction of the Reformation there (1499–1531), part of
which is based on prosopographies of the leading politicians and the
clergy.[118] Rublack employs his data not just to answer specific questions
about the persons whose biographies are reconstructed, but as an
instrument to illuminate an entire historical process in which the biographical subjects were principal actors. Thus, although his prosopographical data are not so extensive as those of Jacob, Rublack successfully makes the transition from the study of structures (prosopography
is, after all, a structural method) to the study of historical events. In this

---

[115] W. Den Boer, "Die prosopographische Methode in der modernen Geschichtsschreibung der Hohen Römischen Kaiserzeit," *Mnemosyne*, 22 (1969), 268–280. On the
method in general, see Lawrence Stone, "Prosopography," *Daedalus*, 100, No. 1
(Winter 1971), pp. 46–79.

[116] *The Social World of the Florentine Humanists, 1390–1460* (Princeton, 1963); *Lawyers
and Statecraft in Renaissance Florence* (Princeton, 1968).

[117] Walter Jacob, *Politische Führungsschicht und Reformation. Untersuchungen zur Reformation in Zürich 1519–1528*, Zürcher Beiträge zur Reformationsgeschichte, 1 (Zürich,
1970). Worth consulting is René Hauswirth's review in *Zwingliana*, 13, No. 4 (1970),
255–260. The principal weakness of this work is the near absence of an historical
sociology and the consequent inadequacy of the stratification scheme used. Building
upon this important work but with a much more developed theoretical sense is Erdmann
Weyrauch's "Paper on Social Stratification. Zur Konzeptualisierung der Forschung
im Unterprojekt Z 2.2" (mimeographed working paper, Tübingen, 1974), working
paper No. 17 of the research group described in note 111 above.

[118] Hans-Christoph Rublack, *Die Einführung der Reformation in Konstanz von den
Anfängen bis zum Abschluss 1531*, QFRG, 40 (= Veröffentlichungen des Vereins für
Kirchengeschichte in der evang. Landeskirche in Baden, 27) (Gütersloh-Karlsruhe,
1971).

respect, his book has few parallels in the current literature on the Reformation in the cities of the Holy Roman Empire.[119] The most massive and most impressive work of this kind deals not with a single city but with an entire diocese; and, although much of the book is clearly based on exhaustive social research at least partly of a prosopographical sort, the data themselves do not, with one exception, appear in the work itself—probably for sound material reasons. The reference is to Francis Rapp's huge *Réformes et Réformation à Strasbourg. Église et Société dans le diocèse de Strasbourg (1450–1525)*.[120] As a social study of the late medieval church on a diocesan level the book is absolutely without parallel or rival, though one hopes it will not remain so. Its most remarkable feature is its deliberate linking of structural and temporal analyses, employing his researches on the social complexion of various sectors of the clergy and religious orders to explain the failures of successive reform efforts in the diocese of Strasbourg.

3. No one can long study the histories of European aristocracies without being impressed by the importance of family ties. The family as a subject of historical study is, at last, receiving the kind of attention it deserves, although there is no agreement on even the most elementary trends in family structure.[121] It is likely that, in their zeal to dispel the traditional view of the progressive nuclearization of the primitive complex stem or joint family through the disintegrating effects of urban life, Peter Laslett and his British colleagues have gone much too far in denying the importance of the complex family at any stage of Western history.[122] There is recent evidence that the complex family flourished

---

[119] Territorial history in Southwest Germany is much better served, although the materials run heavily to pastors and territorial officials. Volker Press promises a volume of data, including a prosopography of the Palatine officials, to accompany his *Calvinismus und Territorialstaat. Regierung und Zentralbehörden der Kurpfalz 1559–1619*, Kieler Historische Studien, 7 (Stuttgart, 1970). We may hope for a study based on Walter Bernhardt's *Die Zentralbehörden des Herzogtums Württemberg und ihre Beamten 1520–1629*, 2 vols., VKLBW, B 70–71 (Stuttgart, 1973), which is modelled on Friedrich Gundlach's treatment of the Hessian regime. Similar repertories of the officials of Baden, Vorderösterreich, and the chief bishoprics would be extremely helpful.

[120] Collection de l'Institut des Hautes Etudes Alsaciennes, 23 (Paris, 1974). See also René Pierre Levresse, "Prosopographie du chapitre de l'église cathédrale de Strasbourg de 1092 à 1593," *AEA*, 18 (1970), 1–39.

[121] There is an excellent survey of the question by Diane Owen Hughes, "Urban Growth and Family Structure in Medieval Genoa," *Past & Present*, No. 66 (February 1975), 3–7.

[122] See Peter Laslett and Richard Wall, eds., *Households and Family in Past Time* (Cambridge, 1972), pp. 1–81, an extended polemic against the historical concept of the extended family.

until very late in at least certain sectors of the Central European peasantry,[123] and, for the other end of the social hierarchy, students of aristocratic social life during the Middle Ages and Renaissance have affirmed the importance of extra-nuclear family bonds.[124]

It is now clear that the thesis of unilinear, progressive nuclearization of family structure in the towns is incorrect on several counts. First, certain historical developments, especially political ones, tended to strengthen or weaken aristocratic family structure both on the land and in the towns. It is likely, for example, that the political decentralization of post-Carolingian France and Italy promoted the growth of large households on the land.[125] In the Italian towns, on the other hand, the political victory of the *popolo* over the old aristocratic clans tended to have a disintegrating effect on the latter.[126] Secondly, the effect of town life on aristocratic family structure varied enormously from city to city. Whereas in Tuscany the traditional picture of progressive nuclearization is probably true, in Genoa quite the opposite happened, as the rise of the commercial aristocracy during the earlier twelfth century produced a situation in which "lineage ties became more clearly defined, more firmly patrilineal, and more frequently invoked; and the bonds of the domestic group, the joint patriarchal family, were tightened."[127] In either case extended family ties among the aristocracy, whether organized into a single or into multiple households, formed a fundamental part of aristocratic self-consciousness and a constant element of urban aristocratic politics. Lauro Martines has summarized this importance:

> The rich urban families, the oligarchical families, tended to monopolize the public forums of the cities of late medieval and Renaissance Italy. Generally speaking, they controlled the institutions of government, and their spokesmen best expressed the politico-social values that we have come to associate with those cities. Whether at Florence or Venice, Padua or Genoa, the affairs and direction of government were bound up with the practical interests of the political families. Indeed, it is not

---

[123] Lutz K. Berkner, "The Stem Family and the Developmental Cycle of the Peasant Household: An Eighteenth Century Austrian Example," *AHR*, 77 (1972), 398–418.

[124] Georges Duby, "Lignage, noblesse et chevalerie au la région maconnaise," *AESC*, 27 (1972), 803–823, for example.

[125] Hughes, "Urban Growth and Family Structure," p. 4, with references.

[126] David Herlihy, "Mapping Households in Medieval Italy," *The Catholic Historical Review*, 58 (1972), 1–22. Any study of aristocratic propertyholding during this era will reveal the importance of the extended family as a social entity. The matter of actual household size is likely to have been of lesser importance to aristocrats because of their great ability to maintain family ties over considerable distances and time.

[127] Hughes, "Urban Growth and Family Structure," pp. 6–7.

wholly metaphorical to say that government and the principal families
were indivisible; and when they were not, then political violence was
profound, men overturned governments and the streets were delivered
to lawlessness.[128]

The strength of extended family structures may not have varied only
between town and land, between town and town, and from one epoch
to another, but also between class and class. Certainly the question has
not been studied systematically with regard to the single most important
determinant of class, property in its various forms. It is not difficult to
understand, however, that some features of aristocratic life tended to
promote the maintenance of family ties beyond the individual aristocratic
household. One such feature was the practice of co-enfiefment, by which
a single male in each generation was the fiefholder (*Lehenträger, porteur à
fief*) for a group of adult males related in the first or second degrees.
Fief-holding in the Upper Rhine Valley, whether by urban or by rural
aristocrats, was overwhelmingly of this kind.[129] Secondly, most aristocratic families of this region possessed a *Stammsitz*, an ancestral residence
which, if a fief, was inalienable and in which each family member had some
stake.[130] The practice of partible inheritance, the general rule in the
German-speaking world, probably helped to weaken family ties in some
cases and some periods (especially after the development of a general
market in land made the liquidation and division of inheritances easy),
but it may also have served to strengthen the family by keeping all
siblings on the same social level. The spread of genealogy meant that
aristocrats, its chief practitioners, knew better than other folks did
(supposing the genealogies to be unfalsified), not only who their
ancestors were, but also how closely they were related to contemporaries
of the same social status. Among aristocrats, property, marriages, and
status might all be considered and conserved as the goods of the complex
family. This is perfectly clear from the story (ca. 1507) of Johann
Werner of Zimmern and his romance with Sophia Bock (d. 1510), a rich,
homely widow of Strasbourg.[131] The match was promoted by Margrave

---

[128] Lauro Martines, "The Historical Approach to Violence," in *Violence and Disorder
in Italian Cities, 1200–1500*, pp. 3–18, here at p. 14.

[129] See Chapter II below, pp. 86ff.

[130] See the case described in Chapter IV below, pp. 129–130.

[131] The story is told in *ZC*, II, 148–151, where the woman is called "Sophia Böcklin."
The Bock and the Böcklin were quite distinct from each other, although tradition and
heraldic evidence give them a common origin; and there is no Sophia in the Böcklin
genealogy for this period, although the Böcklin descent is fairly well known. In the
necrology of the commandery of the Knights of St. John at Strasbourg, however,

Christoph I of Baden (1453–1527), who wanted to help Johann Werner recoup his family's depleted resources. When Johann Werner consulted his brothers and sisters, they advised him to marry Sophia, whose lower status was somewhat enhanced by her wealth and her first marriage to a count, "then, too, he has two brothers, who—even if he damages his own descendants by this marriage—can make good, honorable marriages, fitting and in accord with their ancestry, and maintain the family in such a way that heirs will be eligible for tournaments and for the better ecclesiastical benefices."[132] Although Johann Werner did not feel compelled to follow this advice and did not marry Sophia, still the advice itself is evidence of a policy of collective maintenance and survival in one generation of an aristocratic family.

In the study of aristocracies, then, the concept of "family" must necessarily remain a complex one and not be restricted to the organization of individual households. "Family" was at once a category of familial relationship, of blood and marriage, and of property in the broadest sense of the term. "Family" was not just a household but a community maintained for the preservation and enhancement of all the forms of property that gave the family its social position: real property; capital; and cultural capital in the form of education.[133] This led to the possibility that the aristocratic family could be also a political unit, which did not necessarily mean that related officeholders always pursued together the aggrandizement of the family. It did provide, however, both informal systems of communication and possibilities of cooperation prior to and more intimate than official relationships and paths of political education, by which young aristocrats could be initiated into family political traditions and groomed to take their places in the regime.

---

there is a notice that Sophia Böckin (i.e., Bock) died on 8 January 1510, and she was the wife of the count of Löwenstein and the daughter of Johann Conrad Bock and Hartliebe von Andlau. BNUS, Ms. 752, at 8.I. This woman can only be the rich widow of the story in the *Zimmerische Chronik*, who there marries Count Ludwig von Löwenstein. Hans Conrad Bock was a patrician senator at Strasbourg in 1466/67, 69/70, and 75/76. Hatt, p. 405. The Hans Conrad Bock who was senator in 1435, 37, 41, 43, 45, and 47, and Stettmeister in 1433, 49, 51, 53, 55, 57/58, 60/61, and 63/64 (Hatt, pp. 405, 597) is likely to have been a different, older man. As for the *Zimmern Chronicle*, I have used the older edition by K. A. von Barack, which will be superseded when the indices are complete to Hans Martin Decker-Hauff's fine new edition.

[132] *ZC*, II, 149 lines 5–11.

[133] Education as cultural capital is meant here in the sense developed by Pierre Bourdieu, "Reproduction culturelle et reproduction sociale," *Informations en sciences sociales*, 10, No. 2 (1972), 45–79; now available in German in Pierre Bourdieu and Jean-Claude Passeron, *Grundlagen einer Theorie der symbolischen Gewalt*, trans. Eva Moldenhauer (Frankfurt/M., 1973), pp. 88–139.

D. Problems, Plan, and Purpose of this Study

1. A prosopographical apparatus, provided in Appendix A, lies at the basis of this study of Strasbourg's ruling class and political elite during the Reformation era (ca. 1520–55).[134] The "universe" of the apparatus includes every discoverable person who sat in the town's privy councils (the XV and XIII) during this time span. The lists of names had themselves to be reconstructed, as the privy councils were true *arcanae regiminis*, lists of whose members rarely appear among the registers of officeholders.[135] For a study of the social foundations of Strasbourg's politics, the composition of the "universe" was not difficult, because it has been known for a long time—at least since the work of Gustav Schmoller[136]—that the two privy councils formed, since the middle of the fifteenth century, the inner circle of power at Strasbourg. The reconstructed lists of privy councillors must then contain, as they do, all or nearly all of the principal political figures of the age, though they naturally include a good many smaller fry as well.

Given the importance of the lists as a starting point and as a basis of collection of political and social data for this study, the accuracy and completeness of the lists bear closely upon the integrity of the analysis. As to accuracy, no person has been included in the lists unless a contemporary source designates him as a XVer or a XIIIer, and the dates of service in the privy councils are inclusive rather than exclusive. The problems of name collection have been discussed elsewhere.[137] Suffice here to say that, in most cases, new appointments and notices of resignations and deaths are recorded in the protocols of the Senate & XXI from 1539 onward (the year at which the extant series "XXI" begins). For the preceding years, the names were gathered from a very wide variety of sources, and any lacunae in the lists fall in the 1520s rather than in any later period.

The prosopographical appendix (Appendix A) contains biographies of 105 men who were privy councillors between 1520 and 1555, many of whom served also for one or more years before or after these dates.

---

[134] The entries in Appendix A below are cited throughout this work in the following form: PROSOPOGRAPHY, with Roman numeral denoting entry.

[135] Thomas A. Brady, Jr., "The Privy Councils of Strasbourg (XV and XIII): A Supplement to Jacques Hatt, *Liste des membres du grand sénat de Strasbourg*," *BCGA*, No. 27 (1974), 73–79.

[136] Gustav Schmoller, *Strassburg zur Zeit der Zunftkämpfe und die Reform seiner Verfassung und Verwaltung*, Quellen und Forschungen zur Sprach- und Culturgeschichte der germanischen Völker, XI (Strasbourg, 1875).

[137] Brady, "Privy Councils," pp. 73–74.

The councillors were co-opted for life tenures, the XV from senators and ex-senators, the XIII normally from the XV. Of the 105 known members, the complete terms of service of 85 are known; and these 85 served for an average of just under fifteen years (14.8 yrs.). Of the twenty-eight who were in office at any one time, nine were supposed to be patricians (*Constofler*) and nineteen to be members of the guilds; the actual division of the 105 is 32 (30.5%) patricians and 73 (69.5%) guildsmen—or within several percentage points of the legal ratio. The difference is to be explained by the somewhat longer average length of tenure of the patricians vis-à-vis the guildsmen (16.3 yrs. vs. 14.1 yrs.). Because the total period spanned by the lists reaches 20–25 years backward and forward from the period 1520–55, it is impossible to say theoretically, on the basis of an average service of 15 yrs., how many names the lists *should* contain.

2. The state of the sources at Strasbourg is not particularly favorable. Some of the great staple sources of social history, such as tax registers, court records, and treasury records, are lost nearly without a trace. Others, such as guild archives, are mere fragments.[138] Some riches do remain, especially the under-exploited registers of the Strasbourg notaries (series "KS"),[139] and a wealth of material in both major Strasbourg archives on transfers of feudal and other sorts of real property. The maxim, nevertheless, that the lower down the class structure the more obscure the person, is doubly true in Strasbourg. Just those records which might have allowed a reconstruction of the occupational, income, and even behavioral patterns of the middling folk, and perhaps even some of the lower classes, have disappeared at Strasbourg. The structure of income, for example, and the social complexion of criminality, are topics which cannot be pursued there.

These losses mean not just a loss of information but something far more serious: except for the upper class and a few of the well-to-do middling folk, no social class of medieval and Reformation Strasbourg can be studied systematically by one or another of the tools of modern social

---

[138] Jean Rott, "Artisanat et mouvements sociaux à Strasbourg autour de 1525," in *Artisans et ouvriers d' Alsace,* PSSARE, 9 (Strasbourg, 1965), pp. 137–170, here at p. 160n7.

[139] The Archives Municipales de Strasbourg (=AMS), Chambres des Contrats (=KS). There is no inventory of this enormous series, although some volumes do have contemporary indices (indexed by purchaser or lender). All the more valuable, then, is the superb chart of the first 150 volumes, prepared by Mr. Stephen Nelson, which breaks down these volumes by *étude* and puts them into chronological sequence. A copy of this chart is on deposit in AMS.

history. We are thus left with chance notices of individuals and small groups, which by heroic effort can sometimes be forced to yield a coherent story.[140] What is not possible is to extend the method of the present study to such social classes. The aristocracy thus takes in the following study such a central place that it sometimes may seem that aristocracy was an essential characteristic of a social group rather than a relation of the rich and powerful to those they ruled. At the present time these other urban classes—not to speak of the rural producers—cannot be identified, comprehended, and described with anything like the precision that the aristocracy can. They remain, nonetheless, part of the definition of the aristocracy as an urban *ruling* class.

3. The plan of this work is complex. It begins with the political category of the Strasbourg privy councillors, whose 105 biographies form the initial group of data for the study. From this group, accepted on the basis of earlier institutional studies as a political elite, the study moves to the aristocracy itself as a complex social class composed of two fractions, one rentier and the other mercantile, and divided into two estates, one patrician the other of the guilds. An analysis of the elements of their integration into a single class is followed by an examination of the paths and means of aristocratic political control. This completes the first, structural part of the study, which moves from the political elite to the ruling class and back to political life.

The second, historical part of this study attempts to employ the structural analyses of the first part to reinterpret the policies and political behavior of the regime of Strasbourg, not during the entire Reformation era, but only in what—at least from the local point of view—may fairly be regarded as the two chief political crises of the age (1524–25 and 1547–48). Thereby is employed the unproven assumption that regimes are most likely to reveal their true social character at times of greatest stress. The bridge material (Chapter VII) between the analyses of the two crises is directed at the chief line of argument and is not meant to fill a narrative gap.

4. Several assumptions which guided the preparation of this study deserve to be stated, although no apology for them is intended. The first and most important is that historical societies were organized into social formations which we call classes and the internal structures of which depended *ultimately* upon the ways in which those societies got their livings. These formations differ in structure and complexity from society

---

[140] A notable example is the article cited in note 138 above.

to society and age to age, although they have in common the extraction
of a portion of the social product from those who produce it by those
who rule. The means of extraction vary tremendously, and so do the
accompanying justifications. Taken as a whole, Europe at the end of
the Middle Ages was characterized by social formations whose enduring
characteristics were what may be called "late feudal," although there
already appear tell-tale signs of more modern social formations.

A second assumption has to do with the role of political power in the
preservation of social structures. The aristocrats of aristocratic societies
are by definition those who rule, and the first law of aristocratic politics
is collective survival, just as its mortal sin is the disruption of the state
for factional, familial, or individual gain. The much greater importance
of political control to the economic domination in pre-modern societies
than in the early phases of industrial capitalism finds theoretical expression
in the absence of the distinction between state and society in contemporary
political theory.

Thirdly, there is the principle of social fractions,[141] those fragments
of a class which, at some time in their development, have the potential
either for incorporation into the class from which they sprang or for
breaking away to form the nucleus of a new class formation. Which
alternative realizes itself depends to a great extent on specific conditions.
Hence the possibility for integration of commercial aristocracies into a
larger feudal structure, despite their exhibition of apparently anti-feudal
characteristics.

A fourth assumption has to do with the significance of culture, both
high and low. The very minor role played by cultural phenomena—
chiefly theology—in this study does *not* flow from an assumption of the
total dependence of culture on non-cultural phenomena, either of the
substructure-superstructure or of some other type. Although popular
culture is a difficult enough subject in itself, whose importance is not to
be gauged by the relative paucity of literature devoted to it,[142] its relation
to high culture is even more problematical. Certainly there are times

---

[141] The term "fraction" is here used in the sense defined by Nicos Poulantzas, *Pouvoir
politique et classes sociales de l'état capitaliste* (Paris, 1968), p. 88: "On désigne par *fractions
autonomes* de classe celles qui constituent le substrat de forces sociales éventuelles, par
fractions des ensembles sociaux susceptibles de devenir des fractions autonomes. . . ."
This work now exists in a German version, *Politische Macht und gesellschaftliche Klassen*,
trans. Günter Seib and Erika Hültenschmidt (Frankfurt a. M., 1974). For the historical
use of the term, see Czok, "Die Bürgerkämpfe in Süd- und Westdeutschland," pp. 47–48.
[142] See the wise words of Natalie Z. Davis, "Some Tasks and Themes in the Study
of Popular Religion," in *The Pursuit of Holiness*, pp. 313–314.

when the influence of popular ideas upon high culture can be direct
and measurable, as, for example, in the connection between the pronounced reevaluation of the social image of the German peasant around
1500 and the quasi-egalitarian doctrines of the early Reformation
years.[143] The high culture, on the other hand, is vitally important to a
grasp of the self-understanding of an entire society, together with the
more specific self-consciousness of its ruling class. This covers a great
deal more than direct cultural expressions of domination, although
these are basically important to it. More useful here is perhaps the broader
concept of cultural "hegemony," which allows a certain play to cultural
traditions themselves as well as the possibility of a reciprocal force of
the culture's leading ideas upon social relations and political events.
The leading ideas of Reformation Germany were chiefly theological
ideas, without a firm grasp of which the culture and self-consciousness
of the age simply cannot be understood. That they play a relatively
minor role in this study is due rather to the specific aims of the work
than to an ignorance of their significance.

5. This study has a number of purposes, not all of them of the same
type. There is, first of all, the desire to contribute to the illumination of
the history of one of the Holy Roman Empire's most interesting cities
and one of the chief centers of the German Reformation. Secondly,
there is the purpose of contributing to the setting of urban history back
firmly in its territorial, late feudal context. A third purpose of this work
is to add to the growing basis for a general historical sociology of the
late feudal era. Fourthly, the following study is designed to demonstrate
the utility of the study of social groups to an explanation of the political
aspects of the German Reformation. Finally, this book is meant as a
contribution to the collective effort to liberate the field of Reformation
studies from the dead hand of romantic idealism.

Nothing in this introduction is intended as a disclaimer of the internal
logic of the following chapters and the conclusions to which they lead.
If this book convinces some of its readers that historical investigations
at the microsocial level can stand in the service of dispelling the mystery
surrounding historical change, then it will have achieved its chief aim.

---

[143] Helmut Brackert, *Bauernkrieg und Literatur* (Frankfurt/M., 1975), pp. 25–35.
See the excellent analysis of the peasantry's political self-image by Horst Buszello,
*Der deutsche Bauernkrieg von 1525 als politische Bewegung mit besonderer Berücksichtigung der
anonymen Flugschrift An die Versamlung Gemayner Pawerschafft*, Studien zur europäischen
Geschichte, 8 (Berlin, 1969), pp. 16–91.

It is a window on the workings of an extremely complex, whole society, whose historical wholeness is the analogue and determinant of the holistic understanding we seek. For the whole is ever the truth.

PART ONE

RULING CLASS AND REGIME

"dem got gût beschere, der hette ouch gern ere."
—Hans Armbruster in der Brandgasse, ca. 1477—

"sie sollen ouch vor offenem rat sweren hynnanfürder keinerley koufmanschaft noch antwerck zu triben . . ."
—Ordinance on new patricians, Strasbourg, 1472—

"Dywil vnser handtwerck ein kauffmanschatz vnd darzu auch ein handtwerck ist, . . ."
—The master furriers of Strasbourg, 1529—

"Denique videbam monarchiam absque tyrannide, aristocratiam sine factionibus, democratiam sine tumultu, opes absque luxu, foelicitatem absque procacitate."
—Desiderius Erasmus, 21 Sept. 1514—

INTRODUCTION

Most of what is known about urban aristocracies in Europe at the end of the Middle Ages suggests that the ruling class of a particular town should be sought among one or more of the following types of persons: merchants, rentiers, and merchants becoming rentiers. The basic types do not vary much across western and central Europe around 1500, although one would want to add the lawyers and notaries in the towns of southern Europe. Otherwise, urban notables might be formally noble or not, and they might rule with, through, or in the absence of guilds, but the essential coincidence of wealth and political power marked all urban societies.

For an approach to the aristocracy of Strasbourg in the age of the Reformation we have a more precise base from which to start than theoretical deductions from the general characteristics of European towns—useful as the latter may be. The 105 biographies in the prosopographical appendix, including every known person who reached the privy councils of the regime between 1520 and 1555, may be classified according to estate (*Stand*) and according to social/occupational categories.

Table 1

Classification of 105 privy councillors of Strasbourg (XVers and XIIIers) by estate and by occupation

Category	Status (%)	Occupation (%)
A. Constofler	32(30.5)	
Rentiers		32(30.5)
B. Guildsmen	73(69.5)	
Rentiers		13(12.4)
Big merchants		15(14.3)
Other merchants		18(17.1)
Goldsmiths		4(3.8)
Artisans		14(13.3)
Officials		2(1.9)
Unknown		7(6.7)
	105(100.0)	105(100.0)

Source: Prosopography.

The rentiers, that is, persons living from interest, rents, and dues, comprised 42.9% of all privy councillors; the merchants and goldsmiths another 35.2%; and the artisans only 13.3%—in one of the Empire's most famous guild regimes. Together the rentier-mercantile elements supplied more than three-quarters (78.1%) of all the privy councillors during this era, which justifies the search for Strasbourg's ruling class among their ranks. The patriciate (Chapter II) and the guild aristocracy (Chapter III) are examined separately, followed by an analysis of the two fractions' social unity (Chapter IV) and the structures of their political control of the town (Chapter V).

CHAPTER TWO

STRASBOURG'S PATRICIATE—THE CONSTOFLER

A. "Patrician" and "Patriciate," Problems of Definition

The remnants of Strasbourg's noble aristocracy at the end of the Middle Ages were organized into two corporations, the Constofeln zum Hohensteg and zum Mühlstein, for whom one-third of all high civic offices was reserved. All Constofler were at least armigerous and most were noble, although there were armigerous and even noble families in the guilds as well. In this study, it is for this group—the Constofler—that the term "patriciate" is used.

So long and so extensive is the literature on medieval German urban aristocracies, and so little agreement has been reached on the use of the term "patriciate," that Hanns Hubert Hofmann has called it an "unfortunate, because too broadly conceived term."[1] As Ingrid Bátori has recently written, the term itself is an anachronism when applied to urban elites before the seventeenth century, or at very least it is neither more precise nor more useful a collective term than the dozen or so other names by which they called themselves.[2] Philippe Dollinger is thus properly cautious in choosing to apply the term to groups of wealthy urban families who did not belong to the guilds and who dominated the governments of their towns until some established date—varying with the town.[3] This definition seems broad enough to embrace the commercial aristocracies of the Hanseatic towns as well as the noble and semi-noble aristocrats of many South German ones. It has the added advantage of containing the three chief elements of aristocratic position: wealth, elevated social status, and political power.[4]

"Patrician," like its counterpart "plebeian," is a Roman term resur-

---

[1] Hanns Hubert Hofmann, "Der Adel in Franken," in *Deutscher Adel 1430–1555*, ed. Helmuth Rössler, DFN, 1 (Darmstadt, 1965), p. 107n21.

[2] Ingrid Bátori, "Das Patriziat der deutschen Stadt. Zur Klärung einer historischen Frage," *ZSSD*, 2 (1975), 1–30, here at p. 4. Bátori's excellent notes make it unnecessary to list here the general literature on German urban patriciates.

[3] Philippe Dollinger, "Patriciat noble et patriciat bourgeois à Strasbourg au XIVe siècle," *RA*, 90 (1950–51), 52n1.

[4] Weyrauch, Paper on Social Stratification, p. 4. See the very useful definition of (elevated) social place by Martines, *Social World of the Florentine Humanists*, p. 18.

rected by the classicists of the Renaissance era.[5] Although similarities between the urban, aristocratic civilizations of ancient Rome and Greece and that of the Italian city-states of the fifteenth and sixteenth centuries may seem less clear and less compelling to us than they did to the writers of the Italian (Florentine and Venetian) civic humanist tradition—from Petrarch, or at least from Leonardo Bruni, to Machiavelli—it is just as well to remind ourselves that classical civic ideals and political language seemed useful enough to a broad stream of European political thinkers, not just urban ones, from the civic humanists through the classicizing republicans of the eighteenth century.[6] The similarities perceived by the Italian civic humanists, moreover, had less to do with the origins of civic social formations and institutions than with their structural characteristics. Such writers were thus far more realistic than are those modern historians who attempt to fix and limit a term such as "patrician" to its first historical usage—which is obscure enough—and insist on the need for an unchanging definition of the term.[7]

The word "patriciate" leads straight into the old debate over the origins of European urban aristocracies, a struggle basically between the partisans of feudal origins of the European cities and the ministerial/noble origins of their ruling classes, and those who, seeing the city as the spearhead of bourgeois progress against feudalism, insist on the mercantile origins of the medieval urban patriciates.[8] The tremendous

---

[5] According to Friedrich von Klocke, *Das Patriziatsproblem und die Werler Erbsälzer*, Veröffentlichungen der Historischen Kommission Westfalens, XXIII/7 (Münster/W., 1965), p. 16, who, however, identifies an earlier (1306), isolated example.

[6] Pocock, *Machiavellian Moment*, is an extended analysis of the renaturalization and transformations of classical political language from the Italian Renaissance city-state to revolutionary America. See also Elliott, "Revolution and Continuity," p. 50.

[7] Erwin Riedenauer, "Kaiser und Patriziat. Struktur und Funktion des reichsstädtischen Patriziats im Blickpunkt kaiserlicher Adelspolitik von Karl V. bis Karl VI.," *ZBLG*, 30 (1967), 625–626, who surveys the various views of this kind. The two best studies of individual German patriciates both treat relatively small towns. Alfred Otto Stolze, *Der Sünfzen zu Lindau. Das Patriziat eiber schwänischen Reichsstadt*, ed. Bernhard Zeller (Lindau-Constance, 1956); and Alfons Dreher, *Das Patriziat der Reichsstadt Ravensburg. Von den Anfängen bis zum Beginn des 19. Jahrhunderts* (Stuttgart, 1966), which first appeared in *ZWLG*, 19 (1960), 51–88, 215–313; 21 (1962), 237–386; 23 (1964), 1–140; 24 (1965), 1–131. Of other extended studies, reliable but less certain on social and economic subjects is Ruth Elben, *Das Patriziat der Reichsstadt Rottweil. Von den Anfängen bis zum Jahre 1550*, VKLBW, B 30 (Stuttgart, 1964).

[8] See, in brief, Hanns Hubert Hofmann, "Nobiles Norimbergenses. Beobachtungen zur Struktur der reichsstädtischen Oberschicht," *Untersuchungen zur gesellschaftlichen Struktur*, p. 64. The question of urban aristocratic origins was especially treated by Hans Planitz. See his "Zur Geschichte des städtischen Meliorats," *ZSSR, GA*, 67

variety of origins of European urban aristocratic families makes the issue of "the feudal city" vs. "the bourgeois city" quite impervious to resolution on the basis of social origins. It is no longer possible to argue, with Pirenne, that the northern cities developed under the hegemony of exclusively mercantile ruling classes; while the mixed feudal–mercantile origins of the urban ruling classes in North Italy and South Germany are well-established facts.[9]

Even more telling against the desire for a fixed, substantialist definition of the term "patriciate" is the fact that the cities in Europe and their ruling classes developed within a wider social order which had no classical parallels but which had nevertheless to be understood and dealt with as the wider context of urban life. When Machiavelli, in his brief, brilliant prolegomenon to a political sociology of the Renaissance Italian city (*Discorsi*, *I*, 55), described the lay ruling classes on the land, many of whose members still enjoyed true feudal power over their subjects, he called them "gentlemen"—a term which had no classical equivalent—because the social order he was describing had no classical analogue.

All of this suggests that classical terms, such as "patriciate" and "plebs," can be useful to the modern student of late medieval and Renaissance societies, just as they were to contemporaries, but that the use of the terms has always been analogical in the sense that Renaissance thinkers employed them because they believed their own ruling and lower classes to be in some respects "like" the Roman patriciate and plebs respectively. Such terms should be used by the modern historian in a relational way, depending on the identification of a class's or group's position in an entire social system rather than on the remote historical origins of the group. Once clear of this conceptual hurdle, it becomes much easier to consider in the same or very similar terms the ruling classes of towns so different from one another as Nuremberg, where the patriciate was of relatively recent, mercantile origin and quite separate

---

(1950), 141–175; and "Studien zur Rechtsgeschichte des städtischen Patriziats," *Mitteilungen des Instituts für Österreichische Geschichtsforschung,* 58 (1950), 317–335.

[9] See Karl Frölich, "Kaufmannsgilden und Stadtverfassung im Mittelalter," in *Die Stadt des Mittelalters,* ed. Carl Haase, II, 11–13. On the revision of Pirenne's theory, see A. B. Hibbert, "The Origins of the Medieval Town Patriciate," *Past & Present,* 3 (February 1953), 15–27; and, for the Netherlands, Jan A. Van Houtte, "Gesellschaftliche Schichten in den Städten der Niederlande," in *Untersuchungen zur gesellschaftlichen Struktur,* pp. 259–276, esp. p. 266; Van Werveke, "Les villes belges: histoire des institutions économiques et sociales," pp. 557–558.

from the rural nobility,[10] and Strasbourg—where the patriciate was of mixed origin and had massive ties to the land.[11] The extent, however, to which groups named by contemporaries as "patricians" or "honorables" comprised the entire ruling class of a city, varied enormously with the economic structures and the histories of the individual towns.[12] This is perhaps one more reason to use the term "patriciate" as a less comprehensive term than "urban aristocracy."

In the following pages the terms "patrician" and "Constofler" are used interchangeably. The latter word has to recommend it only the fact that, at Strasbourg and several other South German towns, it was the old and usual term for the portion of the aristocracy that did not belong to the guilds.[13]

B.   The Rehabilitation of the Patriciate

Three sources contributed to the composition of the Strasbourg patriciate at the end of the Middle Ages: former episcopal ministeriales; immigrants from the rural nobility; and mercantile families grown rich in trade.[14] Some of the leading patrician political families of the pre-Reformation period—such as the Kageneck, the Ottfriedrich, the Wetzel von Marsilien, the Spender, the Zorn, and the Mülnheim—descended from the old ministerial core of the patriciate, whose ranks,

---

[10] As Hanns Hubert Hofmann ("Nobiles Norimbergenses," pp. 72–73) puts it, "*Divites* wurden nun also nach einer gewissen schwankenden Übergangsperiode zu *potentes*."

[11] See, for example, Jean Schneider, *La ville de Metz aux XIIIe et XIVe siècles* (Nancy, 1950), pp. 336–346.

[12] Bátori, "Das Patriziat der deutschen Stadt," p. 5.

[13] From: *connestabularii* (=*comes stabuli*). Theo Reintges, *Ursprung und Wesen der spätmittelalterlichen Schützengilden*, Rheinisches Archiv. Veröffentlichungen des Instituts für geschichtliche Landeskunde der Rheinlande an der Universität Bonn, 58 (Bonn, 1963), p. 115n52. On the medieval Constofeln of Strasbourg, see Jacques Hatt, *Une ville du XVe siècle. Strasbourg* (Strasbourg, 1929), pp. 13–14.

[14] Dollinger, "Patriciat noble et patriciat bourgeois," pp. 61–63, derives the Strasbourg patriciate chiefly from wealthy families of non-ministerial, non-noble origin, a position in which he is followed by Alfred Graf Kageneck, "Das Patriziat im Elsass unter Berücksichtigung der Schweizer Verhältnisse," in *Deutsches Patriziat 1430–1740*, ed. Helmuth Rössler, DFN, 3 (Limburg/Lahn, 1968), pp. 380–382. Helga Mosbacher, in her Berlin dissertation of 1972, has reviewed the twelfth- and thirteenth-century evidence and concludes that a major sector of the Strasbourg patriciate stemmed from episcopal ministeriales and in particular from *Kammerhandwerker*. Helga Mosbacher, "Kammerhandwerk, Ministerialität und Bürgertum in Strassburg. Studien zur Zusammensetzung und Entwicklung des Patriziats im 13. Jahrhundert," ZGO, 119 (1972), 33–173, here at pp. 141–161.

continually depleted by family extinctions, emigrations, and at least one mass exile (1419), were steadily replenished from the wealthiest merchant and banking families. There may have once been a separate estate of wealthy, non-patrician "Bürger" or "cives" outside the guilds, a so-called "bourgeois patriciate," but since 1419 there were only two estates at Strasbourg, the Constofler—divided into the two "gesell-schaften" or "ritterschaften" Zum Hohensteg and Zum Mühlstein—and the remainder of the citizenry organized into twenty-eight (since 1482, twenty) guilds. A tripartite division, however, consisting of *nobiles, cives,* and *tribus* (*Adel, Bürger, Handwerker*) survived (for very good reasons, as we shall see) in unofficial political language.

In few other large towns of South Germany had the old urban aristocracy been so thoroughly humbled during the fourteenth and fifteenth centuries as at Strasbourg. Until 1332 the old patriciate had been the sole lords of the city, comparable to the *grandi* of Florence in their great days before the Ordinances of Justice (1293). Thereafter, successive struggles with the mercantile elite and then with the guilds smashed the nobles' monopoly of power and drove the majority of them from the city into the land (1419). After this final defeat, which marked the end of the "guild revolts" at Strasbourg,[15] the reconstituted but diminished patriciate retained only one-third of the civic offices, leaving the lion's share to the victorious guilds, a proportion which did not change during succeeding reductions in the size of the civic senate (*grosser Rat*).[16] After 1419 the patriciate of Strasbourg was not only a politically beaten class, like the Florentine *grandi* after 1293, it had also lost more than two-thirds of its members to the land.[17]

The patriciate was not only smaller, it was also much more closely knit after 1419–20. During the sixty years before 1420, thirty-eight new family names appear among the patrician senators; but, during the following sixty years, only eight new names appear.[18] Slowly, though it could never regain its old glory, the patriciate underwent an impressive rehabilitation. During the second half of the fifteenth century, the two remaining Constofeln acquired enough new members to assure the numerical preservation of the fraction; and they gradually secured

[15] Philippe Dollinger, "La évolution politique des corporations strasbourgeoises à la fin du moyen âge," in *Artisans et ouvriers,* p. 130.

[16] *Ibid.,* pp. 132–133; Hatt, *Une ville,* pp. 12–14.

[17] Dollinger, "La évolution politique," p. 130; *idem,* "Patriciat noble et patriciat bourgeois," p. 121.

[18] Kageneck, "Das Patriziat im Elsass," p. 383.

from the leaders of the guild regime a recognition of the legitimate and even necessary role of the patriciate as the pinnacle of the civic social hierarchy.

The patriciate's renewed strength and prestige depended on two, quite different developments: the steady social pressure of wealthy guildsmen who wanted to become patricians; and the political rehabilitation of the patriciate through its military role in the wars of the mid- and later fifteenth century. The debate over the patriciate's civic utility (1461–1509) fixed the status of the patricians and their societies within the regime, thereby averting their total exclusion from political power—such as had been the fate of the Florentine magnates and would be that of the aristocrats of Basel.[19]

The rage among wealthy merchants for ennoblement and the gentleman's life was as powerful at Strasbourg as elsewhere in Europe.[20] An inquiry in 1457 revealed that a dozen former guildsmen had recently joined the Constofeln; and one successful climber candidly remarked: "He whom God has given riches also wants honor."[21] During the next few decades, there emerged a steady stream of "rich, prosperous persons, who serve in the guilds as their ancestors did, but who now want to join the Constofeln."[22] This pressure posed a genuine problem to the

---

[19] Rudolf Wackernagel, *Geschichte der Stadt Basel,* 3 vols. (Basel, 1907–24), III, 84–86, 283–285.

[20] See Fritz Rörig, *The Medieval Town* (Berkeley–Los Angeles, 1967), pp. 84–86; Erwin Riedenauer, "Kaiserliche Standeserhebungen für reichsstädtische Bürger 1519–1740," in *Deutsches Patriziat 1430–1740,* pp. 27–98. For the same phenomenon in France, see Lewis, *Later Medieval France,* pp. 173–181; Major, "The Crown and the Aristocracy in Renaissance France"; Philippe Wolff, *Commerce et marchands de Toulouse (vers 1350-vers 1450)* (Paris, 1954), pp. 616–617; and Robert Boutruche, ed., *Bordeaux de 1453 à 1715* (Bordeaux, 1966), pp. 167–168. For an overview of this kind of social mobility, see Jacques Heers, *L'occident aux XIVe et XV siècles. Aspects économiques et sociaux,* Nouvelle Clio, No. 23 (Paris, 1970), p. 391; Leopold Génicot, "Naïssance, fonction et richesse dans l'ordonnance de la société médiévale. Le cas de la noblesse du nord-ouest du continent," in *Problèmes de stratification sociale,* ed. R. Mousnier, p. 91. For the sixteenth century, see Pierre Jeannin, *Merchants of the 16th Century,* trans. Paul Fittinghoff (New York, 1972), pp. 139–142. See also Erich Maschke, "Das Berufsbewusstsein des mittelalterlichen Fernkaufmanns," in *Die Stadt des Mittelalters,* III, 200, 200n113.

[21] Dollinger, "La évolution politique," pp. 130–131.

[22] "Nuwe constofler urteil," undated but certainly from the second half of the fifteenth century (perhaps connected with the documents of 1471? and 1472 cited below), printed in Karl Theodor von Eheberg, ed., *Verfassungs-, Verwaltungs- und Wirtschaftsgeschichte der Stadt Strassburg bis 1681,* I: *Urkunden und Akten* (Strasbourg, 1899), pp. 768–770, No. 396.

regime. Some politicians opposed yielding to this pressure, because the passage of the wealthiest guildsmen into the Constofeln would lead to "the decline of the guilds"; but others pointed out that refusal would lead to just as harmful a phenomenon, the emigration of the rich,

> wherefore the entire city and also all the guilds would profit more if such rich, prosperous persons remained in the city as members of the Constofeln than if they emigrated; because their emigration would cause the commune a significant loss in cavalry, toll receipts, taxes, and other incomes.[23]

Despite the survival of anti-patrician sentiments, this opinion held the day.

Military service became, in fact, a crucial element in the willingness of the guild regime to preserve the patriciate. In the wars of the fifteenth century—the Armagnac invasions in 1439–44 and the Burgundian wars in 1471–77—the communal militia of Strasbourg made its last major campaigns. Thereafter, during the sixteenth century, Strasbourg would hire mercenaries to do its real fighting.[24] But the townsmen themselves fought in the fifteenth century wars, and they were led by their own patricians.

The regime's gratitude for the military performance of the patricians expressed itself in small ways. When Adam Zorn became a citizen in 1474, the usual fee was waived, "to the honor of his ancestors and his late father, who lost his life like a true knight in the city's service against the Armagnacs during the storming of the chateau of Marlenheim, which was taken and burned" in 1444.[25] More revealing is the case of Hans von Seckingen. When Seckingen, a descendant of wealthy merchants who had been active at Milan about 1400, was elected to the senate as a Constofler in 1479, someone disputed his right to call himself

---

[23] *Ibid.*, p. 769.

[24] Ulrich Crämer, "Die Wehrmacht Strassburgs von der Reformationszeit bis zum Fall der Reichsstadt," *ZGO*, 84 (1932), 45–95. I refer to major campaigns, not to minor operations. The same process has been established at Überlingen at about the same time. See David Warren Sabean, *Landbesitz und Gesellschaft am Vorabend des Bauernkriegs. Eine Studie der sozialen Verhältnisse im südlichen Oberschwaben in den Jahren vor 1525*, Quellen und Forschungen zur Agrargeschichte, 26 (Stuttgart, 1972), p. 57. See Rainer Wohlfeil, "Adel und neues Heerwesen," in *Deutscher Adel 1430–1555*, pp. 202–233, with abundant references.

[25] Wittmer, No. 2754; *QBLG*, III, 395n; Hatt, p. 613. Adam Zorn (d. ca. 1516), *Ritter*, son of Martin Zorn, commanded troops in Lorraine during the Burgundian wars and served many terms as Stettmeister of Strasbourg.

a patrician. The XV investigated the case and found that during the Burgundian wars,

> Sir Hans von Seckingen aided the defence in the city's service, rode out, risked his life and limb for the common good and did the best thing, persevering into the noble battle of Nancy, . . . where he was dubbed and received into the rank of Knight. . . . And since Sir Hans von Seckingen has specially received his knightly status in the afore mentioned battle of Nancy, ... the XV, for all of the aforesaid sound reasons, and so that others in the future will likewise risk life and limb for the love of honor and the common good, . . . believe that Sir Hans von Seckingen should be admitted to the Constofel by virtue of his knighthood, and that he should henceforth be and be regarded as a Constofler.[26]

A grateful regime allowed Seckingen his "honor," although the fate of the Basel nobles suggests that civic gratitude for service in the field could not be expected to last forever.[27]

The value of nobles as diplomats, a point stressed by Erich Maschke, certainly applies to Strasbourg, where diplomatic missions regularly comprised one patrician and one non-patrician member of the regime.[28]

---

[26] Eheberg, pp. 302–303, No. 112, and p. 455, No. 216. Hans von Seckingen (d. ca. 1509), descended from Hans Fridel von Seckingen, a merchant active at Milan in 1399–1400; he was related to Erhard von Seckingen (d. 21 December 1433), buried at St. Thomas; he married Barbara von Mülnheim (d. 9 April 1486), who was buried "zu den Reuern," and before 1502 Elisabeth Kärling. Stromer, *Oberdeutsche Hochfinanz*, pp. 409–411; Louis Schnéegans, *L'église de Saint-Thomas à Strasbourg et ses monuments historiques* (Strasbourg, 1842), p. 225; Hertzog, II, 129; Manfred Krebs, *Quellensammlung zur oberrheinischen Geschlechterkunde,* I, 1 (Karlsruhe, 1943), pp. 20–24; M. A. Cowie and M. L. Cowie, eds., *Works of Peter Schott (1460–1490),* 2 vols. (Chapel Hill, N.C., 1963–72), II, 758. Hans's son, also Hans, was vicar at Old St. Peter Strasbourg and became a citizen and member of the guild Zur Luzern (though his father had belonged to a Constofel) in 1524. Wittmer, No. 7511. The reason for this social plunge is found in a remark by Jacob Wimpheling in 1508: "Joannes de Seckingen itidem miles sua et suorum bona abliquirivit." The Newberry Library, Chicago, Ms. 63, fol. 114^r, on the dating of which see Otto Herding, "Zu einer humanistischen Handschrift, 63 der Newberry Library Chicago," in *Geschichte, Wirtschaft, Gesellschaft. Festschrift für Clemens Bauer zum 75. Geburtstag,* eds. Erich Hassinger, *et al.* (Berlin, 1974), pp. 153–187, here at p. 165.

[27] Many nobles had been driven from Basel during the wars of 1439–44, and large numbers of them later served Basel against the Burgundians, "umb burgrecht ze verdienen." Hildburg Brauer-Gramm, *Der Landvogt Peter von Hagenbach. Die burgundische Herrschaft am Oberrhein 1469–1474,* Göttinger Bausteine zur Geschichtswissenschaft, 27 (Göttingen, 1957), p. 31.

[28] Maschke, "Verfassung und soziale Kräfte," p. 292. The volumes of *PCSS* show that this was standing policy during the first half of the sixteenth century, but it was no novelty then. See, for example, the mission of Philips von Mülnheim (patrician) and Peter Schott (guildsman) to Charles the Rash of Burgundy in September, 1473, in *QBLG,* III, 429–430.

But the rehabilitation of the Constofler at Strasbourg was basically an accompaniment of the generation of the Burgundian wars, when the pressure of wealthy guildsmen wanting to become gentlemen became acute,[29] and the regime felt compelled to regulate mobility upward into the patriciate. The first law, passed by the assembly of Schöffen on 28 December 1471, laid down the liberal rule that

> any reputable man who has inherited his honor and property from his ancestors should understand that we would gladly increase his honor; [and] whoever he may be, whose grandfather and father served the city mounted at their own expense and who, being a man of property and honor, also serves mounted, wants to become a patrician,

may secure such honor by approval of the Senate & XXI and the assembly.[30] Property, honor, and military service, these were to remain the chief marks of the Constofler in the entire subsequent debate over the status and freedoms of the patriciate and its societies, a debate which began with this law of 1471 and ended only with the decree of 1509.

By the law of 1471 the regime of Strasbourg appropriated the right to declare a citizen a Constofler, a decision which fitted well into the general extension of the regime's authority over the internal affairs of subsidiary corporations during the fifteenth century. Indeed, the right to regulate admission to the Constofeln themselves became the chief point of contention between the Constofeln and those members of the regime who wished to give this power, too, to the regime. Right down through the last quarter of the fifteenth century, the regime contained guildsmen who resented the bleeding of the wealth and power of the guilds through the passage of the wealthiest guild families into the patriciate.

In the beginning, in the law of 1471, the regime simply assumed that the Constofler would admit, "in the manner in which they customarily admit patricians," whoever had met the qualifications and had gotten the approval of the regime and the assembly.[31] When, however, the wealthy former cloth merchant Bernhard Wurmser and his sons applied for patrician status in 1472, having been ennobled twenty years before,[32]

---

[29] Fourteen are named in an undated document (but from the 1470s) in Eheberg, pp. 451–453, No. 215, of whom some were willing to go back to their guilds and others were not.

[30] Eheberg, p. 242, No. 92; an excerpt in *Chroniken der deutschen Städte vom 14. bis ins 16. Jahrhundert*, ed. C. Hegel, IX: *Strassburg*, II (Leipzig, 1871), p. 964.

[31] *Ibid.*

[32] Karl Friedrich von Frank, *Standeserhebungen und Gnadenakte für das Deutsche Reich und die Österreichischen Erblande bis 1806*, 4 vols. (Schloss Senftenegg, Lower Austria, 1967–74), IV, 248.

guildsmen in the regime complained that the Constofler alleged the right to refuse admission to applicants unless each and every old member approved.

> The patricians have an agreement which holds that they will receive no one into their societies as a patrician unless all members agree, and if one member objects, they will not admit such a person. What is worse, it is said that they have a custom that such a veto power is possessed as well by their companions ["ir stubegesellen"] who live on the land and are not even citizens of this city. Some of us think that this is not to be tolerated.[33]

The XV, fearing new quarrels, decided not to challenge the liberty of the *Stuben* to veto new applicants, but they did lay down a new and detailed set of qualifications for new patricians.[34] Such persons must take an oath to reside in Strasbourg for ten years and to serve the commune mounted; and they must swear "henceforth to practice no commerce or craft, though they may participate in partnerships and invest in firms." Although eligible for patrician offices, the new Constofler had to take seats "below the born patricians," and the Constofeln might charge them no more than 15 lb. as an admission fee.

The chief problem, as the XV saw it, was that there were now too few patricians eligible for public office, so the regime ought to strive for controlled augmentation of the Constofeln rather than fight about alleged liberties. Thus, in a judgment issued sometime during the 1470s, the regime admitted the right of the Constofeln to accept or reject new members, but it declared that rich persons who wished to become patricians, including holders of imperial patents of nobility (*Briefadel*), could be so designated by the regime and would be regarded as patricians —whether or not a Constofel would admit them.[35] This meant that Strasbourg's regime took upon itself the right to create patricians out of wealthy guildsmen who met the regime's requirements. The regime, then, and not the emperor or the Constofeln themselves, decided who was and who was not to be considered a patrician of Strasbourg.

Unsurprisingly, the patricians opposed the creation of patricians outside the Constofeln. Their position was expressed in an opinion

---

[33] Eheberg, pp. 243–246, No. 92; excerpt in *Chroniken der deutschen Städte*, IX, 965–966 (15 April 1472).

[34] *Ibid.*

[35] "Nuwe constofler urteil," in Eheberg, pp. 768–770, No. 396, undated, but by language and provisions closely related to the decree of 15 April 1472 (cited in note 33 above).

(undated but around 1482) which recommended barring from patrician offices anyone who had not been admitted to one of the two Constofeln.[36] When this became law, the patricians had won a major victory.[37] Finally, in 1509, the entire matter was regulated by a compromise: resident nobles and other gentlemen had to join a Constofel, and any "Juncker" who could not gain admittance to a Constofel had to join a guild or leave the city.[38] This law conceded the liberty of the Constofeln to veto prospective members, but it also opened the way to regular corporate status, in the guilds, for nobles, armigers, and gentlemen-rentiers of all sorts, who could not or would not join a Constofel. The XV and the regime upheld their power to determine the right of access to public offices, while the Constofeln preserved their control over their own memberships.

Strasbourg's guild regime rested content with this recognition of the liberties and the anomalous status of the Constofeln as urban corporations. The Constofeln were never simply noble equivalents of guilds, for they were never purely urban institutions. Unlike the guilds, they adopted and revised their own statutes without consulting the XV, who held the power to review all guild statutes.[39] Unlike the presiding guild officials, the elected *Stubenmeister* of the Constofeln were apparently not subject to review by the regime, although this office was restricted to members who were citizens of Strasbourg.[40] On at least one occasion, an agreement concerning the office of *Stubenmeister* was submitted for

---

[36] *Ibid.*, pp. 519–520, No. 273, undated. The final paragraph notes approval by the guilds "Uff zinstag Sant Oswaltstag," which places it in 1454, 1465, 1471, 1482, 1493, or 1499. It was probably drafted in 1482, the year of the final constitutional revision, because two of the four drafters, Claus Wurmser (1478) and Hans Erhart von Rotweil (1479), had not yet entered the regime in 1471. It may, of course, date from the 1490s.

[37] *Ibid.*, p. 519: "und alle die wile ein solicher nit uff ein constofelstube entpfangen wurt, so sol derselbe die zit nit gebrucht noch gezogen werden zu den reten den XXI noch schöffen noch amman; aber wann er uff ein stuben entpfangen wurt, so mag man in bruchen wie ein andern constofeler, doch sol derselbe kein koufmanschatz triben durch sin, sin wibe, kynde oder gesynde, aber slechte und ungeverlich gemeinschaft oder verlegung ze thun mag er wol tun."

[38] "Les annales des frères mineurs de Strasbourg, redigées par le frère Martin Stauffenberger, économe du couvent (1507–1510)," ed. Rodolphe Reuss, in *BSCMHA*, N.S. 18, p. 311, dated "vor Michaëlis" (i.e., before 29 September).

[39] See the *Stubenordnung* of the Constofel zum Mühlstein, dated 1492, in AMS, I, 17–19/1.

[40] ADBR, E 1375/(4), dated 23 April 1515, revision of the statues of the Constofel zum Hohensteg: "dass wir sullen erkiessen zwen stuben meyster von der genantten vnser geselschafft jn der Statt sesshafftig die do acht jor die nehsten noch datum diss brieffs aneinander Stuben meister bliben sollen. . . ."

approval not to the regime but to the emperor.[41] Finally, no other civic political corporation at Strasbourg contained members who were not citizens or were not bound by the obligation to maintain a household in the city. All of these characteristics the guilds lacked, and their preservation was a symbol of the guild regime's toleration of the participation by the civic nobility in a status system quite different from the local one.

C. LIBERTIES AND LIMITATIONS OF THE CONSTOFELN AND THE CONSTOFLER

Since the settlement of 1509, the guild regime not only tolerated the liberties of the Constofeln, it actively protected them for at least a generation. This is clear from the regime's support for the Constofel zum Hohensteg through two lengthy suits against the corporation and its liberties during the first half of the sixteenth century. In each case, gentlemen of Strasbourg unsuccessfully appealed a judgment of the Senate & XXI to the *Reichskammergericht*.

In his suit against the Constofel zum Hohensteg (1514–23), Philips Hagen challenged the society's right to admit to and exclude from their social functions as they pleased, a liberty closely connected with the independence of the corporation from interference in its internal affairs. Philips was the grandson of Frantz Hagen, a wealthy merchant of Strasbourg and veteran of the Burgundian wars, who was ennobled by Frederick III in 1478.[42] Neither Frantz nor his son, also Frantz, nor Philips could gain entry to a Constofel. On 5 July 1514, Philips Hagen appeared uninvited at a dance in the hall Zum Hohensteg, where, after the second dance, four prominent members persuaded him that his

---

[41] Osthouse (Bas-Rhin), Fonds Zorn de Bulach, Laden I, Nos. 86 (1510) and 86[bis] (21 May 1522). My thanks to F.-J. Fuchs for allowing me to see photocopies of selected documents from this family archive.

[42] Authenticated copy of the Hagen patent, dated 19 September 1478, in AMS, IX 1/4. AMS, IX 1 contains the *Reichskammergericht* dossier (Koser, Nos. 538–539) of Philips Hagen's appeal of a local judgment against him. See also Riedenauer, "Kaiserliche Standeserhebungen," p. 70. Kageneck, "Das Patriziat im Elsass," p. 389, writes that Frantz Hagen gained admission to the Constofel zum Hohensteg after a nine-year suit and through the intervention of Emperor Maximilian I. This almost certainly refers to the suit of Philips Hagen against the Constofel zum Hohensteg, which lasted nine years (1514–23), but which Hagen lost. Philips Hagen was the grandson, not the son, of the man who was first ennobled by Emperor Frederick III. The grandfather (d. by 1493) could speak French and served in the Burgundian wars. AMS, AA 294, undated; Wittmer, No. 4421. Frantz Hagen, Jr., was armigerous and is last mentioned in 1509. AMS, KS 9, fol. 129.

health would be better served by immediate departure. Depart he did, after some hot words, and promptly brought suit against the society for damage to his honor (*Ehrenverletzung*) and for refusal to acknowledge an imperial patent of nobility.[43] He contended that patrician dances were traditionally open to all resident nobles, while the officers of the Constofel held that the society had the customary liberty to invite and exclude whom it chose. This was by no means an uncontested liberty, as the regime itself had earlier intervened to bar from patrician dances the bourgeois relatives of bourgeois wives of patricians.[44] The Constofel won the case before the court of first instance, the Senate & XXI, supported as it was by the other Constofel, by pleading that its dances had always been open by invitation only—thus skirting the more serious issue as to whether a piece of parchment could make a noble.

The Constofeln certainly had no valid legal argument against Hagen's claim to be noble. Besides his family's patent, Hagen stressed the fact that his father had lived nobly for thirty years and "also through his whole life was regarded and honored as a nobleman."[45] His wife, Barbara von Falkenstein, was a noblewoman, and one of his female relatives, Magdalena Hagen, married successively a Bock von Erlenburg and a Böcklin—families whose noble status was unchallengeable.[46] So good were the Hagen claims that, after the suit was finished, Philips's son, Marx Hagen, joined a Constofel and served in the senate as a patrician.[47] The Hagen had just as honorable a status and just as good a set of credentials as the Wurmser, who were also *Briefadel* of very recent creation and had entered the patriciate without much difficulty.[48] And the Hagen credentials were certainly better than those of the Bietenheim, who in the late sixteenth century moved into the patriciate without formal ennoble-

---

[43] The best account of these events is in the "Liber reconuentionalis hern Adams Zorn . . . contra Philipssen Hagen," received at Worms on 9 May 1516, in AMS, IX 1/4. At the time of the incident, Philips Hagen was not a citizen of Strasbourg, for he had renounced his citizenship on 30 January 1504 and purchased it again on 23 July 1517. Wittmer, Nos. 5398, 6668. He also renounced citizenship again during the suit, for he is found purchasing it once again on 24 July 1522. AMS, KS 13, fol. 167^v.

[44] Eheberg, pp. 520–521, No. 274.

[45] "Articuli et positiones Philipsen Hagen vs. Zorn et consortes," received at Nuremberg on 6 October 1522, in AMS, IX 1/4.

[46] AMS, KS 10, fols. 251^v–252^r; AMS, KS 21, fol. 43^v.

[47] AMS, IX 3/3; Hatt, p. 446; Johannes Ficker and Otto Winckelmann, *Handschriftenproben des 16. Jahrhunderts nach Strassburger Originalen*, 2 vols. (Strasbourg, 1902–05), I, 12: Marx Hagen (ca. 1510–51).

[48] The Wurmser appear in the Senate as guild representatives before 1476 and as patricians from that year onward. Hatt, pp. 575–576.

ment.[49] The conclusion is unavoidable that the Constofel zum Hohensteg excluded the Hagen either because of an old grudge or to teach some *arrivistes* a lesson. At any rate, the case demonstrates that the Constofeln could not be obliged by any formal criterion to admit an applicant; and this position was supported by the regime.

A second suit against the same corporation was pressed by the male members of the Mosung family, who in 1534 were refused admission.[50] The suit dragged on before the Senate & XXI and then, on appeal, before the *Reichskammergericht* for nearly twenty years. The Mosung brothers asked for admission to the Constofel zum Hohensteg on the ground that they were descended from the patrician Mosung of the fourteenth century. The patricians replied that these were different Mosung and were the descendants of guildsmen. As in the Hagen case, the plaintiffs' formal credentials were quite respectable. They were sons of Claus Mosung (d. 1529), of whose patent of nobility ("rittermässiger Adelsstand") from Charles V they were able to secure a confirmation.[51] They now called themselves "Mosung von Schäffolsheim," lived in a chateau like gentlemen, and claimed that because their remote ancestors had been "Wappens genoss vnnd Adels stanndt" the Constofel had to admit them.[52] The Senate & XXI, faithful to the settlement of 1509, upheld the liberty of the Constofel to admit or reject whom it pleased.[53] The only right to membership was hereditary right, and the Mosung genealogical and heraldic proofs were found to be insufficient.[54]

---

[49] Riedenauer, "Kaiserliche Standeserhebungen," p. 97n117. Riedenauer errs when he writes that the same was true of the Ebel. Friedrich Ebel was ennobled on 4 May 1554. BMS, Ms. 936, fol. 5ᵛ.

[50] ADBR, 3B 779, the *Reichskammergericht* dossier (Koser, No. 644). The sewn fascicle of depositions and other evidence from the court of first instance (ADBR, 3B 779/8) is filled with interesting information about the pursuit of genealogy and heraldry in sixteenth-century Strasbourg. It is used by Geneviève Levallet-Haug, "Quelques exemples d'orfèvrerie strasbourgeoise des XVe et XVIe siècles," *ASAVS*, 5 (1975), 41–44, whose transcriptions are frequently inaccurate (e.gg., read "Batt" von Fegersheim on p. 42, Hans Erhart von "Rotwil" on p. 43, and Hans Jacob "Knobloch" on p. 43). The document is incorrectly cited (p. 41) under 3B 7798 rather than the correct 3B 779/8.

[51] Riedenauer, "Kaiserliche Standeserhebungen," p. 70. As information extracted from (now lost) guild records by the defendants proved, Claus Mosung had indeed belonged to the *Küferzunft* during the first decade of the sixteenth century. ADBR, 3B 779/4, fol. 17ʳ, and No. 8, fol. 29ᵛ.

[52] ADBR, 3B 779/4, fol. 26ᵛ.

[53] *Ibid.*, fols. 16ʳ–17ʳ, 27ʳ⁻ᵛ.

[54] Which is why the arguments were largely composed of genealogical and heraldic evidence. See esp. *ibid.*, No. 8, fols. 25ʳ–26ʳ.

The Hagen and Mosung cases complement information from other sources and provide a clearer picture of the contemporary definition of a patrician of Strasbourg: a patrician (Constofler) was a gentleman who was either the son of a patrician or was found by the other patricians to be worthy of membership in their Constofel. Except for demonstrable direct descent from a patrician, no formal qualification conferred a right to admission—not a patent of nobility, nor a noble marriage, nor the reputation of living nobly. The patricians could be very strict with applicants from outside the well-known region of the Upper Rhine valley. Johann Schultheiss (d. 1551) of Schwäbisch Hall moved to Strasbourg around 1544, married a Strasbourgeoise, and was admitted to the Constofel zum Hohensteg on 1 December 1545.[55] Two years later, Schultheiss was still gathering testimony about his family background for the Constofel, and there is reason to conclude that his proofs were not considered sufficient, for by 1549 he apparently had been demoted to the guilds.[56]

One result of the protected liberties of the Constofeln was that, all through the sixteenth century, there were armigerous families, and even a few noble ones, in the guilds. They were not a whit inferior, by the standards of status outside the town, to most of the patrician families. Such families as the Ryff, Drachenfels, Rotweil, Duntzenheim, Jörger, Barpfennig, and Erstein were armigerous, just as were many patrician families. Some, such as the Erstein, called Armbruster, were rentiers and fiefholders and held perfectly valid imperial *Wappenbriefe*.[57] Some other guild families were actually noble. Gottfried von Hohenburg was ennobled by Maximilian I in 1509, and his subsequent service as Ammeister (1509, 15, 21) from the guild Zur Blume proves that this office,

---

[55] AMS, Livre de Bourgeoisie 1543–1618, col. 19, where his wife is named Ursula Mussler. Hans Schultheiss studied at Heidelberg, Tübingen, and Leipzig (1537–42), renounced citizenship at Hall on 23 December 1547, and died at Strasbourg on 27 August 1551. Information on his testament is in AMS, V 132/27. See Gerhard Wunder and G. Leckner, eds., *Die Bürgerschaft der Reichsstadt Hall von 1395–1600*, Württembergische Geschichtsquellen, 25 (Stuttgart, 1956), p. 489; Gerhard Wunder, "Die Sozialstruktur der Reichsstadt Schwäbisch Hall," p. 32. His family was one of the richest at Hall.

[56] AMS, I 17–19/2 (2 December 1547): Heinrich Spiess zu Morstein and Wilhelm von Crailsheim zu Hornburg attest for Hans Schultheiss "seines Adels vnnd herkhomens" for the "Ritterliche gesellschafft zu dem hohensteg zu Straszburgk"; and they affirm that the Schultheiss family "gutte, erliche alte vom Adell sein." This attestation was apparently found by the Constofel to be inadequate, for around 1549 Jacob Sturm classified Schultheiss among the rich guildsmen. AMS, VI 491/3.

[57] That of the Erstein, called Armbruster, (Breslau, 28 February 1420) was a confirmation of the family's right to bear arms (*Wappenbestätigung*). Frank, I, 30.

Table 2

Maintenance of Horses in the Civic Stable as Military Obligation at Strasbourg, ca. 1460–1540
(in persons/horses)

Corporation(s)	1460/75	1473/79	1517	1518	1519	1540
Constofeln	—	67/91	28/37	16/19	17/30	20/31
Guilds	53/71	65/70	16/22	15/19	15/18	14/17
Zum Encker	7/21	8/10	3/4	4/5	2/2	
Zum Spiegel	—	16/17	6/10	5/8	5/8	
Zur Blume	19/21	4/4	1/1	2/2	1/1	
Zum Freiburg	—	11/10	2/3	3/3	4/4	
Tucher	3/4	2/2	1/1	—	—	
Zur Luzern	11/13	8/11	1/1	2/2	—	
Zur Möhrin	—	4/4	—	—	—	
Zur Steltz	—	1/1	1/1	—	—	
Küfer	—	4/4	1/1	1/1	1/1	
Gerber	—	2/2	—	—	—	
Weinsticher	—	2/2	—	—	—	
Schuhmacher	—	3/3	—	—	—	
Gartner	13/13	—	—	—	—	

Sources: 1460/75: AMS, IV 86. 1473/79: AMS, R 28, fols. 100^r–103^r (Eheberg, pp. 227–229, No. 79). 1517–19: AMS, VI 591/1. 1540: AMS, R 29/107.

though reserved to the guilds, was not closed to nobles.[58] The Ingold, ennobled on 21 August 1473, became one of Strasbourg's major merchant-banking families and stayed in the guilds until the end of the next century.[59] Conrad Joham was a merchant-banker and son of a knight, who, though ennobled by Charles V in 1536 as "Joham von Mundolsheim," continued to represent the Tanners' guild in the privy councils until he emigrated in 1548.[60] Friedrich VI von Gottesheim, also a noble by imperial patent, served all his life in a guild and never entered a Constofel.[61] Some of these families and individuals may have joined or remained in the guilds in order to be able to continue their direct engagement in trade. Others may have been rebuffed by the Constofler, as the Hagen were. Whatever the reasons, through the sixteenth century there was a stratum of armigers and nobles in the guilds—some of them rentiers and some merchants—who differed from the Constofler only in that they were not Constofler. There was no other firm distinction

---

[58] Prosopography, No. XLI.
[59] *Ibid.*, No. XLIII; BMS, Ms. 936, fol. 5^r.
[60] Prosopography, No. XLV.
[61] Prosopography, No. XXXIV.

between patricians and gentleman-guildsmen, not even the historic role of the patricians as the commune's cavalry.

It is perhaps ironical that one of the principal justifications for the rehabilitation of the patriciate during the later fifteenth century, their service as cavalry, was of declining importance after 1500 and, indeed, did not distinguish them from the other wealthy families of the town. Table 2 is based on surviving fragments of the registers of the civic stable (*Stall*), which record those who kept horses there as part of their military obligation. Besides revealing the steady decline of the communal cavalry, Table 2 shows that a large portion, sometimes nearly one-half, of the cavalry was supplied by wealthy guildsmen. It also shows the concentration of wealth in certain guilds and the relative decline of the guilds Zur Blume (butchers) and Zur Luzern (grain merchants) and the rise of the guilds Zum Encker (shippers) and Zum Spiegel (merchants). By 1517, nearly all the non-patricians who served "zu Ross" belonged to one of the upper eight guilds in the official guild hierarchy, a point to which we shall return.

The decline of the communal cavalry, the military arm staffed by the rich, was but one aspect of the general decline of the communal militia. Its last great age saw the campaigns against Charles the Rash of Burgundy during the mid-1470s. Although occasionally mustered thereafter, it rarely left town. The militia's last campaign was a ludicrous, one-day outing across the Rhine to Wilstätt (1526) to liberate a Strasbourgeois arrested there. Although the guild militia was mustered with great ceremony in the summer of 1543, during the Smalkaldic War (1546) the regime wisely invested in mercenaries.[62] At Strasbourg as elsewhere, the day of the citizen-soldier, whether patrician horseman or artisan pikeman, was over.

Contemporary with the decline of the patriciate's military role came a transformation of the institution of knighthood. The traditional term for the patriciate had been "Ritter und Knechte," distinguishing not two estates or strata but only those who had undergone the ceremony of knighthood from those who had not. The latter were simply armigerous gentlemen, although every male patrician was certainly eligible for

---

[62] The story of the Willstätt campaign (11 April 1526) is recounted in most of the Strasbourg chronicles, and perhaps with most detail by Johann Jacob Meyer, *Chronique*, ed. Rodolphe Reuss, *BSCMHA*, N.S. 8, p. 231. On the great muster of 1543 (23 April), see Ludwig Schneegans, *Strassburgische Geschichten* (Strasbourg, 1855), pp. 7–11.

knighthood.[63] The Strasbourg material permits a very precise dating of the disappearance of this institution and its accompanying title. The last large group of knights at Strasbourg were the patricians and other well-to do young men who distinguished themselves in the Burgundian wars. On the fields of Murten and Nancy in 1476, twenty-five cavalrymen were knighted—including two Kageneck, a Spender, a Sturm, a Lentzel, a Merswin, a Böcklin, a Wurmser, a Berer, and a Zorn von Bulach—plus two others (Adam Zorn and Ludwig von Kageneck) who served under Duke René of Lorraine.[64] Three more Strasbourgeois were knighted at the Holy Sepulchre in Jerusalem on 17 July 1483.[65] Knights were very scarce, however, in the next generation. According to tradition, Hans Bock von Gerstheim (d. 1542) was the last local noble to be dubbed knight in the old manner, a tradition that may well be true.[66] The dramatic

Table 3

Incidence of Knighthood among Patrician Officeholders (A) and Stettmeister alone (B) at Strasbourg, 1449–1600

Office	1449–86	1487–1524	1525–62	1563–1600
(A) All Officeholders	99	57	72	60
Knights	24	19	3	0
% Knights	24%	33%	4%	—
(B) Stettmeister alone	30	24	22	24
Knights	19	16	3	0
% Knights	63%	67%	14%	—

Source: Derived from Hatt, *Liste des membres.*

[63] From his work on Baden, Bernhard Theil concludes "dass der Begriff 'Ritter' keine feste Standeswürde meint, die erblich war, sondern einen Status, der erst erworben werden musste." *Das älteste Lehnbuch der Markgrafen von Baden (1381)*, VKLBW, A 25 (Stuttgart, 1974), p. 136, with references in p. 133n5. For Alsace, see Dollinger, "Patriciat noble et patriciat bourgeois," p. 57; and Henri Dubled, "L'écuyer en Alsace au moyen âge," *RA*, 92 (1953), 47–56, esp. p. 47.

[64] "Strassburgische Archiv-Chronik," in *Code historique et diplomatique de la Ville de Strasbourg,* eds. A. W. Strobel and Louis Schnéegans, 2 vols. (Strasbourg, 1843, 1848), II, 200, 203; BNUS, Ms. 1223, fols. 35^v, 36^r, 46^v (extracts from the lost Duntzenheim chronicle). The same names appear in a little-known Strasbourg chronicle in NSUG, Ms. Hist. 154, fols. 135^v, 138^r.

[65] *ZC*, I, 477–478.

[66] Johann Daniel Schoepflin, *L'Alsace illustrée, ou recherches sur l'Alsace pendant la domination desceltes, des romains, des francs, des allemands et des français*, trans. L. W. Ravenèz, 5 vols. (Mulhouse, 1849–52), V, 778; PROSOPOGRAPHY, No. XI.

decline in the incidence of knighthood as a personal honor among patricians of Strasbourg and other Lower Alsatian nobles is the subject of Tables 3 and 4. Table 3 gives the numbers of patrician officeholders (total of senators and Stettmeister, and Stettmeister alone), 1449–1600, and shows the declining proportion of knights. Since the figures for the Stettmeister (B) are included in those for all officeholders (A), the table reveals both the decline in the incidence of knighthood among politically active patricians of Strasbourg and the coincidence of the honor of knighthood with the more prestigious office of Stettmeister. In every period down to the 1560s, knights were far more likely to gain the office of Stettmeister than were non-knights. The temporary rise in the proportion of knights due to the dubbings during the Burgundian wars is clearly visible in the second period. The decline of knighthood and its near disappearance around the mid-sixteenth century is confirmed by Table 4, which plots the phenomenon among the episcopal vassals summoned to the meetings of the bishop's feudal court at Molsheim (*Manngericht*), ca. 1516–55. About one-half of these vassals were citizens of Strasbourg, most of them patricians. The first half of the sixteenth century, then, saw the last days of knighthood as a personal honor in Lower Alsace and at Strasbourg. Here, on a local and regional scale, is visible the point of transformation of the institution from a personal honor into a hereditary estate (*Stand*). At Strasbourg the collective term

Table 4

"Ritter" and "Edelleute" among the vassals summoned to the feudal court (Manngericht) of the Bishop of Strasbourg, ca. 1516–55

Year	"Edelleute"	"Ritter"	Total	"Ritter" % of Total
ca. 1516	118	9	127	7.1
1520	107	9	116	7.8
1522	104	6	110	5.4
1523	109	7	116	6.0
ca. 1525	92	4	96	4.2
1532	106	3	109	2.6
1537	83	2	85	2.4
1540	86	2	88	2.3
1551	97	0	97	0.0
1554	104	0	104	0.0
1555	100	0	100	0.0

Source: ADBR, G 503.

"ritterschafft" was already in common use as a synonym for a Constofel.[67] At mid-century came the final change, when the free knights—the members of the lesser nobility who were imperial vassals—of Lower Alsace organized themselves into a political corporation, a *Reichsritterschaft*, which survived until the French Revolution. Twenty-nine patricians of Strasbourg, all vassals of the Holy Roman Empire, entered this new corporation and assumed for themselves and their descendants the hereditary rank of *Reichsritter*.[68]

D. The Numerical Survival of the Constofler

The size of the patriciate of Strasbourg at any one time is difficult to determine. The membership of the Constofeln comprised persons of several different sorts: adult, male patricians who were citizens of Strasbourg; noble widows and spinsters; rural nobles who were associate citizens (*Ausbürger*), exempt from the residence requirement; and, at least by the later sixteenth century, social members (*Stubengesellen*) who were not bound to the city by any form of citizenship.[69] The women, the *Ausbürger,* and the others who were not full citizens (*Grossbürger*), plus citizens of comital and baronial rank, were not eligible for civic

---

[67] In the dossier Mosung vs. Constofel zum Hohensteg appear the following phrases: "die Ritterschafft vnnd Constofler des Hohenstegs zu Strassburg" and "die verordeneten gemeiner Ritterschafft der Constofler zum hohensteg." ADBR, 3B 779/4, fols. 3ᵛ–4ʳ, 12ʳ.

[68] Kageneck, "Das Patriziat im Elsass," pp. 390–392; Alfred Overmann, "Die Reichsritterschaft im Unterelsass bis zum Beginn des dreissigjährigen Krieges," *ZGO*, 50 (1895), 570–637.

[69] Charles Wittmer, "Das Strassburger Bürgerrecht bis zum Jahre 1530," *AJb*, 1961, p. 243; F.-J. Fuchs, "Le droit de bourgeoisie à Strasbourg," *RA*, 101 (1962), 25, 32. The longest list dates from the end of the sixteenth century, "Ritterschafft in Vnder Elsass Beeder Stuben zum Hohensteg vndt Mühlstein, So zum Theil der Statt Strassburg Bürger, zum Theil Verglichene, vnd zum Theil gar Ausslendische," which numbers 82 males and 8 females. AMS, I 17–19/4. Comparing this with the list of 41 males who were full citizens in 1598 (AMS, VI 496) suggests that less than one-half the Constofler were full citizens. Jean-Frédéric Hermann, *Notices historiques, statistiques et littéraires sur la ville de Strasbourg,* 2 vols. (Strasbourg, 1817, 1819), II, 28–30, prints a list of 95 males, representing 89 families and branches of families, who were supposedly enrolled in the Constofeln at the end of the fifteenth century. It is actually a composite which includes a good many persons from the later sixteenth century, and twenty-eight of the men can be identified with persons who flourished after 1550. On the entire subject of citizenship and noble status, see Heinz Lieberich, "Rittermässigkeit und bürgerliche Gleichheit. Anmerkungen zur gesellschaftlichen Stellung des Bürgers im Mittelalter," in *Festschrift für Hermann Krause,* eds. Sten Gagner, *et al.,* (Cologne–Vienna, 1975), pp. 66–93.

Table 5

Numbers of adult male patricians at Strasbourg, 1392–1589

Year*	Number	Source
1392	315	Dollinger, "La évolution politique," p. 130.
1444	100	*Ibid.*
1492	ca. 70	Based on AMS, I 17–19/1.
1497/98	ca. 72	Overmann, "Reichsritterschaft," p. 589.
1524	ca. 55	Based on AMS, IX 1/4.
1535	35	AMS, VI 495.
1541/43	ca. 35	AMS, I 20a/2–3.
1548/49	14	AMS, VI 491/3.
1550	229	Overmann, "Reichsritterschaft," pp. 632–633.
1589	41	*Ibid.*, p. 635.

*The figures for 1492 and 1524 are expanded from lists of just one Constofel, based on a known normal ratio between the two *Stuben* (about 3:2 in favor of the Constofel zum Hohensteg).

office.[70] Table 5 summarizes the few surviving lists of adult male patricians from the late fourteenth until the late sixteenth century, revealing the effects of the patriciate's political defeat in 1419–20. Excluding the sharp decline in 1548, which was due to a temporary emigration of most of the patriciate, the Constofeln numbered at any one point during the Reformation generation about 30–50 adult males, not counting females, *Ausbürger,* and other ineligibles.

The abiding political problem of the Strasbourg patriciate since the later fifteenth century was the provision of enough eligible adult males to fill the patrician share of civic offices. During the early 1470s, long before the Constofeln had declined to their Reformation-era levels, it was already difficult to find enough eligible persons to fill the patrician offices.[71] Approximately twenty-two patricians were required for the Senate (*Grosser Rat*), Lesser Senate (*Kleiner Rat*), and other bodies each year, serving for two-year terms. Half of them were replaced annually, and a former officeholder was ineligible for office for one year after his last term. The eligibility lists drawn up for the Constofeln thus include all male full citizens over twenty-five years old (thirty if unmarried),

---

[70] See Gerhard Wunder, "Ein Verzeichnis des Strassburger Landgebiets aus dem Jahr 1516," *ZGO*, 114 (1966), 57–58, who discusses and lists some citizens of baronial and comital rank. The *Stubenordnung* of the Constofel zum Mühlstein of 1492 refers to those "stubengesellen" who live on the land are are not bound by the residence requirement for citizens. AMS, I, 17–19/1.

[71] *Chroniken der deutschen Städte,* IX, 966 (15 April 1472).

minus: the eleven or twelve men remaining in office for the second year of a term; and the eleven or twelve men going out of office. Table 6 shows the numbers of adult male patricians from the eligibility lists drawn up at the end of each year. The numbers are totals for the two corporations, and each has been increased by twenty-two to account for the exclusions noted above. The results should approximate the actual numbers of patricians eligible for any civic office in the years indicated; and comparable figures from other sources are given in parentheses.

Table 6

Numbers of male patricians eligible for civic office at Strasbourg, 1490–1598

Year	Number	Year	Number	Year	Number
1490	49	1535	(35)	1570	39
1495	46	1541/43	(35)	1575	48
1501	41	1548/49	(14)	1580	54
1506	48	ca. 1550	(29)	1585	65
1508	47	1557	54	1590	51
1520	43	1561	53	1595	59
1524	50?	1565	45	1598	35

Sources: AMS, VI 494–496; sources of numbers in parentheses are given in Table 5 above.

Table 6 confirms the picture in Table 5, showing that the patriciate was numerically weakest during the Reformation generation (ca. 1520–1550), thereafter recovering something like its previous numbers and even a few more. During the years of the nadir, moreover, nearly the entire eligible sector of the patriciate had to hold office, since each January there were needed twenty-two officeholders plus eleven in-eligibles. This means that for about thirty years the patriciate was barely large enough to fill its quota of offices, which, in turn, suggests why there remained no trace of any competition for office among the patricians of this generation and why the rehabilitated patriciate posed no threat to the domination of the regime by the guildsmen. The figures also show that the Reformation occurred when the political position of the patriciate was waning—although it did not cause this wane—and that the few patrician politicians who actually wielded political influence during this generation probably represented nearly the sum total of political ambition and ability in the Constofeln. Above all, these Tables 5 and 6 reveal that the patriciate was not numerically strong enough to have defended its one-third of civic offices, had a threat to its share grown out of the popular phase of the Reformation, and that, therefore, the continued possession of so large a share of civic offices by the patriciate reflects the judgment of the wealthy guild politicians that the patricians were now useful allies rather than rivals.

Very little numerical gain came from the admission of new noble citizens. The flow of nobles in and out of the Constofeln down to 1530 can be followed in the *Bürgerbuch*, from which Table 7 is derived. The first part (A) shows the average annual numbers of admissions and renunciations, 1490–1530, while the second (B) breaks down the admissions, 1510–1530, by sex and by Constofel.[72]

Table 7

(A) Annual average numbers of admissions to and renunciations of citizenship by patricians in Strasbourg, 1490–1530

	1490–1509	1510–24	1525	1526–30
Admissions	3.6/yr.	3.5/yr.	34	5.8/yr.
Renunciations	1.8/yr.			

(B) New admissions of nobles to citizenship, 1510–30, by sex and Constofel

Constofel	Men	Women	Total (%)
Zum Hohensteg	48	18	66 (56.9)
Zum Mühlstein	32	6	38 (32.8)
Undesignated	6	6	12 (10.3)
	—	—	
Total	86	30	116 (100.0)

If the years 1525–30 are excluded from the results of Table 7(A) as reflecting the abnormal conditions during and after the Peasants' War, in normal times the Constofeln had a net gain of 1.8 new patricians per year. If the women, who made up more than one-quarter (25.9%) of the admissions, are excluded as ineligibles, then the average gain of eligibles was probably about one and one-third male patricians per year. Lest it be thought that the sex ratio for the period 1510–30 is badly skewed by the admission of many noble nuns during the year of the Peasants' War, it should be added that the proportion of women in the admissions for

---

[72] Before 1510 the *Bürgerbuch* rarely gives the Constofel of a new patrician citizen.

the entire period 1490–1530 is somewhat higher: 28.4% women and 71.6% men. Table 7(B) also confirms the conclusion from other evidence that the Constofel zum Hohensteg was normally about 50% larger than the Constofel zum Mühlstein.

The foregoing analysis yields a fairly clear picture of the numerical survival of the Strasbourg patriciate during the sixteenth century. First, the combined membership of the two Constofeln declined slowly and steadily from the mid-fifteenth century, whereupon it stabilized at 40–60 members for the next half-century. Secondly, the politically active portion of the patriciate during the Reformation generation was just barely large enough to fill the patrician offices, at least until the crisis of 1548–49. Thirdly, immigration and emigration produced a new gain of members to the two Constofeln of about 1.8 patricians (of whom 1.3 males) per year. Finally, from the defeat of 1419–20 until the mid-sixteenth century, the Strasbourg patriciate was a waning estate, whose continued possession of such a large share of civic offices must be explained by the relationships of the patriciate to the other fraction of the civic aristocracy.

E. THE STRASBOURG PATRICIATE BETWEEN CITY AND LAND

Whereas the centrality of the family as a social and political unit in urban aristocracies was a universal phenomenon in Europe, the strength and density of familial and other social ties between urban and rural aristocracies varied greatly from region to region and from city to city. There are well-known cases of urban exclusiveness, either voluntary as at Venice or involuntary as at Nuremberg. Conditions were very different in Swabia, where the patricians of the principal towns had long enjoyed intimate social connections with the lesser nobility of the surrounding regions.[73] It has been observed that the Strasbourg patricians were relatively closely tied to the rural nobility and that these connections were much stronger during the sixteenth century than they earlier had been.[74] Though it clearly resembled its Swabian counterpart, the aristocratic nexus of city and land at Strasbourg had some peculiar features which may be studied through the principal patrician families.

---

[73] Albrecht Rieber, "Das Patriziat von Ulm, Augsburg, Ravensburg, Memmingen, Biberach," in *Deutsches Patriziat 1430–1740*, p. 329. The same was true at Rottweil, for which see Elben, *Patriziat der Reichsstadt Rottweil*, pp. 102, 110, 131, 151. For the very different situation at Nuremberg, see Hofmann, "Nobiles Norimbergenses," pp. 74–76.

[74] Kageneck, "Das Patriziat im Elsass," p. 386.

As to the absolute size of the Strasbourg patriciate around 1500, Kageneck's estimate of forty to fifty families or households is probably close to the mark, though it is sooner too high than too low. The number of politically active families was certainly lower than that. This is indicated by the following figures for the numbers of families and branches of families who held the offices of patrician senator and Stettmeister during four thirty-eight year periods between 1449 and 1600: 1449–86, forty-eight; 1487–1524, thirty; 1525–62, thirty six; and 1563–1600, thirty.[75] The average for each generation during the sixteenth century was of the order of thirty to thirty-five families. The Strasbourg patriciate was thus larger than that of Ulm, a city of comparable size and social complexion, where the patriciate declined from seventy families (plus thirteen *Ausbürger* families) in 1430 to twenty-nine in 1488 and seventeen in 1552.[76] The decline from the fifteenth century, probably typical for defeated patriciates in towns ruled by guilds, is also to be observed in the much smaller town of Memmingen, where the patriciate declined from about thirty-seven families in 1450 to about twenty-two in 1500.[77] Strasbourg's patriciate stabilized at a level, in number of families, far above that of the largest South German city, Augsburg, where, perhaps due to the late beginning and prolonged character of the guild revolts, the patriciate had so declined in numbers by 1538 that the eight remaining families were augmented, with the regime's approval, by thirty-eight families from the ranks of the wealthy non-patricians.[78]

The inner core of the patriciate—the most politically active and therefore the most deeply engaged in urban affairs—can be identified

---

[75] Derived from the officeholding lists in Hatt, *Liste des membres,* and based on a series of calculations, the results of part of which are given in Appendix B. "Family" is here taken in the broadest sense, all variations on a single surname being grouped under that name. The chronological breakdown is explained in the introductory paragraph to Appendix B.

[76] Rieber, "Das Patriziat von Ulm," p. 307. The Ulm patriciate also resembled that of Strasbourg both in its retention of a substantial share of political power after the victory of the guilds and in its general abstention from trade. *Ibid.,* p. 310; Gottfried Geiger, *Die Reichsstadt Ulm vor der Reformation. Städtisches und kirchliches Leben am Ausgang des Mittelalters,* Forschungen zur Geschichte der Stadt Ulm, 11 (Ulm, 1971), p. 38, who, however, notes that the patriciate was able to block upward mobility from the guilds.

[77] Raimund Eirich, *Memmingens Wirtschaft und Patriziat von 1347 bis 1551. Eine wirtschafts- und sozialgeschichtliche Untersuchung über das Memminger Patriziat während der Zunftverfassung* (Weissenhorn, 1971), pp. 24–27. My calculations are approximate and are based on the dates Eirich gives for each family.

[78] Rieber, "Das Patriziat von Ulm," p. 313.

from the lists of patrician senators and Stettmeister. Appendix B contains ranked lists of the ten most active patrician families for each of four thirty-eight-year periods between 1449 and 1600, based on each family's share of all high civic offices and of the more prestigious office of Stettmeister alone.[79] The most engaged, and probably most powerful, families predictably dominated the office of Stettmeister to a far greater extent than they did the senatorial office.[80] We can detect the passing of old and the coming of new families in the political core of the patriciate: the rise of the Wurmser, the Böcklin, and the Sturm toward the end of the fifteenth century; the weakening of the Mülnheim and the Bock after 1550; and the passing (from politics at least) of the Hüffel and Lentzel after the first period (1449–86), the Spender, Berer, and Völtsch after the second (1487–1524), and the Kageneck and the Ellenhart after the third (1525–62). The latter were mostly old patrician families who never again assumed their former influence in civic politics. The fourth period (1563–1600) is marked by the rise to power of three recently ennobled merchant families, the Joham von Mundolsheim, the Prechter, and the Mieg von Boofzheim. But these lists also show that the Reformation produced no fundamental change in the inner political core of the patriciate; the patricians who participated in the introduction of the reform came from old, well-established families.[81]

The lists in Appendix B also yield the names of six families whose political *engagement* reveals them to have formed the enduring core of the patriciate during the later fifteenth and the first half of the sixteenth century: Mülnheim, Sturm, Wurmser, Böcklin, Bock, and Zorn. In these families, if in any, we should find the true urban nobility, the families who were most "urban," most attached to the city and its structure of power. This is confirmed by some further computations based on the office holding patterns: the six families furnished in each of the four periods between 1449 and 1600 never less than half of the Stettmeister, their share reaching a maximum during the years 1525–62 of more than three-quarters (77.2%); and they never supplied

---

[79] Appendix B below; and see note 75 above.

[80]. Somewhat deceptive in the tables is the appearance of families whose apparent political prominence was in fact due to the career of one member. This is true of the Burggraff and Zum Rust in period 1, the Endingen in periods 1 and 2, the Ellenhart in periods 2 and 3, the Röder von Diersburg in period 3, and the Rechberg and Bock von Erlenburg in period 4.

[81] Of the families who disappeared from political life after the 1520s, the Spender, Berer, and Ottfriedrich became extinct in the male lines in 1534, 1536, and 1536 respectively. Schoepflin, *L'Alsace illustrée*, V, 715, 657, 700.

less than two-fifths of all patrician officeholders in any one of the four periods, their share reaching a maximum of more than one half (54.1%) during the years 1525–62.

Many patricians tended to wear the mantle of citizenship rather lightly, and the frequency with which prominent nobles moved in and out of the city is one way of gauging the strength of their civic commitment. Ludwig Böcklin (d. 1529), the most influential patrician in the regime in the immediate pre-Reformation years, renounced and purchased citizenship three times each between 1483 and 1500, perhaps in connection with military service abroad or for other personal reasons.[82] The champion for fickleness, however, was Jacob Beger von Bleyberg (d. 1522), who renounced citizenship five times and purchased it four times between 1481 and 1503.[83] As citizens were bound by law to maintain households in the city, any kind of pressing personal business might lead even a politically active patrician to renounce his citizenship for a time. Egenolf Röder von Diersburg (d. 1550), for example, was elected Stettmeister for a two-year term at the beginning of 1519. In the autumn, as the plague was raging in Strasbourg, Röder gave up his offices and citizenship (15 September 1519) and left the town—probably for his country seat at Diersburg in the Ortenau—and did not return until the following spring (26 May 1520). His colleagues apparently not only did not resent his going, they reinstalled him in the Senate when he returned.[84]

Röder is a good example of the fact that, apart from the handful of patrician families who perennially supplied officeholders, many "urban nobles" were simply individual members of rural clans who happened to become citizens and live in town. Röder belonged to a powerful noble family of the Ortenau (Middle Baden), lords of Diersburg and principal vassals of the margraves of Baden.[85] He acquired citizenship through marriage in 1507 and kept it all his life (except for the interval in 1519–20), becoming a Stettmeister and a stalwart of the Evangelical party in the regime. None of his male relatives followed his example.

---

[82] Wittmer, Nos. 3557, 3569, 4131, 4084, 4987, 5004.

[83] *Ibid.*, Nos. 3369, 3593, 3740, 3808, 4240, 4187, 4547, 4689, 4988. Beger was a knight. The last male member of this family, Mathis Beger von Geispolsheim, was assassinated by Friedrich Bock von Bläsheim at Geispolsheim in 1532. Schoepflin, *L'Alsace illustrée*, V, 656.

[84] AMS, Livre de Bourgeoisie 1440–1530, fol. 230. See Brady, "Privy Councils," p. 78n2.

[85] Theil, *Lehnbuch*, pp. 84–89; PROSOPOGRAPHY, No. LXXVI.

Much the same is true of Hans Jacob Widergrien von Staufenberg, whose family held a share in the chateau of Staufenberg, a mighty fortress in the Ortenau, visible from the roofs of Strasbourg.[86] Occasional members of other right-bank families—such as the Schauenburg and the Erlin von Rorburg (originally from Strasbourg)—also moved into the city, became citizens, and sometimes held offices.[87] Others wandered in from further abroad. Zeisolf von Adelsheim (d. 1503) was the son of a Palatine official in Lower Alsace and descendant of an old Franconian family of Palatine vassals.[88] He married a Strasbourg widow, Ottilia Schott (d. 1519) in 1477, daughter of Peter Schott the Elder (d. 1504) and mother-in-law of Martin Sturm, settled in at Strasbourg, sold some of his rural properties, and lived the life of an urban gentleman. His family, however, remained on the land. From just as far away, from Swabia, came a branch of the Neuneck family, which flourished briefly at Strasbourg.[89]

Closer to home, many Alsatian families—that is, noble families whose land lay *chiefly* on the left bank of the Rhine—also supplied occasional patrician citizens. The Zuckmantel, for example, had their principal seat at the small town of Brumath, north of Strasbourg, from which they took the name "Zuckmantel von Brumath." Although they appear frequently

---

[86] Theil, *Lehnbuch,* pp. 101–103; PROSOPOGRAPHY, No. XCIX.

[87] On the Schauenburg, see R. von Schauenburg, *Familiengeschichte der Reichsfreiherren von Schauenburg* (n.p., 1954). On the Erlin von Rorburg and their acquisitions in the Ortenau, see A. Ruppert, "Strassburger Adel in der Mortenau, I: Die Erlin von Rorburg," *Strassburger Studien, Zeitschrift für Geschichte, Sprache und Litteratur des Elsasses,* 2 (Strasbourg, 1884), pp. 68–77.

[88] Zeisolf von Adelsheim (Adeltzheim, Adletzheim) (d. 30 December 1503), son of the Palatine *Hofmeister* and sometime *Unterlandvogt* in Lower Alsace, Götz von Adelsheim (d. ca. 1489/90). The family were Palatine vassals with a *Stammsitz* at Adelsheim in Franconia at the southern edge of the Odenwald, by virtue of which they were also *Reichsritter*. They held fiefs in Lower Alsace since 1483, and Zeisolf and his brothers sold their rights to the imperial fief at Wasselonne to the city of Strasbourg for 7,000 fl. in 1496. Zeisolf married in 1477 Ottilia Schott (d. 1519), daughter of the Altammeister Peter Schott, Sr. (d. 1504), and widow of Peter von Köllen; and he became a citizen of Strasbourg in the same year. Their daughter, Aurelia von Adelsheim, married Ludwig Böcklin von Böcklinsau and died ca. 1537. Gerhard Wunder, *Das Strassburger Landgebiet. Territorialgeschichte der einzelnen Teile des städtischen Herrschaftsbereiches vom 13. bis zum 18. Jahrhundert,* Schriften zur Verfassungsgeschichte, 5 (Berlin, 1967), pp. 133–134, where Zeisolf's death should be dated to 1503 rather than 1505; Cowie and Cowie, eds., *Works of Peter Schott, 1460–1490,* II, 700; PROSOPOGRAPHY, No. XII.

[89] Johann Ottmar, *Die Burg Neuneck und ihr Adel. Ein Beitrag zur Geschichte des niederen Adels am Neckar und Schwarzwald,* Göppinger Akademische Beiträge, 84 (Göppingen, 1974), pp. 172, 174, 179–180, 189–190, 194–196. Neuneck lies on the eastern slope of the Black Forest, southeast of Freudenstadt.

in various contexts in the history of Strasbourg, Zuckmantel rarely held office there. Melchior Zuckmantel acquired citizenship through his marriage to Elsa von Mülnheim in 1501 and served frequently in the Senate between 1507 and 1524, when he renounced his citizenship and moved to the land, perhaps because he opposed the ecclesiastical reforms, although he later returned to the city. No other Zuckmantel before him had ever held high office at Strasbourg, and none after him until 1607.[90] This easy movement into and out of the city also supplies the answer to the mysterious disappearance from Strasbourg of patrician families who were formerly active in politics. The Völtsch, for example, held high office as patricians for two hundred years after 1332, during which period they produced one outstanding figure, the knight Peter Völtsch (d. ca. 1512), a favorite of Emperor Maximilian I.[91] With Reimbold Völtsch (Senate 1531/32) they disappear from the regime of Strasbourg, emerge on the land as the "Völtsch von Stützheim," and flourish for another three-quarters of a century.[92] Similar patterns could be worked out for other old patrician families, such as the Lentzel, the Hüffel, and the Wetzel von Marsilien.

Very occasionally there appeared in the Constofeln of Strasbourg a member of a noble family whose seat was in another Alsatian town. The most prominent such person among the privy councillors of the Reformation generation was Bernhard Goss (d. 1580) of Oberehnheim, the last male member of one of that small free city's oldest noble fami-

---

[90] Wittmer, Nos. 5096, 7537; Hatt, p. 581; incomplete genealogy by Paul-Ernest Lehr, *L'Alsace noble, suivie de la livre d'or du patriciat de Strasbourg*, 3 vols. (Paris-Strasbourg, 1870), III, 256–260 (hereafter cited as Lehr, volume and page). He was a vassal of the lords of Fleckenstein and the bishops of Strasbourg ca. 1513–44; in 1540 he asked to be relieved as one of the *Drei auf dem Pfennigthurm* because he was "mit alter beladen." Friedrich Hefele, "Freiherrlich von Gaylingisches Archiv im Schlosse zu Ebnet bei Freiburg," *MBHK*, 39 (1917), Nos. 912–916; ADBR, G 503 (see Appendix C below); AMS, XXI 1540, fol. 520^v.

[91] Peter Völtsch (d. by 1512), *Ritter*, Imperial *Fiskal* and many times Stettmeister of Strasbourg (1486–96); tenant of the chateau and village of Schiltigheim; married Margarethe Böcklin von Böcklinsau (widow of Philips Wetzel von Marsilien), Barbara von Landsberg (d. 1505), and Margarethe von Angelach, by the last of whom he had two daughters, Euphania and Veronica (AMS, KS 13, fol. 44^v); he was the son of Reimbold Völtsch (d. by 28 August 1481) and was knighted at Jerusalem on 17 July 1483. Friedrich Schmidt-Sibeth, "Die Völsch im Niederelsass," *Archiv für Sippenforschung*, 35 (1969), 41–45, here at p. 44; Charles Schmidt, *Histoire littéraire d'Alsace à la fin du XVe et au commencement du XVIe siècle*, 2 vols. (Paris, 1879), I, 45, 45n108; ZC, I, 478 line 25.

[92] Schmidt-Sibeth, "Die Völsch im Niederelsass," pp. 41–44; Hatt, p. 563.

lies.[93] Bernhard and his brother, Landolf, came to Strasbourg in 1524, where Bernhard married a Bietenheim. He became a mercenary soldier, his father's profession, and settled down around 1548. He entered the regime and spent the last thirty years of his long life as a privy councillor.

Some patricians took the ties of citizenship very lightly, indeed, although the behavior of Hans Erhard von Winterthur was perhaps extreme. He was the father of the last male member of a prodigal family;[94] and in the 1480s and 1490s he conducted a long, bitter suit against the Sturm over the seigneurial rights to Breuschwickersheim, a village not far west of Strasbourg. The chateau and the seigneury gradually passed from Winterthur into Sturm hands during the second half of the fifteenth and the first decades of the sixteenth century, as Hans Erhard and his son, Daniel, alternated between selling their rights to the Sturm and conducting lawsuits against them. In the course of this suit against Friedrich Sturm, his son Martin, and Peter Schott the Ammeister, to whose granddaughter Martin Sturm was married, Hans Erhard alleged that he could get no justice at Strasbourg, because Schott had used his office (the most powerful office in the city) in favor of the Sturm. So he moved to Rottweil, southeastward across the Black Forest, where he became a citizen and tried to goad the regime of his new town against his enemies at Strasbourg, an unusual step which availed him little in the end.[95] This is an interesting case of a noble trying to use a new lord against his former lord, except that in this case the lords were regimes of free cities of the Empire.

Except, perhaps, for occasional parvenus, the patrician families of Strasbourg maintained an easy social intercourse with their fellows on the land. They were still *turnierfähig* and presumably jousted with and against their rural cousins. Membership in a Constofel at Strasbourg

---

[93] Joseph Gyss, *Histoire de la ville d'Obernai et ses rapports avec les autres villes ci-devant impériales d'Alsace et avec les seigneuries voisines,* 2 vols. (Strasbourg, 1866), I, 76, 154–155, 308–309, 438–439, 448–450; Kindler, *GBS*, p. 95; PROSOPOGRAPHY, No. XXXIII. The proper form of the name was Goss or Gossmar von Oberehnheim (or: Ehnheim), and only Bernhard, Jr. (d. 1581), appears in his later life as "Goss von Dürckelstein."

[94] On the quarrel and its object, see AMS, III 2/9; Hefele, Nos. 544, 771; Fernand Jaenger, "Zur Geschichte des Schlosses Breuschwickersheim." *CAAAH*, 30 (1939), 81–89. On the Winterthur, see Kindler, *GBS*, pp. 428–430.

[95] AMS, III 2/9, letter of 20 October 1489, in which Hans Erhard von Winterthur appears as "mitburger" of the burgomaster and senate of Rottweil; he had sworn a "gelubde" to obey the judgment at Strasbourg but alleged that the oath was no longer binding, because Peter Schott had put him "in den Stock." Winterthur suggests that Schott had misused his power as Ammeister in favor of the husband of his granddaughter, Martin Sturm.

was not, however, proof positive of *Turnierfähigkeit,* and patricians who wanted to joust had to produce passable credentials. Thus, Adam Zorn, knighted on the field of Murten in 1476, secured in 1480–83 at least three attestations from fellow nobles that he was of sufficient rank and honor to be *turnierfähig.*[96] Eleven Strasbourgeois, probably all experienced soldiers, joined the entourage of Maximilian I on his journey to Rome in 1508.[97] One of them, Sifridt I von Bietenheim, was not a Constofler but a *Stubengeselle* of the guild Zur Luzern.[98] The next generation certainly had less military experience and, if the case of the Sturm brothers is indicative, turned to more bourgeois weapons. Jacob Sturm disclaimed any special expertise with the arquebus, but his older brother, Friedrich, competed in a shooting contest at Speyer during the Imperial Diet of 1529.[99]

The urban nobles also shared with the rural ones the movement into the service of princes, a typical feature of noble life during the later Middle Ages.[100] On the Upper Rhine, this tendency set in with the worsening of the economic position of the rural nobles during the fourteenth century,[101] and it may be that families who had heavy, urban-centered investments (e.g., banking) felt the pressure towards princely service less strongly. Strasbourgeois nonetheless went into the service of princes, both great and small, with great frequency during the later fifteenth century. A large group of local nobles entered the Palatine service: Jacob (1480–94) and Burckhardt (1491) Beger, Claus Berer (1478), Hans Balthasar von Endingen (1492), Caspar Ritter von Urendorf, Jr. (1481), Adam Zorn (1482–92), and Claus Zorn von Bulach (1482) and his two sons, Caspar and Rudolf (1497). Stephan Bock von Bläsheim, father of Hans Bock von Gerstheim and Jacob Bock von Bläsheim, entered Palatine service in 1478 ("sol m. g. h. vnd siner

---

[96] Osthouse (Bas-Rhin), Fonds Zorn de Bulach, Laden IVbis, Nos. 2–4, attestations by Kuntz von Zähringen (1480), Hans Rudolf von Endingen (1483), and Caspar Beger von Geispolsheim (1480).

[97] BNUS, Ms. 1223, fol. 47^v, excerpt from Daniel Specklin's (largely) lost "Collectanea," II, fol. 136.

[98] The father of the subject of PROSOPOGRAPHY, No. IX.

[99] Jacob Sturm's disclaimer in *PCSS,* II, 196, No. 197. The contest of 1529 in *DRA, JR,* VII, 858.

[100] This aspect of the Lower Alsatian and Strasbourg aristocracies has been little studied. The beginnings of the trend lie in the fourteenth century, as can be seen from what is known of the region just across the Rhine, the Ortenau. See Theil, *Lehnbuch,* pp. 131–139. In Upper—and to a much lesser degree in Lower—Alsace the process is connected with the rise and fall of the Burgundian power along the Upper Rhine.

[101] Theil, *Lehnbuch,* pp. 137–143.

gnaden landfaut im Elsas zu allen gescheffden gewarten").[102] Caspar
Böcklin, brother of a Stettmeister of Strasbourg, Wilhelm Böcklin,
served as an official of the counts of Saarwerden from 1485 until 1493.[103]
After 1500 this wave of Strasbourgeois into Palatine service ebbed
permanently.[104] In the service of the bishop of Speyer, too, Strasbourg
patricians are scarcely to be found after 1510.[105]

There are few more decisive signs of mutual social acceptability than
intermarriage, and the Strasbourg patriciate and the rural nobility of the
surrounding region had an almost unqualified *connubium*. Kageneck's
calculations show a higher incidence of intermarriage between patrician
and rural noble families during the sixteenth century than in the previous
century: whereas 65% of the patrician marriages during the fifteenth
century involved a partner from another urban family, only 40% of the
sixteenth-century marriages did so.[106] The data in Appendix A below
contain notices of 165 marriages in which one partner was a patrician of
Strasbourg; and the other partner belonged to another patrician family
in 73 cases (44.2%), to a rural noble family or noble family of another
town in 75 cases (45.5%), and to a non-patrician family of Strasbourg in
17 cases (10.3%). The figures are not markedly different from those of
Kageneck, to which, however, being a selection based on quite different
criteria, they are not strictly comparable.

Several aspects of patrician marriage patterns deserve special notice.
The first is the near absence of marriages between patricians of Strasbourg and aristocrats of other towns. The only apparent exception,
Hagenau, is not a true one. For the ties of the Hagenau aristocrats were
with their emigrant cousins at Strasbourg, who were guildsmen there
rather than Constofler.[107] Aristocrats of other Alsatian towns, such as

---

[102] Manfred Krebs, "Die kurpfälzischen Dienerbücher 1476–1685," *Mitteilungen der
Oberrheinischen Historischen Kommission,* No. 1 (1942), Nos. 128–129, 146, 619, 2838,
3170, 3176–3178, 2756.

[103] Hans Walter Herrmann, *Geschichte der Grafschaft Saarwerden bis zum Jahre 1527,*
2 vols., Veröffentlichungen der Kommission für saarländische Landesgeschichte und
Volksforschung, I (Saarbrücken, 1957–59), I, Nos. 1381, 1382, 1401, 1489, and II,
pp. 163–265, where several members of the Lumbart family appear.

[104]. One exception is Hans Sturm (d. 1536), on whom see PROSOPOGRAPHY, No.
XCII.

[105] Manfred Krebs, "Die Dienerbücher des Bistums Speyer 1464–1768," *ZGO,* 94
(1948), 55–195, here at Nos. 139 (Jakob von Blumenau, 20 June 1469), and 2029 (Claus
Zuckmantel, "Burgfaut" at Windstein, 4 March 1508).

[106] Kageneck, "Das Patriziat im Elsass," p. 386, although he does not tell how he
arrived at this figure.

[107] See Chapter III below, p. 104.

Saverne, Colmar, and Sélestat, hardly appear as patrician marriage partners. The same is true of the aristocracies of cities up—such as Basel —and down—such as Worms and Speyer—the Rhine, as well as the free towns of Swabia. In this the patricians of Strasbourg display an important difference from the comparable classes of the other large free cities of South Germany. Such marriage and business ties as existed between Nuremberg and Augsburg had no counterpart at Strasbourg, and, except for the Hagenau connection, neither did the patrician-mercantile clans who were spread through the free towns of Upper Swabia, such as the Ehinger and the Besserer.[108] Strasbourg families married either into other Strasbourg families or into rural noble families, most of whom resided in a region running from the borders of Lorraine in the West to the eastern slopes of the Black Forest in the East, from the southern boundaries of Lower Alsace and the Ortenau in the South into the Baden–Palatine borderlands in the North.[109] In this respect, as in so many others, the city of Strasbourg and the region of Lower Alsace had far stronger ties to the right bank regions than they did to Upper Alsace.[110] To these patterns there were occasional exceptions, such as the marriage of Richardis Schenck *dit* Missbach of Strasbourg to a Rehlinger of Augsburg (which made the Rehlinger cousins of the Strasbourg Sturm),[111] but they are notable by their rarity.

---

[108] Rieber, "Das Patriziat von Ulm," pp. 309, 327–329; Wolfgang von Stromer, "Reichtum und Ratswürde. Die wirtschaftliche Führungsschicht der Reichsstadt Nürnberg 1348–1648," in *Führungskräfte der Wirtschaft in Mittelalter und Neuzeit 1350–1850*, Teil I, ed. Herbert Helbig, DFN, 6 (Limburg/Lahn, 1973), pp. 1–50, here at p. 17; and in the same volume, Friedrich Blendinger, "Die wirtschaftlichen Führungsschichten in Augsburg 1430–1740," pp. 51–86, here at p. 56.

[109] Roughly the area for which Strasbourg was a chief market center for agricultural products and the major money market.

[110] One meets evidence at every turn, cultural, social, political, economic, and ecclesiastical, that the Rhine formed a very strong bond between the two banks. Especially the economic ties seem to have been stronger across the stream than along it, so that the two right-bank regions, the Ortenau and the Breisgau, were closer to their left-bank partners, Lower and Upper Alsace, than they were to each other.

[111] *Genealogisches Handbuch des in Bayern immatrikulierten Adels,* VIII (Neustadt/Aisch, 1961), p. 292, a notice of the marriage in 1503 of Bernhard Rehlinger to Richardis "Missbeck" of Strasbourg. Jacob Sturm commonly addressed their son, Wolfgang, as "vetter" (e.gg., *PCSS,* IV, 592, No. 547; AMS, XXI 1546, fol. 397ᵛ). Rehlinger's mother came from the family of Schenck *dit* Missbach; and the only Sturm-Schenck connection I have found is the marriage of Agnes Sturm to Peter Schenck, called Missbach (d. 1462). BMS, Ms. 1024 ("Papiers du Chan. Léon Dacheux"), fol. 82 (from the lost collection by Luck). Agnes was the daughter of Friedrich Sturm (d. 1476) and Katharina Wurmser and was therefore the sister of Martin Sturm and the aunt of Jacob

Most patrician families of Strasbourg not only had marriage and other ties to the land, they were themselves lords in the land, where they comprised a significant proportion of the lesser nobility. When the imperial commissioners assembled the free knights of Lower Alsace in 1547, one hundred and thirteen persons were invited, of whom twenty-nine (25.7%) were citizens of Strasbourg, three each (2.7% each) were citizens of Hagenau and Sélestat, and seventy-six (67.3%) were not citizens.[112] What is more interesting, however, is that eight families are found both among the citizens of Strasbourg and the non-citizens. The Bock had three in the city and one on the land, the Böcklin 5 and 3 respectively, the Sturm 4 and 1, the Mülnheim 2 and 2, the Wetzel von Marsilien, the Wurmser, and the Mittelhausen 1 and 2, and the Kageneck 1 and 1. Among the non-citizens, being those families, apparently, whose male co-vassals were not citizens, are all of the families that appear *now and again* as patrician citizens of Strasbourg. Not all of the nobles were seigneurs by virtue of their Imperial fiefs, some of which were fief-rentes or other types of fiefs without seigneurial rights. Such was the case of the Sturm, whose seigneurial rights at Breuschwickersheim were allodial rather than feudal and whose imperial fief was a fief-rente.[113]

The densest network of feudal relations in which patricians of Strasbourg participated was that of the bishops of Strasbourg. The surviving records of the bishops' feudal court (*Manngericht*) provide a graphic picture of the feudal character of the patriciate. Every Settmeister of the period 1520–55 and two-thirds of the patrician senators were vassals or brothers of vassals of the bishop of Strasbourg, together with more than 90% of the patrician privy councillors.[114] The patrician politicians were summoned regularly to the meetings of this court at Molsheim, and, to judge by their letters of excuse, they sometimes attended. Two other princes, both of whom were feudal lords in Lower Alsace, also

and his brothers. ADBR, 12 J 2022/15. Rehlinger's mother was quite possibly a daughter of this Sturm–Schenck marriage.

[112] ADBR, E 1375/1.

[113] PROSOPOGRAPHY, No. XCIV.

[114] Based on Appendix C, collated with data in the PROSOPOGRAPHY. Included are persons who were summoned to the *Manngericht* and males related to such persons in the first degree. Nearly all episcopal fiefs were held in co-vassalage, with the senior male in each generation (*Lehenträger, porteur à fief*) actually doing homage for the fiefs. Such a fief is said to be held "in gemein" or "in gemeinschafft," or (in Baden) "zu gesamter Hand." Theil finds that this form, as opposed to subdivision of fiefs among feudal heirs, had become the usual one in Baden by the mid-fifteenth century. Theil, *Lehnbuch*, p. 171.

counted patricians of Strasbourg among their vassals. Between 1449 and 1560, the Electors Palatine numbered among their vassals at least five families whose members were frequently to be found in the Constofeln at Strasbourg: Wurmser, Mülnheim, Landsberg, Rathsamhausen, and Sturm.[115] The margraves of Baden, on the other hand, granted fiefs between 1471 and 1565 to at least fourteen such families, including the Kageneck, Wetzel von Marsilien, Endingen, Widergrien von Staufenberg, Zorn von Bulach, Röder von Diersburg, Merswin, Marx von Eckwersheim, Mittelhausen, Wolff von Renchen, Wurmser, Böcklin, Sturm, and Beger—plus the Ingold and Mussler who were guildsmen.[116] Among the lesser lords of the region, Strasbourgeois commonly held fiefs from the counts of Hanau-Lichtenberg, Zweibrücken-Bitsch-Lichtenberg, and Mörs-Saarwerden, and the lords of Fleckenstein, Andlau, and Rappoltstein.[117] It was not unusual for a patrician politician to have four or five feudal lords. The Sturm, for example, held during the first half of the sixteenth century fiefs from the Empire, the Elector Palatine, the bishop of Strasbourg, Hanau-Lichtenberg, and Rappoltstein.[118]

---

[115] Based on the surviving feudal registers of the Electors Palatine, in GLAK, 67/1006–1008, 1010–1016, 1022, 1057–1058, which have adequate indices.

[116] Based on the surviving feudal registers of the margraves of Baden, in GLAK, 67/42–46, 48–49, which have adequate indices.

[117] There are no systematic studies of feudal relations on the left bank during the later Middle Ages and into the sixteenth century, although Henri Dubled has written an excellent series of studies of seigneurial institutions and lord-peasant relations in Alsace. See his "Grundherrschaft und Dorfgerichtsbarkeit im Elsass vom 13–15. Jahrhundert und ihr Verhältnis zueinander," *Deutsches Archiv für Erforschung des Mittelalters,* 17 (1961), 518–526; "Les grandes tendances de l'exploitation au sein de la seigneurie rurale en Alsace du XIIIe au XVe siècle," *VSWG,* 49 (1962), 41–121; "Grundherrschaft und Landgemeinde im mittelalterlichen Elsass," *Saarbrücker Hefte,* 18 (1963), 16–28; "Servitude et liberté en Alsace au moyen âge. La condition des personnes au sein de la seigneurie rurale du XIIIe au XVe siècle," *VSWG,* 50 (1963), 164–203, 289–328; "L'administration de la seigneurie rurale en Alsace du XIIIe au XVe siècle," *VSWG,* 52 (1965), 433–484; "Der Herrschaftsbegriff im Mittelalter am Oberrhein, hauptsächlich im Elsass," *AJb,* 1959, pp. 77–91; "La justice de la seigneurie foncière en Alsace aux XIVe et XVe siècles," *Revue d'histoire suisse,* 10 (1960), 337–375. For Baden in the fourteenth and fifteenth centuries, there is Theil, *Lehnbuch*; and Wilhelm Hofmann, *Adel und Landesherren im nördlichen Schwarzwald von der Mitte des 14. Jahrhunderts bis zum Beginn des 16. Jahrhunderts,* Darstellungen aus der württembergischen Geschichte, 40 (Stuttgart, 1954). For the Palatinate, there is much in Henry J. Cohn, *The Government of the Rhine Palatinate in the Fifteenth Century* (Oxford, 1965). Most urban histories ignore the subject, and the standard works on Strasbourg are no exceptions.

[118] Source in PROSOPOGRAPHY, No. XCIV. The Baden fief of the Sturm was a fief-rente yielding "zu einem Rechten Manlehen zweintzig guldin geltz guter" annually on 2

The patricians were lords not only on many of their feudal holdings but often on their allodial lands as well. A unique, incomplete list surviving from 1516 ennumerates the civic military obligations of villages and parts of villages whose seigneurs were Strasbourgeois.[119] The obligations were owed in return for the extension of the city's protection over the holdings of its citizens.[120] As lords of fifty-seven villages are listed twenty-two persons named with both surname and Christian name, plus nine other family names. Every family or individual named belonged to the Constofeln except the Mussler, who resembled the patricians in every other respect.[121] Included are most of the leading political families: Bock, Böcklin, Wurmser, Sturm, Zorn, Zorn zum Riet, Mülnheim, Völtsch, Ramstein, and Landsberg.[122] This list thus reveals not only political ties of the city to half a hundred villages outside its territory proper, but also another series of individual and family interests in the world outside the town.

This framework of description of the external ties of the Strasbourg patriciate may take on some flesh and blood from the biographies of two brothers, Hans Bock von Gerstheim (d. 1542) and Jacob Bock von Bläsheim (d. ca. 1511).[123] The Bock had mercantile origins, perhaps at Rottweil, and had belonged to the anti-noble party in the revolt of 1332,

February; it was first granted to Wernher Sturm, son of Huglin, on 25 January 1391 by Margrave Bernhard, and it was last renewed by Margrave Christoph I to Ott Sturm on 14 May 1508. GLAK, 44/818.

[119] Wunder, "Verzeichnis," pp. 55–69, of which the second part names villages on both banks in which Strasbourgeois possessed seigneurial rights.

[120] Wunder, *Landgebiet,* pp. 44–46. The obligation derived from the extension of civic protection (*Schutz und Schirm*) to citizens' lands.

[121] The exception is Peter Mussler (d. 17 August 1519), son of Reimbolt M. and an armigeous member of the guild Zum Encker, who served six two-year terms in the Senate (1492–1517). His sister, Elisabeth, married Jacob Zorn zum Riet (see PROSOPO-GRAPHY, No. CIV); and he had brothers named Reimbolt, Veltin, and Hans, of whom only Reimbolt survived him. He was a member of the XIII by 1506 and probably served until his death. Hatt, p. 504; AMS, V 137/14, a copy of his testament (29 March 1515); Louis Spach, "Deux hommes d'armes de Strasbourg à Bamberg (1512–1513)," *BSCMHA*, N.S. 8 (1871), p. 49; Brady, "Privy Councils," p. 77. In 1516 Mussler is named lord of Wolfisheim, which his family had begun to acquire by 1439 and which they held from the counts of Lichtenberg (later Hanau-Lichtenberg) until it was partitioned among a variety of heirs in the 1530s. ADBR, E 2775/3–4, 9–23a, 27. Although the Mussler commonly married patricians, they were never Constofler.

[122] Disregarding duplications, these families account for 24 of the 34 individual and family names listed.

[123] This account is based largely on sources given in PROSOPOGRAPHY, No. XI. In the standard genealogical works (Lehr, Kindler), the entries on the Bock von Gerstheim and von Bläsheim are incomplete and riddled with errors.

soon thereafter becoming themselves nobles.[124] Jacob and Hans were the sons of Stephan Bock von Bläsheim, an important political figure of the later fifteenth century, and Engel (or Angela) Bock von Gerstheim.[125] The brothers divided their inheritance in 1507, Hans taking the Imperial fief of Gerstheim and Jacob the allodial chateau and estates at Bläsheim, with complex provisions for keeping the properties in the Bock family should either line fail.[126] The two brothers were knighted, and both joined the Constofel zum Mühlstein,[127] but thereafter their careers took different paths. Jacob took very little part in patrician political life, while Hans became a pillar of Strasbourg's diplomacy, served twenty years as Stettmeister, and became (with Jacob Sturm) one of the two leading patrician politicians of the Reformation generation.[128]

Hans's political career made him an eminent urban figure, but his and his children's marriages tell a rather different story. Hans married Ursula von Fleckenstein, whose family were powerful barons in northern Alsace. One daughter married Jacob Sturm, but the other four all married great families of the surrounding regions: one to an Andlau and another to an Eschau; a third to Hans IV Landschad von Steinach (1500–71), who served successively as an official in Baden, Württemberg, and the Palatinate;[129] and a fourth to Florenz von Venningen (d.

---

[124] Kageneck, "Das Patriziat im Elsass," p. 382; Hatt, pp. 404–405. The possible Rottweil origin of the Bock is supported by a passage in *ZC*, I, 316–317. The Rottweil Bock family drops out of sight after 1444. Elben, *Patriziat der Reichsstadt Rottweil*, p. 186.

[125] A correct genealogy of this line through this marriage is given by Hans Rott, *Quellen und Forschungen zur südwestdeutschen und schweizerischen Kunstgeschichte im XV. und XVI. Jahrhundert*, part III: *Der Oberrhein*, 3 vols. (Stuttgart, 1936–38), Textband, pp. 74–75, 79 (hereafter cited as Rott, *Oberrhein*). It is confirmed by a manuscript family tree listing four generations of the ancestors of Friedrich Bock von Gerstheim (d. 1614), in ADBR, 12J 2022/15.

[126] The partition, which involved other properties as well, is described in the testament of Hans Bock von Gerstheim (9 October 1542), of which a copy is in ADBR, G 841, along with a copy of the testament of his son, Ludwig Bock von Gerstheim (d. 1565).

[127] AMS, I 17–19/1: "würte der stuben zum Mülestein," 1492.

[128] Jacob never held an important office, unless the Jacob Bock who was senator in 1472/73 and Stettmeister in 1476 is the same man (Hatt, pp. 405, 597), which the early dates make unlikely. Jacob Bock von Bläsheim gave up his citizenship between 1489 and 1500. Wittmer, Nos. 4063, 5046.

[129] Apollonia Bock von Gerstheim (d. 29 September 1542), married Philips von Hirschhorn (d. 16 March 1522) and remarried on 22 October 1523 Hans IV Landschad von Steinach (ca. 1500–71), who served successively the margrave of Baden, duke of Württemberg, Elector Palatine, and Count Palatine of Zweibrücken. Robert Irsch-

1538), chancellor of the Palatinate.[130] Hans's only surviving son and chief heir, Ludwig, married Agnes Zorn von Plobsheim, whose mother was Jacob Sturm's sister.[131] Hans was a seigneur and a great man in the land, holding fiefs and other lands on both sides of the Rhine. In 1541, when the old widower was dying, having outlived nearly his entire generation, he retired to his country seat at Gersteim without surrendering his offices; and he was buried there rather than in one of the civic cemeteries.

Much less is known about the marriages of the children of Jacob Bock. One daughter married a Knobloch, a family established both at Strasbourg and Hagenau, while a son married into a parvenu noble family of the Breisgau, the Stürtzel von Buchheim.[132] The history of the brothers Bock illustrates how leading Strasbourg patricians could belong, at one and the same time, to the urban patriciate and to the rural nobility.

Their position between city and land subjected the patricians to different, not always compatible, forms of socialization. On the one hand, they consorted with their friends and relatives on the land, who still possessed much of the brawling contempt for law and violent proclivities of the medieval lesser nobility. In the city, on the other hand, they were subjected to the subtle forces of embourgeoisement, especially now that the nobles dwelt in town at the suffrance of lesser folk. Two stories illustrate very well the different kinds of behavior such contrary pressures might foster. The first shows that the nobles of Strasbourg had not entirely abandoned the ways of their ancestors and their rural cousins. It is the story of Hans Balthasar von Endingen (d. by 1520), scion of the Strasbourg branch of a noble family of the Kaiserstuhl region in the Breisgau.[133] His father, Hans Rudolph II (d. by 1493), and

---

linger, "Zur Geschichte der Herren von Steinach und der Landschaden von Steinach," *ZGO*, 86 (1934), 421–508, here at Table 3; *idem*, ed., "Die Aufzeichnungen des Hans Ulrich Landschad von Steinach über sein Geschlecht," *ZGO*, 86 (1934), 205–258, here at pp. 248–249; Bernhardt, *Die Zentralbehörden . . . Württemberg,* pp. 457–458.

[130] Veronica Bock von Gersteim married Florenz von Vennigen (d. 7 September 1538), former professor of law at Heidelberg and Chancellor of the Palatinate, 1505–38. Although her family were Evangelicals, her children by Venningen were Catholics. The Venningen were also intermarried with the Hirschhorn family. Press, *Calvinismus und Territorialstaat,* pp. 29, 176, 176n28, with references; Bernhardt, *Die Zentralbehörden . . . Württemberg,* pp. 694–696.

[131] Sources in PROSOPOGRAPHY, Nos. XI, XCIV.

[132] ADBR, 3B 122. On this family, see Jürgen Bücking, "Das Geschlecht Stürtzel von Buchheim (1491–1790). Ein Versuch zur Sozial- und Wirtschaftsgeschichte des Breisgauer Adels in der frühen Neuzeit," *Blätter für deutsche Landesgeschichte,* 118 (1970), 239–278, who does not mention this marriage.

[133] Kindler, *OG*, I, 298–302; Hatt, pp. 427–600; ADBR, G 634.

his first-cousin, Hans Ludwig (d. 1548), were long-time patrician officeholders at Strasbourg. Hans Balthasar was made of more traditional stuff. In 1515 he ambushed some merchants from St.-Nicolas-de-Porte in Lorraine at a spot near Hagenau and grabbed their goods to the sum of 15,000 fl. For this deed, the typical act of a *Raubritter,* he eventually submitted to the civic regime's arbitration and came away with very little loss.[134] Jacob Wimpheling might preach to the nobles of Strasbourg the virtues of education, good Latin, and civic duty and tell them that the old days of high living, feuding, and plundering were over;[135] but Hans Balthasar von Endingen proved to his fellows that they did not necessarily have to submit to law, order, and embourgeoisement.

The second story illustrates an easy social intercourse between nobles and Strasbourgeois of much lower status. It tells of Jörg von Hohenstein, of the same family that had lost so much of its patrimony to the upstart Jörger, and his "gesellschafft."[136] Jörg promised these twenty-four drinking companions a *fuder* (ca. 1,100 liters) of wine if they could move it without aid from Bergbietenheim to Strasbourg in a single day. If not, they would each pay him 12 fl. The men piled the wine on a wagon, harnessed themselves to it, and pulled it to Strasbourg in about three hours (16 August 1529). Some of the wine was presented to the *Blatterhaus* (the hospital for syphilitics), a great deal more went down dusty throats, and the chroniclers got another good tale to record. The composition of Jörg's "gesellschafft" was a real cross-section of local society. There were eight nobles, including a Hüffel, Jacob Bock, a Landsberg, two Erlin von Rorburg, and a Zorn, and the sixteen others were all commoners. They included a number of men of good family: Conrad Meyer, son-in-law of an Ammeister and himself a future XVer; Lux Messinger, son of a XIIIer and himself a future Ammeister and privy

---

[134] ADBR, 3B 711; AMS, III 71/3.

[135] *Jacobi Wimpfelingi Opera selecta,* I: *Jakob Wimpfelings "Adolescentia,"* ed. Otto Herding (Munich, 1965), pp. 155–156, 333–339. See my comments in "The Themes of Social Structure, Social Conflict, and Civic Harmony in Jakob Wimpheling's *Germania,*" *Sixteenth Century Journal,* 3 (1972), 65–76, here at p. 71.

[136] The story of the "Weinzug" of 16 August 1529 appears in nearly identical form in two chronicles: Rudolf Reuss, ed., "Strassburg im sechzehnten Jahrhundert, 1500–1591. Ausszug aus der Imlin'schen Familienchronik," *Alsatia,* 10 (1873–74), 363–476, here at pp. 415–416 (hereafter cited as "Imlin Chronik."); and Johannes Städel, "Chronica Aller Denckwürdigsten Historien . . .," 4 vols., III, 178–179 (hereafter cited as Städel, "Chronik"). This chronicle is in the Musée historique de la Ville de Strasbourg, and I am grateful to the director, Jean-Pierre Klein, for making it available to me. An independent version of the story is in Nicolaus Gerbel's diary, AST 38, fol. 63[r]. On the Hohenstein and the Jörger, see Chapter IV below, pp. 129–130.

councillor; Martin Hug von Ottenheim, son of an Ammeister; and Michael Heuss, a future privy councillor and Ammeister.[137] There were also the Hag brothers, Martin and Claus. But the society also included humbler men, such as Hans Hollinger, an artisan who would nearly twenty years later become a radical opponent of the regime, and Veltin, "der fuhrknecht" at Unser Lieben Frauen Haus, and several others about whom nearly nothing or nothing at all is known.[138] Although it is not clear just what the nature of this "gesellschafft" was, still nobles, guild aristocrats, and artisans pulled in the harness together, apparently all in good fun.[139] The story displays an easy social intercourse between social classes which cannot but have owed something to the urban milieu.

F. Conclusion

The conclusions that may be drawn from this analysis of the position of the Strasbourg patriciate during the late fifteenth and the sixteenth century agree, with important variations, with the special literature's picture of the patriciates of other South German cities in which the patrician political monopoly had been broken by the guild revolts. The patriciate, defined as the membership of the two Constofeln, were all armigerous and roughly of the same status as the lesser nobility on the land. The Constofeln did not include, however, all of the citizen nobles and armigers, some of whom joined, voluntarily or involuntarily, the guilds.

---

[137] See PROSOPOGRAPHY, Nos. LVI, LV, XLII, XXXIX.

[138] Hans Hollinger (or: Holinger) of Gosheim (d. ca. 1571) purchased citizenship at Strasbourg on 23 October 1520 and joined the guild Zum Spiegel although he was probably an embroiderer (*Seidensticker*); that he was not a poor man is shown by the fact that in 1549 a man of Lindau owed him 200 fl. A Georg Hollinger, also a Seidensticker, was active at Strasbourg in 1545; and Paul Hollinger (1569–73) and Bartholomeus Hollinger (1576), both goldsmiths, were later active there. Wittmer, No. 6977; Rott, *Oberrhein*, I, 284, 291; AMS, KS 63/II, fols. 50^r–52^r (27 July 1549); ADBR, E 1356/1. For Hollinger's involvement in anti-government agitation after the Smalkaldic War, see AMS, XXI 1547, fols. 232^{r-v} (7 May), 255^r (18 May), 261^{r-v} (21 May).

[139] The full membership of Hohenstein's "gesellschafft" was eight nobles ("die Edlen") and sixteen commoners ("die burger"). The nobles were Jacob Hüffel, Jacob Bock, Dietrich von Landsberg, Wolff Erlin von Rorburg, Adolph Erlin von Rorburg, Wolff Zorn (von Duntzenheim), Georg Blicker, and Oswald von Baden. The commoners were Conrad Meyer, Lux Messinger, Martin Hug von Ottenheim, Hans Hag, Claus Hag, Moritz Pfaff, Hans Hollinger, Blasön Hans, Michael Heuss, Jörg Chrisman, Conrat Stoffler, Zentz Duncker, Mathis Landvogt, Mathis Gerbott, Asimus Geissbrecht, and Veltin, "der fuhrknecht" at Unserer Frauen Haus.

After their final political defeat in 1419, the patricians were gradually rehabilitated in the eyes of the regime because of their military service in the Armagnac and Burgundian wars and the regime's recognition of their utility as cavalry and diplomats. During the struggle over the liberties of the Constofeln in the period 1471–1509, the Constofeln bowed to the regime's establishment of qualifications for the patriciate but retained, with the regime's acquiescence, the right to veto prospective members.

The patriciate's chief political problem since the later fifteenth century was their declining numbers, which reached a low point during the Reformation generation, and the consequent mounting difficulty of supplying their share of the civic offices with qualified persons. Even with the stabilization of their numbers at about thirty to forty families after 1500, the patriciate was never in a position to reconquer lost privileges and thus formed no threat to the guild aristocrats. The political core of the patriciate during the first half of the sixteenth century comprised about six families—Mülnheim, Sturm, Wurmser, Bock, Zorn, and Böcklin—and its composition was not significantly affected by the events of the Reformation generation.

Most patricians of Strasbourg were vassals of one or more lords and seigneurs in the land. Their relations with the rural nobility of Lower Alsace and Middle Baden were extremely fluid, and many patricians were simply town-dwelling members of predominantly rural families. Finally, the conception of the Strasbourg patriciate as a coherent *urban* nobility, exclusively committed to urban life and urban politics, is very badly in error. The city was only one of several social systems in which the patricians lived.

The patricians of Strasbourg were not a class, much less a caste. They may be regarded as the most feudal fraction of the urban aristocracy, or as the urban fraction of the lesser nobility. They were also an urban estate, albeit of a peculiar kind. Together with families of similar status in the guilds, they were Strasbourg's sector of the aristocracy of the region. Secondly, they were a privileged estate within the corporation of the commune of Strasbourg, constitutionally entitled to exclusive enjoyment of civic offices and honors vastly greater than the share of any other corporation of comparable size in the city.

The legal position of the Strasbourg patriciate is thus to be explained by the achievement, during the middle half of the fifteenth century, of a successful solution to the intra-aristocratic struggles known as the guild revolts. By contrast, in towns which entered the critical years of the

sixteenth century with this struggle unsettled, such as Basel and Esslingen, the patriciate suffered in a way that the Strasbourg nobles did not.
One of the secrets of Strasbourg's vaunted political stability during the
sixteenth century is that, long before the patriciate had formed a common
political front, based on common interests, with the mercantile aristocracy of the guilds.

CHAPTER THREE

THE GUILD ARISTOCRACY OF STRASBOURG

The primacy of large-scale trade as the milieu of accumulation of new fortunes was common to most medieval and Renaissance cities; and the great period of transformation which set in about 1480, when the European economies were incorporated into a new type of "world economy," giving urban merchants—at least in favored regions—access to vast new sectors of profit-making outside the bounds of their own, local economies, made possible the building of mercantile and banking fortunes on a hitherto unknown scale.[1] In South Germany in particular, the ninety years after 1480 were a boom time of commercial expansion and profit-taking, a wave of wealth which merely accentuated the principle of German urban life that newly-made families were newly made in trade.[2]

No force in urban society could long have kept new wealth away from political power—this was the lesson the old urban patricians had learned to their discomfort and loss during the "civic struggles" of the fourteenth and fifteenth centuries.[3] Either the newly rich merchants were admitted to the city halls or they would force their ways in, usually with the backing of the lower classes. The only alternative, the Venetian way—in which a closely defined ruling class also monopolized large-scale trade—had the immense advantage of enabling a ruling class to defeat upstart guilds; but, except at Nuremberg, it was a path rarely trod in South Germany. Most cities had guilds, often containing merchants

---

[1] Wallerstein, *Modern World System,* chapter II.

[2] Bátori, "Das Patriziat der deutschen Stadt," p. 24. The contrary thesis of Werner Sombart (1902), that the great capitalist fortunes of the early modern era derived from ground rents rather than from trade, was thoroughly confuted by Jakob Strieder and his students. See Blendinger, "Die wirtschaftlichen Führungsschichten in Augsburg 1430–1740," p. 53.

[3] Bátori, "Das Patriziat der deutschen Stadt," p. 14 and 14n59; Karl Czok, "Städtische Volksbewegungen," in *Die Stadt des Mittelalters,* III, 311. A classic case is Cologne, where the merchants successfully challenged the rule of the *Geschlechter* in 1396. Franz Irsigler, "Soziale Wandlungen in der Kölner Kaufmannschaft im 14. und 15. Jahrhundert," *Hansische Geschichtsblätter,* 92 (1974), 59–78. For a contrast, see Stromer's analysis of the coincidence of economic and political power in Nürnberg, in "Reichtum und Ratswürde," pp. 10–15.

who were as rich as or richer than the old patrician families; and, where such conditions obtained, the mercantile aristocracy in the guilds almost inevitably came to share power with the remnants of older ruling groups.

The social place of merchants and their role in the guilds varied widely among South German towns, corresponding to the multiplicity of civic economies and social orders. The big merchants might all be guildsmen and might share power with a patriciate that was barred from trade, as at Ulm and Strasbourg; or the merchants might themselves form a patriciate and have a political monopoly, as at Nuremberg; or the merchants might be divided between patriciate and guilds, as at Augsburg. Whatever their corporate status, the big merchants could always be found in the inner ruling circles, sooner or later. Wealth, after all, whether old or new, honorable or tainted, from land or from trade, was the single *sine qua non* for the acquisition and maintenance of high status and access to power.[4]

The social order at Strasbourg at the end of the Middle Ages had this peculiarity, that great wealth was relatively widely distributed through the corporate hierarchy and that no single aristocratic social type could be exclusively identified with any single corporate institution. Rentiers, both amigerous and noble, were found in a number of guilds as well as in the Constofeln. Nor were the big merchants concentrated in one or two merchant guilds. One of the great internal strengths of the social order was a reasonably wide distribution of important wealth—mercantile and landed wealth—through the entire guild hierarchy. This is not to say that there was no definable guild aristocracy; it is merely to say that the guild aristocracy cannot be looked for all in one place. Big merchants and smaller traders had different characteristics and different social horizons, but they cooperated politically not only between themselves but also with the patricians and the wealthier stratum of artisan masters. The consequent relative social insignificance of corporate boundaries, though often puzzling to the modern historian, provided inner lines of control which helped to make the social order very solid. Strasbourg was a city in which there was room for the more eminent of the "little people"—the tradesmen, shopkeepers, and artisans—in the chambers of government, although such men could never dominate the regime. There were nonetheless many lines of family and other social interests running from the mansions of the true aristocrats through these middling people into the shops and ateliers of the city.

---

[4] Bátori, "Das Patriziat der deutschen Stadt," pp. 4–5.

The mercantile elements in Strasbourg's regime, identifiable in the lists of privy councillors, divide fairly clearly into a group of big merchant families, a cluster of merchant-rentier families, and a group of inter-related families of lesser merchants and well-to-do artisans. The relative sizes of and the relationships among the groups can be understood by placing them into the context of the economic structures of the city and its region. The rentier guildsmen, closely related to the big merchant families, were in other ways so like the patrician rentiers that they may safely be relegated to the following chapter.

A. The Commercial Economy of Strasbourg at the End of the Middle Ages

Hans Baron, in a pioneering study written nearly forty years ago, emphasized the regional basis of Strasbourg's economy and the pre-dominance of agricultural products in the town's exports as factors in the city's notoriously independent foreign policy during the Reformation era.[5] His sketch of Strasbourg's mercantile economy is in the main confirmed by more recent studies.[6] The economy of the city around 1500 was shaped by four basic characteristics: 1) the city's role as a center of transportation and transshipment of goods; 2) its role as a collection and export center for wine and grain from both sides of the Upper Rhine; 3) the relatively unspecialized structure of its crafts; and 4) the relatively modest share of its principal merchants in the South German mercantile and banking boom after 1480.

1. Trade and travel moved through Strasbourg along two major axes. Along the north-south axis, the Rhine and its adjacent, parallel roads, Strasbourg was the only large riverine town between Basel and Speyer; and the local shippers enjoyed a chartered monopoly of the carrying trade downstream.[7] Along the east-west axis, roads coming

---

[5] Hans Baron, "Religion and Politics in the German Imperial Cities during the Reformation," *The English Historical Review*, 52 (1937), 405–427, 614–633, here at pp. 621–622.

[6] Two studies are fundamental: Peter Hertner, *Stadtwirtschaft zwischen Reich und Frankreich, Wirtschaft und Gesellschaft Strassburgs 1650–1714*, Neue Wirtschaftsgeschich-te, 8 (Cologne–Vienna, 1973), esp. pp. 1–196; and F.-J. Fuchs, "L'espace économique rhénan et les relations commerciales de Strasbourg avec le sud-ouest de l'Allemagne au XVIe siècle," in *Oberrheinische Studien, 3: Festschrift für Günther Haselier aus Anlass seines 60. Geburtstages am 19. April 1974*, ed. Alfons Schäfer (Karlsruhe, 1975), pp. 289–325.

[7] Hertner, *Stadtwirtschaft*, pp. 7–10; Alexander Dietz, *Frankfurter Handelsgeschichte*, 4 vols. in 5 (Frankfurt/M., 1910–25), I, 304–307; Jean-François Bergier, *Genève et*

through the Burgundian Gate from southern France and the entire western Mediterranean region converged at Strasbourg with the roads from northern France and the Low Countries that came through the Saverne Gap from Lorraine. Travel then moved eastward over the Rhine bridge, up the Kinzig or the Rench valleys into the Black Forest, and down into the Neckar basin towards Heilbronn, Ulm, Augsburg, and Nuremberg.[8] The north–south route was always the most important for Strasbourg merchants, who traded in the Rhine basin from central Switzerland to Frankfurt, where they regularly attended the fairs.[9] The shippers of Strasbourg were a rich, influential group, many of whom were merchants as well; and their guild stood first in the official hierarchy of the guilds.[10] The pronounced transit character of Stras-

---

l'économie européene de la renaissance, École Pratique des Hautes Études, VIe section, série "Affaires et gens d'affaires," 29 (Paris, 1963), pp. 154–159. On the shippers, see Carl Loeper's very old *Die Rheinschifffahrt Strassburgs in früherer Zeit und die Strassburger Schiffleut-Zunft* (Strasbourg, 1877).

[8] Hertner, *Stadtwirtschaft,* pp. 3–7; F.-J. Fuchs, "Les relations commerciales entre Nuremberg et Strasbourg aux XV et XVIe siècles," in *Hommage à Dürer. Strasbourg et Nuremberg dans la première moitié du XVIe siècle,* PSSARE, Collection "recherches et documents," 12 (Strasbourg, 1972), p. 77.

[9] The best study of the economic history of medieval Alsace is by Hektor Ammann, *Von der Wirtschaftsgeltung des Elsass im Mittelalter* (Lahr/Schwarzwald, 1955), also in *AJb,* 1955, pp. 95–202. On Strasbourg's commerce during the later Middle Ages, see Freddy Thiriet, "Sur les relations commerciales entre Strasbourg et l'Italie du Nord à la fin du moyen âge," *RA,* 100 (1961), 121–128; Georges Lévy-Mertz, "Le commerce strasbourgeois au XVe siècle," *RA,* 97 (1958), 91–114; Philippe Dollinger, "Marchands strasbourgeois à Fribourg en Suisse au XIVe siècle," *L'Alsace et la Suisse à travers les siècles,* PSSARE, 4 (Strasbourg, 1952), pp. 75–84; *idem,* "Commerce et marchands strasbourgeois à Fribourg en Suisse au moyen âge," in *Beiträge zur Wirtschafts- und Stadtgeschichte. Festschrift für Hektor Ammann,* ed. Hermann Aubin, *et al.* (Wiesbaden, 1965), pp. 124–143; Stromer, *Oberdeutsche Hochfinanz,* pp. 52, 61–62, 69–70, 79. For the sixteenth century there are numerous basic studies by François-Joseph Fuchs, of which, besides those cited in notes 6 and 8 above, see "Une famille de négociants banquiers du XVIe siècle, les Prechter de Strasbourg," *RA,* 95 (1956), 146–194; "Richesse et faillité des Ingold, financiers et commerçants strasbourgeois du XVIe siècle," in *La bourgeoisie alsacienne. Études d'histoire sociale,* PSSARE, 5 (Strasbourg, 1954), pp. 203–233; and "Heurs et malheurs d'un marchand-banquier strasbourgeois du XVIe siècle. Israël Minckel (vers 1522–1569), bailleur de fonds du Roi de France et des Huguenots," *RHPR,* 54 (1974), 115–127.

[10] The Shippers' Guild (Zum Encker) began in the 21st rank of 25 guilds (1332), moved to 7th (1333–34), 11th (1335–39, 1341–1470), and to 1st of 24 guilds in 1472, a position it maintained until the end of the guild regime in 1789. Hatt, *passim.* The principal shippers of Strasbourg were also merchants, because the boats they took downstream to Frankfurt were normally sold there for firewood or building timber. The unsuitability of the banks of the Upper Rhine for towpaths meant that upstream traffic normally came by land routes. Strasbourg shippers also traded in other goods on

bourg's commerce was to remain a distinguishing mark of the civic economy through the early modern era.[11]

2. The special place of agricultural products in the trade of Alsatian towns is suggested by the proliferation there of urban guilds composed of producers of or traders in foodstuffs, especially wine.[12] Wine and grain were the chief exports of the densely populated economic region comprising Lower Alsace and Middle Baden, of which Strasbourg was the chief market center. The market structures for the two products differed significantly from one another. After three centuries of high demand in northern Europe, Alsatian wine began to yield about 1500 to the competition from wines of the Middle Rhine.[13] The share of the Strasbourgeois in the historic market region for Alsatian wine—downstream to Cologne, the Netherlands, and North Germany—declined with the demand, although the two-way trade in wine and herring between Strasbourg and Antwerp was still lively during the first half of the sixteenth century.[14] Grain from Lower Alsace, on the other hand, was sold at Strasbourg chiefly to buyers from Alsace and nearby, less favored regions, such as Swabia and Switzerland.[15] Besides these two

---

their own accounts, although to do so legitimately they were supposed to join the Merchants' Guild (Zum Spiegel) as well. Dietz, *Frankfurter Handelsgeschichte*, I, 304–305.

[11] Hertner, *Stadtwirtschaft*, pp. 115–116.

[12] Noticed by Maschke, "Verfassung und soziale Kräfte," p. 296. Guilds of the "Ackerleute," "Gartner," and "Rebleute" developed in six, four, and fourteen Alsatian towns respectively. Anne Marie Imbs, "Tableaux des corporations alsaciennes, XIVe–XVIIIe siècles," *Artisans et ouvriers d'Alsace*, pp. 35–45, here at pp. 38–42.

[13] Medard Barth, *Der Rebbau des Elsass und die Absatzgebiete seiner Weine. Ein geschichtlicher Durchblick*, 2 vols. (Strasbourg–Paris, 1958), I, 353–407, and esp. the Colmar export figures on p. 412. See now, above all, Fuchs, "L'espace économique rhénan," pp. 291–294, 299–304, 311–317, 325.

[14] Fuchs, "L'espace économique rhénan," pp. 301–303; Alexander Dietz, "Strassburg und Frankfurt a. M. Eine Städtefreundschaft," *ELJb*, 1 (1922), 49–67, here at pp. 52–54; Philippe Dollinger, *The German Hansa* (Stanford, 1970), pp. 225–226; Herman Van der Wee, *The Growth of the Antwerp Market and the European Economy*, 3 vols. (The Hague, 1963), II, 63. Balthasar König, whose agents were active at Antwerp between 1512 and 1555, shipped wine downriver to Antwerp and imported herring into Alsace. Jakob Strieder, *Aus Antwerpener Notariatsarchiven. Quellen zur deutschen Wirtschaftsgeschichte des 16. Jahrhunderts*, DHMN, IV (Stuttgart–Berlin–Leipzig, 1930), pp. 228, 231–232, 234; Émile Coornaert, *Les français et le commerce international à Anvers, fin du XVe–XVIe siècle*, 2 vols. (Paris, 1961), I, 393, who dates König's Antwerp activities; Fuchs, "L'espace économique rhénan," p. 308; and Fuchs, "La paiement de la rançon des paysans prisonniers due Duc de Lorraine," in *La Guerre des paysans 1525. Etudes alsatiques*, ed. A. Wollbrett, pp. 127–128, here at p. 128n2.

[15] Miriam U. Chrisman's criticism (*Strasbourg*, p. 6n12) of Hans Baron's emphasis on Strasbourg as a center of the grain trade is misplaced. This is clear from Fuchs,

products, in which there was undoubtedly a brisk casual trade as well, Strasbourgeois traded in imported goods, especially spices, fine cloth, and metals, along with foodstuffs and timber from the surrounding region.[16]

3. Specialized manufacturing for export was not very highly developed at Strasbourg. This was an age of rapid development of specialized production for export in and around the chief towns of South Germany; and the rising market for such wares as the metal products of Nuremberg and Augsburg and the fustians of Augsburg and other Swabian towns induced important social changes in these towns. Besides a rapid accumulation of capital in the hands of entrepreneurs and merchants, there was a growing gap between urban rich and poor, together with the beginnings of an invasion of the craft system of production by proto-capitalistic forms of organization. Such forces, while not absent in the cities which retained a more balanced structure of crafts, were much less powerful there, and the tendency toward separation of productive and controlling forces in manufacturing was correspondingly weaker.[17]

"L'espace économique rhénan," pp. 310–317, 325. See also Rapp, *Réformes et Réformation*, p. 454n116; Bergier, *Genève*, p. 137; Jacques Ungerer, *Le pont du Rhin à Strasbourg du XIVe siècle à la Révolution*, Publications de l'Institut des Hautes Études Alsaciennes, VII (Strasbourg–Paris, 1952), p. 44; and Franz Irsigler, "Kölner Wirtschaftsbeziehungen zum Oberrhein vom 14. bis 16. Jahrhundert," *ZGO*, 122 (1974), 1–21, here at pp. 6–8.

[16] See the lists by Lévy-Mertz, "Le commerce strasbourgeois au XVe siècle," pp. 101–102; Ungerer, *Le pont du Rhin*, pp. 46–53.

[17] A relative matter, of course, and a very large subject which has received no systematic treatment, at least for the South German towns. Two studies, one for the North and one for the South, suggest these differences between "industrial" and "commercial" towns: Ernst Pitz, "Wirtschaftliche und soziale Probleme der gewerblichen Entwicklung im 15./16. Jahrhundert nach hansisch-niederdeutschen Quellen," *Jahrbücher für Nationalökonomie und Statistik*, 179 (1966), 200–227, reprinted in *Die Stadt des Mittelalters*, III, 137–176, here at pp. 172–176; and Peter Eitel, "Die politische, soziale und wirtschaftliche Stellung des Zunftbürgertums in den oberschwäbischen Reichsstädten am Ausgang des Mittelalters," in *Städtische Mittelschichten*, pp. 78–93, here at pp. 88–89. That the difference was *not* mainly a function of size may be seen in the example of Isny im Allgäu, a tiny free city in which cloth production for export was very highly developed. Hermann Kellenbenz, "Isny im Allgäu. Von den wirtschaftlichen Möglichkeiten einer Reichsstadt zwischen Mittelalter und Neuzeit," *JGOR*, 12/13 (1966/67), 100–123, esp. pp. 106–111. Important figures are supplied by Erich Maschke, "Mittelschichten in den deutschen Städten des Mittelalters," in *Städtische Mittelschichten*, p. 9; and Peter Eitel, *Die oberschwäbischen Reichsstädte im Zeitalter der Zunftherrschaft. Untersuchungen zu ihrer politischen und sozialen Struktur unter besonderer Berücksichtigung der Städte Lindau, Memmingen, Ravensburg und Überlingen*, Schriften zur südwestdeutschen Landeskunde, 8 (Stuttgart, 1970), p. 126. Against this evidence, see the (unsupported) skepticism of Wolfgang Zorn, "Sozialgeschichte 1500–1648," in *Handbuch der deutschen*

Strasbourg was an old-fashioned town with a balanced craft structure, where artisan guilds, with their drive to eliminate competition through qualitative and quantitative restrictions on production, retained much of their early strength.[18] The one urban product which commanded a market outside the region was "Strasbourg gray," a cheap woollen cloth which was rarely exported farther away than central Switzerland.[19] There were also the newer industries. Like their counterparts in Augsburg and Nuremberg, for example, rich Strasbourgeois invested in mines and foundries and conducted a lively trade in metals, especially in silver and copper from the mines in the Black Forest and the Vosges.[20] They were also a controlling force in the production and marketing of paper through much of the Upper and Middle Rhine.[21] Unlike locally produced cloth, metals and paper had the common advantage of being produced outside the city, in the uplands and mountains on both sides of the Rhine, where production relations could develop in greater freedom than was possible in a craft economy and where, on the other hand, the separation of capital and labor did not swell the class of propertyless wageworkers *within the city.*

4. A fourth characteristic of Strasbourg's mercantile economy, the relatively modest share of the Strasbourgeois in the explosive growth of South German commerce and banking between 1480 and 1550, was

---

Wirtschafts- und Sozialgeschichte, ed. Hermann Aubin and Wolfgang Zorn, I: *Von der Frühzeit bis zum Ende des 18. Jahrhunderts* (Stuttgart, 1971), p. 458. On the entire subject, see Jean Schneider, "Les villes allemandes au moyen âge: les institutions économiques," in *La ville,* vol. 2, pp. 471–474.

[18] Fundamental on industry is Gustav Schmoller, *Die Strassburger Tucher- und Weberzunft* (Strasbourg, 1879). Recent literature includes Jean Rott, "Artisanat et mouvements sociaux à Strasbourg autour de 1525," in *Artisans et ouvriers d'Alsace,* pp. 137–170; Anselme Schimpf, "Les tailleurs de pierre strasbourgeois," *ibid.,* pp. 97–126; Adolphe Riff, "La corporation des maréchaux de la ville de Strasbourg de 1563 à 1789," *ibid.,* pp. 171–184; F.-J. Fuchs, "L'immigration artisanale à Strasbourg de 1544 à 1565," *ibid.,* pp. 185–198; and Jean-Robert Zimmermann, *Les compagnons de métiers à Strasbourg de début du XIVe siècle à la veille de la Réforme,* PSSARE, Collection "recherches et documents," 10 (Strasbourg, 1971).

[19] Dollinger, "Commerce et marchands," p. 126; Ammann, *Von der Wirtschaftsgeltung des Elsass,* p. 71, who shows that Strasbourg produced perhaps 1,800–2,000 pieces of cloth annually, whereas the leading German cloth centers each produced around 10,000 pieces annually. See also Fuchs, "L'espace économique rhénan," p. 294.

[20] Fuchs, "L'espace économique rhénan," pp. 323–324; and, on investment opportunities in the extensive mining and foundry operations in the Black Forest, see Eberhard Gothein, *Wirtschaftsgeschichte des Schwarzwaldes und der angrenzenden Landschaften,* ed. by the Badische Historische Kommission, vol. I: *Städte- und Gewerbegeschichte* (Strasbourg, 1892), pp. 617–645, 657–667.

[21] Dietz, *Frankfurter Handelsgeschichte,* II, 108–110.

recognized already by Baron.[22] At the major centers of international commerce and banking in sixteenth century Europe, the numbers of Strasbourgeois lagged, both relatively and absolutely, far behind those of the Augsburgers and the Nurembergers. Table 8 illustrates their relative shares in terms of the numbers of merchants active at various dates in three leading centers.

Table 8

Merchants of Strasbourg, Augsburg, and Nuremberg established at Venice, Antwerp, and Lyons, ca. 1488–1579

Place and Date	Strasbourgeois	Augsburgers	Nurembergers
Venice, ca. 1500	5	62	232
Antwerp, 1488–1514[23]	24	47	73
Lyons, ca. 1550	6	35	24
Lyons, 1579	6	35	26

Sources: Baron, "Religion and Politics," p. 616; Doehaerd, *Études anversoises*, I, 86–97, 103–104; Braudel, *La méditerranée*, rev. ed., I, 202n1; Gascon, *Grand commerce*, II, 916–917.

Strasbourgeois were not engaged at all in the lucrative German loans to the French crown about 1553, though the Augsburgers and Nurembergers were well represented.[24] No Strasbourg firm rivalled in wealth, activities, or reputation the greatest houses of Augsburg and Nuremberg: the Prechter, agents of the Fugger on the Upper Rhine, were much smaller fish than the Welser, the Höchstetter, the Imhoff, or the Rem; while Conrad Joham, one of the richest Strasbourgeois of his generation, is barely known to the historians of South German commerce and banking.[25]

---

[22] Baron, "Religion and Politics," p. 616.

[23] Forty-six Strasbourgeois are known to have been active at Antwerp, 1480–1590. Coornaert, *Les français et le commerce international à Anvers*, I, 393–394.

[24] Richard Ehrenberg, *Das Zeitalter der Fugger. Geldkapital und Creditverkehr im 16. Jahrhundert*, 3rd ed., 2 vols. (Jena, 1922), II, 99n46. Strasbourg financiers of the following generation did invest heavily in French royal debt. See Fuchs, "Israël Minckel," p. 119; Gaston Zeller, "Deux capitalistes strasbourgeois du XVIe siècle," *Etudes d'histoire moderne et contemporaine*, 1 (1947), 5–14. Documents on the Strasbourg–Lyons trade in 1519–20 are in HStAS, A 149/1.

[25] On the Prechter network, see Fuchs, "Prechter," pp. 163–176, and the map on p. 175. On their ties to the Fugger, see *ibid.*, pp. 187–188; Götz Freiherr von Pölnitz, *Jakob Fugger. Kaiser, Kirche und Kapital in der oberdeutschen Renaissance*, 2 vols. (Tübingen, 1949–51), I, 540, and II, 144–145, 149, 230, 238, 270, 441, 451, 522, 540.

The loss of Strasbourg's tax rolls means that we shall never know much about the mercantile fortunes in the town. Gottfried von Hohenburg, who belonged to the upper stratum in the guilds, deposed in 1522 that he was worth about 9,000 Rhenish florins.[26] This certainly made him "very rich" by the standards of his day, though he would not have been a really big man at Augsburg, where in 1509 at least fifty-three men had more than 10,000 fl. in taxable wealth.[27] Very large fortunes were not unknown at Strasbourg. Balthasar König, a big merchant heavily engaged in the Antwerp and Cologne trades, was said to have left an estate worth 150,000 fl., which would have made him a big man anywhere.[28] Veronika Prechter, a daughter of Friedrich II Prechter and wife of Sebastian Mieg von Boofzheim, left a sizeable estate: 12,433 lb. of capital invested at interest; 1939 lb./yr. from her chief rural properties; 646 lb. worth of household goods; 3,156 lb. in cash; and two houses in Strasbourg. Even after deducting her considerable debts (8,272 lb.), this was a very large estate,[29] most of which was invested in interest-bearing debt or real property. Not all aristocrats were so well fixed. Hans Erhard von Rotweil, Jr. (d. 1559), last male member of a prominent family of guild rentiers, left his two unmarried daughters a modest income of slightly more than 100 lb./yr., and they had to pay substantial sums to redeem both his house and rents at Marlenheim and the family silver from the civic treasury.[30] Except for a handful of great families, the wealth of the guild aristocrats of Strasbourg seems to have been rather modest, judged by the standards of Augsburg or Nuremberg.

---

[26] AMS, IX 2/6; PROSOPOGRAPHY, No. XLI.

[27] Walter Jacob (*Politische Führungsschicht*, pp. 60–61, 102–103) classifies any Zürcher having more than 5,000 fl. in taxable wealth as "very rich," a category which contained only five persons in 1519–28. The Augsburg figures, which are notoriously difficult to relate to other figures, are in Jakob Strieder, *Zur Genesis des modernen Kapitalismus. Forschungen zur Entstehung der grossen bürgerlichen Kapitalvermögen am Ausgange des Mittelalters und zu Beginn der Neuzeit, zunächst in Augsburg*, 2nd ed. (Munich-Leipzig, 1935), p. 22. Hohenburg's 9,000 fl. would have put him in the "obere Schicht" at Augsburg. See Blendinger, "Versuch einer Bestimmung der Mittelschicht in der Reichsstadt Augsburg," pp. 47, 68.

[28] HABW, Ms. 2. Aug. 2°, fol. 105ᵛ (30/31 December 1560). My thanks to Jean Rott for bringing this chronicle to my attention and allowing me to peruse his photocopy of it. König's fortune made him a millionaire by modern standards, but fortunes of this magnitude were not extremely rare. The Humpiss family at Ravensburg had in 1473 *taxable* wealth worth at least 130,000 fl. Dreher, "Das Patriziat der Reichsstadt Ravensburg," *ZWLG*, 21 (1962), 385.

[29] AMS, V 152/5.

[30] AMS, V 138/25, accounts (1560–61) of their guardian, Georg Mieg.

5. These four salient characteristics of Strasbourg's economy had important implications for the place of the merchants in the social and political life of the town. Compared with the big merchants of other South German towns of this era, the Strasbourgeois were closely tied to their own region and surrounding ones. The principal export goods were rural rather than urban products, which meant that changes in levels of production would not significantly affect the urban craft system. In Strasbourg itself, "growth" was to some extent sacrificed to the preservation of the city's social peace, an arrangement which had two consequences for the solidity of the aristocratic regime. On the one hand, the artisan masters tended to be staunchly loyal to the regime and to cooperate in using the guild structures as a system of political control. On the other hand, commercial and banking profits flowed away from the crafts and towards finance and real property, facilitating and even promoting the social alliance of the guild aristocracy with the patriciate.

B.   THE BIG MERCHANTS

1. The tendency of urban historians to seek the ancestors of new merchant families among the successful artisans of the same city has begun to yield to the realization that the migration of merchants and other prosperous persons from smaller towns and villages was an important source of new urban merchants.[31] This was certainly true around 1500 at Strasbourg, where the core of the richest merchant stratum was a cluster of immigrant families centered on the Prechter and the Ingold.[32] Whereas the new patricians came mainly from rural Alsace, Baden, and the Palatinate, and the immigrant artisans came mainly from other South German cities as far eastward as Nuremberg, the big merchants migrated from smaller free towns of Alsace.[33] The big merchants of the Reformation era were mostly members of families who had come to Strasbourg during the last third of the fifteenth century: from Hagenau came the Ingold (1440), the Prechter (1473), the Ebel (1499), the Kips (1488), and the Gottesheim (1505); from Saverne the Joham (1486); and from Mulhouse the Mieg (1454); while the Jörger

---

[31] See Herlihy, *Medieval and Renaissance Pistoia,* pp. 183–185; and Jacques Le Goff, "The Town as an Agent of Civilisation," in *The Fontana Economic History of Europe,* ed. Carlo M. Cipolla, I: *The Middle Ages* (London, 1972), pp. 92–94.

[32] Fuchs, "Prechter," p. 147, first noticed this fact.

[33] Fuchs, "L'immigration artisanale à Strasbourg de 1544 à 1565," pp. 186–188, based on his study of the second (1543–1618) and third (1559–1730) surviving *Bürgerbücher.* On the patriciate, see Kageneck, "Das Patriziat im Elsass," p. 386.

came from an unknown place, perhaps Buchsweiler (1460).[34] They began very soon to intermarry with established merchant families, such as the Duntzenheim, the Rotweil, the Arg, and the Mussler, whom they were destined in the main to replace as the pinnacle of the guild aristocracy.

With a few exceptions, this cluster of families monopolized Strasbourg's share of international trade and banking during the first half of the sixteenth century. Friedrich I Prechter became an agent of the Great Ravensburg Company, and his son, Friedrich II, represented the Fugger on the Upper Rhine.[35] The Prechter alone at Strasbourg secured a privilege of exemption from the Imperial anti-monopoly laws, such as was possessed by a number of Nuremberg and Augsburg firms.[36] It is possible that the activities of these recent immigrants added to the popular anti-monopoly sentiment at Strasbourg, for it was certainly against such families that Johann Geiler von Kaysersberg (d. 1510) thundered from his pulpit in the cathedral: "Monopoly exists when someone has, or wants to have, exclusive rights to sell something. Such men secure a charter, a letter, or a seal from a prince or a king. They stand alone in the trough like an old sow and won't let the other hogs in."[37]

2. The big merchants traded in most of the chief commercial centers of sixteenth–century Europe. Not many Strasbourgeois went to Italy to trade, and those who did traded chiefly in luxury goods. The Ingold, for example, were buying saffron at Aquila in 1514, a commodity they had handled since 1500, and they shared space in the Venetian *Fondaco dei*

---

[34] The dates are those at which the first members of these families became citizens of Strasbourg. Fuchs ("Prechter," p. 147) remarks that "La ville de Haguenau fut au XVe et au début du XVIe siècle une véritable pépinière du patriciat strasbourgeois."

[35] Aloys Schulte, *Geschichte der Grossen Ravensburger Handelsgesellschaft 1380–1530*, 3 vols., DHMN, I–III (Stuttgart, 1923), III, 347, No. 64, dated 8 April 1507. The earliest notice of Strasbourgeois in the company's records concerns a shipment of goods from Geneva consigned to "dem Ingold und Andreas Byschoff" for transportation downstream to Frankfurt a. M., dated 1478. *Ibid.*, III, 339, No. 61.

[36] Cited by Jakob Strieder, *Studien zur Geschichte kaptalistischer Organisationsformen. Monopole, Kartelle und Aktiengesellschaften im Mittelalter und zu Beginn der Neuzeit*, 2nd ed. (Munich–Leipzig, 1925), pp. 78–79, 79n1. See the references on the Prechter–Fugger connection in note 25 above.

[37] Quoted in *ibid.*, p. 190. On the anti-monopoly movement during the first half of the sixteenth century, see Fritz Blaich, *Die Reichsmonopolgesetzgebung im Zeitalter Karls V. Ihre ordnungspolitische Problematik,* Schriften zum Vergleich von Wirtschaftsordnungen, 8 (Stuttgart, 1967), pp. 10–81. For its polemical side, there is still no better collection of texts than in Johannes Janssen's *Geschichte des deutschen Volkes seit dem Ausgang des Mittelalters*, I: *Die allgemeinen Zustände des deutschen Volkes beim Ausgang des Mittelalters,* 7th ed. (Freiburg/Br., 1881), pp. 392–403, who quotes other Geiler texts (p. 394).

tedeschi with Friedrich I Prechter and Anshelm Joham.[38] Joham's son, Conrad, had agents at Genoa, Venice, Milan, Antwerp, and Lyons during the 1530s and 1540s and was a major dealer in silk and silver.[39] Friedrich I Prechter established himself at Antwerp by 1512, and the Mieg and Ingold were there several decades later.[40] The same families took part in the massive shift of South German capital in the 1540s to Lyons, where the Strasbourgeois shared trade privileges with the Augsburgers, Nurembergers, and Ulmers. The protection of this trade became a significant element in Strasbourg's foreign policy during the 1540s, although Strasbourgeois became big creditors of the French crown only in the next generation.[41] The major Strasbourg firms also traded with and had factors in the two chief metropoles downstream, Frankfurt am Main and Cologne.[42]

---

[38] "Driffas von Kauffmannschaft (1514/1515)," in *Welthandelsbräuche 1480–1540*, ed. K. O. Müller, DHMN, V (Wiesbaden, 1962), p. 246; Schulte, *Geschichte der Grossen Ravensburger Handelsgesellschaft*, III, 347, No. 64; Henry Simonsfeld, *Der Fondaco dei Tedeschi in Venedig und die deutsch-venezianischen Handelsbeziehungen*, 2 vols. (Stuttgart, 1887), II, 188. A list of Strasbourg spice merchants ca. 1510 is in BLBK, Hs. Ettenheim–Münster 17, fol. 35^r.

[39] *PCSS*, II, 497, 560, and III, 383; and the references in PROSOPOGRAPHY, No. XLV. Joham's daughter, Christina, married Daniel Stallburger (1515–53), a silk dealer of Frankfurt/M. and son of Claus Stallburger "der Reiche" (1469–1524); and Georg Joham von Mundolsheim (d. 1584) married in 1556 Claus's daughter, Agnes. Dietz, *Frankfurter Handelsgeschichte*, I, 282. Joham's factor at Frankfurt, Hieronymus Mengershausen of Nordheim (d. 1557), became a citizen of Frankfurt in 1539 and an independent merchant in Italian silks and satins; at death he was worth about 18,000 fl. *Ibid.*, p. 250.

[40] See note 14 above. On the Mieg and their business network, see Philippe Mieg, "Note sur les négociants strasbourgeois Muege au XVe siècle," *RA*, 98 (1959), 138–145; and Etienne Juillard, *L'europe rhénane. Géographie d'un grand espace* (Paris, 1968), p. 27.

[41] Richard Gascon, *Grand commerce et vie urbaine au XVIe siècle. Lyon et ses marchands (environs de 1520-environs de 1580)*, 2 vols., École Pratique des Hautes Études, série "Civilisations et Sociétés," 22 (Paris–The Hague, 1971), I, figures 9–11 between pp. 110–111, where the inconsequence of Strasbourg for Lyons' *commerce* is clear, proving that the financial activities of Strasbourgeois there were not based on a strong trade connection. See Gerhard Pfeiffer, "Die Bemühungen der oberdeutschen Kaufleute um die Privilegierung ihres Handels in Lyon," *Beiträge zur Wirtschaftsgeschichte Nürnbergs*, I, 408–423; Marcel Brésard, *Les foires de Lyon aux XVe et XVIe siècles* (Paris, 1914), pp. 121–122; Fuchs, "Israël Minckel," pp. 118–120. On the protection of trading privileges, see further AMS, XXI 1547, fols. 311^v–313^r, 357^v; AMS, XXI 1548, fol. 37^r; Antoine Kentzinger, ed., *Documents historiques rélatifs à l'histoire de France, tirés des archives de la ville de Strasbourg*, 2 vols. (Strasbourg, 1818–19), I, 31–32; Franziskus Petri, "Strassburgs Beziehungen zu Frankreich während der Reformationszeit," *ELJb*, 10 (1931), 168–169.

[42] On Strasbourg's trade with other German-speaking cities, see in general Fuchs, "L'espace économique rhénan," pp. 289–325, who discusses trade with Frankfurt/M. and Cologne in the sixteenth century. On the Strasbourg–Frankfurt trade there is also

Large-scale trade went hand-in-hand with banking; and "even when trafficking in money became their principal activity, the big businessmen kept up their merchandising operations."[43] One important link between banking and merchandising was the trade in metals, for precious and semi-precious metals were both media and objects of exchange. Then, too, the mining districts provided attractive sites of investment for wealthy urban folk, far from the watchful eyes of the artisan masters of their own towns. Through the trade in metals, the goldsmiths, who have been classified with the merchants rather than the other artisans, moved into a business they shared with merchant firms.[44] The Prechter and several allied families were among the heavy investors in the silver mines at Sainte-Marie-aux-Mines in the Liepvre valley during the 1530s and 1540s;[45] and among their leading customers were Conrad Joham and Anton von Sigolsheim, the stepfather of the XVer Conrad Meyer, along with a couple of prominent goldsmiths, Martin Kroschweiler and Erasmus Krug, Jr. Kroschweiler married a daughter of Herbart Hetter, a XVer whose son, Erasmus Hetter, was later a partner of Erasmus Krug, Jr., in a copper-refining enterprise.[46] Through the Hetter there was a tie to the great goldsmith family of Sebott, for Erasmus Hetter's mother was a Sebott. Erasmus Krug, Jr., a goldsmith and son of an immigrant goldsmith from Nuremberg, became one of Strasbourg's major entrepreneurs. Besides his copper refinery in the Vosges, he invested important sums in the exploitation of mines in the Grisons and in the canton of Uri.[47] These entrepreneur–goldsmiths shared the trade in metals with the great trading firms of the town.

In banking, too, the biggest operators were the Prechter and Ingold firms, Conrad Joham, and the Mieg.[48] These firms, except for the Mieg,

---

Dietz, "Strassburg und Frankfurt a. M.," pp. 49–67, which brings together material scattered through his *Frankfurter Handelsgeschichte*. For the Strasbourg–Nuremberg trade, there is Fuchs's study cited in note 8 above; and, for the Strasbourg–Cologne trade, see Irsigler, "Kölner Wirtschaftsbeziehungen zum Oberrhein vom 14. bis 16. Jahrhundert," pp. 1–21.

[43] Jeannin, *Merchants,* p. 55.

[44] Maschke, "Verfassung und soziale Kräfte," pp. 450–451.

[45] Fuchs, "Prechter," pp. 169–172, esp. p. 170.

[46] F.-J. Fuchs, "Une usine de raffinage de cuivre dans la vallée de la Bruche (Alsace) au XVIe siècle," in *Festschrift für Hermann Heimpel,* I, 719–740; and PROSOPOGRAPHY, No. XXXVIII.

[47] F.-J. Fuchs, "Un orfèvre strasbourgeois du XVIe siècle à la recherche de métaux precieux, Erasme Krug, exploitant de mines à Disentis (Grisons), et à Silenen (Uri)," in *Hommage à Hans Haug=CAAAH,* N.S. 11 (1967), 77–88.

[48] Fuchs, "Prechter," pp. 178–187; Fuchs, "Ingold," p. 204.

were named as the desired guarantors of an enormous war loan which the Smalkaldic League tried to raise at Lyons in 1546.[49] In the next decade, two Strasbourgeois, Israel Minckel and Georg Obrecht, became major creditors of the king of France.[50] In banking as in trade, the documents mention again and again the same small group of names.

3. The composition of the richest stratum of guildsmen can be established with some precision. Fragments of the *Stallbuch*, which contained the names of citizens who were rich enough to serve the commune "zu Ross" and were therefore obliged to maintain horses in the civic stable, show that the richest men of the years 1517–19 mostly came from big merchant families:[51] Friedrich II Prechter maintained three horses—the same number as the richest patricians—and Peter Mussler (d. 1519) and Daniel Mieg each maintained two. No less than six Mieg appear, along with Friedrich V von Gottesheim (uncle of the future privy councillor), Herbart Hetter, Batt von Duntzenheim, Gottfried von Hohenburg, Mathis Pfarrer, Claus Braun, and Diebold Sebott—all future privy councillors—a mixture of big merchants, rentiers, and goldsmiths.

An unexpected source at the end of the Reformation generation provides a more comprehensive list of the richest Strasbourgeois. At the end of 1548 or in early 1549, Jacob Sturm was seeking a way to save the patrician share of civic offices despite the shortage of eligible patricians. He apparently toyed with the idea of creating a new estate, or rather of resurrecting an old middle estate, of *Bürger* (*optimates, cives*), rich, non-patrician families standing between the patricians (*Adel, nobiles*) and the guildsmen (*Handwerker, tribus*).[52] Each of the three estates would have one-third of the civic offices. Sturm also noted the names of families and individuals he thought suitable (i.e., rich enough) to be designated *optimates*. He wrote down three lists:

---

[49] HStAM, Politisches Archiv des Landgrafen Philipp von Hessen (=PA), 2915, 2917; *PCSS*, II, 100, 210, 210n2, and III, 487n1, and IV, 398, 401–402; AMS, VII 11/3. See now Jean-Daniel Pariset, "Les relations des rois de France et des princes protestants allemands 1541–1559," Thèse de l'École des Chartes, 2 vols. (Paris, 1972), I, 110.

[50] Fuchs, "Israël Minckel."

[51] AMS, VI 591/1 (1517–19); AMS, R 29/107 (1540).

[52] AMS, VI 491/3, unsigned but in Sturm's hand. Sturm uses both German and Latin terms for all three "estates," leaving no doubt that he intended to establish (or re-establish) an estate of *Bürger* as a legal/constitutional category separate from the guilds. This conclusion is inescapable from Sturm's proposed reorganization of the Senate: "x vom adel, dorunder 4 stettmeister. x von bürgern die ein eygen stuben. x von handtwerken, je zwo zunfft einen vnd ye ein jar vmb das ander."

Table 9

Prospective "Optimates"/"Bürger" selected by Jacob Sturm, 1548–49

List I: "cives"	List II	List III: "Bürger"
Arg	Mieg	Ingold, Philips
Ingold	Ingold	— , Jacob
Ebel	Ebel	— , Hans, Sr.
Prechter	Prechter	— , Florentz
Gottesheim	Joham	— , Jerg
Joham		— , Hans, Jr.
Mieg		Mieg, Andreas
Erstein-Armbruster		— , Carl, Jr.
Meyer (Conrad)		— , Sebastian *et fratres*
Nidbruck		von Gottesheim, Friedrich VI
Rotweil		von Duntzenheim, Jacob
		— , Hans
		Minckel, Israel
		von Nidbruck, Philips
		Schultheiss von Hall, Hans
		Joham, Conrad *et filii*
		— , Heinrich
		— , Sebastian
		Varnbühler, Ulrich
		Meyer, Conrad

Source: AMS, VI 491/3.

A few of these men were immigrants, such as Hans Schultheiss of Schwäbisch Hall, Philips Nidbruck of Metz, and Ulrich Varnbühler, a Swabian who had married one of Conrad Joham's daughters. Israel Minckel, born and educated at Strasbourg, was the son of a wealthy immigrant from Frankfurt am Main.[53] The others are the names of the big merchants and rentier guildsmen of the Reformation era. With the addition of a few older families, either extinct in the male lines or fallen onto evil days by the 1540s, such as the Mussler and the Jörger, the lists would have sufficed for the 1520s as well. Sturm's notes not only confirm the composition of the stratum of richest guildsmen at Strasbourg, they also reveal the persistence of the concept of a category of citizens who were in the guilds but, by virtue of their wealth, not of them.

4. The cohesiveness of the big merchants was based on intermarriage

---

[53] Fuchs, "Israël Minckel"; AMS, KS 70/I, fols. 48ʳ–49ʳ.

patterns and often cemented with business partnerships.[54] The children of Friedrich I Prechter married into the Mieg, Duntzenheim, and Ebel families, while his grandchildren married partners from the Mieg, the Gottesheim, and the Joham. The most lively exchange occurred between the Ebel and Ingold families: in one generation, five Ebel siblings married five Ingold siblings.[55] Table 10 summarizes the Ingold marriage network over three generations from about 1475 to about 1575.

Table 10

Ingold marriages, ca. 1475–ca. 1575

---

1) Older merchant families: Rotweil, Arg, Duntzenheim, Messinger, Gerbott.
2) Newer merchant families: Joham (3), Ebel (7), Prechter, Mieg (2), König, Widt.
3) Patrician families: Mülnheim.

Source: Fuchs, "Ingold."

These families of the Prechter–Ingold–Ebel–Mieg–Joham–Arg–Duntzenheim–Gottesheim complex formed the core of the guild aristocracy. They, plus a few allied families, were the "haute bourgeosie" of sixteenth-century Strasbourg.[56]

C.   THE LESSER MERCHANTS

1. Lesser merchants, mainly cloth merchants, make up the largest identifiable group of guild privy councillors in the Reformation generation—nearly one-quarter of the total. The distinction between greater and lesser merchants has more to do with the scale of wealth than with the type of business operations, while "even the dichotomy of whole-sale–retail is, in part, fictitious."[57] Although the political importance of

---

[54] A point stressed by Fuchs, "Israël Minckel," pp. 116–117; and, in a Nuremberg context, by Hellmut Haller von Hallerstein, "Grösse und Quellen der Vermögen von hundert Nürnberger Bürger um 1500," in *Beiträge zur Wirtschaftsgeschichte Nürnbergs*, I, 173. This is particularly striking with the Prechter, for whom see Fuchs, "Prechter," pp. 147–149, 157–159.

[55] Fuchs, "Ingold," p. 204; Christian Wolff, "Les Ingold aux XVIe et XVIIe siècles. Essai de mise au point de leur généalogie," *BCGA*, No. 9 (1970), 112–118, here at pp. 114–115.

[56] This is Fuchs's term ("Israël Minckel," p. 115). If I do not employ its English equivalent, "big bourgeoisie" or "upper bourgeoisie," it is because the terms are rather clumsy. I thoroughly agree with Fuchs's identification of this stratum.

[57] Jeannin, *Merchants*, pp. 30–31.

these middling elements in the urban social order is well recognized,[58] very little is known about them in detail. It is nevertheless clear that they shared much with the big merchants, for business operations even at the relatively humble level of the shopkeeper involved problems of credit and partnership "that were not basically very different from those confronting big business."[59]

Among the cloth merchants who appear so frequently as privy councillors, no very clear division between merchants and shopkeepers can be discerned. The Ammeister Mattheus Geiger (d. 1549), for example, is called both a "merchant" (*mercator*) and a "retailer" (*Krämer*); and although he is known to have kept a shop in the Münstergasse, he was also involved in the French trade.[60] The marriages in his family during three generations involved partners from mercantile families, such as the Bischoff and the Hammerer (also cloth merchants), professional men such as the physician, Johann Fuchs, and the civic syndic, Michel Han, and the armigerous family von Rotweil. The Ammeister Martin Herlin (d. 1547) was also a merchant (*mercator*), though next to nothing is known of his business, and the Herlin marriages show a similar pattern of partners from merchant, goldsmith, and rentier families.[61] A whole series of privy councillors came from similar families: Pfarrer, Braun, Stösser, Hammerer, Messinger, and Kniebis. Some may have descended from old families of local artisans, but other privy councillors of this group were immigrants, such as Caspar Hoffmeister, a native of Weil der Stadt in Swabia.[62]

2. While it is quite true, as Gustav Schmoller discovered long ago,[63] that by the end of the fifteenth century the cloth entrepreneurs had gained control both of the cloth industry and the Cloth Guild at Strasbourg, the cloth merchants were by no means confined to this guild. Mathis Pfarrer and Hans Hammerer were cloth merchants and partners in the cloth trade for nearly twenty years, but neither ever belonged to the Cloth Guild, Pfarrer having originally belonged to the guild Zum

[58] Herlihy, *Pistoia*, pp. 183–191; *idem*, "Some Psychological and Social Roots of Violence in the Tuscan Cities," *Violence and Civil Disorder in Italian Cities*, pp. 138–139.

[59] Jeannin, *Merchants*, pp. 32–35.

[60] PROSOPOGRAPHY, No. XXXI. See Eitel, "Die politische . . . Stellung des Zunftbürgertums," p. 86.

[61] PROSOPOGRAPHY, No. XXXVII. Other such families represented in the PROSOPOGRAPHY are the Heuss, Lindenfels, Franck, Pfarrer, Hammerer, and Stösser families, plus perhaps the Braun, the Storck, and the Kips.

[62] PROSOPOGRAPHY, No. XL.

[63] Schmoller, *Strassburger Tucher- und Weberzunft*, pp. 495–496, 500.

Freiburg and Hammerer to the guild Zum Encker.[64] Caspar Hoffmeister belonged to the guild Zur Blume, the old Butchers' Guild, while Herbart Hetter belonged to the rich guild Zum Spiegel, formerly the Merchants' Guild. Martin Betscholt (d. 1546) stayed in the guild of his forefathers, the guild Zur Blume, but he traded in Lorraine and probably in cloth.

Of such men it can be said they were almost certainly less wealthy than the big merchant families with whom they occasionally inter-married, and that their economic horizons were certainly more circum-scribed geographically than those of the big merchant-bankers. This is probable just from the nature of the Alsatian cloth trade.

It is difficult to exaggerate the social significance of the small merchants, who in many ways formed a bridge between the upper level of the guild aristocracy and the world of the shopkeepers and artisan masters. Like the former, they were businessmen and men of affairs, able to manage their own time and money; and, like the latter, they were men of little experience outside their own and neighbouring regions, were usually not armigerous, were inexperienced in war, and were solidly attached to the region in which their civic regime was a relatively major power.

D.   MASTER ARTISANS AND ARTISAN GUILDS

1. The absence of quantifiable sources and the fragmentary state of the guild archives at Strasbourg make the world of the crafts and the shops a dim and somewhat mysterious one, into which surviving records throw occasional, welcome beams of light. The number of shopkeeper and artisan masters was so large[65] that the few men of this sort who became privy councillors cannot be taken as representative of the entire stratum. Lacking any very precise information about them, one yields easily to the temptation to identify "artisans" with the "lower classes," a step which leads only to confusion. For, as humble as they might appear from the vantage point of the aristocrats, the masters of even very ordi-nary crafts were genuine *masters,* both in the sense of commanding the tools and lore of their crafts and in the sense of commanding the labor and loyalty of the journeymen and apprentices. If the civic population is divided into masters and servants, those who commanded and those who obeyed, then most of the master artisans fall into the former cate-

---

[64] PROSOPOGRAPHY, Nos. XXXVI and LXXIII.
[65] Rott, "Artisanat," p. 160n7.

gory. This is all the truer because of the oligarchical tendencies in late medieval guilds and the relative decline of the position and chances of the journeymen due to the steady decline in real wages and the emergence of the "perpetual journeyman."[66] The romantic image of the master as surrogate father can be misleading, because by the end of the Middle Ages the use of wage labor was extremely common in some trades, particularly the metalworking crafts and the building trades (except the stonemasons).[67] Although Strasbourg never became a major center of highly specialized export industries, in which the use of wage labor was elsewhere common, the employment even of master artisans as wage laborers was well known there by the fifteenth century.[68]

The gulf between master artisans and merchants, on the other side, was not necessarily great, because, in some trades at least, successful artisan masters were more likely to move into commerce than into new or larger-scale forms of craft organization. The craft guild system, as is well known, managed its markets, and thus the relative prosperity of its members, by controlling the quality and quantity of the goods produced. Since the system of craft regulation operated to discourage or even prohibit major increases of fixed capital investment and the size of shops, successful masters were more likely to seek the higher, surer profits of commerce than to risk their capital in ventures likely to provoke their comrades' wrath.[69] The men who appear as masters in many of Strasbourg's guilds were actually as much merchants as they were artisans. This was true of some guilds which, though embracing relatively humble occupations, were not artisan guilds in the classic sense.

Largest of all was the enormous Gardeners' Guild, whose 600 members made it thrice as large as the city's next largest guild, and which was subdivided into three sub-guilds corresponding to the three old suburbs in which the members were concentrated.[70] Although notorious as one of the city's poorer guilds, it actually contained some relatively wealthy men whose livelihood rested on the chief occupation of the guild, truck-gardening for the urban market. Such were the leading families of Graff and Drenss, who supplied most of the guild's prominent politicians

---

[66] Sylvia L. Thrupp, "Medieval Industry, 1000–1500," in *The Fontana Economic History of Europe*, I, 265ff.

[67] *Ibid.,* p. 265.

[68] Zimmermann, *Les compagnons de métier*, pp. 50–52.

[69] Maschke, "Verfassung und soziale Kräfte," pp. 440–444; Wallerstein, *Modern World System,* pp. 122–124; Thrupp, "Medieval Industry, 1000–1500," p. 269.

[70] See Rott, "Artisanat," p. 167n117.

during the Reformation era.[71] The same is true of another occupationally homogeneous, relatively humble guild, the Fishermen, in which the well-to-do stratum was made up of fish merchants. Anshelm Baldner, the Fishermens' XVer from 1536 until 1563, is known to have kept a shop, although he is always called a fisherman ("vischer," "piscator").[72] The Baldner and two other families furnished most of the guilds privy councillors during the period 1488 to 1585: five Baldner served a total of sixty years as XVer; two Ulrich (Roettel) served twenty years; and two Lamp served eight years.[73] That many butchers were also dealers in livestock and hides is known from numerous South German examples, and it was probably the case in Strasbourg as well. An official inquiry in 1521 discovered that eight butchers were keeping a total of 284 head of cattle in reserve and that the biggest operator, Hans Volmar, had more that a quarter of them (74).[74]

Some of the richest master artisans were to be found in the metal-working trades, and the goldsmiths have already been singled out in this respect. They were the dominant craft in the guild Zur Steltz, which they shared with the glaziers (*Glaser, Glasmaler*), painters, and printers, plus a cluster of smaller crafts. A list of masters from the early 1530s contains thirty-nine names, of whom at least sixteen are those of goldsmiths.[75] During the Reformation era, the senator from this guild was a goldsmith nearly two-thirds of the time, and every privy councillor of this generation but one from the guild was a goldsmith (all XVers).[76] Some of the other metalworking trades were much smaller, and their masters were not, one suspects, nearly so rich; but the small size of the mastership undoubtedly made the police of production much easier. Such was the

---

[71] PROSOPOGRAPHY, Nos. XVIII, XIX, XXXV. Andreas Graff (d. 15/16 January 1557) was also a XVer from the *Gartnerzunft*. Hatt, p. 658; AMS, XXI 1557, fol. 3ʳ.

[72] PROSOPOGRAPHY, Nos. III, IV, V.

[73] A (unique) list of the XVers from the *Fischerzunft*, 1470–1654, is in AMS, VI 488/3.

[74] AMS, IV 102/4: "Die nochgeschriben sint die Rinder so die metziger hinder jnen habent," 1521. On the traffic in livestock, see Fuchs, "L'espace economique rhénan," pp. 317–320, with references.

[75] AMS, IV 102/9, checked against the lists of Strasbourg artists in Rott, *Oberrhein*, I, 185–307, and Textband, pp. 273–368. The latest possible date is 1534, the year of Diebold Sebott's death. My thanks to Miriam U. Chrisman, who checked this list against her files of Strasbourg printers.

[76] Thomas A. Brady, Jr., "The Social Place of a German Renaissance Artist: Hans Baldung Grien (1484/85–1545) at Strasbourg," *Central European History*, 8, (1975), 306–307.

case with the master tinsmiths (*Kannengiesser*), who through much of the sixteenth century numbered only seven or eight persons.[77]

These considerations support the view that the term "master artisan" had no fixed social content. In a single craft a master might be a prosperous employer and merchant or he might be a wageworker—both types would be masters of the same corporation and have, at least formally, equal rights in the government of the guild. The mastership thus combined in a single status persons of truly different social classes; and this is yet another case of estate categories overlapping the boundaries between classes.

2. It is common enough to see in the well-to-do artisan and shopkeeper masters the fiercest defenders of protected privilege and the most militant enemies of freer labor relations and more advanced technology.[78] While this view is in the main correct, several other characteristics of this stratum are worth mentioning. In the first place, the artisans were probably the most thoroughly urban of all social strata in Strasbourg, because immigrant artisans to Strasbourg came almost exclusively from other cities and towns and not from the villages or the land.[79] There were also larger craft organizations which represented the professional and economic interests of the crafts in many cities. Best known and most important of these was the great brotherhood of the stonemasons, which stretched across the entire southern half of the German-speaking world and had its headquarters in the richly endowed construction and maintenance organization of Strasbourg's cathedral (*Unserer Lieben Frauen Werk*).[80] Thither came periodically representatives of masons' corporations from dozens of towns to revise the brotherhood's statutes. At such an assembly at Strasbourg in 1516, the delegates included thirty-eight masters from twenty-seven different cities and forty-one journeymen from thirty-two different cities.[81] Such ties strengthened the char-

---

[77] Riff, "La corporation des maréchaux de la ville de Strasbourg de 1563 à 1789," p. 177, figures confirmed by lists (1519, 1521) of tinsmiths containing seven names each, in AMS, III 12/10.

[78] Kofler, *Zur Geschichte der bürgerlichen Gesellschaft,* pp. 123–124.

[79] Fuchs, "L'immigration artisanale," pp. 185–198.

[80] Schimpf, "Les tailleurs de pierre strasbourgeois," pp. 125–126.

[81] BNUS, Ms. 741 ("Der Steinmetzen Bruoderschafft vnnd Ordnungen jr hanndtwerckh Betreffende, etc."), fols. 17^r–18^r; and the articles of 1459 and 1563 are edited by Schimpf, "Les tailleurs de pierre strasbourgeois," pp. 99–111, 112–119. Strasbourg masters and journeymen participated in many such supra-regional artisan organizations, some of which are described by Gothein, *Wirtschaftsgeschichte des Schwarzwaldes,* pp. 373, 380, 390–391, 410; and Lucien Sittler, "Les associations artisanales en Alsace au moyen âge et sous l'ancien regime," *RA,* 97 (1958), 36–80.

acter of the artisans as perhaps the most urban stratum of the urban population.

It is thus quite correct to see in the artisan and shopkeeper masters the most locally oriented of those strata of the citizenry that counted politically and the group to whom civic regulation of production and market conditions meant the most. Here was a perennial source of potential conflict between them and the big merchants and, indeed, any group wanting to practice "freie Kaufmannschaft." This is clear enough from the frequent complaints by prominent masters against illegal sales of goods by merchants—Friedrich I Prechter was an oft-cited offender—and against the refusal of some merchants to pay the fee (*Hausgelt*) levied on any goods sold from private shops rather than from the civic *Kaufhaus*.[82]

The merchandizing rivalry between big merchants and artisan-merchants in the fur trade came to a head at Strasbourg around 1513, when the furriers called upon a peculiar survival from the city's past to aid them in their struggle against the big fellows. The grand mastership of the furriers of Strasbourg had its origins as an office before the late twelfth century in a group of privileged but legally unfree artisans who were episcopal ministeriales (*Kammerhandwerker*).[83] Like other ministerial offices, it underwent a process of feudalization; and, by the mid-fifteenth century, the grand mastership of the furriers ("das ober kursener meisterthüm by üch zü Strassburg") was an episcopal fief customarily granted to a noble of the town, most often to a Mülnheim.[84] Well into the sixteenth century, the real master furriers of Strasbourg (for the office had long ago ceased to have anything to do with the craft) fought against interference by enfiefed grand masters and against taking an oath of loyalty to them. This quarrel lasted more than half a century. When the furriers proceeded against Conrad Joham and his firm around 1513, however, they called on the grand master, Bläsi von Mülnheim (d. 1526), to represent their case against the free sale of furs.[85] Mülnheim

---

[82] AMS, IV 101/5 (ca. 1506–10); Lévy-Mertz, "Le commerce strasbourgeois," pp. 96–99.

[83] Mosbacher, "Kammerhandwerk, Ministerialität und Bürgertum in Strassburg," pp. 97–104.

[84] AMS, III 20. Like so many other feudal offices, this one became an item of sale and was, for instance, sold by Hans Nollisheim to Adam Bock for 4 fl. before 1445. The documents in this dossier should be added to those printed by Mosbacher, "Kammerhandwerk, Ministerialität und Bürgertum in Strassburg," pp. 163ff.

[85] AMS, III 11/25, first document undated, but the following extract from the protocols of the Senate & XXI is dated 10 March 1513.

charged that Joham and his (unnamed) partners sold furs "vsswendig dem koufhuss . . . vnd aber Cunrat Joham vermeint des selben als einer freyn koufmanschafft güt macht zu haben etc." The Senate & XXI as court of first instance struck a compromise between the protectionist, corporate interest of the furriers and Joham's right to "freie Kaufmann-schaft." They ruled that Joham might continue to sell furs, because he was not selling finished, ready-to-wear furs or locally worked furs, but he would have to sell them from the *Kaufhaus,* under the eyes of civic inspectors, rather than from his own shop. This case involved alleged mercantile competition between locally produced goods and imported goods, between artisans in their merchant role and one of the biggest international merchants of Strasbourg. It is perhaps symptomatic of the relative power of Strasbourg's artisan masters and the relatively balanced character of the local economy that the quarrel ended in an officially-sponsored compromise. The master furriers did not stand against Conrad Joham as producers vs. a seller but as one sort of merchant against a (in this instance) competing sort.

That the independent master artisans were true merchants is not just a deduction based on a modern point of view but was believed by the masters themselves. On August 26, 1529, the journeymen furriers petitioned the regime of Strasbourg against their own masters, charging them with using the new religion as a disguise for their selfish purposes, and the journeymen submitted new articles to govern their craft.[86] The master furriers replied that "since our craft (*handtwerck*) is a mercan-tile pursuit (*ein kauffmanschatz*) as well as a craft, it is impossible to conduct the business with so few persons" as three, the number of underlings proposed as a maximum by the journeymen.[87] Here it was the journeymen who wanted the size of shops limited and the masters who balked at setting the maximum so low. The artisan mentality was here defended by the journeymen against the mercantile interests of their masters.

---

[86] AMS, III 11/25 (26 August 1529): "Welches aber zu besorgenn bey ettlichenn mer zu eynem deckmantel oder eygenn nutze zu fürderen dan gegen menigklich ausz der liebe zu handlenn angenomenn werde."

[87] *Ibid.,* articles of the masters: "Zum Ersten, Dywil vnser handtwerck ein kauff-manschatz vnd dar zu auch ein handtwerck ist, so ist es nit moglich das es mit so wenig oder lutzel personen mag getriben worden, Wie dann solchs von jnen vermeint will werden." The journeymen had wanted the size of shops restricted to three persons besides the master. The journeymen's articles, according to a note by Peter Butz, were submitted to the Senate & XXI on 17 February 1529 and then referred to "die alten herren," a phrase which normally refers to the XIII but in this case may mean the XV.

3. It is extremely difficult to establish average levels of wealth for any groups at Strasbourg, and for groups of modest social position, such as artisan masters and the civil servants, it is impossible. Some precious and fairly precise figures are nonetheless occasionally yielded by the depositions of witnesses in court suits. Thirty-eight witnesses were questioned for a suit before the *Reichskammergericht* in 1522, some of whom were civic officials and master artisans.[88] At the top of the officials were the *Ungelter,* collectors of the indirect tax on foodstuffs: Nicolaus Hammerer (age 33 yrs.) estimated his own worth at 3,500 fl. and Caspar Stoffler (age 54 yrs.) at 2,000 fl. Hieronymus Schlapp (age 59 yrs.), a secretary at the mint, admitted to a worth of 500 fl., while Peter Wolff (age 59 yrs.), the *Schuldvogt,* admitted to 600 fl. Much poorer was Martzolff Stoltz (age 48 yrs.), a judge in the *Burggrafengericht,* who was worth only 200 fl. The messengers of the regime (*Laufboten, Ratsboten*) gave estimates ranging from 50 to about 400 fl. Among the artisans, Johannes Bart (age 52 yrs.), master furrier, admitted only that he "lives from his craft and has nothing otherwise except what God gives him each day." Other master artisans were more candid: Veit Kindtweiler (age 70 yrs.), a tanner (*Weissgerber*), ca. 400 fl.; Wernher von Westhoven (age ca. 69 yrs.), a cooper ("der Statt kuffer"), 300–400 fl.; Master Albrecht (age 55 yrs.), the tinsmith ("kannengiesser"), ca. 1,000 fl. As meager as these figures are, they are nearly the only estimates of the wealth of artisans ever recovered from the records of sixteenth–century Strasbourg. According to them, a master artisan who was worth around 500 fl. was a person of real substance, while several thousand florins ranked a man with the lesser merchants.

E. GUILD GOVERNMENT AND GUILD HIERARCHY

1. The gradual subordination of the guilds to the XV (established 1433) had two important consequences. First, during the latter two-thirds of the fifteenth century the new (1433) regulation requiring guild councils (*Schöffenräte*) of uniform size (fifteen persons each) was gradually enforced, so that by 1500 the desired uniformity was achieved.[89] Secondly, the poorer guilds were suppressed and their crafts (*Handwerke*) incorporated into the wealthier guilds, so that by 1482 the number had been reduced from twenty-eight to twenty.[90] This change converted some

---

[88] AMS, IX 1/6 (1522).

[89] Philippe Dollinger, "Notes sur les échevins de Strasbourg au moyen âge," *CAAAH*, N.S. 11 (1967), 65–72, here at pp. 70–72.

[90] *Ibid.,* Hatt, pp. 6–7.

guilds into collections of unrelated or barely related crafts. In the guild Zur Möhrin, for example, one of the real hodge-podges among the Strasbourg guilds, were to be found the merchants of salt fish, the rope-makers, secondhand dealers, and the grain merchants.[91]

The development of such *Sammelzünfte* lacking any economic integrity made the forms of guild government all the more important. The guild Schöffen were coopted for life and formed the ruling group of the guild, although they did not, as a corporation, oversee the everyday life of the guild and its crafts. This was the task of the guild court (*Zunftgericht*) and series of other guild officials. In the *Kürschnerzunft*, whose lists of officials for this era have survived, the court comprised nine members, of whom seven were Schöffen, headed by the guildmaster (*Zunftmeister*) and including the rotating office of *Schaffner*.[92] Two Schöffen held office as supervisors of the journeymen (*Zu den Gesellen*), but only one of the other six officials (four "Sün leutt," two "Fürsprechen") was a Schöffe, the others being presumably younger men in training and therefore probably future Schöffen. This was a relatively simple guild, comprising only the single craft of the furriers, and the internal structures of larger, more complex guilds may have been considerably more complicated.

In the Furriers' Guild, too, the records permit the examination of the political career of a guild master who never became an important political figure in the town, a case which may be more instructive—at least from the point of view of the political structures of the guilds—than the career of someone who rose swiftly into the upper levels of the civic regime would be. Barthel Keller (d. ca. 1584) had a long career in guild offices, although his experience in civic offices was limited to three two-year terms as a senator (1547/48, 51/52, 77/78) of the furriers.[93] Perennially in office within the guild, Keller held most offices several times:

> Zunftmeister, 1538, 43, 49
> Alter Meister, 1539, 44, 50
> Zunftgericht, 1529, 31 (Schaffner), 32, 35, 36, 53 (alter Ratsherr), 54, 79
>   (alter Ratsherr)
> Sün leutt, 1534, 62
> Zu den gesellen, 1537, 40, 45.

---

[91] Chrisman, *Strasbourg,* p. 309.

[92] AMS, Archives des tribus, Pelletiers, No. 6, a register of guild offices, "Schöffen-vnd Gerichtsbuch," 1500–1659.

[93] *Ibid.*; Hatt, p. 467.

During slightly more than half a century, Keller spent fourteen years in the guild court and five years in other offices, which means that he held some guild office every other year.

2. If the guilds varied in internal structure, they also varied in prestige, for they were ordered in an official hierarchy the order of which was not haphazard. Every guild town had such a hierarchy, which was scrupulously followed in official documents and which was "a hierarchy according to the norms of social eminence."[94] A rough distinction existed between merchant and artisan guilds, although occupational boundaries and guild boundaries did not always coincide, and there were often artisans in merchant guilds and vice versa. At Strasbourg the top of the hierarchy belonged to the rich guilds Zum Encker and Zum Spiegel, the medieval guilds of the shippers and the merchants respectively. At the bottom were the Gardeners and the Masons. The gentlemen-guildsmen (*Juncker*) seem to have preferred the guild Zum Encker, where a number of them belonged around 1500.[95]

The twenty guilds of Reformation Strasbourg divided fairly neatly into seven or eight upper and twelve or thirteen lower guilds. Seven of the first eight guilds in the hierarchy—all except the *Tucherzunft*—abandoned their occupational names during the later fifteenth century and took their new names from the names of their guild halls (e.gg., Zum Blume, Zum Freiburg, Zur Möhrin, etc.); and these new names came into official use around 1500. The most plausible reasons for the changes are that these guilds were now collective guilds which contained several unrelated crafts each, and that the merchants in these guilds wanted to imitate the Constofler, whose corporations had never had occupational names.[96] The upper eight guilds in 1517–19 contained 95%

---

[94] Maschke, "Verfassung und soziale Kräfte," pp. 284–286, 294–296; Eitel, "Die politische . . . Stellung des Zunftbürgertums," pp. 88–89; Rublack, *Einführung der Reformation in Konstanz,* pp. 139–142. For the grouping of the trades into twenty guilds at Strasbourg, see Ulrich Crämer, *Die Verfassung und Verwaltung Strassburgs von der Reformationszeit bis zum Fall der Reichsstadt (1521–1681), SWIELR,* N.S. 3 (Frankfurt/M., 1931), pp. 86–101.

[95] AMS, VI 591/1: "Stubengesellen zum Encker," 1501. The *Junker* include two Mussler, a Jörger, and a von Berss. At Freiburg im Breisgau, rich *Müssiggänger* could become citizens without joining either the patricians or a guild, or they could join any guild but the *Rebleute.* Gothein, *Wirtschaftsgeschichte des Schwarzwaldes,* p. 383.

[96] Hatt, p. 7, gives the dates of name changes as between 1512 and 1518, and he is followed by Chrisman, *Strasbourg,* p. 307. Hatt's source was the *Ratslisten* in AMS, Livre de Bourgeoisie I. The muster lists of 1501 and 1507 already use the new names (AMS, VI 591/1), and at least some of them were in use by the 1460s. See, for example, *Kleine Strassburger Chronik. Denckwürdige Sachen alhier in Strassburg vorgeloffen und begeben*

of the guildsmen who served the commune as cavalry ("zu Ross"), an indication of the concentration of wealth at this end of the hierarchy of guilds. The greatest number by far came from the guild Zum Spiegel, followed by that Zum Encker.[97]

The true center of social life for the rich from all the guilds of Strasbourg was the guild hall Zum Spiegel, the richest guild of all. Like Basel, Ulm, and Zürich, Strasbourg permitted double guild membership, and wealthy men—mostly merchants—from other guilds routinely joined the guild Zum Spiegel as well.[98] This guild hall thus served the same purpose as did the social clubs of merchants in other South German towns and the *Trinkstuben* of the Constofler at Strasbourg and elsewhere.[99] While maintaining a membership in some other guild, whether for economic or for political reasons, the merchants from the entire guild structure belonged to this merchants' club (the "Gesellschaft" of the phrase "Zunft und Gesellschaft") as "Stubengesellen zum Spiegel." The spreading of the rich through the guild hierarchy formed, as we shall see (Chapter V), one of the chief lines of aristocratic control of the entire guild regime.[100]

F. Conclusion

The guild aristocracy of Strasbourg during the first half of the sixteenth century contained big merchants, rentiers, lesser merchants, and some artisan masters and shopkeepers. The big merchant-bankers were mostly recent immigrants and formed a smaller group, and were

---

1424–1615, ed. Rodolphe Reuss (Strasbourg, 1889), pp. 1–2. A similar change occurred in most of the Upper Swabian towns; but in Ulm even the richest guilds retained their old occupational names. Eitel, *Die oberschwäbischen Reichsstädte*, pp. 37–50; Geiger, *Die Reichsstadt Ulm*, pp. 30–31.

[97] See Table 2 in Chapter II above. In 1517–19 only one guildsman furnished a horse (Hans Conrat, *Küfer*, one horse) and belonged to one of the twelve lesser guilds.

[98] Maschke, "Verfassung und soziale Kräfte," p. 445.

[99] Eitel, "Die politische . . . Stellung des Zunftbürgertums," p. 86. The basis of this description of the guild Zum Spiegel is a surviving account book for the *Stube*, kept by Conrad Meyer (PROSOPOGRAPHY, No. LVI) in 1530–31. It is now in ADBR, E 1356/1: "Diss ist ein Rechnung der Ersamen gesellschafft vnnd Zunfft zum Spiegel . . . von dem Schwertag ann Anno XV^c XXX bitz widder vff dem schwertag Anno XV^c XXXI." This guild at least kept its accounts by the political year (year begins on the first Tuesday in January) rather than the fiscal year (year begins on St. John the Baptist's Day, 24 June).

[100] The situation was similar, if not so pronounced, at Ulm. Geiger, *Die Reichsstadt Ulm*, pp. 32–35.

probably less rich, than analogous groups at Nuremberg and Augsburg. Opportunities for investment of commercial profits in one or another sector of the craft system were severely limited or non-existent; and the crafts were consequently not badly invaded by entrepreneurs. There was no clear economic separation between the big merchants and the lesser ones, but the social eminence of the big merchants and the rentiers was recognized.

Successful artisan masters could very well identify more closely with the merchants, some of whose characteristics they shared, than with their fellow guildsmen who worked for wages. The guild hierarchy was socially significant, and, though less clearly, so was the distinction between upper and lower guilds (eight and twelve respectively after 1482). The greatest concentrations of wealth lay in the guilds Zum Spiegel and Zum Encker, although there were rich men in most of the guilds and well-to-do men in all of them; and the guild hall Zum Spiegel served as the social center for the non-patrician rich of the city.

With its balanced, well-protected craft system, Strasbourg around 1500 offered tempting prospects for investment of commercial profits only in real estate and in money-lending. The city's political economy is the basis for understanding the high degree of amalgamation and integration of the guild aristocracy with the noble patriciate. This phenomenon, the subject of the following chapter, was well expressed by a fifteenth–century Strasbourgeois who said: "He whom God has given riches, also wants honor." [101]

---

[101] For the source of this quotation, see Chapter II above, note 21.

CHAPTER FOUR

THE UNITY OF STRASBOURG'S ARISTOCRACY

From separate analyses of the two fractions of Strasbourg's aristocracy, we move now to an examination of their economic and social integration into a single, solid ruling class. The historic result of this process of integration was the transformation—past, present, and potential—of successful guild families into gentlemen—men of leisure and property and, finally, nobles. No more than elsewhere was this process at Strasbourg a change in class, though it did mean a rise in status from the guilds into the patriciate.[1] The process moved not without tension and not without running against the lines of estate-consciousness and concrete social ties of each fraction to its own estate—the patricians to the rural nobility and the rich guildsmen to the world of the guilds. In the last analysis, however, the solidarity of the aristocracy reached right across estate lines, because it was built upon a massive economic and social foundation, a foundation which made possible their political cooperation.

A. Estates and Social Mobility

European societies of the late medieval and early modern eras had multiple status hierarchies. At Strasbourg, as in other free towns, all members of the commune (*Grossbürger*) were *cives*, which dictated a *certain* legal equality among them and a distinction between them and all other persons.[2] On the one hand, townsmen or citizens comprised a

---

[1] Wallerstein, *Modern World System*, p. 124: "Bourgeois and feudal classes, in an explanation which uses class categories to explain social change, should not be read, as it usually is, to mean 'merchants' and 'landowners.'"

[2] Although extreme forms of this view still appear, far more common is the moderate form expressed by Karl Kroeschell, "Stadtrecht und Stadtgeschichte," *Die Stadt des Mittelalters,* II, 281–299, reprinted from *Studium Generale,* 16 (1963), 481–488. At the opposite end of the historiographical spectrum, by virtue of their use of social categories, are the Marxist urban historians. See Karl Czok, "Zur Stellung der Stadt in der deutschen Geschichte," *JRG,* 3 (1968), 9–33; Karlheinz Blaschke, "Qualität, Quantität und Raumfunktion als Wesensmerkmale der Stadt vom Mittelalter bis zur Gegenwart," *ibid.*, pp. 34–50; and, for the view of an outsider, Erich Maschke, "Deutsche Stadtforschung auf der Grundlage des historischen Materialismus," *JGOR,* 12/13 (1966/67), 121–141.

distinct estate in a more comprehensive estate structure; on the other hand, they were themselves divided into an urban estate structure. At Strasbourg this structure contained two estates, patricians (*Constofler*) and guildsmen (*Handwerker*).[3]

The two urban estates did not exhaust the estate memberships of Strasbourgeois. The categories of noble and armiger, for example, were not coterminous with any internal estate boundaries, especially not that between patricians and guildsmen. There were nobles and armigers in the guilds as well as in the Constofeln. And families who got new patents might join a Constofel, or they might be refused admittance (e.g., the Hagen). Or they might choose to join or stay in a guild and remain in trade, as the Gottesheim did, who by all formal criteria were eligible for the Constofeln. The guilds, on the other hand, contained a great many armigerous families, such as the Duntzenheim, Bietenheim, Mieg, Ingold, Berss, and Rotweil families. In such families, some of the men were rentiers, others were merchants and bankers.[4]

Nearly the entire complex of the Prechter–Ingold–Ebel–Mieg group of big merchant families climbed into the patriciate by the end of the sixteenth century. They were the last large group of families to do so. It has often been noticed that the Strasbourg patriciate was relatively open to new families from the guilds;[5] but this condition began to change during the second half of the sixteenth century, perhaps because of the heightened noble estate consciousness produced by the incorporation of the Lower Alsatian *Reichsritterschaft*.[6] The richest families got in, however, while the door was still open. Conrad Joham, a noble since 1536, never joined a Constofel, but his sons did and became leading patrician politicians.[7] Friedrich Ebel was ennobled in 1554 and Wilhelm Prechter two years later, although it was not until 1584 that Prechter's son, Friedrich, agreed to leave trade and the guild Zum Spiegel and join a Constofel.[8] The Ingold had been nobles all along, since 1473 when

---

[3] "Handwerker" means not an artisan but a guildsman. Maschke, "Verfassung und soziale Kräfte," p. 294.

[4] Such as Hans von Berss (PROSOPOGRAPHY, No. VII), a "Herr und Müssiggänger."

[5] Most recently by Kageneck, "Das Patriziat im Elsass," p. 389. Nurembergers, on the other hand, acquired many more patents of nobility than did Strasbourgeois. Riedenauer, "Kaiserliche Standeserhebungen," p. 32.

[6] Kageneck, "Das Patriziat im Elsass," pp. 392–393.

[7] PROSOPOGRAPHY, No. XLV; Hatt, pp. 463, 601.

[8] BMS, Ms. 936, fol. 5ᵛ. On the Prechter, see Fuchs, "Prechter," p. 149; Riedenauer, "Kaiserliche Standeserhebungen," p. 70; and André-Marcel Burg, "Grandeur et décadence de la bourgeoisie haguenauienne. Deux familles, les Brechter et les Hoffmann," in *La bourgeoisie alsacienne*, pp. 181–196.

Claus Ingold (d. 1474) had secured a patent from Frederick III, but they entered the Constofeln only at the end of the sixteenth century.[9] The Botzheim, a widespread family also of Hagenau origin, entered the patriciate at about the same time.[10] As for the Mieg, Sebastian Mieg was ennobled as "Mieg von Boofzheim" in 1577, and the family were patricians by the 1580s.[11] Finally, there is the case of Sifridt von Bietenheim, an armigerous member of the guild Zur Luzern, whose descendants entered the patriciate by 1586—apparently with no further elevation in rank.[12]

Some newly ennobled families stayed in the guilds. Such were the Türckheim, of whom the brothers Nicolaus and Ulrich were ennobled by Wilhelm Böcklin von Böcklinsau, Provost of Magdeburg, at Freiburg im Breisgau in 1552.[13] The Türckheim stayed in the guilds, and Nicolaus subsequently served as a senator from his guild. Much the same is true of the Gottesheim and Hohenburg families, nobles who remained guildsmen.[14]

Most of the merely armigerous guild families never reached the patriciate. Such were the Duntzenheim and the Münch and a large

---

[9] BMS, Ms. 936, fol. 5^r, ennoblement of Claus Ingold (d. 24 March 1474), dated Niederbaden, 21 July 1473; he had been granted arms in 1466. Riedenauer, "Kaiserliche Standeserhebungen," p. 97n117, should be corrected on this point. This Claus Ingold was the progenitor of the main Strasbourg line. See Wolff, "Les Ingold," pp. 114–116.

[10] Riedenauer, "Kaiserliche Standeserhebungen," p. 70; Hatt, p. 408.

[11] Riedenauer, "Kaiserliche Standeserhebungen," p. 70; Hatt, p. 499; Kageneck, "Das Patriziat im Elsass," p. 389; Schoepflin, L'Alsace illustrée, IV, 583.

[12] PROSOPOGRAPHY, No. IX. The Bietenheim do not appear in the records of ennoblements and grants of arms (BMS, Ms. 936, fols. 3^v–7^r). The most extensive record of ennoblements of Strasbourgeois during the later sixteenth century is in "Die pfalzgräfliche Registratur des Dompropstes Wilhelm Boecklin von Boecklinsau," ed. by Julius Kindler von Knobloch, ZGO, 45 (1891), 263–282, 645–662, which is now largely superseded by August Roth, "Wilhelm Böcklin von Böcklinsau 1555–1585," in Hofpfalzgrafen-Register, ed. by the HEROLD, Verein für Heraldik, Genealogie und verwandte Wissenschaften zu Berlin, I (Neustadt/Aisch, 1964), pp. 9–23.

[13] BMS, Ms. 936, fol. 3^v; H. Neu, "Freiherrlich von Türckheimisches Archiv auf Schloss Mahlberg, Bezirksamt Ettenheim," and "Freiherrlich von Türckheimisches Archiv in Altdorf, Bezirksamt Ettenheim," in MBHK, 29 (1907), m40–m82, here at pp. m50, No. 12, p. m53, No. 1, and p. m55, No. 1, of which the second document contains extracts from "dem ältesten Memorial des Gerichts zur Blume zu Strassburg," now lost, and the third is the testament of Nicolaus von Türckheim (4 May 1569). He was senator from the guild Zum Spiegel in 1567/68, 79/80, and 83/84. Hatt, p. 559.

[14] PROSOPOGRAPHY, Nos. XXXIV, XLI. On the Gottesheim, see Franz Batt, Das Eigenthum zu Hagenau im Elsass, 2 vols. (Colmar, 1876–81), II, appendix, xxxx–xxxxi; André-Marcel Burg, "La famille de Gottesheim, remarques sur sa généalogie publiée par Hertzog," BCGA, No. 18 (1972), 47–48.

number of other guild families who secured patents of arms during the sixteenth century,[15] although on at least one occasion during the previous century armigerous status had been recognized as the equivalent of ennoblement.[16] Many of the armigerous guild families, such as the Jörger, the Erstein *dit* Armbruster, the Arg, the Rumler, and the Barpfennig, either died out in the male lines during the sixteenth century or disappeared from politics.

The upward movement of big merchant families into the patriciate may have been encouraged by the financial crisis and depression of the 1570s. This is probably true of the Ingold, and it is worth noting that most of the influx of merchant families occurred during the two decades following the crisis.[17] After two or three generations in large-scale commerce and banking, they became rentiers, a longevity in commerce that conforms roughly to the patterns elsewhere.[18]

They intermarried with the patricians long before they sat in the Constofeln. Strasbourg patricians may have taken relatively fewer marriage partners from other urban families during the sixteenth century than their ancestors had done,[19] but they nonetheless continued to arrange marriages with partners from rich guild families with some regularity. Such marriages established important family bonds among patrician and non-patrician privy councillors. A series of marriages before 1500, for example, formed a Sturm–von Köllen–Schott–Mieg connection and made Jacob Sturm and his brothers cousins of their colleagues, Daniel, Carl, and Andreas Mieg.[20] Especially in the Mieg and Joham families were patrician marriage partners common before the families themselves climbed into the patriciate. The Mieg took during the years ca. 1480 to 1550 marriage partners from no less than seven patrician clans: von Köllen, Mülnheim, Wurmser, Zorn von

---

[15] The chief records of grants of arms are cited in note 12 above, to which should be added a notice in the *Hofpfalzgrafen-Register,* II (1971), 7, No. 7, that Hans Braun of Strasbourg, citizen of Eichstätt, received arms on 7 May 1590.

[16] Riedenauer, "Kaiserliche Standeserhebungen," p. 90n35 (Voltz von Altenau).

[17] On the economic crisis of the 1570s at Strasbourg, see Fuchs, "Ingold," pp. 215–218; *idem,* "Israël Minckel," pp. 123–126.

[18] See Thrupp, *The Merchant Class of Medieval London,* pp. 279–297; Wolff, *Commerce et marchands de Toulouse,* pp. 616–617; and, in general, Braudel, *La méditerranée,* 2nd ed., II, 68–75. In the Empire, of course, ennoblement did not necessarily mean withdrawal from trade. On the process and prices of ennoblement, see G. Benecke, "Ennoblement and Privilege in Early Modern Germany," *History,* N.S. 56 (1971), 360–370.

[19] Kageneck, "Das Patriziat im Elsass," p. 386.

[20] Alexandre Straub, "Notes généalogiques sur une ancienne famille patricienne de Strasbourg [Schott]," *BSCMHA,* N.S. 9, pp. 80–88.

Plobsheim, Kippenheim, Bock von Gerstheim, and Wetzel von Marsilien.[21] Conrad Joham, whose father had been a knight, married Susanna von Mülnheim; and two of their sons married daughters of Nicolaus Ziegler, lord of Barr, while other children married into the Zorn von Bulach and Böcklin von Böcklinsau families.[22] Of the marriages recorded in Appendix A in which one partner was a patrician, the other partner was from a guild family in roughly one marriage out of ten.

B. The Feudal Bonds

That the patricians of Strasbourg were nearly all vassals is predictable, that many rich guildsmen also were vassals is rather less so—although fief-holding by armigerous bourgeois was common enough in late medieval Germany. The penetration of urban wealth into the nexus of specifically feudal relationships was not a new phenomenon in Lower Alsace around 1500. Its precondition was the political disintegration and commercialization of seigneurial power from the mid-fourteenth century onwards, in the wake of which many seigneurs gradually sacrificed direct exercise of their rights and prerogatives as a mode of power over the land and its people to their need for larger cash incomes.[23] This Europe-wide development of the fourteenth and fifteenth centuries[24] was doubtless heightened in Lower Alsace by the absence of a single dominant prince. Until around 1550 the lesser nobility lacked any

---

[21] Philippe Mieg, *Histoire généalogique de la famille Mieg* (Mulhouse, 1934), pp. 3–20.

[22] Hertzog, VI, 250–251; Lehr, II, 255.

[23] Dubled, "L'administration de la seigneurie rurale en Alsace du XIIIe au XVe siècle," p. 451; *idem*, "Der Herrschaftsbegriff im Mittelalter am Oberrhein," pp. 88–90. The resultant fragmentation has been called "Der . . . am meisten beherrschende Zug der elsässischen Agrarwirtschaft...," by Clemens Bauer, "Probleme der mittelalterlichen Agrargeschichte im Elsass," *AJb*, 1953, 238–250, here at p. 247. The process has not been studied in detail for Alsace, but there is a superb study of selected right-bank families by Hans-Peter Sattler, "Die Ritterschaft der Ortenau in der spätmittelalterlichen Wirtschaftskrise. Eine Untersuchung ritterlicher Vermögensverhältnisse im 14. Jahrhundert," *Die Ortenau*, 42 (1962), 220–258; 44 (1964), 22–39; 45 (1965), 32–57; 46 (1966), 32–58.

[24] See, for example, Georges Duby, "Le grand domaine de la fin du moyen âge en France," in *First International Conference for Economic History, Stockholm 1960. Contributions, Communications,* École Pratique des Hautes Études, VIe section, série "Congrès et colloques," I (Paris–The Hague, 1960), pp. 333–342. For southwestern Germany, see Friedrich Lütge, *Geschichte der deutschen Agrarverfassung vom frühen Mittelalter bis zum 19. Jahrhundert,* 2nd ed. (Stuttgart, 1967), pp. 159–182, 192–194; Rolf Sprandel, "Sozialgeschichte 1350–1500," *Handbuch der deutschen Wirtschafts- und Sozialgeschichte,* I, 372–374.

corporate institutions through which collective discipline might have worked to encourage families to maintain direct seigneurial control and to construct legal barriers against parvenus. Lower Alsace thus lacked the two chief protections of the social integrity of the feudal order in the land, a strong territorial state and a firm corporate organization.

The nobles themselves were partly responsible for the lack of a territorial government, for they—with the towns—had joined the struggle against the Burgundian "tyranny" on the Upper Rhine during the later fifteenth century, the one serious attempt before 1681 to incorporate Alsace into a state.[25] The feudal political order had always rested on the tension between a centralizing moment and a centrifugal one, and the lack of the former in Lower Alsace tended to petrify the seigneury as a political and administrative unit and leave it open to the penetration of commercial forces flowing outward from the towns.[26] This situation would change slightly during the early modern era, when the lesser nobles were able to exert some control through the corporation of the *Reichsritterschaft*,[27] but in the meantime many feudal rights fell into the hands of upstarts.

The market in seigneurial rights was, if not completely free, yet very open to urban money by the mid-fifteenth century. Seigneuries could be secured intact through enfiefment, but they could also be acquired piecemeal. The half-century effort through which the Sturm acquired Breuschwickersheim from the Winterthur began before 1465, when

---

[25] Brauer-Gramm, *Der Landvogt Peter von Hagenbach,* is the best study.

[26] Dubled, "L'administration de la seigneurie rurale en Alsace du XIIIe au XVe siècle," p. 482. Of the penetration of the land by wealthy urban families in France, Marc Bloch wrote: "But it is true that such penetration *en masse* was confined to the sixteenth century, never to be repeated. By the seventeenth century the nobility was already a semi-closed caste." *French Rural History. An Essay on its Basic Characteristics,* trans. Janet Sondheimer (Berkeley–Los Angeles, 1966), p. 125. There were, nonetheless, regions where little or no such penetration took place, for example, the Baden portion of the Breisgau. Albrecht Strobel, *Agrarverfassung im Übergang. Studien zur Agrargeschichte des badischen Breisgaus vom Beginn des 16. bis zum Ausgang des 18. Jahrhunderts,* Forschungen zur oberrheinischen Landesgeschichte, 23 (Freiburg/B.-Munich, 1972), p. 47.

[27] Formed to protect noble privileges and regularize Imperial taxation, this corporation conducted a struggle against the Strasbourg regime's requirement that all citizens maintain a residence in the city. Overmann, "Reichsritterschaft," pp. 630–637. Such institutions are conventionally seen as protections for the lesser nobility against the princes, but they could just as well be used against threats from below. See, for example, the corporation formed in Upper Swabia in the early fifteenth century, in Herbert Obenaus, *Recht und Verfassung der Gesellschaften mit St. Jörgenschild in Schwaben,* Veröffentlichungen des Max-Planck-Instituts für Geschichte, 7 (Göttingen, 1961), pp. 13–16.

Friedrich Sturm was already part-owner of the chateau.[28] His son, Martin, slowly bought up land and rights in and around the village during the next three decades.[29] In 1503, already deeply in debt to the Sturm, Daniel von Winterthur (the last of his line) sold Martin Sturm half of the chateau and the seigneurial rights ("obrigkheit," "herrschafft") over the village for 600 rhenish florins.[30] Although the chateau then became the Sturm's country seat until the family died out in 1640,[31] they did not get it without a fight. Daniel von Winterthur's mother, Brigitta Rebstock, tried to sell the seigneurial rights again to Jacob and Ludwig Zorn zum Riet. The ensuing suit raged for six years and was carried by the Zorn brothers to the *Reichskammergericht*, before an arbitrated settlement in 1522 left the Sturm in possession of the seigneury and the chateau.[32]

If seigneurial tenures and rights could be purchased, it is not difficult to comprehend how wealthy Strasbourg guildsmen could work their ways into the feudal system on the land. The rise of the Jörger brothers, Hans (d. ca. 1487) and Claus (d. ca. 1514), one of the genuine success stories of fifteenth–century Strasbourg, illustrates one path upward.[33] Hans, a wealthy merchant-banker, and his brother began to acquire feudal tenures in 1476, when Bishop Ruprecht of Strasbourg admitted them to fiefs of the Hohenstein family, including one-half each of the villages of Bietenheim and Achenheim and the chateau of Hohenstein.[34] Three years later, when Hans Jörger was episcopal chief bailiff (*Oberschultheiss*) at Strasbourg, Bishop Albrecht granted the brothers a large number of fiefs formerly held by families now extinct, plus some

---

[28] Hefele, No. 544; and see Jaenger, "Zur Geschichte des Schlosses Breuschwickersheim," pp. 81–89.

[29] Hefele, Nos. 671, 720, 730, 765, 771; PROSOPOGRAPHY, No. XCIV.

[30] Hefele, No. 792.

[31] Jacob Friedrich (d. 19 May 1640) was the last male Sturm. ADBR, 12J 2022/1–3.

[32] ADBR, 3B 1484, with a record of arbitrated settlement (24 October 1522) in AMS, KS 20, fols. 53^r–54^v, in which the Sturm were to make over certain properties and revenues to the heirs of the Winterthur (Rebstock, Zorn zum Riet) in return for clear title to the chateau and seigneury.

[33] When Hans Jörger became a citizen of Strasbourg on 6 February 1460 (Wittmer, No. 1510), he joined the Gardeners, one of the poor guilds; but his brother, Claus, and his son, also Hans, in 1501 belonged to the guild Zur Luzern, and they were two of the three persons in this guild rich enough to serve the commune as cavalry. AMS, VI 591/1. Claus Jörger was in fact a cloth merchant, as is shown by a list (30 January 1490) of cloths he sold to the lords of Rappoltstein. *RUB*, V, 405, No. 994. His brother, Hans, was a merchant and banker. Fuchs, "Droit de bourgeoisie," p. 39.

[34] ADBR, G 675/(1), and the first document in the dossier dated 1525.

formerly held by Hans von Hohenstein. Both grants were co-enfief-
ments with Jakob von Hohenstein.[35] Behind this apparently effortless
rise of the Jörger was a dreary story of the long slide of the Hohenstein
into financial ruin.[36] Jakob's father, Anton von Hohenstein, had
borrowed 1,200 fl. from the Jörger brothers, which he secured by
agreeing to take them into his tenures as co-vassals. Jakob von Hohenstein's (d. 1480/81) heirs fell still more deeply into the Jörgers' debt, to
whom they sold (1489) their rights in several villages and their half of the
village of Orschweiler.[37] The Jörger now controlled most of the
Hohenstein fiefs, including the *Stammsitz* at chateau Hohenstein, and
Claus Jörger was followed by Hans's son and by his own son, Maximilian, as episcopal tenants. By 1511, however, Claus Jörger was
himself in deep trouble, and Jerg von Hohenstein, Jakob's son, took
advantage of Claus's troubles to get back the family seat.[38] The bishop's
feudal court ruled that the Hohenstein *Stammsitz* could not be alien-
ated, but that the Jörger should remain in possession until the debts
were paid—which they did at least until 1517.[39] The other fiefs of
the Hohenstein, however, could not be saved, and they remained in the
Jörger family until 1570.[40] The judgment for Jerg von Hohenstein,
then, did not mean that the Jörger, who were not noble, could not
hold fiefs but only that their tenancy was by virtue of mortgage only,
a mortgage which conferred *usus* rather than *possessio* in the full sense.
Claus's son, Maximilian, moved to Basel, whence he conducted a series
of suits against his Strasbourg cousins over the remaining fiefs. The
Jörger thus held fiefs and brought suits in feudal court like other vassals,
although they were armigerous (since 1473) rentiers and guildsmen.
Their brief rise shows what an ambitious urban family could do in a
world in which the rural nobles needed money and the urban merchants
had it.

---

[35] *Ibid.*, Nos. (1) and (2).

[36] As revealed by the records of a suit of Jerg von Hohenstein, son of Jakob, against
Claus Jörger and the heirs of Hans Jörger, heard before the episcopal *Manngericht* at
Molsheim. ADBR, G 675; AMS, IV 22, 1; ADBR, 1G 158/34 (9 November 1538).

[37] Wunder, *Landgebiet,* pp. 142, 142n39, 183. Hans Jörger had lent 2,000 fl. to Jakob
von Hohenstein in 1476, taking in pledge the Hohenstein half of Orschweiler. Hans's
son paid 1,800 fl. more for clear title to the Hohenstein rights.

[38] Claus Jörger's debts in ADBR, G 675 (1516); and AMS, KS 20, fols. 8ʳ–10ᵛ. On
Claus's ruin, see Wunder, *Landgebiet*, p. 11; and The Newberry Library, Chicago,
Ms. 63, fol. 114ʳ: "Familia georgianorum in magno flore fama et pompa fuit iam eorum
bona propre distrahuntur ut creditoribus satisfiat."

[39] ADBR, G 675/(4), *Lehenrevers* of 23 March 1517.

[40] *Ibid.*, No. (7), dated 10 April 1570.

Less spectacular but more enduring was the success of the Kips family. Hans Kips migrated to Strasbourg in 1488 from Buchsweiler, where he had probably been in the service of the counts of Zweibrücken–Bitsch–Lichtenberg.[41] Five years earlier he received in fief lands and rents at Kindweiler and Geisweiler, formerly held by the noble Baltram family, from Count Simon Wecker of Zweibrücken.[42] Hans married a Messinger of Strasbourg; and their son, Veltin, married Han's ward, Margarethe von Gottesheim, represented the Bakers' guild in the XV of Strasbourg (1541–51), and succeeded his father as tenant of this fief (1520–51).[43] The Kips, too, remained a guild family, connected with the Gottesheim, Messinger, and Duntzenheim—all aristocratic guild families.

Rich families of the guilds appear most frequently as vassals of the chief prince of the land, the bishop of Strasbourg. Episcopal tenants during the sixteenth century included, besides the Jörger and the Kips, such families as the Joham, Rotweil, Erstein *dit* Armbruster, Mussler, Bietenheim, and Barpfennig.[44] The Rotweil held the hereditary office of *Pedell* in the episcopal feudal court as tenants of the so-called "Bottenlehen" from the bishop until the male line failed in 1559. Though armigerous the Rotweil were never patricians, and they held numerous offices as representatives of the guilds Zum Encker and Zum Spiegel.[45]

The story of another family of non-patrician episcopal vassals, the Bietenheim, illustrates another path to vassaldom. Sifridt von Bietenheim (d. ca. 1553) was an armigerous guildsman and professional soldier, who was connected by marriage to the merchant families von Saltzburg and Rumler and to the patrician Sturm, and who served in the XV of Strasbourg from the guild Zur Luzern from 1539 until his expulsion in 1544.[46] Sifridt gained control of an episcopal fief in the Sulz-

---

[41] BMS, Ms. 936, fol. 6ʳ; AMS, IX 1/6.

[42] Hans Kips was *Altmarschalk* at Hagenau in 1479. Hefele, No. 632; Wittmer, No. 3979 (19 November 1488); ADBR, E 5948/2–13 (formerly ADBR, 16 J 56/1–11, 14), records of the Kips fief.

[43] ADBR, E 5948/5–9. The fief remained in the family until 1594. On Veltin Kips (d. 1551), see PROSOPOGRAPHY, No. XLIX.

[44] ADBR, G 503, registers of summonses to the episcopal *Manngericht* (see Appendix C below); and lists in Hertzog, IV, 65–66.

[45] ADBR, G 503, where Hans Erhard von Rotweil, Sr. and Jr., appear through 1559; ADBR, G 821/1, 3–4; ADBR, G 853/6. The line died out with Hans Erhard, Jr., in 1559. See PROSOPOGRAPHY, No. LXXVIII; Hatt, p. 526.

[46] PROSOPOGRAPHY, No. IX. The family became extinct in the male line in 1680. Kindler, *GBS*, pp. 34–35. On Sifridt's career as a soldier, see *ZC* (ed. Barack), II, 124, and III, 286, 416. He was the half-brother of Stephan Sturm (PROSOPOGRAPHY, No. XCVI). ADBR, 3B 92.

mattertal through a complicated series of marriages. The fief, which included the forest of Pfingstberg and a share of the toll in the valley, had been granted in 1479 to an episcopal secretary, Andreas Bauholzer.[47] As Bauholzer died without male heirs, the tenure passed to his son-in-law, Adam von Saltzburg, a wealthy merchant and partner in the Prechter firm, and, through Agnes von Saltzburg (Adam's daughter by Maria Bauholzer) to Agnes's husband, Sifridt von Bietenheim (1523). Seven years later, Bietenheim, with his lord's permission, subinfeudated the fief for 101 years to Hans von Rixheim, who had leased the nearby chateau of Orschweier from the bishop in 1524. This tenure did not run its course, for by 1542 the Bietenheim had got the fief back and remained its tenants until 1680. A curious sidelight on the feudal tenures of Strasbourg guildsmen appears with the death of Sifridt von Bietenheim, who left only minor sons. Actual tenant until Claus von Bietenheim reached his majority in 1565 was his guardian, Abraham Held, son-in-law of Sifridt von Bietenheim and later (1568–92) Ammeister of Strasbourg from the Tailors' guild.[48] Sifridt von Bietenheim was never a patrician, although he was an armiger and rentier, and he was socially acceptable enough to be a gambling and drinking crony of Count Wilhelm von Fürstenberg.[49] He and his children married mostly into mercantile families rather than patrician ones, but such marriages, too, could open paths to new gains. Sifridt's own marriage is proof of that.

A third path to vassaldom and seigneurial status, besides mortgages and marriages, was outright purchase. The Mieg, a rich merchant family from Mulhouse, began acquiring parts of the village of Boofz-

---

[47] This history is reconstructed from ADBR, G 704; ADBR, G 526; and Theobald Walter, "Burgen und Adel im Sulzmattertal," *JGSLEL*, 30 (1914), 194. Sifridt von Bietenheim's marriages in AMS, KS 15, fol. 165^{r-v}; AMS, KS 19, fol. 109^r; AMS, KS 22, fol. 83^{r-v}, which is the marriage settlement with his second wife. His first marriage, with Agnes von Saltzburg, occurred in 1522, his first enfiefment in 1523. On Adam von Saltzburg, see Fuchs, "Prechter," p. 158.

[48] ADBR, G 704, *Lehnbrief* of Bishop Erasmus of Strasbourg for Abraham Held as guardian (*Vogt*) of Nicolaus, Hans, Ruprecht, and Christoph von Bietenheim, minor sons of Sifridt von Bietenheim, 27 March 1553. Abraham Held, son of Melchior, was Ammeister from the *Schneiderzunft* in 1568, 74, 80, 86 and 92. In 1569 he was guardian of Hans Georg Armbruster, son of Conrad Armbruster and Salome von Bietenheim, one of Sifridt's sisters. AMS, KS 63/I, fol. 5^r; Hatt, p. 622; AMS, Livre de Bourgeoisie 1559–1713, col. 244 (6 August 1569).

[49] In *ZC*, III, 416 lines 12–16, is told the story that Bietenheim was a guest for gambling at the chateau of Breuscheck, where he witnessed Count Wilhelm von Fürstenberg's unsuccessful attempts to seduce the two daughters of Nicolaus Ziegler, lord of Barr. The girls later married two sons of Conrad Joham.

heim in 1501, when Ludwig Mieg bought one-quarter of it.[50] His heirs bought up the remainder, including the seigneurial rights, in 1567 and 1573, on which basis the Mieg von Boofzheim were admitted to the Lower Alsatian *Reichsritterschaft*. In another case, Conrad Joham paid 5,000 fl. to Mathias Held for rights to the Imperial fiefs of Mundolsheim and Mittelhausbergen, whose former tenant, Mathias Beger, had conveniently been killed by Friedrich Bock von Bläsheim in 1532; and Joham's children also joined the corporation of free knights.[51]

The Ingold were noble guildsmen who could boast of greater success on the land than most of their fellows could. Hans Ingold (d. 1507), son of Claus and progenitor of the entire Strasbourg line, acquired no less than four Baden fiefs, one in the Baden–Hochberg lands and three in the properties which went to the Baden–Baden line.[52] In three of the fiefs, Hans succeeded noble families which had died out in the male lines; and in the other he was co-enfiefed with the noble Neuenstein family at Nussbach. At Kolbsheim the Ingold succeeded a line of the Zorn, at Bledesheim (= Bläsheim?) the Schaup family. The fiefs passed to Hans's sons, Mathis (1508) and Friedrich (1521). The Ingold were thus leading vassals of the margraves of Baden all during the period of their greatest commercial activity and prosperity.

A rather unusual fief was controlled for several generations by the Mussler, armigerous guildsmen of Strasbourg. From 1516 onwards for nearly three decades, the Mussler were principal partners in and then sole tenants of the iron foundries ("Ysen schmitten," "yssenwerck") at Kandern which Peter (d. 1519) and Reimbold (d. ca. 1528) Mussler and their cousin, Peter Münch ("kaiserlicher Zügwarter" at Breisach), held in fief from Baden–Durlach.[53] In 1528, when there was no adult male Mussler to do homage, it was rendered by the guardian of Anna Mussler,

---

[50] Schoepflin, *L'Alsace illustrée*, IV, 583, recounts the story of how the Mieg acquired this village which lies near the Rhine south of Strasbourg. See also Philippe Mieg, "L'établissement de la Réforme et les premiers pasteurs à Boofzheim," *Bulletin de la Société d'histoire du protestantisme français*, 78 (1929), 84–85.

[51] Schoepflin, *L'Alsace illustrée*, V, 790–791; AMS, IV 110; Hatt, p. 463. Beger, called "der unsinnige Beger," was the last male member of the family, and Bock apparently killed him in self-defense. Kindler, *OG*, I, 51; *ZC*, I, 329 ll. 31–37.

[52] GLAK, 67/42, fols. 18^r–19^r; 67/43, fols. 22^r–24^v, 26^r–29^v, 249^r–254^r; 67/44, fols. 170^r–177^r, 245^r–247^v; 67/46, fols. 168^v–181^v, 218^v–223^r; 67/48, fols. 319^r–321^r, 323^v–329^v.

[53] GLAK, 67/45, fols. 168^r–169^r; 67/49, fols. 12^r–15^v, 93^r–94^r. Kandern was the site of an integrated iron works in the lordship of Sausenberg, which came under Baden control in 1503 and was a fief of the Baden–Durlach line. The Mussler and Münch gained control of the works by lending money to their operator, Wilhelm Bond of Roskopp. Krieger, ed., *Topographisches Wörterbuch des Grossherzogtums Baden,* 2nd ed., I, 1122;

Bläsi Baumgartner of Strasbourg; and in 1544 the fief was declared in escheat and reverted to the margrave. This case is uncommonly interesting as involving the conveyance of an industrial operation by means of the ancient institution of the fief. It is unusual, but certainly not unique, for the list of objects of enfiefment is endless, including produce of all kinds, tithes, rents, seigneurial rights, cash incomes, and—quite frequently—capons.

It would be incorrect to conclude from these success stories that any rich commoner could simply buy a fief or a seigneury. These tenants were all armigerous except for the Ingold, who were nobles. Simple commoners rarely got so far. Caspar Hoffmeister, a cloth merchant and immigrant to Strasbourg from Weil der Stadt, loaned 625 fl. to Margrave Christoph I of Baden in 1508 and received in return a fief-rente of 15 fl./yr.—but only for life.[54] This act provided an easy means of paying a creditor without creating another family of Baden vassals.

Of the seventeen Strasbourg families who were vassals of the margraves of Baden during the last quarter of the fifteenth and the first half of the sixteenth century, only two were guild families; of the Palatine vassals at Strasbourg, none were guildsmen. What was true, then, of the Strasbourg vassals of the bishop of Strasbourg was also true of the Strasbourg vassals of Baden and the Palatinate: 1) most were from well-established patrician families; 2) most fiefs were held by a number of related men as co-vassals; 3) the occasional non-patrician vassals were all at least armigerous; 4) it was not difficult for a wealthy armiger to secure some claim to a fief, through mortgage, marriage, or purchase of the succession to extinct families; and 5) the vassal's status at Strasbourg —Constofler or guildsman—had not the slightest bearing on a family's ability to move into the great web of feudal relations on the Upper Rhine, to its own pleasure and profit.

Other types of feudal dues were also subject to purchase and subdivision. The *Bede* was a basic peasant obligation to the seigneur which was often transformed into a general property tax collected by the prince.[55] In the absence of real territorial government, however, the

---

Gothein, *Wirtschaftsgeschichte des Schwarzwaldes,* pp. 657–658; Fuchs, "L'espace économique rhénan," pp. 323–324; and AMS, V 137/14, where Peter Münch is named as a cousin ("vetter") of the Strasbourg Mussler. Another case of enfiefment of a Strasbourgeois with mines, Frantz Hagen (Jr.?) by Count Heinrich von Fürstenberg in 1488, is in *FUB,* IV, 80, No. 93.

[54] GLAK, 67/43, fol. 630ʳ; PROSOPOGRAPHY, No. XL.

[55] In the Palatinate, for example. Cohn, *Government of the Rhine Palatinate,* pp. 85–91, 101.

Bede could become simply an income, divisible and mortgageable like other incomes and devoid of direct political significance. The village of Neuweiler, for example, had passed from the hands of the abbey of the same name into those of the counts of Lichtenberg, later Hanau–Lichtenberg.[56] In 1524 the *Bede* of Neuweiler, whose annual yield was about 226 lb., was divided among twenty-six different owners, mainly patricians and ecclesiastical corporations of Strasbourg; while from 1540 until 1547, Count Philip IV of Hanau–Lichtenberg mortgaged $2\frac{1}{2}$ *fuder* of wine from this *Bede* to the patricians, Claus Zorn zum Riet and Martin Wetzel von Marsilien.[57]

Tithes were handled similarly, and there is the striking case of the greater tithe at Dorlisheim (about $12\frac{1}{2}$ miles west of Strasbourg), which in 1531 was divided into 234ths among nine owners, including the city of Strasbourg, the convent of St. Arbogast, and a number of patricians and other nobles.[58] Seigneurial rights, too, could be held in shares, as they were at Allmannsweier and Wittenweier (near Lahr in Baden), where around 1550 six Strasbourg families owned the *Ortsherrschaft* in fractions ranging from two to nine 24ths.[59]

One final, fabulous example will complete this story of the common participation of patricians and guild aristocrats in the purchase and acquisition of feudal rights and tenures and will illustrate to what lengths of fragmentation the commercialization of feudal institutions could lead. The village of Neuhof lay on the left bank of the Rhine a few miles south of Strasbourg, and it had been in the hands of Strasbourgeois since about 1370.[60] From about 1500 the property and seigneurial rights over the district were split and split again: first into halves (before 1504), then into 12ths (1504), 24ths, 48ths, and 96ths. In 1566, one owner possessed two and one-half 96ths ($=5/192$) of the district's revenues. Even stranger is the partitioning of a small separate part of the district, the Gansau, of which Aurelia Stösser owned 77/78 of 1/8 ($=77/624$) shortly before 1578.[61] The list of families and persons who participated

---

[56] Johannes Fritz, *Die alten Territorien des Elsass nach dem Stande vom 1. Januar 1648*, Statistische Mittheilungen über Elsass-Lothringen, 27 (Strasbourg, 1896), p. 138.

[57] ADBR, E 2024; PROSOPOGRAPHY, Nos. XCVIII, CIV.

[58] Wunder, *Landgebiet*, p. 102, from AMS, VII 57/1, fol. 8. The great tithe was here paid in grain; and the small tithe (in wine) belonged to the city of Strasbourg.

[59] Wunder, *Landgebiet*, p. 112. Owners were the Landsberg, Lentzel, Rathsamhausen, Böcklin, von Böcklinsau, and Widergrien von Staufenberg families, plus Susanna Spender, wife of Adolf von Mittelhausen (PROSOPOGRAPHY, No. LXIV).

[60] The entire account is based on Wunder, *Landgebiet*, pp. 33–38.

[61] Daughter of Hans Stösser (PROSOPOGRAPHY, No. XC).

in the corporate ownership of the Neuhof district during the sixteenth
century reads like a roll-call of the local and regional aristocracy: noble
families from the land, such as the Röder von Diersburg, the Pfau von
Rüppur, the Blumeneck, the Lichtenfels, the Klett von Uttenheim,
the Wolf von Renchen, and the Voltz von Lahr; Strasbourg patricians,
such as the Böcklin von Böcklinsau, the Zorn zum Riet, the Endingen,
the Wetzel von Marsilien, and the Zorn von Bulach; and prominent
guild families of Strasbourg, such as the Duntzenheim, the Mieg, the
Kirchhofer, the Mussler, the Stösser, and the Schenckbecher. Shares in
the district were inherited, bought and sold, traded, and given as dowries,
changing hands much like shares in a modern business corporation.
One is hardly surprised to learn, then, that in 1573 Johann Schenckbecher and his wife, Dorothea Pfeffinger, marketed 1/12 of 5/6 of 1/4
(= 5/288) of the collective income of the district of Neuhof.

Fiefholding by wealthy guildsmen of Strasbourg created an embarrass-
ing political problem during the 1540s. The Ammeister of Strasbourg
could not take oaths to foreign lords and could not hold fiefs.[62] This law
apparently caused no difficulties until January, 1543, when Claus
Kniebis was excused from serving a fifth term as ruling Ammeister
because of his failing health.[63] What followed was scandalous: four of the
next five persons elected—Andreas Mieg, Caspar Rumler, Conrad
Meyer, and Veltin Kips—declined to surrender their fiefs and had to
refuse the commune's highest office.[64] At six o'clock in the evening on
January 4, the Senate & XXI finally persuaded Simon Franck to become
Ammeister, although Franck lay then in his sickbed, to which he had
been confined for the past eight months.[65] Late in the same year the XV
were asked to review the law and recommend a remedy for the situation
in which "everyone excuses himself from the office of Ammeister for the

---

[62] Eheberg, p. 86, No. 23 (1433): "Es soll dehein ammeister hyanfürder noch dehein
lehen noch ampten, es syent vögtien, schultheissenampt, steblerpfrunen oder desglich
werben, stellen empfohen noch haben ungeverlich, es sy von herren, stiften, clöstern
oder derglich, die lehen oder ampt zů lihen hant zů geben," by pain of a fine of 100 marks
of silver.

[63] Often retold, but there is a good version in Hertzog, VIII, 97. Some details are
from AMS, XXI 1542, fols. 533ʳ–539ᵛ; AMS, XXI 1543, fol. 2ʳ.

[64] The fifth man, Martin Betscholt, was excused because of ill health. PROSOPO-
GRAPHY, Nos. VIII, XLIX, LVI, LX, LXXX.

[65] PROSOPOGRAPHY, No. XXX. He had returned very ill from Hungary on 2 May 1542,
where he had served as paymaster (*Seckelmeister*) to the Strasbourg troops. Hertzog,
VIII, 97, describes the effects of this election upon the people: "vnnd diese vielfeltige
Wahlen haben bei der Gemeinde zu Strassburg gross verwundernuss gebracht / dann
zuvor dero gleichen niemals beschehen."

sake of some small fief."[66] The XV did recommend changing the law, but the Senate & XXI decided to administer the existing law somewhat more generously.

To what extent this prohibition of fiefholding by Ammeisters was still politically necessary during the sixteenth century is very difficult to determine, for no easy conclusion can be reached about the political significance of the bonds of vassalage in this region of extreme political fragmentation.[67] Whether any Strasbourgeois of this era served a margrave of Baden, an elector Palatine, or one of the numerous counts and barons in a military capacity as a direct result of the bond of vassalage, may be doubted. Setting aside the financial transactions made in feudal form, it may be doubted that the lords received any service or any other benefit from continuing enfiefments, although, in the highly fragmented condition of property and seigneurial rights on both sides of the Rhine, enfiefment was certainly preferable to the possibility of losing the rights altogether. On the other hand, princes maintained a certain amount of good will among the Lower Alsatian nobility and maintained points of entry into the politics of the region.

With the bishops of Strasbourg, the situation was certainly different. Each episcopal vassal was called to each meeting (*Tagung*) of the bishop's feudal court (*Manngericht*), which met at Molsheim thirty-three times between 1510 and 1573, or slightly more often than once every two years.[68] The chief business of this court, which staunchly refused to permit any form of written procedure to be introduced,[69] was the settle-

---

[66] AMS, XXI 1543, fol. 497^v (17 November 1543). The XV's recommendation to the Senate & XXI in *ibid.*, fols. 536^r–537^r (8 December 1543). In 1558 Bastian Münch (PROSOPOGRAPHY, No. LXX) declined to be Ammeister because he wanted to retain his fief. Successful refusals of the Ammeister office for reasons of health were not uncommon, as Felix Erstein-Armbruster and Simon Franck in 1549. PROSOPOGRAPHY, Nos. XXIX, XXX.

[67] This was due less to the status of the vassals as citizens of a free city than to the absence of a strong territorial principality which might have transformed the knights of Lower Alsace into a service nobility. Volker Press finds precisely this process at work in the Kraichgau, where the young men from the families of free knights went to the Palatine court, rose in service, and ended their careers as *Diener vom Haus aus*: "Das Lehensband, wenn auch in seiner Bedeutung gemindert, spielte im Verhältnis der Ritter zur Pfalz eine erhebliche Rolle." Volker Press, "Die Ritterschaft im Kraichgau zwischen Reich und Territorium 1500–1623," *ZGO*, 122 (1974), 35–98, here at pp. 40–41.

[68] ADBR, G 502, "Tagbuch dess Manngerichtss" (1510–1573). See the introduction to Appendix C below.

[69] ADBR, G 502, at 21 April 1517 (Tuesday after Quasimodo): "Vff disem mantag ist aberkannt das man nit in schrifften handeln lass auch nit vss schrifften zulesen gestatt, Es were dann das einer ein schlechten gedenckzedtel hett daruss er sich erinnern mocht." Hence the paucity of extant records.

ment of suits between vassals or between lord and vassals over feudal rights and property. Yet, the older, political function of the assembly of vassals was not entirely dead, and the bishop still expected some kind of military service from his vassals in case of threat to the region in the form of invasion. At least Bishop Erasmus asked the vassals in 1537:

> as the situation is somewhat threatening . . . Then His Grace asks that his vassals, according to their feudal obligations, return home, make military preparations, and hold themselves ready at home, and, when His Grace calls, join him [in arms], and help to overcome any invasion.

On the other hand, he continued, he had called them up some time ago, and "very few obeyed this call."[70] Bishop Erasmus, then only a few years in office, may well have had illusions about his power as feudal lord. If so, he soon learned that little military aid was to be had from the corps of his vassals. During the troubled early 1550s, he called instead the Imperial estates (*Landstände*, but here only the direct subjects of the Empire) to organize and carry out the defense of Lower Alsace against invasions.[71]

What was actually going on among the bishop's vassals during this era was open surfacing of the tendency—implicit at least in feudal structures across Europe since several centuries before—to convert the feudal tenure into a form of true property. The one customary aspect of the feudal tie that was strictly adhered to was the requirement that homage be performed and received anew with every change of lord or vassal, that is, upon the death of each prince or each vassal. The stately volumes of Baden and Palatine feudal registers (*Lehnbücher*) are witnesses to the regularity with which this act was performed and the charters renewed, even by vassals whose fiefs lay deep in Lower Alsace, far from the central territories of the two houses.[72] In the feudal structures of a weaker lord, however, such as an ecclesiastical prince, the pressure to transform tenures into property could express itself more easily. Bishop Erasmus of Strasbourg contended—or thought he had to contend—with just such

---

[70] ADBR, G 502, Instruction of Bishop Erasmus, 21 April 1537, inserted after the entry for 1521: "wie die louff . . . ist etwas sorglich . . . Darumb seiner gnaden gnedigs begern sey, sie hiemit bey jren lehenpflichten erforderend, das sie sich dar zu schicken, gerusst machen, vnd anheimisch hallten, so bald sie von siner f. g. erfordert werden, das sie sin g. dann zuziehen, eynissolchen vberfalls rettung thun zuhelffen." When he last called them, "aber derzeyt gar wenig solcher erfordrung gehorsam befunden."

[71] *PCSS*, V, 404–407, No. 303 (28.X.1552); p. 432, No. 333 (22.III.1553); pp. 434–436, No. 337 (12.IV.1553); pp. 530–531, No. 428 (4./5.V.1554).

[72] GLAK, 67/42–46, 47–49 (Baden, both lines, ca. 1471–1565); 67/1006–1008, 1010–1016, 1022, 1057–1058 (Palatinate, ca. 1477–1559).

pressures among his own vassals. In 1548 he instructed his *Lehnrichter*, Sebastian von Landsberg, to announce to the assembled vassals of the *Manngericht* that, although some vassals have been heard to allege that they are no longer obliged to render homage anew when the lord or the vassal has died, he insists on the maintenance of the old forms—that homage be rendered and received, and that the charters and acknowledgments (*Lehenreverse*) be renewed after each installation of a bishop and after a vassal has been succeeded by another.[73] On this occasion, the vassals promised to obey. Nevertheless, most vassals, including the Strasbourgeois, submitted plausible excuses in writing if they could or would not attend the Molsheim assemblies, and the absentees might sometimes amount to one-third of the entire assembly.[74] This suggests that they took somewhat seriously their roles as episcopal vassals, to the extent, at least, of taking some care to maintain good relations with this feudal lord.

An understanding of the involvement of the Strasbourg aristocracy in the regional networks of feudal relations casts a new light on the character of the patrician–guildsman aristocracy and the regime it controlled. The literature on Strasbourg in the age of the Reformation is almost totally innocent of the subject. No treatment of Jacob Sturm, for example, includes the fact that he was a vassal of the Holy Roman Empire, the bishop of Strasbourg, and the elector Palatine. The more general literature is equally innocent of feudal involvements of nearly every patrician family and most of the wealthier guild families. The political significance of these connections is difficult to gauge. None of these aristocrats seems to have ever performed military or any other kind of service as vassals. When Strasbourgeois went to war, they went as citizens or as mercenaries, not as vassals.[75] The overall weight of this web of social relations cannot, however, be entirely discounted. In

---

[73] ADBR, G 502, Instruction of Bishop Erasmus, 12 June 1548, inserted after the entry for 1521.

[74] ADBR, G 503, at 9 June 1551, where fully one-third of the vassals excuse their absence from the *Manntag,* with excuses ranging from official duties to a trip to the baths.

[75] Examples in PROSOPOGRAPHY, Nos. IX, XXXIII, LXXVI, CII. Six of the twenty commanders and advisers supplied by Strasbourg in the Smalkaldic War were members of the Böcklin family, and another was a Zorn (Jerg Z.). Harry Gerber, "Die Kriegsrechnungen des Schmalkaldischen Bundes über den Krieg im Oberland des Jahres 1546," *ARG*, 33 (1936), 239, and 34 (1937), 273; *PCSS*, IV, 265–266, No. 245. Jacob Böcklin also fought in the war of 1552, when he took part in the siege of Frankfurt a. M. Rochus von Liliencron, ed., *Die historischen Volkslieder der Deutschen*, 4 vols. (Leipzig, 1865–69), IV, 55, No. 601, at stanza 10. The Strasbourg nobles were not new at the mercenary business then. On 16 April 1528 "ist graff wilhelm von Fürstenberg mit

judging the regime's policies towards the other powers of the region and its attitudes toward peasant disturbances, it is useful to know that the ruling aristocracy of Strasbourg was a thoroughly feudal aristocracy as well, that the lords of the town were also lords in the land.

C. THE BONDS OF REAL PROPERTY

The attractiveness of land ownership to the urban rich seems to have been nearly universal in late medieval Europe. In his study of *Medieval and Renaissance Pistoia*, David Herlihy writes that by the early fifteenth century "investments in land were much preferred over commercial ventures" by the patricians of this small Tuscan town.[76] It doubtless is true that both the prestige of land ownership and the security of investment in land heightened the attractiveness of real property to urban investors all over Europe during the fourteenth and fifteenth centuries.[77] Due to lack of space and the fragmentary state of the sources (the Strasbourg sources do not flow freely until about 1550[78]) not much more can be done here than to suggest the patterns of ownership of urban, suburban, and rural property in and around Strasbourg.

The leading property owners within the city walls during the fifteenth century were the great patrician families, the Zorn, Mülnheim, Kageneck, and Sturm; and they still owned much of the city during the following century.[79] The eastern part of the island which formed the core of Stras-

---

ettliche knechten die er zu Strassburg hatt angenomen gehn Meran bescheiden, vnd ist vil adel von Strassburg mit im zogen." The survivors came home after St. James's Day (25 July), "das mehrtheil kranck vnd gross geschwollen." "Imlin Chronik," Ms. in BNUS, Ms. 1266, fol. 67ᵛ. Nobles were in great demand as mercenary cavalry, though most were recruited in the North. Wohlfeil, "Adel und neues Heerwesen," pp. 225–226.

[76] Herlihy, *Medieval and Renaissance Pistoia*, p. 194, basic on town and land. For the Italian cities in general, see Enrico Fiume, "Sui rapporti tra città e contado nell'eta communale," *Archivio storico italiano*, 114 (1956), 18–68. By far most advanced is the French literature, of which I cite Guy Fourquin, *Les campagnes de la région parisienne à la fin du moyen âge (du milieu du XIIe siècle au début du XVIe)* (Paris, 1964); Emmanuel Le Roy Ladurie, *Les paysans de Languedoc,* 2 vols. (Paris, 1964); and Jean Schneider, *La ville de Metz*. The German literature is still heavily engaged in juridical studies of civic territories, though this is less true of Gerhard Wunder's *Das Strassburger Landgebiet* than of most others. See Kiessling, *Bürgerliche Gesellschaft und Kirche in Augsburg,* esp. pp. 197–201, who, however, treats only feudal tenures.

[77] Kiessling, *Bürgerliche Gesellschaft und Kirche in Augsburg*, p. 198.

[78] The chief group of sources is the notarial registers (series KS in AMS), although there is also much information in ADBR, series E.

[79] Hatt, *Une ville*, pp. 40–41, 472–476.

bourg, the oldest section of the city, was studded with the houses of the old families.[80] Along the Bimpernanzgasse, for example, were the houses of the Kageneck and the Zorn von Bulach around 1530, together with the residences of such leading guild politicians as Claus Münch, Jacob von Duntzenheim, and Mattheus Geiger. Around the Rossmarkt, which marked the northern boundary of the oldest quarter of the town, were the mansions of the Landsberg, the Mülnheim, and the Wurmser; and in the fashionable Brandgasse just south of the Rossmarkt, there lived the Sturm brothers, Friedrich von Gottesheim, the wealthy gold-smith Erasmus Krug, Veltin Kips, some of the Bock and the Marx von Eckwersheim, several noble cathedral canons, and the well-to-do painter Hans Baldung Grien.[81] In the Judengasse, the next street southward, Conrad Joham built his mansion on the site of the Jewish baths. Several houses had to be torn down to make space for this great, elegant *Hof*, which his colleagues in the regime obligingly permitted him to extend out over the street farther than the law allowed. Here Joham and his sons entertained high noble and royal visitors to Strasbourg.[82]

Besides their own dwellings, the rich families also owned rental houses in every quarter of the town. Appendix A contains numerous examples of persons who owned several buildings, based on the very incomplete material collected by Adolph Seyboth and on the notarial registers. Some families owned rental properties in the newest sections of Strasbourg, the three former suburbs on the southeastern, northern, and western sides of the town, where the poorest sectors of the popula-

---

[80] The following lines are based on the extensive, though necessarily incomplete, house-by-house survey of the city of Adolph Seyboth, *Das alte Strassburg vom 13. Jahrhundert bis zum Jahre 1870* (Strasbourg, 1890), and on Jean-Pierre Kintz, "La société strasbourgeoise du milieu du XVIe siècle à la fin de la guerre de trente ans 1560–1650," Thèse presentée pour le doctorat és lettres, Strasbourg, 1977, pp. 16–22. My thanks to M. Kintz for permission to read this part of his thesis and for photocopies of it. Kintz's work is based on the most thorough kind of research into the parish registers of Strasbourg and should yield the first portrait of a German-speaking population during this era, using French methods of historical demography. His work on the social complexion of the parishes clearly shows the rich to have been concentrated in the Cathedral parish and in St. Thomas (*ibid.*, p. 20).

[81] Seyboth, pp. 20–23. There were also many wealthy families in the Himmelreich-gässchen, Maurergässchen, and esp. the Judengasse.

[82] *Ibid.*, pp. 27–28; AMS, XXI 1544, fols. 133[r], 159[v]–160[r], 162[v]–163[r]. The house later passed to the Mieg, and there is a description of it by a subsequent owner, Sebastian Mieg von Boofzheim, in *Fragments de diverses vielles chroniques*, ed. Léon Dacheux, in *BSCMHA*, N.S. 18 (1900), No. 4278. On the visitors, see Seyboth, p. 27; Büheler, *Chronik*, No. 293.

tion lived.[83] They also often owned garden and pasture land just within or just outside the walls, or they rented such land from the city—presumably to supply their own tables.[84]

Judging from Seyboth's data, urban and suburban property changed hands with great frequency; and, although the land market at Strasbourg during the sixteenth century has never been studied, one example will show that such a market existed and that persons of relatively modest wealth could speculate in real estate. Hans Baldung Grien (1484/85–1545) was Strasbourg's most famous artist during the sixteenth century.[85] He came back to Strasbourg in 1509, fresh from his journeyman years in the atelier of Dürer at Nuremberg, and married the niece of Martin Herlin, who was then merely a local merchant and not yet one of the city's most powerful politicians.[86] From the mid-1510s onward, the Baldungs invested surplus income in annuities (*Leibgedinge*), so that by the mid-1520s they were already getting more from this source annually than would be earned by a master artisan who worked for wages. They bought a residence in the fashionable Brandgasse and lived among the notables of the town. What is less generally known about Baldung is that he was also a speculator in real estate. In 1525 he sold to Frantz Bertsch, a well-to-do apothecary, a small plot just outside the Judentor which he had owned for at least four years.[87] In 1528–29 the Baldungs made a series of deals which reveal their methods. They owned a small property at Schiltigheim, just northwest of the city, valued at 60 fl. In 1528 they traded this land to a patrician couple, Ludwig von Yberg (d. 1536) and Katharina von Kageneck, for another property at Illkirch (southwest of the city) worth 160 fl. To pay the difference between the Illkirch and Schiltigheim properties, they constituted a rente on the Illkirch plot yielding 4 fl./yr. and redeemable at 400 fl. Ten months later, they sold the Illkirch property for 200 fl., a profit of 140 minus the debt of 4 fl./yr. Except for the original purchase of the Schiltigheim land, which they may have financed by borrowing

---

[83] The three suburbs corresponded to the three divisions of the enormous Gardeners' Guild: "in der Steinstrasse" (present Faubourg de Pierre), "in der Krutenau," and "unter den Wagner" (present Faubourg National). Rott, "Artisanat," p. 158; Kintz, "La société strasbourgeoise," p. 19; Chrisman, *Strasbourg*, pp. 138–140, 303–306.

[84] Many examples in the surviving *Allmendbücher* in AMS, VII 1436 and 1438.

[85] See Brady, "Social Place of a German Renaissance Artist," pp. 298ff.

[86] PROSOPOGRAPHY, No. XXXVII.

[87] This and following deals are described in detail in Brady, "Social Place of a German Renaissance Artist," pp. 300–302.

from her uncle, Martin Herlin the Ammeister, the Baldungs completed this series of transactions with no cash outlay. The case suggests that a systematic study of the urban land market at Strasbourg would have to extend quite far into the middling ranks of the guilds—at least into those of the wealthier master artisans. It was a market in which status distinctions were meaningless, in which only cash or credit counted.

The once common belief that Alsatian townsmen were relatively in-different to the acquisition of rural property is now known to be quite false.[88] The researches of F.-J. Fuchs and Jean Vogt have revealed a very lively tempo of investment in rural land by Strasbourgeois after 1550, and there is no reason to suppose that it began suddenly at this date.[89] The notarial registers permit the question to be studied from about 1500 onwards, and the following account—though not systematic—will provide sufficient examples to show that many Strasbourgeois were rural landowners during the earlier sixteenth century.

The biggest owners in the city, the patricians, were also the biggest individual owners in the countryside. A useful kind of document for this subject is the land survey conducted by local village officials (*Schöffen*) at the request of owners, usually carried out after an important group of parcels changed hands (*renovatio bonorum, Erneuerung der Güter*). Indi-vidual parcels were identified in these surveys by naming the owners of adjoining parcels or landmarks; and when a large amount of property in a single bannlieu was surveyed, a large percentage of the district's owners would be named. Table 11 analyzes three such surveys: the first made at Vendenheim in April, 1526, for the heirs of Bläsi von Mülnheim; the second at Osthofen and Ergersheim in May, 1524, for Carl Mieg, Sr.; and the third made for the three surviving daughters of Lorentz Schott at Lampertheim around 1532/33.

The big corporate owners in all three districts were the collegial chapters and hospitals of Strasbourg, while the chief noble owners were families of the Strasbourg patriciate—the Wurmser, Mülnheim, Knobloch, and Böcklin at Vendenheim, and the Mülnheim and Beger at

---

[88] Etienne Juillard, "Indifférence de la bourgeoisie alsacienne à l'égard de la pro-priété rurale aux XVIIIe et XIXe siècles," in *La bourgeoisie alsacienne*, pp. 377–386, here at pp. 377–378. He is followed by Michel Rochefort, *L'organisation urbaine de l'Alsace*, Thèse presentée à la Faculté des Lettres de l'Université de Strasbourg (Stras-bourg, 1960), p. 24.

[89] F.-J. Fuchs, "Bourgeois de Strasbourg propriétaires ruraux au XVIIe siècle," *Paysans d'Alsace*, PSSARE, 7 (Strasbourg, 1969), pp. 99–120; Jean Vogt, "A propos de la propriété bourgeoise en Alsace (XVIe–XVIIIe siècles)," *RA*, 100 (1962), 48–66.

Osthofen and Ergersheim.[90] Among the non-patrician citizens appear the Ammeister Claus Kniebis and Hans Schott, former senator from the Furriers' guild, at Osthofen and Ergersheim, plus, of course, the Schott daughters at Lampertheim.[91] The properties surveyed at Lampertheim had passed through the hands of several wealthy guildsmen of Strasbourg. They had belonged to Hans Jörger by 1481, from whom they passed to the Rotweil; and Lorentz Schott, a tanner ("weissgerber") of Strasbourg, bought them from Hans Erhard, Sr., and Margarethe von Rotweil in 1512 and left them "jnn Eygenthums wyse" to his three daughters. The three women all married leading guild politicians: Hans Lindenfels, Christoph II Städel, and Georg Leimer.[92]

None of these villages lay in the civic territory. Vendenheim was an Imperial fief (of the Wurmser), Ergersheim belonged to the episcopal territory, Lampertheim belonged partly to the bishop and partly to the cathedral chapter, and Osthofen was partly an Imperial and partly an episcopal fief.[93] The villages were all relatively close to Strasbourg, Vendenheim lying nearly seven miles and Osthofen slightly more than nine miles westward (seigneurial rights belonging to the Wurmser and the Bock respectively), while Ergersheim lay next to Osthofen and Lampertheim just south of Vendenheim. If the surveys are accurate indicators of ownership patterns, about 70% of the land was owned by individuals, families and corporations of Strasbourg, most of it by patricians and collegial chapters.

The Schott sisters' extensive holdings at Lampertheim were not an isolated case of rural proprietorship by a guild family. The amount of land in the hands of ordinary citizens was undoubtedly increased at Strasbourg, as elsewhere in Europe, through the Reformation's release of much land from mortmain. The traditional view, deriving from the work of Otto Winckelmann, is that the properties of liquidated religious corporations at Strasbourg were turned en bloc to the support of hospitals, schools, and the welfare fund.[94] There likely *was* far less leakage

---

[90] Twelve patrician families appear in the Vendenheim survey and ten in the Osthofen survey.

[91] PROSOPOGRAPHY, No. L. Hans Schott, senator from the *Kürschnerzunft* in 1518, 21/22 (Hatt, p. 538). The biggest owner at Osthofen who was also a guildsman of Strasbourg was Lehenmans (or Lehemans) Veltin of Osthofen; he purchased citizenship and joined the *Weinsticherzunft* on 17 February 1524 (Wittmer, No. 7667).

[92] AMS, IV 105a; PROSOPOGRAPHY, Nos. LII, LIII, LXXXVIII.

[93] Fritz, *Territorien*, pp. 93, 95, 105–106, 108, 111.

[94] I refer to Otto Winckelmann's *Das Fürsorgewesen der Stadt Strassburg* (1922).

Table 11

Property-owners mentioned in surveys at Vendenheim (April, 1526), Osthofen & Ergersheim (May, 1524), and Lampertheim (ca. 1532/33)

Type of Owner	Vendenheim		Osthofen and Ergersheim		Lampertheim		Total	
	Owners	Parcels	Owners	Parcels	Owners	Parcels	Owners	Parcels
1. Ecclesiastical and other Corporations	18 (26%)	134 (37%)	25 (27%)	150 (38%)	12 (31%)	50 (41%)	55 (28%)	334 (39%)
2. Nobles and Noble Families	20 (29%)	154 (43%)	17 (18%)	82 (21%)	8 (20%)	20 (19%)	45 (22%)	256 (30%)
3. Other Strasbourg Citizens	3 (4%)	15 (4%)	6 (7%)	10 (3%)	5 (13%)	15 (14%)	14 (7%)	40 (5%)
4. Peasants	25 (36%)	52 (14%)	37 (40%)	121 (21%)	10 (26%)	15 (14%)	72 (36%)	188 (22%)
5. Others	3 (4%)	4 (1%)	7 (8%)	27 (7%)	4 (11%)	7 (6%)	14 (7%)	38 (4%)
Total	69 (100%)	359 (100%)	92 (100%)	390 (100%)	39 (100%)	107 (100%)	200 (100%)	856 (100%)

Sources: AMS, KS 17, fols. 219ʳ–225ᵛ, 37ʳ–44ᵛ; AMS, IV 105a. In each case, the person(s) for whom the survey was made is/are omitted.

of ecclesiastical property into private hands at Strasbourg than in some other places, but some well-placed persons did realize quick gains from the dissolution of the convents, especially in the earliest phase. One of them was the Ammeister Claus Kniebis, the chief of the most ardent Evangelicals in the regime, to whom and to whose associates the secularization of St. Clara auf dem Wörth—one of Strasbourg's two houses of Poor Clares—proved a bonanza. Kniebis picked up no less than 150 parcels of land around Mommenheim from the holdings of St. Clara, while his brother-in-law, Dr. Michael Rot, a graduate of the University of Ferrara, and his ward, Margarethe von Truchtersheim, got other parcels from the same source.[95] At Mommenheim, a village in the *Reichslandvogtei* of Hagenau, most of the other urban owners were citizens of Hagenau, the closest city.[96] Kniebis, whose social place has always been something of a mystery, seems to have been a rentier, for the lists of his rural properties are very long, and most of them seem to have been leased to peasant tenants.[97]

So common did rural landownership by guildsmen of Strasbourg become during the next generation (after 1550) that Jean Vogt has called the process an "invasion."[98] The new proprietors were not always rich merchants, for artisans also appear in the lists of buyers. Such absentee owners often made unwelcome neighbors for the local peasants, such as those of Dambach, who complained in 1551 that Michael Schwencker, a notary and XVer of Strasbourg, was abusing the village commons.[99] Strasbourgeois frequently invested in rural lands in the districts of the Ried and the Kochersberg, north of Strasbourg. Sometimes they

---

[95] AMS, KS 17, fols. 270^r–275^r, "Renovatio bonorum" for Claus Kniebis at Mommenheim, 30 November 1526; AMS, KS 18, fols. 1^r–15^r, records of sales of convent land by Elisabeth Mussler, prioress of St. Clara auf dem Wörth.

[96] Fritz, *Territorien*, p. 130. Several of Strasbourg's ecclesiastical corporations had properties there, plus Hans Jacob Zorn von Plobsheim, son of Adam Zorn and son-in-law of Martin Sturm (PROSOPOGRAPHY, No. XCIV), and Michels Martzolf, a gardener and native of Mommenheim, who purchased citizenship at Strasbourg and joined the Gardeners' Guild on 31 August 1519 (Wittmer, No. 6846).

[97] AMS, KS 15, fols. 176^r–177^r; AMS, KS 19, fols. 279^v–280^r, lands around Pforzheim and near Rastatt, all inherited from his mother, who was a sister of Hugo Meyer, "vicarius chori ecclesie maiore argentinen." AMS, KS 63/I, fol. 195^r–v, lands at Offenheim rented for 22 *Viertel* of wheat and a *Viertel* of legumes ("erbsen") annually; AMS, KS 63/II, fol. 107^r–v, lands at Königshofen leased to a peasant; and AMS, KS 63/II, fols. 126^r–127^r, lands in the bannlieu of Strasbourg, leased to Hans Schott of Wasselonne.

[98] Vogt, "A propos de la propriété bourgeoise," p. 49.

[99] AMS, VI 393/1, quoted by *ibid.*, p. 65n1, and see p. 51; PROSOPOGRAPHY, No. LXXXV.

acquired them from patrician sellers, as was the case with lands owned by Jacob Braun, son of the XVer Claus Braun, at Eckwersheim around 1570.[100] But the bulk of bourgeois acquisitions in the districts around Strasbourg during the sixteenth century doubtless resulted from the piling up of peasant debts to urban usurers—one more feature of the invasion of the land by urban money.[101]

D. THE BONDS OF USURY

The invasion of the countryside by urban moneylenders was probably as old around Strasbourg as it was in the region of Metz, where Jean Schneider has documented the process from the late thirteenth century onward.[102] Jean Vogt has studied moneylending by Strasbourgeois to peasants during the later sixteenth century and has established the principal characteristics of the business at that time by examining commodity rentes (*rentes en nature*) constituted by peasants for Strasbourgeois.[103] The purchase of constituted, redeemable rentes in grain and wine by Strasbourgeois was very common within a 15–20 mile radius of the city, especially in the Kochersberg district, north of the city, and in the lower valley of the Breusch.[104] The latter region, lying west of the city along the edge of the Vosges, was a rich area long beloved of the Lower Alsatian religious houses and foundations as a place to invest surplus income.[105] As in so much else, lay Strasbourgeois of the sixteenth

---

[100] Vogt, "A propos de la propriété bourgeoise," p. 51; PROSOPOGRAPHY, No. XV.

[101] Vogt, "A propos de la propriété bourgeoise," pp. 49–50. Fuchs, "Bourgeois de Strasbourg propriétaires ruraux," finds the same process around 1636.

[102] Schneider, *La ville de Metz*, pp. 321–407, and esp. pp. 384–407, basic for the entire question. The process may have begun somewhat later at Strasbourg, where economic growth began somewhat later than at Metz; but the basic types of rentes were certainly well known at Strasbourg by the High Middle Ages. Henri Dubled, "Aspects de la vie économique de Strasbourg aux XIIIe et XIVe siècles: baux et rentes," *AEA*, 6(1955), 23–56. In general, see Georges Duby, *Rural Economy and Country Life in the Medieval West*, trans. Cynthia Postan (Columbia, S.C., 1968), pp. 252–259, on urban investment in peasant debt.

[103] Jean Vogt, "Remarques sur les rentes en nature rachetables payeés par les campagnards aux prêteurs strasbourgeois (deuxième moitié du XVIe siècle)," *RHMC*, 15 (1968), 662–671.

[104] Fuchs finds similar concentrations of investment in the Kochersberg district during the first half of the seventeenth century. Fuchs, "Bourgeois de Strasbourg proprietaires ruraux," p. 100. On the constituted rente, see Bernard Schnapper, *Les rentes au XVIe siècle. Histoire d'un instrument de crédit*, École Pratique des Hautes Études, VIe section, série "Affaires et gens d'affaires," 12 (Paris, 1957), p. 42.

[105] Rapp, *Réformes et Réformation*, p. 531; Fritz Kiener, "Zur Vorgeschichte des Bauernkriegs am Oberrhein," *ZGO*, 58 (1904), 479–507, here at pp. 497–498. On the

century here trod paths long ago blazed by their clergy. Such commodity rentes, constituted by peasants in return for cash loans, were bought by a wide variety of Strasbourgeois, including cloth merchants and artisans, for whom the purchase of peasant debt was often the first step toward the acquisition of permanent rural property interests.

The purchase of property right in the peasants' produce by means of cash loans differed from the exploitation of peasant agriculture through traditional seigneurial institutions in two ways. First, the ownership of peasant debt, now separated from its political and judicial accompaniments, could become and did become the object of a relatively free market. Secondly, wholesale usury in the land was open to all lenders, merchants and artisans as well as ecclesiastical houses and noble families. Usury, perhaps even more than land ownership, bound the ruling classes of town and land into a solid social phalanx. The incomes from constituted rentes complemented those from more traditional means of tapping the product of the land, feeding an enormous casual market in commodities. In this sector, all creditors were "merchants," and the prohibition against the direct engagement of patricians in trade did not apply. Some patricians, such as Adolf von Mittelhausen, Sr., seem to have made a regular business of loaning capital in very small sums to peasants.[106] The big lenders, whether patricians or guildsmen, must have been heavily engaged in the trade in grain and wine. This is certainly true of Jacob Zorn zum Riet, who in 1522 received 110 quarters (*Viertel*) of grain from a group of peasants who owed him 33 lb./yr.[107] Zorn thus acquired in one transaction more than 12,000 liters of grain, far more than the consumption of his household.[108] From the creditor's side the

---

Kochersberg region, see Francis Rapp, "Die bäuerliche Aristokratie des Kochersberges im ausgehenden Mittelalter und zu Beginn der Neuzeit," in *Bauernschaft und Bauernstand 1500–1970*, ed. Günther Franz, DFN, 8 (Limburg/Lahn, 1975), pp. 89–102.

[106] AMS, KS 15, fols. 31ʳ, 75ʳ, 77ʳ, 84ᵛ, 87ʳ, 104ʳ, 108ʳ, 125ᵛ, 234ʳ, all in 1522. He was just as active in 1524–25, as can be seen in AMS, KS 17, fols. 22, 24, 26, 30, 45, 53ʳ, 57ʳ, 61ʳ, 78ʳ, 94ʳ, 103ʳ⁻ᵛ, 115ʳ, 125ᵛ, 126ʳ, 128ᵛ, 129ᵛ, 130ʳ. This is Adolf von Mittelhausen, Sr., first-cousin to the younger man of the same name (PROSOPOGRAPHY, No. LXIV).

[107] AMS, KS 15, fol. 96ʳ; PROSOPOGRAPHY, No. CIV. At Strasbourg a *Viertel* was equal to 111.5 liters, which means that the payment to Zorn yielded 12,265 liters. Crämer, *Verfassung und Verwaltung Strassburgs,* p. 101. Fuchs, "Prechter," p. 177, finds that the Prechter rarely bought peasant debt.

[108] Zorn was a partner of Conrad Kirchhofer, a merchant, and others. AMS, KS 17, fol. 31ʳ⁻ᵛ, where are mentioned "Jacobo Zorn zum Riet et Conrado Kirchofer suorumque consortibus," and a little later (fol. 49ʳ), a document mentions only Kirchhofer "et suis consortibus." Many rich Strasbourgeois and, before the Reformation, many of the ecclesiastical corporations possessed large reserves of grain with which they

business can be traced in the few surviving account books of aristocratic households, a series for the household of Maria von Duntzenheim, Conrad's daughter (1521ff.), and a series for various members of the patrician Büchsner.[109] In 1550–51 Friedrich Büchsner's accounts were kept by Jacob Hügel, who recorded that his master in this year collected 113.2 of the 131.8 quarters owed him.[110] This grain, of which the quantities of rye, wheat, barley and oats were related as 5 to 1.5 to 1 to 1, must have formed a very large share of his incomes, for only 82 lb. of his more than 647 lb. in incomes were the yield of cash rentes. The grain prices were apparently quite high in 1550–51, for Büchsner sold a total of 327.7 quarters, mostly rye, from his granary in town during the year. He paid his smith and his tailor in grain and kept 11 quarters of oats for his own horses, selling the remainder in fairly large amounts (10–106 quarters). The three Sturm brothers got wine and grain from an ancient fief-rente held by the Sturm from the Palatine Elector, and they seem to have sold their surplus grain to a local baker—a common and regular source of demand.[111] There is nothing specifically noble or patrician about these activities of the Büchsner and the Sturm, for this vast market system in agricultural produce was open to all. Here great noble and social-climbing artisan master could meet on a level of relative equality vis-a-vis the peasantry.

Rural commodity rentes were usually redeemable and so, on this ground at least, not technically usurious, although, as Vogt has pointed out, one cannot trust that the redemption clause in a constituted rente was actually operative.[112] The rural debtors had the great disadvantage

---

undoubtedly conducted speculations. Fuchs, "L'espace économique rhénan," p. 312, mentions Hans Stösser (PROSOPOGRAPHY, No. XC), Jacob Putlinger, Christoph Wegrauft, and the patrician Peter Ellenhart (PROSOPOGRAPHY, No. XXV) as being among the Strasbourgeois who commanded large grain reserves.

[109] AMS, V 137/32 (1527–31), 24 (1520–21), 25 (1522–23), and 139/4 (1560, 1562, 1572), household accounts prepared by Jacob Schütz, Johann Hackfurt, and Diebold Fagius. There is also an incomplete set of accounts prepared for members of the Büchsner family for various years from 1548 to 1596, in AMS, V 137/26, 138/12–13, and 139/2, 14, 20–21. It is likely that Anna von Duntzenheim's husband, *Junker* Hans Münch, was related to Claus Münch (PROSOPOGRAPHY, No. LXIX), because Claus Münch was once guardian of Jacob von Duntzenheim. AMS, KS 15, fol. 100ᵛ.

[110] AMS, V 137/6.

[111] GLAK, 44/818; AMS, XXI 1546, fols. 547ᵛ–548ʳ; AMS, KS 27/I, fol. 63ᵛ. The Sturm were apparently not major lenders to peasants.

[112] Schnapper, *Les rentes,* pp. 55–56, 104–106, who finds that Parisian rentes before 1530 were mainly of the type discussed here, that is, constitutions by peasants to their urban creditors.

that, unlike their urban counterparts, they could exert no consistent political pressure for relief from their urban creditors. The urban poor formed a debtor class in the power of the same creditors, for the urban rich lent evenhandedly to rural and urban borrowers.[113] The urban debtors, however, received definite if modest relief in the form of a law of 1523 which regulated perpetual rentes (*ewig Zins*). Undoubtedly a response to the mounting popular unrest of the early 1520s, this law enacted a redemption schedule for perpetual rentes—always excepting fief-rentes ("die eigen zins als Erb vnd Manlehen") and lease-rentes (*Erbleihen, baux à l'héritage*)—at rates varying from 2,000% to 3,000% of the annual yield.[114] The regime, a government of usurers, thus moved to enforce the papal condemnation of true perpetual rentes (i.e., redeemable at the will of the creditor only) at the very moment when the movement to destroy the old ecclesiastical order was getting under way in Strasbourg.

On the land no one and nothing intervened to save the debtor from the quagmire of debts to urban usurers. For this we have the testimony of one of the notaries, Fridolin Meyger (d. 1533/36), whose daily task it was to draw up contracts for rentes and acknowledgements of other forms of usurious debt by which the urban lenders kept much of the peasant population in their financial power.[115] Meyger was involved on-and-off with the local Anabaptists, whose teachings condemned his daily collaboration with usurers and gave him a bad conscience. "In order to secure my modest living," he wrote in 1529,

> I am plagued by this devilish curse of usurious loans. Persons, who nevertheless consider themselves good Evangelicals and hear sermons daily, engage in this activity: they want most of all to make a pile of money, as though they were immortal and might live here on earth forever. I know very well that this usurious practice is the support, the very lifeblood of the nobles who go about town—although God has often and strictly forbidden it. Is not idleness a bad thing? What then of

---

[113] Fuchs, "Prechter," pp. 177–178, on the Prechter, who preferred to lend to artisans.

[114] AMS, R 29/92a, of 17 July 1523, on which see Rott, "Artisanat," pp. 150–151. The law is to be classified with the other measures taken by the regime to still unrest on the eve of the revolution of 1524–25.

[115] Fridolin Meyger, son of Johann Meyger of Säckingen and Elisabeth Gottfried, was "clericus, phil. baccalaureus et notarius"; on 1 February 1524, when he was "notarius contractuum des vordern geistlichen hoffs," he purchased citizenship at Strasbourg and joined the guild Zur Steltz. He married Agnes Huber, and they had one surviving son, Hilarius, a notary. BNUS, Ms. 1058, fol. 129ʳ; Wittmer, No. 7369; *TQ Strassburg*, I, 132n8.

the root from which it grows? All courts and law deal with usury, which nourishes all manner of rascals. Indeed, I cannot spare myself, for I am guilty of it as well. Come to the courts if you would see it; look how the courts and the law treat widows and orphans—or how they mistreat them—all because of usurious interests, rentes, and tithes.[116]

Meyger describes "a rich man, member of the regime here at Strasbourg and well thought of by others," who bought wine rentes from peasants; but he admits that "it is not he alone who does such things, but the whole world does them."[117]

The testimony of Meyger the notary provides valuable information about the characteristic features of the traffic in rentes purchased by urban usurers from peasants. Such rentes, he writes, commonly yield either cash or wine, other types of commodity rentes being rather less common.[118] He also testifies that all constituted rentes contained clauses which made the debtor liable with all of his property and income to the creditor (unlimited liability) and not just with the property on which the rente was specifically constituted—a clause clearly usurious according to the papal declarations of the fifteenth century.[119] Unlike ordinary ground rents, finally, constituted rentes were not subject to the rule, derived from Roman law, whereby the sums owed could be reduced in years of poor harvest.[120] Combined with other literary evidence,[121] Fridolin Meyger's document confirms the existence of a very lively traffic in usurious rentes and suggests that the urban usurers who thereby brought peasants into their power included some of the prominent members of the regime.

---

[116] *TQ Strassburg*, II, 222–223, No. 172.

[117] *Ibid.*, pp. 218 lines 29–34.

[118] *Ibid.*, pp. 220 lines 37–38: "Fruchtenzinss zu kouffen oder also mit wuchern nitt also gemeinlich jm bruch als gelt vnnd wynzinss." Vogt finds, however, that grain rentes were very common during the *later* sixteenth century. Vogt, "Remarques sur les rentes," p. 662.

[119] *TQ Strassburg*, II, 220 lines 5–12. This concerns general or specific assignment of liability. According to papal declarations, a rente was not usurious if it yielded a specific portion of the income of a *specified* property to the creditor, while assignment of a debt to all of the debtor's properties was usurious. See Schnapper, *Les rentes,* pp. 55–56, 65–67, who finds that by the end of the fifteenth century nearly all Parisian rentes were assigned generally (i.e., involved unlimited liability of the debtor), although this fact was usually disguised.

[120] *TQ Strassburg*, II, 221–222; Schnapper, *Les rentes,* p. 86.

[121] *TQ Strassburg*, II, 224–225, Beilage zu Nr. 172. The number of prominent Strasbourgeois who engaged in this business was very large and included the painter, Hans Baldung Grien. Brady, "Social Place of a German Renaissance Artist," p. 303.

That Strasbourg was ruled by usurers can hardly be doubted. What is further striking about the business of usury among the aristocrats is that even extremely wealthy individuals loaned money in relatively small amounts to peasants, and that this was a business in which big money and small money were alike engaged. The heavy investment in peasant debt needs a great deal more study, and will likely be found to have been an important ingredient in the regime's attitude towards the revolution of 1524–25 in Lower Alsace.

E.   The Bonds of Banking and Finance

Petty usury was an investment sector open to all, but large-scale moneylending to princes, nobles, and urban regimes was open only to the rich. Even during the heyday of South German banking, Strasbourg never developed into a major financial center on the order of Augsburg or Nuremberg; but it maintained a position as a leading regional center of finance from the fifteenth through the first three-quarters of the sixteenth century.

The most common instrument of moneylending to princes and nobles was the interest-bearing annuity sold for a principal sum in cash, secured by specific revenues of the borrower but not hypothecated on them or on his lands.[122] This replaced the older form, the fief-rente, sometime during the later Middle Ages; and although it may be correct that the fief-rente declined rapidly in popularity after 1400, yet it continued to exist and to be paid all through the period and into the sixteenth century.[123]

Such fief-rentes might consist of cash, commodities, or a combination of the two. The Sturm family, for example, held for many years from the lords of Rappoltstein a fief yielding cash, rye, and oats.[124] First granted in 1312 to a Blumeneck, this fief-rente passed to the Sturm by 1397 and was still being paid when the family became extinct in the male line in 1640. The Sturm also held a fief-rente yielding 20 fl./yr. ("zu einem Rechten Manlehen") from the margraves of Baden (1412–1508) and a fief of grain from the "leygen korne vnd Etter zehenden" owed the elector Palatine by the village of Nordheim (1417–1617).[125]

---

[122] Cohn, *Government of the Rhine Palatinate,* p. 117.

[123] *Ibid.,* p. 114.

[124] ADBR, E 578/1 (1312–1666).

[125] GLAK, 44/818; 67/1007, fols. 30ᵛ–31ʳ; 67/1011, fol. 215ʳ⁻ᵛ; 67/1013, fol. 243ʳ⁻ᵛ; 67/1016, fol. 485ʳ⁻ᵛ; 67/1023, fols. 190ʳ–191ᵛ, 382ᵛ–383ʳ; 67/1057, fols. 257ʳ–258ʳ; 67/1058, fol. 297ʳ⁻ᵛ.

It is nonetheless quite true that, from the later fifteenth century onward, new loans raised by princes and nobles at Strasbourg were paid
through interest-bearing annuities rather than new fief-rentes. The
change had advantages for both sides—for the lenders, because annuities
were alienable and not just heritable as fief-rentes were, and for the
borrowers, because incomes encumbered by annuities in times of need
could be unencumbered in good times. The electors Palatine, long-time
big customers of Strasbourg lenders, borrowed almost exclusively
against redeemable, heritable annuities from the later fifteenth century
onward.[126]

Except in years when money was very scarce, during the sixteenth
century long-term money could be had at Strasbourg at 4–5%. In his
study of the Palatine debt, Henry J. Cohn has noted that the rates of
interest at Strasbourg began to rise from 4% around 1485 and reached
5% by the end of the century, falling back thereafter to around 4%.[127]
This picture is only partly confirmed by the debts of the counts of Mörs–
Saarwerden, who were frequent borrowers at Strasbourg. They borrowed there between 1481 and 1523 at least 12,800 fl. from a variety of
creditors. They paid 5% on annuities sold in 1481 and 1485, but from
1489 onward only 4% until 1523. In the latter troubled year, they
borrowed 5,300 fl. at Strasbourg at rates varying from 3.75% to 6%.[128]

---

[126] Cohn, *Government of the Rhine Palatinate,* pp. 117–118.

[127] *Ibid.,* p. 118.

[128] Herrmann, *Saarwerden,* I, Nos. 1306, 1382, 1433, 1563, 1694, 1837–1841. Further
confirmation comes from records of moneylending by Strasbourgeois to other princes
and regimes during the later fifteenth and the sixteenth centuries. The counts of
Hanau–Lichtenberg contracted debts totalling about 14,500 fl. on which the counts paid
interest at rates ranging from 4% to 5.3% annually; the last loan at 4% was taken up in
1526, and thereafter the counts paid 5–5.3% for Strasbourg money. AMS, VI 296/19.
The counts of Fürstenberg owed a total of 16,550 fl. to Strasbourgeois, corporations,
and the regime (41.4%, 40.5%, and 18.1% respectively) in 1493, on which the debt
service came to 740 fl./yr., plus 95 fl./yr. paid in *Leibgedinge.* 4,100 fl. of this sum bore 4%
interest, 9,450 fl. bore 4.5%, and 3,000 fl. bore 5%; the largest creditors were Jacob
and Florentz Mieg. *FUB,* VII, 304–308. The fourth group of evidence comes from rentes
purchased by Strasbourgeois from the regimes of Basel and Solothurn, 1494–1524.
Two rentes sold to Bartholomäus Widergrien in 1494 and 1502 bore 4% interest; but
nine rentes sold to Strasbourgeois in 1523–24 for a total of 5,748 fl. also bore 4%. This
all suggests that the basic price of long-term money at Strasbourg did rise to 5% by the
later 1520s at the latest, but the interest rate at any particular time probably depended
on the scarcity of money at the moment and on the reputation of the borrower. It is
thus not surprising that the regime of Basel could still get 4%-money during the 1520s,
while others were paying somewhat higher rates. The Basel data is from *UBB,* IX, 136,
No. 158, and p. 207, No. 276; X, 22–23, No. 32. Other evidence also suggests that 5%

The rate of interest paid on annuities is a deceptive gauge of indebtedness, for one advantage of the redeemable annuity was that the debtor could raise new money in good times to repay annuities sold at high rates of interest in hard times. The electors Palatine did precisely this during the reign of Elector Philip (1448–1508), who in 1479 proposed to raise 60,000 fl. at 4% to retire 41,200 fl. in annuities he had sold in Alsace at 5%.[129] Strasbourg's regime resorted to the same device, coupled with a form of intimidation of creditors, to replace part of the war debt raised during 1546–47 at 5% (the price of money at Basel and Strasbourg during the war) with instruments bearing 4%.[130]

The supercession of the fief-rente by the redeemable annuity also had advantages for the lender. The annuity was freely heritable and not restricted as to descent. An annuity of 100 fl./yr.—probably purchased for 4,000 fl.—was bought by Wilhelm Bock from Count Simon Wecker of Zweibrücken in 1494, passed by inheritance to the Mittelhausen family, and rested by 1540 in the hands of Hilteprant von Mülnheim.[131] Annuities were also negotiable. Adolf von Mittelhausen held a 4%-rente, yielding 4 fl./yr., from the bishop of Speyer, which he tried to sell to the Great Hospital of Strasbourg in 1526.[132] Thirdly, annuities—unlike fiefs—were partible, a great advantage in the division of estates. Margrave Christoph of Baden sold an annuity, yielding 56 fl./yr. and redeemable for 1,350 fl., to Diebold von Mülnheim (d. 1496). By 1526. 18 fl./yr. each had passed to Diebold's brother, Ludwig von Mülnheim (d. 1526), and Jacob Sturm, while the remaining 20 fl./yr. was in the hands of Diebold's six children. By selling their portion to Jacob Sturm, the Mülnheim children, the three girls of whom were already married, could realize their shares of this part of their father's estate.[133] Finally, although annuities were redeemable and lenders could therefore be forced to accept payment of the principal and a loss of the income, annuities were in fact often paid for a very long time. Ludwig Wolf von Renchen bought an annuity of 30 lb./yr. for 600 lb. in 1534 from Count Philip of Hanau–Lichtenberg; and the annuity was still being paid during the 1670s,

---

was the usual rate during the sixteenth century. See Dieter Kreil, *Der Stadthaushalt von Schwäbisch Hall im 15./16. Jahrhundert,* Forschungen aus Württembergisch Franken, 1 (Schwäbisch Hall, 1967), p. 108.

[129] Cohn, *Government of the Rhine Palatinate,* p. 118.

[130] *PCSS,* IV, 702–703, 765, 1102–1103; AMS, XXI 1547, fols. 112ᵛ, 113ᵛ, 156ʳ–157ʳ, 275ᵛ–279ʳ; *UBB,* X, 330, No. 303.

[131] ADBR, E 815(3).

[132] AMS, H 589, fol. 73ᵛ.

[133] AMS, Fonds Mullenheim, document dated 4 January 1526.

when the count and his heirs had paid in interest nearly $7\frac{1}{2}$ times what Philip had borrowed.[134]

Princes and nobles came from all the surrounding regions to borrow money at Strasbourg. Besides the electors Palatine and counts of Mörs–Saarwerden already mentioned, regular customers for Strasbourg money were the counts of Zweibrücken–Bitsch–Lichtenberg and their cousins of Hanau–Lichtenberg, the counts of Fürstenberg, the lords of Rappoltstein, the margraves of Baden, and members of the Hapsburg family.[135] Philip, elector Palatine, was the major princely borrower of the pre-Reformation era. The rise of the Smalkaldic League attracted new customers in the persons of Landgrave Philip of Hesse and Duke Ulrich of Württemberg. From 1530 until the collapse of the Smalkaldic League in 1547, Philip was a regular borrower of large sums, beginning with a loan of 10,000 fl. handled by Conrad Joham in 1530. Joham also brought together 20,000 fl. in 1534 to help finance Philip's restoration of Ulrich in Württemberg, and a substantial sum was raised at Strasbourg in 1541 to make possible the grab of Brunswick by the Protestant princes.[136] Ulrich, who was an Alsatian lord as well as duke of Württemberg, began borrowing at Strasbourg after he recovered his duchy (1534), and his successors remained good customers for generations.[137]

The regime's attitude toward prospective borrowers often determined or at least influenced the willingness of local lenders to open their purses to borrowers. Badly indebted rulers, such as the notoriously involvent Hapsburg brothers, Charles and Ferdinand, found it ever more difficult to raise new money in the town.[138] Not even the closest allies always found paths into the local money market greased by government subscriptions to loans. When Landgrave Philip tried to raise a new loan at Strasbourg for the Brunswick operation in 1542, the regime, whose leaders were against the campaign, refused to subscribe to the loan, and

---

[134] ADBR, E 2775/4.

[135] AMS, VII 11/1; AMS, VII 10/4; AMS, VII 80; AMS, VII 84/1–6; AMS, II 93/2–3; and see note 128 above. The dukes of Lorraine do not seem to have been regular customers at Strasbourg, although Duke René did borrow 8,000 fl. there in 1505. AMS, VII 10/25.

[136] HStAM, PA 326, fols. 3, 4a, 34ʳ, 42, 53ʳ, PA 330, fol. 3ʳ, PA 359, fol. 54ʳ, PA 2915, fols. 250ʳ, 290; AMS, VII 11/3; HStAS, A 104/2, fol. 138ʳ; *PCSS*, II, 100, 210, 210n2; Lenz, ed., *Briefwechsel*, I, 311–312, and II, 7, 10, 19.

[137] *PCSS*, II, 210, 210n2, 212–213, 215, 215n1; AMS, VII 11/2.

[138] See the documents on two Hapsburg loans in AMS, VII 84. When Archduke Ferdinand tried to raise 30–40,000 fl. at Strasbourg in 1525, the most he could get was 10,000 fl. AMS, II 93/2.

Philip got only "a few thousand florins" from private sources.[139] The regime's role as lender and guarantor was often not crucial, for the private lenders sometimes had much better credit connections than their government did. When the leaders of the Smalkaldic League tried to float an enormous loan at Lyons at the start of the Smalkaldic War (1546), the bankers of Lyons spurned the civic regimes as guarantors and demanded guarantees from the chief bankers at Strasbourg (the Ingold, the Prechter, Conrad Joham, and Wolfgang Rehlinger), Augsburg, and Ulm.[140] Rarely did civic policy and the interests of the major lenders diverge to the extent that they did on the Lyons loan, when the local bankers simply refused to guarantee the loan. For the chief private sources of big money at Strasbourg were men and families who were part of the aristocracy and deeply involved in the civic regime. Strasbourg was ruled by creditors.

Not all of the sources of big money were individuals. Of the 55,000 fl. owed by the elector Palatine at Strasbourg in 1508, 8.9% was owed to the clergy and ecclesiastical corporations, 55% to the civic treasury, and 36.1% to aristocrats of the town.[141] The relative shares of these types of lenders were rather different in the loans to the counts of Mörs–Saarwerden between 1481 and 1525: 21.6% from corporations (mostly ecclesiastical ones), 18.8% from the civic treasury, and 59.9% from local aristocrats (27.4% from Constofler, 32.1% from guildsmen).[142] Some very large individual loans appear in this list, the biggest being the 5,000 fl. that Carl Mieg, Sr., loaned in 1519 against an annuity of 200 fl./yr.[143]

The patricians were especially active moneylenders, an activity which, unlike direct engagement in commerce, was completely open to them.

---

[139] *PCSS*, III, 218, 218n1.

[140] This is the famous Strozzi loan, on which see *PCSS*, IV, 401–403, No. 378; and Pariset, "Les relations des rois de France et des princes protestants allemands," I, 110.

[141] Cohn, *Government of the Rhine Palatinate,* p. 162, Table IV. Approximately one-fifth of the electoral debt was owned at Strasbourg, after Cologne but before Speyer and Frankfurt/M. The distribution of the debt at Strasbourg conforms to the general pattern of electoral debt: 12.5% owed to clergy, 53% owed to civic and other regimes, and 34.5% owed to nobles.

[142] Herrmann, *Saarwerden,* I, Nos. 1304, 1306, 1382, 1433, 1477, 1519, 1563, 1590–91, 1631, 1687–89, 1694, 1734, 1747, 1769, 1775, 1780–82, 1794, 1818, 1826, 1837–41, 1873, 1880; ADBR, 25J 23, 28–28b, 33, 36–36a, 344k–n, 388, 388b, 290a, 667. The total sum is 46,570 fl. and the total interest 2,055.5 fl./yr. (at 2 fl. = 1 lb.). See also HStAS, A 26, p. 403.

[143] Herrmann, *Saarwerden,* I, No. 1780.

They worked individually and, for large loans, in syndicates, such as the syndicate of the elector Palatine's creditors in 1505, which comprised members of the Zorn von Bulach, Landsberg, Völtsch, and Bock families.[144] The Wurmser, the Böcklin, and the Sturm all appear among the Mörs–Saarwerden creditors. An idea of the scale of holdings of a prominent patrician family may be gleaned from a *censier* (1536–95) of the Bock von Bläsheim, a branch of the Bock descended from Jacob Bock von Bläsheim, brother of Hans Bock von Gerstheim.[145] This line of the Bock took in approximately 294 fl./yr. from loans of about 6,970 fl. to the margraves of Baden, the bishops of Strasbourg, the counts of Zweibrücken, and the government of the small free city of Rosheim. It should not be supposed, however, that rich patricians dealt in larger sums than those to which the big merchants were accustomed. The latter commonly lent and borrowed sums in multiples of a thousand florins. The really big merchants, such as Israel Minckel, Wilhelm Prechter, and the Ingold routinely borrowed 3,000–6,000 fl. at a time from the civic treasury.[146] The merchants who raised money for the counts of Mörs–Saarwerden—the Mieg, the Joham, the Jörger, and the König—did so on the same scale as the patrician creditors.

The most desirable financial information for this study would be the registers of subscribers to the public debt. Evidence on the public debt and public finance at Strasbourg is so fragmentary, however, that no very clear picture can be gained from it. Examples from smaller South German cities suggest that, unlike the great Italian urban republics whose mammoth and ever-expanding public debts provided safe, lucrative investments for the rich and doubtless drew much capital away from trade and industry, the smaller South German urban regimes tried to control and even (when possible) reduce the state debt.[147]

---

[144] AMS, VIII 197/83.

[145] ADBR, Fonds Landsberg, "Censier des Bock de Blaesheim," here at fols. 7ʳ–11ʳ. This interesting document covers the last two-thirds of the sixteenth century and bears entries by a number of members of the Bock family.

[146] AMS, VII 10/27–40, records of loans to merchants, 1555–63.

[147] At Schwäbisch Hall, from the late fifteenth century until the Smalkaldic War (1546–47), service of the public debt normally required only 4–5% of civic expenditures. Kreil, *Stadthaushalt von Schwäbisch Hall*, pp. 104–113. At Basel during the same period, the service of the public debt required an average of one-quarter of all public outlays. Josef Rosen, "Prices and Public Finance in Basle," *Economic History Review,* 2nd series, 25 (1972), 1–17, here at pp. 6–8. The situation was much worse at Cologne, where the Neusser War (1474) drove the public debt to a fantastic level. Despite major efforts to reduce the debt and debt service costs, the latter still ran in 1513 to 93,830 Mark or

The state debt thus probably played a lesser role in the economic life of such towns than it did in the city-states of North Italy.[148] Some German cities nonetheless carried very sizeable public debts. Basel, for example, paid 8,000–10,000 lb./yr. in debt service during the later fifteenth and the first half of the sixteenth century.[149]

One surviving document *may* yield a picture of the size of the public debt at Strasbourg and the social complexion of its owners during the Reformation generation. It is a small book of twenty-two pages in which are noted thirty-five dates between St. John the Baptist's Day, 1533, and the same day one year later (the fiscal year, running from summer fair to summer fair) and with lists of names and sums under each date. Though untitled, the book is probably a register either of subscribers to a loan, in which case the sums are principal sums, or of payments of interest on loans, in which case the sums are interest. If the former, then the principal involved is the total of the sums listed, or about 9,697 fl.; but in the latter case the principal represented by 9,697 fl. at 4% would be about 242,400 fl., assuming a standard rate of interest.[150] If the entries represent payments of interest, the principal sum is so large—nearly a quarter of a million florins—that the borrower can only have been the civic regime. The figure itself is a believable one for the size of the standing public debt at Strasbourg. Though we have no direct evidence about the level of permanent debt there, the contemporary public debt of Basel was between a fifth and a quarter of a million pounds (based on debt service charges of 8,000–10,000 lb./yr.), or about one-fifth smaller than a quarter of a million florins (1 Strasbourg fl. = 1.1956 Basel lb.).[151] Basel was slightly smaller than Strasbourg and had a similarly structured economy; and the figure of 242,425 fl. is therefore not an unreasonable sum for the public debt of Strasbourg in

---

about 23,450 rhenish florins, while in the same year another 54,953.4 Mark (= 13,738 fl.) were spent for debt redemption. Here, as apparently in most South German towns, the popularity of life-term annuities (*Leibrente, Leibgedinge*) declined drastically during the second quarter of the sixteenth century in favor of perpetual rentes (*Erbrente*). Hermann Kellenbenz, "Die Finanzen der Stadt Köln 1515–1532," in *Wirtschaftliche und soziale Strukturen im saekularen Wandel. Festschrift für Wilhelm Abel zum 70. Geburtstag,* eds. Ingomar Bog, *et al.,* 3 vols. (Hannover, 1974), II, 366–376, here at pp. 366–368, 373–374.

[148] See Becker, "Some Common Features of Italian Urban Experience," pp. 192–195.

[149] Rosen, "Prices and Public Finance in Basle," p. 8.

[150] AMS, IV 98/1 (1533–34), analyzed in Appendix D below.

[151] Rosen, "Prices and Public Finance in Basle," p. 8; Auguste Hanauer, *Etudes économiques sur l'Alsace ancienne et moderne,* 2 vols. (Paris–Strasbourg, 1876), I, 497, 499, figures for values of moneys of account from 1532 and 1533 respectively.

1533–34. Annual service charges on the public debt in German cities of this era commonly absorbed 25–30% of the budget and sometimes went much higher.[152]

Several features of the register speak for its being a record of interest payments. First, the dates are all major feast days, with the largest numbers of entries grouped under feast days on which debts were commonly paid, such as St. John the Baptist's Day in the summer and St. Martin's Day in the fall.[153] Secondly, the regular spacing of the entries through the year suggests a record of obligations rather than a (more irregularly spaced) record of subscriptions. Thirdly, most of the sums are multiples of 4 fl., which at 4% interest would yield principal sums in multiples of 100 fl., a common feature of redeemable annuities. Fourthly, the very large share (19.9%) held by or paid to widows and groups of heirs suggests relatively old debt, perhaps even standing debt. Fifthly, payments to two persons, Clara Eckhart and the widow of Andres Degenbeck, a goldsmith, are noted "zu lypgeding," meaning that they are life-annuities (*Leibgedinge*) and thus are definitely long-term financial commitments.[154] Sixthly, a considerable number of names appear more than once, under different dates, suggesting multiple payments of interest rather than multiple subscriptions to a loan. Each of these features speaks for the register being a record of interest paid or owed to individuals and corporations—in which case the borrower was almost certainly the civic regime.

Several other features tell against this interpretation of the register. The total sum of 9,536 fl. is very close to a common size (10,000 fl.) of Landgrave Philip of Hesse's borrowings at Strasbourg. The difficulty in identifying the register with a subscription list to a Hessian loan is that none of Philip's loans fits the register chronologically. He borrowed 10,000 fl. at 6% in June 1530, 10,000 fl. in March 1534, another 10,000 in June 1534, and 15,000 in the same month.[155] The near absence of a

---

[152] Winfried Trusen, "Zum Rentenkauf im Spätmittelalter," *Festschrift für Hermann Heimpel*, II, 140–158, here at p. 158.

[153] There are 252 entries distributed among 35 dates, with the greatest numbers falling on Martini (November 11) 26, Johannis Baptistae (June 24) 24, Urbani (May 25) 21, Georgii (March 12) 19, Purificationis Mariae (February 2) 12, Weihnachten (December 25) 11, and Gregorii (March 12) 10.

[154] AMS, IV 98/1, fols. 2ʳ, etc. Kreil, *Stadthaushalt von Schwäbisch Hall,* pp. 107–108, finds that *Leibgedinge*—annuities for the life of the purchaser (or lives of purchaser and spouse)—declined in popularity in this generation. See note 147 above.

[155] *PCSS,* II, 210n2, 210, 215n1; HStAM, PA 2915, *passim.*

public subscription also tells against this being a register of one of the Hessian loans. "Near absence," because there is a puzzling entry which forms the strongest argument against the booklet being a record of service payments on the public debt: on the feast of St. Matthew the Apostle (24 February), 1534, "Jtem der statt Strasburg 12 fl."[156] The sum is a bagatelle for the civic treasury, but it is improbable that the regime would borrow from itself.

Whether a record of loans or of interest, whether the borrower was the civic regime or another power, the register of 1533–34 provides a look at the relative ranking of Strasbourg lenders and an important insight into the corporate and individual sources of interest-seeking capital at Strasbourg in the middle of the Reformation generation. Table 12 summarizes the shares of corporate and individual lenders. Except for the absence of any significant participation by the civic treasury, the corporate share in the register is not much lower than in the loans to the counts of Mörs–Saarwerden (35.2% and 40.4% respectively). But the composition of the corporate share is here quite different. Foremost in the list are the collegial chapters (New St. Peter, Old St. Peter, St. Thomas), the convents (Carthusians, Commandery of St. John, St. Magdalena, St. Clara auf dem Wörth, St. Catherine) and the endowed corporation for construction and maintenance of the cathedral (*Unserer Lieben Frauen Werk*). The Great Hospital is well represented, as are nearly all of the religious houses—most of which had been dissolved during the later 1520s and now existed only as funds under civic control.[157] This in itself suggests that the registers record long-term (probably civic) debt rather than princely debt of some sort. Several extra-urban ecclesiastical corporations are represented, such as those of Haslach and Surburg, along with the beguines "im Giessen," and the bakers' confraternity. Among the secular corporations are the "Gesellschaft zum grossen Spiegel" (of the guild Zum Spiegel) and the civic poor house (*Elendenherberge*).

Nearly two-thirds (65.4%) of the sums recorded belong to individuals

---

[156] AMS, IV 98/1, fol. 16ᵛ.

[157] The history of the properties of the convents is one of the important untold stories in this generation. The funds were assigned to various civic schools and welfare institutions, but they also tended to serve as a financial reserve for the civic regime and were called upon for contributions in times of need. See Winckelmann, *Fürsorgewesen*, for details. The use of such funds to support the schools may be studied in the school accounts recently discovered at St. Thomas and provisionally catalogued as AST, Supplementa.

Table 12

Lenders of money at Strasbourg, 24.VI.1533–24.VI.1534

Class of Lender	Sum (%)	Principal*	No.
(a) Corporations			
Chapters and Churches	1,236 fl. (12.8%)	30,900 fl.	15
Religious Houses	1,656 fl. (17.1%)	41,400 fl.	16
Other	459 fl. (4.7%)	11,475 fl.	6
Subtotal	3,352 fl. (34.6%)	83,775 fl.	37
(b) Individuals and Families			
Nobles and Patricians	4,796 fl. (49.5%)	119,900 fl.	75
Merchant and Guild			
Rentiers	1,118 fl. (11.5%)	27,950 fl.	29
Other Guildsmen	431 fl. (4.5%)	10,775 fl.	15
Subtotal	6,345 fl. (65.4%)	158,625 fl.	119
Total	9,697 fl. (100.0%)	242,400 fl.	156

Source: AMS, IV 98/1. *Principal, if "sums" listed are payments of interest at 4%.

or families, including a number of groups of heirs. The really big figures all belong to patricians. All the persons listed at more than 100 fl. (nine men, three women, and two groups of children) are nobles and patricians, except for Daniel Mieg, a wealthy rentier–guildsman. These fourteen leaders account for more than one-third of the individual total. Another third of the individual total is accounted for by those in the 51–100 fl. range (twenty-four men, three women, and two groups of children), of whom all but ten are patricians. The non-patricians in these first two groups (over 100 fl. and 51–100 fl.) are nearly all from well-known families: Daniel, Andreas, Carl, and Jerg Mieg, Conrad Joham, Wernher König, and the heirs of Jacob Gerbott (d. 1519). In these two upper groups, then, forty-two (36.5%) of the individuals listed are registered for more than two-thirds (68.8%) of the total sum for individuals.

Hans Bock von Gerstheim's name stands first in the non-corporate list, the only person who is listed for more than 200 fl. (at 348 fl.). Next in this list are Bernhard Wurmser and Bernhard Ottfriedrich, while Peter Ellenhart and Jacob and Hans Sturm also stand above 100 fl. These are all patrician privy councillors. The share of the contemporary and future privy councillors in the register is, in fact, very large: twenty-two of them (patricians and guildsmen) held 1873 fl. or nearly one-fifth (19.6%) of the entire sum and nearly one-third (30.3%) of the total for individuals. Another fifth (19.9%) belongs to widows (11.1%) and groups of children (8.8%). In summary, this register reveals the concentration of liquid wealth in the collegial chapters and the religious houses (most of them now only financial accounts) and documents the relatively large amounts of liquid capital in the hands of the leading patrician families and a few wealthy guild families. More than one-fifth (20.9%) of the privy councillors included in Appendix A below are entered in this single register. If the register records interest payments, then some of the capital sums are handsome indeed, such as Hans Bock von Gerstheim's 7,700 fl. The predominance of the patricians over the big merchants is easily explained by merchants' need for working capital in their firms. Whichever interpretation of the register is correct, it confirms the impression of aristocratic wealth, especially on the part of the patricians.

F. CONCLUSION

The social and economic integration of the two fractions of Strasbourg's ruling aristocracy was a fabric woven of many threads: of feudal bonds and seigneurial lordship, of urban proprietorship and rural landlordship, of estate mobility and intermarriage, of banking to lords and usury to peasants. The rentiers and rich merchants in the guilds emerge as Constofler *de potentia,* the next levy of families climbing up from the guilds into the Constofeln. Families which never became Constofler as well as those who did shared most of the basic economic and social interests of the rentier patriciate. They held fiefs, bought urban and rural property, lent money at interest in sums both large and small, and married with some regularity into Constofler and rural noble families. The estate barrier which separated them from the patriciate was, during this age at least, thoroughly permeable.

Strasbourg's ruling class before and during the Reformation generation was thus a class of creditors, vassals, landlords, and usurers, tied together by marriages, some of whose members engaged in trade. Their investments and properties spilled far over the boundaries of the civic territory, and their purchase of peasant and noble debt extended their vision far beyond the immediate region and into the courts and capitals of neighboring principalities. To the service of these relatively far-flung interests, as well as in the maintenance of a healthy climate for persons like themselves at home, their control of the urban regime was indispensable.

CHAPTER FIVE

THE OLIGARCHY OF STRASBOURG AND ITS STRUCTURES OF POLITICAL DOMINATION

The political machinery through which the rentier-merchant aristocracy ruled Strasbourg may fairly be called an oligarchy, a "government
where only the few have a voice and where among these the rich tend to
hold the most authoritative position."[1] The office-holding members of
these families formed the political elite of the town,[2] that sector of the
aristocracy that gave its time and energies to public affairs in the interests
of the whole, their families, or themselves. In the following pages on the
structure and practices of the oligarchy of Reformation Strasbourg, an
analysis of the institutional structure of political power introduces a
detailed analytical treatment of the men who actually ruled the city.
Two questions guide the analysis: How was the city ruled? Who ruled
the city?

A. The Political Forms—The Constitution

The constitution of Strasbourg at the end of the Middle Ages was a
variant of the type found in most South German towns where guild
revolts had been largely successful.[3] The permanent regime was made
up of an executive, a senate, and several privy councils,[4] plus an assembly.

---

[1] Martines, *Social World of the Florentine Humanists*, p. 387.

[2] Walter Jacob (*Politische Führungsschicht*, p. 6) employs the term "politische Führungsschicht," which implies a stratum of the population, whereas the members of the
government were actually representatives of wider family units and social groups and
were in no sense a *Schicht*. By "political elite" I mean what is often called a "classe
politique." See Eitel, *Die oberschwäbischen Reichsstädte*, p. 156.

[3] The classic constitutional study is Hans Planitz, *Die deutsche Stadt im Mittelalter*,
2nd ed. (Weimar, 1965), see esp. pp. 295–342. For the later Middle Ages, there are
excellent surveys in *La ville*, vol. 1: Philippe Dollinger, "Les villes allemandes au moyen
âge: leurs statuts juridique, politique et administratif," pp. 445–466; and Jean Schneider,
"Les villes allemandes au moyen âge: compétence administrative et judiciaire de leurs
magistrats," pp. 467–516.

[4] The term "regime" here is a collective designation for the permanent part of the
political system; and I prefer it to the term "Magistrat" used by most writers on
Strasbourg (e.g., Chrisman, *Strasbourg*, pp. 23, 23n1). The basic studies of Strasbourg's
constitution in this era are: Otto Winckelmann, "Strassburgs Verfassung und Verwaltung im 16. Jahrhundert," *ZGO*, 57 (1903), 493–537, 600–642; and Ulrich Crämer,

The office of Stettmeister, held by four of the ten incumbent patrician senators and rotated at three-month intervals during the year, brought prestige rather than direct power to its holders. The real head of the regime was the Ammeister, an office from which the patricians were barred. The Senate & XXI elected the six Ammeister, each of whom once elected served one year of a sexennium as ruling Ammeister and five as Altammeister. An Ammeister normally served for life, and the ruling Ammeister presided over the Senate and the Senate & XXI, though not over the privy councils individually.[5] The Ammeister was also barred from the privy council of the XV. He dined in public in his own guild hall (from 1522 at the hall of the guild Zur Luzern) and in all things stood at the head of the regime. In all things, that is, except in the formula at the head of official documents: "Meister und Rat," which referred, as of old, to the Stettmeister.[6]

The Senate (grosser Rat) was much the oldest college of the regime and had once been the commune's supreme deliberative body.[7] During the sixteenth century it sat on Tuesday and Thursday mornings as the high court of the city and on Monday, Wednesday, and Saturday mornings in joint session with the privy councils, forming with them the highest legislative body of the city (Rat und XXI). The thirty senators, ten patricians (including the four Stettmeister) and twenty guildsmen, held office for two years, at the completion of which each was ineligible for one year. Half the body was renewed each January; and the old senators

---

Verfassung und Verwaltung Strassburgs. See also Chrisman, Strasbourg, pp. 14–27, and the sketch on p. 25. A good brief guide to the evolution of the constitution is Dollinger's "La évolution politique des corporations strasbourgeoises à la fin du moyen âge," pp. 127–135.

[5] I retain the terms "Ammeister" and "Stettmeister" because the lack of consistent Latin equivalents makes it difficult to render them satisfactorily into English. Jacob Sturm translated them as "Magister scabinorum seu burgmaister" and "Magister civitatis" respectively (AMS, VI 491/3), a usage met with elsewhere in sixteenth century documents (e.g., in a document inserted between AMS, XXI 1540, fols. 194 and 195). Also common is the term "consul" for the Ammeister, undoubtedly under humanist influence. See Jean Sturm, Quarti Antipappi tres partes priores (Neustadt an der Hardt, 1580), p. 6.; Théodore de Bêze, Icones (Geneva, 1580), fol. Fii; TQ Strassburg, II, 5 l. 25. Heinrich Pantaleon, Prosopographiae heroum (Basel, 1566), p. 361, uses "consul" for the Ammeister and "praetor" for the Stettmeister. An example of the rare use of "dictator" for the Ammeister is in the colophon of a book printed in 1505, in Schmidt, Histoire littéraire, II, 397, No. 216.

[6] Hermann, Notices historiques, II, 32–33; Crämer, Verfassung und Verwaltung Strassburgs, pp. 20–21.

[7] Ibid., pp. 25–26; "Senate" here from the usual Latin "senatus."

selected the new patrician senators, while the new guild senators were appointed by the ruling Schöffen of each guild.

The heart of the regime by the later fifteenth century were the two privy councils, the XV for domestic affairs and the XIII for war and diplomacy.[8] The XIII also exercised appeals jurisdiction and high civil and criminal jurisdiction within certain limits. The XV, established 1433, was composed of five patricians and ten guildsmen, none of whom might be Ammeister, Altammeister, or XIIIers. The province of the XV was the entire internal life of the city, except for military affairs, including the courts, finance, supervision of the guilds, police, the inspectorates, and the entire system of economic regulation.[9] The senior privy council, the XIII, functioned since the first half of the fifteenth century as the inner ruling circle of the city. In it sat four patricians (normally all of them Stettmeister or Altstettmeister), four of the five Altammeister, and four other guildsmen, plus the ruling Ammeister.

The XXI in the formula "Senate & XXI" were not a separate council.[10] The term appears normally as a collective name for the XV and the XIII, plus three or four extra "simple members of the XXI" (ledige XXIer), when they all met in common session with the Senate. The origin of the term is obscure,[11] but during the sixteenth century there were still designated each year "die Herren der Einundzwanzig." The solution to this riddle seems to be as follows. The two privy councils, plus the normal three to four simple XXIers, made thirty-one or thirty-two persons, depending on whether or not the ruling Ammeister was already a XIIIer. Subtracting the four Stettmeister and the ruling Ammeister leaves twenty-six or twenty-seven persons. It was also the custom to have five or six members of the privy councils in the Senate each year, and if they are subtracted, the total of twenty-one or twenty-two remains. This figure, attained by counting only those XVers, XIIIers, and simple XXIers who were neither Stettmeister, the ruling Ammeister, nor senators in a given year, agrees with the extant lists.[12]

---

[8] Ibid., pp. 21–24.

[9] Schmoller, "Strassburg zur Zeit der Zunftkämpfe," in his Deutsches Städtewesen, pp. 214–215.

[10] Crämer, Verfassung und Verwaltung Strassburgs, pp. 24–25.

[11] Otto Winckelmann, "Zur Entstehungsgeschichte der Strassburger Einundzwanzig und Dreizehen," ZGO, 75 (1921), 112–114.

[12] I devised this explanation using the list of "Dye Herren die ain vnd zwantzig" for 1540 (AMS, XXI 1540, before fol. 1), which lists 22 persons, checked against my records of known members of the XV and XIII and the lists of senators by Hatt, pp. 206–207; and it is supported by analyses of the lists of the XXI at the heads of AMS,

"Die Herren der Einundzwantzig" were thus all those privy councillors who held no other office in a given year by virtue of which they would have a right to sit in the sessions of the Senate & XXI. In practice, in most years all four of the Stettmeister would be members of the XIII or the XV. Once selected as a simple XXIer, one served in the privy councils for life. The XVers and XIIIers were coopted for life from lower bodies, so that the normal sequence of a successful political career at Strasbourg was: service in minor offices; a term or two in the Lesser Senate (*kleiner Rat*), a body with purely judicial functions; one or more terms in the Senate; simple XXIer; XVer; and XIIIer. In the meantime a patrician might become a Stettmeister and a guildsman Ammeister.

The institution least well understood in the modern literature is the assembly of the 300 Schöffen of the guilds.[13] By 1500 or so, conforming to a law of 1433, each guild had fifteen Schöffen, whose membership largely overlapped, but was not identical, with that of the *Zunftgericht,* the everyday ruling body of the guild.[14] Here, as in the privy councils, the principles of cooptation and life-tenures were the norm. A running list of the Schöffen of the guild Zum Spiegel, 1554–75, suggests that each corporation of Schöffen changed its membership completely every 18–20 years, which provided a political continuity analogous to that of the privy councils.[15] At the head of each extant list of guild Schöffen stand the names of the guild's privy councillor(s), who was normally the president (*Oberherr*) of the guild as well, and the current and former senators.[16]

XXI 1542 and 1543. I then read that Winckelmann ("Strassburgs Verfassung," pp. 535–536) had come to the same explanation but doubted its validity because he could find no reason for the practice. Nor can I. The size of the XXI was fixed at a maximum of 32 persons in the mid-fifteenth century (Eheberg, pp. 446–447, No. 212). Hermann (*Notices historiques,* II, 32) notes that by 1542 there were complaints against allowing privy councillors to sit in the Senate. It was even the custom until around 1520 to permit one Altammeister—one who was not a XIIIer?—to sit as a senator. The latest example I have found is that of Altammeister Andreas Drachenfels (PROSOPOGRAPHY, No. XVII), senator from the guild Zur Möhrin in 1521. Hatt, p. 193

[13] Crämer, *Verfassung und Verwaltung Strassburg,* p. 27.

[14] Dollinger, "Note sur les échevins de Strasbourg au moyen âge," pp. 70–72. Chrisman's contention (*Strasbourg,* p. 24), that the Schöffen were "popularly elected from the craft guilds," is wrong; for they were coopted by their peers.

[15] BNUS, Ms. 626, fols. 158^v–159^r, interesting notes in a *Stadtrechtsbuch,* written by Jerg Ingold (d. 1576/77) (*ibid.,* fol. 165^r), son of Friedrich Ingold and Margarethe Arg and Schöffe of the guild zum Spiegel.

[16] There are two complete lists of guild Schöffen for this generation. The first (AST 45, fols. 485ff.) was drawn up in 1533 for use of the door guards during the synod; and the other (AMS, IV 48) was drawn up on 7–8 June 1552 and is now bound into a small volume.

The guild Schöffen had no formal constitutional role except when they were called together—all 300 of them—to the city hall (*Pfalz*) on the Martinsplatz (now place Gutenberg) to hear and vote on a proposition put to them by the regime. The proposition might contain a new law (such as that forbidding burials within the city, 9 February 1527), a request by a foreign power for a loan (such as that to the Hapsburg, 2 September 1525), a major change in domestic institutions (such as the abolition of the Mass, 20 February 1529), or a new external treaty (such as the Swiss alliance, 5 January 1530).[17] Such a decision was said to be taken "bey Scheffel und amman," that is, by the Schöffen under the presidency of the Ammeister—the most solemn form of legislative activity and the one major constitutional act from which the Constofler were excluded.

In a city of 20,000 or so inhabitants, the assembly of 300 guild Schöffen was the largest body that ever took part in formal political decisions. The "democratization" of the guild movement had never reached the point of producing an assembly of all citizens, and the oligarchy of the sixteenth century had no intention of encouraging movements in that direction. When, on 30 August 1548, a number of Schöffen asked that the proposition (acceptance of the Interim of Augsburg) be put to the entire citizen body, the regime replied: "But if it were to be brought before the commune, that would be an innovation, for it has never before happened that the Schöffen referred something to the commune; but the decision in weighty affairs has always been taken by the Schöffen and the Ammeister (*bey schoffel und aman*)."[18]

Voting on propositions was not the only function of the Schöffen, nor were they always assembled in the Pfalz. Sometimes they gathered in their own guild halls to hear an announcement of policy or an admonition to obey a certain law, which they were then to pass on to their fellow guildsmen. Frequently during the Reformation era the Schöffen were told to admonish the guildsmen to obey the prohibition against seeking foreign military service.[19] The Schöffen were sometimes polled when the regime wanted their opinion on an issue or wanted to use them as a sample of public opinion.[20] Finally, the plea that every important matter

---

[17] Specklin, *Collectanées*, No. 2281; AMS, II 93/3.

[18] *PCSS*, IV, 1065, No. 818.

[19] As, for example, on 24 November 1530, for which the announcement "durch zwen verordenten von den alten herrn" (= the XIII) exists in Peter Butz's hand in AMS, II 93/4.

[20] The notable poll of January 1547 is analyzed in Chapter VIII below, pp. 259–269.

had to be put to the Schöffen was a useful delaying tactic for Strasbourg's diplomats during the negotiations of the Reformation generation.[21]

It is sometimes assumed that the calling together of the Schöffen was a fairly unusual act during this era, limited to crisis situations such as the Peasants' War, the abolition of the Mass, the Swiss alliance, or the Interim of Augsburg. In fact, the Schöffen were called together with some regularity and for rather more ordinary matters. Between 16 August 1540 and 8 August 1548, for example, the Schöffen met at least eleven times, for matters ranging from an announcement of the episcopal election of 1541 to approval of a new law on the taxation of inheritances (1548).[22]

In the ordinary political life of the town, the Schöffen played a crucial role. Every privy councillor, every senator, and every ex-senator was a Schöffe of one of the guilds—excepting always the Constofler. They and their colleagues formed the normal nexuses of mediation between the regime and the guildsmen of the town—mediating the lines of political control downward and the lines of information upward from the masters to the regime. These processes were neither so formal nor so regular as they may sound in an analytical description, especially not in a small city of 20,000 or so inhabitants, in which everyone knew who was a man of property, influence, and respect, and who was not. The three hundred Schöffen of the guilds were certainly, at least in the vast majority, such men.

B. The Oligarchical Trend and the Descending Lines of Control

One aspect of the growth of oligarchy was the increasing concentration of officeholding. Miriam U. Chrisman has offered the first quantitative evidence for the trend at Strasbourg during the first half of the

---

[21] *PCSS*, I, 550, No. 844, Claus Kniebis and Conrad Joham to Peter Butz, Basel, (19 November?), 1530: "wir von den trien stetten unserm bevel noch mit den gesandten des landgrafen uns vereiniget und alle zugesagt, wie die angestellet notel des verstands das vermag, doch das wir von Straszburg uns das uf unserer schoffel bewilligung vorbehalten, und angezeigt, warumb wir die schoffel nit haben vorhin umb bewilligung angesucht." The subject here is the Strasbourg–Swiss–Hessian alliance, and the "notel des verstands" is the proposed alliance agreement.

[22] BNUS, Ms. 626, fols. 163ᵛ–164ʳ, lists assemblies on 16 April 1540, 19 June and 12 August 1541, 10 February 1543, 14 February 1544, 19 July 1546, ? February, 19 April, and 24 October 1547, and 8 August 1548. The last assembly noted approved a new law on taxation of foreign inheritances and inheritances by resident foreigners (text on fol. 143ᵛ). For the basis of the following paragraph, see Chapter III above, pp. 118–120.

sixteenth century, based on a study of the offices of Stettmeister and senator over a forty-year period:

> ... analysis of the membership of the Magistrat at ten-year intervals from 1508 to 1548 shows a high degree of stability and continuity in the membership of the Stettmeister and Rat, from whom all positions in the major committees were filled. The same men were elected and reelected for periods of ten to twenty years.[23]

Chrisman's findings should be viewed in the light of the fact that frequent service in the Senate was no very reliable index of an individual's political importance. On the contrary, the really successful prominent politicians tended to serve only a few terms in the Senate before moving on to the privy councils.[24]

Chrisman's figures for the office of Stettmeister do not give precisely the concentration of holders of the office, because senior patrician members of the privy councils sometimes ceased to serve as Stettmeister well before the ends of their careers.[25] The trend toward concentration in this office and that of Ammeister was nonetheless real enough and began much earlier than Chrisman suggests. Table 13 shows the average number of terms served by Stettmeister and Ammeister from the mid-fourteenth until the mid-sixteenth century. The Stettmeister and Ammeister of the Reformation era tended to serve on the average twice as many terms as their fourteenth-century predecessors had done. The figures for the Stettmeister certainly reflect the shrinkage of the patriciate, but those for the Ammeister are not open to a similar qualification. The

---

[23] Chrisman, *Strasbourg,* p. 309, and her tables on pp. 311–317, based on the lists published by Hatt. Fundamental on the growth of oligarchy in the South German free cities is Naujoks, *Obrigkeitsgedanke, Zunftverfassung und Reformation,* esp. chapter 1. The connection of the oligarchical trend to the Reformation in the cities was well formulated by Gierke: "dies Alles stellte es ausser Zweifel, dass die Reformation mit der religiösen Selbstbestimmung die bürgerliche Selbstverwaltung nicht zurückführen, sonder vielmehr selbst das obrigkeitliche Princip in ausserordentlichem Grade verstärken sollte." *Das deutsche Genossenschaftsrecht,* I, 702. For more recent views, see Otto Brunner, "Souveränitätsproblem und Sozialstruktur in den deutschen Reichsstädten der frühen Neuzeit," *Neue Wege der Verfassungs- und Sozialgeschichte,* 2nd ed., pp. 294–321, reprinted from *VSWG,* 50 (1963), 329–360; and Erich Maschke, "'Obrigkeit' im spätmittelalterlichen Speyer und in anderen Städten," *ARG,* 57 (1966), 7–23.

[24] The PROSOPOGRAPHY contains many examples: Jacob Sturm served one year; Claus Kniebis, two years; Martin Herlin, one year; Hans Bock von Gerstheim, one year; Jacob Meyer, two years.

[25] Jacob Sturm and Egenolf Röder von Diersburg did not serve as Stettmeister in 1538–48 and 1540–48 respectively; but both men resumed the office in 1549, due to the shortage of eligible patricians.

Table 13

Average numbers of terms (=years) served by Stettmeister and Ammeister of Strasbourg,
1332/49–1550

Period	Average Number of Terms
(a) Stettmeister	
1349–1419	2.4 terms
1420–1499	4.2 terms
1500–1550	7.0 terms
(b) Ammeister	
1332–1399	1.6 terms
1400–1449	2.4 terms
1450–1499	2.6 terms
1500–1550	3.2 terms

Source: Hatt, *Liste des membres du grand sénat de*
Strasbourg.

trend towards concentration was steady and was uninterrupted either by the events of 1419–20 or by the Reformation of the 1520s.

Far more important than these quantitatively summarizable symptoms of the growth of oligarchy were the structural features of the regime that strengthened the descending lines of control from the privy councils to all sectors of the civic administration. The supervision of the affairs of the guilds by the XV was very close, extending to the approval of new guild regulations and the confirmation of new Schöffen.[26] The XIII, for their part, gradually assumed direct control over the city's diplomatic agents and its spies.[27] But these were only the more general areas of privy conciliar control. Central to their power was the placement of one member of each council on the (mostly three-member) administrative boards which oversaw every aspect of the social and economic life of the city and its territory.[28] There were boards for the poorhouse (*Almosen-*

---

[26] Schmoller, *Strassburger Tucher- und Weberzunft,* pp. 484–486, is the best analysis; and there are examples in AMS, XXI 1546, fols. 607ʳ, 613ᵛ, 616ʳ, 624ʳ, 629ʳ, and 635ʳ–636ᵛ.

[27] I discuss this change in "Jacob Sturm of Strasbourg (1489–1553) and the Political Security of German Protestantism, 1526–1532," unpublished Ph.D. dissertation, University of Chicago (Chicago, 1968), pp. 180–181.

[28] On the competences of these and other boards, see Crämer, *Verfassung und Verwaltung Strassburgs,* pp. 44f. The *Almosenherren* for this period are listed by Winckelmann, *Fürsorgewesen,* I, 88, 88n3. There is a list of the *Carthauspfleger,* 1525–1771, in BLBK, Ms. Ortenau 1, fol. 92ʳ.

herren), the fair (*Messherren*), the arsenal (*Zeugherren*), and the hospitals (*Pfleger der Blatterhus, Spitalpfleger*); for the schools (*Scholarchen* or *Schulherren*), construction (*Bauherren*), and civic property (*Allmendherren*); for each district (*Amt*) of the civic territory (*Landherren, Landpfleger*); and since the Reformation for the religious houses (*Klosterherren, Pfleger* of individual houses), for each parish (*Kirchspielpfleger*), and for the suppression of the sects (*Wiedertäuferherren*). Every privy councillor would have to serve on several, and sometimes as many as five, of these boards, and some held their posts for very long periods of time. The post of chief curator (*Oberkirchenpfleger*) at New St. Peter, for example, was for thirty-seven years in the hands of only two men, both privy councillors: Bernhard Ottfriedrich (1531–37) and Mathis Pfarrer (1537–68).[29] The three original *Scholarchen* were appointed in 1526 and served an average of nearly thirty years apiece.[30] A regular part of ritual performed in the regime after the death of a privy councillor was the redistribution of his administrative positions.[31]

Temporary committees followed much the same pattern, although there was no uniform size for such bodies; they were *ad hoc* bodies to prepare reports for the Senate & XXI on specific questions. Most of the members were drawn from the privy councils. Every one of the temporary committees formed at each step of the ecclesiastical reform of the 1520s, for example, contained several privy councillors.[32]

The lines between the privy councils and the ruling Schöffen of the guilds are particularly interesting, because the guild Schöffen mirrored the regime in the growth of oligarchy. At Strasbourg as in other South

---

[29] Johann Philipp Lambs, *Die Jung St. Peter Kirche zu Strassburg* (Strasbourg, 1854), p. 102.

[30] The *Scholarchen* of this era are listed by Oseas Schad, "Kirchengeschichte" (AST, 70/1), fols. 52^r–53^r; and the curators of Unserer Frauen Haus by O. Schad, *Summum argentoratensium templum* (Strasbourg, 1617), pp. 106–109.

[31] Examples in AMS, XXI 1546, fols. 15^v, 52^r, 325^r, 651^v; AMS, XXI 1547, fols. 19^v, 20^v; AMS, XXI 1548, fols. 10^v, 154^v, 228^r, 252^r, 265^r, 293^r, 446^v, 468^v, 469^r, 471^r; AMS, XXI 1549, fols. 3^r, 3^v.

[32] Examples in Adolf Baum, *Magistrat und Reformation in Strassburg bis 1529* (Strasbourg, 1887), pp. 17n2, 28, 35n1, 37, 42n1, 46n4, 48n4, 54n2, 56n3, 67, 87n2, 91n2, 96n3, 103n5, 109, 114, 119n4, 173n5, 197n1. Other types of committees in *Ann. Brant,* Nos. 3541 (fortifications), 4634 (schools), 4728 (chancellery reorganization). *PCSS* contains dozens of examples of committees formed to advise the Senate & XXI on aspects of foreign policy and defense. There is also the appointment of four lay presidents of the synod of 1533 (*Ann. Brant*, No. 4992). For the first half of the 1520s, see the comprehensive summary by Jean Rott, "Magistrat et Réforme à Strasbourg: les dirigéants municipaux de 1521 à 1525," *RHPR*, 54 (1974), 103–114.

German towns of this period, the rule of wealth and the growing ascendance of small groups of well-to-do masters over the mass of artisans were quite normal phenomena.[33] The guild Schöffen were also the pool of non-patrician notables from whose ranks the regime was supplied with new members.[34] In normal times they acted as the paths of control reaching from the regime into the guilds and the nexuses of information and communication from the guilds into the halls of the Senate and the privy councils. Only once during the Reformation generation did the Schöffen really fail to perform their political function. During the struggle over the Interim of Augsburg (1548), the Schöffen, fearing the rebellious mood in their guilds, tried to persuade the regime to put the question to the entire commune, an unprecedented proposal which the regime immediately rejected.[35] The Schöffen, after all, stood in much more direct relationship to the guild memberships than did the privy councillors, and they were correspondingly subjected to more pressure.

One sector of the civic administration, the financial, was not administered directly by privy councillors. Historically the most sensitive sector of civic government,[36] the financial administration was in the hands of several three-member boards drawn from persons nominated by their guilds (*Zumänner*) but who were neither senators nor privy councillors. Young men coming into the government often began their careers, which they could begin at twenty-five (thirty if single), with a three-year term on the treasury board (*Drei auf dem Pfennigthurm*), the mint board (*Münzherren*), or the property tax board (*Drei auf dem Stall, Stallherren*). The first and third of these were by far the most important, and they were regularly staffed by young men of good family (and, presumably, sufficient education to supervise the keeping of accounts), one of the three members being replaced each year.[37] These men dealt

---

[33] See in general Hans Mottek, *Wirtschaftsgeschichte Deutschlands*, I, 5th ed. (Berlin, 1968), 201–212; Josef Kulischer, *Allgemeine Wirtschaftsgeschichte des Mittelalters und der Neuzeit*, 3rd ed., 2 vols. (Munich–Vienna, 1965), I, 213–215. For Strasbourg, see Schmoller, *Strassburger Tucher- und Weberzunft*, pp. 495–496; Rott, "Artisanat," pp. 138–143.

[34] During the assembly of 30 August 1548, the regime's spokesmen addressed the Schöffen as follows: "Diweil nun ir, die schöffel, die do die furnembsten der zunften und gemeinden seind, ..." *PCSS*, IV, 1066. See Winckelmann, "Strasburgs Verfassung," pp. 520–522.

[35] On 27 August 1548. AMS, XXI 1548, fol. 431ʳ; *PCSS*, IV, 1063–1065.

[36] Crämer, *Verfassung und Verwaltung Strassburgs*, pp. 127–132.

[37] List of the "Dreyer der Stadt Stall," 1466–1656, in AMS, VI 493/5. The list of the Drei auf dem Pfennigthurm (AMS, VI 493/6) has a gap for 1438–1598.

with the holiest of civic holies, the solvency of the commune, and a term on one of these boards was a common preparation for a political career.[38]

The sinews of Strasbourg's oligarchic regime were the institutions of life tenures and cooptation in the privy councils and in the ruling corporations of the guilds; and the links between the privy councillors and senators and their fellow Schöffen were perhaps the most vital in the entire system. To reach the privy councils, a Strasbourgeois had to have experience in the ruling group of his guild or Constofel, some service in the civic financial administration or other subordinate offices, and, normally, a few terms in the Senate. The very hallmark of this system was the careful screening of politicians, permitting very few into the inner councils of the regime and able to screen out any whose ambitions outran their willingness to obey the majority. Those few who did attain the privy councils, barely more than one hundred (105) during the years 1520–55, shared a background of experience in municipal affairs. They were amateurs, it is true, if "amateur" is taken as one who has no specialized formal training for his office. But experience they had, along with, barring occasional exceptions, membership in the city's social aristocracy.

C. THE POLITICAL MEANING OF GUILD REPRESENTATION

The discussion of the guild hierarchy (Chapter IV) established a rough distinction between the first eight and the other twelve guilds in the official order of precedence. The wealthy merchants and rentiers were concentrated in the guilds Zum Encker, Zum Spiegel, Zum Freiburg, and Zur Luzern. There were rich men in every guild, but fewer in the guilds at the bottom of the official list, especially the Fischer, the Gartner, and the Zimmerleute. Social distinctions were aggravated by a quite regressive tax system. As in all urban states ruled by the rich, the chief

---

[38] Though not indispensable. Jacob Sturm, for example, entered the Senate immediately after resuming his lay status. Some men served on both boards. Mathis Braun von Reichenberg, for example, was a *Stallherr* in 1537–39 and at the Pfennigthurm in 1547. AMS, 493/5; AMS, XXI 1546, fol. 651ᵛ. Friedrich Sturm, however, entered the Senate in 1520 and first served as *Stallherr* in 1544–46. AMS, VI 493/5; PROSOPOGRAPHY, No. XLI. The (lost) Stall records were confidential, and only the Senate & XXI could divulge information from them. ADBR, 3B 779/4, fols. 17ʳ–18ᵛ. The Pfennigthurm was just as secretive, and the protocols of the Senate & XXI note only the facts of their semi-annual reports. Examples in AMS, XXI 1541, fols. 283ᵛ (27 June 1541), 545ʳ⁻ᵛ (6 January 1542).

source of public revenue was indirect taxes, mainly excises on items of everyday consumption; but the direct property tax, the *Stallgeld,* was also rigged in favor of the rich.[39]

Despite these social distinctions, the really wealthy guild families tended to concentrate in a few guilds; and from this concentration stemmed a potential political problem. It was customary within the regime not to allow a concentration of privy council seats in a few guilds, just as patrician offices were not to be concentrated in the hands of one family. The ideal was that each guild should supply a privy councillor, a realizable ideal given twenty to twenty-one offices in the XV, XIII, and simple XXIers. If the principal had been followed strictly and honestly, the privy councils would have mirrored fairly closely the social complexion of the guild masters. That was not how the system worked.

A close study of the guild memberships of the Ammeister and other privy councillors of the Reformation era reveals a widespread political practice of invasion, that is, changes of guild memberships for political reasons. A young man automatically acquired (*wird zünftig*) at majority membership in his father's guild; but he was not bound to remain in it, and simultaneous membership in two guilds was also permitted.[40] What happened all through this era was that young men of well-to-do families joined a poorer guild (where, presumably, there was less competition for office because fewer men of leisure) before beginning a political career. Or, in the interests of maintaining the appearance of fair representation in the privy councils, new councillors would be ordered to join and represent some guild, almost always a poorer one, than their own. Table 14 presents the numbers of guild privy councillors during the years 1520–55, first by the guilds they represented in the regime and then by the guilds in which they had originally been inscribed. A comparison of columns (A) and (B) demonstrates the extent of the practice of invasion in the privy councils. Slightly more than half of

---

[39] Crämer, *Verfassung und Verwaltung Strassburgs,* pp. 128–132; and esp. Rott, "Artisanat," p. 142. The upper limit, above which the surplus was not taxed, was raised in 1504 from 16,000 fl. to 30,000 fl. The opposition of the urban rich to direct taxes seems to have been, for obvious reasons, a universal phenomenon. See Gene A. Brucker, *Florentine Politics and Society, 1343–1382,* Princeton Studies in History, 12 (Princeton, 1962), pp. 92–96.

[40] Double guild membership (*Doppelzünftigkeit*) was permitted at Strasbourg, as it was at Basel and at Freiburg im Breisgau. Maschke, "Verfassung und soziale Kräfte," p. 452; Gothein, *Wirtschaftsgeschichte des Schwarzwaldes,* p. 378.

Table 14

Members of the XV and XIII of Strasbourg, 1520–55, by guild represented (A) and by original guild membership (B)

Guild	(A) Guild Represented			(B) Original Guild		
	XV only	XIII	Total	XV only	XIII	Total
1. Zum Encker	2	4	6	2	6	8
2. Zum Spiegel	5	3	8	7	8	15
3. Zur Blume	1	4	5	1	4	5
4. Zum Freiburg	0	2	2	3	6	9
5. Tucher	3	2	5	1	1	2
6. Zur Luzern	3	2	5	3	3	6
7. Zur Möhrin	1	3	4	0	2	2
8. Zur Steltz	4	0	4	4	0	4
	19 (50.0%)	20 (57.1%)	39 (53.4%)	21 (55.3%)	30 (85.7%)	51 (69.9%)
9. Brotbecker	1	2	3	0	0	0
10. Kürschner	0	1	1	0	0	0
11. Küfer	1	1	2	1	1	2
12. Gerber	1	2	3	1	2	3
13. Weinsticher	3	2	5	3	0	3
14. Schneider	0	3	3	0	0	0
15. Schmiede	1	1	2	2	1	3
16. Schuhmacher	3	1	4	1	0	1
17. Fischer	4	0	4	4	0	4
18. Zimmerleute	1	1	2	1	0	1
19. Gartner	4	0	4	4	0	4
20. Maurer	0	1	1	0	1	1
	19 (50.0%)	15 (42.9%)	34 (46.6%)	17 (44.7%)	5 (14.3%)	22 (30.1%)
Totals	38 (100%)	35 (100%)	73 (100%)	38 (100%)	35 (100%)	73 (100%)

Source: PROSOPOGRAPHY, Appendix A.

those who reached the XIII and those who reached only the XV represented the eight upper guilds; but 85% of the XIIIers and 55% of the XVers had originally belonged to one of the eight upper guilds. These same eight guilds enrolled in 1537 only 37.3% of the citizenry, while the other twelve guilds, enrolling 62.7% of the citizens, supplied less than one-third (30.1%) of the privy councillors and only five of thirty-five XIIIers.[41] The domination of the privy councils by the upper guilds appears even more striking if only five of the top six guilds (excluding the Tucher) are considered: collectively they supplied 42.1% of the XVers, 77.1% of the XIIIers, and 58.9% of all privy councillors.

---

[41] Rott, "Artisanat," p. 158, gives the census of 1537, broken down by guild.

Table 15

Ammeister of Strasbourg (in annual terms), 1450–1580, by guild represented in office (A, B, D) and by original guild (C, E)

Guild	(A) 1450–1518	(B) 1519–49	(C) 1519–49 adjusted	(D) 1550–80	(E) 1550–80 adjusted
I. 1. Zum Encker	11	1	0	5	11
2. Zum Spiegel	11	0	8	1	2
3. Zur Blume	9	2	3	4	3
4. Zum Freiburg	9	5	12	0	4
5. Tucher	2	0	0	3	3
6. Zur Luzern	10	0	0	0	4
7. Zur Möhrin	8	3	3	1	4
8. Zur Steltz	3	0	0	0	0
	63 (87.5%)	11 (34.4%)	26 (81.2%)	14 (45.2%)	31 (100%)
II. 9. Brotbecker	0	4	1	2	0
10. Kürschner	0	5	0	0	0
11. Küfer	6	1	1	0	0
12. Gerber	0	0	0	0	0
13. Weinsticher	0	4	0	3	0
14. Schneider	2	3	0	5	0
15. Schmiede	0	4	4	0	0
16. Schuhmacher	1	0	0	4	0
17. Fischer	0	0	0	0	0
18. Zimmerleute	0	0	0	3	0
19. Gartner	0	0	0	0	0
20. Maurer	0	0	0	0	0
	9 (12.5%)	21 (65.6%)	6 (18.8%)	17 (54.8%)	0
Totals	72 (100%)	32 (100%)	32 (100%)	31 (100%)	31 (100%)

Even the reconstructed lists of the privy councillors are too incomplete for the period before 1520 to permit a conclusion about how recently the practices of voluntary and involuntary changes in guild memberships had begun. Fortunately there is a solution to this question in applying the same sort of analysis to the Ammeister. Table 15 shows the guilds represented by the Ammeister for the years 1450–1518, 1519–49, and 1550–80 [columns (A), (B) and (D)], while columns (C) and (E) adjust the figures for the second and third periods to show the known guild of origin of the Ammeister.[42] In the Ammeister's office

---

[42] The years 1519 and 1524, when ruling Ammeister died in office, are each counted twice. NSUG, Ms. Hist. 154, fols. 168ʳ–171ᵛ ("Verzeichnus was ein jede Zunfft fur Ammeÿster gehabt," through 1583), shows that running calculations were kept of the shares of the various guilds in the highest office. This list shows that during the period

invasion was a sixteenth century phenomenon. During the seventy years before 1519, the twelve lower guilds supplied the Ammeister during only nine years. In the Reformation generation, however, this pattern underwent an apparent, striking reversal, as the representation in office of the eight upper and twelve lower guilds was divided almost in proportion to the relative numbers of citizens each group enrolled (about 2:3). When the figures are adjusted to show guild of origin, the apparent democratization of the Ammeister's office is shown to have been a sham, a political concession probably to the popular movement of this generation, but only a political device. The practice was continued during the following generation, when the upper guilds actually produced all of the Ammeister—although fewer than half the Ammeister officially held office from one of the upper eight.

The essential aspects of this political pattern are that it was commonly practiced by the wealthy merchant families in rich guilds and that the transfers, with very few exceptions, took place downward in the guild hierarchy, presumably from richer to poorer guilds.[43] The two most dramatic examples are the Duntzenheim and Mieg families. The Duntzenheim belonged to the guild Zum Freiburg, from which Conrad, Sr. (1484), and Conrad, Jr. (1505, 11, 17, 23, 29), served as Ammeister; but the sons of Conrad, Jr., Batt and Jacob, became Ammeister from the Tailors' guild and the guild Zum Encker. The Mieg belonged to the guild Zum Spiegel, but Carl, Sr., and Carl, Jr., both represented the Tucher in the privy councils, and Daniel Mieg represented the Bakers. Caspar Rumler, an armigerous rentier, left the guild Zur Luzern, from

---

1349–1583, only two lesser guilds—Brotbecker (7) and Schneider (5)—had supplied more than three Ammeister each; three guilds had had only one each; and one guild, the Fischer, had never had an Ammeister. Manuscript lists of the Ammeister, often adorned with their arms, were commonly kept. Some of them are noted in Brady, "The Privy Councils," p. 78n3. Such a book, prepared for Martin Herlin (PROSOPOGRAPHY, No. XXXVII) and his son-in-law, Jacob Braun, is now in WLBS, Ms. 580 2⁰ (1333–1558). Two others are in the Bibliothèque Municipale de Sélestat, Mss. 386 (1333–1672) and 257 (1333–1719). See Paul Adam, *L'humanisme à Sélestat. L'école, les humanistes, la bibliothèque*, 2nd ed. (Sélestat, 1967), pp. 134–135. Such books are evidence of the pride families took in maintaining a record of holders of high office. On the other hand, the pride of being elected could well be tempered by a realistic view of the burdens of office. Nothing displays this better than the following story about Philips Hug von Ottenheim (PROSOPOGRAPHY, No. XLII) upon his election as Ammeister in 1520: "Man sagt das diser Ammeister, nach den er gekosen war, soll gasagt haben (dan er seiner handtwercks ein Metzger war) jn meinen jungen tagen hab ich bei meinen elteren den Schaff gehietet, jtzundt aber in meinen alter mass ich der geiss hieten." HABW, 2 Aug. 2⁰, fol. 99ʳ.

[43] The following examples are all documented in the PROSOPOGRAPHY.

which his father had served as Ammeister, to sit for thirty-eight years as privy councillor from the *Zimmerleutzunft* which enrolled the carpenters and the draymen. The extent of this invasion of the lower guilds by merchants and sons of merchants may be gauged by the fact that nearly one-third (31.4%) of all privy councillors from the guilds, 1520–55, was composed of men who at one time or another were members of the Merchants' guild (Zum Spiegel).

Certain guilds resisted political invasion better than did others. Most resistant of the lower guilds were the Fishermen, the Gardeners, the Masons, and the Coopers, and among the upper guilds the guild Zur Steltz, which enrolled the painters, goldsmiths, and other trades but was dominated by the goldsmiths.[44] Easily invaded guilds, on the other hand, were the Bakers, the Tailors, and the *Zimmerleute*. It is difficult to determine what controlled the relative vulnerability of a guild to invasion from the rich, but it may be supposed that guilds which were still composed of economically related trades would produce their own social hierarchy and hence their own political leadership. This certainly seems to have been the case with the Fishermen and Gardeners, neither of which was a craft guild and neither of which was invaded.

The manipulation of guild representation and guild membership enabled the wealthiest guilds and the big merchant families to dominate the regime while preserving the apparent corporate equality of guilds that conformed to the political traditions of the guild regime. It was a point at which the interests of individual families and the collective interest of the guild aristocracy coincided. Although this domination was not interrupted or disrupted by the Reformation, the popular movement of the 1520s is the most plausible reason why the regime began to strive for greater official equality of the guilds in the government. This suggests in turn that, whatever its ultimate political consequences, the Reformation of the 1520s tended to be antagonistic to the oligarchical trend in the regime and to force the regime to revive, however superficially, a connection with its broader political origins. As to the trend itself and the social complexion of the regime, there was little real change. This conclusion conforms in the main to recent findings on the political elites and the Reformation in the towns of Upper Swabia and at Zürich.[45]

---

[44] Every privy councillor from the guild Zur Steltz during this era was a goldsmith, except Ludwig von Mörssmünster (PROSOPOGRAPHY, No. LXV), who was a *Glasmaler*.
[45] Eitel, *Die oberschwäbischen Reichsstädte*, pp. 156–160; Jacob, *Politische Führungs-*

D.   The Men Who Ruled Reformation Strasbourg

On the bases of occupation, status, and other social criteria, the 105 privy councillors of Strasbourg, 1520–55, may be analyzed into social categories as shown in Table 16. Consolidation of the patrician and non-patrician rentiers and of all of the merchants and goldsmiths[46] yields a simplified picture: 42.9% rentiers, 36.2% merchants and goldsmiths, 14.3% artisans, and 6.7% others. The share of the merchants and rentiers in the privy councils as a whole thus attained nearly 80%. If the

Table 16

Social Composition of the Privy Councils of Strasbourg, 1520–55

Category		Number	Total (%)	Guildsmen (%)
1. Patrician rentiers		32	30.5	
2. Other rentiers		13	12.4	17.8
3. Merchant-bankers		15	14.3	20.5
4. Cloth merchants		8	7.6	11.0
5. Other merchants		11	10.5	15.1
6. Goldsmiths		4	3.8	5.5
7. Officials		2	1.9	2.7
8. Artisans		15	14.3	20.5
Gardeners	4			
Fishermen	3			
Saddler	1			
Weaver	1			
Blacksmith	1			
Tinsmith	1			
Windowmaker	1			
Leatherdyer	1			
Butcher	1			
Soapmaker	1			
9. Unknown		5	4.8	6.8
Total		105	100.0	100.0

Source: Prosopography, Appendix A.

---

schicht, pp. 39–53. The analyses are not entirely comparable, because Jacob treats such a short time span—only ten years. Eitel shows how thoroughly high offices were the province of the rich: the higher the office, the greater the gulf between the average wealth of incumbents and the average wealth of the guilds they represented (see the table on pp. 156–157). The Reformation, which won out in most of the towns Eitel studies, had no apparent effect on these patterns. Not entirely comparable, but leading to similar conclusions, is Rublack's treatment of Constance in *Einführung der Reformation in Konstanz,* pp. 106–113.

[46] Maschke, "Verfassung und soziale Kräfte," pp. 450–451. The four goldsmiths among the privy councillors are Veit Beinheim, Caspar Engelmann, Diebold Sebott, and Christoph II Städel. Prosopography, Nos. VI, XXVII, LXXXVI, LXXXVIII.

analysis is limited to the fifty-three men who reached the XIII, the picture is even more dramatic: 94.3% of the XIIIers were merchants and rentiers. The single "artisan" XIIIer, Michael Heuss, although his occupation is given as "soapmaker" ("seiffensieder"), was in fact a university man and a substantial propertyowner. Of the two XIIIers whose occupations are "unknown," Jacob Meyer (Masons) married a sister of Lux Messinger, a well-to-do cloth merchant, and was well enough educated to serve on the school board (*Scholarchen*), while the other, Philips Hug von Ottenheim, was the father of a merchant, Martin, who married into the prominent Braun family.[47] It is highly probable, therefore, that not a single artisan served in the XIII between 1520 and 1555.

The seventeen men who headed the regime as Ammeister between 1520 and 1555 show a heightened version of the same pattern. With the possible exceptions of Michael Heuss and Philips Hug von Ottenheim, they were all rentiers or merchants, and probably none of them were artisans. A guild regime in which no artisans sat in the inner councils is, of course, only an apparent paradox.

The distinction between rentiers and merchants among the guild aristocrats is not very exact. Among the rich families some members doubtless lived from investments and rents while others pursued trade and banking. Among the Mieg, for example, it is difficult to determine which members of the family were and which were not in business; but it is also difficult to believe that Daniel Mieg, who spent nearly his entire adult life in political office and was held to be one of Strasbourg's richest citizens, devoted very much of his time to trade.[48] Another borderline case is that of the Rotweil. They tended to marry into merchant families, such as the Geiger, the Hammerer, and the Ingold, but the career of Hans Ludwig von Rotweil (d. ca. 1531), who was for a while a territorial administrator, suggests that he was a rentier.[49]

If Michael Heuss, the university-educated soapmaker, is excluded, none of the genuine artisans in the privy councils ever entered the XIII. The men whose occupations tend to conform to the crafts which made up their guilds also tend, naturally enough, to be the artisans (or at least

---

[47] PROSOPOGRAPHY, Nos. XXXIX, LVIII, LV, XLII. Hug is now known to have been a butcher (Metzger) (see note 42 above).

[48] During an interrogation of suspected sectaries at Strasbourg on 22 October 1530, one Martin Suter of Freiburg/Br. was reported to have grumbled, "wo kumpt Daniel Mügen vnd Brechternn jr gut har?" *TQ Strassburg*, I, 274, No. 224; PROSOPOGRAPHY, No. LXIII.

[49] PROSOPOGRAPHY, Nos. LXXVIII, LXXIX.

to have artisan crafts as occupational designations). Such men are found most frequently representing the guilds which were most immune from political invasion, such as the Fishermen and the Gardeners, none of whose privy councillors ever rose higher than the XV or became Ammeister. But they tended to come from a few prominent families in such guilds. The Baldner family in the Fishermen's guild and the Drenss (or Trenss) family in the Gardeners' guild, who supplied two and three XVers respectively, seem to have stood at the head of their guilds' political structures.[50] Veltin Storck was a saddler from another politically active family, and his sons were rich enough to buy a patent of arms.[51] Hans Schütz, Sr., seems to have practiced two trades, leatherdyer and tailor, and was thus a genuine artisan; but his son, Hans, Jr., became a *Stubengeselle* of the guild Zum Spiegel.[52] Only one XVer, Claus Schetzel, bore clear marks of lower-class origin: he was often called by his patronymic, Bocks Claus, a typical nominative form among the peasants and the urban lower classes; and his death inventory reveals him to have been a man of very modest means and no real property. On the other hand, he certainly was not a "hab nits," for his daughter married a wealthy immigrant goldsmith, Erasmus Krug of Nuremberg.[53] Taken together, then, there is no doubt that the artisan privy councillors came from the upper social strata in their respective guilds, that they rarely if ever got into the XIII, and that they tended to emerge from the guilds that were least subject to political invasion by the rich.

Given the preponderance of wealthy men in the privy councils, it was natural enough that the councillors should also have been men of property. Table 17 displays the (admittedly incomplete) data of Appendix A on the feudal, urban (= Strasbourg), and other properties of the councillors. Although further research would pile up more data and probably eliminate the category of "none" altogether, it would not alter the basic picture provided by this table. The incidence of real property of all sorts was (expectedly) greater among the patricians than among the guildsmen. Fiefholding was also less frequent among the guildsmen,

[50] Hatt, pp. 395, 557.

[51] PROSOPOGRAPHY, No. LXXXIX; BMS, Ms. 936, fol 4ʳ, a grant of arms to Valentin and Peter Storck by Wilhelm Böcklin von Böcklinsau, 12 July 1579. Four Storck sat in the Senate between 1484 and 1591, including Veltin's father, his brother, Hans, and his son, Peter. Hatt, p. 550.

[52] PROSOPOGRAPHY, No. LXXXIV. The Schütz are esp. interesting, because Hans's niece was Katharina Schütz, wife of the preacher Mathis Zell.

[53] PROSOPOGRAPHY, No. LXXXII. On Erasmus Krug, Sr., see Fuchs, "Nuremberg et Strasbourg," p. 87; *idem*, "Une orfèvre," *passim*.

Table 17

Feudal, urban (=Strasbourg), and other properties of the privy councillors of Strasbourg,
1520–55

Type of Property	Patricians*	Guildsmen*	Total*
Fiefs	29 (90.6%)	16 (21.9%)	45 (42.9%)
Urban	23 (71.9%)	43 (58.9%)	66 (62.9%)
Other	27 (84.4%)	39 (53.4%)	66 (62.9%)
None	—	13 (17.8%)	13 (12.4%)

*100% = Patricians, 32; Guildsmen, 73; Total, 105.
Source: PROSOPOGRAPHY, Appendix A.

although the number of guild privy councillors who were vassals (16) is quite respectable. Isolation of the XIIIers in this table would simply heighten the picture by virtually eliminating the remaining contrasts between the patricians and the guildsmen. As in the preceeding analyses, the higher up the political structure, the more marked are the aristocratic characteristics.

Instructive also is a breakdown of the privy councillors by family. Most of the patricians came from a few families, more than half (56.2%) from the Sturm, the Böcklin von Böcklinsau, the Mülnheim, the Wurmser von Vendenheim, the Zorn zum Riet, and the Wetzel von Marsilien.[54] Eleven of the seventeen patrician XIIIers came from just four families: the Sturm (4), the Mülnheim (3), the Böcklin (2), and the Wurmser (2). This agrees quite closely with the analysis of all patrician officeholders (Chapter II), in which these four families, plus the Zorn and the Bock, were found to have formed the political core of the patriciate during the late fifteenth and the sixteenth centuries.[55] The most politically active family during the Reformation generation was the Sturm, who supplied nearly a fifth of all patrician privy councillors and nearly a quarter of the patrician XIIIers.[56]

Among the guild families, of course, the familial patterns are nothing like so neat. Most active were the Mieg (4) and the Duntzenheim (3), followed by those who supplied two apiece: Ingold, Münch, Prechter, Rotweil, Rumler, Baldner, and Drenss—a total of 21 of the 73 (28.8%).

---

[54] The Sturm lead with six, followed by the Böcklin and Mülnheim with three each, and the Wurmser, Zorn zum Riet, and Wetzel von Marsilien with two each.

[55] See Appendix B and Chapter II above, pp. 78–79.

[56] Six of thirty-two (19%) and four of seventeen (24%) respectively.

Eliminating the artisan families of Baldner and Drenss, who furnished no XIIIers, the remaining seven families supplied nearly two-fifths (38.2%) of the XIIIers. A rather clearer picture may be obtained through the isolation of two main clusters of guild aristocrats: a mercantile cluster consisting of the Prechter, Ingold, Duntzenheim, Gottesheim, Mieg, Ebel, Arg, Drachenfels, Messinger, Kips, Joham, and Braun families; and a tentier cluster of the Münch, Rotweil, Rumler, Hohenburg, Erstein *dit* Armbruster, Jörger, and Bietenheim families.[57] Nineteen privy councillors (18.1%) came from these two clusters, while twenty-three others (21.9%) were related to one or more families in the clusters. Twenty-nine (27.6%) of all privy councillors came from these two clusters, while twenty-three others (21.9%, including nine patricians) were related to one or more families in the clusters through their own marriages or those of a parent, sibling, or child. Of the guild privy councillors the two clusters supplied two fifths (39.7%) of all councillors and nearly three-fifths (55.9%) of the XIIIers.

Analysis by family groupings also uncovers another complex of guild families of great political significance during the Reformation era. The core was the Pfarrer–Kniebis–Herlin–Hammerer–Geiger cluster, to which were associated the Lindenfels, the Franck, the Leimer, the Messinger, and the Stösser. The male members of this complex were, except for Claus Kniebis (who was probably a rentier), cloth merchants and not big merchant-bankers.[58] Secondly, the complex produced a remarkable number of the most powerful guild politicians of the Reformation era. The families of this cluster were distinct from the wealthiest stratum in the guilds in several ways. They and their children rarely or never married into the patriciate or the rural nobility, although connections with the big merchants and guild rentiers—such as Pfarrer–Mieg, Franck–Mieg, and Messinger–Mieg marriages—did exist. These families seem to have been long settled at Strasbourg, unlike the *homines novi* who dominated international commerce and banking. The fact that the men were almost all cloth merchants also suggests that they were not so rich as the big merchants and that their trading activities were geographically more restricted—corresponding to the fairly limited market for Strasbourg cloth.[59] Although some of them, such as Mathis Pfarrer, Hans Hammerer, and Mattheus Geiger traded into Lorraine and

[57] Following the analysis in Chapter III above.
[58] See Chapter III above, pp. 111–112.
[59] See Chapter III above, p. 101.

perhaps even into France, none of them are known to have had agents in the major centers of international trade. Very few were armigerous, none ever rose into the patriciate, and none were fief-holders. These families thus represented a stratum of the guild aristocracy quite distinct from the big merchant-bankers.

The political record of the cloth-merchant complex was truly extraordinary. The ten families produced nine Ammeister who ruled for a total of twenty-nine years between 1520 and 1571,[60] and each of whom sat in the XIII. No family in the complex produced more than one prominent politician. A similar number of big merchant families, by contrast, produced fewer Ammeister but many more privy councillors, and it was common for a single family of this type to supply several prominent politicians—sometimes simultaneously. The Mieg, for example, for nearly a decade had three privy councillors, each from a different guild. From the cloth-merchant stratum came the "Zealots" of the 1520s, the men who led Strasbourg into the Evangelical camp. The group was certainly more remote in every way from the patriciate and the rural nobilities and their far-flung interests than were the privy councillors from rentier and big merchant families. The cloth merchants were correspondingly closer in political mentality, religious outlook, and economic interests to the broad mass of artisan and shopkeeper guild masters, whose world was defined by the city walls and the immediately surrounding region.

E.   The Virtues of Age and Education

The strength of sixteenth–century Strasbourg seemed to foreign observers to lie in its material attributes. Niccolò Machiavelli, writing during the first decade of the century, marvelled at the (probably overestimated) wealth of the city; and Michel de Montaigne, reflecting perhaps on Henry II's failure to take the city in 1552, called it "the strongest place" in Germany.[61]

---

[60] Claus Kniebis (1519, 25, 31, 37), Martin Herlin (1522, 28, 34, 40, 46), Mathis Pfarrer (1527, 33, 39, 45, 51, 57, 63), Hans Lindenfels (1532, 38, 44), Mattheus Geiger (1535, 41, 47), Simon Franck (1543), Lux Messinger (1552), and Georg Leimer (1556, 62).

[61] Niccolò Machiavelli, "Rapporto delle cose della Magna. Fatto questo di giugno 1508," *Arte della guerra et scritti politici minori*, ed. Sergio Bertelli (Milan, 1961), p. 202; Michel de Montaigne, "Journal de voyage en Italie par la Suisse et l'Allemagne en 1580–1581," in *Oeuvres complètes*, eds. Robert Barral and Pierre Michel (Paris, 1967),

The humanists of the pre-reform generation were less prosaic. Erasmus, who repaid his reception at Strasbourg in 1514 with a well-known piece of flattery, pretended to see in its citizens "Roman discipline, Athenian wisdom, and Spartan moderation"; which explained, he went on, why the old folks were not sad, the rich were not arrogant, the magnates not haughty, the plebs patriotic, and all manner of persons lived together in peace.[62] "What could be happier than this harmony?" he concluded, just as if the divine Plato himself had instructed the Strasbourgeois. Taking his cue perhaps from his Dutch friend, the Alsatian humanist Hieronymus Gebwiler (1473–1545) described the regime of the city in classical terms as a *status mixtus*, in which the Ammeister, the Senate & XXI, and the assembly represented respectively the monarchial, aristocratic, and popular principles.[63] Jacob Wimpheling (1450–1528), who of all these writers knew the city best, praised Strasbourg for its absence of factions and the citizens' love of the common good ("res publica," "gemein Nutz").[64]

1. Of all Strasbourg's learned flatterers, Jean Sturm, the fiery rector of the Latin school (1538ff.), knew the regime and its personnel best and saw the strengths of the political system most clearly. Strasbourg, he wrote, is a republic in which the old educate the young men just as parents educate their children.[65] The regime did in fact place a high premium on age and experience. A bachelor could enter the Senate at the age of thirty, a married man at twenty-five. The average privy councillor

---

p. 469. Compare the impression of an Englishman, Thomas Tebold, in a letter to the earl of Wiltshire, Tübingen, 12 March 1536: "Strosborough, an imperial city, has not great country nor possessions, but there is no city in Almain so strong, and they are rich enough to support 30,000 men for two years, and have victuals to keep the city for four years." *Letters and Papers, Foreign and Domestic, of the Reign of Henry VIII, 1509–42*, X, 186, No. 458.

[62] Erasmus to Jacob Wimpheling, 21 September 1514, in *Opus epistolarum Des. Roterodami denuo recognitum et auctum*, eds. P. S. Allen and H. S. Allen, 12 vols. (Oxford, 1906–46), II, No. 305, pp. 17–24, here at p. 19 ll. 85–97.

[63] *Die Strassburger Chronik des elsässischen Humanisten Hieronymus Gebwiler*, ed. Karl Stenzel, SWIELR (Berlin–Leipzig, 1926), p. 66 (composed ca. 1521–23).

[64] "Germania," lib. II, cap. "De concordia," in Emil von Borries, ed., *Wimpfeling und Murner im Kampf um die ältere Geschichte des Elsasses. Ein Beitrag zur Charakteristik des deutschen Frühhumanismus*, SWIELR (Heidelberg, 1926), pp. 110–111. On Wimpheling's concept of "gemein Nutz" and its place in his social thought, see Kohls, *Die Schule bei Martin Bucer*, p. 38; and my critique in "The Themes of Social Structure, Social Conflict, and Civic Harmony in Jakob Wimpheling's *Germania*," *Sixteenth Century Journal*, 3 (1972), 65–76, here at pp. 74–75.

[65] Sturm, *Quarti Antipappi*, p. 40.

of the Reformation generation spent a very long time in office—just how long is shown by Table 18.

Table 18

Average number of years in office of 1905 Privy Councillors of Strasbourg, 1520–55

Office	Patricians		Guildsmen		Total	
	No.	Average years	No.	Average years	No.	Average years
XV & XIII	32	15.8	73	13.6	105	14.3
XVers only	14	11.6	38	8.5	52	9.3
XIIIers[66]	18	16.7	35	19.0	53	18.2
Stettmeister	31	6.8				
Ammeister			23	3.0		

Source: PROSOPOGRAPHY in Appendix A below.

These figures show the average longevity in the offices specified and not the average lengths of total political careers. Entire political careers, from first entry into the Senate until leaving the privy councils (by death or resignation), averaged 23.3 years for patricians, 18.9 years for guildsmen, and 20.2 years overall. This means that patrician political careers average something like five years longer than non-patrician ones, a finding conformable to, for example, the greater longevity of patrician careers at Constance.[67]

Some of the prominent politicians of the Reformation generation enjoyed very long political careers. Mathis Pfarrer was the champion with 49 years, followed by Caspar Rumler with 46, Jacob Meyer (Masons) with 43 years, Friedrich and Stephan Sturm with 42 years each, and Heinrich von Mülnheim with 41. The five Sturm of this generation in the councils (Friedrich, Hans, Jacob, Peter, and Stephan) were in politics for an average of thirty-two years, while the two Rumler (Florentz and Caspar, father and son) spanned with their careers a period of nearly three-quarters of a century (74 years). Thirteen other privy councillors were in the regime between thirty and forty years

---

[66] This is the only category of longevity in office in which the guild privy councillors exceeded the patrician ones.

[67] See Rublack, *Einführung der Reformation in Konstanz*, p. 13 and p. 201n43. The greater length of patrician careers at Strasbourg may well have been due to the small size of the patriciate and the consequent absence of competition for offices.

each, and another thirty-seven served between twenty and thirty years each. As the absolute minimum age for entering the Senate was twenty-five, the usual average age of the privy councillors must have been around 45–50 years and was probably higher.

The career profiles of the privy councillors and the central position of the council of XIII suggest a partial explanation for the famed vigor and boldness of Strasbourg's foreign policy during the Reformation era. The leading political figures of this era were men who, with a few exceptions, began their careers during the decade 1512–22 and rose into the XIII by 1530. The following men made up the XIII during most of the 1530s and, with some losses in 1539–42, the 1540s:

Hans Bock von Gerstheim	(1512)	1518–42
Claus Kniebis	(1512)	1520–52
Egenolf Röder von Diersburg	(1515)	1530–50
Martin Herlin	(1519)	1523–47
Jacob Meyer	(1519)	1525–62
Bernhard Ottfriedrich	(1519)	1533–39
Mathis Pfarrer	(1519)	1525–68
Daniel Mieg	(1520)	1522–41
Bernhard Wurmser von Vendenheim	(1520)	1532–40
Conrad Joham	(1521)	1530–48
Jacob Sturm	(1524)	1526–53
Mattheus Geiger	(1529)	1533–49

The dates of beginnings of political careers (in parentheses) and of service in the XIII show that this core of the regime was composed of men who entered politics before the Reformation and most of whom spent their entire adult lives in political offices. They served an average of more than twenty-two years in the XIII, and their days of power fell squarely in the great era of German political Protestantism.

The concentration of age and experience in the privy councils may have been, as Jean Sturm wrote, one of the regime's great strengths, but it was also a weakness. It meant that privy councillors frequently asked to be relieved or replaced for reasons of health. This was especially true of the Ammeister, who during their terms as ruling Ammeister were expected to spend nearly every waking hour on duty. The refusals of Heinrich Ingold in 1520 and Andreas Drachenfels in 1524 to accept another term seem to have caused no special difficulties. It was different by the 1540s, when the generation of men who had sponsored the reforms of the 1520s were becoming less and less physically capable of discharging their duties. Claus Kniebis, who had been born before 1480, had to decline a fifth term as ruling Ammeister in 1543 "because of age and other incapacities," and Martin Betscholt, elected in his place, was excused on the same ground.[68] Simon Franck, who had been drafted from his sickbed in 1543, refused to serve again in 1549 "because he is sick."[69] Hans Bock von Gerstheim, who was probably the oldest man in the regime in 1540, could not take his seat in the XIII during the spring of the year because of an injured leg. In the following January he begged to be relieved of his offices, "in view of his age and failing sight."[70] His colleagues did not excuse him, although during 1542 he was living in the country and came infrequently into the city. On March 15 Bock was summoned from Gerstheim to come to Strasbourg "as an old, experienced man . . . because the business and events are so rapid and so weighty."[71] This time he could not come, and the matter was dropped. Seven months later, Bock was dead.

The plea to be excused "leibs halb" was a powerful appeal to one's colleagues and could not always be ignored. Occasionally the colleagues did permit a temporary relief from duties, though rarely a permanent one. When Conrad Joham was summoned to return from a spa (probably in Baden) and resume his duties in June, 1542, he wrote back "that he is still in the baths and still feels weak, and he asks that my lords allow him to stay until the time of the fair; for to leave sooner would endanger his health."[72] Three days later, Caspar Rumler, a XVer and member of the fair board (*Messherr*), was relieved of the latter post because he was ill "and will not be able to go out [of his house] during this fair."[73] Very rarely, however, did the councils permit one of their members to resign completely from his posts. On December 27, 1544, the pious, good-hearted, old cloth merchant, Bastian Erb, asked to be allowed to resign from the XV. By his own account, he had served in one office or another during more than twenty of the past twenty-eight years; and now, at the

---

[68] Hertzog, VIII, 97.

[69] AMS, XXI 1548, fols. 639^r–640^v (3 January 1549).

[70] AMS, XXI 1540, fol. 139^v (4 April 1540), and fols. 531^v–532^r (3 January 1541). Bock was probably born around 1470 and was old enough to have entered the university in 1491 and to be the father-in-law of Jacob Sturm (b. 1489). PROSOPOGRAPHY, No. XI. On the day that Bock asked to be relieved of his offices, Egenolf Röder von Diersburg also asked to be allowed to resign, because of "sein lÿbs beschwerden."

[71] AMS, XXI 1542, fol. 102^r (15 March 1542).

[72] AMS, XXI 1542, fol. 220^v (14 June 1542); he returned by 11 July.

[73] AMS, XXI 1542, fol. 224^r (17 June 1542). His replacement, Conrad Meyer, pleaded that he had to help his father-in-law, Anthonj von Sigolsheim, in his shop during the fair; but he was told that "he shall serve my lords in this way."

age of sixty-five, his sight, hearing, and mental faculties were failing.[74] Despite this plea, only death granted Erb the desired relief, more than three years later.

2. What surplus of practical experience the privy councillors of Strasbourg may have had, they made up for in the formal education they lacked. The level of advanced (i.e., university) education among them compares, nonetheless, rather favorably with the levels of education among contemporary office-holders in Ulm and in the smaller towns of Upper Swabia.[75] Twelve of the 105 privy councillors attended a university, of whom five never completed a degree. Among the university men the patricians and guildsmen are represented in precisely the ratio 1:2. Only three men of the Reformation generation, Claus Kniebis and Jacob and Peter Sturm, completed a law degree, and only Jacob Sturm had studied theology.[76] The only man to move directly from the

---

[74] Erb's petition is printed from AMS, H 5767, by Winckelmann, *Fürsorgewesen*, II, 68–70, No. 30. It was read to the Senate & XXI on 27 December 1544. AMS, XXI 1544, fol. 554[r].

[75] Geiger, *Die Reichsstadt Ulm*, pp. 58–59; Eitel, *Die oberschwäbischen Reichsstädte*, pp. 160–161, although, again, the groups are not entirely comparable. Jacob, *Politische Führungsschicht*, does not study this question; and Paul Guyer, "Politische Führungs-schichten der Stadt Zürich vom 13. bis zum 18. Jahrhundert," *Deutsches Patriziat 1450–1740*, p. 408, discusses only the study of law. The general subject of levels of education among urban ruling groups remains open, but there are some shrewd suggestions in Heinrich Kramm, "Besitzschichten und Bildungsschichten der mittel-deutschen Städte im 16. Jahrhundert," *VSWG*, 51 (1964), 454–491. In particular there are Kramm's findings (p. 464) that it is an error to believe that matriculation in a university is evidence of an intention to pursue a career based on professional education, and that a large percentage of the matriculants never completed the course for even the B.A. James H. Overfield has recently argued that the proportion of aristocrats among students at German universities rose during the sixteenth century, while the numbers of paupers fell accordingly. James H. Overfield, "Nobles and Paupers at German Universities to 1600," *Societas*, 4 (1974), 175–210. In his study of Strasbourgeois attending four Rhenish universities (Basel, Freiburg, Heidelberg, and Cologne), 1450–1520, Francis Rapp finds that about 7% of the students came from patrician families, 16% from guild families who also produced members of the government, and 32% from the strata of artisans, small merchants, and shopkeepers. The nobles and wealthy guild families thus did not attend universities in numbers out of proportion to their shares of the citizen population. Francis Rapp, "Les Strasbourgeois et les Universités rhénanes à la fin du Moyen Age jusqu'à la Réforme," *ASAVS*, 4 (1974), 11–22, here at pp. 14–15. My own study of the university matriculation lists for the pre-Reformation era has led me to a similar conclusion. The picture after 1560 or so is quite different and re-quires a special study. See note 80 below.

[76] I owe my knowledge of Kniebis's law degree to Jean Rott. Hans Winterberg, *Die Schüler von Ulrich Zasius*, VKLBW, B 18 (Stuttgart, 1961), pp. 71–72, has revived the tradition that Jacob Sturm studied law under Zasius at Freiburg i. Br. I cannot confirm this, although Otto Winckelmann once wrote that he had seen a source in Stuttgart in

university into one of the free professions was Michael Schwencker, a notary public and graduate in arts from Heidelberg. Of the younger men, Carl Mieg, Jr., was the only other privy councillor to have studied law. Heidelberg, to which half of the twelve university men had gone, was the most popular university before the Reformation, followed by Freiburg im Breisgau with four; and no other university was represented by more than one graduate or former student. The principle that university education was an instrument of social mobility, especially for townsmen, has little or no applicability to this group of Strasbourgeois.[77] As in contemporary Nuremberg, there were no practicing professionals, and in particular no lawyers, in the inner circles of the regime.[78]

Not until the end of the sixteenth century did university-educated men enter the privy councils in significant numbers. Before the Reformation, members of well-to-do Strasbourg families rarely attended the university unless they were destined for the Church, and the Strasbourgeois who attended such popular universities as Heidelberg, Freiburg im Breisgau, and Basel before 1520 mostly came from families about whom very little is known. Nor did the brief flowering of literary humanism during the 1510s make much lasting impression, particularly on lay education, for the members of the Strasbourg literary group (or sodality) were mostly clerics.[79] The principle change, that is to say the rise of professional advanced education in lay circles at Strasbourg, came during the second half of the sixteenth century, when sons of prominent Strasbourg families began to attend various German, French, and Italian universities. At the University of Padua alone during the second half of the sixteenth century there studied the sons of five privy councillors of the Reformation generation, the nephews of three others, and the two grandsons of a ninth (Schenckbecher–Drachenfels)—most of whom studied law.[80]

---

which Sturm was designated as having a licentiate in law. "Jakob Sturm," *ADB*, 37 (1894), 5–20, here at p. 7.

[77] Excluding professional employees, of whom at least three capitalized very well on their educations. Sebastian Brant (d. 1521), Bernhard Botzheim (ca. 1520–91) and Ludwig Gremp von Freudenstein (1509–83), all jurists. To them should be added Michel Han of Kenzingen, who studied law at Freiburg i. Br. and became syndic of Strasbourg and chancellor of Pfalz-Zweibrücken. Ficker–Winckelmann, I, 14, 20, 28.

[78] Gerald Strauss, *Nuremberg in the 16th Century* (New York, 1966), p. 58.

[79] Rapp, *Réformes et Réformation*, pp. 446–447.

[80] Gustav Knod, "Oberrheinische Studenten im 16. und 17. Jahrhundert auf der Universität Padua," *ZGO*, 54 (1900), 197–258, 432–453, and vol. 55 (1901), 246–262, 612–637. The students in question are: Sebastian Mieg, son of Carl M., Sr. (*ZGO*, vol. 55, pp. 452–453, No. 183); Johannes Beinheim, nephew of Hans Hammerer (p. 433, No. 107); Joshua Geiger, son of Mattheus Geiger (vol. 54, p. 231, No. 1); Johann and

University-trained lawyers, who were very rare in the regime in 1550, were very common by 1600.

The vastly increased tempo of diplomacy and the transfer of ecclesiastical authority to the lay regime—plus the more general tendency to greater specialization and enhanced bureaucracy common to all Renaissance regimes—placed ever greater strains on the abilities and capacities of Strasbourg's amateur rulers during the Reformation generation. These conditions also fostered the growth of the professional staff. Sebastian Brant (d. 1521), who had been both City Advocate and City Secretary, was replaced by two secretaries, and by the mid-1530s the city employed two advocates as well.[81] The increase of civic business required a thorough reorganization of the civic chancellery (1537), and by the next decade the intricacies of civic finance seem to have strained the capacities of the young men who staffed the financial committees.[82] Each of these developments points to the increasing inability of the oligarchy to meet its tasks and obligations without more professional help.

Of no aspect of civic government was this truer than of ecclesiastical affairs. The regulation of parish affairs and the recruitment and supervision of clergy posed no problems, for these were tasks which the Reformation merely expanded. The problem of doctrine was quite different. Of all the privy councillors of this era, only Jacob Sturm had studied theology formally, and although he led the diplomatic corps

---

Lorentz Schenckbecher, grandsons of Andreas Drachenfels (pp. 232–233, Nos. 4–5); Heinrich Joham, nephew of Conrad J. (p. 233, No. 6); Ludwig Böcklin von Böcklinsau, son of Ulman B. v. B. (p. 234, No. 7); Carl Heuss, son of Michael H. (p. 240, No. 22); Heinrich Baumgartner, nephew of Hans Hammerer (p. 240, No. 23); Peter Storck, son of Veltin S. (p. 241, No. 26); and Nicolaus Jacob Wurmser von Vendenheim, nephew of Wolf Sigismund W. v. V. (p. 243, No. 34). Nearly all of them had attended German universities, and many also attended other Italian and French universities as well.

[81] The secretaries were Peter Butz (d. 1531) and Wendelin von St. Johann (d. 1554). Ficker–Winckelmann, I, 16–17; Eheberg, p. 558, No. 297. Jacob Kirser, Dr.iur., was employed as an advocate in 1529 (Eheberg, pp. 559–560, No. 299). By the mid-1530s were employed as advocates two pupils of Zasius, Franz Frosch (d. 1540) of Nuremberg and Wendelin Bittelbronn (d. 1541). Winterberg, *Die Schüler von Ulrich Zasius*, pp. 16, 38–39; Ficker–Winckelmann, I, 23–24. There is a list of advocates employed by the city in AMS, VI 493/2. It would be very valuable to have a study of the Strasbourg lawyers along the lines of Gerhard Gansslen's *Die Ratsadvokaten und Ratskonsulenten der Reichsstadt Ulm, insbesondere ihr Wirken in den Bürgerprozessen am Ende des 18. Jahrhunderts*, Forschungen zur Geschichte der Stadt Ulm, 6 (Ulm, 1966).

[82] This is clear from the provisions of the *Münzordnung* of 1544 and the *Pfennigthurmordnung* of 1558. Eheberg, pp. 579–583, No. 306, and pp. 392–395, No. 311. The chancellery reorganization of 1537 is in *ibid.*, pp. 562–571, No. 302.

all through the Reformation era, he confessed his own incompetence to deal expertly with doctrinal questions.[83] The preachers, to be sure, were available as experts and were so employed—like the lawyers—but the Reformation placed all ecclesiastical matters, including the establishment of official norms of belief, ultimately in the hands of the laymen who made up the regime. The regime dealt with this question in the wake of the synod of 1533, when the Senate & XXI had to choose between the Tetrapolitan Confession, a relic of the negotiations at Augsburg in 1530, and the freshly made "XVI Articles."[84] Jacob Sturm, the senior lay president of the synod, reminded his colleagues that they had come to the crux of the entire business:

> so we must finally decide which of the doctrines we heard is to be considered the Word of God. It will be fruitless to proceed to other matters until one can know what is to be considered the divine Word. One way to proceed is as follows. Because the confession submitted at Augsburg is so long that it would take more than a whole day to read it in the Senate chamber—plus the fact that with coming and going no one will sit still to hear it through, and everyone will forget the early parts by the time we get to the later ones—we can buy some of the printed copies and distribute them, so that each can read it closely and diligently and decide for himself whether we should stay with this document or not. Then, eight days or so later, a discussion will be held, in which each can express his own opinion and view. And, since the preachers have offered their expert aid, they can be called and consulted to the degree that they are needed.[85]

Sturm presumably knew the abilities of his colleagues. The surviving fragment of the record of discussion of doctrine in the Senate & XXI casts no very rosy light on the intelligence and learning of the privy councillors and demonstrates dramatically how unequal to the task they really were.[86] Jacob Meyer (Masons), a XIIIer who had been a stalwart

---

[83] Thomas A. Brady, Jr., "Jacob Sturm of Strasbourg and the Lutherans at the Diet of Augsburg, 1530," *CH*, 42 (1973), 183–202, here at p. 187 and note 17.

[84] *Ibid.*, pp. 191–192; and Chrisman, *Strasbourg*, pp. 211–224, for the literature on the Tetrapolitan Confession and on the synod of 1533. Fundamental on the synod is François Wendel, *L'église de Strasbourg, sa constitution et son organisation, 1532–1535*, Études d'histoire et de philosophie religieuses, 38 (Paris, 1942); and the sources in *TQ Strassburg*, II.

[85] *TQ Strassburg*, II, 271–273, No. 503 (8 February 1534), approved nearly verbatim on 16 February (*ibid.*, pp. 279–280, No. 508).

[86] *Ann. Brant*, No. 5042, also in *TQ Strassburg*, II, 294, No. 523 (20 March 1534). The remarks of individual councillors are taken from this document. There is simply not enough extant documentation to support an analysis of the extent to which the doctrinal formulations of the Strasbourg reformers reflected the opinions of the regime itself or the political mood of its members. See the brilliantly suggestive study by Gerald Strauss, "Protestant Dogma and City Government: The Case of Nuremberg," *Past & Present*, No. 36 (1967), 38–58, who argues for a correspondence between the thoroughly

of the "Zealot" faction during the mid-1520s, said "that he has always accepted the decision of the majority, and he will do so now." Carl Mieg, Sr., a XVer and scion of a great merchant family, promised that "he will not oppose whatever my lords decide; but he hopes that, being a layman, he won't be snared into something he doesn't understand and then be forced to confess and believe." Hans von Blumenau, a patrician XVer, agreeably confessed that "what pleases my lords will please him," a position duly seconded by the Stettmeister Philips von Kageneck. The only university man whose comments have survived was Peter Sturm, Jacob's younger brother and a graduate in law. He pleaded that "due to the heavy workload, he doesn't know what he believes and has no opinion to express on this matter, except that he doesn't like the factionalism and believes that the preaching is too violent." Nothing in the backgrounds, education, or experience of these men suited them to the task of deciding what others should believe. It is not remarkable, therefore, that they tended to shy away from the task and that, except as a weapon against the sects, public norms of belief were never much enforced at Strasbourg in this generation.

3. The keystone of aristocratic control of the regime of Strasbourg was not the demand for age and experience but the fact that a political career was quite expensive. At Strasbourg, as in other towns, the salaries of office-holders were always very low.[87] Career politicians had therefore almost necessarily to be men of leisure.[88] Whereas the rentier could well afford to spend much of his time in government business—five mornings per week plus the time spent in committee meetings—and the merchant could either hold office occasionally or enter politics after a successful career in trade,[89] the shopkeeper and the artisan could ill afford to spend

---

aristocratic form of the Nuremberg regime and the Lutheran view of the essential futility of all works. Of Strasbourg it may be suggested that perhaps its reformers' departures from Lutheran teaching in the direction of greater ethical activism (thus reducing substantially the Lutheran separation of salvation from everyday life) reflects the freer political life and the broader basis of political power at Strasbourg.

[87] The salary schedules of 1506 are printed by Eheberg, pp. 544–546, No. 289. The salaries were raised substantially in 1566, for which see "Städel Chronik," III, 463.

[88] Maschke, "Verfassung und soziale Kräfte," pp. 330–331, 335, 336.

[89] Ludwig von Mörssmünster, a senator in 1549, was coopted into the XV on 14 May 1552, but he asked to be excused because of his advanced age. AMS, XXI 1552, fol. 151ʳ. Anshelm Baldner asked his colleagues in the XV (on 15 June 1545) to vacate the sentence of banishment against his son, "die weill er beÿ mein herrn den funffzehen vnd ein vnd zweintzig seyen vnd sein geschefft versamen muss, den son harein zü lassen jm jn seiner handel . . . mogen beratlich vnd hilfflich sein." AMS, XXI 1545, fol. 242ᵛ.

almost half of each working day away from his shop or atelier. He certainly could not do so for a period of fifteen to twenty years. Even for the lesser merchants the demands of public office could be burdensome. When he was coopted into the XV on August 12, 1551, Georg Leimer asked to be excused, "for not only is he unsuited for the post, he is not a rich man and also has living children to support."[90] The expense of public office, especially the loss of income to men whose incomes depended directly on the amount of time they spent in their occupations, was clearly an important guarantee of the continued monopoly of the regime by rich men of leisure. The same condition, by robbing the regime of men of ambition and ability, exacerbated the chronic shortage of able privy councillors.

In critical situations, when a privy councillor was no longer willing to pay the costs—to his income and to his health—of his offices, his colleagues would appeal to his sense of duty and obligation. They reminded him that he had bound himself by oath to place the public good before his private welfare, or, in their words, he must "do the best thing" ("das beste thun"). This phrase was a very old element in the political language of Strasbourg[91] and a key symbol of the collective discipline of the civic political elite. When the Stettmeister Bernhard Wurmser tried to resign his offices because of rumors that he was aiding his brother, Nicolaus, dean of St. Thomas, to resist the regime's reforms, his colleagues asked "that he continue to hold and bear his offices in the government and help to do the best thing."[92] Wurmser stayed on. Such pleas became quite common during the 1540s, when age and waning enthusiasm for diplomatic service made it increasingly difficult to staff

---

[90] AMS, XXI 1551, fol. 260ʳ: "derselbig der bit vndertheniglich jne zuerlassen dan neben dem das er vngeschickt zu sachen sy er mit geringer narung versehen, hab auch lebendiger kind das er dinst nötig."

[91] It appears in the *Dreizehnerordnung* of 1448 (Eheberg, p. 161, No. 45): "das er darinne ouch alzit das beste und wegeste tůge." Also in the regulation for the Ammeister-stube, 1468 (*ibid.,* p. 230, No. 82 para. 2): "und welhe dann also kuchenmeister wurdent, soltent sweren der statt und der stuben nutz und ere und das beste und wegeste zu tun." It appears commonly in oaths taken by the leading civic employees, as, for example, in the oath sworn by the new advocate, Jacob Wetzler, on 2 December 1489 (*ibid.,* p. 339, No. 137): "oder anders zů thůnde, des besten, so ich mich verstande oder vermag"; and in the oath taken by Wendelin von St. Johann on 1 November 1520 (*ibid.,* p. 558, No. 297): "und alle zit das beste und wegste thun und furnemen noch nutz und notturft der stat Straszburg."

[92] *Ann. Brant,* No. 4574 (27 January 1525): "dasz er fürther im Regiment sine empter besitz und trag und helff das best thun. . . ."

embassies. When Jacob Meyer begged for relief from the long journey to Regensburg for the Imperial Diet of 1541, he was told: "because he can see himself that so few men are available, he cannot be excused; and he will have along Sir Jacob Sturm, who will do the best thing."[93] The insistence that each councillor "do the best thing" was more than just an appeal to patriotism, for it reminded each man that he had sworn to serve the regime even at great cost to himself. The very survival of the oligarchy at Strasbourg, as in every aristocratic republic, depended on the willingness of some aristocrats to sacrifice their own convenience and their own direct economic interests to the collective purpose and survival of the entire regime.

F.   The Oligarchy of Strasbourg—A Balance Sheet

Reformation Strasbourg was ruled by a rentier–merchant aristocracy, whose common economic interests and social bonds overrode nearly all distinctions of estate. The rentier fraction comprised the entire patriciate plus a significant element in the guilds; while the merchant fraction in the guilds was divided into two distinct, but not opposed, strata. The big merchant families were chiefly recent migrants from smaller Alsatian towns, and the lesser merchants were mainly dealers in cloth. The big merchants, who inter-married both with the patricians and with the lesser merchants, formed the social cement of the entire ruling class.

The oligarchy, the aristocracy's political domination of the commune, was both institutional and social. On the one hand, very few persons outside the aristocracy possessed the wealth, and thus the leisure, required for reaching the inner councils of the regime; and the shopkeeper and artisan elements, with few significant exceptions, thus rarely played an important political role. On the other hand, the power of the privy councils and the administrative boards, which the councillors controlled, enabled a small number of career politicians to exercise daily surveillance over all aspects of civic life. The practice of political invasion of poorer guilds by rich young men from richer guilds assured that the constitutional distribution of offices among the guilds could be manipulated to the benefit of the wealthiest stratum of guild families. A structure which apparently provided access to political power to a wide variety of Strasbourgeois thus actually served to strengthen the domination of the

---

[93] AMS, XXI 1541, fol. 514^{r-v}.

regime by rentiers and merchants. The easy movement of politicians from guild to guild also provided important lines of political influence down into the entire range of crafts. This invasion from above was resisted only by a few, apparently relatively homogeneous guilds, whose offices then remained in the hands of their own leading families.

The aristocracy of Strasbourg produced a political elite whose abilities and experience were adequate to the ordinary tasks of internal police and external relations, but whose age, educations, and leisure provided no protection against the forces, external and internal, unleashed by the Reformation.

PART TWO

REGIME AND REFORMATION

"das man in der lutherischen sachen nit so hitzlich gegen einander im Rath handelte, . . ."
—Bernhard Wurmser von Vendenheim, 1523—

"sind also zu beyden theylen Christen, des Gott erbarm etc."
—Jacob Sturm, August, 1525—

"So seÿ er leibs halben blod, kunds nit thun."
—Peter Sturm, 20 November 1540—

"er woll sich in khein rachtung begeben, wöll jn den keiser jm hymel vertruwen, vnd bey gottes wort vnd der burgerschaft halten vnd ston."
—Sebastian Erb, 19 January 1547—

"Wo nhun vngnad vf ein statt solte gelegt werden, vnd er nicht mocht haben hin weg zu ziehen, hett er jn acht tag zu besorgen, das er vnnd seiner brueder vmb alle jre Narung khemen, vnnd muessten doruber verderben."
—Philips Ingold, 18 August 1548—

INTRODUCTION

What follows is neither a history of Strasbourg during the Reformation era nor a history of the Reformation in Strasbourg. It is a study of the behavior of the city's ruling class and political elite during the two principal crises of the age. In the first crisis, conventionally called "The Peasants' War," the hegemony of the old ecclesiastical system was smashed, along with much that was dear to the aristocrats, but the oligarchy itself retained its inner integrity and its collective will to rule. The second crisis developed in the wake of the Smalkaldic War (1546–47) and the Interim of Augsburg (1548) and sent an already weakened oligarchy into headlong dissolution and a large part of the aristocracy into temporary exile. In each crisis the aristocracy responded through its political elite to mounting pressure from below; but the responses differed dramatically. The aristocracy survived the events of 1524–25, the deepest social crisis in pre-modern German history, with a minimum of apparent damage, while the less general crisis of 1547–48 brought the entire structure of aristocratic hegemony at Strasbourg to the brink of collapse. In Chapters VI–VIII, which represent the full transition from structural to properly historical analysis, the understanding of the aristocracy and its oligarchy achieved in the foregoing chapters supplies the tools for study and explication of the behavior of Strasbourg's ruling class in the critical phases of the Reformation.

CHAPTER SIX

THE ARISTOCRACY AND A CRISIS WITHSTOOD,

1523–1525

Just five hundred years ago took place the events, commonly called "the German Peasants' War," that formed the watershed of the German Reformation.[1] For a few years the movement that went down to bloody defeat in 1525 *was* the Reformation, the climax of a great popular surge of protest, resentment, and hope aimed at the entire structure of social domination. The movement of the little people in the cities, in the small towns, and on the land absorbed the propaganda of Luther and his disciples into a pre-existing program of social transformation in which the restoration of the true Christian gospel was to ring in a new order of divine justice, peace, and brotherhood. From this same movement against the feudal order came the pressures which, despite the defeat in

---

[1] Most historians now accept that the "Peasants' War" involved the "common man" in South Germany and not just the peasants, and that it was a social revolution rather than just a war. How deeply this profounder, wider vision of the events has penetrated the historical literature may be seen in this characterization: "Dass die historische Erinnerung dennoch vom Bauernkrieg nicht loskommt, sondern immer wieder auf ihn zurückkommt und auf ihn zurückgelenkt wird, ist zunächst wohl darin begründet, dass hier Geschichte und Politik nicht allein in fürstlichen Kanzleien und Rathäusern gemacht wurden, die das Volk dann eben auszuhalten und zu tragen hatte, sondern dass hier die Initiative von unten ausgegangen und zur Sachen vieler geworden ist. Wie wir an den Reaktionen ablesen können, war schliesslich dann das Ganze der Gesellschaft mit all ihren Gruppen betroffen: das flache Land und die Städte, die einfachen Leute und die Gelehrten, ja selbst die Künstler, der gemeine Mann und die Regierungen, die Laien und die Kirchen. Was auf dem Spiegel stand, war nicht wenig: Wohl und Wehe der Gesellschaft, Ordnung, Frieden, Gerechtigkeit, persönliche Freiheit, das Heil, das elementare Auskommen." Martin Brecht, "Die Bedeutung des Bauernkrieges in Südwestdeutschland," *Schwäbische Heimat. Zeitschrift zur Pflege von Landschaft, Volkstum, Kultur,* 26 (1975), 297–301, here at p. 297. On the wide acceptance that has been gained by these two aspects of Marxist interpretation of the events of 1525, see Heiko A. Oberman, "The Gospel of Social Unrest: 450 Years after the so-called 'German Peasants' War' of 1525," *Harvard Theological Review,* 69 (1976). The present state of scholarship may be gauged in Rainer Wohlfeil, "Einleitung: Der Bauernkrieg als geschichtswissenschaftliches Problem," in *Der Bauernkrieg 1524–26. Bauernkrieg und Reformation,* pp. 7–50, with rich references. Of the flood of commemorative literature in 1974–75, see esp. Günter Vogler, *et al.,* eds., *Illustrierte Geschichter der deutschen frühbürgerlichen Revolution* (Berlin, 1974); and *Deutscher Bauernkrieg 1525,* ed. H. A. Oberman.

1525, gradually forced the German ruling classes to liquidate the lord-ship of priests in exchange for the release of properties accumulated over the past five centuries from the clerical dead hand. This exchange formed the material heart of the Reformation after 1525; and thus the question as to whether the post-1525 reform was chiefly a popular or chiefly an official reform ("Volksreformation oder Ratsreformation?") has only one answer: it was both![2] 1525 decided, once and for all, what kind of reform the lords of Germany would tolerate: it was not that the (often effective) popular pressure for changes in religious practices, norms of belief, and status of the clergy would cease; but that the Reformation was to be confined to religion and ecclesiastical life, and that any further attempt to force society to conform to the true gospel would meet swift, instinctive, and merciless retribution.

Yet 1525 did not entirely rob the German movement of its revolu-tionary nature. Every ecclesiastical reform either touched the permanent interests of one or more classes or exposed the points of tension and conflict between classes and therefore threatened the society's political order. To obscure or deny this political character of the reforms by appealing to the dualistic aspects of Luther's doctrine of the "two realms," as sometimes is done, is to falsify both the history of the Reformation and Luther's opinions.[3] Every practical reform proposal impinged on either the symbolic forms or the material substance of aristocratic domination. Two examples, one very direct and the other less so, will clarify this point. The issue of tithe refusal touched the social order at its most sensitive point, property rights. This was especially true where, as

---

[2] The major argument for a continuing *Volksreformation,* based chiefly on central and northern German sources, is by Franz Lau, "Der Bauernkrieg und das angebliche Ende der lutherischen Reformation als spontaner Volksbewegung," *Luther-Jahrbuch,* 26 (1959), 109–134, reprinted in *Wirkungen der deutschen Reformation bis 1555,* ed. Walther Hubatsch, Wege der Forschung, 203 (Darmstadt, 1967), pp. 68–100. Supporting Lau but based on South German sources is Moeller, *Reichsstadt und Reformation,* pp. 20–22. Kohls, "Evangelische Bewegung und Kirchenordnung," pp. 110–134, tries to over-come this dichotomy through a phase hypothesis ("evangelische Bewegung," "poli-tische Reformation," and "Rückbesinnung"), the chief fault of which is the curious notion that the reform movement became political only when the regimes intervened to protect and control property and restore order. There is a good discussion of the phases of reform in cities by Winfried Becker, *Reformation und Revolution,* Katholisches Leben und Kirchenreform im Zeitalter der Glaubensspaltung, 34 (Münster/W., 1974), pp. 86–92.

[3] I refer here to the tendency to call upon the "two realms" doctrine as support for the contention that there existed two, objectively distinct spheres of life, namely, "religion" and "politics."

in Southwest Germany, ecclesiastical tithes had frequently been secularized into divisible, heritable incomes in the hands of laymen.[4] Attacks on the wealth and property rights of the church necessarily cast doubt upon the justice of rents and dues in general and on the accumulation of vast amounts of property in aristocratic hands. More pointedly, attacks on ecclesiastical lordship would not balk at the line between clerical and lay lordship unless, as happened in 1525, they were forced to do so. The Bible, it was widely believed, not only did not approve the great tithe, it did not justify serfdom—as the third of the "Twelve Articles" of Upper Swabia duly explained.[5] The second example is iconoclasm, to the religious significance of which some scholarly attention has been devoted.[6] Iconoclastic riots and laws destroyed what were not only objects of devotion but also public, material witnesses to the piety, wealth, and eminence of generations of aristocratic donors. The blows of hammers on statues, funeral tablets, shrines, and retables struck directly at the bonds between aristocratic family glory past and aristocratic family power present. Such attacks were no less dangerous for being directed at the *symbolic* forms, rather than the material substance, of aristocratic power.

Against the threatening character of any ecclesiastical reforms must be set the particular complex of tensions and resentment faced by each urban regime. Strasbourg, it is true, is famed for the swiftness and apparent ease with which the reforms of the 1520s were achieved.

---

[4] The social significance of the tithe is well analyzed by Kamen, *The Iron Century*, pp. 332–333. On the subject of tithes and their economic significance, a theme widely ignored by historians of the Reformation, see *Les fluctuations du produit de la dîme. Conjoncture décimale et domaniale de la fin du moyen âge au XVIIIe siècle*, eds. Joseph Goy and Emmanuel Le Roy Ladurie, Cahiers des études rurales, 3 (Paris–The Hague, 1972), and esp. therein Jean Vogt, "Pour une étude sociale de la dîme. Esquisse de la tenure de la dîme en Alsace, XVIe–XVIIIe siècles," pp. 103–133. Fundamental for Alsace is the analysis by Luzian Pfleger, *Die elsässische Pfarrei. Ihre Entstehung und Entwicklung. Ein Beitrag zur kirchlichen Rechts- und Kulturgeschichte*, Forschungen zur Kirchengeschichte des Elsass, 3 (Strasbourg, 1936), pp. 286–324.

[5] The notion of the biblical origin of the tithe was under attack in South Germany before the Reformation, for example by Conrad Summenhart, whose Tübingen disputation on the subject was held in 1497 and published in 1500. *Tractatulus bipartitus de decimis defensivus opinionis theologorum adversus communiter canonistas de quotta decimarum, si debita sit iure divino vel humano* (Hagenau, 1500). I owe this reference to Heiko A. Oberman, who edits and analyzes this treatise in his forthcoming book on the University of Tübingen before the Reformation.

[6] See Hans von Campenhausen, "Die Bilderfrage in der Reformation," *ZKiG*, 68 (1957), pp. 96–128, who, however, treats only the views of the principal reformers; and Moeller, *Reichsstadt und Reformation*, pp. 23–25.

Unlike Nuremberg, where the even swifter (though less radical) reforms
flowed easily from the advanced state of lay power over the church, at
Strasbourg the two generations before 1525 had witnessed the failure of
every major reform effort and of each attempt, from whatever side, to
control the ecclesiastical system and put it in order. Such failures left the
local church of the city and diocese of Strasbourg wallowing in a sea of
anti-clericalism and mired in a swamp of apparently untouchable
fiscality and private interest.[7] While it is true that the Reformation was
largely a fruit of the failure of reform, it is also true that the enduring
interest of the urban aristocracy inclined against major change rather
than for it—which makes the changes of the 1520s all the more remarkable.

The reforms of the 1520s form the backdrop for two principal themes
in the following pages. First, the responses and reactions of the oligarchy to the reform movement are explored and the tendencies toward
party-formation within the oligarchy examined. Then, the aristocracy
itself is portrayed at the center of the crisis; and the chapter concludes
with a balance-sheet of the reforms for the ruling aristocracy.

A.   The Reform at Strasbourg and the Crisis of the Mid-1520s

1. The history of ecclesiastical reform from above in the diocese of
Strasbourg, marked by conflict and failure, slips into a lull with the
death of the clergy's most indomitable clerical critic, Johann Geiler von
Kaysersberg, in 1510. One year earlier, in an act which Rapp has called
"the last illusion," the new bishop, Count Wilhelm von Honstein
(reigned 1507–41), had issued his ill-fated reform ordinance, which
won him only a public humiliation.[8] If the official efforts at reform ebbed
during the decade before 1520, the tide of popular discontent did not.
Fueled at least partly by the rising average costs of loans and a series of
mediocre harvests, rural rebellion in Lower Alsace broke out in 1493.[9]
A second rising erupted in 1502, and a third, truly serious one, the
Bundschuh, in 1517.[10] The danger in these revolts was that beyond the

---

[7] Rapp, *Réformes et Réformation,* pp. 421–434.

[8] *Ibid.,* pp. 376–381.

[9] *Ibid.,* pp. 246, 406–407, 436–437.

[10] *Ibid.,* pp. 407–410, 437–440. The Bundschuh of 1517 involved about 100 villages,
forming at large circle centered on Strasbourg, of which a number belonged to aristocrats
of Strasbourg: Schnersheim (Marx von Eckwersheim), Düppigheim (Martin Sturm),
Fessenheim (Mülnheim), Bläsheim (Hans Bock von Gerstheim), Hindisheim (Zum

targets of choice, the clergy and religious, stood the lay ruling classes. The economic grievances which gave color and substance to an anti-clericalism becoming ever more modish in the town were directed against practices—chiefly various forms of direct appropriation and of usury—which were as widespread among the lay aristocracy as among the clergy.[11] Lurking behind the tide of anticlericalism was a complex of grievance, resentment, and social hatred which, although its first home was on the land, was increasingly at home in the cities as well. It was into this menacing situation that the Lutheran movement broke in the early 1520s. And although it did not create the crisis, Lutheranism contained ideological material and symbols which could and did help bring the complex of resentment, grievance, and hope to a powerful focus.

Lutheran or quasi-Lutheran preaching began at Strasbourg in 1521.[12] As in other South German towns, its earliest adherents were young clergymen, most of them at least dabblers in the fashionable culture of humanism.[13] Important conversions and clerical immigrations occurred in 1522 and 1523, the year of the first popular disturbances in the churches, including acts of violence against priests, popular demonstrations of support for the appointment of preachers of "the gospel," and moves to back preachers whose positions were threatened by the bishop or by their patrons. The year 1524 opened with a decree (January 25, 1524) that liquidated the ancient immunity of the clergy by forcing them (except cathedral canons, high nobles who could not be coerced) to become citizens and join guilds. This move merely brought to a conclusion the century-old trend toward greater lay control of the churches and convents.

Trübel), Matzenheim (Jacob Bapst), Schäffolsheim (Wurmser), and Niederhausbergen (Jacob Beger). Albert Rosenkranz, *Der Bundschuh. Die Erhebung des südwestdeutschen Bauernstandes in den Jahren 1493–1517*, 2 vols., SWIELR (Heidelberg, 1927), I, 452–457; II, 273, 275–276, 285–287.

[11] Rapp, *Réformes et Réformation,* pp. 440–441.

[12] These events are described in detail by Adam, *EKSS*, pp. 25–108; and Chrisman, *Strasbourg,* pp. 98–117, 131–154; but what is there written about the beginnings of the Evangelical movement at Strasbourg must be revised in the light of the study by Marc Lienhard and Jean Rott, "Die Anfänge der evangelischen Predigt in Strassburg und ihr erstes Manifest: der Aufruf des Karmeliterlesemeisters Tilman von Lyn (Anfang 1522)," in *Bucer und seine Zeit. Forschungsbeiträge und Bibliographie*, eds. Marijn de Kroon and Friedhelm Krüger, VIEGM, 80 (Wiesbaden, 1976), pp. 54–73.

[13] Bernd Moeller, "Die deutschen Humanisten und die Anfänge der Reformation," *ZKiG*, 70 (1959), 46–61 (Engl. trans. in *Imperial Cities and the Reformation*, pp. 19–38).

Rather more at variance with tradition were the first steps toward liquidation of the convents, beginning with the most vulnerable, the friars' houses, and toward assumption of direct control of the city's parishes. Both processes were well underway by the autumn of 1524, when the tempo of violence mounted sharply in tune with the waxing wave of revolt in the land. By January, 1525, the gardeners, the largest, most radical, and one of the poorest groups of artisans in the city, were demanding a total expropriation of the church. While their fellows were refusing all rents and tithes to ecclesiastical lords, a group of the gardeners attacked the inner sanctum of the regime, the treasury. Ostensibly to protect the city against peasant bands but actually to defend itself against its own citizens, the regime made military preparations in early 1525 and moved to take control of the chief foci of potential violence. How far it was willing to go in this self-defense is shown by an edict issued at the height of the rural revolt, just after Easter, which abolished the Mass in all but four churches of the town; and it even considered total abolition of the Mass, a step not actually taken until 1529.

Preparedness, the willingness to act, and a fine nose for danger carried the oligarchy through the crisis. A poll of the guild Schöffen on the eve of the slaughter at Saverne, where Duke Antoine of Lorraine crushed the Lower Alsatian peasantry (May 18, 1525), revealed that the majority of them firmly supported the regime. With the end of the revolt in the land, the incidence of popular violence subsided in the city as well, and the further progress of ecclesiastical reform became a matter of negotiation, of push and pull, between the leading preachers—who had preached law and order during the crisis—and the regime.[14]

By a historiographical tradition of long standing, "the Reformation" was victorious at Strasbourg in the year 1524, a view which no longer enjoys the support it once did.[15] The problem lies not with the identifica-

---

[14] Kittelson, *Wolfgang Capito*, pp. 120–122; Jean Rott, "La Guerre des Paysans et la Ville de Strasbourg," *La Guerre des Paysans 1525*, ed. A. Wollbrett, pp. 23–32, here at p. 29.

[15] See, for example, Robert Stupperich, "Strassburgs Stellung im Beginn des Sakramentsstreits (1524–1525)," *ARG*, 38 (1941), 249–262, here at p. 249. His romantic picture of the regime, preachers, and people basking in the harmony and peace of "the gospel" from 1524 onward has been translated to a slightly later time (with little more justice) by Peter F. Barton, "Das Jahr 1525 und die Abschaffung der Messe in Strassburg," in *Reformation und Humanismus. Robert Stupperich zum 65. Geburtstag*, eds. Martin Greschat and J. F. G. Goeters (Witten, 1969), pp. 141–157, here at pp. 150–151. The notion that the issue of "the Reformation" was settled at Strasbourg by 1524 is rejected by Chrisman, *Strasbourg*, pp. 158–161, and Kittelson, *Wolfgang Capito*, p. 134n53, who are certainly correct on this point.

tion of a particular year but with the meaning of the term "the Reformation." Commonly enough, by the term is meant a unitary, normative, meta-historical principle or set of principles derived solely from the authentic theology of Luther. According to this idealistic conception, such a principle broke through to a sudden, decisive victory at Strasbourg in 1524. The truth is, however, that the doctrines peculiar to Luther never dominated local religion at Strasbourg during the Reformation generation; and the Strasbourgeois must therefore be added to those groups of early adherents of the Evangelical movement, who, as the idealist historians are forced to argue, must have "misunderstood" Luther because they did not submit to his judgment on every point.[16] Actually, the "reform movement" contained from the first a variety of tendencies which would eventually differentiate themselves as Anabaptism, Zwinglianism, Lutheranism, etc.,[17] although neither the precise forms nor their principles of variation and antagonism were predictable at the beginning. At Strasbourg, the regime moved from a state of division in 1523 to a pro-reform position in 1525, although the meaning of "reform" depended more on local issues—within the larger framework of the movement against clerical lordship—than it did on the teachings of Luther.

2. The extant evidence speaks for a badly split regime in 1523. Mathis Zell (1477–1549), the deposed cathedral preacher, alleged that half of the members of the regime were attending his lectures out of love for the (Evangelical) truth; but, about the same time (summer 1523), Martin Bucer judged the strength of the reform faction in the regime much less favorably.[18] The direct testimony of an insider, Bernhard Wurmser von Vendenheim, reveals the heat of the debates:

> Sir Bernhard Wurmser says that he believes that my lords should take care that they do not attack one another so violently in the Senate concerning the Lutheran affair, that provocative speeches should be avoided, and that no one should twist another's words against him.[19]

---

[16] This misconception is discussed by Moeller, "Problems of Reformation Research," p. 10.

[17] On the original unity of the Evangelical movement, which later differentiated itself along lines determined partly by internal tensions and partly by events, I agree entirely with the formulation by Gerhard Brendler, *Das Täuferreich zu Münster 1534/35*, Leipziger Übersetzungen und Abhandlungen zum Mittelalter, B2 (Berlin, 1966), pp. 166–167.

[18] A. Baum, *Magistrat und Reformation*, p. 20, citing Zell's *Verantwortung*, fol. 62, and Bucer's letter to Zwingli, 9 June 1523.

[19] *Ann. Brant*, No. 3476. See *ibid.*, No. 4473 (12 December 1523): "Erk.: Dass man über die luther. Sachen im Rath nit so hitzig deliberiren soll."

The deadlock was not complete in 1523, for the regime began then to evolve a program of ecclesiastical and secular concessions designed to help bring the movement under control. One such measure was the edict (14 July 1523) which declared that all perpetual rentes, with certain exceptions, were now redeemable at fixed rates.[20] Although directed at the collegial chapters in favor of their debtors,[21] the measure was socially ambiguous, for the chapters were only a few major usurers in a city ruled by usurers.[22] The law thus represents a considerable sacrifice by the aristocracy and a (to them) unwelcome restriction of property rights, features which suggest how seriously the regime took the popular movement even at this early stage. The regime also founded a civic welfare fund (*Almosen*) to replace the haphazard, clerically administered poor relief and to provide closer supervision of the lives of the poor.[23] The culmination of this pattern was the enactment of a tax reform in favor of the poorer classes during the height of the rebellion of 1525.[24]

Aristocratic regimes in pre-modern Europe had a finely developed sense for what was dangerous and what was not; and the wisdom of the day held that religious disturbance was something of which rulers had to be "infinitely afraid," being a force "sufficient of itself to bring mutation to a state."[25] The recognition of the danger posed by religious

---

[20] AMS, R 29/92a, signed by Peter Butz, which begins: "Nochdem ein gemeine Stat vnnd Burgerschafft diser stat Strassburg mit ewigen zinsen hochbelestiget vnd beschwert worden, do durch dan konnfftiger abgangk zubesorgen ist, Solchem vorzusein, so habent vnser hern Meister vnd Ratt, Schöffen vnd Aman in chrafft einer stat gegebenen fryheiten je von vil heyligen Bapsten, keysern vnd konigen verluhen jrer gemeine stat vnd burgerschafft zu gut vnd vffgang, Erkant vnd verordnet das man solche ewige zinse wol ablösen möge. . . ." See Rott, "Artisanat," pp. 150–151.

[21] *Ann. Brant,* Nos. 4488, 4496, 4498 (January–February 1524).

[22] Rapp, *Réformes et Réformation,* pp. 440–441.

[23] On this development, see Winckelmann's massive *Fürsorgewesen,* although his belief that civic poor relief was a product of Lutheranism is a casualty of modern scholarship. As Natalie Z. Davis puts it: "Perhaps the trouble is that we have not sufficiently convinced ourselves of how and why European religious sensibility had changed in regard to begging and the charitable act even without the impact of Reformed teachings on these subjects." "Poor Relief, Humanism, and Heresy," in her *Society and Culture in Early Modern France,* pp. 17–64, here at p. 19. See also Kamen, *The Iron Century,* pp. 403–410, an excellent general interpretation; and Brian Pullan, *Rich and Poor in Renaissance Venice. The Social Institutions of a Catholic State, to 1620* (Cambridge, Mass., 1971), pp. 216–238, 254–257, 636–637, 641–642.

[24] Rott, "Artisanat," pp. 148, 156.

[25] Etienne Pasquier, *Lettres historiques (1556–1594),* ed. Dorothy Thickett (Geneva, 1969), p. 100, quoted by Elliott, "Revolution and Continuity," p. 45. Also dangerous, according to Pasquier, are "huge debts" and "a royal minority."

disturbance itself—quite apart from the possibility or probability of accompanying sedition—undoubtedly kept the regime of Strasbourg unified from 1523 through the crisis of 1525, despite the existence of acute personal and party differences. This unity was expressed in the combined effort at secular as well as ecclesiastical reforms, an effort which preceded the emergence of a solid Evangelical majority in the oligarchy.

A giant step toward bringing the disturbances under control, and a move which seems to have met with no significant lay opposition, was the liquidation of clerical immunity and the incorporation of the clergy into the political commune. Much has been written about this step as an attainment of the ultimate social–spiritual unity of the city.[26] It was also a step of great practical utility, for it brought the main agitators and their chief targets into the network of ordinary political life, where they were subject to the political controls that touched the lives of all citizens. This is illustrated by the case of Sifridt Keller, a vicar at Old St. Peter, who became a citizen and joined the *Weinsticherzunft* on 31 January 1525. Six months later, when he was agitating against the regime and threatening its members, the government could have him arrested and jailed without worrying about the consequences of violating clerical immunity.[27]

From 1523 to 1524 the regime became willing to go to almost any lengths to bring the popular movement under control. The most serious expression of this will was the beginning of the liquidation of the convents, a step which not only cut deeply into aristocratic self-understanding and pride but also formed a serious violation of property rights. To this extent, the traditional view is correct in seeing 1524 as a turning point—that is, to the extent that the regime now contained a majority which was willing to take extreme, even dangerous steps to bring the movement under control. There was still in 1523 an important party which believed that no major changes were necessary. This was no longer true in 1524, when the regime took steps clearly forbidden by the Edict of Worms (1521). In a walled city, where there was no secure place of refuge from internal rebellion, it was probably not difficult to convince all but the most militant Catholics that to fail to yield some would mean to lose all. In just this process the regime learned well and correctly that the reformers' reform was not only not dangerous to

---

[26] Moeller, "Kleriker als Bürger," the fullest treatment; and Ozment, *The Reformation and the Cities*, pp. 32–38.

[27] Wittmer, No. 7696; *Ann. Brant,* No. 4627.

established order, it was itself the best antidote to revolution.[28] In later years the regime would justify its actions by appealing to the twin necessities of "the love of truth" and the need to "maintain civil peace." [29] Such arguments, unlike the more partisan cry against idolatry, could and probably did appeal to the political wits of senators and privy councillors of various shades of opinion during the 1520s. Although friends of the old church fought each major change right down to 1529, and although the Evangelicals were never of a single mind about reform, the basic path of reform pursued a logic which transcended party feelings and forced itself on the oligarchy as a whole.

B.   The Zealots, the Politiques, and the Old Guard

Nearly ninety years ago, Adolf Baum confessed that "we know almost nothing" about the religious convictions of members of the regime during the mid-1520s.[30] Although Baum was the first historian who did not rely entirely on Jean Sturm's second-hand account of the religious divisions in the regime, he was unable to add much to Sturm's picture.[31] The state of the sources is so lamentable that we shall never get a very precise picture of the factional alignments, but the main outlines of the parties can be ascertained and some of their leaders and members identified.

The party names employed in this account are modern inventions,

---

[28] Martin Luther and Philip Melanchthon wrote at the end of December, 1529: "Das zu besorgen war, wo des Luthers lere nicht drein komen were, . . . Es were ein iamerlich verderben ynn deudschen lande entstanden. . . . Es were ein unordige, sturmissche, fahrlich mutation odder enderung worden (Wie sie der Muntzer auch anfieng), wo nicht eine bestendiger lere darzwisschen komen were, und on zweifel die gantze religion gefallen und lauter Epicurer worden aus den Christen." *WaBr*, XII, No. 4235, pp. 106–110, here at ll. 16–24 on pp. 107–108. The notion of Luther's reform as a specific against revolution is at least as old as 1526, when Landgrave Philip of Hesse expressed it in his instruction for the Diet of Speyer. Walter Friedensburg, *Der Reichstag zu Speyer 1526 im Zusammenhang der politischen und kirchlichen Entwicklung Deutschlands im Reformationszeitalter,* Historische Untersuchungen, 5 (Berlin, 1887), pp. 497–498.

[29] The apologies composed at Strasbourg in 1529–30 are filled with such phrases. These are taken from *BDS*, III, ed. Robert Stupperich (Gütersloh–Paris, 1969), 370 ll. 22–23, from "Rathschlag D" composed for the embassy to the Diet of Augsburg in 1530.

[30] A. Baum, *Magistrat und Reformation,* p. 11.

[31] Sturm, *Quarti Antipappi,* pp. 3ff., whose comments are the basis of almost all subsequent sketches of the political leaders of Strasbourg in this generation. Ficker and Winckelmann (1902–05) were the first to add information from manuscript sources.

but they correspond well enough to the groups to which they are attached. The "Zealots" are the militant Evangelicals of the 1520s, those who demanded reform regardless of the external consequences and who tended to favor Zwinglianism in ecclesiastical policy and a pro-Swiss foreign policy. The "Politiques" are the moderate Evangelicals and their allies, who were inclined to consider the effects of reforms on the city's reputation abroad and to seek security for their city in alliance with the Lutheran powers in the Empire. Finally, those Catholics who defended the old faith until the bitter end in 1529 are here called the "Old Guard." The assignment of individuals to one party or another is based on individuals' opinions and reputations as well as on policies supported at one time or another from the mid-1520s through the 1540s.

1. The chief of the Zealots was Claus Kniebis, a university-educated rentier, who spent his entire adult life in civic office and who converted to the new religion by 1522.[32] During the next two years he was joined by a series of prominent figures from the ranks of both patricians and guildsmen.[33] From the former came Egenolf Röder von Diersburg, still smarting from his father's excommunication, Bernhard Ottfriedrich, and Hans Bock von Gerstheim, who had opposed Luther personally at the Diet of Worms (1521) but converted by early 1524. Bock's later actions cast some doubt on his classification as a Zealot, but he was certainly a devout, militant Evangelical at an early date. Of the guildsmen, Martin Herlin, a merchant, Daniel Mieg, a wealthy rentier, and Jacob Meyer (Masons) were Zealots from an early date; Hans Lindenfels, a cloth merchant, joined them by the later 1520s; and Mathis Pfarrer,

---

[32] Jean Rott, "La Réforme à Nuremberg et à Strasbourg. Contacts et contrastes (avec des correspondances inédites)," in *Hommage à Dürer*, pp. 91–142, here at pp. 88–100; *idem*, "Un recueil de correspondances strasbourgeoises du XVIe siècle à la bibliothèque de Copenhague (ms. Thott 197, 2°)," *Bulletin philologique et historique (jusqu'à 1610) de la Comité des travaux historiques et scientifiques*, année 1968 (1971), pp. 749–818, here at pp. 759–764; *idem*, "Magistrat et réforme," pp. 103–114.

[33] All in the PROSOPOGRAPHY. Zwingli wrote to Claus Kniebis on 6 August 1524 and sent greetings to Hans Bock, "quem domino fidelem esse omnes praedicant." *ZW*, VIII, No. 343, here at p. 215 ll. 4–7 (wrongly assigned to 1526 by Johann Wilhelm Baum, *Capito und Butzer, Strassburgs Reformatoren* [Elberfeld, 1860], p. 365). He wrote on 28 September 1524 to Kniebis, Herlin, and Daniel Mieg, urged them to work harder for the common cause, and revealed his Strasbourg informant to be Wolfgang Capito. Oskar Farner, ed., "Ein unveröffentlichter Zwinglibrief," *Zwingliana*, 9 (1950), 248 (not yet in Zwingli's collected correspondence). Jörg Frey, the young Strasbourgeois whose pulpit-stimulated hysteria led him to the block in 1529, named as leading Evangelical politicians Egenolf Röder von Diersburg, Bernhard Ottfriedrich, Daniel Mieg, Claus Kniebis, and Martin Herlin. The fullest account of this pitiful story is in the "Imlin Chronik," pp. 412–414.

another cloth merchant and son-in-law of Sebastian Brant, may also have supported this group. These men dominated the drafting of reform measures during 1524–25, a fact which may be seen in the surviving records of committee assignments for these years.[34] Table 19 Lists the

Table 19

Members of the regime of Strasbourg most frequently assigned to committees on ecclesiastical (A)
and non-ecclesiastical (B) affairs, 1521–25

Name	(A) Eccles. (Rank)		(B) Non-eccles. (Rank)		(C) Total (Rank)	
Kniebis, Claus	36	(1)	33	(1)	69	(1)
Herlin, Martin	28	(3)	25	(2)	53	(2)
Meyer, Jacob	29	(2)	11	(7)	40	(3)
Bock v. Gerstheim, Hans	21	(5)	18	(4)	39	(4)
Mieg, Daniel	14	(10)	25	(2)	39	(4)
Böcklin, Ludwig	20	(6)	9	(10)	29	(6)
Hug v. Ottenheim, Philips	17	(7)	10	(8)	27	(7)
Pfarrer, Mathis	22	(4)	5	(14)	27	(7)
Ottfriedrich, Bernhard	16	(9)	9	(10)	25	(9)
Hoffmeister, Caspar	13	(11)	10	(8)	23	(10)
Ellenhart, Peter	17	(7)	4	(16)	21	(11)
Sturm, Jacob	13	(11)	7	(12)	20	(12)
Wurmser, Bernhard	7	(17)	12	(6)	19	(13)
Spender, Reimbold	3	(24)	13	(5)	16	(14)
Zuckmantel, Melchior	12	(14)	4	(16)	16	(14)
Röder v. Diersburg, Egenolf	12	(14)	4	(16)	16	(14)
Lindenfels, Hans	13	(11)	1	(27)	14	(17)
v. Rotweil, Hans Ludwig	3	(24)	7	(12)	10	(18)
Joham, Conrad	8	(16)	1	(27)	9	(19)
Spender, Jacob	7	(17)	2	(22)	9	(19)

Source: Rott, "Magistrat et réforme," p. 113.

men most frequently assigned to committees in 1521–25. Nearly nine-tenths (88%) of the ecclesiastical committees fall in 1523–25 and more than two-thirds in 1524–25, compared with 38% and 34% of the non-ecclesiastical committees respectively;[35] and although the records are fragmentary, they are thus likely to afford a fairly reliable picture of the

---

[34] Rott, "Magistrat et réforme," pp. 113–114.

[35] The disparity is due to a certain bias for ecclesiastical affairs in the excerpting of the protocols of the Senate & XXI, although the same is not true of Peter Butz's list, published by Rott, *ibid.*, pp. 107–112.

relative levels of participation of councillors in the reforms. The Zealots thoroughly dominated the committees which drafted the major reforms. Five of them stand in the first five places both in total assignments and in ecclesiastical assignments, and two others stand in the eighth and ninth places. The table also reveals that Jacob Sturm, who is conventionally assigned a major role in the reforms at Strasbourg,[36] actually played a modest role, as befitted a junior patrician senator.

The Zealots were all men who had entered the regime before the Reformation, most of them by 1519–20, and did not owe their access to public office to their advocacy of the new religion. Their way upward may have been speeded, however, by the movement of 1523–25. The most remarkable feature of Table 19 is the mysterious absence of nearly the entire older generation. To be sure, the eldest politicians were mostly XIIIers and were perhaps less likely to be assigned to ecclesiastical committees than were the younger XVers, in whose competence ecclesiastical affairs directly rested. But that is not the entire story. Although more than half (eleven of twenty) of the men in Table 19 are patricians, only two—Hans Bock von Gerstheim and Ludwig Böcklin— appear among the six men most often assigned to ecclesiastical committees, and neither appears in the top four. Also missing are nearly all of the prominent guild politicians of the older generation, men such as Conrad von Duntzenheim, Andreas Drachenfels, and Gottfried von Hohenburg, all Altammeister. With the sole exception of Hans Bock von Gerstheim, whose membership in the Zealots is not entirely certain, the Zealots were younger non-patricians, mostly XVers. A closer analysis of the religious complexion of the regime may throw some light on their role.

2. The members of the Old Guard are difficult to identify. Jean Sturm named four men who led the Catholic resistance: Andreas Mieg, Gottfried von Hohenburg, Conrad von Duntzenheim, and Hans Ebel.[37] They all belonged to the wealthiest stratum in the guilds, and all were merchants except Hohenburg, who was a rentier. Hohenburg and Duntzenheim were Altammeister and XIIIers and belonged to the true inner circle, while Ebel and Mieg were neophyte senators in 1524 and

---

[36] This conventional error is repeated by Konrad Fuchs, "Zur Politik der protestantischen Reichsstände vor der Eröffnung des Augsburger Reichstags von 1530," *ZGO*, 118 (1970), 170.

[37] Sturm, *Quarti Antipappi*, pp. 9–10, information that is likely to be correct, as Sturm married Ebel's granddaughter.

1525 respectively, and neither was a privy councillor at this time. At least two other men belonged to the Catholic party, the merchant Martin Betscholt and the cloth merchant Caspar Hoffmeister. Betscholt had entered the Senate in 1522 and was not yet a prominent figure in the regime, while Hoffmeister had been a XVer at least since 1518.[38] Another Altammeister, Andreas Drachenfels, almost certainly belonged to this party, but he refused a fifth term as ruling Ammeister in 1524 and apparently resigned his offices shortly thereafter.

Drachenfels resigned his offices in January, 1524, and Hohenburg in September of the same year. A number of other, mostly older, privy councillors disappeared from government affairs in 1524 or 1525 for (unknown) reasons other than death. Herbart Hetter (d. ca. 1542), son of an immigrant from Recklinghausen, is known to have tried to protect the Dominicans against an attack on their house; but he dropped out of sight in 1525. Two years earlier, Claus Schetzel (1453–1530) ceased to play a role in the regime. In 1524 disappeared several prominent patricians, Hans Ludwig von Endingen (1474–1548) and Ludwig Zorn zum Riet (d. 1529), plus Hans Ludwig von Rotweil (1458–1531). Some or all of these men are likely to have left office because they disagreed with the steps their colleagues took in 1524–25. The same may be true of Melchior Zuckmantel von Brumath, a patrician senator who renounced his citizenship while in office (3 July 1524).[39] This all suggests that by 1525 or so the Catholics knew that the cause of the old faith was lost. A few prominent Catholics stayed on and continued the struggle from within: Martin Betscholt, who defended the Mass during the struggle over abolition in 1528 but eventually conformed to the new order; and Conrad von Duntzenheim, who resigned his offices in 1530. Duntzenheim's departure may be said to mark the end of the Old Guard as a party in the regime of Strasbourg.

3. The Zealots and the Old Guard account for only a small fraction of the privy councillors and senators. Of the majority nearly nothing is known about their religious leanings or commitments. What is certain is that by 1524 at the latest the Senate & XXI contained a majority willing to enact some ecclesiastical reforms in order to preserve the peace of the city. In 1524 and 1525, as Table 19 shows, the known defenders of Catholicism simply were not appointed to sensitive committees. Caspar Hoffmeister may be an exception, but the date of his conformity to the

---

[38] His place in Table 19 bears out Hoffmeister's greater prominence.
[39] On Melchior Zuckmantel von Brumath, see Chapter II above, p. 81.

new order is unknown. This did not mean that the Senate & XXI contained by 1524 a majority of strongly committed Evangelicals. The speed of the reforms at Strasbourg reflects the strength of the popular movement more than it does the progress of the new religion within the aristocracy; and this is the reason why, once the popular pressure eased, as it did by 1526, the pace of reform slowed nearly to a standstill.[40] The Evangelicals did have by 1524 control or near-control of the XV, where they were stronger than in the Senate & XXI as a whole.[41] They were greatly aided by the difficulty of stopping the granting of reforms once the process had begun. By the spring of 1525, when the regime came very close (one vote, it is said) to abolishing the Mass, a step not actually taken until 1529, it needed an intransigent traditionalist to oppose all changes in the properties, institutions, and ceremonies of the old church.[42]

The oligarchy did not, however, act out of fear alone. Although it is true enough that the Zealots tended to be of somewhat lower social rank than the privy councillors as a whole, it is also true that the new faith made important inroads into the upper classes by the end of 1524 and continued to attract aristocrats during the following years. Jacob Sturm entered the regime as a fresh convert and ex-cleric in January, 1524. Some months before, the public conversion of Wolfgang Capito (1478–1541), provost of St. Thomas and a spectacularly successful ecclesiastical climber from Hagenau, gave the local movement a clerical figure who, if not exactly an aristocrat, was at least very well connected.[43] Jacob Zorn zum Riet converted by 1525 and Egenolf Röder von Diersburg by 1527, two of the commune's most eminent aristocrats.

---

[40] Kittelson, *Wolfgang Capito,* pp. 132–135.

[41] This is clear from action taken on 10 November 1524, when the XV reported on a proposal to abolish "die fünff kriegs messen." A majority recommended their abolition and a minority "das man solche messen hinfurtter, wie die von den alten vffgesetzt halten sol." The Senate & XXI approved the minority position. AMS, R 29/253, by Peter Butz. See Luzian Pfleger, "Die Stadt- und Ratsgottesdienste im Strassburger Münster," *AEKG,* 12 (1937), 1–55.

[42] See Capito's letter quoted by Chrisman, *Strasbourg,* p. 150. The chronology and tempo of popular agitation at Strasbourg in 1525 are well described by Rott, "Artisanat," pp. 143–148. The rumor of a plot to open the gates, whether true or false, spread far and wide and was reported by Johannes Cochlaeus, "Ein kurzer Begriff von Aufruhren und Rotten der Bauern in hohem Deutschland," in *Quellen zur Geschichte des Bauernkriegs in Oberschwaben,* ed. Franz Ludwig Baumann, Bibliothek des Litterarischen Vereins in Stuttgart, CXXIX (Tübingen, 1876), p. 786.

[43] Kittelson, *Wolfgang Capito,* p. 108, who dates the conversion to the beginning of August, 1524.

Friedrich Ingold, head of the merchant-banking clan, vassal of the margrave of Baden, and probably a "lediger XXIer," participated in the first eucharistic service in German (19 February 1524) and became a strong partisan of the new faith.[44] This faith, whether it flew the banner of "the Lutheran affair," or that of "the pure Word of God," did not first appear at Strasbourg—as it did in some places—as the cause of social revolution. By 1524 it was welcome in some of the most elegant parlors as well as in humble workers' dwellings, having become respectable before the general crisis of the Reformation developed.

As hot as the words became in the chamber of the Senate & XXI, the oligarchy never lost its public face of unity. When the need for a united policy was especially acute, as during 1525,[45] there appeared a definite reluctance to press the internal division to an open breach— which would have destroyed the regime's ability to command obedience from either party. We need not take literally Jean Sturm's second-hand picture of the gentlemanly tolerance and politeness that reigned in the Senate & XXI during the mid-1520s[46]—Bernhard Wurmser's plea[47] is proof that we should not—but no party took its case to the people. Unofficial partisan acts by members of the regime are very rare. Hans Lindenfels "and his gang" did stage an iconoclastic riot at Old St. Peter on 22 February 1529,[48] and Claus Kniebis occasionally skirted the bounds of legality or tradition in working for his cause. But the defeated Catholics were not forced from office or subjected to any other forms of vengeance, and no one inquired too carefully into the personal beliefs of the senators and privy councillors. This solidarity reflects once more the fact that the general crisis of 1524–25 broke in on an aristocracy at Strasbourg within which old and new wealth lived in firm alliance; and it is a sign that the social struggles of the Middle Ages were over.

---

[44] Friedrich Ingold (d. by 1540) was the son of Hans Ingold (d. 1507) and Brigitta Dedinger (d. 1496) and the brother of Claus Ingold (PROSOPOGRAPHY, No. XLIII); he married Margarethe Arg. He represented the guild Zum Spiegel in the Senate in 1519/20 and 1529/30. The supposition that he was a "lediger XXIer" rests on the fact that, although he was active in the regime in years when he was not a senator (and was thus in the XXI), he nowhere appears among the XVers or the XIIIers. TQ Strassburg, I, 60, No. 65; Fuchs, "Ingold," p. 204; Wolff, "Les Ingold," p. 115 (with wrong death date); Hatt, p. 461.

[45] See, for example, Ann. Brant, No. 4630 (24 July 1525).

[46] Sturm, Quarti Antipappi, p. 10: "Haec erat illius temporis, in vtraque parte Senatus aequitas: nullius conscientiam compellere: non solum superiori suffragiis patri: sed etiam inferiori, si periculum videbant ciuitatis, cedere."

[47] See above, p. 205.

[48] Fragments de diverses vieilles chroniques, No. 4011.

There was also a pronounced unity of domestic and foreign policy in the oligarchy's reaction to the Reformation. Through the year 1523, the regime tried to remain within the limits set by the Edict of Worms.[49] During late 1524 and 1525, however, the context of foreign relations was not the Imperial situation but the revolt on both sides of the Rhine. In its stance toward the peasant armies, the regime repeated its internal policy of pacification.[50] Whatever their individual tendencies and beliefs, the members of the regime were united in wanting the restoration of peace and business as usual in the countryside, although it is entirely possible that some of the nobles, themselves lords on the land, found the violent intervention by Duke Antoine of Lorraine not entirely unwelcome. The internal cohesion of the regime may have been strained by the struggles over domestic reforms, but the oligarchy did not behave in 1525 like the political arm of an aristocracy that felt itself in mortal danger. It pursued rather a policy of internal and external pacification with great determination and consistency right through the grimmest weeks of the revolution. The peace it gained in 1525, with vital assists from princes who were less fastidious about the methods of pacification, vindicated the regime's solidarity. The true gauge of the seriousness of the situation in 1525 and of the regime's realistic, correct apprehension of the situation, are the sacrifices that the aristocracy made in the interest of survival.

C.   Aristocratic Losses and Gains in the Reforms of the Mid-1520s

1. It may well be true that certain changes in piety and religious culture in the South German towns around 1500 prepared the ground for the reception of the Lutheran message two decades later.[51] At Strasbourg the austere moralism and acidic pulpit sarcasm of Johann

---

[49] This was the basis of the regime's refusal (December 1523) to support the preacher at St. Thomas, Anton Firn, against the dean and chapter. *Ann. Brant,* No. 4465.

[50] Fundamental on the regime's policy toward the revolution in the region is Jean Rott, "La guerre des paysans et la ville de Strasbourg," in *La Guerre des paysans 1525*, ed. Alphonse Wollbrett for the Société d'histoire et d'archéologie de Saverne et environs (Saverne, 1975), pp. 23–32, a volume which is relevant to all aspects of the revolution in Alsace and the Ortenau, with a fine bibliography on p. 141. To the works there listed should be added Francis Rapp, "Die soziale und wirtschaftliche Vorgeschichte des Bauernkriegs im Unterelsass," in *Bauernkriegs-Studien,* pp. 29–46.

[51] See Bernd Moeller, "Frömmigkeit in Deutschland um 1500," *ARG,* 56 (1965), 5–31; Kohls, "Evangelische Bewegung und Kirchenordnung," pp. 112–116.

Geiler certainly fanned the endemic local anticlericalism; and it was with good reason that some local Evangelical preachers looked on him as a forerunner.[52] Well before the news of Luther's early blows could have spread among the common folk at Strasbourg, Hans Lamprecht, an innkeeper, declared that "the indulgence is nothing, and, if he had enough money to span from here to Colmar, he wouldn't give a farthing for an indulgence."[53] Jacob Sturm, too, attributed his alienation from the old church to indigenous influence when he told his old teacher and friend, Jacob Wimpheling, "if I am a heretic, you made me one."[54] Strasbourg in 1520 was nonetheless not just a ripe plum waiting to fall into the hands of Luther's disciples, for the ties of the aristocracy to the economy, institutions, and the very physical sites of the old church were very old and very strong.

That the urban governments in South Germany, possibly excepting that of Nuremberg, did not take the lead in promoting reform is a commonplace of the literature on the urban reform.[55] Explanations range from a reluctance to violate Imperial law to Kohls's hardly supported suggestion that the regimes were deeply engaged in a political

---

[52] This is not to say that he anticipated Luther's doctrine of justification, a point settled by E. Jane Dempsey Douglass, *Justification in Late Medieval Preaching. A Study of John Geiler of Keisersberg,* SMRT, 1 (Leiden, 1966), p. 208. Granted Douglass's definition of "Protestant" (Protestant=someone who adheres to Luther's doctrine of justification), it is undoubtedly true that Geiler was "by no means a fifteenth-century Protestant." But this assertion does not touch the fact that Geiler (and Wimpheling) was regarded as a forerunner by the reformers of Strasbourg. Caspar Hedio once remarked: "so mehr ich D. Kaisersperg lesse, ie mer er mir gefaellt, dann ich less etwan sein geschrifft, so find ich dass ers wol hat verstanden und gemerckt, aber es ist die zeit noch nit gewessen." "Les éphémérides de Jacques de Gottesheim, docteur en droit, prébendier du Grand-Choeur de la Cathédrale (1524–1543)," ed. Rodolphe Reuss, in *BSCMHA,* N.S. 19, p. 271 (24 July 1526). Mathis Zell's very similar judgment is cited by Chrisman, *Strasbourg,* p. 78. On the growth of anticlericalism at pre-Reformation Strasbourg, see now Rapp, *Réformes et Réformation,* pp. 431–479, which should be compared with Kiessling's account of anticlericalism in Augsburg, in *Bürgerliche Gesellschaft und Kirche in Augsburg,* pp. 306–315.

[53] *Ann. Brant,* No. 4396 (3 April 1518). Hans Lamprecht, innkeeper Zum goldenen Schaff, bought citizenship on 17 January 1513 and joined the guild Zum Freiburg. The outcome of his case is unknown, but he did renounce his citizenship on 3 March 1519. Wittmer, Nos. 6260, 6887.

[54] Jacob Wimpheling to Sixt Hermann, Sélestat, 2 November 1524, printed by Ficker–Winckelmann, II, 48. Wimpheling accused Sturm of Wyclifism, a charge he had made also against Capito. Kittelson, *Wolfgang Capito,* pp. 15, 101, 145, 243, shows that Wimpheling knew what he was talking about.

[55] Lau, "Der Bauernkrieg und das angebliche Ende," p. 119; Moeller, *Reichsstadt und Reformation,* pp. 25–28; Kohls, "Evangelische Bewegung und Kirchenordnung," p. 127; and, for Strasbourg, Chrisman, *Strasbourg,* p. 116.

reform of their own, to Moeller's argument that the regimes feared that toleration of religious diversity would damage the unity and spiritual welfare of the commune as a sacral body. Moeller, it is true, draws on social considerations, such as "the natural opposition of the aristocrat to the passions of the multitude and the general conservatism of the rich and privileged" and the fact that "the old church reserved very pleasant rewards for nobility and wealth, like entry into economically comfortable positions and into offices guaranteeing salvation."[56] Gerald Strauss, on the other hand, has argued that Luther's pessimistic anthropology suited perfectly the Nuremberg aristocracy, which recognized its solid political stake in a doctrine that taught the fundamental futility of human action.[57] None of these arguments recognizes the extensive and profound *familial* ties between the urban ruling classes and the old ecclesiastical order. These attachments, compounds of material interest, symbolic satisfaction, and family tradition, meant that only a terrible shock—such as the revolution of 1524–25—could induce the oligarchies to undertake a wholesale dismantling of the old order. A reform could be undertaken, it is true, which would satisfy the Evangelical clergy and still preserve nearly all the benefits the aristocracy had had from the old faith—the case of Nuremberg proves the point. At Strasbourg, however, where the reforms were considerably more radical and the popular movement very strong, the ruling class had to sacrifice very much in order to protect its domination. The following discussion is meant to outline the principal facets of this theme rather than to exhaust it. First come the churches as physical incorporations of aristocratic family pride, piety, and position. Next is the living web between the aristocratic families and clerical and religious personnel, the juridical separateness of whom from the commune is a favorite theme of the "sacral corporation" tradition of scholarship.[58] The third theme is the complex of aristocratic financial interest, and the last the ties to the traditional cultus.

2. Pre-reformation Strasbourg had at least nineteen convents, five collegial churches, seven parish churches, and about 180 chapels.[59] Some of these structures were pulled down during the sixteenth century,

---

[56] Moeller, *Reichsstadt und Reformation*, p. 27, quoting from the English version, p. 62, although I am not convinced that "guaranteeing salvation" is what is meant by "Sicherstellung des Seelenheils."

[57] See above, p. 192n86.

[58] See the references in note 26 above, and Chrisman, *Strasbourg*, p. 45.

[59] Specklin, *Collectanées*, Nos. 2135–2136.

and the survivors lost the bulk of their internal decoration either then or during the French Revolution. Some of these establishments were physical monuments in wood, paint, glass, and stone to the piety and pride of generations of aristocratic Strasbourgeois. The panoply of tombs, funeral tablets, altars, and retables, mostly donated by the great families, made the churches and chapels living museums dedicated to the ancestors of the civic ruling class.

The destruction of so much religious art means that the full pattern of donations cannot be reconstructed systematically, but enough fragments and records remain to yield an impression of the scale of donation before the Reformation. The ancient church of St. Thomas, for example, was adorned by the epitaphs of patrician ancestors of such families as the Merswin, Ellenhart, Zorn zum Riet, and Lentzel, plus such wealthy guild families as the Mieg, Ingold, Ryff, and Gerbott.[60] The cathedral, as befitted its greater dignity and size, was a showcase of graves of and memorials to patricians, wealthy guildsmen, and members of the regional nobility.[61] The Reformation put an end to the practice of displaying the memories of one's ancestors in the local churches. In 1527 the regime forbade further burials in the churches and chapels of the town; and thereafter aristocrats were buried, along with other citizens, in designated cemeteries outside the walls.[62] Early in the next year, the government moved to protect "the gravestones of the nobles and the burghers" from the depradations of iconoclasts and purifiers.[63] Not even the ancestral tombs of the aristocracy were safe from popular depradations, and Mathis Beger, who abhorred what was happening at Strasbourg, rescued his father's bones from the Carmelite convent and reinterred them at his chateau at Geispolsheim.[64] Although the official legislation ending the practice of church burial altogether dates from several years after 1525, it was the fruit of popular pressure for the purification of the churches and the damage done to existing monuments.

---

[60] Schnéegans, L'église de Saint-Thomas, pp. 225–234.

[61] On the old decoration of the cathedral and its removal or destruction during the Reformation, see Johannes Ficker, Das Bekenntnis zur Reformation im Strassburger Münster, Theologische Studien und Kritiken, 109/1 (Leipzig, 1941); and, on the funeral monuments in particular, Joseph M. B. Clauss, "Das Münster als Begräbnisstätte und seine Grabinschriften," Strassburger Münster–Blatt, 2 (1905), 9–26, and 3 (1906), 11–31.

[62] Specklin, Collectanées, No. 2281.

[63] Ann. Brant, Nos. 3512, 4711 (6 January 1528), cited by Clauss, "Das Münster als Begräbnisstätte," Strassburger Münster–Blatt, 2 (1905), 11–12.

[64] Matern Berler, "Chronik," in Code historique, II, 98.

As with the tombs and funeral monuments, so with the altars, retables, shrines, and windows. Many but not all disappeared during the 1520s; and the conventional wisdom about the iconoclasm of those years is that the iconoclasts were the very persons who had earlier made the donations ("die Bilderstifter wurden Bilderstürmer").[65] This hypothesis, which has never been tested empirically, involves the highly improbable implication that the iconoclasts of the Reformation era were urban aristocrats whose fathers and grandfathers had been the donors. At most, it is likely that members of the urban regimes—who, even if convinced Evangelicals, were not likely to help destroy their own families' pasts—realistically yielded to popular pressure in purging the city's churches.

Donations to the churches, as we know from histories of towns where far less was destroyed than at Strasbourg, occurred on a lavish scale during the generations just before the Reformation.[66] At Strasbourg there were major individual gifts, such as the large Mount of Olives in stone which Nicolaus Röder von Diersburg (d. 1511) donated to St. Thomas.[67] Certain families also had traditional attachments to particular convents and churches. The Sturm and their guildsman allies, the Schott, for example, favored the Dominican houses.[68] Peter Schott the Elder (d. 1504) had daughters in both parts of the Dominican double convent of Ss. Margarethe and Agnes, where, at one daughter's request, he donated in 1494 200 fl. for a retable. The Sturm had numerous Dominicans in the family. Martin Sturm's daughter, Clara, entered Ss. Margarethe and Agnes in 1508 with a dowry of 200 fl.; and his two brothers, Ludwig and Ott, were buried "zu den Predigern" just before

---

[65] This phrase of Hermann Heimpel's is cited with full approval by Moeller, *Reichsstadt und Reformation*, p. 24 (*Imperial Cities and the Reformation*, p. 60), who admits that donors and iconoclasts were not actually the *same* persons but maintains that this makes no difference, because they belonged to the same urban communities. This naive view should be compared with the rich insights in Natalie Davis's "The Rites of Violence," *Society and Culture in Early Modern France,* esp. pp. 173ff.

[66] See Kiessling, *Bürgerliche Gesellschaft und Kirche in Augsburg,* pp. 246–251; Geiger, *Die Reichsstadt Ulm,* pp. 167–170.

[67] Walter Hotz, *Handbuch der Kunstdenkmäler im Elsass und Lothringen* (Berlin, 1965), p. 230; Roland Recht, "Nicolas de Leyde à Strasbourg. L'épitaphe dite 'du chanoine de Busnang,'" *ASAVS,* 4 (1974), 23–39, here at pp. 29, 39.

[68] On the Sturm and Schott connections to the Dominicans, see *Fragments de diverses vieilles chroniques,* No. 4235; Philippe A. Grandidier, *Nouvelles oeuvres inédites,* ed. A. Ingold, 5 vols. (Colmar, 1897–1900), V, 366–367; Kraus, *Kunst und Alterthum im Unter-Elsass,* p. 516; Rapp, *Réformes et Réformation,* p. 520; J. A. Riegger, *Amoenitates litterariae friburgenses,* 3 parts (Ulm, 1775–76), p. 172; Straub, "Notes généalogiques," *BSCMHA,* N.S. 9, p. 86; Schmidt, *Histoire littéraire,* II, 29, 29n78, 9n20.

the Reformation. One of the collegial churches, All Saints', went back to a Mülnheim foundation, while the Knights of St. John owed their residence, the great establishment "zum grünen Wörth," to the generosity of a Merswin.[69]

The retable as an art form reached its high point just before the Reformation, and retables were frequent gifts from wealthy Strasbourg donors. One such gift was made to a rural church by Conrad von Duntzenheim, Sr., Ammeister and father of Conrad, Jr.[70] A truly grand gift was the great retable for the shrine of St. Margaret, painted in the same Strasbourg shop that produced the Duntzenheim retable, which Stephan Bock von Bläsheim, Hans Bock's father, commissioned. This was a princely gift by one of the great local figures of the generation of the Burgundian Wars.[71]

Grander than retables were glass windows, which set the arms of the donor families high above the congregations, where they gleamed in permanent superiority. One of the great glass monuments of the last pre-Reformation generation was a magnificent group for the convent of the Penitentials, St. Magdalena, created in the shop of Peter of Andlau in 1476–85.[72] These windows, which survived the Reformation, were donated by a large group of interrelated aristocrats, including several Wurmser and Böcklin, a non-patrician Erstein–Armbruster, and several members of the Ryff family, whose arms were prominently displayed in the windows.

Whole crafts depended for their livelihood largely on the generosity of aristocratic donors and thus experienced a sharp depression with the cessation of local patronage for ecclesiastical art.[73] Much of the work of Strasbourg painters, sculptors, and glaziers fell prey to the iconoclastic riots of 1524 and 1525. At first the regime tried to protect the retables and altars with legislation, but soon after (spring, 1525) it bowed to popular pressure and ordered such objects removed from the churches.[74]

---

[69] *Chroniken der deutschen Städte*, IX, 732–733, 732n6, 733n2.

[70] Originally at Weyersheim, now in the Maison de l'Oeuvre Notre-Dame, Strasbourg, it portrays St. Conrad with the donor at his feet. Rott, *Oberrhein,* Textband, p. 75.

[71] The wings of this retable are preserved at Dijon and Langenbrück (Baselland). *Ibid.*, pp. 74–75.

[72] Hans Haug, "Notes sur Pierre d'Andlau, peintre-verrier à Strasbourg, et son atelier," *AAHA*, 15 (1936), 91–105.

[73] Rott, *Oberrhein*, I, 304–305.

[74] *Ibid.*, p. 304. The first decree is dated 18 March 1525; the second is undated but assigned by Rott to 1525.

The regime recognized the residual property rights of the descendants of donors in the objects donated and permitted them to rescue and take home the material fruits of ancestral piety.[75] The funeral tablets and retables saved in this way presumably found their ways into private chapels. In return for taking part in the orderly purification of the churches, the aristocracy received one paltry compensation: permission to hang heraldic shields in the cathedral.[76]

3. As the churches and chapels contained physical links to aristocratic families past, so the personnel of the convents and collegial chapters contained living links to aristocratic families present. Such family ties to the old church are often ignored by historians who take a strictly juridical view of the handling by urban regimes of the problem of eliminating the *privilegium fori* and the immunities of the clergy and religious. Such scholars tend to see only the elimination of a foreign body from the commune, while, in fact, the "foreignness" of the clergy was a very relative matter, because of familial ties between citizen families and the local clergy and religious. It is certain, on the one hand, that the percentage of native-born persons among the Strasbourg clergy and religious was lower during the two generations before the Reformation than it earlier had been.[77] The cathedral chapter, of which Erasmus once joked that Jesus Christ could not have become a canon for lack of sufficient quarterings, admitted mostly counts and dukes during the sixteenth century and had no Alsatian canon after 1455. The other four chapters—St. Thomas, Old and New St. Peter, and All Saints'—contained many fewer Strasbourgeois (less than 30%) and fewer Alsatians than they had before 1450. At the Dominicans', a "bourgeois" rather than a noble house, the percentage of natives had fallen to about 25%. Only in the women's houses of the mendicant orders did the children of local families still predominate, and here, as in the other houses and chapters (except All Saints'), the share of the patricians lagged far behind that of the wealthy guild families. In this

---

[75] *Ibid.*: "Damit sich aber nyemands zu beclagen hab, das ime das syn, so von ime oder sinen voreltern in die kirchen geben worden, genomen oder entwert werde, das man dann eim yeden, so tafeln in den kirchen stan hatte . . ., verkunden und sagen lassen soll, dieselben in acht tagen den nehsten hinweg zu nemen; dann wo nit, werde man im sonst abweg nemen."

[76] Schad, *Summum argentoratensium templum*, p. 77, who lists forty-one families, some Constofler and some guildsmen, whose arms hung in the cathedral in his day. They are long gone, but their like can still be seen in the Münster at Ulm.

[77] Rapp, *Réformes et Réformation*, pp. 298–305, 451–452; *idem*, "Haut et bas clergé dans le diocèse de Strasbourg à la vielle de la réforme," *RA*, 103 (1965), 11.

respect it is correct to speak of an "alienation" between the local population and their clergy and religious during the two generations before the
Reformation, a growing distance which was only indirectly connected
with the existence of clerical immunities.

Despite this important erosion of the living social bonds between
aristocracy and clergy during the decades before 1520, much remained.
Nearly one-quarter of the clergy and religious who acquired citizenship
at Strasbourg in 1523–25—mostly pursuant to the law of 1524—
received their citizenship from a parent.[78] Some prominent families
had strong ties to individual houses and chapters. Claus Braun, a
merchant and XVer, had two brothers who were canons at Old St.
Peter and two daughters who were nuns at St. Nicolaus in Undis, one
of the five houses that survived the Reformation more or less intact.[79]
His canon brothers continued to hold benefices from the bishop and
received new benefices well after the reforms at Strasbourg, which
suggests that the family did not become Evangelicals. At the two houses
of the Poor Clares, St. Clara auf dem Wörth and St. Clara auf dem
Rossmarkt (both pulled down at the Reformation)—the prioress came
from prominent old guild families, the Ryff and Mussler respectively.[80]
The Stettmeister Egenolf Röder von Diersburg had one sister, Magdalena (d. 1531), who was abbess at St. Stephan, two others who were
nuns at St. Marx, and a third who had been a nun at Andlau.[81] Alexius

---

[78] Based on a study of 256 admissions of clergy, religious, and ecclesiastical officials
in the *Livre de bourgeoisie 1440–1530* for the years 1523 (23), 1524 (31), and 1525 (198).
Ten were patricians, of whom five were women. The lists do not include, of course,
minors taken from the convents and restored to their families; and the number of women
in the lists (6) is extremely low.

[79] Jacob and Johann, who acquired their citizenship from their deceased father on
31 January 1525. Wittmer, Nos. 7691, 7695. See PROSOPOGRAPHY, No. XV. On the
fates of the convents, see Robert Schelp, *Die Reformationsprozesse der Stadt Strassburg am
Reichskammergericht zur Zeit des schmalkaldischen Bundes (1524)/1531–1541/(1555)*,
2nd ed. (Kaiserslautern, 1965), pp. 60–62.

[80] St. Clara auf dem Wörth, just outside the walls on the southeast side of the city,
was partially torn down in 1525 and entirely so in 1526, the nuns being transferred to
the other St. Clara; but both congregations were dissolved in 1529. Specklin, *Collectanées*, Nos. 2270, 2277, 2303; *Ann. Brant*, No. 4799. The prioresses were Beatrix Ryff at
St. Clara auf dem Rossmarkt and Elisabeth Mussler (not the one who married Jacob
Zorn zum Riet) at St. Clara auf dem Wörth. AST 35: "St. Clara vff den Rossmarkt," at
31 March 1526; AMS, KS 18, fols. 1ʳ–4ʳ, dated 14 November 1524. On the Ryff family,
see Lehr, III, 458; on the Mussler, see above, p. 88n121.

[81] PROSOPOGRAPHY, No. LXXVI; "Les éphémérides de Jacques de Gottesheim,"
pp. 273–275; Schelp, *Reformationsprozesse*, 2nd ed., p. 104; Rapp, *Réformes et Réformation*, p. 390n142.

Büchsner, a patrician senator in 1525/26, had a brother, Balthasar, who was canon at All Saints'.[82] In all probability, scarcely a patrician family at Strasbourg, and very few prominent guild families, lacked at least one member in a convent or chapter in 1520.

The family ties between the convents and aristocracy at Strasbourg had always been a powerful barrier against all-too-hasty interference by the regime in the internal affairs of the houses. During the fifteenth century, in fact, the regime seems to have usually sided with the regulars in their quarrels with the secular clergy, a natural stance if one considers that parishes could never answer to the demands of aristocratic familial piety to the degree that the convents did or supply the places for their children as the convents did.[83] It was largely due to such connections that Johann Geiler's campaign (1492) to restore discipline in some of the women's houses was so unsuccessful.[84] As for the Reformation, these family ties probably helped to cool the ardor for reform in the breasts of all but the most zealous Evangelicals among the aristocracy. The latter showed their colors by removing their female relatives from the convents. Claus Kniebis took his thirteen-year-old daughter from St. Nicolaus in Undis against her will in 1522 (22 June); and Jacob Spender followed his example five months later.[85] The Sturm brothers, whose parents had died several years before, took their sister, Clara, from St. Margarethe in the following year.[86]

For waverers and men in the middle of the struggle, ties to the clergy could be troublesome. They were for Bernhard Wurmser, whose brother, Nicolaus (1473–1536), was dean of St. Thomas, a staunch Catholic, and a major foe of the regime's effort to subjugate the collegial chapters.[87] Rumors ran through the town that Bernhard and another

[82] Wittmer, No. 7687; Gustav Knod, "Elsässische Studenten in Heidelberg und Bologna," *ZGO*, 46 (1892), 338, No. 133. He became a canon at St. Thomas in 1538 and died on 28 March 1541.

[83] This seems to have been the case in the regular-secular quarrel over the *ultimum vale* during the 1450s and sporadically thereafter. Rapp, *Réformes et Réformation*, pp. 333–337.

[84] Specklin, *Collectanées*, No. 2164: "Darzu hatten vil vom adel und im regiment, toechter, schwestern, bassen und mehr freunde darinnen, wolten auch ohne des pabst erlaubniss solches nit angreiffen."

[85] AMS, II 7/20, quoted in *La ville libre de Strasbourg au carrefour des courants de pensée du XVIe siècle. Humanisme et Réforme à Strasbourg*, Exposition du 5 mai au 10 juin 1973 (Strasbourg, 1973), pp. 51–52, No. 108. A similar case is that of Adolf von Mittelhausen, Sr., who in May, 1525, tried to remove his sister from St. Margarethe. AST 37, fols. 48ʳ, 59ᵛ.

[86] Rapp, *Réformes et Réformation*, p. 520, from ADBR, H 3325, fols. 24–25.

[87] Ficker–Winckelmann, II, 53; Rapp, *Réformes et Réformation*, p. 161.

brother were helping Nicolaus against the regime, which so distressed Bernhard that he asked to be relieved of his offices, which his colleagues refused to allow.[88] At New St. Peter, the provost was Wolfgang Böcklin von Böcklinsau (d. 1530), a cousin of the regime's most influential patrician figure, Ludwig Böcklin.[89] It may be significant that none of the many Wurmser and Böcklin who held office between 1520 and 1555 was ever to be found among the staunch Evangelicals, that several members of each family renounced citizenship during the crisis of 1548, and that members of each family returned to Catholicism.[90]

The reform at Strasbourg did not abolish, and it probably did not much restrict, the access of the aristocratic families to endowed canonries in the collegial chapters, whose existence was not threatened by the ecclesiastical changes. It may, in fact, have enhanced the availability of benefices to *local* aristocrats. Only the chapter of St. Thomas has been studied for this period, and a comparison of the appointments before and after the regime took control of nominations does not indicate that the Reformation restricted aristocratic access to the benefices there.[91] During the 1530s, a Büchsner, a Wetzel von Marsilien, a Wurmser, and a Mieg became canons at St. Thomas; and the numerous canons from local aristocratic families who got their benefices before the Reformation, continued to enjoy their revenues whether or not they converted to the new religion. It is likely that studies of Old and New St. Peter and of Allerheiligen would yield similar results.

4. The early Reformation cut fairly deeply into aristocratic property

---

[88] *Ann. Brant,* No. 4574 (27 January 1525).

[89] Kindler, *OG,* I, 131–132; PROSOPOGRAPHY, No. XII; Sturm, *Quarti Antipappi,* p. 4. On Wolfgang Böcklin, see Rapp, *Réformes et Réformation,* p. 506; *Ann. Brant,* No. 4496.

[90] As Wolf Sigismund Wurmser von Vendenheim (PROSOPOGRAPHY, No. CIII), and Wilhelm Böcklin von Böcklinsau (d. 14.X.1585), on whom see Hermann Kopf, *Ritter Wilhelm Böcklin von Böcklinsau. Hofmarschall–Dompropst–Stifter in Freiburg* (Freiburg/Br., 1974), pp. 8–9, 17, 36, and the references in Chapter IV above, note 12.

[91] Gustav Knod, *Die Stiftsherren von St. Thomas zu Strassburg (1518–1548)* (Strasbourg, 1892), pp. 17–46. Canons appointed before the Reformation who were closely related to privy councillors were: Nicolaus Wurmser (1473–1536), 1510–36, brother of Bernhard W.; Daniel Messinger (d. 1527), 1499–1527, brother of Lux M.; Johann Wetzel von Marsilien (d. 1538), 1510–38, brother of Jacob W. v. M.; Theobaldus Baldner (d. 1530), 1501–17, brother? of Heinrich B.; Caspar Wurmser, 1521–39; Sebastian Wurmser (d. 1541), 1522–41; Heinrich Ebel (d. 1563), 1518–32; Wolfgang Böcklin (d. 1530), 1509–30. Appointed during the 1530s were: Balthasar Büchsner, (d. 1541), 1538–41, brother of Alexius B.; Heinrich Wetzel von Marsilien, 1536–45, son of Philips W. v. M.; Wolfgang Wurmser, 1534–48; and Mathis Mieg (d. 1581), 1532–55.

rights, especially the rights of lay patronage of ecclesiastical posts and lay ownership of ecclesiastical tithes. In the long run, of course, the Reformation probably strengthened lay control of both clergy and ecclesiastical property on the land in Lower Alsace, just as it did at Strasbourg.[92] In the short run, however, it was by no means clear that the movement would respect lay property rights in ecclesiastical posts and revenues, any more than it respected the property rights of ecclesiastical owners. Secularized tithes were extremely common in the diocese of Strasbourg on both sides of the Rhine, as was lay patronage of the village pastorates.[93] Although the question has not been studied systematically in Lower Alsace, a study of analogous forms of patronage in Upper Swabia shows that the share of lay patronage rights owned by citizens of the free cities there was climbing at the expense of the lower nobility on the land ever since the fourteenth century.[94]

Some families suffered directly as a result of government intervention to pacify the popular movement. The Marx von Eckwersheim were lay patrons of the church of St. Andreas at Strasbourg, where they held patronage and tithe in fief from the bishop.[95] By early 1525, the Catholic pastor was finding it ever harder to collect the tithe and deliver it to his lords, the Marx. The regime, in order to assuage the growing clamor at St. Andreas for an Evangelical preacher, asked the Marx to oust their own man from the parish, which they refused to do. A few weeks later, the church was closed forever.[96] The Marx were apparently never

---

[92] This is true not only because the ecclesiastical structures of Protestantism made the clergy naturally more dependent on the lords, but more specifically because the installation of Evangelical clergy often required a direct violation of rights of patronage by the seigneur. This is clear in the account of the movement of Evangelical clergy into the seigneuries of the Lower Alsatian *Reichsritter,* in Adam, *EKET,* pp. 501–550. See Marie-Joseph Bopp, "Evangelische Geistliche und Theologen aus Deutschland und der Schweiz im Elsass. Ein Beitrag zur oberrheinischen Geistes- und Familiengeschichte," *AJb,* 1961, pp. 175–234, here at pp. 214–216.

[93] For Alsace, see Pfleger, *Die elsässische Pfarrei,* esp. pp. 95–103 (lay patronage), and 306–308 (lay ownership of tithes); and, for the right bank, Dieter Kauss, *Die mittelalterliche Pfarrorganisation in der Ortenau,* Veröffentlichungen des Alemannischen Instituts, 30 (Bühl/Baden, 1970), examples at pp. 256, 249–250 (Röder von Diersburg), 235 (Windeck), 240 (Mülnheim), and 263 (Schauenburg).

[94] Gerhard Kallen, *Die oberschwäbischen Pfründen des Bistums Konstanz und ihre Besetzung (1275–1508). Ein Beitrag zur Pfründgeschichte vor der Reformation,* Kirchenrechtliche Abhandlungen, 45/46 (Stuttgart, 1907), pp. 188–189.

[95] AST 134 ("Historische Umstände der Kirchen St. Andreae in Strassburg welche auss der Statt Archiv gezogen worden"); Luzian Pfleger, *Kirchengeschichte der Stadt Strassburg im Mittelalter,* Forschungen zur Kirchengeschichte des Elsass, 6 (Colmar, 1941), p. 53; Adam, *EKSS,* p. 70.

[96] *Ann. Brant,* Nos. 4571–4572, 4585.

compensated for this invasion of their property rights, and no Marx ever served in Strasbourg's regime after this incident.

The oligarchy tried, of course, to protect aristocratic property rights during the liquidation of the convents, thereby recognizing the permanent property rights of aristocratic families in their donations to the houses. As noted above,[97] some laymen bought up properties of the Poor Clares during the early days of the liquidation, and Kniebis's position suggests that he took advantage of his office to aggrandize himself and his friends.[98] The curators (*Pfleger*) of the convents were frequently petitioned by former nuns, monks, and friars, and by their relatives, who sought to recover properties donated to the convents. They were often successful. Ottilia von Rotweil recovered 100 fl. and 4 lb. her father had given when she entered St. Marx.[99] Jacob zur Megde, a noble related to many patrician officeholders, asked for restoration of the Mass stipend his father had donated to St. Clara auf dem Rossmarkt, "since, now that the Mass and stipend are no longer fulfilled, . . . he will employ the money elsewhere."[100] At the same house of the Poor Clares, the prioress, Beatrix Ryff, asked for several items, including the lead she had given to cover a roof of the convent.[101] Heirs, too, made claims and had them recognized. Margarethe Pfeffinger was the widowed second wife of Ott Sturm (d. 1521), Martin's brother, and heiress of Jacob von Bietenheim, a deceased monk of the aristocratic convent of St. Arbogast. In 1528, her guardians, Hans von Blumenau and Sifridt von Bietenheim, both members of the regime, asked the curators to affirm her right to Jacob's estate, which would otherwise fall to the monastery.[102] Through

---

[97] See Chapter IV above, p. 146. The traditional view is repeated by Kohls, "Evangelische Bewegung und Kirchenordnung," p. 128: "In den oberdeutschen Städten wurde das Kirchengut nahezu ohne Ausnahme als Eigentum der Kirche nicht angetastet. Die Magistrate fungierten hier lediglich als Treuhänder."

[98] A clear picture will require intensive study of the volumes of AMS, KS, for the mid-1520s.

[99] AST 35: "S. Marc," at Simonis et Judae (28 October) 1524.

[100] *Ibid.*: "St. Clara vff dem Rossmarkt," at 8 June 1527. Jacob zur Megde, from an old patrician family of Strasbourg, became a citizen there on 1 June 1513 and renounced his citizenship in 1522; he was the son of Caspar zur Megde and related to the Vegersheim and the Erstein–Armbruster. Wittmer, Nos. 6295, 7199; Kindler, *OG*, III, 46; Wunder, *Landgebiet,* p. 97.

[101] AST 35: "St. Clara vff dem Rossmarkt," at 31 March and 12 May 1526.

[102] *Ibid.*: "S. Arbogast," at 16 January 1528, where she is wrongly named "Maria." Margarethe's first husband was Sifridt von Bietenheim (d. ca. 1487), father of Sifridt II v. B. (PROSOPOGRAPHY, No. IX) and Jacob v. B. On the fate of St. Arbogast, see Schelp, *Reformationsprozesse,* 2nd ed., pp. 67–101. The existence of residual property right of

such requests, a good deal of the property of the convents probably found its way into aristocratic hands. The most interesting feature of the attitude toward ecclesiastical property, however, is that although the regime itself clearly claimed succession to the ecclesiastical owners, it also affirmed the continued existence of property rights on behalf of the donors and their heirs.

5. Another type of bond between an aristocrat and a religious house, a bond of sentiment involving the aristocratic notion of honor, is illustrated by the story of the fate of the Knights of St. John at Strasbourg. The commandery of the Knights at Strasbourg owned a tremendous establishment in whose precincts the emperors lodged during their infrequent visits to the town.[103] By the terms of the will of the donor, Rulman Merswin (1307–82), two nobles of Strasbourg served as lay curators of the house; and, during the late 1520s, the curators were two of the oldest and most powerful patrician privy councillors, Ludwig Böcklin von Böcklinsau and Hans Bock von Gerstheim.[104] Böcklin's religious loyalty is unknown, but Bock was a zealous Evangelical. In January, 1529, began a struggle between Bock and his colleagues in the regime, who wanted to regularize the civic supervision (*Pflegerei*) of the commandery by appointing non-noble curators on the same basis as for the other religious houses. Bock pleaded that he had given his oath as a knight to uphold the terms of Rulman Merswin's will, and he fought his colleagues at every step. He seems to have won his point, as the curators during the following two decades were all nobles.[105] That Bock himself placed his conception of honor above his feelings against the old church, largely explains why the commandery of St. John survived the Reformation.[106]

---

donors and heirs of donors in capital and other objects of pious foundations was widely recognized. See Rublack, *Einführung der Reformation in Konstanz*, p. 303n245; Becker, *Reformation und Revolution*, p. 97.

[103] Specklin, *Collectanées*, No. 2196; and see above, note 69.

[104] Based on the records of the *Klosterherren*, two dossiers in AST 35: "St. Johans zum Grünen Werd" (copy in a seventeenth–century hand) and "Johaniter." The quarrel began on 8 February 1529, although the innovation was contemplated as early as 1527.

[105] Curators (*Pfleger*) at St. Johann were: Hans Jacob Zorn von Plobsheim, 1527; Ludwig Böcklin von Böcklinsau, 1527–29; Hans Bock von Gerstheim, 1527–42; Jacob Zorn zum Riet, 1529–31; Jacob Sturm, 1533–53; Ulman Böcklin von Böcklinsau, 1534–48. The list is derived from the two dossiers in AST 35; and no guildsmen appear as curators of the Knights of St. John.

[106] There is also the fact, of course, that the Grand Master of the order in the Empire was a member of the Imperial Diet.

There is another reason why the commandery of St. John survived. In 1548, when the commandery had only one member left, its chief curator, Jacob Sturm, made the case for a revival of the community through permission to take in new members.[107] His reasoning was a piece of pure calculation. Although the house had declined to a single member, the commandery was an important moneylender in the city, and its customers included prominent and humble Strasbourgeois, some of whom were Evangelicals. The latter did not shun the house's banking services just because the commandery remained loyal to the old church.[108] Sturm reasoned, with good sense, that the provincial of the order at Freiburg im Breisgau would have a legitimate claim to the property of the order at Strasbourg if the local house died out, and that it was therefore much in the interest of the Evangelical regime and city that the Catholic Knights of St. John flourish again.

6. The old religious ceremonies, and especially the Masses which the Evangelical preachers called idolatry, contained entire webs of bonds between living aristocrats and their familial pasts. The foundation of Mass stipends, providing for the regular reading of Masses for the families' dead, bound the living donors and the dead beneficiaries into a familial community analogous to the union of the Church Triumphant and the Church Militant. It is highly probable that every well-to-do family in Strasbourg had established Mass stipends in one or more churches and convents into whose necrologies their dead were entered. An illuminating example is the necrology of the Red Church, the church of the Strasbourg lazarhouse.[109] Here were entered as donors or beneficiaries of Mass stipends members of many patrician and wealthy guild families, including one-quarter of all the families who supplied privy councillors between 1520 and 1555. This was a relatively humble church, and the necrologies of the great collegial churches of Strasbourg would give an even more impressive picture of private Masses as a bond between the present and the past of aristocratic families.

The gradual abolition of the Mass also struck at much of the public ritual which represented the great deeds of the communal past and bestowed divine blessing upon the present structure and leadership of

---

[107] ADBR, H 1408 (1548). My thanks to Jean Rott for supplying me with a copy of his transcription of this document.

[108] ADBR, H 1630, a notarial register which gives a running account of the house's lending business.

[109] Charles Wittmer, "L'obituaire de l'Eglise Rouge de Strasbourg," *AEA*, 1 (1946), 87–131, with an index on pp. 129–131.

the social order. Public Masses celebrated the most glorious events in civic history, such as war memorial Masses in memory of the victories of the Burgundian Wars. Such ceremonies were abolished fairly early in the reform movement and never restored. As part of the regime's sacred panoply, the ceremonial expression of the *arcanae regiminis*, of course, they could hardly be truly replaced by Evangelical preaching services.[110]

In abolishing another type of Mass, the public funeral Mass for a dead Ammeister, the regime reluctantly swept away one of the few rewards it could bestow upon an Ammeister's family, the public funeral customarily given the most eminent servants of the commune. When Heinrich Ingold died, just before Christmas, 1523, it was asked in the Senate & XXI whether or not, in view of the recent anticlerical disturbances, they should allow the usual High Mass in the cathedral for a dead Ammeister. It was decided that they should, and Ingold was the last Ammeister of Strasbourg to be buried in the old way.[111] When Florentz Rumler died, just over two years later, his former colleagues decided to send a delegation to console the family (Rumler's son was a XVer) but to dispense with the funeral Mass.[112]

7. Acceptance of the principal demands of the reform movement by the aristocracy and its regime in Strasbourg entailed the loss of much that had been precious to the great families of the town. In a certain sense, the assault on the old church was also an assault on the aristocracy itself, for, just as the physical city belonged in a peculiar sense to the aristocrats— its landlords—so the old church belonged, again in a peculiar sense, to the aristocracy. Many of the attacks on the Catholic clergy, on the traditional ceremonies, on the decoration of the churches, and on the forms and uses of ecclesiastical property and jurisdiction, were also assaults on the symbolic forms, and occasionally on the material substance, of aristocratic power. To specific institutions the movement and the reforms it engendered were dangerous only to a point, for the most aristocratic ecclesiastical institutions were hardly damaged, even at

---

[110] Pfleger, "Die Stadt- und Ratsgottesdienste," pp. 16–21.

[111] *Ann. Brant,* No. 4480 (24 December 1523); and a more detailed account in the "Imlin Chronik," pp. 391–392, where it is noted that the funeral Mass was held at the *Stadtaltar* in the Münster *after* Ingold (on whom see PROSOPOGRAPHY, No. XLIV) was actually buried at St. Thomas, whereas the usual practice was to sing the Mass over the body. The current disturbances at St. Thomas probably prompted the decision not to hold a solemn funeral Mass there.

[112] *Ann. Brant,* No. 4658 (7 February 1526); PROSOPOGRAPHY, No. LXXXI.

Strasbourg. It was the most aristocratic convents, such as St. Stephan, St. Nicolaus in Undis, that survived while the mendicant orders were disappearing, and the only ecclesiastical body closed to all Strasbourgeois—the most "foreign" in the terms of the juridically minded historians —the cathedral chapter, was also the only one that was virtually untouched by the reforms.[113]

In 1524–25 the regime bought social peace at a certain cost, some of which was paid by the aristocracy itself. In the absence of a special study it is impossible to even guess at the material losses to individual families as the church ceased to be a vast system of relief for the aristocracies; and, as this analysis has suggested, the direct material losses were probably less significant than the damage done to cultural capital, that is, the pride, prestige, and social rank of aristocratic families. On the one hand, the closing of the convents meant the cutting off of the aristocracy from one of the chief grazing grounds for the support of its children; and, on the other hand, the purification of the churches destroyed the public symbols of the glory and pride of aristocratic families.

D.   Accommodation to the New Order

There may have been other aristocrats whose reaction to the destruction of so much tradition resembled that of Mathis Beger, the noble who liberated his father's bones from the heretics at Strasbourg. Antipathy for or even total rejection of the reforms may have been largely or partly responsible for the disappearance from public life of so many old families after the mid-1520s, such as the Lentzel, the Ryff, the Marx von Eckwersheim, the Mussler, the Völtsch, and the Arg. The overwhelming impression offered by the aristocracy before and after the Reformation, however, is one of great continuity; and this suggests that, in one way or another, most of the great families reached an accommodation with the new order.

Most of the leading patrician and guild families continued in government through the reforms and afterward without interruption, such as the Sturm, Mülnheim, Zorn zum Riet, Wurmser von Vendenheim, and Böcklin von Böcklinsau in the one category, and the Rumler, Sebott,

---

[113] Schelp, *Reformationsprozesse,* pp. 60–61, with references. See also Levresse, "Prosopographie du chapitre de l'église cathédrale de Strasbourg"; and, for the historical background, the unpublished thesis of Jean Rott, "Histoire du Chapitre cathédrale de Strasbourg du XIVe et au XVe siècle," Thèse de l'Ecole des Chartes, 2 vols. (Paris, 1933).

Ingold, Duntzenheim, Messinger, Mieg, and Rotweil in the other. In most cases we do not know when or by whom a family was reconciled to the new order. The sons of Conrad von Duntzenheim, Jr., Jacob and Batt, did decline to follow their father's defense of Catholicism, became Evangelicals, and enjoyed long political careers.[114] The three Sturm brothers and the two Böcklin brothers were also Evangelicals who stepped smoothly into the political legacies of Catholic fathers. If there was an exodus of aristocrats at Strasbourg in response to the reforms, as there was in some other towns,[115] it was so minute that no historian has been able to document it.

The crisis of 1523–25 nonetheless left deep scars within the ruling class. From Bernhard Wurmser's pleas, quoted above, we know that bitter words flew up and down the benches in the chambers of the Senate and the privy councils. Two other incidents bear special mention, both of which involved Claus Kniebis and cannot but have damaged his reputation inside the regime. On May 14, 1524, Augustin Drenss, subsequently the Gardeners' XVer and a member of the politically most powerful family in that guild, charged that Kniebis and his brother-in-law, Dr. Michael Rot, had deceived Drenss's sister, Margarethe, into an agreement to marry Caspar Hedio, a scholar-preacher and protégé of Wolfgang Capito.[116] Drenss, who seems not to have been a lover of priests of any kind, objected to the marriage as contrary to both civil and canon law, "as Christendom has known them for a thousand years and more, and also because no little disadvantage, disgrace, and dishonor might accrue to me and mine from this affair."[117] Here was yet another case of a wayward priest seducing a young girl away from her family, a common enough grievance of the pre-Reformation era. That Hedio did not consider himself a priest and regarded himself as free to marry did not matter in the least to Drenss, who saw in the prospective brother-in-law simply one more lustful clerical seducer of the daughters of honest citizens:

> If it should come to the point at which every priest and monk could find it proper to deceive and seduce the child or relative of an upright fellow and

---

[114] Noted by Sturm, *Quarti Antipappi*, p. 10.

[115] Moeller, *Reichsstadt und Reformation*, p. 27.

[116] Documents now in AST 69/2–6, fols. 5ʳ–15ᵛ; PROSOPOGRAPHY, No. XVIII.

[117] AST 69/2–6, fol. 5ᵛ: "dero sÿ die Cristenheit dúsent jar vnnd noch lenger gebrucht hatt vnnd ouch darusz mir vnnd denn meinern nit kleiner nachteÿll schandt vnnd schmach erwachsen möcht."

citizen, secretly and against his will, then that would be a terrible thing; and my lords can well imagine the consequences.[118]

Drenss was outraged at the involvement of Kniebis, Kniebis's relatives, and his own and the girl's mother in the affair, and he appealed to his colleagues as fathers and husbands, men whose power over their closest female relatives was endangered by this clerical deceit, to forbid the marriage. They did not. Under heavy pressure from his colleagues, which suggests just how influential Kniebis was, Drenss withdrew his complaint, and his sister married her preacher on 24 June 1524.[119] Many of Drenss's colleagues attended the wedding banquet,[120] and Kniebis and Rot got away without a reprimand.

The second incident also occurred during 1524. A noble named Hans Jacob Schütz von Trubach tried to rouse the commons of Sélestat to overthrow the civic regime and introduce Lutheranism.[121] Wolfgang Capito at Strasbourg was suspected of complicity, and Claus Kniebis was also thought to be involved. Rumors lingered on, though nothing was proven, and added to Kniebis's reputation as a zealot and disrupter.[122]

The principal male actors in these incidents, Drenss and Kniebis, served as privy councillors until their respective deaths. So did Martin Betscholt, one of the last privy councillors to defend the Mass, along with Bernhard Wurmser, who in 1523 had been so anxious about his own reputation. The reforms at Strasbourg happened so quickly and under such great popular pressure that the movement carried along with it a great many persons, including aristocrats, who were either conventionally religious Evangelicals, unperturbed conformists, or even clandestine

---

[118] *Ibid.*, fol. 6ʳ: "Dan solt es je do hin khomen das ein ÿeden pfaffen vnnd munch zÿmmen vnnd geburen wolt onn witter engeltnusz einem frumen Bÿderman vnnd burger sine khindt oder verwanten wider wissen vnnd willen zu betriegen vnnd zu beschlÿssen were wollich schimpflich zu hören vnnd was dar vszs erwachsen möcht jr meine gnädigen herren wol ermessen."

[119] *Ann. Brant*, No. 4521; Büheler, *Chronique*, No. 206; Specklin, *Collectanées*, No. 2240.

[120] J. W. Baum, *Capito und Butzer*, p. 160. Kniebis's son, Nicolaus Hugo, was Margarethe Drenss's guardian after Hedio's death. AMS, V 14/112.

[121] Paul Adam, *Histoire religieuse de Sélestat*, I: *Des origines à 1615* (Sélestat, 1967), pp. 187–192; Lina Baillet, "Deux villes de la Moyenne Alsace: Sélestat et Colmar, face aux conflits religieux et sociaux," in *La Guerre des paysans 1525*, ed. A. Wollbrett, pp. 93–102, here at pp. 94–95.

[122] *Ann Brant*, No. 4529; "Les éphémérides de Jacques de Gottesheim," p. 271 (17 February 1527). It was believed that the true dimensions of the plot had never been uncovered.

Catholics. The regime was outwardly a solid phalanx on the side of the new religion, but there was no internal agreement on the meaning of the reforms, no ideological unity; and there was to be no *enforced* public norm of belief at Strasbourg until the coming of ultra-Lutheranism during the second half of the sixteenth century. The remarkable flexibility and unity of the oligarchy at Strasbourg during the crisis of 1523–25 concealed many a partial accommodation to the new religion, along with many complete ones.

E. CONCLUSION

From a purely institutional point of view, it is true enough that the measures against the clergy, the convents, and the pious foundations in the South German free cities during the 1520s moved along paths marked out long before the Reformation. In such actions, "the town government could feel in harmony with the ideas and institutions of the late Middle Ages."[123] From the aristocratic point of view, however, this vision of thoroughgoing continuity is misleading and even false, for the Reformation destroyed much that was dear to urban aristocratic families and not a little that was politically important to them. This was true of civic religion, whose ritual gave religious sanction to the conserving conservatism so vital to aristocratic regimes. The assault on ritual in the Reformation was a potential danger to the entire social order, because the ritual of the old religion and the political ritual and symbols of the commune were so intimately tied together. Whether the Evangelical clergy, with all of their obedience and good will, ever made good this loss, is the subject of another study.

It may well be true that "Catholicism at the end of the Middle Ages was in large part a cult of the living in the service of the dead,"[124] whose souls were prayed for and memories preserved through the pious donations of living descendants. But only "in large part," for the religious relation between living and dead was a reciprocal one, and the dead repaid the prayers of the living by enhancing the prestige and marital value of the living. A family tree loaded with eminent figures, whose

[123] Moeller, *Reichsstadt und Reformation*, p. 32 (*Imperial Cities and the Reformation*, p. 68).
[124] A. N. Galpern, "Late Medieval Piety in Sixteenth-Century Champagne," in *The Pursuit of Holiness*, pp. 141–176, here at p. 149. See Davis, "Some Tasks and Themes in the Study of Popular Religion," pp. 326–336.

wealth, glory, and piety could daily be displayed to one's fellows in various public forms, was a definite social and even political asset, a form of cultural capital peculiar to the aristocratic ruling classes of pre-capitalist society.[125] Anyone who visited or attended regularly the churches and chapels of pre-Reformation Strasbourg would learn the eminence of the great families whose donations and arms looked out on or down on the worshipers from the windows, retables, altars, and funeral monuments with which each place of worship was studded. Here were displayed the genealogies which legitimated the political power of the aristocrats.[126] The Reformation severely damaged, if it did not destroy, these bonds to the past, for it severed the ties of family history to civic religion and relegated this form of cultural capital to the private, non-political sphere.

More immediate and more concrete was the loss of wide sectors of the extensive systems of endowed livings for the children of the rich through the liquidation of so many convents and foundations. In judging the significance of these losses, however, one must remember that even in so thoroughly reformed a city as Reformation Strasbourg, the most aristocratic houses survived the longest, and the collegial chapters were not invaded at all.

If what was lost impresses, it is dwarfed by what was saved. In satisfying popular demands at clerical expense the regime cut dangerously into the structure of property rights, a clear indicator of the crisis's seriousness. One must remember that obligations of the most various origins—tithes, patronage, fiefs, seigneurial dues, etc.—had been fairly thoroughly transformed into property in the modern sense, and that, except for the institution of mortmain which hindered the development of a completely free market in property and rights, the forms and institutions of property did not much differ between ecclesiastical and lay owners. When, therefore, the rulers yielded to the argument that ecclesiastical property should be administered for the public good regardless of historic rights and the intentions of donors, not far beyond this idea lay the position that all property should be so administered.

---

[125] The concept of "cultural capital" is developed by Pierre Bourdieu, who applies it chiefly to education, the primary system for transmitting symbolic goods in modern society. See Bourdieu, "Reproduction culturelle et reproduction sociale," pp. 47–48 (German version, pp. 91–96).

[126] Keith Thomas, "History and Anthropology," Past & Present, No. 24 (April 1963), pp. 7–8, discusses the symbolic importance of genealogy to aristocratic systems of power.

Property, after all, was still a socially contingent concept, not yet enshrined as one of the holiest elements of nature and natural law. This is why the regime's invasions of ecclesiastical property rights was truly dangerous: there was no fundamental reason why all property should not be socialized as ecclesiastical property was. In this light, the actions of the regime seem graver and more consequential. What the aristocrats sacrificed in 1523–25 suggests what the Reformation might have become. What was saved in 1523–25 suggests how that potential was thwarted.

Scarred but still in possession of its social cohesion and its political unity, the aristocracy and oligarchy of Strasbourg weathered the crisis of the mid-1520s. They had altered as little as possible but as much as necessary and had survived the storms with hegemony intact. But the Reformation was not over, and in the ensuing difficulties the regime would never again display quite the full political nerve and the will to act, the qualities which had borne it through the terrible months of the lost revolution.

CHAPTER SEVEN

THE REGIME OF STRASBOURG IN THE HALCYON DAYS OF THE GERMAN REFORMATION, 1526–1546

For two decades after the revolution of 1525, the Evangelical party in the Holy Roman Empire grew stronger with each passing year. The formation of the Smalkaldic League (1531), the peace wrested from Charles V (1532), and the settlement of intra-Evangelical quarrels in the Wittenberg Concord (1536) ushered in a period of peace and relative relief from the execution of Imperial laws against the new religion.[1] At Strasbourg the respite from external pressure enabled the regime to begin reconstructing the lines of ecclesiastical control,[2] while the regime played a crucial role externally in the gradual incorporation of the South German free towns (always excepting Nuremberg) into the Smalkaldic League.[3] Despite the apparent success of the regime, the oligarchy of Strasbourg continued to be divided into parties that reflected the unresolved accommodation of the various sectors of the ruling class to the reforms of the mid-1520s. This tension, plus the mounting burden of political business created by Reformation politics, the declining powers of the generation of the 1520s, and the failure to recruit adequate successors prepared an internal disintegration long before the disastrous confrontation of the League with Charles V in 1546–47.

A. Zealots and Politiques: The Unity of Foreign and Domestic Policy

1. The foreign policy of the late 1520s and early 1530s, the era of new alliances for Strasbourg, was shaped in large measure by the commanding figure of Jacob Sturm, who by 1530 had emerged as the most powerful figure in the regime.[4] He prepared the regime's submission

---

[1] Ekkehart Fabian, *Die Entstehung des Schmalkaldischen Bundes und seiner Verfassung 1529–1531/33. Brück, Landgraf Philipp von Hessen und Jakob Sturm*, 2nd ed., SKRG, 1 (Tübingen, 1956).

[2] Chrisman, *Strasbourg*, pp. 201–226.

[3] Baron, "Religion and Politics," p. 406.

[4] See Brady, "Jacob Sturm of Strasbourg and the Lutherans," pp. 184–185.

to the Saxon conditions for the formation of a united Protestant front —abandoning the Zwinglian allies in Switzerland—and remained to the last one of the League's strongest partisans.

These facts are well known. What is not well known is that Sturm's policy won through at Strasbourg against powerful and dogged opposition from men who were closely identified with the reforms of the mid-1520s, the "Zealots" around Claus Kniebis, who may be identified with Zwinglian religion and a pro-Swiss foreign policy. Around Sturm, on the other side, gathered the "Politiques," those who supported his pro-Lutheran, pro-Saxon policies.

The conflict between Zealots and Politiques did not end either with the formation of the Smalkaldic League or with the defeat of Strasbourg's Swiss allies at Kappel in 1531.[5] The issue was more than a disagreement over the best way to assure Strasbourg's security or a personal rivalry between Sturm and Kniebis. Sturm's "Saxon solution" strove to overcome the unresolved contradiction at the heart of the Strasbourg Reformation, a contradiction between the enthusiastic, purifying, corporatist-congregationalist movement of the "little people" in the 1520s and the begrudging acceptance of the reforms by most of the civic ruling class. The oligarchy's relationship to those whom it ruled was shaped by the fact that it had been pressured into the reforms. Just as the "Swiss solution" was the analogue in foreign policy to the popular movement, so Sturm's "Saxon solution" was an analogue to the aristocracy's ambiguous response to that movement. It is in this light that the connections among Sturm's foreign policy, the reconstruction of the church under lay control, the rise of sectarianism at Strasbourg, and the inner disintegration of the oligarchy during the 1540s must be judged. The very success of the oligarchy in damming and channeling the movement of the 1520s prepared the ground for the struggle of 1547–48.

There were good enough reasons to identify reformed Strasbourg with the Zwinglian cause. The reform movement in the Alsatian city had exhibited marks well known in the Evangelical towns of Switzerland: virulent anticlericalism, iconoclasm, hostility to the economic

---

[5] The Strasbourg–Swiss connection is analyzed by René Hauswirth, *Landgraf Philipp von Hessen und Zwingli. Voraussetzungen und Geschichte der politischen Beziehungen zwischen Hessen, Strassburg, Konstanz, Ulrich von Württemberg und reformierten Eidgenossen 1526–1531*, SKRG, 35 (Tübingen, 1968), esp. pp. 139–160.

apparatus of the church (e.g., the tithe), and the desire for popular, lay control over parish life.[6] The conformity to type was completed during the mid-1520s, when the Strasbourg reformers moved into the orbit of Zwingli's theological influence.[7] The Saxon Lutherans and the Nurembergers thus branded reformed Strasbourg as a Zwinglian or "sacramentarian" town, especially after its regime suppressed the Mass on 20 February 1529. This reputation was correct, provided that "Zwinglian" does not necessarily mean a close formal conformity to the opinions of the Zürich preacher.[8]

Zwinglianism swept through the South German towns during the 1520s and possessed, despite its many variations, common social and political roots and tendencies. Wherever the political struggle between old and new wealth, between entrenched patricians and guilds, had not yet reached a final settlement, Zwinglianism went hand-in-hand with anti-patrician, anti-aristocratic sentiments and provocations—thus tying the age of the guild revolts to that of the Reformation—and sometimes ended in a wholesale flight of the urban aristocracy.[9] Though early bound up with radical, popular tendencies that later flowed into the sectarian movement, Zwinglianism was essentially the religion not of the totally dominated but of the "little people," the small merchants, shopkeepers, and artisans, whose relationship to the aristocratic regimes was everywhere ambivalent. Such groups often had some participation in civic political life but rarely any power. The most characteristic ideological expression of this stratum during the Reformation was the sacral corporatism, that traditional ideal which the Rhenish reformers clothed anew in Evangelical theology.[10] This ideology aided the urban regimes in shearing the movement of its potentially dangerous features.

---

[6] Chrisman, *Strasbourg,* chapter 7; Kohls, "Evangelische Bewegung und Kirchenordnung," pp. 117–124.

[7] The influence of Zwingli on Bucer and Capito during the second half of the 1520s is a commonplace in the literature. See, most recently, Kittelson, *Wolfgang Capito,* p. 147: "Under Capito's direction, the Strasbourg reformers were in Zwingli's camp before there was such a thing." On Bucer, see James M. Kittelson, "Martin Bucer and the Sacramentarian Controversy: The Origins of his Policy of Concord," *ARG,* 64 (1973), 166–183.

[8] See, for example, Philipp Melanchthon to Elector Johann of Saxony, 6 March 1530, in *CR,* II, 21–22, No. 666.

[9] For example, at Ravensburg. Dreher, "Das Patriziat der Reichsstadt Ravensburg," *ZWLG,* 21 (1962), 380–382.

[10] Moeller, *Reichsstadt und Reformation,* pp. 34–67. See Kittelson, "Wolfgang Capito, the Council and Reform Strasbourg," pp. 136–137.

The congregationalist tendency expressed in the practice of adult baptism was scotched by bringing church life under governmental supervision; while radical spiritualism fell victim to the Bible as wielded by its learned interpreters, the reformers. Thus harnessed, Zwinglianism became an orderly, acceptable form of ecclesiastical life.

Zwinglianism also had problematical political tendencies. In keeping with its enthusiastic exaltation of the commune as a fellowship of priests, Swiss Zwinglianism was republican, anti-feudal, anti-princely, and anti-Imperial.[11] The assault on hierarchy in the church could never be utterly shorn of its potential against all hierarchy; and the Lutheran preachers quickly and with much justice constructed the equation, Zwinglian = rebel. The charge was perfectly understood by the Rhenish Zwinglians such as Martin Bucer, who racked his brain for arguments and produced only pleas for fraternity against the ominous chain of reasoning which led from Strasbourg over Zwingli to the arch-rebel himself, Thomas Müntzer.[12] Sturm, with his pro-Saxon policy, worked with might and main to bury this reputation of opposition to every sort of aristocratic hegemony.

2. The social and political fabric of popular urban religion in South Germany during the 1520s forms the backdrop for the struggle over foreign and domestic policy at Strasbourg. Broadly speaking, the Zealots favored and fostered a political-military alliance with Zürich, Bern, and Basel during the years 1524 to 1530. Only the leaders of this party can be identified with certainty: Claus Kniebis (its undisputed head), Martin Herlin, Daniel Mieg, and perhaps Hans Bock von Gerstheim.[13] Secret negotiations with the Evangelical Swiss towns went on during 1524 and 1525, apparently motivated by the disturbances in the land, and were broken off when the threat subsided.[14] When they were resumed in 1527, the common pattern of reforms and the desire to defend it were prime motives for alliance. By the end of 1529, the four

---

[11] Norman Birnbaum, "The Zwinglian Reformation in Zurich," in *Toward a Critical Sociology* (New York, 1971), pp. 133–161; Josef Macek, *Der Tiroler Bauernkrieg und Michael Gaismair,* trans. R. F. Schmiedt (Berlin, 1965; Czech ed., 1960), pp. 492–493.

[12] A very bald statement by Melanchthon to Friedrich Myconius, ca. February, 1530, in *CR,* II, 17–18, No. 664. Bucer was quite aware of the formula and tried to defend himself and his masters against the implication that they were tainted by "the spirit of Müntzer." *BDS,* III, 334–335. See also, for the Zwinglianism–Müntzer connection, Melanchthon's report on the Marburg colloquy, ca. 5 October 1529, in *CR,* I, 1099, No. 637.

[13] On the parties and party names, see Chapter VI above, pp. 208–215.

[14] Hauswirth, *Landgraf Philipp von Hessen und Zwingli,* pp. 139–160, gives the best account of these negotiations.

regimes had worked out the terms for a "Christian federation," which contained an element of political federation as well as a mutual defense pact. This came at the end of December, 1529, when the regime of Strasbourg, betrayed by the Saxon elector and his tame allies, faced prosecution in the Imperial courts for its internal reforms.

The first round of Swiss negotiations had been conducted under the auspices of the ruling Ammeisters, Daniel Mieg (1524) and Claus Kniebis (1525), and they were resumed under Mathis Pfarrer (1527) and Martin Herlin (1528). In a drama filled with minor but bitter irony, the alliance was voted through the Senate & XXI and the assembly of Schöffen during the last days of Conrad von Duntzenheim's final term as ruling Ammeister. He tried to stave it off, although the popular mood in that famine winter of 1529 must have already been quite menacing. Neither he nor his opponents pretended that the Swiss alliance was anything but an outgrowth of the community of interest created between Strasbourg and the Swiss towns, "on the basis of faith," through their common experience of reform.[15] The pact would produce, Duntzenheim warned the Schöffen, "a great danger to the city of Strasbourg . . . disturbances [and] heavy expenses," because war between Archduke Ferdinand and the Evangelical Swiss was inevitable. Just as strongly *for* the alliance spoke the incoming ruling Ammeister, Daniel Mieg, who extolled the probable political advantages of federation with brethren in faith.[16] On 29 December, the Schöffen approved the treaty: 184 of 220 voting Schöffen voted for the treaty, four against, and thirty-four for Sturm's policy of delaying a decision until after the coming Diet. In the Senate & XXI, the division was nearly as decisive, as thirty-eight members voted for and only eleven against the treaty.[17] Coming as it did less than one year after the symbolic purifying act of abolishing the Mass, this decision was the last major victory of the Zealots, in which they were able temporarily to harmonize the city's foreign policy with the internal reforms of the preceding half-decade.

Strasbourg's resumption of relations with the Lutheran princes was not due solely to Zürich's military defeat in 1531.[18] In early 1530, within

---

[15] AMS, AA 1808/11, fols. 27–28.

[16] AMS, AA 1808/15, fol. 36. Fols. 35 and 37 contain a signed address by Peter Butz in favor of the alliance, perhaps also addressed to the Schöffen. Butz was not, however, a consistent supporter of the Zealots, for he had opposed on political grounds the abolition of the Mass during the debate of the summer of 1528. *BDS*, II, 427n18.

[17] *Ann. Brant*, No. 4836.

[18] Hauswirth, *Landgraf Philipp von Hessen und Zwingli*, pp. 214–215; Brady, "Jacob Sturm of Strasbourg and the Lutherans," pp. 184–185.

months of the vote for the Swiss alliance, Sturm began planning a reconciliation with the Saxon elector. Viewed realistically, the Swiss pact had obvious defects: the high price exacted by the Swiss; their shortage of cavalry; and their reputation for selfishness. Even more weighty was the fact that the Swiss could supply no support in the main arenas of Imperial politics, the Diet and the *Reichskammergericht*. The political logic of the "Christian federation," then, contained a strong presumption for ever closer political ties to the Swiss and ever weaker ones to the Empire, a pressure in the direction of the path taken by Basel in 1501 and more recently by Mulhouse and Rottweil.[19] Strasbourg's failure to follow was due partly to geography, partly to Swiss reluctance to have such a large, rich city as a confederate, and, perhaps most important, partly to the efforts of a party at Strasbourg, led by Jacob Sturm, which aimed at reconciliation with the Lutheran princes.

The Politiques were not only former Catholic diehards and the conformists, they were also a genuinely Evangelical party of a conservative cast. The core of their policy was the promotion of internal unity and, while accepting the reforms of 1524–25, avoidance of further internal changes that might worsen the regime's relations with the emperor and the princes. Thus, they opposed the abolition of the Mass at Strasbourg until this step could no longer be resisted. In foreign affairs, they supported a policy, evolved by Jacob Sturm during 1528, of abandoning the historic alliance of free cities in South Germany for a league led by the Lutheran princes. Leader of the Politiques from first to last was Jacob Sturm, and the victory of his policy in 1530 marked his ascent to a position of premier influence in the regime.[20]

The Politique counterpart to the Zwinglian activism of the Zealots was Sturm's spiritualist, thoroughly laic religious position, which, though in essence quite un-Lutheran, fitted a conservative Lutheran view of church and state better than it did a Zwinglian one. In his opinion on the public cultus written just after the Peasants' War (August, 1525),[21] Sturm urged that both Catholics and Evangelicals were

---

[19] Adolf Gasser, *Die territoriale Entwicklung der schweizerischen Eidgenossenschaft 1291–1797* (Aarau, 1932), pp. 140–144, 152–159.

[20] I have treated the genesis of Sturm's policy in "Jacob Sturm of Strasbourg and the Political Security of German Protestantism," chapters IV–V; and more briefly in "Jacob Sturm of Strasbourg and the Lutherans," p. 185.

[21] Sturm's memorial (AST, 166, fols. 265–267) is edited and analyzed in my "'Sind also zu beyden theylen Christen, des Gott erbarm.' Jacob Sturm's Memorial on Public Worship at Strasbourg (August, 1525)," in the forthcoming *Mélanges Jean Rott*. Kniebis's and other unpublished opinions are listed in *ibid.*, note 21.

Christians and should live together in tolerance and patriotic unity—a far cry from Kniebis's denunciations of the Mass as idolatry. As a known opponent of the preachers' campaign against the Mass in 1525-28, Sturm was at one point (September, 1526) suspected of having provided the decisive vote against abolition.[22] On the eucharistic issue, that splintery bone of intra-Evangelical contention, Sturm's view approached the anti-sacramentalism of Caspar Schwenckfeld.[23] Most of all, he hated the preachers' meddling in politics, and he lacked all sympathy for their self-image as charismatic, prophetic leaders of the community.[24] On the place of doctrine in the formation of the Evangelical military front, Sturm believed that precise doctrinal formulae were a matter of relative indifference and that what mattered among allies was a fraternal recognition of common interests and common partisanship for a good cause.[25]

Who else were Politiques? Certainly Bernhard Wurmser, whose anxiety about the reform movement touched his own reputation more that it did the issues. Probably Conrad Joham, the banker and international merchant, whose business connections gave him a wideness of outlook and a love of order. Probably also those Catholics who conformed after 1529, such as Andreas Mieg and Martin Betscholt. Possibly Mathis Pfarrer, to whose temperament any bold action was foreign. Possibly also Sturm's brother, Peter, who seems to have spent his entire political career in his brother's shadow. Among the latecomers, judging by their actions and those of their families in 1548, were Ulman and Wolfgang Böcklin von Böcklinsau, Carl Mieg, Sr., and perhaps Batt von Duntzenheim, whose younger brother, Jacob, was almost certainly a Zealot. If these identifications are correct or nearly correct, then the

---

[22] *Ann. Brant*, No. 4701 (24 September 1526): "Daruff erkannt, dass man die mess halten soll, bis dass die verordnete bottschafft von kais. Maj. wider zu land kompt, und Ir Maj. gemüt gehört werd. Solches haben etliche Jacob Sturmen bedacht, das er der messen halb ein mehr [Mähre] gemacht. Erkannt: zu inquiriren, wer der schwetzer; auch den Predicanten sagen, die überflussigen reden der mess und anderer sachen halb zu underlassen."

[23] Johannes Ficker, ed., "Jakob Sturms Entwurf zur Strassburger reformatorischen Verantwortung für den Augsburger Reichstag 1530," *ELJb*, 19 (1941), 152. See Brady, "Jacob Sturm of Strasbourg and the Lutherans," p. 186.

[24] *PCSS*, I, 264, No. 464 (15 July 1526), where Sturm writes to Peter Butz that the preachers' political agitation "bringt argwon, als ob si sich mer uf ein fleischlichen arme dan uf Christum allein verliessen." The reading of this text by Baron ("Religion and Politics," p. 412) is not correct.

[25] This is the sense of Sturm's comments on the Schwabach Articles, ed. by Hans von Schubert, *Bekenntnisbildung und Religionspolitik (1524–1534). Untersuchungen und Texte* (Gotha, 1910), pp. 169–182.

social differences between the leaderships of the two parties are highly revealing. The Zealots, except for Kniebis, were not university men and tended to come from the milieu of the lesser merchants, especially cloth merchants; while the Politiques came from both fractions of the aristocracy proper, the patriciate and the guild aristocrats.

The social characteristic corresponded in several ways to the diplomatic engagement of the two parties. The Zealots were mainly men of local family and, except for Daniel Mieg, local outlook and interests. After 1530–32 Kniebis, Mieg and Herlin withdrew almost entirely from diplomacy on the levels of the Empire and the Smalkaldic League. They were deeply involved, on the other hand, in the Swiss negotiations, conducted in good Alemannic German rather than Latin or the artificial speech of the chancelleries. After his exclusion from Strasbourg's seat in the *Reichsregiment* in 1529, Mieg rarely engaged in diplomacy of any kind.[26] Herlin, too, undertook few major embassies after the Diet of 1526. And Kniebis's swan song in Imperial politics was the Diet of Regensburg in 1532, where he found his presence fruitless and expensive.[27] Thereafter the entire burden of diplomacy on this scale rested on the shoulders of Jacob Sturm, Mathis Pfarrer, and Batt von Duntzenheim, with occasional, grudging service from Jacob Meyer.

Jacob Sturm, on the other hand, although he was the rising star of the diplomatic corps during the later 1520s, played next to no role in the negotiations with the Swiss. He rebuffed Ulrich Zwingli's schemes for a great anti-Hapsburg alliance and for a league of Swiss and South German cities in 1529–30; he manipulated Zwingli without scruple in his negotiations with the Lutherans at the Diet of Augsburg in 1530; and he engineered the eventual subscription of Strasbourg and other "Zwinglian" towns of South Germany to the thoroughly Lutheran Confession of Augsburg.[28] As a university man, a noble, and a former servant of a prince, Sturm was thoroughly at home in the world of Imperial diplomacy in a way that Herlin and Mieg could never be.

Claus Kniebis never abandoned his opposition to Sturm's alliance policy. Good Zwinglian and republican that he was, Kniebis hated all princes and feared their designs on urban liberties. This view, which is

---

[26] *DRA, JR*, VII, 621, 628; and Mieg's account in *PCSS*, I, 347, No. 593. The most humiliating aspect of the affair was that the elector of Saxony's man, Hans von Planitz, entered the complaint against Strasbourg.

[27] Claus Kniebis to Jacob Sturm and Jacob Meyer, Regensburg, 22 and 27 June 1532, in *PCSS*, II, 154, 156, Nos. 148, 151.

[28] Brady, "Jacob Sturm of Strasbourg and the Lutherans," pp. 185–201.

connected with the Zealots' pro-Swiss foreign policy during the 1520s, Kniebis expressed time and again during the early 1540s in his letters to Bernhard Meyer, Basel's powerful burgomaster.[29] Kniebis believed that Sturm had led Strasbourg into a union that left the city defenseless against the princes' exploitation of the towns through the system of Imperial taxation, their ultimate object being the total subjugation of the cities. "We have been betrayed and robbed of our money," he wrote to Meyer, and the princes "want the lion's share and treat us neither fairly nor justly. May Almighty God help us to free ourselves from these raging wolves!"[30] His solution was the old one, the "good old friendship and unity" between Strasbourg and the Swiss, "especially [but not only?] those who are of our religion."[31] In effect, he wanted the old Swiss–South German urban league proposed by Zwingli in 1529.[32] Although his pleas to Meyer came to nothing, he never surrendered his hope that Strasbourg could be extracted from the Smalkaldic League and pushed into a new urban union. In July, 1546, on the eve of the Smalkaldic War, Kniebis was still dreaming of Swiss aid,[33] and, had circumstances allowed, he would have been willing to give the German princes "the Swiss treatment."[34] This was the main line of the old Zealot foreign

---

[29] Kniebis's views and his mounting anxiety about the consequences of Sturm's foreign policy may be followed during 1542–44 in his letters to Bernhard Meyer of Basel. *PCSS*, III, Nos. 290, 293, 297, 318, 324, 364, 368, 440. The initiative to discussion of a new Swiss alliance was Kniebis's alone (*ibid.*, p. 302). When Meyer did come to Strasbourg in December, 1542, he talked with Kniebis, Martin Herlin, and Jacob Meyer (Masons)—but not with Jacob Sturm, who was probably still at Strasbourg, as his first report from Nuremberg is dated 14 December (*ibid.*, p. 343, No. 330). The talks came to nothing (*ibid.*, p. 337).

[30] Kniebis to Meyer, Strasbourg, 13 August 1542 (*ibid.*, p. 302, No. 290).

[31] Kniebis to Meyer, Strasbourg, 30 August 1542 (*ibid.*, p. 309, No. 297).

[32] Most detailed in *ibid.*, pp. 309–310: "wo nün die andern stett als Strassburg, Costenz, und Lindow und etlich derglichen, die nit so gar in iren herschaften gelegen, sich nit darin schicken, wann die fursten daruf verharren und in unlidlich ding uflegen, das sie mogen sagen, wir konnen und wollen das nit thun, und das sie dessen sich ouch mit dem ernst widersetzen und gut frind haben, die in darin beraten und beholfen sin, ..." On Zwingli's project for a league of Strasbourg and the Swiss towns with the Upper Swabian and Lake Constance towns, see Hauswirth, *Landgraf Philipp von Hessen und Zwingli*, pp. 129–137.

[33] C. Kniebis to B. Meyer, (Strasbourg), 26 July 1546: "ob sich begeb, dass die find der cristliche[n] religion sich ouch zu uns nehern wurden, das ir des ingedenk wurden und thun, was sich darzu zu thun gebürt." *PCSS*, IV, 260, No. 239.

[34] The phrase is from a French writer, François de l'Alouete, *Des affaires d'estat* (Metz, 1597), p. 218, quoted by Davis Bitton, *The French Nobility in Crisis, 1560–1640* (Stanford, 1969), p. 25. That such a solution would have pleased Kniebis is clear from

policy to which Kniebis, aging and failing in health, remained true to the end of his days.

Claus Kniebis's views are an expression, uncommon in so blunt a form outside Switzerland, of the republicanism that marched hand-in-hand with the radical moment in urban reformed religion in Upper Germany and in the political theology of Martin Bucer[35]—although this tendency rarely overcame for long Bucer's abiding reverence for legitimate authority.[36] Only in the Swiss towns did this complex of ideas truly flourish, and even there its revolutionary potential never quite overcame the corporate myth of communal spirituality which was the principal ideological content of the Rhenish urban reform. At Strasbourg, the only "saints" who challenged the oligarchy's ecclesiastical hegemony were sectaries and a few schoolteachers, and most of them came to bad ends. As for Kniebis, his patriotism was as strong as that of his opponents. Although defeated by Sturm, and although forced to witness the failure and humiliation of the local reformed church, Kniebis worked in the governmental harness until his death.

---

his letter to B. Meyer, (Strasbourg), 12 November 1542, after he had heard of Duke Ulrich of Wurttemberg's latest oppression of Esslingen: "denn die bosheit und untreu der hern ist so gross, das ich gloub, gott unser her werd einmal ein endrung machen. si haben der getrowen straf gottes in der ufrur anno etc. 25 vergessen. der Türk wer schier so lidlich zu tülden als ir etlich." *PCSS*, III, 337, No. 324.

[35] Hans Baron, "Calvinist Republicanism and its Historical Roots," *CH*, 8 (1939), 30–42.

[36] The confusion in most studies of Bucer's social and political thought stems from a failure to recognize two, potentially antagonistic moments: an individualistic moment of freedom based on the Spirit; and an ecclesiastical, corporate moment based on clerical mediation of the gospel. The first was dominant in his early writings; the second began to emerge after 1525 and dominated during the struggle against the sects; and the first moment revived during his period of deepest disillusionment in the 1540s—only to be submerged again in the *De regno Christi*. This dialectic was already suggested by August Lang, *Der Evangelienkommentar Martin Butzers und die Grundzüge seiner Theologie*, Studien zur Geschichte der Theologie und der Kirche, II, 2 (Leipzig, 1900), esp. pp. 205–206, since whose study little progress has been made toward a synthetic interpretation of Bucer's theology consistent with the facts of his biography. Most writers are stymied by the co-existence of a sectarian (his kinship with the sects is usually granted) with an authoritarian-Erastian current. See, most recently, W. P. Stephens, *The Holy Spirit in the Theology of Martin Bucer* (Cambridge, 1970), who is aware of the need for an historical approach (see chapter 7, on Bucer's ecclesiology), but who nonetheless organizes his study doctrinally. Similarly, although Bucer's relationship to Calvin is fairly well understood, few scholars have followed the lead of Hans Baron, who argued in 1924 that the same two, dialectically related moments shaped the thought of Calvin. Hans Baron, *Calvins Staatsanschauung und das konfessionelle Zeitalter*, Beiheft 1 der *Historischen Zeitschrift* (Berlin–Munich, 1924), esp. pp. 82–87.

B.   THE CAUSE OF ORDER

The Politiques' victory in foreign policy found its internal complement in the reconstruction of Strasbourg's ecclesiastical order during
1533–34.[37] The immediate occasion was the rise of the sects since 1526.
The revolution and its aftermath split the Evangelical movement at
Strasbourg into three competing streams. One stream was the official one,
bedded in the preachers' agreement to preach a purely religious reform
in return for the regime's backing. A second was the path of isolation,
either in the Nicodemite spiritualism of the schoolteacher Otto Brunfels
or in the mystical dreamings of the gardener–preacher of the Ruprecht-
sau, Clement Ziegler, sobered veterans of a lost revolution.[38] A third
stream was formed by the enthusiastic bearers of a gospel of individual
rebirth whom history groups under the name of "Anabaptists" and
who found early and fertile soil in the inns, ateliers, and back streets of
Strasbourg. The rise of the sects was a standing rebuke to Bucer and his
comrades, who called on the oligarchy to defend them against the sects
as they had once called on the same men for aid against the entrenched
Catholic clergy. On this issue clerical and lay leadership was at one: the
Anabaptists were separatists, stubborn heretics, and, so report had it,
communists.[39] They were identified during the synod of 1533, purged
from the town, and banished downriver to evangelize on the Lower
Rhine.

There was a price for saving the preachers and their movement from
the sects. What Bucer and his colleagues wanted was a system of ecclesiastical government and police in which the clergy would have at least an
equal role with the regime; but what they got was a thoroughgoing
system of lay government of the church. Beginning with the institution
of parish boards (*Kirchenpfleger*) in 1531, parish life at Strasbourg was

---

[37] Chrisman, *Strasbourg,* chapters 11–12.

[38] On Brunfels, see Carlo Ginzburg, *Il nicodemismo. Simulazione e dissimulazione religiosa
nell'Europa del '500,* Biblioteca di cultura storica, 107 (Turin, 1970); and on Ziegler,
Peter, "Le maraîcher Clément Ziegler," pp. 274–281, and Jean-Michel Boehler,
"Clément Ziegler, un prédicateur populaire au pied du Mont Sainte-Odile," *La Guerre
des Paysans 1525,* ed. A. Wollbrett, pp. 15–19.

[39] Literature in *TQ Strassburg,* I, "Vorwort," notes 6–9, 19. To it may be added two
American Ph.D. dissertations: Charles Buell Mitchell, "Martin Bucer and Sectarian
Dissent: a Confrontation of the Magisterial Reformation with Anabaptists and
Spiritualists," Yale University, 1961; and Henry George Krahn, "An Analysis of the
Conflict between the Clergy of the Reformed Church and the Leaders of the Anabaptist
Movement in Strasbourg, 1529–1534," University of Washington, 1969. Neither
adduces new sources. See now the treatment by Kittelson, *Wolfgang Capito,* chapter VII.

brought under the regime's direct control and particularly that of the privy councillors, who dominated the parish boards.[40] The church ordinance of 1534 rejected the institution of excommunication, a proposal to enforce compulsory church attendance, and a rigorous police of morals—all standing objectives of Bucer and his party among the clergy. The oligarchs did not need the advice of the anti-Bucerians in the schools, the "Epicureans," to tell them that Bucer's proposal amounted to "a new papacy," a reconstruction of clerical power.[41] As for doctrine, although the regime did approve formal standards of belief for its church, it rejected every proposal that it police the *beliefs* of its citizen-subjects. The single permanent element of coercion in the new order was the requirement, aimed at the sects, that all children born to citizens must be baptized as infants. Otherwise, down to the Interim, the regime resisted the continuing clerical efforts to goad it into promoting a more godly society at Strasbourg.

This ecclesiastical settlement was not chiefly the work of the Zealots such as Kniebis, who was known to cast a mild eye even on the sects.[42] It was rather the work of the Politiques, men who recognized and even embodied the incomplete, partly coerced conversion of the aristocracy as a whole to the new faith, and who stood for easy tolerance in religion and firm laicism in ecclesiastical government.[43] Their leader, Jacob Sturm, was the commanding personality among the four lay presidents of the synod of 1533. His colleagues were Martin Herlin, a Zealot, Andreas Mieg, lately a Catholic and now a conformist, and Sebastian Erb, a devout, good-hearted cloth merchant of no particular distinction.[44] Sturm, an early leader in the campaign against the sects,[45] redacted the church ordinance of 1534 and expunged certain aspects of clerical

---

[40] Wendel, *L'eglise de Strasbourg*, p. 46.

[41] I mean the "Epicureans," a significant, never entirely vanquished opposition among the intelligentsia. See now Werner Bellardi, "Anton Engelbrecht (1485–1558), Helfer, Mitarbeiter und Gegner Bucers," *ARG*, 64 (1973), 188–191, 197.

[42] Kniebis was said to have told a local sectary, Hanns Borst, that he would not be forced to have his children baptized. *TQ Strassburg*, II, 441, No. 649 (17 March 1535). Kniebis, despite his leading position in the regime, is nowhere specifically identified with repression of the sects.

[43] See Philippe Dollinger, "La tolérance à Strasbourg au XVIe siècle," in *Hommage à Lucien Febvre*, 2 vols. (Paris, 1953), II, 241–249, with whose interpretation—that the easy-going treatment of doctrinal matters at Strasbourg had laic, not clerical, origins—I thoroughly agree.

[44] PROSOPOGRAPHY, Nos. XCIII, XXVIII, XXXVII, LX; *TQ Strassburg*, II, 353, No. 577. Herlin was replaced by Mathis Pfarrer, a more temperate man.

[45] *TQ Strassburg*, I, 122–123, No. 92 (27 July 1527).

control which Bucer had written into the draft.[46] Sturm's colleagues in the regime were neither equipped nor willing to serve as learned doctors of the church, an incapacity perfectly evident in the "opinions" of several of them on the proposed statements of doctrine.[47] The regime was composed, after all, of persons of varying, even antagonistic views on religion—and perhaps even a few with few or no opinions about it. Paulus Baldner had participated in the irregular baptism of his own child, and Caspar Hoffmeister had allowed sectarian preaching at the *Blatterhaus*.[48] That there were others whose sympathies lay with the old church is clear from the report in 1540 that some of them slipped out to village churches to make their Easter duties; and many of the seigneurs among them were slow enough in introducing reformed religion into their seigneuries.[49] There can be no doubt that the vast majority of the councillors and senators were clearly "Evangelical," but it is just as clear that "Evangelical" included a goodly variety of beliefs, ranging from crypto-Catholicism to occasional sympathy for the sectaries. The real separatists and the preachers of the apocalypse had to go, of course, but even here the oligarchs showed that they were quite able to distinguish the dangerous from the merely annoying. Melchior Hoffman

---

[46] Typical is his comment on compulsory church attendance: "Gebott machen glissner." *Ibid.*, p. 354n2. The various redactions of the church ordinance show that Sturm's was the guiding hand, and no other layman is represented among the extant papers of the synod. *Ibid.*, pp. 353–361, No. 577.

[47] The extant ones are quoted on p. 193 above; and they do not lend credence to Chrisman's statement (*Strasbourg*, p. 221) that the doctrinal statements "were seriously studied and discussed."

[48] PROSOPOGRAPHY, No. XL; *TQ Strassburg*, I, 132, No. 109. There were other politicians who had connections with the sectaries. Martin Betscholt (PROSOPOGRAPHY, No. VIII) was related to the ex-priest and baiter of Bucer, Jörg Betscholt (*TQ Strassburg*, I, 276, No. 224 and note 51, and II, 176, No. 440). Gregorius (Gorius, Jörg) Pfitzer, who hosted Wilhelm Reublin in the spring of 1526, was a furrier who became senator from the *Kürschnerzunft* between 1525 and 1544, and who married (by 1530) Sophia Hellin; he was appointed "lediger" XXIer on 30 October 1541 (AMS, XXI 1541, fols. 456ᵛ–457ʳ), but although Gerber (*PCSS*, IV, 1442) lists him as a XVer, the text he cites (*ibid.*, p. 679, No. 604) does not so designate him; and, when he and Jacob Meyer were sent on mission in 1552, Meyer was given his proper title as XIIIer but Pfitzer was given no title at all (*ibid.*, V, 341n3, quoting AMS, XXI 1552, fol. 217ʳ). On Pfitzer, see AMS, KS 18, fol. 251ᵛ; AMS, KS 20, fol. 60ᵛ; AMS, KS 25, fol. 114ʳ; AMS, KS 26, fol. 103ʳ; Hatt, p. 513.

[49] The Ammeister reported "das ettlich herren des Regimentss dise kar woch zu Eschaw zum sacrament gangen. . . ." AMS, XXI 1540, fol. 118 (5 April 1540). On the survival of Catholicism at Strasbourg after 1529, see F.-J. Fuchs, "Les Catholiques strasbourgeois de 1529 à 1681," *AEA*, 23 (1975), 141–169, here at pp. 143–147. On the seigneuries of the Strasbourg nobles, see Chapter VIII below, note 111.

rotted in a Strasbourg jail, plagued by the damp and the cold, for the last decade of his life, while Caspar Schwenckfeld, who had also disobeyed the command not to return to Strasbourg, was politely asked to leave town.[50] Hoffman presumably was not more heretical than Schwenckfeld, but his millenarian vision of a new age of the saints was certainly a good deal more disturbing than the nobleman's quiet instruction in the parlors of the town.[51] Ignorant of Latin and barely acquainted with academic theology the councillors may have been, but generations of political experience guided their instinctive judgment as to who was dangerous and who was not.

A corollary to the ecclesiastical settlement was the gradual establishment and outfitting of a system of civic schools. The original school board (*Scholarchen*) of 1526 was composed of Jacob Sturm, Claus Kniebis, and Jacob Meyer. Kniebis and Sturm were university men, and Sturm was always the leading figure on the board.[52] The most important feature of the organization of the schools was their direct control by privy councillors, all laymen, and their consequent independence from clerical control.[53] Here, too, the regime scotched every move to introduce clerical control; and the tension between church and school, a legacy of the 1530s but reflecting the ambiguous character of the previous decade's reforms, was to prove troublesome and even explosive to the councillors of the next generation.

---

[50] *TQ Strassburg*, II, 367–368, No. 588: Schwenckfeld shall be told to leave Strasbourg, "und sollen die präsidenten ihm solches freundlich untersagen, dass m. h. h. ihm da mit nichts unehrlichs wollen zumessen; lassen ihm darum desto freundlicher sagen." As gentlemen to gentleman! Hoffman might have wished that the regime had been half so solicitous of his health as it was of Schwenckfeld's honor. For Hoffman's fate, see *ibid.*, II, Nos. 395–396, 400, 417, 428, 452, 461, 467–468; and Klaus Deppermann, "Melchior Hoffmans Weg von Luther zu den Täufern," in *Umstrittenes Täufertum 1525–1975*, ed. Hans-Jürgen Goertz (Göttingen, 1975), pp. 173–205, here at pp. 200–202.

[51] Schwenckfeld's Strasbourg friends seem to have been mostly aristocrats, though his partisans included Katharina Schütz, wife of Mathis Zell. Jacob Bernays, "Zur Biographie Johann Winthers von Andernach," *ZGO*, 55 (1901), 47–52; Roland H. Bainton, "Katherine Zell," *Medievalia et Humanistica*, N.S. 1 (1970), 11–12, 17–18, and in his *Women of the Reformation in Germany and Italy* (Minneapolis, 1971), pp. 66–73. The lists of Schwenckfeld's "co-believers" and "most devoted friends and lieutenants" collected by Selina Gerhard Schultz, *Caspar Schwenckfeld von Ossig (1489–1561)* (Norristown, Pa., 1946), pp. 357–358, are not trustworthy.

[52] Jean Rott, introduction to Jean Sturm's *Classicae epistolae sive scholae Argentinenses restitutae* (Paris–Strasbourg, 1938), viii.

[53] See Kohls, *Die Schule bei Martin Bucer*, pp. 95–99. On the rise of the academy, see now Anton Schindling, *Humanistische Hochschule und freie Reichsstadt—Gymnasium und Akademie in Strassburg 1538 bis 1621*, VIEGM, 77 (Wiesbaden, 1976).

The seemingly so solid ecclesiastical settlement at Strasbourg began to weaken during the early 1540s. By 1544, Bucer and his closest clerical colleagues were so frustrated by the oligarchy's restraints and the refusal to introduce a stricter moral regimen that they began once again to agitate against the regime's total control of church life.[54] Bucer returned at least partly to the congregational principle, having temporarily lost faith in the ideal of the Christian magistrate.[55] He thereby laid the groundwork for a conventicle movement which would try, in the wake of the defeat of 1546–47, to build a new, purer fellowship behind the lay-controlled facade of official Christianity.

From the humble, clandestine meeting places of the banned sects to the elegant parlors where Schwenckfeld was welcome, from the schools that sheltered Jean Sturm's protégés from clerical critics to the highest levels of the city's new ecclesiastical establishment, the oligarchy's work checked, dammed, and channelled the forces of piety, ambition, solidarity, and resentment which formed the wake of the incomplete revolution. Checked, perhaps, but not scotched. The very swiftness and forced character of the Reformation at Strasbourg plunged the aristocracy into a series of new obligations and tensions to which—by the early 1540s—the personnel of the regime were ever less equal.

C. THE FAILURE OF THE DIPLOMATIC CORPS, 1540–45

The oligarchy's principal works during the halcyon days of the Reformation era were the Politique foreign policy which led Strasbourg into the Smalkaldic League and the construction of the new church order. This work began to crumble on both fronts during the early 1540s, but especially on the former. The ageing veterans of the first Reformation crisis found no reliable replacements in the diplomatic corps. The most serious aspect of this inner decay of political will was the mounting refusal of young aristocrats to sacrifice time, money, and health to the city's service. The losses of Daniel Mieg to the plague of 1541, of Hans

---

[54] Werner Bellardi, *Die Geschichte der "christlichen Gemeinschaft" in Strassburg (1546/1550). Der Versuch einer "zweiten Reformation,"* QFRG, 18 (Leipzig, 1934), pp. 10–22, esp. p. 22.

[55] Deppermann, "Melchior Hoffmans Weg von Luther zu den Täufern," p. 205: "Die Illusion seines Lebens war der Glaube an eine 'fromme Obrigkeit', die seinen apokalyptischen und spiritualistischen Ideen zum Siege verhelfen sollte." The illusion was certainly shared by most of the urban reformers. See Moeller, "Die Kirche in den evangelischen freien Städten Oberdeutschlands," pp. 159–162.

Bock in 1542, and of Batt von Duntzenheim in 1543 were not supplied by younger men of similar stature and commitment. The Smalkaldic League had proved a sinkhole into which good Strasbourg money flowed without return and without end. Thousands of florins were paid out for the princes' conquest of Braunschweig in 1542, but nothing came back—at least not into the coffers of the cities. This expensive campaign, conducted in the name of the defense of the gospel, was, as Sturm and his colleagues had later to admit, "basically not a matter of religion."[56] Meanwhile, the interests of the big merchant-bankers were changing, shifting away from Antwerp and the Netherlands and toward Lyons and France.[57] By the eve of the Smalkaldic War, the oligarchy no longer had much stomach for the course into which Sturm had led it. It was expensive, time-consuming, and much too complicated for most amateur statesmen.

1. Two problems arose in the area of diplomacy and foreign policy. On the one hand, the tempo and amount of diplomatic activity in Reformation Germany placed physical and intellectual burdens on the Strasbourgeois that they could not shoulder.[58] On the other hand, the foreign policy of the Reformation generation drew Strasbourgeois into serious ties to powers with whom the city had no tradition of contacts, introduced them to a whole new level of politics concerning the *Reichskammergericht*, pitted them seriously against the emperor for the first time in history, and in general complicated external affairs to an extent hitherto unknown.

The physical demands of diplomacy may be judged by the record of Jacob Sturm, Strasbourg's diplomatic workhorse. His brothers recorded on his epitaph that he had made ninety-one diplomatic missions

---

[56] Opinion by Jacob Sturm, Mathis Pfarrer, and Conrad Joham, 26 October 1546 (*PCSS*, IV, 446, No. 422): "wie treulich man inen gegen Brunswick geholfen, das im grund kein religionsache gewesen. . . ." On the Braunschweig adventure from the Strasbourg side, see Rudolf Mattausch, "Die Reichsstadt Strassburg im Schmalkaldischen Bund am Vorabend des Krieges von 1546/47," dissertation Freiburg i. Br., 1954, pp. 33–56. A history of the Braunschweig campaign is a pressing need.

[57] Pfeiffer, "Die Bemühungen der oberdeutschen Kaufleute," pp. 413–415; Hermann Kellenbenz, "Les foires de Lyon dans la politique de Charles-Quint," *Cahiers d'histoire*, 5 (1960), 18–21.

[58] Had Strasbourg been an entirely independent state, the problem would probably have arisen much earlier, as it did at Venice. See Donald E. Queller, ed., *Early Venetian Legislation on Ambassadors*, Travaux d'Humanisme et Renaissance, 88 (Geneva, 1966), pp. 30–39; idem, *The Office of Ambassador in the Middle Ages* (Princeton, 1967), pp. 149–160, esp. pp. 158–160.

during his twenty-nine years of service.[59] From the year of the great revolution until just before his death (1553), Sturm attended nearly every Imperial Diet, meeting of the Smalkaldic League, and assembly of South German free cities, plus numerous minor assemblies. It was custom at Strasbourg, as in some other towns, that each embassy should be made up of one patrician and one guildsman.[60] The first problem was that of finding Sturm a regular partner from among the guild politicians. During the years 1526–35, he was accompanied sometimes by Martin Herlin or Jacob Meyer and more regularly by Mathis Pfarrer. Claus Kniebis went on mission rarely and with great reluctance,[61] and Batt von Duntzenheim emerged as Sturm's most usual companion.

Most councillors lacked the linguistic skills and social experience proper to a diplomat. Very few could speak Latin, although a know-ledge of French was fairly common among the merchants.[62] More serious was that the average guild politician who was sent on mission, including the Strasbourgeois, felt lost in or intimidated by the great assemblies of notables. Mathis Pfarrer, for example, never rid himself of the tendency to start at every rumor, threat, and proposal that swam through the murky atmosphere of an Imperial Diet.[63] He was probably the equal of most of the amateur urban diplomats of the era, whose average quality, according to the princes who had to deal with them,

---

[59] Sturm's epitaph by Hermann, *Notices historiques,* II, 401. What follows is drawn from my research on Sturm's career.

[60] At Ulm, for example. Geiger, *Reichsstadt Ulm,* p. 37.

[61] Typical of Kniebis's impatience is the note he sent home from the Diet of Regens-burg, 22 June 1532: "dann ich numer auch gern zu haus wölt, dieweil ich doch sorge, ich verthue vil und richt dargegen wenig aus." *PCSS*, II, 154.

[62] PROSOPOGRAPHY, Nos. VIII, XXXIII, XXXIV, XLV, LX, XC.

[63] See his letter to Peter Butz, 12 August 1530, in *PCSS*, I, 511–512, No. 807. Otto Winckelmann, editor of *PCSS*, II–III, wrote of Pfarrer's report on the League meeting at Frankfurt in December, 1531: they "sind bei aller Weitscheifigkeit so nichtssagend, dass selbst mit einem Auszug aus denselben niemandem gedient sein dürfte. Sie geben, so zu sagen, nur das Gerippe der Verhandlungen, d.h. die äusseren Umstände und Formalitäten, unter denen sich die Beschlüsse der Versammlung vollzogen, und gehen nur selten auf den sachlichen Kern der Verhandlungen ein." I can only commend the gentleness of Winckelmann's judgment. How little impact Pfarrer made on those who met him during the Diet of Augsburg, 1530, may be seen from the fact that, though Pfarrer sat through several important meetings between Sturm and Count Albrecht of Mansfeld on 12–13 October 1530, Mansfeld did not even remember his name properly. See Brady, "Jacob Sturm of Strasbourg and the Luther-ans," p. 200n67.

was not very high.[64] By the early 1540s Duntzenheim was dead, and Pfarrer could rarely be persuaded to ride on mission.[65] No able guild politician could be found for regular diplomatic service, as one-by-one the older, experienced men fell into ill health or died.

The situation with the patrician diplomats was not much better. Hans Bock von Gerstheim had retired from diplomacy with the rise of Sturm, and Bernhard Wurmser undertook only occasional missions.[66] Wurmser's successor in the XIII, Ulman Böcklin von Böcklinsau, was the man marked to share with Sturm the diplomatic duties from the patrician side.[67] He had for some years served as Strasbourg's delegate (*Kriegsrat*) to the war council of the League, a post he held until the dissolution of the alliance in 1547.[68] Never did he live up to his colleagues' expectations. Before his cooptation into the XIII, he was already (June, 1541) complaining of the unreasonable expenses he incurred as delegate to the war council.[69] Some months later he tried to resign, pleading that the meetings were pointless and expensive.[70] Hans Bock and Hans Lindenfels begged him "to consider that each man must do something in this matter for the honor of God and the common weal," but Böcklin replied

---

[64] For example, Landgrave Philipp of Hesse, whose complaints about the Augsburg diplomatic corps were relayed to the regime by Sebastian Schertlin von Burtenbach in a letter of 12 December 1545: "Her Landgraf offtermals geclagt, das die von Augspurg jre gesante offter verenderen, vnnd nit solche leut die er gern hette schicken, vnnd so es zu ernstlichem thun kumm, so müessen die stett ander leut senden." Theodor Herberger, ed., *Sebastian Schertlin von Burtenbach und seine an die Stadt Augsburg geschriebene Briefe* (Augsburg, 1852), p. 40. Even more to the point is the story of the bumbling envoys sent by the Swiss Evangelical towns to the French court in 1537, for which see Johannes Volker Wagner, *Graf Wilhelm von Fürstenberg, 1491–1549, und die politisch-geistigen Mächte seiner Zeit,* Pariser Historische Studien, 4 (Stuttgart, 1966), pp. 119–120, 122, 122n302.

[65] See, for example, his refusal on 17 July 1542, in AMS, XXI 1542, fol. 271ᵛ. See also the process of selecting a companion for Sturm to the Diet of 1544, when Jacob Meyer and Mathis Pfarrer declined because of ill health, and Mattheus Geiger was appointed. *PCSS,* III, 451n1. Geiger, inexperienced in diplomacy on this level, had successfully pleaded ill health in refusing a mission in June, 1542. AMS, XXI 1542, fol. 266ᵛ, 271ʳ.

[66] Wurmser was sent during November, 1535, to Westphalia to interview Jan of Leyden, "dem widdertäufferischen vermeinten künig," in order to ascertain the connections between Jan and Melchior Hoffman, then a prisoner at Strasbourg. *TQ Strassburg,* II, 481–484, No. 700.

[67] PROSOPOGRAPHY, No. XIII.

[68] Gerber, "Die Kriegsrechnungen, II," *ARG,* 32, pp. 52, 67, 68, 80n2, 246; and "Die Kriegsrechnungen, III," *ARG,* 33, p. 232; *PCSS,* IV, 395–396, No. 372, and p. 439, No. 415n1.

[69] AMS, XXI 1540, fols. 231ʳ, 232ʳ ⁻ᵛ (18 June 1540).

[70] AMS, XXI 1540, fols. 390ʳ ⁻ᵛ, 391ᵛ–392ʳ, 399ᵛ–400ᵛ (18, 20, and 30 October 1540).

that his entourage ("vff pferdt, knecht vnd buben") had cost him 600 fl. over the past three years, that the other urban war councillors were much better paid than he, and that the post was "damaging and burdensome" to him. His colleagues refused to accept his resignation, and Jacob Wetzel von Marsilien, a patrician XVer from a much more ancient noble family than the Böcklin, sneered that the post wouldn't be so expensive if Böcklin didn't insist on travelling like a great lord. Böcklin continued to begrudge every mission during the following years and sometimes flatly refused to ride.[71]

Ulman Böcklin may simply have been a bad choice. After all, he neglected other civic duties, such as rental payments on the public properties he leased,[72] and in 1548 he renounced his citizenship and never again resided in the city.[73] Much the same sort of resistance to diplomatic service, however, came from Peter Sturm, Jacob's younger brother. Four times Hans Bock and Claus Kniebis asked him to ride to the Imperial Diet of 1540, and four times he begged to be excused. He ran the gamut of possible excuses: "he has no rhetorical ability and knows nothing about the business"; for some time "he has been so weak that he could not do it even if the affair were a personal one"; and "it would be terribly burdensome, and, if he were paid 200 fl., he still wouldn't recover the expenses."[74] Amateurs, even rich amateurs, became increasingly reluctant to make the sacrifices diplomacy demanded. They pleaded ill health, expensiveness, ignorance, and lack of skill— but they pleaded and continued to plead.

By 1545 Jacob Sturm recognized that the situation had become truly serious, and he warned his colleagues to find able, young men to take up the burden of diplomacy:

> You should reflect whether it is good to have everything in one man's head. When reports are made to the Senate, the senators don't sit still and pay attention, for nobody takes such things seriously. During such deliberations, each one complains that he knows nothing about the business and says that the XIII should handle it. If the affair goes well, they say: "How could it have gone otherwise?" If it goes badly, they say: "It is not good that the whole city's welfare lies in the hands of one man."[75]

---

[71] Which he did at least twice during 1545. *PCSS*, III, 640n1, 675n5.

[72] In 1540–48 he rented the "vogellgrien ann dem nidern mucken wadell," for which he owed the city 18 s./yr. and paid nothing. AMS, VII 1436, fol. 19^v.

[73] He was later active as an envoy of the Lower Alsatian *Reichsritterschaft* at the Diet of Augsburg, 1550. *PCSS*, V, 78–79, Nos. 49–50.

[74] AMS, XXI 1540, fols. 468^{r-v}, 469^v, 470^v–471^r (20 and 22 November 1540).

[75] AMS, XXI 1545, fol. 453^r; *PCSS*, III, 675n5.

Everything stayed in one man's head. The younger patrician privy councillors, men such as the cousins von Mülnheim, Hilteprant and Heinrich, never acquired sufficient experience to be of much value as diplomats—at least not during Sturm's lifetime.[76]

2. During the 1540s the regime came to depend ever more heavily on its professional employees, a trend that Sturm himself encouraged when he complained that he was forced to spend more time on diplomacy than the city's full-time civil servants did.[77] This may have been true, but it was also true that, from about 1540 onward, the regime's professional servants spent ever more time on diplomatic missions.

Much of the new burden fell upon Michel Han, the city syndic and Mattheus Geiger's son-in-law, who was no very strong reed on which to lean. As his diplomatic duties grew, Han warned his masters that he couldn't live on a salary of 150 fl./yr. and that an unnamed prince had offered him a post as chancellor.[78] Early in 1541, while Sturm was engaged in the colloquy of Worms and Batt von Duntzenheim in a meeting at Regensburg, Han was ordered to accompany Mathis Pfarrer to a diet of the League at Naumburg, one of the first significant breaches of the rule that embassies should be composed of one patrician and one guildsman.[79] Five days after his return to Strasbourg, Han was sent *alone* to a meeting of the southern League towns at Esslingen— perhaps the first occasion on which a Strasbourg embassy included *no* privy councillor.[80] Han often rode on mission with Ulman Böcklin, the reluctant war councillor, who usually left the arduous work of drafting reports entirely in the syndic's hands. Finally, when he was told to ride to Nuremberg to join Sturm at the Diet in January, 1543, Han balked. He first complained that he was so ill he could not ride, and then he broached

---

[76] PROSOPOGRAPHY, Nos. LXVI, LXVII. Heinrich von Mülnheim, who was Jacob Sturm's cousin, was an uncertain quantity. When he replaced Ulman Böcklin temporarily as war councillor in 1545, Martin Bucer wrote to Landgrave Philipp: "Es solt ein verwanter herr Jacobs, Heinrich von Mülen, sein geritten, gar ein feiner, bestendiger junger man, wurdt mit der zeit einzogen werden. Weil er aber der bundtnuss nach kein erfarnuss hatt, ..." Lenz, ed., *Briefwechsel des Landgrafen Philipps . . . mit Bucer*, II, 378. In fact, von Mülnheim was the first privy councillor to renounce citizenship during the political crisis of 1548. See below, p. 281.

[77] In July, 1543. *PCSS*, III, 414, 414n5, 504n2.

[78] AMS, XXI 1540, fol. 386[r–v] (16 October 1540). The prince may have been the Count Palatine of Zweibrücken, whose chancellor Han later became. Ficker–Winckelmann, I, 19; *PCSS*, IV, 448, No. 425n1.

[79] AMS, XXI 1541, fols. 35[v]–40[r], 42[r]–45[v], 47[v]–48[r].

[80] *Ibid.*, fol. 50[v].

the whole matter frankly to his masters:

> he recognizes that he is bound to do what is commanded, so far as he is physically able. But the city's reputation would be much better served if a member of the regime were sent to join Sir Jacob.

When Han eventually agreed to ride, the XIII confessed their own incapacity which put so much work on Han's shoulders: "that, since he is one of those experienced in the business, he will be more helpful to Sir Jacob than anyone else would be."[81] Late in the same year, when he was asked to go down to Frankfurt for a meeting of the League, Han issued a final, frank, and accurate analysis of the regime's weakness in handing over its diplomacy to its employees:

> He is neither able enough nor skilled enough; his head and mind simply can't grasp the business. For this is a weighty matter, especially the Braunschweig affair; and he cannot speak well enough to represent the cities' position in an orderly and effective manner. . . . Especially when he has no master, such as Sir Jacob Sturm, who can speak to the questions by himself, he cannot do the job. The Saxons and the Hessians both have much greater authority than he has; and Sir Ulman [Böcklin] puts the whole burden on him. If his lords only want him to agree tamely to the proposals of the Saxons and Hessians, then he can do that well enough. . . . If he must go, then he will ride, come what may.

"He is able enough," was the XIII's reply.[82]

The crisis years 1546–49 simply speeded up the disintegration of which Han had complained. The guildsmen who accompanied Sturm in the tangled negotiations after the Smalkaldic War were mostly either non-entities or utterly inexperienced, while the salaried employees played ever greater roles in diplomacy.[83] The ablest, perhaps, of the lawyers who were conducting more and more of Strasbourg's diplomacy was Dr. Ludwig Gremp, a Swabian graduate of the University of Tübingen, who entered the city's service in 1541.[84] Gremp made himself

---

[81] AMS, XXI 1543, fol. 23ᵛ.

[82] *Ibid.*, fol. 407ʳ⁻ᵛ (14 September 1543); also *PCSS*, III, 434, No. 409.

[83] I refer chiefly to Hans von Odratzheim and Michael Schwencker, on whom see *PCSS*, IV, *passim*; and PROSOPOGRAPHY, Nos. LXXI, LXXXV. An exception to this characterization may be Friedrich von Gottesheim (*ibid.*, No. XXXIV), but he renounced his citizenship in August, 1548.

[84] Ludwig Gremp von Freudenstein (1509–83), son of Onophrius II Gremp (1487–1551) of Vaihingen and Anna Besserer of Ulm; he was teaching law at Tübingen when hired by Strasbourg in 1541; he was ennobled as Gremp von Freudenstein, 19 August 1551. Ficker–Winckelmann, I, 28; Riedenauer, "Kaiserliche Standeserhebungen," p. 70; *PCSS*, III, 188, No. 195; Bernhardt, *Die Zentralbehörden . . . des Herzogtums Württemberg*, pp. 329–330.

indispensable as an envoy and became a major figure in the civic diplomatic corps—so much so that by the time of the Diet of Augsburg in 1555, Gremp and another lawyer, Jakob Hermann, actually dominated the embassy and conducted the correspondence with the XIII at home.[85] By this time it was quite common for the XIII to send salaried lawyers alone on mission.[86]

With the death of Jacob Sturm in 1553, Strasbourg's diplomacy lay largely in the hands of the lawyers. The old system, in which the business of the regime was conducted by the politically active sector of the aristocracy itself, broke down completely under the strains of the second crisis of the Reformation era. The aristocracy itself was not producing privy councillors of sufficient education, ability, and commitment to meet the new political conditions.

This transformation of the diplomatic corps formed an analogue to what had earlier happened in the sector of warfare and defense. Whereas the Strasbourgeois of the fifteenth century had fought their own battles, led by the patrician warriors of the town, the Strasbourgeois of the sixteenth century were defended by mercenaries. So in diplomacy, the privy councillors—who had always supplied the city's envoys—gradually gave way to salaried, university-trained lawyers. Jacob Sturm was the last of a breed at Strasbourg, the last great aristocratic amateur diplomat the oligarchy produced.

D. CONCLUSION

How different the world looked from the chamber of the XIII of Strasbourg in 1546, on the eve of the Smalkaldic War, than it had on the morrow of the great Peasants' War. Then the oligarchy had stood up to a movement of immense destructive potential, steered it away from dangerous paths, and struck a compromise with it that left most of the aristocracy's power intact. The oligarchy had acted when it had had to act, conceded when concessions seemed necessary, and carried the aristocracy through the greatest upheaval in the history of the Empire with no loss of power and little of prestige, and without major losses from its own ranks. Now, in the mid-1540s, the oligarchy stood once

---

[85] This is perfectly clear from the delegation's correspondence, in *PCSS*, V, 582–652.

[86] Gremp represented Strasbourg alone at a meeting in Ulm, July, 1554 (*ibid.*, pp. 546–550, No. 446, recess dated 15 July 1554); and Jakob Hermann was sent alone to the *Kreistag* at Worms during the same month (*ibid.*, p. 551, No. 445, of 25 July 1554).

more before the prospect of war, begrudging the money it had poured into the bottomless treasury of the League, wary of further sectarian outbursts, uncertain of the loyalty of its clergy, and unable to produce the personnel who could shore up the sagging web of diplomacy in which the city's security lay ensnared. Had the great myth of the city as a godly community mirrored more truly the social and political realities of reformed Strasbourg, the coming war might have welded the commune into a grim band of saints, prepared to sacrifice goods, kin, and selves for the gospel. That is precisely what did not happen.

CHAPTER EIGHT

EXODUS—THE COLLAPSE OF THE OLIGARCHY IN THE CRISIS OF 1547–1548

The war, begun with elevated hopes during the previous summer, ended for Strasbourg and the other South German Evangelical towns in early 1547 in an atmosphere of mistrust, fear, and failure. Except for native-born mercenaries, the Strasbourgeois had not done any campaigning, but they had paid, paid again, and paid once more the war levies of the League.[1] To the Strasbourgeois, some of whom had greeted the war as a defense of the gospel, others as a strike for civic liberties against tyranny, the autumn months of 1546 had brought only report and rumor of the endless military maneuverings in the Upper Danube valley. By the new year, the southern front had collapsed: Ulm and Frankfurt accepted humiliating terms; Ulrich of Württemberg, the gouty old sinner, had sued Charles for peace; and Augsburg was invested by Imperial troops. Now began a new political crisis at Strasbourg, which, during the next eighteen months, would bring the city to the brink of social war and drive the aristocracy from the town.

A. War and Peace Parties at Strasbourg, 1547

1. The collapse of the League left Strasbourg without allies and its regime without a policy. On 19 January 1547, it took a step taken only once before in living memory—at the height of the revolution of 1525—and polled the Schöffen of the guilds as to whether the regime should treat with Charles or prepare the city for a siege.[2] Two privy councillors and a clerk visited each guild hall and recorded the opinions, while the

---

[1] There is no modern history of the Smalkaldic War. For Strasbourg's role, see Alcuin Hollaender, *Strassburg im Smalkaldischen Krieg* (Strasbourg, 1881), written too early to take advantage of *PCSS*, IV. On the military side, see Crämer, "Die Wehrmacht Strassburgs," pp. 53–55. Nearly twenty aristocrats of Strasbourg served as officers in the League army, chiefly in Hessian units. Gerber, "Die Kriegsrechnungen, I–V," *ARG*, 32–34, *passim,* including three Böcklin, a von Baden, a von Kippenheim, and a Zorn.

[2] Chrisman, *Strasbourg,* p. 151.

patrician officeholders were called to the city hall to offer their views.[3] The result was a document of seventy-four folio sides of opinions, recommendations, complaints, and avowals of loyalty by the notables of Strasbourg.[4] Two-hundred-eighty Schöffen and twenty-three patricians gave their views, a sampling of political opinion which has no rival in the extant records of Reformation Strasbourg.

The poll of 1547 poses a number of problems of interpretation. Most detailed and most individual are the statements by the aristocrats, the patricians and the wealthy merchants in such guilds as Zum Spiegel and Zum Freiburg, while the remarks by Schöffen in some of the craft guilds tend to be brief and repetitious. The first speakers were always the privy councillors, senators, and ex-senators (*Altratsherren*), and the other Schöffen sometimes simply agreed with the views of these notables. But not always, and especially not in guilds whose representation in the regime was in the hands of invaders from wealthier guilds. The Tanners' guild (*Gerber*) shows that agreement with the notables was not just a matter of docility. They had two privy councillors, Conrad Joham, a XIIIer who had long ago moved over from the guild Zum Spiegel, and Veltin Storck, a XVer and saddler who belonged to the guild by virtue of his craft.[5] Joham, the guild's president, spoke first and urged "peace with honor" ("eim eherlichen vertrag") with guarantees of the city's liberties and religion. This, as we shall see, was the majority position of the aristocracy. A Duntzenheim, another invader from the guild Zum Spiegel, agreed with Joham, as did one other Schöffe.[6] But then spoke

---

[3] On 8 January 1547, after a committee report from Jacob Sturm, Mathis Pfarrer, Hans Lindenfels, and Conrad Joham, it was decided to poll the Schöffen (*PCSS*, IV, 558, No. 515n3); the committee's report is in Joham's hand (*ibid.*, pp. 556–557, No. 514). Originally scheduled for 13 January, it was actually held on the 19th; and the documents are described in *ibid.*, p. 558, No. 515n3. I use the fair copies in AMS, AA 564, fols. 15–34, 38–42, 45–46, 49–52, 55–61, 86–89, 91–92, prepared from the clerks' protocols in AMS, AA 565. See Hollaender, *Strassburg im Schmalkaldischen Krieg*, pp. 51–53, 94n2, the only historian besides Gerber (editor of *PCSS*, IV) who has evaluated the poll. Among the patricians, only the officeholders were polled. AMS, XXI 1547, fols. 1–2, by Gerber in *PCSS*, IV, No. 515n3.

[4] I write "notables," because this was not a poll of the guilds but of the ruling Schöffen of the guilds, a point sometimes forgotten in evaluating the earlier poll of 15 May 1525 (e.g., by Chrisman, *Strasbourg*, p. 151).

[5] AMS, AA 564, fols. 56ᵛ–58ʳ.

[6] *Ibid.*, fol. 56ᵛ: "Jst der meynung wie h. Conradt Joham." This Jacob von Duntzenheim was normally called "Jacob von Duntzenheim in Dorngasse" to distinguish him from the other Jacob von Duntzenheim, the son of Conrad, Jr., and brother of Batt (PROSOPOGRAPHY, No. XXII). He was undoubtedly related to the better known Ammeister; and he was senator from the *Gerberzunft* in 1525/26, 29/30, 41/42, 47/48.

Veltin Storck, who said that now he would approve no treaty, because the emperor had never kept his word in the past; if an honorable treaty were secured ("zu gemeinen eherlichen vertrag khomen"), however, he would vote for it. Eight other Schöffe supported Storck, no others supported Joham, and two wanted no treaty at all.[7] Something similar happened in the Cobblers' guild (*Schuhmacher*), where Conrad Meyer, the XVer and president and an invader from the guild Zum Spiegel, a Messinger, and two other Schöffen voted for "peace with honor," but ten others voted for resistance.[8] In the Carpenters' guild (*Zimmerleute*), Caspar Rumler, a rentier XVer and an invader, advised seeking "peace with honor" and resistance only as a last resort, but seven other Schöffen saw "defense as the only way, because the emperor has never kept his word."[9] The loss of the war seems to have brought to the surface the normally latent conflict between the aristocratic invaders and the masters of the guilds they invaded.

In guilds retaining some measure of economic integrity and in which the political leadership came from the guilds' own crafts, the political consciousness was both more militant and more nearly unanimous. Most striking is the Cloth guild (*Tucher*), whose masters were mainly cloth merchants and entrepreneurs. The privy councillor was the XVer Bastian Erb, a man of deep Evangelical piety and a generous and devoted friend of the afflicted, though not an especially influential man in the regime.[10] As president of his guild, Erb said that he "will agree to no reconciliation and will trust the emperor in heaven but not here; and he

---

Hatt, p. 424. On Conrad Joham and Veltin Storck, see PROSOPOGRAPHY, Nos. XLV, LXXXIX.

[7] AMS, AA 564, fols. 57ᵛ–58ʳ. Peter Gerber "Will gar jnn kheinen vertrag willigen," a position shared by Georgius Schurer.

[8] *Ibid.*, fols. 19ᵛ–20ᵛ. Typical of the majority in this guild was Conrad Fenchel: "woll helffen dem keÿser ein widerstandt thun, vnd sein vermögen zusetzen."

[9] *Ibid.*, fols. 50ᵛ–51ʳ. Rumler: "rath zu einem vertrag, wo man den vnuerletzlich der religion vnd statt Freiheitten bekhommen mocht, wo not, die gegenwer." Most of the Schöffen in this guild, however, supported their long-time senator, Thoman Lehen: "rath zur gegenwer, dan der keÿser halt khein glauben." Lehen was senator in 1539/40, 43/44, 47/48, 53/54, 57/58, and 61/62. Hatt, p. 482.

[10] AMS, AA 564, fols. 58ʳ–59ᵛ, where the unanimity of the Schöffen is quite remarkable and the religious motive appears more frequently than in any other guild. On Bastian Erb, see PROSOPOGRAPHY, No. XXVIII. My estimate of the character of this guild is based on Schmoller, *Die Strassburger Tucher- und Weberzunft*, and on the absence —except for several Mieg, interlopers from the guild Zum Spiegel (PROSOPOGRAPHY, Nos. LXI, LXII)—of genuine aristocrats among its Schöffen.

will stand by and hold to the Word of God and the people."[11] Every other Schöffe in this guild stood behind Erb. In the Masons' guild (*Maurer*), the Schöffen stood united behind the demand of their long-time president, the XIIIer Jacob Meyer, to seek no treaty with Charles and to prepare for war.[12] The Bakers (*Brotbecker*) stood almost as solidly behind their president, the XVer Veltin Kips, who also called for resistance.[13]

The Schöffen of other guilds were badly divided. Mathis Pfarrer, a cloth merchant, XIIIer, Altammeister, and one of the regime's most powerful figures, was also president of the Winetasters' guild (*Weinsticher*), which comprised the wine merchants and several other trades. Pfarrer advised "defense if we cannot secure an honorable treaty in which the religion and civic liberties are guaranteed"—the "peace with honor" position.[14] The two other notables were divided: Hans von Odratzheim, a rentier, urged the militant position of defense and no trust in the emperor; while Diebold Gerfalck supported Pfarrer's position. Eight others supported Pfarrer, three Odratzheim, and one left the decision to the regime. The division in the Fishermen's guild (*Fischer*) was rather different. This guild had never been subject to political invasion and during this era was usually represented in the privy councils by members of the Baldner family. Old Anshelm Baldner, the XVer and president, urged the militant position on his colleagues, but only six of them supported him.[15] Eight others refused to take one position or the other. Gilg Baldner, for example, advised that "it is better to follow God's guidance"; while Hanns Lehenman confessed that "the matter is important and too elevated for him; he will trust my lords, as those who know best, to find the best way; and, whatever they decide, he will stand by them and not abandon them."[16] In the Gardeners'

---

[11] AMS, AA 564, fol. 58^r: "Beschleusst er woll sich in khein rachtung begeben, wöll jn den keiser jm hymel vertruwen, vnd bey gottes wort vnd der burgerschaft halten vnd ston."

[12] *Ibid.*, fols. 21^v–24^v, the longest protocol and the one containing the largest number of genuinely individual responses.

[13] *Ibid.*, fol. 52^v, one of the shortest protocols, with most of the Schöffen simply agreeing with Kips. Only one, Jacob Schefer, the *Schaffner* at St. Margarethe, qualified his stand for resistance: "rath zur defension, wo man nit zu einem leidlichen vertrag vnuerletzt der Religion vnd statt Freiheitten khommen mag."

[14] *Ibid.*, fol. 49^r–v.

[15] *Ibid.*, fols. 45^v–46^v.

[16] *Ibid.*, fol. 46^r. Baldner: "dweil er nichts halt, ob man dann schon dann ein friden macht vnd Religion vssdingt, so hielt ers nit, weger ists, Man lass got walten." The *Fischerzunft* was full of Baldner, and I cannot establish a relationship between Gilg and

guild (*Gartner*), five Schöffen echoed the militancy of their XVer, Andreas Drenss, four simply expressed support for the regime, several others were willing to treat if civic liberties could be secured,[17] and Thoman Obrecht—no gardener but a civic employee—rejected both paths and agreed to leave the entire matter to the regime.[18]

When Alcuin Hollaender examined this poll, he concluded that a majority of the Schöffen was willing to accept a treaty with the emperor if it guaranteed the city's religion and liberties.[19] This is close to the truth, although the poll contains five basic positions rather than just majority and minority ones. First was the unqualified view that a treaty should be gotten from Charles, a path recommended by only three Schöffen. Secondly, there was the "peace with honor" view, strong among the aristocracy but also well represented elsewhere, being advocated by nearly one-quarter (24.3%) of all the Schöffen.[20] Thirdly, a

---

the three Baldner who were privy councillors. Hans Lehenman: "die sach sei wichtig vnnd jm zu hoch, wols mein herren als den hochverstendigen gewalt geben, das best dorin zu Roten. Vnnd was sie thun, do beÿ wollen sie ston vnnd halten vnnd mein herren nit verlassen."

[17] *Ibid.*, fols. 59ᵛ–61ʳ. The position of the Drenss in this guild was similar to that of the Baldner in their guild. If this division seems strange in view of the belligerent reputation of the Strasbourg gardeners, it should be noted that these are the views of the Schöffen, not all of whom were gardeners.

[18] Thoman Obrecht (d. 11 August 1560), son of Mattheus Obrecht and Jacobe von Rotweil, was *Oberschreiber* of the treasury (*Pfennigthurm*) from 1519 until his death, although he tried to resign as early as 1546. He and Elisabeth Rot had at least two sons: Heinrich, Ammeister in 1596 and 1602, XVer 1585–94 and XIIIer 1594–1606, who married Johanna, daughter of Wolfgang Schütterlin; and David (or Daniel) (d. 1592), M.D., who married Barbara, daughter of Hans Stösser (PROSOPOGRAPHY, No. XC). AMS, VI 493/6; BNUS, Ms. 1058, fols. 139ʳ, 176ᵛ; AMS, XXI 1546, fol. 595ᵛ; AMS, XXI 1547, fols. 127ʳ–128ᵛ.

[19] Hollaender, *Strassburg im Schmalkaldischen Krieg*, p. 53, who analyzes in detail only the views of the patricians. See Gerber, in *PCSS*, IV, No. 515n3.

[20] My calculations differ somewhat from those of Gerber, although I agree with him that the anti-treaty position was a majority one. A great deal depends on how one evaluates individual words and phrases. If a Schöffe said he wanted a treaty if an acceptable one could be gotten, I put him in the peace party. Wilhelm Prechter (Spiegel), for example, said that "wo man zu einem sollichen vertrag komen mocht, das man die Religion vnnd freiheit erhielt, wolt er Rahten, wo nit so woll er das sein mit vffsetzen." AMS, AA 564, fol. 16ʳ. If, however, a Schöffe counselled resistance unless a treaty could be gotten, I put him in the moderate resistance party. Caspar Hennicken (Schneider), for example, said that he "rath auch zur gegenwer, doch wan der keÿser ein ansuchen thet, vnd man zu billichen erlichen vnd leidlichen mitteln könte khommen, möcht erleiden, das vertragen wurd." Combining the moderate resistance party (position 3) with the strong resistance one yields 63% for resistance. This means that 176 Schöffen were basically against treating with Charles, which agrees well with Gerber's count of 180. *PCSS*, IV, 515n3.

small minority (8.9%) favored defense but also advocated negotiation. Fourthly, the majority (53.9%) simply voted for resistance or did so "because the emperor has never honored his word." Fifthly and finally, a tenth (10.4%) of them chose no policy but left the question in the regime's hands. The differences between the second and third positions are rather subtle, being often just a matter of a few words; and sometimes the words of those who spoke first were simply echoed and repeated by later speakers.[21] It is nonetheless possible to rank the guilds according to an index of militancy. In Table 20 a rating of 10.0 means that every

Table 20

Militancy Rating of ruling Schöffen of the guilds of Strasbourg, 19 January 1547.
(10.0 = 100% of Schöffen voted for that position)

Column A = Resistance (Rank) Column C = Trust regime (Rank)
Column B = Negotiation (Rank) Column D = B + C (Rank)

Guild	A (rank)	B (rank)	C (rank)	D (rank)
Tucher	10.0 (1)	— (20)	— (20)	— (20)
Kürschner	10.0 (1)	— (20)	— (20)	— (20)
Schneider	10.0 (1)	— (20)	— (20)	— (20)
Zur Luzern	9.3 (4)	— (20)	0.7 (6)	0.7 (15)
Brotbecker	9.2 (5)	0.8 (8)	— (20)	0.8 (13)
Küfer	9.2 (5)	0.8 (8)	— (20)	0.8 (13)
Maurer	8.7 (7)	— (20)	0.7 (6)	0.7 (15)
Zur Blume	8.6 (8)	0.7 (11)	0.7 (6)	1.4 (11)
Gerber	8.6 (8)	1.4 (7)	— (20)	1.4 (11)
Zimmerleute	8.6 (8)	0.7 (11)	— (20)	0.7 (15)
Zum Encker	8.3 (11)	0.8 (8)	0.8 (5)	1.6 (10)
Schuhmacher	6.7 (12)	2.7 (6)	0.7 (6)	3.4 (9)
Gartner	5.7 (13)	— (20)	4.3 (3)	4.3 (8)
Fischer	5.3 (14)	— (20)	4.7 (2)	4.7 (7)
Schmiede	4.6 (15)	5.3 (5)	— (20)	5.3 (6)
Zum Freiburg	3.1 (16)	6.9 (2)	— (20)	6.9 (4)
Zur Steltz	2.8 (17)	0.7 (11)	5.7 (1)	6.4 (5)
Weinsticher	2.7 (18)	6.7 (4)	0.7 (6)	7.4 (3)
Zur Möhrin	1.3 (19)	8.6 (1)	— (20)	8.6 (2)
Zum Spiegel	0.8 (20)	6.9 (2)	2.3 (4)	9.2 (1)
Constofler	1.3	7.8	0.8	8.6

Source: AMS, AA 564, fols. 15–34, 38–42, 45–46, 49–52, 55–61, 86–89, 91–92.

---

[21] Such was the influence of Adam von Wehrstein (Zur Möhrin), a senator; of Diebold Hass and Hans Neff (or Neve) (Zur Blume), a senator and an ex-senator respectively; of Jacob von Duntzenheim (Zum Encker), a XIIIer; of Anselm Baldner

Schöffe in that guild gave an unqualified vote for the position rated in the column indicated (in column A, e.g., resistance); so that a rating of 10.0 means that every Schöffe voted for resistance (column A), for treating with Charles V (column B), or for leaving the matter to the regime (column C). Column D combines columns B and C into a total peace party, for a vote to support the regime was, in effect, a vote for negotiation.[22]

Table 20 confirms roughly the identification of the peace party with the rich.[23] The guilds in which the rich were most heavily concentrated—Zum Spiegel, Zur Möhrin, Zur Steltz, and Zum Freiburg—were all among the least militant; while the most militant guilds included, with few exceptions, guilds retaining a high degree of economic homogeneity and little subject to political invasion, such as the *Tucher, Kürschner, Brotbecker, Küfer,* and *Maurer.* The butchers of the guild Zur Blume were nearly as militant, and so were the tanners (*Gerber*). The guild Zur Luzern, though it descended from the old grain merchants' guild, included a large number of barber-surgeons (*Scherer*), relatively humble people, among its Schöffen. Some relatively humble guilds, such as the gardeners, the carpenters, and the fishermen, lacked the militancy of some more prestigious ones. The entire analysis, of course, deals with the Schöffen only, the guild notables, and does not represent the views or the mood of the city's population as a whole.

The aristocracy as a whole wanted a negotiated peace with the emperor, although expressions of a desire for peace *at any price* were rare. The twenty-three patrician polled were overwhelmingly for peace, although their reasons differed slightly from those of the peace party in the guilds. Only one noble, Heinrich von Mülnheim, spoke for militant resistance:

(Fischer), a XVer; of Simon Franck (Küfer), Altammeister; and of Veltin Storck (Gerber), a XVer. The clerks can very well have emphasized or obscured the degree of influence of an important man simply by the way they recorded the opinions. In the *Brotbeckerzunft,* for example, most persons are noted with the phrases "in simili forma" or "rath wie jtzgmelt." AMS, AA 564, fol. 52ᵛ.

[22] Positions 2 and 3 are here combined into a treaty party (column B).

[23] The index of militancy correlates fairly well but inversely with the index of influx of new clerical members into the guilds in 1523–25, which is suggestive, because the influx of a large number of new clerical members would tend to weaken the social solidarity of the guild. Eight of the ten most militant guilds in 1547 were also among the ten guilds that received the fewest new clerical members in 1523–25. The exceptions are the guild Zur Luzern and the Schneider, which received large numbers of clerics and were also very militant in 1547.

He hates to hear that we won't and shouldn't honor letter and seal [the League treaty], as some have said, perhaps because the emperor has also broken his word. He finds it terrible, because the cities should hold to the true faith; and perhaps just because Strasbourg maintains its league with Saxony and Hesse, God may grant peace. He would neither seek a treaty nor agree to one, for *the common people will lose heart if they hear of a treaty*. If we decide to treat, there may still be a good way, but first we should send to the princes, Saxony and Hesse, for if salvation is to be had with them, we should prefer to maintain our league with them. But if no aid is possible and the princes together negotiate a peace, that would be the best course; and we should enter into no treaty except together with the princes and the other cities. He would much rather die honorably than have a dishonorable peace.[24]

Mülnheim's was a specifically aristocratic resistance view, based as much on his honor as a noble as on religious and patriotic considerations. Jacob Sturm stated what became the regime's own policy:

If Strasbourg can or may secure a treaty, through whatever paths are open to us, which is neither against God nor honor nor ruinous to the city, then he will aid in getting it accepted. But if no such treaty can be had, then we should rather prepare for a siege. He therefore wants the honorable Senate to be empowered to seek a peace that is neither ungodly, dishonorable, nor unbearable, that it be able to act on its own—for he can say nothing now about mediators. He doesn't know what such negotiations will produce, but he fears that failure to seek peace now will make peace impossible to achieve, and we may end by fleeing the possibility of peace. Therefore, he proposes that we consider whatever the enemy may propose to us.[25]

Seven other patricians announced their agreement with Sturm, and most of the others, at greater or lesser length, spoke for the same basic position. One of the peculiarities of the patrician opinions is the concern for the typically noble quality of honor. As Ulman Böcklin put it, "[He] would rather die honorably than live without honor."[26] He and others wanted to keep faith with the princes and the few towns that had not yet made peace. As Assmus (Erasmus) Böcklin said, "We know that both princes are still in the field."[27] But the insiders, the XIIIers, knew that no hope lay in that direction. Jacob Sturm did not even mention the League or the princes in his speech, and his brother, Peter, bluntly said

---

[24] AMS, AA 564, fols. 28ᵛ–29ʳ [emphasis added].
[25] *Ibid.*, fol. 25ᵛ.
[26] *Ibid.*, fol. 26ʳ: "Will lieber erlich sterben dan vnerlich leben."
[27] *Ibid.*, fol. 30ʳ.

that "though he would prefer nothing so much as the maintenance of the League," in the present situation "no one else can help us, and we shall get no aid."[28] Some other patricians wanted at least to notify the princes of the regime's peace feelers, and only one, the senator Mathis Braun von Reichenberg, flatly stated that under no circumstances should the war continue.[29]

The guild aristocracy spoke through the Schöffen of the guild Zum Spiegel and the big merchants and rentiers in other guilds. Andreas Mieg, XIIIer and president Zum Spiegel, said that he couldn't choose a policy, "but, because the situation is always changing and my lords are always better informed than are the common people, he wants the Senate to be empowered to do whatever is best for the city and the people."[30] Friedrich VI von Gottesheim wanted to inform the princes and wait for further developments before suing for peace. Philips Ingold advised seeking peace through mediators, and he was seconded by Martin Hug von Ottenheim. Only Frantz Bertsch, the apothecary, among the Schöffen zum Spiegel, "does not want to seek a peace but to remain by God's Word," while the rest of his colleagues agreed either with Andreas Mieg or with Gottesheim. Aristocrats in other guilds spoke in similar veins: Conrad Meyer, XVer and president of the Cobblers' guild; Conrad Joham, XIIIer and president of the Tanners' guild; and Mattheus Geiger, Lux Messinger, and most other Schöffen Zum Freiburg.[31] They and many other Schöffen who wanted negotiation and peace repeated the formula that a treaty must guarantee the religion and liberties of the city—as Geiger expressed it, "that we keep our religion and our liberties"—and, almost as frequently, that no Imperial garrison be put into Strasbourg. There were exceptions. Felix Erstein-Armbruster, an armigerous rentier of an old Strasbourg family, echoed the militancy of much humbler men: "He will stick by God and the gospel, and if he must fall, better by the hand of man than that of God."[32] Veltin Kips and Jacob von Duntzenheim, both merchants, and the wealthy goldsmith Christoph II Städel, were of the same mind.[33] In the main, however, the rich of Strasbourg wanted peace with honor.

---

[28] *Ibid.*, fol. 26[r–v].
[29] *Ibid.*, fol. 29[v]: "kan zu keinen krieg rathen."
[30] *Ibid.*, fol. 15[r].
[31] *Ibid.*, fols. 16[v]–17[v], 19[v], 56[v].
[32] *Ibid.*, fol. 42[v].
[33] *Ibid.*, fols. 42[r], 52[r], 52[v].

That the Schöffen were polled at all suggests that the regime itself was badly divided over the issue of peace or war, which is confirmed by an analysis of the views of the privy councillors and senators. This information is summarized in Table 21.[34] In both the estate hierarchy and in the hierarchy of colleges, sentiment for negotiation was strongest at the top and weakest at the bottom, that is, strongest in the XIII and among the patricians and weakest among the senators and the guildsmen. Of the patricians in the regime, only the senators Hans Jacob Schorp von Freudenberg and Marx Hag gave even qualified support to Heinrich von Mülnheim's militant position. Only in the XIII did a majority of the guildsmen favor treating with Charles.

Table 21

Division of the Senate & XXI of Strasbourg on Negotiation or Resistance, 19 January 1547

Council	Patricians	Guildsmen	Total
XIII			
Negotiate	3	6	9
Resist	0	3	3
XV			
Negotiate	3	2	5
Resist	1	8	9
Simple XXI			
Negotiate	0	0	0
Resist	0	2	2
Senate			
Negotiate	7	6	13
Resist	2	14	16
All Senate & XXI			
Negotiate	13	14	27
Resist	3	27	30
Total	16	41	57

Source: AMS, AA 564, fols. 15–34, 38–42, 45–46, 49–52, 55–61, 86–89, 91–92; PROSOPOGRAPHY, Appendix A.

Here in the XIII sat the veterans of the great days of the 1520s, and only three of them spoke for resistance: Jacob von Duntzenheim, Jacob Meyer (Masons), and Martin Herlin, of whom the latter two had

---

[34] Those who said, "stellt es meinen Herren heim," are here combined with those who favored a treaty. Two patrician privy councillors, Egenolf Röder von Diersburg and Alexius Büchsner, are missing from the poll.

belonged to the Zealot faction led by Claus Kniebis. The major surprise is that Kniebis himself counselled his colleagues to seek an honorable peace: "if we may keep our religion and liberties and are assured that the emperor will not garrison the city, he favors a treaty; if not, he will cooperate and await what God may send, and he will give my lords authority in this matter."[35] The old, now sobered Zealot carried only half the Schöffen in his own guild, the others voting for resistance. Kniebis's position, which may reflect his advanced age and numerous physical afflictions, is not consistent with his long-time militancy. For the rest, it may be noticed that resistance sentiment was markedly weaker in the Senate & XXI (47%) than among the Schöffen as a whole (62%), and that in the regime as well, the patricians and big merchants were overwhelmingly for peace.

2. The poll of 19 January 1547 provides some clues to the social sources and endurance of the anti-treaty party during the next two years. Some responses suggest how strongly the new religion had become an ingredient of civic patriotism. Schöffe after Schöffe stated his desire "to retain our religion and civic liberties" and his willingness "to engage life and goods" for their sake. Such phrases occur among the responses of wealthy merchants as well as those of humbler folk, and they occur in the statements of patricians and merchants who would later choose exile over the sacrifices required by the defense of religion and liberties.[36] Most united and most militant in voicing the ideal of the civic "sacral corporation," however, were the Schöffen of those guilds that were ruled by small merchants and masters from relatively ordinary trades: butchers and cloth merchants, tanners and saddlers, tailors and furriers, bakers and masons. Here, one is pressed by the evidence to conclude, among these folk was the proper social home of the ideal of the commune as a religious corporation in its Reformation form. One may call them petty bourgeoisie, guild bourgeoisie, middling folk, the shopkeeper-artisan element, or what one will. They were in fact the lowest social stratum of the ruling class of the city, the lowest group that enjoyed some direct access to political power and from whose midst most of the Zealots of the 1520s had come. Claus Kniebis, the university-

---

[35] AMS, AA 564, fol. 18^r.

[36] Such as Wilhelm Prechter (see note 20 above). Friedrich Ebel: "Woll leib vnd gut bey einer stat lassen." Wolfgang Böcklin von Böcklinsau: "will er leib vnd gut bey der stat Strassburgk lassen." Claus Zorn zum Riet: "Aber vf gnad vnd vngnad sich zuergeben, das woll er nit thon, ehe leib vnd gut darob lassen." *Ibid.*, fols. 16^r, 27^r.

educated rentier, was probably less typical of them than was the merchant Martin Herlin. They were, to express their place in technical terms, the dominated fraction of a dominant class, just those persons to whom the regime of control, regulation, discipline, and corporate consciousness—the essence of the guild order—meant the most: in the shop, in the guild, and in the church. Strasbourg, the city, its territory, and the economically tributary region around it formed the boundaries of their entire lives and consciousness; and the city's corporate order preserved their regulated but substantial independence and preserved their superiority over the wageworkers, servants, and perpetual journeymen who formed the broad mass of the plebs.

Men from this stratum had probably supported most strongly the introduction of a corporate ecclesiastical discipline for which Bucer and his colleagues had striven in vain for the past two decades. One occasionally finds among their responses a nearly pure form of the reformers' ideal of the city as sacral corporation and the collective responsibility for sin and virtue (the feature that differentiates it decisively from Lutheranism). Bastian Erb lamented that

> if the grave sins and offenses are suppressed, such as usury, arrogance, and blasphemy, he hopes that God will grant grace. If not, we will have to submit to the yoke, for nothing will be accomplished with these mercenaries and scoundrels—but only with pious citizens and peasants, and he has often talked with his fellow Schöffen about this.[37]

He had indeed! Wolff von Brompt (Brumath), a Schöffe of the same guild and also probably a cloth merchant, agreed with "herr Bastian," "and if everyone else falls away and he alone remains, he will refuse a treaty with the emperor or with anyone else; but he will stand by God and His Word. Christians must suffer!"[38] Luther, too, had preached that Christians must suffer, but these respectable Strasbourgeois were not counselling mere passive resistance. They wanted internal moral reform and external militancy. As Lorentz Graff, a gardener and former XVer, said, "each must transform his own life and the sins must be punished, just as in Ninive—otherwise all is in vain."[39] Such men called

---

[37] *Ibid.*, fol. 58ʳ.

[38] *Ibid.*: "vnd ob sie schon abfellig wurden vnd nur ainer allein plib, wolt er leib vnd seel am selben hallten, darumb woll er jn kheinen vertrag weder gegen keiser noch nyemandt bewilligen, Sonder bey Gott vnd seinem Wort halten. Christen muessen leiden."

[39] *Ibid.*, fol. 60ᵛ. Graff had resigned his offices in 1542.

upon the regime to restore godly discipline in the commune as a preparation for defending the gospel.

There were other militants among the Schöffen whose consciousness was less corporate and more class oriented. These were the Schöffen who did not trust the regime to stand fast. In the Cloth guild, six Schöffen warned that the regime must accept no treaty without prior approval by the Schöffen.[40] Georg Büheler of the Masons' guild demanded that "the whoredom so prevalent among rich and poor must be punished, and it would not hurt to purge the regime of evil-doers, both nobles and non-nobles."[41] Five men—three barber-surgeons in the guild Zur Luzern, one Schöffe in the guild Zur Blume, and the truculent, redoubtable mason, Conrad Kruss—urged the government to take the question of peace and war to the people.[42] This demand was to recur more than once during the following two years; but no matter how desperate the outlook, the regime never took a question beyond the Schöffen to the commune.[43] What gave such views an ominous edge was their combination of religious zeal, virulent hatred for the emperor, resentment over the lost war, and a latent mistrust of the aristocrats and their regime. Two leaders of the subsequent guerilla action against the official peace policy, the masons Conrad Kruss and Claus von Andlau, shared views of this sort. Kruss demanded that the civic leaders "undertake, with deeds rather than just with words, to rule according to the gospel," while Andlau described the regime's alternatives as "placing us between God and the Devil."[44] This spirit, far more disturbing to the aristocrats than the corporatist piety of the cloth merchants, had a certain smell of Münster, of a godly reign of the saints, something which, although it never came to pass at Strasbourg, lay dormant in the social order and in the hearts of the little folk of the town.

---

[40] *Ibid.*, fols. 58^r–59^v. They were Jacob Schöttel, Claus Wagner, Hanns Keller, Gottfried Wolff, Görg Vberreuttern, and Lazarus Berner.

[41] *Ibid.*, fol. 24^r: "vnd schade nichtz ob man schon Edell vnd vnedell vmb das vnrechten willen vss dem Rath satzte." This sort of Donatism is a rather natural deduction from sacral corporatist ideology and its doctrine of the "Christian magistrate."

[42] *Ibid.*, fols. 23^{r-v}, 31^r, 32^r. Michael Schwencker (PROSOPOGRAPHY, No. LXXXV), *Oberherr* Zur Luzern, XVer, and an immigrant, said: "will wie die alten Strassburger dabey bleiben, gut vnd blut daran setzen, sonderlich die weill es die Religion belangt, Got werde gnad geben!" *Ibid.*, fol. 30^r. Conrad Kruss acquired citizenship on 4 February 1525 "von wegen Anna, Hans Schultheiss von Wurtzburg, des schumachers seligen, dochter, siner hussfrawen, vnd dient mit den murern." Wittmer, No. 7719.

[43] See, for example, *PCSS*, IV, 685–686, No. 601n1.

[44] AMS, AA 564, fol. 23^{r-v}. Kruss submitted a long statement of his views.

That such fears were not nugatory is shown by the agitation during the spring months against the regime, while Jacob Sturm and the lawyers negotiated with Charles's agents the submission of Strasbourg. When the first set of terms was read to the Schöffen on February 3, Conrad Kruss charged that the regime had illegally disposed of ecclesiastical properties; and Hans Mennlich, the Tailors' Schöffe, threw in Sturm's face the pro-war, anti-Imperial opinions which Sturm himself had expressed as the war began.[45] Mennlich was told to "shut his mouth," and Kruss was jailed for two months, banished for five years, and then pardoned after one year. But the agitation continued among the artisans. Nearly all of the dozen or more men who were investigated or prosecuted for "subversive talk" ("unnutze reden") during the spring and summer of 1547 were artisans: tailors, butchers, a furrier, an embroiderer (*Seidensticker*), barber-surgeons, and gardeners. No less than three Schöffen were involved, Kruss and Andlau of the masons and Hans Mennlich of the tailors.[46] A certain Arbogast Keller, a cooper (*Kübler*), was heard to say that the aristocrats in the regime had secret letters from the emperor, which they would post on their houses when his troops took the city and thus save their goods and themselves. If it came to that, Keller said, he would put some fir trees under the city hall and burn it to the ground.[47]

Two features of the mounting political agitation among the artisans during the first half of 1547 were especially ominous: the oft-expressed need to search out those responsible for the loss of the war; and the attempts of some of the preachers to manipulate popular resentment to their own purposes. Resentful talk found natural targets in the emperor and the bishop, but it spilled over onto the French and other resident foreigners.[48] The chief target, however, was always the regime, whom

---

[45] *PCSS*, IV, 656, No. 586n8; Hollaender, *Strassburg im Schmalkaldischen Krieg*, pp. 78–79. The masons were a special center of militancy. When a certain Jörg Murer of Colmar asked for permission to renounce his citizenship, "das er sich hie nit nehren moge," the regime decided to investigate him for sedition. AMS, XXI 1547, fols. 333ᵛ–334ʳ (22 June 1547).

[46] AMS, XXI 1547, fols. 215ᵛ–217ʳ, 221ʳ, 231ᵛ, 232ᵛ, 252ʳ, 253ᵛ, 255ʳ, 292ʳ⁻ᵛ, 419ʳ⁻ᵛ; AMS, R 29/110; *PCSS*, IV, 646ff. One of the more curious characters was "die lange Naglerin, so abermals jnn der predig gejauchzet, sich sonsten seltzame gesprech gehabt, der kaiser kome, man muess die Altaria vnd die Mess widerumb auffrichten etc." AMS, XXI 1547, fols. 363ᵛ–364ʳ (13 July 1547).

[47] AMS, XXI 1547, fol. 419ʳ⁻ᵛ (3 August 1547).

[48] *Ibid.*, fol. 4ʳ⁻ᵛ (13 January 1547). Reported to Jacob Sturm by the pastor of the French congregation, who explained: "villeicht der vrsach das die welschen jetzo gegen den Teutschen handlen. do man kein vnderscheid zwischen Hispaniern Italienern

the militants charged with seeking peace at any price and, in particular, of negotiating a secret treaty with Charles which compromised the religion and liberties of Strasbourg. Already in January there had been voiced the accusation that the regime had not fully supported the war.[49] During the months of negotiation of the treaty (February–April), the suspicion spread among the people that their lords were betraying them, giving rise to a current story that the regime and the people of Strasbourg were at odds with one another.[50] By April there were rumors that leading political figures, XIIIers especially, and other nobles and aristocrats were leaving the city—a false rumor, but one which accurately represented the mounting tendency for the struggle between war and peace parties to become a conflict between the "common man" and the aristocracy.[51] A special target of popular wrath was Wolfgang Rehlinger. He was a former burgomaster of Augsburg, where he had resigned his citizenship in 1543. Rehlinger then migrated to Strasbourg, his mother's home city, where his cousin, Jacob Sturm, nominated him for citizenship.[52] Rehlinger played a key role in the regime's reconciliation with the emperor, for which activity the militants in the war party branded him "a traitor to this city."[53] Word ran through Strasbourg that Rehlinger would be killed if he returned to the city. He was a perfect target: a foreigner, rich, and a chief mediator of the treaty—but he was also Jacob Sturm's cousin. He was a very suitable focal point for the process by which the struggle over the issue of war and peace was gradually

---

vnd Franzosen mach. Nuhn seyen sie jrs vatters lands vmbs Euangelium verlossen, wolten gern jr leib vnd leben bey einer stat Strassburgk lassen. Wo sie aber gemeiner stat vnd der burgerschaft beschwerlich oder vberlestig sein solen, so wolte sy ehe sich anderswo hin thun." See also AMS, XXI 1546, fol. 610[r] (15 December 1546).

[49] *Ibid.*, fol. 653[r] (8 January 1547).

[50] *PCSS*, IV, 672, No. 597; p. 680, No. 604n1; p. 683, No. 608n1; p. 692, No. 614n2; p. 694, No. 615; p. 695, No. 616.

[51] *Ibid.*, p. 695, No. 616; p. 692, No. 614n2.

[52] Wolfgang Rehlinger (d. 18 June 1557), son of Bernhard Rehlinger and Richardis Missbach (i.e., Schenck gen. Missbach) of Strasbourg; married 13 February 1528 Anna Wieland (d. 29 August 1551), by whom he had five children; burgomaster of Augsburg in 1534, 36, 37, 39, 41; Baumeister in 1535, 37, 40, 42; XIIIer 1534–37, 39–43; renounced citizenship 1543 and admitted as a *Schirmbürger* at Strasbourg 1545; emigrated 28 August 1548; readmitted at Strasbourg 30 January 1555. *Genealogisches Handbuch des in Bayern immatrikulierten Adels*, VII (Neustadt a. d. Aisch, 1961), pp. 292, 294; Bernays, "Zur Biographie Johann Winthers von Andernach," p. 36n1; AMS, R 26/29, fols. 104[r]–108[v], 109[r], 110[r]–119[v]; AMS, XXI 1555, fols. 35[v]–36[r]; and the data on his offices at Augsburg from manuscript sources, communicated by James E. Mininger. On the Sturm–Rehlinger connection, see chapter II above, note 111.

[53] AMS, XXI 1547, fols. 255[r]–256[v], 297[r–v].

transformed into a popular struggle against the aristocracy and its oligarchy.

Just as serious, from another side, was the anti-treaty campaign which some of the preachers conducted from the pulpits of the town. Martin Bucer was a stalwart of the resistance party, believing as he did that the Strasbourgeois should be prepared to sacrifice life, liberty, and property for the defense of the gospel: "Look how God made and kept the Swiss free! But this requires biblical courage and struggle; no need to worry about money, provisions, and supplies—God will provide!"[54] Most militant of the clergy was Paul Fagius, the young pastor of the volatile parish of New St. Peter, where he thundered from his pulpit against peace and the treaty.[55] Mathis Zell, ever the most popular man among the town's clergy, joined in from his pulpit in the cathedral.[56] Again and again Jacob Sturm pleaded with his colleagues to gag these preachers, "so that they cease to preach to the people against the treaty and cause mistrust between the common man and the regime."[57] Through the spring and summer months of 1547, the regime tried, with indifferent success, to still the anti-treaty, anti-Imperial and, often enough, anti-government preaching.

For Bucer and Fagius at least, the mounting unrest was a golden opportunity to force a "second reformation" at Strasbourg. They were emboldened to attempt what was perhaps the most subversive path of action they could have taken: the formation of conventicles, private associations of "saints"—complete with the discipline and power of excommunication which the regime had always refused to allow.[58] Here began the clerically-led conventicle movement which flourished especially in 1549 before its merciless suppression by the regime.[59]

---

[54] (Martin Bucer) to (Landgrave Philipp of Hesse), (Strasbourg), 29 March 1547, in Lenz, ed. *Briefwechsel des Landgrafen Philipps . . . mit Bucer,* II, 490, No. 250.

[55] AMS, XXI 1547, fols. 63ᵛ–64ʳ; *PCSS,* IV, 656, No. 586n7. On Fagius (1504–49) of Rheinzabern (Pfalz), since 1544 pastor at New St. Peter, see Richard Raubenheimer, *Paul Fagius aus Rheinzabern. Sein Leben und Wirken als Reformator und Gelehrter,* Veröffent-lichungen des Vereins für Pfälzische Kirchengeschichte, 6 (Grünstadt/Pfalz, 1957).

[56] AMS, XXI 1547, fols. 41ʳ, 345ʳ⁻ᵛ, 347ᵛ–348ᵛ.

[57] Jacob Sturm, Marx Hagen, Friedrich von Gottesheim, and Ludwig Gremp to the XIII of Strasbourg, Nördlingen, 19 March 1547, in *PCSS,* IV, 655–656, No. 586.

[58] AMS, XXI 1547, fols. 63ᵛ–64ʳ: "das die prediger zu St. Thoman und zum Jungen St. Peter die leut insonderheit beschicken und understanden der bann fur sich selbs ufzurichten." Also in *PCSS,* IV, 656, No. 586n7. On this movement and its meaning, see Bellardi, "*Christliche Gemeinschaft*", pp. 30–37. It reached a climax on 9 November 1547, when the clergy split over the issue of obedience to the regime. *Ibid.,* pp. 38–48.

[59] *Ibid.,* chapter IV.

By the spring of 1547, these preachers had lost faith in the regime they had so faithfully served, and they began to try to reconstruct the alliance between the gospel and the people which had carried them and their reform to victory during the great days of the 1520s.

The post-war unrest and agitation was thus already marked by anti-oligarchical sentiment and class feeling against the rich, the powerful, and the influential. One year later, the conflict would burst into full bloom in the struggle over the Interim. The social character of this political unrest is visible both in the division of the ruling class into war and peace parties and in the leaders and targets of agitation during the post-war months. The preachers' campaign, though largely a fight for their own survival and directed chiefly against the government, had a similar social character both in the membership of its conventicles and in renewal of the memories of the great days of the Reformation.

B.   POPULAR AND CLERICAL RESISTANCE BETWEEN TREATY AND INTERIM, 1547–48

1. The signing of the peace treaty with the emperor in late April, 1547, dampened but could not still entirely the anti-treaty forces. They quickly pointed out that the treaty contained no guarantee of civic religion and thus no real insurance against a new conflict with Charles, an invasion of the Southwest, a siege, and perhaps the restoration of Catholicism. It was quite true that Sturm's treaty averted the dual threat of an Imperial garrison and a dictated expulsion of the guilds from the regime—the fate of Augsburg, Ulm, and other southern free towns.[60] But the remaining political question, the general ecclesiastical settlement and its local application, was also a source of acute internal danger because of the resistance an unfavorable decision would certainly produce. Charles's determination to issue and enforce an "interim" ecclesiastical order assured the continuation of the internal political-social crisis at Strasbourg.

Strasbourg's aristocracy wanted and needed peace, for the war had cost too much and done too much damage to commerce for them to have much stomach for a new war.[61] The war debt and the indemnities to

---

[60] Hollaender, *Strassburg im Schmalkaldischen Krieg*, pp. 82–92.

[61] *PCSS*, IV, 668–670, No. 593 and note 11, on the disruption of commerce and confiscation of goods. The Ingold had some goods "aufgehauen" near Nuremberg (*ibid.*, pp. 694–695, No. 615).

Charles and his brother caused further political difficulties in addition to burdening the public finances. The war and the treaty added nearly a third of a million Rhenish florins to the public debt: 220,000 fl. paid in levies to the Smalkaldic League; 43,000 for the mercenaries to garrison the city; and 43,000 fl. in indemnities.[62] Charles also demanded and got an indemnity in cannon, the fetching of which by his agents occasioned an ugly incident of threats and insults.[63] A small part of the war costs had been raised through interest-free loans taken or forced from the surviving ecclesiastical corporations and the funds of the liquidated religious houses; but most of it came from Basel and elsewhere at 5% and had to be serviced. In October, 1547, the regime resorted to a new tax, choosing to raise the wine excise.[64] This unpopular measure merely added to the grumbling about mal-administration of civic finances. Drawing on an ancient tradition of complaint, Blesi Nessel, an immigrant cooper, muttered that "civic finances are badly administered."[65] The war debt and the need to service it were yet another way in which the war and its loss had poisoned the political atmosphere of the town.

The chief question, however, remained the ecclesiastical settlement, and with each passing month was waning the prospect of holding the loyalty of the little people, if the price of peace were to be paid at the cost of their new church. This dilemma inspired Jacob Sturm's work at the great "armored Diet" of the Empire in the conquered city of Augsburg (October, 1547–June, 1548).[66] The emperor's price for peace was a document known as the Interim of Augsburg, which would require Strasbourg to transform its church order into a modified version of Catholicism. That would probably mean social war within, if the regime introduced the Interim, or war and a siege from Charles, if it did not. Jacob Sturm knew that the commune lacked the internal solidarity and

---

[62] *Ibid.,* p. 1102, No. 842. The war debt deserves a special study.

[63] The cannon were not fetched until September, 1548. *Ibid.,* pp. 1073–1074, No. 821; pp. 1074–1075, No. 823 and notes 1–4; pp. 1082–1083, No. 828. See Sebald Büheler, *Chronique,* No. 310, whose father as head of the arsenal (*Zeugmeister*) supervised the transfer.

[64] Büheler, *Chronique,* No. 306; AMS, VI 493/4, fol. 9ᵛ; *PCSS,* IV, 702–703, No. 626, p. 765, No. 668 and note 4. The wine excise (*Umgelt*) was increased and the standard measure decreased, in effect a double increase.

[65] AMS, XXI 1547, fols. 215ᵛ, 222ʳ⁻ᵛ, 231ʳ. Blesi Nessel, a cooper of Obernai, purchased citizenship at Strasbourg on 29 February 1524. Wittmer, No. 7372. In 1555, he and his daughter asked the regime to punish her husband, who, they alleged, had been living in adultery since 1548. AMS, XXI 1555, at 12 January 1555.

[66] See Harry Gerber, "Jakob Sturms Anteil an den Religionsverhandlungen des Augsburger 'geharnischten' Reichstags von 1547/48," *ELJb,* 8 (1929), 166–191.

willingness to sacrifice which a successful resistance to Charles would require. If Strasbourg refused the Interim, he warned, it would involve "not only the pious Christians, who are ready to die for the cause, but also those who are not prepared to be thrown into the greatest danger and, to speak humanly, into certain ruin in a hopeless cause."[67] This realism left him only the hope that private negotiations with the Imperial chancellor, Cardinal Granvelle, might win a moderation of the Interim's terms.

2. During the summer of 1547 the political mood in Strasbourg had been threatening enough that the regime had forbidden the customary parades of the apprentices through the streets.[68] But the city to which Sturm and Hans von Odratzheim returned on 9 July 1548 was seething with rumor of revolt and threat of violence. The preachers, who saw in the Interim the crack of doom, agitated tirelessly against it. Fagius preached at New St. Peter on the regime's power of the sword and cursed all who supported the peace.[69] During the previous winter the regime had tried to pacify the clergy by taking steps toward a stricter system of ecclesiastical discipline.[70] This gesture was now swept aside, and the clergy shouted with one voice against the Interim and for a police of morals—compulsory church attendance, reconstruction of clerical authority, punishment of sins—it is no wonder that a contemporary pamphlet charged that "the preachers want to make a Münster of this city."[71] Everyone knew what that meant. There were new arrests and investigations of persons hitherto not known to have been involved in the popular movement, men of substance, such as Jacob Bötzel, a Schöffe in the Coopers' guild.[72] As in the previous year, the agitators,

---

[67] *PCSS*, IV, 1018–1020, No. 792 (29 June 1548).

[68] As on 16 May 1547, when the regime cancelled the annual parade of the bakers' apprentices. AMS, XXI 1547, fol. 250[r–v].

[69] AMS, XXI 1548, fol. 364[r] (16 July 1548), and 236[r–v] (5 May 1548). On the Interim struggle, see now the Berlin thesis of Erdmann Weyrauch, "Konfessionelle Krise und soziale Stabilität. Versuch der Beschreibung und systemtheoretischen Analyse des Interims in Strassburg (1548–1562) mit einer methodologischen Einleitung" (1976), 2 vols., here at I, 63–68, where Weyrauch surveys critically both the general literature on the Interim and the special literature on Strasbourg. See also Werner Bellardi, "Bucers 'Summarischer Vergriff' und das Interim in Strassburg," *ZKiG*, 85 (1974), 64–76.

[70] AMS, XXI 1548, fols. 22[v], 35[r], 36[r], 63[r].

[71] AMS, XXI 1548, fol. 312[v]; and see fols. 319[r], 324[r–v], 333[v].

[72] *Ibid.*, fol. 368[r–v] (18 July 1548). Jacob Bötzel, perhaps related to the Peter Bötzel of Landshut, a cooper who purchased citizenship at Strasbourg on 12 November 1493 (Wittmer, No. 4405), had been of a different opinion during the poll of the Schöffen on 19 January 1547. Then he had favored a treaty, "Dan wo das Landt verderbt, sey die

rumormongers, and organizers were all artisans—weavers, coopers, gardeners, cobblers, and barber-surgeons. Some old faces were back, such as Conrad Kruss and Claus von Andlau, together with many new recruits.

Spurred by a growing pile of reports on plots, rumors, and sedition, the government reported on the Interim to the Schöffen on 23 July 1548. They assured the Schöffen that they were doing all possible to secure an ameliorated set of terms.[73] On August 16 arrived the emperor's negative decision, forbidding any alterations to the Interim and precluding further negotiations. Again the regime went to the Schöffen and pleaded with them to calm the people and trust their rulers.[74] The rumor ran through Strasbourg that the regime had made a secret treaty with Charles. The truth was that Charles had given the Strasbourgeois one month from 16 August to accept the Interim or be placed under the Imperial ban. There were secret meetings of Fagius and a schoolteacher, Michael Toxites, with some of the leaders of the popular opposition; and there were rumors of a secret meeting of the notables in the Gardeners' guild.[75]

The opposition was crippled by its failure to find a leader. Certainly, many of the oligarchs hated the prospect of restoring Catholicism in any form. "It is grievous to many good men," Egenolf Röder von Diersburg told a Württemberg agent, "to have to abandon the confessed truth and go back to idolatry."[76] But neither Röder nor any other noble was willing to turn on his own kind, as Salvatore de' Medici had done in Florence in the days of the Ciompi, and as Giano della Bella had done in the same city nearly one hundred years before. The remaining Zealots were sorely pressed. The logical leader of the opposition was Claus Kniebis. We must pray to God, he wrote Bernhard Meyer, "that we will not have to submit to the obedience of the Antichrist, against the doctrine which has come to us from God's Word."[77] "I believe," he wrote a few days later to Meyer,

---

Statt auch nichtz." AMS, AA 564, fol. 56^r. He may be counted as one who was radicalized by the movement of 1547–48. Other investigations and arrests in AMS, XXI 1548, fols. 164^v, 233^v, 368, 396, 411^v–412^r, 426^r, 431–432, 440^v.

[73] *PCSS*, IV, 1035–1037, No. 800.

[74] *Ibid.*, pp. 1053–1054, No. 811.

[75] AMS, XXI 1548, fols. 411^v–412^r (18 August 1548). A good deal of attention was devoted during these days to the security of the walls and gates. See, for example, *ibid.*, fol. 396^{r-v}.

[76] *PCSS*, IV, 1022, No. 794n4 (4 July 1548).

[77] *Ibid.*, p. 1022, No. 793n5 (5 July 1548).

that for a hundred years never have we been in such great danger as we are now. If we refuse the emperor's will and reject the Interim, we will call down his wrath on us. Then we would be in the greatest danger; for we have many Papists here and also many others who would not sacrifice much for religion and God. . . . The emperor wants his answer, yes or no. We haven't yet consulted our Schöffen. If only the Almighty, for the honor of His name, would relieve us of these tribulations and grant that we could be and remain in His divine grace and yet not anger the emperor.[78]

Bowed with age, nearly blind and deaf, the old Zealot had not exactly become a Politique, but he at least saw the situation realistically and recognized that Strasbourg's great weakness lay not in its walls and guns but in its people. Once cultivated because of its obvious utility, the myth of the sacral commune was now a dangerous political illusion. Kniebis, like the great Politique, his colleague of more than a quarter of a century, Jacob Sturm, recognized that the city was no godly band of saints but a society badly divided by class feeling and by religious loyalties. At this point the entire Reformation at Strasbourg was unmasked in the preachers' compromise with the oligarchy's determination not to tolerate the transformation of the people into a disciplined, united, godly band of defenders of the gospel. And Kniebis knew it. On August 13, two weeks before the crisis attained its climax, Kniebis withdrew. Appointed to the committee that was to recommend a course of action, he pleaded to be left alone, "because he is physically unable to do it. And he asks that another be appointed in his place."[79] They let him go, and Jacob Meyer, another veteran Zealot, served in his stead. The opposition found no leader.

In these days, the last of July and the month of August, 1548, the entire inner solidarity and nerve of the aristocracy and the regime were crumbling. Confidence in the regime fell to a low point. When the regime tried to borrow 24,000 florins in mid-July, only 3,000 could be found.[80] On the 8th or early on the 9th of August, there came the terrible news of the fate of Constance,[81] the only other city in South Germany

---

[78] *Ibid.,* pp. 1034–1035, No. 799 (16 July 1548).

[79] AMS, XXI 1548, fols. 396ᵛ–397ʳ.

[80] *Ibid.,* fol. 359ʳ.

[81] *PCSS,* IV, 1048, No. 808n2. See Paul Fagius to Johann Ulstetter, Strasbourg, 10 August 1548, in BNUS, Thesaurus Baumianus (=Thesaurus Epistolicus Reformatorum Alsaticorum), XIX, 93; an extract in German in Wilhelm Horning, ed. & trans., *Briefe von Strassburger Reformatoren ihren Mitarbeitern und Freunden über die Einführung des "Interims" in Strassburg (1548–1554)* (Strasbourg, 1887), p. 13.

which had held out against the Interim, taken by surprise and stormed by Imperial troops. Daily came to the privy councils reports of the deep impression made by the fall of Constance; and it is a measure of the regime's impotence at this point that Fagius, though warned to silence, praised Constance's staunchness from his pulpit.[82]

C.   THE EXODUS OF THE ARISTOCRACY, AUGUST–SEPTEMBER, 1548

1. Only the aristocrats of Strasbourg acted with decision as the political crisis approached its peak during the late summer. The first to leave the city, Heinrich von Mülnheim, had advocated resistance in 1547. He gave his colleagues as his not-very-candid excuse his desire to retire to Mutzig, for "he has no residence here. And he has more revenues and interests there than here."[83] About the motives of those who began to leave the city in mid-August, on the other hand, there can be no doubt. The first to go was Wolfgang Rehlinger, who declared on the 15th that he was in such personal danger at Strasbourg that he had to emigrate.[84] On the 18th, the first of the great merchant families took its leave: Philips Ingold, a XXIer and head of his clan, renounced his offices and citizenship for himself, his brother, his nephews, and their families.[85] When his colleagues urged him to reconsider, he frankly explained that "he has goods in German and French ('welsch') territories which might easily be confiscated." When further pressed, he admitted that he had heard stories in the streets that he, Ingold, had spoken secretly with the Neapolitan cavalry in the countryside and that "he was a better Imperial subject than a Strasbourgeois." If Strasbourg shared Constance's fate, and if he couldn't leave the city, "he and his brother would lose all their substance within eight days and would be ruined." The flight of the Ingold began a general emigration, and Caspar Hedio reported on the 22nd that "the rich, the nobles, and the merchants are leaving the city in great numbers."[86]

This entire process reached its climax on 27 and 28 August. On the

---

[82] AMS, XXI 1548, fols, 416, 417, 429; *PCSS*, IV, 1059, No. 816n1.

[83] AMS, XXI 1548, fols. 353ᵛ–354ʳ.

[84] *Ibid.,* fols. 398–400.

[85] *Ibid.,* fols. 409ᵛ–410ᵛ, 423ʳ⁻ᵛ (18 August 1548).

[86] Caspar Hedio to Matthaeus Erb, Strasbourg, 22 August 1548, an extract in German in Horning, ed. & trans., *Briefe,* p. 14. Bucer wrote to Ambrosius Blaurer from Strasbourg, 7 September 1548: "(. . . Diverso nos premit tentatio; maior pars plebis cupit Christum, senatus metuit Caesarem; extorserunt ergo tandem assensum, ut Caesari

27th, the regime went a second time to the Schöffen and asked for authority to send another embassy to the emperor to ask for better terms. For the first time in living memory the majority of the Schöffen refused their lords' proposal. One hundred thirty-two Schöffen voted for the proposition, but 134 refused it and demanded that the issue be put to the entire commune—a step which, as the deeply shaken regime acknowledged, was without precedent in civic history.[87] On the following day, the emigration of the rich became a flood. Some of the city's most prominent men now left their offices, their colleagues, and their homes: Ulman and Wolfgang Böcklin von Böcklinsau, Claus Zorn zum Riet, Conrad Joham, and Conrad Meyer.[88] On the 30th, now sustained almost completely by the determination of Jacob Sturm, the regime went once more to the Schöffen for authority to resume negotiations with Charles V. This time they won, as 206 Schöffen voted to grant such authority, and only four still voted against it. The opinion of the other ninety absent or abstaining Schöffen is unknown, but they were almost certainly solidly against the Interim and the regime's policy.[89] Symbolic perhaps of the

Table 22

The Strasbourg Emigrés (August–September, 1548) according to status/social group and sex[90]

Status/Social Group	Adults		Children		Total
	M	F	M	F	(%)
Patricians	25	9	—	—	34 (31)
Merchant/rentier families	36	5	5	10	56 (51)
Artisans	5	—	—	—	5 (5)
Others	12	2	—	—	14 (13)
Total	78	16	5	10	109 (100)

supplicent et pentat). . . ." *Briefwechsel der Brüder Ambrosius und Thomas Blaurer 1509–1548/67,* ed. for the Badische Historische Kommission by Traugott Schiess, 3 vols. (Freiburg/Br., 1908–12), II, 734–735, No. 1568, here at p. 734 (from AST 9/27). See also A. Blaurer to Heinrich Bullinger, (Constance), 10 August (1548), in *ibid.,* pp. 726–727, No. 1558, here at p. 727.

[87] *PCSS,* IV, 1059, 1063, No. 816, and esp. p. 1063n9.

[88] AMS, XXI 1548, fols. 432^v, 434^r–435^r; PROSOPOGRAPHY, Nos. XIII, XIV, XLV, LVI, CIV.

[89] *PCSS,* IV, 1065–1068, No. 818, and esp. p. 1068n11. On 27 August 266 Schöffen voted; on the 30th only 210. There would always have been a few Schöffen absent, but ninety at one time reflects abnormal circumstances. The poll of 19 January 1547 had mustered 280 of them.

[90] Based on a comparison of the emigré list with the composition of the privy councils (PROSOPOGRAPHY) and of the Senate (Hatt, pp. 212–213).

peace party's victory, on the next day came the report that a partisan of the regime had beaten Paul Fagius in the streets. Although aristocrats continued to leave the city for a few more days, the regime's victory reduced the flood to a trickle.

Those who said that the rich and the eminent were leaving the city were perfectly correct. The several lists of emigrés during the Interim struggles are combined in Appendix E below,[91] which is summarized analytically in Table 22.[92] Citizenship was also renounced for a (not individually named) group of Böcklin children. Together the two fractions of the aristocracy accounted for more than four-fifths (82%) of the exiles. Some families contributed especially heavily: three male Bock; four male, one female, and one group of Böcklin children; three male and one female Ebel; six male Ingold; four male and one female Joham; the children and widow of Carl Mieg, Sr.; one male and two female Prechter; one male and three female Wurmser. In short, the cream of Strasbourg society loaded up its valuables and streamed out of the city within a week. Since the renunciations by adult males usually embraced an entire household, the number of actual emigrés was much larger than Table 22 shows.

---

[91] An official record of persons who formally renounced citizenship in 1548 is in AMS, KS 63/I, fols. 1^r–5^r. A second, very important manuscript list of persons who renounced, or were contemplating renouncing, their citizenship at the end of August, 1548, was sent to Basel from Strasbourg on 31 August 1548. The text of the covering letter is printed in *PCSS*, IV, 1069–1070, No. 819. The list and the letter were copied and sent to the Evangelical members of the Swiss Confederation, as is clear from a letter of the regime of Basel to that of Bern, 4 September 1548, in Bern Staatsarchiv, UP 67, No. 267. Copies of the lists of exiles are extant in Mulhouse (AMM, I, No. 4447, from which copy Gerber printed the letter in *PCSS*), in Bern (Staatsarchiv, UP 67, Nos. 265–266), and Schaffhausen (Staatsarchiv, Korrespondenzen 1548, No. 8). I owe my knowledge of the documents in Bern and Schaffhausen to Jean Rott, who kindly permitted me to see his notes and copies. From this and other sources, a longer list was compiled which is printed by Johann Martin Pastorius, *Kurze Abhandlung von den Ammeistern der Stadt Strassburg* (Strasbourg, 1761), pp. 169–172; to which corrections from the Mulhouse copy are printed by Bernays, "Zur Biographie Johann Winthers von Andernach," p. 36n1, and in *PCSS*, IV, 1070, No. 819n5. A fourth list is in an excerpt from Daniel Specklin's lost "Collectanea," II, 292, preserved in BNUS, Ms. 1223, fols. 48^v–49^r. These lists are collated and the names arranged alphabetically in Appendix E below.

[92] In the table I have included persons from list 3 (AMS, KS 63/I, fols. 1^r–5^r) who renounced citizenship between 15 July and 10 September. Perhaps a few persons are included who renounced their citizenship for reasons having nothing to do with the Interim, but the average number of renunciations during the first six months of 1548 was only three to four per month. The identification of the patricians is quite easy, that of the merchant and rentier elements from the guilds not much more difficult.

The emigration devastated the oligarchy. Two XIIIers left, along with four patrician and four guildsman XVers, one simple XXIer, two of four Stettmeister and five of the other six patrician senators, and three of the twenty senators from the guilds: taken together, nearly one-third of the Senate & XXI and not a few of its oldest and more prestigious members. No privy councillor who had ever been associated with the Zealot party emigrated, and patrician officeholders emigrated in much higher ratio to their numbers than the guildsmen did. Along with current office-holders, other former and future officeholders left the city, such as Caspar Barpfennig, a former senator and Simon Franck's brother-in-law, and seven younger men who would one day sit in the privy councils. Only one privy councillor who was a veteran of the regime in the days of the first crisis emigrated, Conrad Joham, but among the XVers and senators were sons, sons-in-law, and cousins of men whose political careers were closely tied to the Reformation at Strasbourg: the brothers Ulman and Wolfgang Böcklin von Böcklinsau, both privy councillors, who had served as the city's agents with the armies during the Smalkaldic War; Stephan Sturm, first-cousin to Jacob and his brothers and son of a man who had been knighted for service during the Burgundian Wars; Sebastian Münch, a XVer and son of Claus Münch; Martin Hug von Ottenheim, a senator and son of an Ammeister; and Claus Zorn zum Riet, Stettmeister and son of Jacob Zorn zum Riet.

One scholar has attributed the emigration to "the mercantile spirit,"[93] which, although itself a bit ridiculous, does suggest one of the two chief reasons for emigration: fear of financial ruin. Philips Ingold testified that the Imperial ban laid on Strasbourg would ruin his firm within a few days.[94] The city and its citizens would be outlaws, whose persons, goods, and funds would be fair game to every predatory power—damaging enough to the ordinary citizen, but fatal to the merchant-bankers, whose goods and capital were spread up and down the Rhine, in Italy, in France, and in the Netherlands—thereby swelling their already con-siderable losses in the war of 1546–47.[95] Nor could the patricians protect their rural properties from plunder, their fiefs from forfeit, or their rural incomes from default. Troops of Italian cavalry prowling both banks of

---

[93] Karl Hahn, *Die katholische Kirche in Strassburg unter dem Bischof Erasmus von Limburg 1541–1568*, SWIELR, N.S. 24 (Frankfurt/M., 1941), p. 151: "Der Kaufmannsgeist machte sich bemerkbar. Einzelne liebten ihren Mammon mehr als das Evangelium und gaben mit solche einem Verhalten ein unruhmliches Beispiel." I note that Chrisman's (*Strasbourg*, p. 256n53) identification of Hahn as "a Catholic historian" is incorrect.

[94] AMS, XXI 1548, fols. 409ᵛ–410ᵛ, 423ʳ⁻ᵛ.

[95] See above, note 61.

the Upper Rhine assured that the losses would be considerable. In short, all of the property and property relations which the revolution of 1525 had not damaged permanently now stood open to invasion by powers capable of carrying out a permanent expropriation. During the crisis of the mid-1520s the common interests of all the ruling classes of South Germany had protected the aristocrats from great losses; while in 1548 the aristocrats stood alone, open to the predatory character of the same classes.

No less severe was the threat within. An anonymous witness remarked that "through their departure they . . . cause the greatest unrest . . . among the entire citizenry, who say that these fellows must know about some planned attack, else they would not run away."[96] Wolfgang Rehlinger testified that he could not feel safe in Strasbourg, and Philips Ingold reported threats and insults, along with rumors of his supposed treason.[97] During the last days of August, then, the aristocratic support for peace and reconciliation with the emperor—for Jacob Sturm's policy, that is—came back to haunt them. The mood in the streets grew uglier, and threats to aristocrats grew more frequent. A chronicler of the next generation left a precious description of the political mood of those days:

> each day the Senate was deep in deliberation about the Interim, while two or three thousand citizens were gathered constantly before the city hall, and nobody knew what to do. The regime again and again asked the people to trust them and to go home. At last [August 30] the Schöffen, having received authority from the guilds to treat, passed these powers to the regime. But the people wanted no change in religion. When the Senate & XXI met, many of them, fearing for their own skins and afraid of the emperor, wanted to flee; but Sir Jacob Sturm stood at the door and wouldn't let anyone out until a decision had been reached. Since some of them had Imperial sympathies and held Imperial fiefs, they were afraid of the people, realizing that they would be the targets of a possible rebellion. They decided to accept the book or Interim, for the rumor was true that the emperor intended to come, just as he had said. The fate of Constance was well noted. For the sake of civic peace, these men renounced their citizenship and went abroad until the crisis was over. The people cursed them and charged them with cowardice, following them through the streets with insults.[98]

---

[96] *PCSS*, IV, 1069, No. 819.
[97] See above, note 85.
[98] Specklin, *Collectanées*, No. 2387.

This account by Daniel Specklin, a Protestant, is confirmed by Sebald Büheler, a Catholic Strasbourgeois of the same generation: "many of the big men left the city of Strasbourg, XIIIers and XVers, . . . for they feared a negative reply from the emperor or a revolt in the city itself."[99] The city, their city, no longer belonged to them, and they were no longer safe in its streets. The Böcklin brothers, both privy councillors, said that they had heard of a plot to hang them from the city walls if it came to a siege; and Conrad Joham reported warnings from the milieu of the civic slaughterhouse (*Metzig*).[100] No other incident from those days expresses the bitterness of the militant resistance party against the peace-minded aristocrats as does the story that the ruling Ammeister, Jacob von Duntzenheim, raged to his long-time colleague, Conrad Joham: "I would love to stick a dagger through your heart."[101] Conrad Meyer, a long-time XVer and son-in-law of an Ammeister, pleaded that "he has his money invested with lords and princes and might easily lose it; and he knows no trade,"[102] although lurking in the background of his testimony as well was the fact that aristocrats could no longer walk the streets in safety. All the popular resentment against the treaty and the Interim, all the frustrated patriotism after a lost war, all the fruits of pulpit agitation, and the entire sensibility that Jacob Sturm and his colleagues were willing to sell away the one positive fruit the little people had gained from the Reformation—a religious solidarity and conscious-ness more nearly suitable to their own lives—boiled up in class hatred and political mistrust. It was too much, even for some who were not really aristocrats. Bastian Münch, XVer and son of a XVer, tried to resign his offices, promising to remain in the city if he had no official responsibilities. His colleagues refused, noting the bad impression such special treatment would make, and Münch, too, availed himself of the right of every Strasbourgeois to "free emigration."[103]

Just because they *were* aristocrats and not ordinary folk, the emigrés had refuges to which to flee: the mercantile families had their relatives in smaller towns of the region and business connections everywhere; while the nobles had their country seats. Most did not go far away. The

---

[99] Büheler, *Chronique*, No. 314.

[100] AMS, XXI 1548, fol. 432[v].

[101] *Ibid.*, fol. 434[r].

[102] *Ibid.*, fols. 434[r]–437[r].

[103] *Ibid.*, fols. 396[v]–397[r], 436[v]–437[r]. The right of *freier Zug* entered into all the discus-sions between the regime and the emigrés.

two chief sources[104] agree that many went to Offenburg, the tiny free city in the lower Kinzig valley, and to the Alsatian towns of Hagenau and Sélestat. One writer adds the names of three larger cities downstream, Speyer, Mainz, and Frankfurt am Main.[105] The natives of these towns did not receive them well:

> and they are not very well regarded by the people at Sélestat and Hage-
> nau, who say that these people were Evangelicals and are now running
> back to papism, leaving the poor folk at Strasbourg in the lurch ...
> And it is feared that they would do the same to the people [in these other
> towns], hence the common folk treat them badly.[106]

About the nobles it is known only that Heinrich von Mülnheim told his colleagues that he was moving to his country seat at Mutzig; but it is highly probable that many of the other nobles also went to the country. Like the merchants but in their own way, the noble patricians were in the city but not entirely of it, for they had always lived between city and land.

2. It was not to be expected that the exiles would stay away forever. Within a little more than two months of the main exodus, the Senate & XXI began to consider the problem of readmission. The mood among the members of the regime who had stayed, while their fellows had fled, was naturally enough somewhat punitive. On 10 November 1548, they decided to raise the price of citizenship for the exiles, and some refused to pay the inflated price.[107] By the next summer, when the crisis was over, negotiations with Bishop Erasmus well underway, and Martin Bucer and Paul Fagius sent on their way into exile, the aristocratic emigrés began to trickle back into the city. In May and June, Wilhelm Prechter and Friedrich von Gottesheim, two of Strasbourg's richest men, decided to return to the city.[108] Their former colleagues wanted to punish them with back taxes on their properties and compensatory payments of the excises, but Prechter reminded them of his father's services to the commune and of their failure to punish other exiles with these burdens; and he won his case.[109]

---

[104] The anonymous informant in *PCSS*, IV, 1069, No. 819; and Büheler, *Chronique*, No. 314, who names Offenburg, Hagenau, and Sélestat.

[105] *PCSS*, IV, 1069, No. 819. The editor notes that Simon Sulzer wrote to Jean Calvin on 3 September 1548 that some emigrés went to Freiburg im Breisgau. *CR*, XLI, col. 48.

[106] *PCSS*, IV, 1069, No. 819.

[107] AMS, XXI 1548, fol. 555.

[108] Fuchs, "Prechter," pp. 152–153.

[109] *Ibid.*, p. 153; AMS, XXI 1549, fols. 251ᵛ–257ᵛ.

Some never came back. Conrad Joham apparently died at his country seat at Mundolsheim. It is possible that his decision to emigrate reflected a certain broadmindedness in religion, for in 1550 he is found presenting a Catholic priest to Bishop Erasmus in his capacity as lay patron of a chaplaincy at the cloister of Hohenberg on Mont Ste.-Odile.[110] In this, however, he hardly differed from the dozens of other Evangelical aristocrats of Strasbourg who continued to tolerate Catholic pastors in their seigneuries long after the urban Reformation was finished.[111] Like Joham, Ulman Böcklin von Böcklinsau never returned, although he did repeatedly send to the Senate & XXI about his back pay as the city's delegate to the war council of the Smalkaldic League.[112]

The emigration's effects on the internal structure and workings of the regime were extensive and uniformly detrimental to the smooth continuation of the old system. Most serious was the severe shortage of adult male patricians in the city. At the turn of 1548–49, Jacob Sturm counted only fourteen such men in the city and contemplated proposing a constitutional reform that would create a new estate of rich non-patricians, his apparent object being to protect the patrician share of offices from inroads by the guilds.[113] Sturm himself and Egenolf Röder von Diersburg had to resume the office of Stettmeister, which they had long ago given over to younger men.[114] Friedrich Sturm, eldest of the Sturm brothers and veteran of a long, undistinguished political career, suddenly found himself a Stettmeister and a XVer.[115] So few patricians were available for office, however, that the Schöffen agreed to a reduction of the number of Stettmeister from four to two (1551–53) until such

---

[110] Medard Barth, ed., "Der Liber investiturarum sub Erasmo episcopo argentinensi datarum (1541–1568)," *AEA*, 6 (1955), 69–102, here at p. 82, No. 66.

[111] This is clear from a survey of the seigneuries of the *Reichsritter* in Lower Alsace and the attempts to introduce Evangelical clergy into their parishes. See Adam, *EKET*, pp. 501–550. The patronage rights, of course, often lay with the ecclesiastical patrons and not with the seigneurs; but truly militant Evangelical nobles might well have tried to sweep away the rights of ecclesiastical lords (much as the city government had done) and install their own men as pastors, something that happened rarely in Lower Alsace. I do not mean to suggest that the failure to act in this way is suggestive of crypto-Catholicism. On the contrary, it suggests the tremendous conservatism of the reform on the land.

[112] PROSOPOGRAPHY, No. XIII; AMS, XXI 1553, fol. 140^v (5 April 1553); AMS, XXI 1555, fol. 87^r (4 March 1555).

[113] See AMS, VI 491/3; and Chapter III above, pp. 108–109.

[114] Hatt, p. 213.

[115] PROSOPOGRAPHY, No. XCI.

time as the full complement of patrician offices could be filled.[116] The emigration had actually disrupted the entire fabric of patrician political life, and the Constofel zum Hohensteg simply ceased to function for more than half a decade. Friedrich Reiffsteck, Strasbourg's advocate at the *Reichskammergericht*, wrote to the court's president on 13 February 1549 that "one *Stubenherr*, Claus Zorn zum Riet, has died, and almost all the Constofler have left the city of Strasbourg for other places; the society itself is scattered, and no two are left together."[117] More than half a decade later, two patricians reported to the Constofel's counsel that "a few years ago the patricians of our society Zum Hohensteg . . . moved away, and they can hardly be brought together again."[118]

There was no absolute shortage of guildsman officeholders, of course, although some novices and neophytes found themselves rocketed through the hierarchy of offices during 1548–50. Georg Leimer entered the Senate for the first time in 1552, when he was already a XVer; and four years later he was ruling Ammeister.[119] Jacob Meyer "zum Heroldt" of the guild Zur Blume became a XVer in 1548 and Ammeister the next year without ever having been a senator.[120] Felix Erstein-Armbruster, a rentier who had served one term as senator in 1542/43, found himself whipped through the XV into the XIII within a few months in late 1548.[121] Lux Messinger, a cloth merchant who had spent four two-year terms in the Senate between 1527 and 1546, was coopted directly into the XIII in 1548.[122] The emigration of eight XVers and several XIIIers, whose places were filled with other XVers, meant that nearly the entire XV had to be replaced during late 1548 and that only a couple of experienced XVers, such as Peter Sturm, remained.

The regime's need for experienced personnel was urgent but not so desperate that it had to court the exiles. When Heinrich Hüffel, a patrician emigré, petitioned the Senate & XXI in early 1550 to keep his office as *Amtmann* at Wasselonne although he was no longer a citizen, he was refused.[123] The regime did begin to take in the exiles, however, as soon as the latter returned to the city and repurchased citizenship.

---

[116] Hatt, p. 214n; Winckelmann, "Strassburgs Verfassung," pp. 515–516.
[117] ADBR, 3B 779/12 (Mosungs v. Constofel zum Hohensteg).
[118] ADBR, 3B 779/15 (at 22 September 1554).
[119] PROSOPOGRAPHY, No. LII.
[120] PROSOPOGRAPHY, No. LIX.
[121] PROSOPOGRAPHY, No. XXIX.
[122] PROSOPOGRAPHY, No. LV.
[123] AMS, XXI 1550, fols. 63ᵛ, 68ʳ.

The exiles of 1548, in fact, included a number of prominent political figures of the next generation; and, apart from temporary difficulties due to a certain residual desire to punish them for their flight, the exiles were reintegrated into their rightful places in the aristocracy and the oligarchy with little fuss. The truth is that the regime of Evangelical Strasbourg during the 1550s, 1560s, and 1570s was to a great extent led by men who had abandoned the city and the defense of the gospel in 1548. Some slipped right back into their political careers. Stephan Sturm received permission to repurchase his citizenship during the second week of September, 1550; and, when the government changed on the next Schwörtag (January, 1551), Sturm was a new patrician senator.[124] Friedrich von Gottesheim reappeared in the XV in 1551 and moved up to the XIII in the same year.[125] Diebold Joham von Mundolsheim (d. 1578), Conrad's son, came back to Strasbourg after his father's death in exile, entered a Constofel, and became one of Strasbourg's leading patrician politicians of the next generation.[126]

In the end, those of the exiles who wanted to return, did return; and those who wanted to resume or begin political careers, did so. Whatever resentment lingered in the hearts of the little people of Strasbourg, whatever vengeful feelings were harbored in the councils of government, the aristocrats who stayed readily readmitted their friends, cousins, in-laws, and business partners who had fled. The oligarchy, despite the desertion of so many aristocrats, simply had not been attacked from below with sufficient strength, organization, and tactical leadership to threaten seriously the endurance of the regime. The aristocrats, on the other hand, had, by "voting with their feet," shaped the regime's policy as surely as they might have by remaining in their Strasbourg mansions and sitting in their accustomed seats in the chambers of government. Their going endangered the economic future of the commune and truncated its traditional social pyramid. Their nearly effortless resumption of their places in the social life and regime of Strasbourg shows, better than any other event during this generation, just how strong the structure of aristocratic power was.

---

[124] PROSOPOGRAPHY, No. XCVI; AMS, XXI 1550, fols. 387^r, 389^v, 390^v.

[125] PROSOPOGRAPHY, No. XXXIV.

[126] Diebold Joham von Mundolsheim, Conrad's eldest son: senator 1556/57, 59/60, 62/63; Stettmeister 1565/66, 68/69, 71/72, 74/75, 77; XVer 1559–72. Hatt, pp. 463, 601, 661.

D. Conclusion

The crisis of 1547–48 differed from that of 1524–23 most radically in its social character. In the first crisis, the general threat to all established powers in South Germany—with the possible exception of the emperor —had forged a united front of princes, prelates, lords, and urban regimes against the common foe. The lords of Germany stood, just as they later would at Münster (1534), in a solid array, regardless of confession, against the forces of revolution. After the Smalkaldic War, by contrast, only those rulers were threatened who refused to accept Charles's terms; and they were threatened not so much by direct military action (though that threat, too, existed) as by the greed of other urban regimes, princes, and lords, who could plunder the citizens of a banned city with impunity. Fiefs could be declared escheated, properties and incomes seized, goods and capital confiscated, and payments of interest and other debts refused; and the *banniti* could be joyfully and righteously plundered by Catholics and Evangelicals alike.

Under these conditions, the choice between war and peace during the summer of 1548 was for the aristocrats of Strasbourg the choice between certain social extinction and possible survival. This was why, despite the insults and threats from their social inferiors, they did not give in to the resistance movement and oppose the introduction of the Interim. In the late fall of 1546, when the war in Upper Germany was lost for the Smalkaldic allies, Jacob Sturm had predicted that the decision to offer up one's goods, livelihood, and life for the gospel would prove to be a very individual matter. He had never been more right.

CHAPTER NINE

CONCLUSIONS AND REFLECTIONS

Because most of the chapters of this book have their own final paragraphs entitled "Conclusions," an extensive summing up is not necessary
here. A brief recounting of the findings and their implications is nonetheless in order.

A. Conclusions

1. The structural part (Part I) yields several firm conclusions about
the character and tendencies of Strasbourg's ruling class before and
during the Reformation generation. First, there is the nature of that
class as a rentier–merchant aristocracy with relationships to both rural
and urban class systems and estate structures. The rentier nobles were
nearly indistinguishable from, and often simply the town-dwelling
sector of, the lesser nobility of Lower Alsace. The merchants divided
fairly neatly into the big merchant-bankers, whose families were mostly
recent migrants from other Alsatian free towns, and lesser merchants,
mostly of cloth, who tended to come from native families. The distinction between rentiers and merchants cut right across the estate line
between the Constofler (patricians) and the guildsmen and, indeed,
sometimes right across families.

A second finding is the very high degree of social solidarity between
the rentier nobles and the merchants. They shared the various forms of
propertyholding and, except for direct engagement in commerce, the
forms of investment. They held fiefs from a great variety of lords and
intermarried with great frequency. Above all, together they formed the
wealthiest stratum of the urban population. Both fractions of the
aristocracy had widespread economic interests outside the city and the
urban territory, which made them of all urban strata the most sensitive
to political shifts and trends beyond the Vosges and the Black Forest.
These characteristics are much less noticeable among the lesser merchants and well-to-do artisan masters, although they, too, were bound to
the aristocracy through occasional family ties and, above all, by their
positions among the dominant economic elements of the town. More
fundamental than any status distinction was the line between those who

had the freedom to aggrandize, or simply to manage, their own fortunes and lives, and those who lived permanently at the mercy of others.

Thirdly, this social solidarity within the ruling class formed the foundation of the political unity of its fractions. The most important political fact in pre-Reformation Strasbourg was not the constitutional division of offices between patricians and guildsmen but the cessation of the complex of social forces that had energized the guild revolts of the past 200 years. Strasbourg, unlike some other towns, entered the Reformation with a politically united ruling class. The structural expressions of this unity were the commanding positions of the privy councils (XV and XIII) within the regime, into which men were coopted for life, and the continuing political invasion of the poorer guilds by rich ambitious young men. Far from forming a democratizing factor in the regime, the political representation of the guilds turns out to have been, next to the Schöffen of the guilds, a principal line of political influence reaching from the aristocracy right down into the everyday life of the guilds. Of the classic elements of oligarchy, only the monopoly or near-monopoly of offices by a specific group of *Geschlechter* was missing at Strasbourg, and even this possibility was proposed by Jacob Sturm after the crisis of 1547–48.

2. The historical section (Part II) presents a new way of looking at the process and outcome of the Reformation at Strasbourg, a way built upon the preceding structural study. It is a way of conflict and tension only partly veiled by the harmonizing ideology of the leading reformers, a story of attack and threat from below, of judicious retrenchment, yielding, and timely conversion from above. There turn out to have been substantial reasons, beyond simple conservative instincts, for the aristocracy to have been wary of major changes in the old ecclesiastical order. But they changed, when the pressure from below was greatest in 1524–25, very rapidly and without major losses from their own ranks. There were benefits in the new religion as well: on the one side, the release of much property from mortmain and its employment either for private benefit or for welcome supplements to public revenues; on the other, the elimination of the weakest and most vulnerable sector—the clerical one—of the entire structure of lordship. In the long run, such benefits far outweighed the immediate financial gains or losses, the gains or losses of access to benefices, and the disruptions of family relations which lay in the Reformation's wake. If there was one important, permanent loss, it was the destruction of the public, sacralized incorpora-tion of aristocratic family history into communal history and into salva-

tion history—an incorporation for which the new religion had no tolerance. In this respect, at least, Evangelical religion was far less friendly to specifically feudal forms of aristocratic power than the old faith had been. The accommodation of most of Strasbourg's ruling class to the Reformation rested nonetheless on rational grounds, if—and on this *if* rests the social essence of the Reformation after 1525—the transformation could be accomplished without damaging the lay analogues to the sacrificed ecclesiastical structures. Although the preachers played their own significant role in this accommodation, it was the aristocrats in the oligarchic regime who, with confidence and little loss of unity, launched the concessions which dulled the edge of the movement in the streets and churches of the town. 1524–25 was a time for all aristocrats to stand together; and—Evangelical and Catholic, Zealot and Politique—at Strasbourg they did so.

The unity in crisis covered, however, an incomplete commitment of the ruling class to the new religion, while the heightened pace of Imperial politics in the wake of the Reformation created a level of diplomatic burdens to which the aristocracy was ever less equal and which it was ever less willing to meet. Neither tradition nor education equipped these nobles, merchants, and artisans either to govern a church or to conduct a far-flung system of diplomacy. Thus, well before the outbreak of the Smalkaldic War (1546), the aristocracy's political will began to fail.

Its failure is the background to the aristocracy's behavior in the crisis of the post-war period. The crisis of 1547–48 differed from that of 1524–25 both internally and externally: internally, because the absorption of an intense, corporatist form of religion by the "little people," the shopkeepers, traders, and artisan masters, threw them into opposition to the regime and thus severed the lines of control running through them into the guilds; and externally, because the later threat stemmed from within the ruling classes of the empire and, instead of uniting the ruling classes against assault from below as in 1524–25, threatened to make Strasbourg's aristocrats the victims of their fellows' greed. This fundamental social difference between the two crises largely explains why an urban ruling class which had firmly withstood the crisis of 1524–25, crumbled before that of 1547–48.

B. REFLECTIONS

1. If it is to be compared fruitfully with the fates of other urban societies in the same era, this mini-cycle of endurance, decline, collapse,

and reconstruction of aristocratic power at Strasbourg during the generation of the Reformation must be set in the larger context of the fundamental stability of urban aristocratic power in the sixteenth–century Empire. The collapse of the aristocracy's political nerve in 1548 is perhaps less surprising than the fact that the structure of aristocratic oligarchy, then at one of its weakest moments between 1419 and the French Revolution, was not forcefully attacked from below, although for a few months it was tended only by Jacob Sturm and a few other stalwarts. The oligarchy's survival in this severely weakened state suggests that the neo-feudal rentier-mercantile ruling class corresponded in a basic way to the economic situation of the time.

The ruling class was not only neo-feudal, however, for it comprised also merchant and artisan elements which, by the ordinary canons of social classification, one could hardly call "aristocratic" and probably not "feudal." These strata possessed a certain economic independence, social prestige, and access to political power, giving them a considerable stake in the existing social order. This "dominated fraction of a dominant class" occupied the political crossroads between the aristocracy proper and the broad mass of guildsmen and their kinfolk. More than any other urban stratum, their mental horizons and material interests were circumscribed by the city walls. The upper part of this stratum—in the persons of such politicians as Mathis Pfarrer, Claus Kniebis, and Martin Herlin—probably exerted more political influence during the Reformation generation than at any other time in recent history, and this prominence of middling elements coincided with the nadir of patrician strength in the city. Thus, the Reformation coincided with—though it certainly did not cause—a certain broadening of the social complexion of the inner circle of the regime.

2. The findings have, in turn, implications for the interpretation of the character and pace of the Reformation at Strasbourg. The relative prominence of less aristocratic elements within the ruling class helps to account for the relatively radical and swift introduction of reforms. It was not only that such men had far less financial and emotional investment in the religious houses, Mass foundations, and benefices than the true aristocrats had; but they were also far more receptive to the refurbished communitarian religion preached by the Strasbourg reformers. The Strasbourg material suggests the social specificity of the various forms of Reformation religion. The noble and merchant aristocrats as groups were comfortable either with the old religion, with the highly private spiritualism of Schwenckfeld (for the more forward

looking), or with the Lutheran dualism. The less feudal elements of the ruling class, on the other hand, tended to the highly communitarian form of Evangelical religion represented by a Zwingli or a Bucer, plus the republican politics it normally accompanied. Here, among the small independent artisans and tradespeople, the idea of the commune as the Christian collective found its proper social home. From this vantage point, the great Lutheran reaction of the 1560s and 1570s represents the return to full dominance of the most aristocratic elements of the city, symbolized and reinforced by the ascendancy of the most nearly feudal form of Evangelical religion. An investigation guided by such an analysis may yet decipher the failure of the Zwinglian cause in South Germany.

3. A final implication of this study's findings is that the proper relation between structural and narrative approaches to history is not serial but dialectical. That structural studies should serve as the foundation for the explanation of events is the conventional wisdom of the modern historian, and it also happens to be true. What is less widely appreciated is the importance of rapid change and of threatening conditions—in short, of crisis—in illuminating the real nature of social systems. It is more than just a consideration of collective behavior, although this is an essential element especially of the movement from historical change back to social structure. One can no more choose between structural and narrative history than one can between theory and practice. This belief is reflected in the structure of this book, in its movement from the structure of a society to its history and back toward a transformed understanding of the enduring characteristics of the whole society. For the whole, first, last, and always, is the truth.

APPENDIX A
PROSOPOGRAPHY

Members of the Privy Councils (XV and XIII) of Strasbourg, 1520–55

Appendix A contains reconstructed biographies, organized after the "Key to the Prosopographical Categories" which follows these paragraphs, of 105 men who belonged to one or both of the two privy councils of Strasbourg between 1520 and 1555. I have described elsewhere (Brady, "The Privy Councils [XV and XIII] of Strasbourg") some of the problems of collection and orthography, and I repeat here only the observation that although the terms in office are inclusive and could in some cases be lengthened by new sources, few *new* names of XVers or XIIIers are likely to turn up for the years after 1514. The magnitude of the reconstruction problem may be judged by the following facts: 1) there are no running lists of privy councillors; 2) the protocols of the Senate & XXI are extant only from 1539 onward; and 3) approximately ninety volumes of genealogical manuscripts went up in smoke in 1870.

The forms of citation employed in this appendix differ slightly from those in the rest of the book's apparatus. The sigla used elsewhere are also used here, but the short forms of other titles are here reduced to just the name(s) of author(s) or editor(s). All works cited are contained in the general bibliography (pp. 393–427 below), in whose entries the short forms are provided in parentheses after the other data wherever confusion might arise. Personal and place names are treated according to the principles discussed at the end of the Preface (p. xvii above).

KEY TO THE PROSOPOGRAPHICAL CATEGORIES

The biographical data in Appendix A appears in the following twenty categories which are arranged alphabetically (the letters "I" and "O" are not used) within each entry. The entries are themselves arranged alphabetically by family name.

A. Constofel *or* Guild(s)
B. Citizenship, Acquisition/Renunciation
C. Senate (*Grosser Rat*), with years in office
D. Stettmeister *or* Ammeister, with years in office
E. XV, with inclusive dates
F. XIII, with inclusive dates
G. Family Background
H. Parents

J. Siblings
K. Spouse(s)
L. Children
M. Occupation(s)
N. Business Connections
P. Other Indications of Wealth
Q. Fiefs
R. Other Real Property
S. Education
T. Religion/Attitude to Reformation
U. Relationships to Other Politicians
V. Other Information

I.   *ARBOGAST, Hans Claus*

A. Zimmerleute (Hatt, p. 393).
C. 1502, 05/06, 09/10 (Hatt, p. 393).
E. 1514–20 (AGCS, Comptes in Heilewog; AMS, VI 495: "1518," "1520").
R. Rented a garden from the city (AMS, VII 1436, fol. 9ʳ).

II. *ARG, Peter*   d. 1521 (Lehr, III, 425)

A. Zum Encker, *Oberherr* 1504–21; armiger (Hatt, p. 393; Loeper, p. 306;
     Kindler, *GBS*, p. 19).
C. 1498/99, 1502/03, 08/09 (Hatt, p. 393).
D. Ammeister 1504, 10, 16 (Hatt, p. 620).
E. 1500–03 (*Schriften Geilers,* p. 1).
F. 1505–21 (AGCS, Comptes in Heilewog: "1514"; Hatt, p. 620).
G. Prominent guild family, politically active 1363–1531 (Kindler, *GBS*,
     p. 19; Hatt, p. 393).
H. Heinrich A. (d. 1481), Ammeister 1465, 71, 77; Margarethe v. Walten-
     heim (*Fragments,* Nos. 4226, 4380; Lehr, III, 425).
J. Caspar (d. 1501), m. Ursula Liebinger; Ursula (d. 1521), m. 1) Valentin
     Mussler, and 2) Jacob Schenck (BNUS, Ms. 1058, fols. 4ᵛ–5ʳ;
     AMS, V 1/52).
K. 1) Katharina Münch, 2) Ursula Messinger, and 3) Katharina Ryff (BNUS,
     Ms. 1058, fol. 4ᵛ; AMS, KS 15, fol. 37ʳ; Lehr, III, 425).
L. Lienhart; Diebold, m. 1) Rosa v. Duntzenheim, daughter of CONRAD v.
     D., and 2) Margarethe Löwe, daughter of Conrad L.; Katharina, m.
     Friedrich Wydt (Wittmer, No. 7565; AMS, KS 17, fol. 276ʳ; AMS,
     KS 21, fol. 34ʳ; AMS, VI 145/3; BNUS, Ms. 1058, fols. 4ᵛ–5ʳ;
     Fuchs, "Israël Minckel," pp. 116–117).
M. Merchant (Fuchs, "Israël Minckel," p. 117).
N. Diebold A., his son, was an employee of the Ingold firm 1522–40 (AMS,
     KS 15, fol. 22ʳ; AMS, XXI 1540, fol. 197ᵛ).
R. Strasbourg (Seyboth, pp. 59, 116, 239).
U. Related through various marriages to CONRAD, BATT, and JACOB v.
     DUNTZENHEIM, CLAUS and SEBASTIAN MÜNCH, and LUX MESSINGER.

III. *BALDNER (Balthener, Paldner), Anshelm*
d. 2.IX.1563 (BNUS, Ms. 626, fol. 162ᵛ)

A. Fischer (Hatt, p. 395).
C. 1537/38 (Hatt, p. 395).
E. 1535–63 (AMS, VI 488/3; Hatt, p. 634).
G. The BALDNER were a prominent political family in the *Fischerzunft* (AMS, VI 488/3; Hatt, p. 395).
J. Augustin (d. by 1543), whose widow married Christman Romersheim (AMS, XXI 1543, fol. 152ᵛ).
L. Sixt, XVer 1565–83 (AMS, XXI 1545, fol. 242ᵛ; AMS, VI 488/3).
M. Fisherman ("piscator," "vischer"), shopkeeper (AMS, KS 15, fol. 131ʳ; AMS, XXI 1545, fol. 242ʳ).
R. Strasbourg (AMS, KS 15, fols. 131ʳ, 152ᵛ).
U. Related to HEINRICH and PAULUS BALDNER.

IV. *BALDNER, Heinrich*   d. I. 1526 (AMS, VI 488/3)

A. Fischer (Hatt, p. 395).
C. 1517/18 (Hatt, p. 395).
E. 1522–26 (AMS, VI 488/3).
G. See under ANSHELM BALDNER.
U. Related to ANSHELM and PAULUS BALDNER.

V. *BALDNER, Paulus*   d. by 21.XII.1535 (AMS, VI 488/3)

A. Fischer (Hatt, p. 395).
C. 1521/22, 29/30 (Hatt, p. 395).
E. 1526–35 AMS, VI 488/3; AMS, VI 495; *TQ Strassburg*, I, 191, No. 161).
G. See under ANSHELM BALDNER.
K. 1) Agnes Gunthersheim, and 2) Susanna Beck, widow of Diebold Dingsheim, a miller (AMS, KS 13, fols. 192ʳ–195ʳ; AMS, KS 20, fols. 247ʳ–248ᵛ).
L. Agnes; Merg; Michel; Asma, all by his first wife (AMS, KS 20, fol. 247ʳ).
M. Fisherman ("piscator") (AMS, KS 10, fol. 89ʳ).
P. 1525 he pledged 400 fl. as *Nachwidem* to his second wife (ADBR, E 5589/[2]).
R. Strasbourg (AMS, VII 1436, fol. 22ᵇ; AMS, VI 210/6).
T. The first Strasbourgeois to baptize a child without clergyman or godparents (*TQ Strassburg*, I, 191, No. 161).
U. Related to ANSHELM and HEINRICH BALDNER.

VI. *BEINHEIM, Veit*   d. 3./4.IX.1541 (AMS, XXI 1541, fol. 386ʳ⁻ᵛ)

A. Zum Spiegel 1530/31; Zur Steltz (Hatt, p. 397; ADBR, E 1356/1).
C. 1539/40 (Hatt, p. 397).
E. 1540?–41 (AMS, XXI 1541, fol. 386ʳ⁻ᵛ).
H. Veit B. (d. 1508); Apollonia Mondschein, daughter of Conrad M. (BNUS, Ms. 1058, fol. 13ᵛ; ADBR, 3B 62/5).
J. Hans, notary, m. 1) Agnes Wilen, daughter of Paul W., goldsmith, and 2) Magdalena Vogler, daughter of Lux V., apothecary; Jacobe and

Apollonia, who died young (BNUS, Ms. 1058, fol. 13ᵛ; Wittmer, No. 7647; ADBR, 3B 62/8).

K. 1532 Margarethe Conradj (d. 1579), daughter of Wilhelm C.; she subsequently remarried 2) Johann Meyer *dit* Motzbeck, City Secretary, and 3) HANS HAMMERER (BNUS, Ms. 1058, fol. 13ᵛ; BMS, Ms. 1024, fol. 80; AMS, KS 17, fol. 132ᵛ).

L. Veit, ennobled 1582, m. Anna v. Bietenheim, daughter of SIFRIDT v. B. (BMS, Ms. 1024, fol. 80; BNUS, Ms. 1058, fol. 13ᵛ).

M. Goldsmith (ADBR, 3B 62/3; Rott, *Oberrhein*, I, 283).

P. He and his brother inherited 1,300 fl. and half a house at Strasbourg (ADBR, 3B 62/8).

T. Possibly an Evangelical sympathizer by 1522/23 (Baumgarten, pp. 255–256).

U. His son married a daughter of SIFRIDT v. BIETENHEIM.

VII. *v. BERSS (Boersch), Hans*   d. 27.I.1569 (BNUS, Ms. 626, fol. 161ᵛ)

A. Zum Encker, *Oberherr* 1554ff. (Hatt, p. 399; Loeper, p. 306).

C. 1552/53 (Hatt, p. 399).

D. Ammeister 1554, 60, 66 (Hatt, p. 620).

E. 1551–54 (BNUS, Ms. 626, fol. 162ʳ; AMS, XXI 1554, fol. 161ʳ).

F. 1557–69 (BNUS, Ms. 626, fol. 161ᵛ; Hatt, p. 652).

K. Magdalena Hauswürt (Lehr, III, 428).

M. Rentier ("Herr und Müssiggänger") (Moeder, pp. 60–61).

T. Probably a supporter of conservative Lutheranism (Horning, p. 189).

V. An alternative death date is 1.III.1569 ("Imlin Chronik," p. 444).

VIII. *BETSCHOLT, Martin*   d. 27.XI.1546 (AMS, XXI 1546, fol. 580ʳ)

A. Zur Blume (Hatt, pp. 400–401).

C. 1522, 26/27, 32/33, 36/37 (Hatt, pp. 400–401).

D. Ammeister 1543, refused due to ill health (Hertzog, VII, 97).

E. 1523–32 (*PCSS*, I, 108; Rott, "Magistrat," p. 113; AMS, VI 488/10).

F. 1532–46 (AMS, VI 495; *PCSS*, II, 158; AMS, XXI 1546, fol. 580ʳ).

G. The B. came from the Ortenau, where another branch rose into the lesser nobility; the Strasbourg branch furnished 3 Ammeister during the 14th–15th centuries, all from the guild Zur Blume/Metzger (Kindler, *GBS*, p. 33; Kindler, *OG*, I, 69; Lehr, III, 423, 432, 468).

H. Possibly Friedrich B. (d. 1501); Adelheid Rothschild (d. 1513) (Kindler, *OG*, I, 69).

J. Martha? (d. by 1567), m. 1) Georg v. Bernshofen, and 2) N. Marschall v. Zimmern; Ursula, m. Peter Mieg (Kindler, *OG*, I, 69).

K. Elisabeth Schütz (d. 1511) (BNUS, Ms. 1058, fol. 17ᵛ).

L. Jacob; N., m. Lienhardt Lupen (AMS, XXI 1540, fols. 45ᵛ, 215ᵛ–216ʳ).

M. Merchant (*ZC*, III, 219, lines 4–6).

N. St.-Nicolas-de-Porte in Lorraine (*ZC*, III, 219, lines 4–6).

S. Spoke and read French (*PCSS*, III, 331n1).

T. Roman Catholic at least until abolition of the Mass 1529, after which he apparently conformed to the new religion (Baum, p. 179; Ficker–Winckelmann, I, 3, is misleading).

U. Related in unknown degrees to EGENOLF RÖDER V. DIERSBURG and to
    CARL MIEG, Sr., whose mother was a Betscholt.

IX. *v. BIETENHEIM, Sifridt II* d. ca. 1553 (*BCGA*, No. 27 [1974], p. 86)
A. Zur Luzern; armiger (Hatt, p. 401; AMS, KS 11, fol. 198; Kindler, *GBS*,
    pp. 34–35).
C. 1523/24, 27/28, 31/32, 35/36 (Hatt, p. 401).
E. 1539–44 (AMS, VI 496; AMS, XXI 1544, fol. 329^r; Hatt, p. 634).
G. The B. were a family of professional soldiers; SIFRIDT's son, Nicolaus,
    served in the Senate as a Constofler 1586ff. (Kindler, *GBS*, p. 34;
    Hatt, p. 401).
H. Sifridt I v. B. (d. 1483/87 or after 1508); Margarethe Pfeffinger, daughter
    of Bernhard P. and Ursula Vollmar; she remarried Ottman Sturm,
    father of STEPHAN STURM (BNUS, Ms. 1058, fol. 21^r; Kindler, *GBS*,
    p. 35; Wittmer, No. 7856; *BCGA*, No. 10 [1970], p. 141, and No. 27
    [1974], pp. 85–86).
J. Hugo, m. Katharina Ryff; Hans, unmarried; Ursula, m. FLORENTZ
    RUMLER; Katharina, m. 1487 Heinrich Karricher "von Muenichen";
    Jacob (d. 1528), monk at St. Arbogast Strasbourg (BNUS, Ms.
    1058, fol. 21^r; Wittmer, Nos. 3850, 7856; AST 35: "S. Arbogast").
K. 1) Agnes v. Saltzburg, daughter of the merchant Adam v. S. (d. ca. 1522),
    and 2) 1530 Anna Berger v. Blochberg, daughter of Hans B. v. B.
    and Anna v. Utzingen (AMS, KS 15, fol. 165^r; AMS, KS 22, fol. 83^r;
    BNUS, Ms. 1058, fol. 21^r; *BCGA*, No. 27 [1974], p. 86).
L. Nicolaus, m. 1) Susanna v. Kageneck, daughter of PHILIPS v. K., and
    2) Anna Maria v. Kippenheim, daughter of Claus Bernhard v. K.
    and Beatrix v. Ehingen; Johann Robert (d. before 1565); Christoph,
    m. Ursula Surger; Maria, m. Abraham Held, Ammeister 1568–92;
    Agnes, m. BERNHARD GOSS V. OBEREHNHEIM; Ursula, m. Eckhardt
    zum Trübel; Anna, m. Bernhard Kröder; Cleopha; Margarethe;
    Kunigunde (BNUS, Ms. 1058; fol. 21^r; *BCGA*, No. 27 [1974],
    pp. 86–87).
M. Rentier; soldier (*ZC*, II, 124–125).
Q. Fief from Bp. of Strasbourg at Orschweier; fief from lords of Flecken-
    stein (ADBR, G 503 and G 704; AMS, XXI 1545, fol. 442^{r-v}).
R. Strasbourg; rented the "schlösslin am hägelin" from the city (AMS, KS
    12, fol. 228^v; AMS, KS 15, fol. 59^v; AMS, KS 22, fol. 83^{r-v}; Saladin,
    Chronik, p. 39; AMS, VII 1436, fol. 14^r).
S. Evangelical perhaps by XII. 1522 (*Ann. Brant*, No. 3470).
U. Brother-in-law of FLORENTZ RUMLER and uncle of CASPAR RUMLER;
    father-in-law of BERNHARD GOSS V. OBEREHNHEIM; half-brother of
    STEPHAN STURM; related to PHILIPS v. KAGENECK.
V. S. v. B. was arrested, convicted, and stripped of his offices 1544 for
    harboring a Strasbourgeois who had illegally gone to France as a
    soldier and returned for illegal recruiting (AMS, XXI 1544, fols.
    316^v–317^r, 329^{r-v}, 339^v–340^r).

X. *v. BLUMENAU, Hans* d. VIII.1536 (*Ann. Brant,* No. 5129)
A. Constofel zum Mühlstein (AMS, VI 495).
B. Purchased 21.II.1502 (Wittmer, No. 5172).
C. 1510/11, 14/15, 21/22, 26/27, 29, 31/32, 34/35 (Hatt, p. 404).
E. 1523–36 (*Ann. Brant,* Nos. 4444, 5129; Winckelmann, I, 88; AMS, VI 495; Rott, "Magistrat," p. 113).
G. The last member of his family to serve in the regime of Strasbourg; the male line became extinct 1593 (Kindler, *GBS,* pp. 38–39).
K. Ursula Drachenfels, daughter of ANDREAS D. (AMS, KS 21, fols. 74^r–75^v; BNUS, Ms. 1058, fol. 192^v).
M. Rentier.
R. Strasbourg; Wasselonne (AMS, KS 16, fols. 230^r–232^r; AMS, KS 21, fols. 74^r–75^v).
T. Evangelical since early 1524 (Lambs, p. 28).
U. Son-in-law of ANDREAS DRACHENFELS.

XI. *BOCK v. GERSTHEIM, Hans*
d. 12.X.1542 (AMS, XXI 1542, fols. 411^r, 414^r)
A. Constofel zum Mühlstein; *Ritter* (AMS, VI 495).
C. 1512/13 (Hatt, p. 404).
D. Stettmeister 1506/07, 09/10, 15/16, 18, 22/23, 25/26, 29/30, 32/33, 35/36, 39, 41/42 (Hatt, p. 590).
E. 1510–15 (AMS, VI 495; Winckelmann, I, 24; AGCS, Comptes in Heilewog: "1514").
F. 1518–42 (AMS, VI, 495; *Ann. Brant,* Nos. 4410, 4451; AMS, XXI 1542, fol. 414^r; Rott, "Magistrat," p. 113).
G. The B. were an old Strasbourg patrician family, perhaps of Rottweil origin; the B. v. Gerstheim and v. Bläsheim both descend from Stephan B. v. Bläsheim, and their genealogies by Kindler (*GBS,* pp. 39–40) and Lehr (I, 93) are untrustworthy.
H. Stephan Bock v. Bläsheim (d. 1485/94); Engel Bock v. Gerstheim (d. after 1514) (ADBR, E 842; Rott, *Oberrhein,* Textband, p. 79).
J. Jacob B. v. Bläsheim (d. after 1510); Agathe, m. 1480 Burkhardt Beger, episcopal *Hofrichter*; Adelheid, m. Jakob v. Landsberg (AMS, I 17–19/1; ADBR, E 841–842; Hefele, Nos. 827, 924; Rott, *Oberrhein,* Textband, p. 79; AMS, KS 20, fol. 114^r).
K. By 1507 Ursula v. Fleckenstein, daughter of Jakob v. F., Sr., (d. 1514) (ADBR, E 841–842; Hefele, Nos. 841, 843).
L. Jacob, Jr. (d. ca. 1541), m. Ursula Stürtzel v. Buchheim; N.N. (d. by 1530), m. JACOB STURM (1489–1553); Veronika, m. Florentz v. Venningen (d. 1538), Palatine chancellor; Christina (d. 2.IV.1575), m. Alexander v. Andlau; Apollonia (d. 1542), m. 1) Philips v. Hirschhorn, and 2) 1523 Hans IV Landschad v. Steinach (d. 1571); Petronella, m. Ludwig v. Eschau; Ludwig B. v. Gerstheim (d. after 1565), m. 1) Agnes Zorn v. Plobsheim, daughter of Hans Jakob Z. v. P. and Anna Sturm, and 2) Elisabeth v. Lützelburg (ADBR, E 841–842; AMS, XXI 1539, fol. 245^r; AMS, AA 407a; ADBR, 12J

2022/15; AMS, Livre de Bourgeoisie 1559–1713, col. 140; *BCGA*, No. 10 [1970], p. 145).

M. Rentier; seigneur.
Q. Bläsheim, a fief of the H.R.E.; Obenheim, fief of the Cathedral Chapter of Strasbourg; several other fiefs of the Bp. of Strasbourg (ADBR, E 842, G 501, G 503).
R. Gerstheim; 1/2 of Schmiegheim and rents at Benfeld; Zutzendorf; Mulhouse; Strasbourg (Wunder, "Verzeichnis," p. 65n75; AMS, VI 279/1; Büheler, *Chronique*, No. 248).
S. Univ. of Freiburg i. Br. 1491; his testament lists Latin books (*Matrikel Freiburg*, I, 102; ADBR, E 841).
T. Evangelical by 1524; avid reader of theological books; did not introduce Evangelical religion at Gerstheim (*ZW*, VIII, 215, No. 343; Sturm, p. 9; Adam, *EKET*, p. 520).
U. Father-in-law of Jacob Sturm.

XII. *BÖCKLIN v. BÖCKLINSAU, Ludwig* d. II.1529 (AST 37, fol. 84)

A. Constofel zum Mühlstein, *Ritter* (AMS, VI 495: "1510").
B. Renounced 28.IV.1483, 27.II.1490, and 15.I.1499; purchased 31.I.1484, 6.III.1490, and 4.II.1500 (Wittmer, Nos. 3557, 4131, 4987, 3569, 4084, 5004).
C. 1498/99, 1504/05, 07 (Hatt, p. 406).
D. Stettmeister 1508, 10/11, 13/14, 16/17, 19/20 (Hatt, p. 590).
F. 1514–29 (AGCS, Comptes in Heilewog: "1514"; AMS, VI 495: "1518"; AST 37, fol. 84; Rott, "Artisanat," p. 167n15; Rott, "Magistrat," p. 113).
G. See under Ulman B. v. B.; the B. bore the name "von Böcklinsau" by a privilege from Emperor Maximilian I, 2.II.1513 (Kindler, *OG*, I, 130).
H. Friedrich B. (d. 1474), *Ritter*; Gertrud Bock (Wittmer, No. 3557; Kindler, *OG*, I, 131; Lehr, I, 101).
J. Margarethe (d. by 1501), m. 1) Philips Wetzel v. Marsilien, 2) Peter Völtsch (d. 1512), *Ritter*; Andreas (Kindler, *OG*, I, 131).
K. Aurelia v. Adelsheim (d. after 1537), daughter of Zeissolf v. A. (d. 1503) and Ottilia Schott (d. 1519) (ADBR, 12J 2022/15; AMS, KS 20, fols. 204^v–206^v).
L. Georg, childless (Kindler, *OG*, I, 131).
M. Rentier; seigneur.
P. Rente yielding 20 fl./yr. from counts of Mörs–Saarwerden 1506–31 (ADBR, 25J 28; Herrmann, I, Nos. 1605, 1818).
Q. Fief of 1/4 of Kehl from counts of Mörs–Saarwerden, margraves of Baden, and counts of Hanau–Lichtenberg; fief from Bp. of Strasbourg (Wunder, *Landgebiet*, p. 22; Herrmann, I, No. 1492a; HStAD, B 2, 60, 5; ADBR, G 503).
R. Schmieheim, Stützheim; Rust, Hipsheim; Strasbourg (Wunder, "Verzeichnis," pp. 61, 64; Fuchs, *Documents*, Nos. 981, 1200; Seyboth, p. 19).

T. Apparently a moderate and conciliator (Sturm, p. 4).
U. His wife was half-sister to MARTIN STURM and aunt of FRIEDRICH, JACOB, and PETER STURM; related to ULMAN and WOLFGANG B. v. B. and to JACOB and MARTIN WETZEL v. MARSILIEN.

XIII.   *BÖCKLIN v. BÖCKLINSAU, Ulman* d. ca. 1565 (Kindler, *OG*, I, 132)

A. Constofel zum Hohensteg (AMS, I 20a/3).
B. Renounced 28.VIII.1548 (AMS, KS 63/I, fol. 3ʳ).
C. 1529/30 (Hatt, p. 406).
D. Stettmeister 1532, 34, 37/38, 40/41, 43/44, 46/47 (Hatt, p. 598).
E. 1532–39 (AMS, VI 488/10; AMS, XXI 1539, fol. 250ʳ).
F. 1539–48 (AMS, XXI 1539, fol. 250ʳ; AMS, KS 63/I, fol. 3ʳ).
G. The B. v. B. were a noble family well established in Lower Alsace and the Ortenau (Kindler, *OG*, I, 130–135; Lehr, II, 99–108); patrician senators of Strasbourg 1333–1781 (Hatt, pp. 405–407, 598, 652).
H. Claus B. v. B. (d. after 1524), *Amtmann* at Wilstätt; Ursula Wurmser v. Vendenheim, sister of BERNHARD W. v. V. (Kindler, *OG*, I, 132).
J. Magdalena (d. after 1566), m. Jacob v. Dettlingen (d. by 1546); Jacob (d. 1569); Maria, m. Joachim v. Westhausen; Sebastian, Knight of St. John; Ursula, m. Johann Werner Truchsess v. Rheinfelden; WOLFGANG, m. Jacoba Ritter v. Hagenau (Kindler, *OG*, I, 132).
K. 1) Anna Ritter v. Hagenau, and 2) Juliana Susanna Joham v. Mundolsheim, daughter of CONRAD JOHAM (Kindler, *OG*, I, 132; Hertzog, VI, 250).
L. Ludwig, *Amtmann* at Wilstätt and Balbronn, m. Maria Salome Marx v. Eckwersheim; Martha, m. Gabriel zum Trübel; Magdalena, m. Johann Caspar v. Baden; Heinrich, m. Beatrix v. Landsberg; Hans Konrad, m. Richardis Völtsch v. Stützheim (Kindler, *OG*, I, 132).
M. Rentier; seigneur.
P. 1520–57 moneylender to counts of Mörs–Saarwerden (ADBR, 25J 34; Herrmann, I, No. 1794).
Q. Schloss Moersburg, fief of counts of Mörs–Saarwerden; 1/4 of Kehl as fief of Mörs–Saarwerden and Baden; fief of Hanau–Lichtenberg; fief of Bp. of Strasbourg (ADBR, 25J 795; Kindler, *OG*, I, 132; Wunder, *Landgebiet,* p. 22; HStAD, B 2, 60, 5; ADBR, G 503).
R. Strasbourg, in the Krutenau (AMS, VII 1436, fols. 19ᵛ, 35ʳ).
U. Brother of WOLFGANG B. v. B.; related to LUDWIG B. v. B.; son-in-law of CONRAD JOHAM; nephew of BERNHARD WURMSER v. VENDENHEIM.
V. After his emigration 1548 from Strasbourg, ULMAN B. v. B. was active in the Lower Alsatian *Reichsritterschaft* (*PCSS*, V, 78–79, 86).

XIV.   *BÖCKLIN v. BÖCKLINSAU, Wolfgang*

A. Constofel zum Hohensteg (AMS, I 20a/3).
B. Renounced 28.VIII.1548 (AMS, KS 63/I, fol. 3r).
C. 1539/40, 44/45 (Hatt, p. 406).
D. Stettmeister 1547/48 (Hatt, p. 598).
E. 1545–48 (AMS, XXI 1545, fol. 519v; Pastorius, p. 170).

G. See under ULMAN B. v. B.

H. Claus B. v. B.; Ursula Wurmser v. Vendenheim, sister of BERNHARD W. v. V. (Kindler, *OG*, I, 132).

J. See under ULMAN B. v. B.

K. Jacoba Ritter v. Hagenau (Kindler, *OG*, I, 132).

L. Philipp Jacob, m. Clara Elisabeth Marx v. Eckwersheim; Eva (d. 1600), m. Georg v. Venningen; Wilhelm (d. 1587), m. Lucia v. Reinach (Kindler, *OG*, I, 132).

M. Rentier; seigneur.

Q. See under ULMAN B. v. B., the family *Lehenträger*.

U. Brother of ULMAN B. v. B.; nephew of BERNHARD WURMSER V. VENDENHEIM.

XV. *BRAUN, Nicolaus (Claus)* d. 1541 (BNUS, Ms. 1058, fol. 29^v)

A. Zur Luzern (Hatt, p. 410).

C. 1525/26, 33/34, 39/40 (Hatt, p. 410).

E. 1525–41 (AMS, KS 18, fol. 32^v; AMS, VI 495; AST 75, fol. 499).

H. Adolph B. (d. before 1518), XVer 1514; Apollonia Lamb (d. 1531) (BNUS, Ms. 1058, fol. 29^v; AGCS, Comptes in Heilewog: "1514").

J. Johann, *prepositus* at New St. Peter Strasbourg 1526; *Meister* Jakob (d. 1535), canon at Old St. Peter Strasbourg; Georg, m. 1) Salome Lechler, and 2) Susanna Meyer; Maria, m. Martin Hug v. Ottenheim; Anastasia (d. 1528), m. Balthasar König, merchant; Jacobe, m. Jakob Kips (BNUS, Ms. 1058, fol. 29^v; AST Supplementa 35, fol. 10^r).

K. Elisabeth Seidensticher (d. 1541) (BNUS, Ms. 1058, fol. 29^v).

L. Adolph, merchant, m. Margarethe v. Duntzenheim (d. 1577), daughter of Philipp v. D.; Jacob, merchant, m. Katharina Heiler; Susanna, prioress at St. Nicolaus in Undis Strasbourg; Katharina, nun at St. Nicolaus in Undis Strasbourg (BNUS, Ms. 1058, fol. 29^v; AMS, VII 10/28).

M. Probably a merchant.

N. 1530 member of a credit syndicate with HANS HAMMERER, Onophrius Brant, and HERBART HETTER (AMS, KS 27/I, fol. 18^v).

Q. His son, Adolph, held a fief from the Bp. of Strasbourg 1557 (ADBR, G 503: "1557").

U. Related by marriages to PHILIPS HUG V. OTTENHEIM and VELTIN KIPS; his son married a niece of CONRAD V. DUNTZENHEIM.

V. B.'s sons were important merchant-bankers (AMS, III 85/1; AMS, II 16/39).

XVI. *BÜCHSNER, Alexius* d. 19./20.V.1547 (AMS, XXI 1547, fol. 257^r)

A. Constofel zum Mühlstein (AMS, I 20a/3).

B. Renounced 31.VIII.1496; purchased 16.IX.1504 (Wittmer, Nos. 4725, 5378).

C. 1520, 25/26, 29/30, 34/35, 41/42, 44, 46/47 (Hatt, p. 412).

E.   1543 (AMS, VI 496; Hatt, p. 634); he was a "lediger XXIer" 1547 (AMS, XXI 1547, fol. 257^r).

G.   An old and widespread Alsatian noble family, the B. died out in the early 17th century (Kindler, *GBS*, p. 51).

H.   Thoman B. (d. by 1496) (Wittmer, No. 4725).

J.   Ulrich (d. by 1521), m. Petronella v. Hammerstein, who remarried Simon Wecker v. Mittelhausen (d. after 1567); Balthasar?, canon at Allerheiligen and St. Thomas Strasbourg (AMS, KS 13, fols. 92^v–93^r; Kindler, *OG*, III, 94; G. Knod, in *ZGO*, XLVI [1892], 338, No. 13).

K.   Ursula Berer, daughter of Claus B. and sister of the wife of BERNHARD WURMSER v. VENDENHEIM (AMS, KS 27/I, fols. 170^r–172^r).

L.   Ursula, m. Philips v. Nidbruck of Metz (?) (Hefele, No. 1045).

M.   Rentier.

N.   Moneylender to peasants (AMS, KS 12, fols. 4^v–5^r, 32^v, 121^r, 166^r, 213^v, 218^r; AMS, KS 15, fol. 95^v; AMS, KS 17, fols. 12^r, 13^{r-v}, 16^r, 92^r, 123^v, 125^v).

P.   Several large rentes from counts of Zweibrücken–Bitsch–Lichtenberg and Hanau–Lichtenberg (AMS, KS 16, fols. 172^v–176^r, 224^r–227^r); his wife inherited a large sum (AMS, KS 27/I, fols. 170^r–172^r).

R.   Ittenheim, Mundolsheim, Lampertheim, Vendenheim; Strasbourg (AMS, KS 12, fols. 232^v–236^r; Hefele, Nos. 918–919; Seyboth, p. 236; AMS, VII 1436, fol. 6^r).

U.   Related through the Berer to BERNHARD WURMSER v. VENDENHEIM.

XVII.   *DRACHENFELS (Trachenfels, Drache), Andreas*
                                    d. ca. 1530 (BNUS, Ms. 1058, fol. 192^v)

A.   Zur Möhrin, *Oberherr*, 1518ff.; armiger (Hatt, p. 556; *Kleine Strassburger Chronik,* p. 5; Kindler, *GBS*, p. 374).

C.   1490/91, 1510/11, 14/15, 20/21 (Hatt, p. 556).

D.   Ammeister 1500, 06, 12, 18, refused 1524 due to illness (Hatt, p. 616; Sturm, p. 6; Meyer, *Chronique,* p. 38).

F.   1501–24 as Altammeister (Rott, "Magistrat," p. 113; AGCS, Comptes in Heilewog: "1514"; Sturm, p. 6; Baum, p. 48n4).

G.   Andreas was the last male D.; the D. were a leading guild family during the 15th and early 16th centuries (Kindler, *GBS*, pp. 373–374; Lehr, III, 467–468).

H.   Hans D., Ammeister 1452, 58; Katharina Hapmacher, daughter of Andreas H. (Kindler, *GBS*, pp. 373–374; Lehr, III, 467–468; Hatt, p. 616).

J.   Lienhart (d. 1501), senator 1484–97; Matern (d. 1491), Ammeister 1483, 89, m. Ottilia v. Künheim (Kindler, *GBS*, p. 374; Lehr, III, 467–468; Hatt, p. 616).

K.   Irmelina Schenck v. Isenheim (d. 1511) (BNUS, Ms. 1058, fol. 192^v; AST 1655, fols. 103^v–104^r; Lehr, III, 468).

L.   Ursula, m. 1518 HANS v. BLUMENAU; Katharina (d. 5.II.1552), m. Paulus Mieg, armiger; Beatrix, m. Lorentz Schenckbecher; Aurelia, m. 1) Mathis Wurm v. Geudertheim, 2) *Junker* Wolff Ryff, 3) Jerg

Junckern of Mainz (AST 1655, fols. 103ᵛ–104ʳ; BNUS, Ms. 1058, fol. 192ᵛ; AMS, KS 8, fol. 12ᵛ; AMS, KS 25, fols. 123ᵛ–124ᵛ).

M. Probably a merchant or a shipper-merchant.

R. Offenburg 1526 (AMS, KS 17, fol. 218ᵛ).

T. Roman Catholic, resigned offices 1524 (Sturm, p. 41; AST 38, fol. 7ᵛ).

U. Father-in-law of HANS V. BLUMENAU.

V. The death date 1535 by Kindler is probably incorrect, that of 1524 by Lehr is certainly so.

XVIII. DRENSS (Trenss), Augustin
d. 3.V.1552 (BNUS, Ms. 626, fol. 162ʳ)

A. Gartner "unter den Wagner" (Hatt, p. 557; AMS, KS 19, fol. 292ᵛ).

C. 1536/37 (Hatt, p. 557).

E. 1542–52 (AMS, XXI 1542, fol. 360ʳ; AMS, XXI 1552, fol. 151ʳ; Hatt, p. 634).

G. The D. were a leading senatorial family in the Gartnerzunft (Hatt, p. 557).

H. Andres D. (d. by 1524); Agnes N. (AST 69/5, fol. 12ʳ).

J. Magdalena, m. Gallus Müller, "ortulanus"; Margarethe, m. 1524 Dr. Caspar Hedio (AMS, KS 19, fol. 292ᵛ; AST 69/2; Ann. Brant, No. 4521).

K. Aurelia Rot (AMS, KS 19, fol. 292ᵛ).

L. Agnes, m. VELTIN STORCK (BNUS, Ms. 1058, fol. 183ʳ).

M. Gardener (AMS, KS 19, fol. 292ᵛ).

P. Moneylender to other gardeners (AMS, KS 23/II, fols. 170ᵛ–171ʳ); his father served the commune "zu Ross" (AMS, IV 86).

R. Königshofen; rented land from PHILIPS V. KAGENECK 1529 (AMS, KS 14, fol. 154ʳ; AMS, KS 23/II, fol. 143ᵛ).

T. 1524 he strongly objected to his sister's marriage to Caspar Hedio, the preacher (Ann. Brant, No. 4521; AST 69/6, fol. 14ʳ).

U. Father-in-law of VELTIN STORCK.

XIX. DRENSS, Jacob
d. 1571 (AMS, V 14/49)

A. Gartner "unter den Wagner" (Hatt, p. 557; AMS, KS 19, fol. 176ʳ).

C. 1546/47 (Hatt, p. 557).

E. 1552–57 (AMS, XXI 1552, fol. 151ʳ; AMS, VI 492/1; AMS, XXI 1557, fol. 493ʳ⁻ᵛ).

G. See under AUGUSTIN D.

H. Hans D. (d. ca. 1555) (AMS, H 4688).

K. 1525 Barbara Leckgewender, daughter of Georg L., gardener (AMS, KS 12, fol. 137ᵛ).

M. Gardener (AMS, KS 19, fol. 176ʳ; AMS, H 4688).

P. Moneylender to other gardeners (AMS, KS 12, fols. 137ᵛ, 245ʳ⁻ᵛ; AMS, KS 20, fol. 306ᵛ).

R. Owned agricultural land near Strasbourg and rented public land; 1571 his house at Strasbourg sold for 1,100 fl. (AMS, KS 15, fol. 91ᵛ; AMS, VII 1436, fols. 5ᵛ–6ʳ; AMS, H 4688).

U. Related to AUGUSTIN D.

V. Not to be confused with "Jacobus Drens iun. cler. arg. vicarius eccl. S.
    Thomae" 1518ff., who studied at Heidelberg 1512–14 (Knod, in
    ZGO, XLVI [1892], 338).

XX. *v. DUNTZENHEIM, Batt* d. 22.XI.1543 (Ficker–Winckelmann, I, 10)

A. Zum Spiegel 1530; Zum Freiburg to 1533; Schneider 1533–43; armiger
    (ADBR, E 1356/1; AMS, VI 591/1; Hatt, pp. 423, 617; AMS, KS 12,
    fol. 13ʳ).
C. 1533/34 (Hatt, p. 423).
D. Ammeister 1542 (Hatt, p. 617).
E. 1533–38 (AMS, VI 495; *PCSS*, II, 508).
F. 1538–43 (*PCSS*, II, 508; Hertzog, VIII, 96).
G. See under CONRAD v. D.
H. CONRAD v. D.; Agnes Ingold (AMS, KS 16, fol. 95; Wolff, "Ingold,"
    p. 117).
K. 1) Margarethe Medinger (d. 1530), and 2) Clara Gerbott (AMS, KS 20,
    fols. 18ʳ–19ʳ; Lehr, III, 432; BNUS, Ms. 1058, fol. 41ᵛ).
L. None (AMS, KS 20, fols. 18ʳ–19ʳ).
M. Merchant (Fuchs, "Israël Minckel," p. 118; HStAS, A 149/1).
N. Lyons (Fuchs, "Israël Minckel," p. 118).
R. Strasbourg and suburbs (AMS, VII 1436, fol. 7ᵛ; AMS, KS 12, fols. 87ʳ,
    195ʳ, 207ᵛ, 210ᵛ, 216ᵛ–217ʳ, 268ᵛ–269ʳ).
T. Evangelical (Sturm, p. 10).
U. Son of CONRAD v. D.; brother of JACOB v. D.

XXI. *v. DUNTZENHEIM, Conrad "der Jung"*
                              d. Venice 1532 (Ficker–Winckelmann, I, 2)

A. Zum Freiburg, *Oberherr* 1523–32; Zum Spiegel 1530–31 (Hatt, p. 424;
    Kleine Strassburger Chronik, p. 5; ADBR, E 1356/1).
C. 1501/02 (Hatt, p. 424).
D. Ammeister 1505, 11, 17, 23, 29 (Hatt, p. 616).
F. 1506–30 as Altammeister (AMS, VI 495: "1518"; AMS, VI 493/4,
    fol. 8ʳ; Rott, "Magistrat," p. 113; AGCS, Comptes in Heilewog:
    "1514").
G. This family, of whom four members were Ammeister 1484–1554, served
    in the Senate 1368–1576; it is perhaps a bourgeois branch of a
    patrician family who appear in Strasbourg 1308–98 (Kindler, *GBS*,
    p. 66; Hatt, pp. 424, 621).
H. Conrad v. D., Sr. (d. 1486), Ammeister 1484; Ursula Bürdin (Lehr, III,
    432; BNUS, Ms. 1058, fol. 41ʳ).
J. Philips, m. Ursula Sebott (BNUS, Ms. 1058, fol. 41ʳ).
K. Agnes Ingold, sister of CLAUS I. (AMS, KS 16, fol. 95; Wolff, "Ingold,"
    p. 117).
L. BATT, m. 1) Margarethe Medinger (d. 1530), and 2) Clara Gerbott;
    Ursula (d. 1580), m. FRIEDRICH II PRECHTER (d. 1528); Anna, m.
    Claus Bohem; JACOB, m. 1) Anna Kips, and 2) Elisabeth Löwe;
    Hans; Wolfgang, m. Anna Wörlin; Maria, m. *Junker* Hans Münch

(d. ca. 1521) (AMS, KS 14, fol. 152^r; AMS, KS 25, fol. 7b; AMS, KS 20, fols. 18^r–19^r; Lehr, III, 432; Wittmer, No. 8221; Winckelmann, II, 258, No. 167; Fuchs, "Prechter," p. 148; AMS, V 137/23, 25).

M. Merchant (Ficker–Winckelmann, I, 2).

N. Venice (Hertzog, VIII, 94; Specklin, *Collectanées*, No. 2307).

R. Strasbourg; Willstätt; Neuhof (AMS, V 137/23; AMS, KS 15, fol. 203^v; Wunder, *Landgebiet*, p. 34; AMS, VII 1436, fol. 35^r).

S. University of Heidelberg 1483 (*Matrikel Heidelberg*, I, 373; Knod, in *ZGO*, XLVI [1892], 338n).

T. Roman Catholic and opponent of the reforms; resigned offices 1530 (Sturm, p. 10; Specklin, *Collectanées*, No. 2307).

U. Father of BATT and JACOB v. D.; father-in-law of FRIEDRICH II PRECHTER and the sister? of VELTIN KIPS; related to DIEBOLD SEBOTT; brother-in-law of CLAUS INGOLD.

XXII. *v. DUNTZENHEIM, Jacob* d. 16.IV.1554 (Meyer, *Chronique*, p. 161)

A. Zum Freiburg to 1534; Zum Spiegel 1530–31; Zum Encker, *Oberherr* 1548–54; armiger (ADBR, E 1356/1; Hatt, p. 424; Loeper, p. 306; AMS, KS 17, fol. 15^v).

C. 1534/35, 40/41 (Hatt, p. 424).

D. Ammeister 1548, 54 (Hatt, p. 617).

E. 1539–46 (Hatt, p. 654; AMS, XXI 1546, fol. 580^r).

F. 1546–48, 1549–54 (AMS, XXI, 1546, fol. 580^r; AMS, XXI 1547, fol. 700^v; AMS, XXI 1549, fol. 510^v; Meyer, *Chronique,* p. 161).

G. See under CONRAD v. D.

H. CONRAD v. D.; and Agnes Ingold (AMS, KS 16, fol. 95; Wolff, "Les Ingold," p. 117).

J. See under CONRAD v. D.

K. 1) Anna Kips, sister? of VELTIN K., and 2) Elisabeth Löwe (AMS, KS 14, fol. 152^r; Winckelmann, II, 258, No. 167).

M. Merchant ("mercator") (AMS, KS 25, fol. 163^v).

N. Frankfurt; Switzerland; member of a firm with his brother, Philipp, "et aliorum ipsorum consortium in negocio mercatoris" 1528 (Dietz, p. 60; AMS, KS 26, fols. 58^r–60^v; AMS, KS 23/II, fols. 88^v–89^r).

R. Strasbourg; Molsheim; rented land from the city (AMS, KS 15, fol. 154^v; *PCSS*, V, 400; Specklin, *Collectanées*, No. 354; *PCSS*, I, 173; AMS, VII 1436, fols. 9^r, 19^v).

T. Evangelical (Sturm, p. 10).

U. Son of CONRAD and brother of BATT v. D.; brother-in-law (?) of VELTIN KIPS.

XXIII. *v. DÜRNINGEN, Veltin*   d. 1530/31 (Schadeus, ch. 16)

A. Küfer; *Junker* (Hatt, p. 424; Specklin, *Collectanées*, No. 2224).

C. 1504/05, 08/09, 12/13, 16/17, 20/21, 24/25 (Hatt, p. 424).

E.   1507–28 (Brant, p. 279; AGCS, Comptes in Heilewog: "1514"; AMS, VI 495: "1518"; AST 35: "Ste.-Claire en Woerth").
L.   Dorothea, m. Johann Krieg (d. by 1523) of Barr, clockmaker (Rott, *Oberrhein*, I, 225).
M.   Weaver ("textor"); soap merchant (Rott, *Oberrhein*, I, 225; AMS, IV 101/5, fols. 2^r, 4^r).

XXIV.   *EBEL, Friedrich*   d. 1564 (BNUS, Ms. 626, fol. 162^r)

A.   Zum Spiegel (father's guild); Küfer 1554–55; ennobled 4.V.1554 (AMS, IV 48; BNUS, Ms. 626, fol. 162^r; BMS, Ms. 936, fol. 5^v).
B.   Renounced ca. 30.VIII.1548 (AMM, I, No. 4447).
E.   1554–55 (AMS, XXI 1554, fol. 161^r; AMS, XXI 1555, fol. 488^r).
G.   The E. were a wealthy merchant family from Hagenau, who intermarried with the Ingold and the Prechter (Wolff, "Ingold," pp. 117–118; Fuchs, "Prechter," pp. 148–149).
H.   Hans E. (d. 1543); Susanna Prechter (d. 1551), daughter of FRIEDRICH II PRECHTER (BNUS, Ms. 1058, fol. 46^v; Fuchs, "Prechter," pp. 148–149).
J.   Anna, m. 1531 Jacob v. Hohenburg, son of GOTTFRIED v. H.; Hans Heinrich, m. Margarethe Ingold; Katharina, m. Philips Ingold; Salome, m. Jacob Ingold; Martha, m. ca. 1546 Hans Ingold (BNUS, Ms. 1058, fol. 46^v).
K.   Ursula Ingold (d. 1586) (BNUS, Ms. 1058, fol. 46^v).
L.   Ursula (d. 1585), m. Carl Lörcher; Veronika, m. 1590 Daniel v. Molsheim; Daniel, m. Salome Franck, granddaughter of SIMON FRANCK; Susanna, m. Balthasar Mieg; and 3 others (BNUS, Ms. 1058, fol. 46^v).
M.   Merchant–rentier.
P.   His father was a member of the Prechter firm of 1527 and was engaged in the silver mines at Sainte-Marie-aux-Mines (Fuchs, "Prechter," p. 158).
Q.   Fiefs of the *Obervogtei* of Hagenau and of Ludwig Bock, son of HANS BOCK v. GERSTHEIM (AMS, XXI 1555, fol. 488^r).
T.   His father was a defender of Catholicism during the 1520s (Sturm, p. 10).
U.   Nephew of FRIEDRICH II PRECHTER; first-cousin of WILHELM PRECHTER; related to GOTTFRIED v. HOHENBURG, CLAUS INGOLD, SIMON FRANCK, and the MIEG.

XXV.   *ELLENHART (Elnhart), Peter*
                              d. 17.IX.1533 (AMS, VI 495: "1533")

A.   Constofel zum Mühlstein; armiger (AMS, VI 495; AMS, KS 8, fol. 37^v).
C.   1494/95, 1500/01, 05/06, 08/09, 11/12 (Hatt, p. 427).
D.   Stettmeister 1517/18, 21/22, 24/25, 28/29 (Hatt, p. 590).
E.   1507–33 (Brant, p. 266; AGCS, Comptes in Heilewog: "1514"; *Ann. Brant*, No. 5607; AMS, VII 1438, fol. 7b; Rott, "Magistrat," p. 113).

G. The last male E., a family which held patrician offices at Strasbourg since 1359 (Hatt, p. 427; Kindler, *GBS*, p. 72).

K. Susanna Spender (d. by 1531), daughter of Hans S. (AMS, KS 26, fols. 89^r–90^v; Kindler, *GBS*, p. 72).

L. Dorothea, m. Jakob v. Schauenburg; Susanna, m. Hartmann v. Wangen; Salome; Apollonia (d. by 1531); Elisabeth, a nun at St. Magdalena Strasbourg; Ursula, unmarried 1531 (AMS, KS 20, fol. 125^r; AMS, KS 26, fols. 89^r–90^v; AMS, II 69/9; Kindler, *GBS*, p. 72).

M. Rentier.

P. An important dealer in grain; creditor of a Wurmser 1506; owner of a rente from the Bp. of Strasbourg secured at Still 1531 (Fuchs, "L'espace économique," p. 312; AMS, KS 8, fol. 82^r; AMS, AA 1555a/43–44, 66).

Q. Fief from Bp. of Strasbourg (ADBR, G 503).

R. Strasbourg (Seyboth, p. 112).

T. Buried 1533 among the Schauenburgs at Lautenbach in a Catholic church (*KDBadens*, XII/1, p. 201).

XXVI. *v. ENDINGEN, Hans Ludwig*   d. ca. 1474 (AMS, IX 1/4)
                                          b. 1548 (Kindler, *OG*, I, 301)

A. Constofel zum Hohensteg (AMS, VI 495: "1510").

C. 1501/02 (Hatt, p. 427).

D. Stettmeister 1504/05, 07/08, 10/11, 13/14, 16/17, 19/20, 22/23 (Hatt, p. 600).

F. 1507–24 (Brant, p. 280; Spach, p. 49; AGCS, Comptes in Heilewog: "1514"; AMS, VI 495: "1518"; Rott, "Magistrat," p. 113).

G. Family armigerous since 1403; E. were patrician senators at Strasbourg 1375–1523 (Frank, I, 275; Hatt, pp. 427, 600).

H. Thoman v. E. (d. by 1513); Barbara Bettschold; Thoman v. E. remarried Elisabeth Mussler, who later married JACOB ZORN ZUM RIET (Kindler, *OG*, I, 301).

J. Thoman (d. after 1545); Clara Anna, m. 1) Hans Jacob Knobloch, and 2) Hans Christoph von Baden; Anna (d. by 1516), m. Ludwig Sturm, brother of MARTIN S.; Philipp (d. 1505), canon of New St. Peter Strasbourg (Kindler, *OG*, I, 301).

K. Barbara Marx v. Eckwersheim (Kindler, *OG*, I, 301).

M. Rentier; seigneur.

P. Creditor of counts of Mörs–Saarwerden 1508–12 (Herrmann, I, No. 1631).

Q. Altdorf (Baden), Ettenheim, and Walburg, held from the Bp. of Strasbourg; Rust, held from Bp. of Strasbourg; fief from counts of Zweibrücken–Bitsch–Lichtenberg; Hundsfelden, held in pledge from Lichtenberg; Strasbourg (Fuchs, *Documents*, No. 1805; ADBR, G 634/4–5; Wunder, "Verzeichnis," p. 61 and n49; Kindler, *OG*, I, 301; Wunder, *Landgebiet*, p. 31).

R. Strasbourg (Seyboth, pp. 49, 293).

T.   The fact that he seems to have resigned his offices in 1524 suggests that he opposed the reform.

U.   Uncle of Jerg Marx v. Eckwersheim; brother-in-law of Martin Sturm; his step-mother remarried Jacob Zorn Zum Riet.

V.   The date of birth, taken from a legal deposition made in 1524, proves that he was not the Hans Ludwig v. E. who became a citizen in 1481 and senator in 1488 (Kindler, *OG*, I, 301; Wittmer, No. 3309; Hatt, p. 427).

XXVII.   *ENGELMANN, Caspar*
                     d. 11./12.XII.1539 (AMS, XXI 1539, fol. 375^v)

A.   Zum Spiegel (ADBR, E 1356/1).

E.   1537?–39 (AMS, XXI 1539, fol. 375^v).

G.   The E. were a cloth-merchant family from Hagenau (*BCGA*, No. 9 [1970], p. 112n3, and No. 31 [1975], pp. 66–67).

H.   Christoph E. of Hagenau, cloth merchant (3.VII.1450–23.VIII.1522); Dorothea von Dalheim (ca. 1468–29.IX.1515) (*BCGA*, No. 31 [1975], p. 67); or possibly Nicolaus E. and Dorothea N., both of Frankfurt/M. (AMS, KS 70/III, fols. 25^r–26^r).

J.   Christoph (26.IX.1494–20.III.1541), cloth merchant, m. 1517 Margarethe Surgant (1498–18.I.1540) (*BCGA*, No. 31 [1975], p. 66; AMS, KS 8, fol. 35^r).

K.   1525 Margarethe Kniebis, daughter of Claus K. (AMS, KS 19, fol. 115; Kindler, *OG*, II, 313–314).

M.   Goldsmith (Winckelmann, II, 257, No. 155; Rott, *Oberrhein*, I, 284).

P.   1529 purchased a *Leibgeding* yielding 12 lb. 12s. per year for 158 lb. from the city (AMS, V 55/4).

U.   Son-in-law of Claus Kniebis.

XXVIII.   *ERB, Sebastian (Bastian)*
                     b. 1478 (Winckelmann, I, 159; ADBR, 3 B 1357)
                     d. 22.II.1548 (AMS, XXI 1548, fol. 108^r)

A.   Tucher; Zum Spiegel 1530–31 (Hatt, p. 423; ADBR, E 1356/1).

C.   1517/18, 1525/26, 1531/32, 1539/40 (Hatt, p. 428).

E.   1542–48 (AMS, XXI 1541, fol. 537^r; AMS, VI 495–496; AMS, VI 492/1; AMS, XXI 1548, fol. 108^r; Hatt, p. 634).

K.   1) Ottilia Treger (d. 1542), and 2) Ursula Siedler (d. 1567) (AMS, KS 27/I, fol. 111^r; Winckelmann, I, 160, 160n5).

L.   The first marriage was childless (AMS, KS 27/I, fol. 111^r).

M.   Cloth merchant ("venditor pannorum") (AMS, KS 15, fol. 18^v).

P.   A leading philanthropist, he succeeded Caspar Hoffmeister as administrator of the *Blatterhaus* 1532–48 and willed the bulk of his fortune to a trust for the poor (AMS, XXI 1548, fols. 127^v, 276^v, 292^v–293^r; AMS, II, 79a/1; Winckelmann, I, 159–160, and II, 251, No. 68).

R.   Bought part of the Carthusian convent; lived in a house rented from the city (Seyboth, p. 175; AMS, VII 1438, fol. 59^r).

T. Evangelical at least since early 1524; in 1527 he signed a petition against the Mass (Lambs, p. 28; AST 80, fols. 65^r–66^r).

XXIX. *ERSTEIN gen. ARMBRUSTER, Felix*
d. 24.XI.1559 (Kindler, *GBS*, p. 19)

A. Zum Encker 1525–48; Tucher 1548–59; armiger (Hatt, p. 430; AMS, XXI 1548, fol. 108^r).
B. Purchased 26.I.1525 (Wittmer, No. 7598).
C. 1542/43 (Hatt, p. 430).
D. Ammeister 1549, refused (AMS, XXI 1548, fols. 640^v–641^r).
E. 1548 (AMS, XXI 1548, fol. 108^r).
F. 1548–52 (AMS, XXI 1548, fol. 441^r; AMS, XXI 1552, fols. 277^v–278^r).
G. Family armigerous since 1420; also "Erstheim"; Felix was the last male E. (Frank, I, 30; Kindler, *GBS*, p. 19).
H. Ulrich E., "edelknecht"; Clara v. Colmar (AMS, KS 15, fol. 153^{r-v}; Kindler, *OG*, I, 20).
J. Jacobe, m. Georg v. Routenheim, armiger; Martha; Salome (AMS, KS 15, fols. 157^r, 222^r).
K. 1) 1524 Anna v. Eich, and 2) N. Mieg (d. 1547/48) (AMS, KS 15, fols. 4^v–5^r; Saladin, *Chronik*, p. 379; ADBR, G 503).
M. Rentier.
Q. Fief of the Bp. of Strasbourg; fief of Count Georg v. Hohenstein (ADBR, G 503; AMS, KS 15, fols. 130^r, 153^r–154^r).
T. Evangelical (AMS, XXI 1541, fol. 163^{r-v}).
V. Afflicted with leprosy, he resigned his offices on 13.VIII.1552 (AMS, XXI 1553, fols. 116^v–117^r, 169^v, 182^v–183^r).

XXX. *FRANK, Simon*
d. 26./27.IX.1557 (AMS, XXI 1557, fol. 383^v; Ficker–Winckelmann, I, 11)

A. Küfer (Hatt, p. 432).
C. 1534/35, 38/39 (Hatt, p. 432).
D. Ammeister 1543, 49 refused (Hatt, p. 621; AMS, XXI 1548, fols. 639^r–640^v).
E. 1533–42 (AMS, VI 495; Hatt, p. 634).
F. 1548–56 (AMS, XXI 1548, fol. 230^r; AMS, XXI 1556, fol. 186^v).
G. His son "hielt sich adlig" (Kindler, *GBS*, p. 86).
H. N. Franck; Elisabeth Kniebis, sister of CLAUS K.; she remarried Bartholomeus Barpfennig (d. 1518) (AMS, KS 19, fol. 291^r; Kindler, *OG*, I, 382).
K. Katharina Barpfennig, daughter of Bartholomeus B. and sister of Caspar B., armiger (AMS, KS 19, fol. 291^r; AMS, V 79/20; Lehr, II, 175).
L. Simon, a mercenary captain, m. 1) Katharina Mieg, and 2) Gertrud von Schauenburg (Kindler, *GBS*, p. 86).
M. Merchant (BNUS, Ms. 1058, fol. 52^r).
P. Moneylender to peasants; his rentals of civic pastures suggest that he may have been a livestock dealer (AMS, KS 25, fol. 305^v; AMS, VII 1436, fol. 17^v; AMS, VII 1438, fol. 18^v; Lehr, II, 175).

R. Rural lands; Strasbourg (AMS, KS 11, fols. 147^v–148^r; Seyboth, p. 65).
U. Nephew of CLAUS KNIEBIS; related to CARL, ANDREAS, and DANIEL MIEG; brother-in-law of Caspar Barpfennig, a wealthy senator.
V. Paymaster ("Seckelmeister") to Strasbourg contingent of troops sent to Hungary 1542 (BNUS, Ms. 1018, fols. 226–227).

XXXI. *GEIGER (Gyger), Mattheus*　　　b. 1485 (Himly, *Chronologie,* p. 68) d. 27.XII.1549 (Lehr, III, 438; Ficker–Winckelmann, I, 11).

A. Zum Freiburg; Zum Spiegel 1530–31 (Hatt, p. 437; ADBR, E 1356/1).
C. 1529/30 (Hatt, p. 437).
D. Ammeister 1535, 41, 47 (Hatt, p. 617).
E. 1532–33 (AMS, VI 488/10; AMS, VI 495).
F. 1533–49 (AMS, VI 495; AMS, XXI 1549, fol. 510^v).
H. Nicolaus G. (d. by 1502); Sibilla Bischoff (BNUS, Ms. 1058, fol. 64^r; Lehr, III, 438).
J. Helene (d. 1525), m. 1) Steffan Thoman, and 2) HANS ERHARD "senior" v. ROTWEIL (Hefele, No. 791; AMS, KS 17, fol. 155^r).
K. 1) Anna Günter (d. 1512), and 2) Agnes Hammerer, sister of HANS H. (Lehr, III, 438).
L. David (1530–89), m. Katharina Fuchs, daughter of Dr. Johann F.; Lucretia (d. 1586), m. Michael Lichtensteiger, Ammeister 1569–87; Anna, m. Hans Erhard "junior" v. Rotweil; N.N., m. Michel Han, city syndic; and 17 other children (Lehr, III, 449; BNUS, Ms. 1058, fol. 64^r; PCSS, III, 505n2).
M. Merchant ("institor," "mercator," "Krämer") (AMS, KS 17, fol. 18^r; AMS, KS 19, fol. 331^r; Büheler, *Chronique,* No. 262).　　　　　·
N. His shop was in the house called "Zum Winden" in the Münstergasse; he was one of the merchants who pressed for trade privileges in France 1548; partner of Melchior Bischoff 1523 (Büheler, *Chronique,* No. 262; Seyboth, p. 150; AMS, XXI 1548, fol. 37^r; AMS, KS 16, fol. 15^v).
P. David G., his son, was wealthy enough to be able to pull down the house "Zum Winden" and build a new residence on the site 1567–68 (Büheler, *Chronique,* No. 262).
R. Strasbourg (Seyboth, pp. 19, 150; AMS, VII 1436, fol. 19^v).
U. Brother-in-law of HANS HAMMERER; brother-in-law of HANS ERHARD v. ROTWEIL; related to HANS WILHELM v. ROTWEIL.
V. Guardian 1534ff. of Israel Minckel, later a very wealthy merchant-banker (Fuchs, "Israël Minckel," p. 116).

XXXII. *GERFALCK, Diebold*　　d. 7.IX.1564 (BNUS, Ms. 626, fol. 162^r)

A. Weinsticher (Hatt, p. 439).
C. 1538/39, 46/47, 52/53, 56/57, 60/61 (Hatt, p. 439).
E. 1539–?, 1558–64 (AMS, XXI 1539, fol. 375^v; AMS, XXI 1558, fol. 432; Hatt, p. 657; BNUS, Ms. 626, fol. 162^r).

H.   Jacob G., "der glaser" of Münster im Gregoriental; Agnes v. Andlau, daughter of Peter v. A., "der glaser" (Wittmer, No. 3778; Rott, *Oberrhein*, I, 282).
K.   Margarethe Kochersperg (AMS, KS 21, fol. 53).
S.   University of Heidelberg 1520, bacc. art. 1521, mag. art. 1523 (*Matrikel Heidelberg*, I, 522, 522n4, and II, 441).

XXXIII.   *GOSS (Gossmar) v. OBEREHNHEIM, Bernhard*
                              d. 4.V.1580 (AMS, VIII 186, fol. 23^r)

A.   Constofel zum Mühlstein 1524; Constofel zum Hohensteg 1550–80; armiger (Wittmer, No. 7530; AMS, VI 496; Gyss, I, 448).
B.   Purchased 20.VII.1524 (Wittmer, No. 7530).
C.   1548/49, 51/52, 55/56, 58/59, 61/62, 64/65, 67/68, 70/71, 73/74, 76/77 (Hatt, p. 441).
E.   1551–80 (BNUS, Ms. 626, fol. 163^r; AMS, XXI 1550, fol. 503^v; Hatt, p. 658).
G.   An old noble family of Obernai, extinct in the male line with this man, who is often called "Goss von Dürckelstein" (Gyss, I, 76, 438–439; Kindler, *GBS*, p. 95); the notice by Hertzog (VI, 171) contains several errors.
H.   Diebold G. or Bernhard G. (d. 1509) (Kindler, *GBS*, p. 95; Gyss, I, 438).
J.   Landolf (d. by 1532) (Wittmer, No. 7515; ADBR, G 503).
K.   1) N.N., and 2) 1565 Agnes, daughter of SIFRIDT V. BIETENHEIM (Hertzog, VI, 171; Kindler, *GBS*, p. 95).
L.   Ursula, m. 1585 Hans Andreas Wurmser; 1 other daughter (Kindler, *GBS*, p. 95).
M.   Rentier; mercenary soldier in France (AMS, V 1/14; *ZC*, III, 219).
Q.   Imperial fief called "Bannschatz" at Obernai; fiefs from Bp. at Hagenau and Rimlenheim (AMS, XXI 1559, fol. 34^v; ADBR, G 503, and G 911/2–3, 6–8; Gyss, I, 76, 154–155, 308).
R.   Obernai; Werde, Saint-Hippolyte/St. Pilt, Châtenois, Hindisheim, Kertzfeld; chateau at Obernai, rented from Jakob v. Oberkirch (Gyss, I, 308–309, 438–439; Kindler, *GBS*, p. 95).
S.   Spoke French (*ZC*, III, 219).
U.   Son-in-law of SIFRIDT V. BIETENHEIM.

XXXIV.   *v. GOTTESHEIM, Friedrich VI*
                              b. 1506 (Lehr, II, 218; AMS, 852/105)
                              d. 3./4.II.1581 (AMS, VIII 186, fol. 23^r).

A.   Zum Spiegel to 1548; Zur Blume 1549–81; noble (Hatt, p. 441; ADBR, E 1356/1; AMS, XXI 1548, fol. 4^r; Riedenauer, p. 72).
B.   Purchased 18.II.1528; renounced 30.VIII.1548; repurchased 1549 (Wittmer, No. 8560; AMS, KS 63/I, fol. 4^r; Fuchs, "Prechter," pp. 152–153).
C.   1547/48 (Hatt, p. 441).
E.   1548, 1551 (AMS, XXI 1548, fol. 460^v; AMS, XXI 1551, fol. 318^r).
F.   1551–81 (AMS, XXI 1551, fol. 318^r; Hatt, p. 658).

G. Wealthy merchant family of Hagenau, ennobled 1513 by Emperor Maximilian I (Riedenauer, p. 72; Burg, pp. 361–362; Batt, II, Anhang, pp. xxxx–xxxxi).

H. Philips I v. G. (1471–1528), *mag. artium*; Margarethe, daughter of Mathis v. Kirspach of Hagenau (AMS, 852/105; AMS, KS 23/II, fol. 224^v; Lehr II, 219).

J. Mathis (1503–30), *mag. artium,* of Hagenau, m. Margarethe, daughter of Dr. Caspar Baldung; Jacob (1512–72) of Hagenau, m. Maria v. Landsberg; Philips II (1522–ca. 1596), Stettmeister at Hagenau, m. Ursula Schultheiss; Margarethe, m. VELTIN KIPS; Katharina, m. Diebold v. Sessolsheim of Hagenau; Anna, m. after 1532 Conrad Breuning of Hagenau; Susanna, m. after 1532 Jacob Wurm (AMS, 852/105; Batt, II, Anhang, pp. xxxx–xxxxi).

K. Agnes, daughter of CONRAD V. DUNTZENHEIM (AMS, KS 15, fol. 233^r).

L. None (AMS, 852/105).

M. Merchant-banker (Fuchs, "Prechter," pp. 147, 159).

N. Partner of the Prechter; Besançon, Augsburg, Saverne, Frankfurt/M. (Fuchs, "Prechter," p. 159; AMS, V 21/1; AMS, VII 12/5; AMS, V 1/82; Dietz, p. 60).

P. His testament disposes of over 18,000 fl. in cash (AMS, II 76a/1).

Q. The "Bruch zu Surburg" in fief from Fleckenstein 1543 (Hefele, No. 975; Batt, II, 604–605).

R. Strasbourg; Bernolsheim, Wahlenheim, Brumath, Oberhofen (Seyboth, pp. 20, 109; AMS, VI 146/2).

S. Spoke and read French; *Kirchenpfleger* of the French parish; Scholarch 1553–81 (AMS, II 84a/27; AMS, II 84b/6; AST 70/1, fols. 52^r–53^r).

U. Son-in-law of CONRAD and brother-in-law of BATT and JACOB V. DUNTZENHEIM; brother-in-law of VELTIN KIPS; related to FRIEDRICH II and WILHELM PRECHTER.

XXXV. GRAFF (Graue), Lorentz
             d. 8./9.VII.1553 (AMS, XXI 1553, fols. 237^r, 239^r)

A. Gartner (Hatt, p. 442).

C. 1522/23, 30/31 (Hatt, p. 442).

E. 1524–42, resigned 1542 (*Ann. Brant,* Nos. 4490, 4947; Rott, "Magistrat," p. 113; AMS, VI 495–496; AMS, XXI 1542, fol. 360^r; Hatt, p. 635).

J. Margred, m. Jacob Rodlin, a gardener (AMS, KS 20, fol. 307^r).

K. 1534 Katharina Apt (ADBR, H 1622, fol. 11^v).

M. Gardener (AMS, KS 20, fol. 307^r).

R. Rented agricultural land from the city (AMS, VII 1436, fols. 9^r, 12^v).

T. Apparently an Evangelical by I. 1524 (*Ann. Brant*, No. 4490).

V. The name "Lorentz Gemüss" in *Ann. Brant*, No. 4947, is an error for "Lorentz Graff."

XXXVI. HAMMERER, Hans d. 26.X.1572 (BNUS, Ms. 626, fol. 162^r)

A. Zum Encker; Weinsticher 1536–58; Schuhmacher 1548–72; armiger (Wittmer, No. 5095; Hatt, p. 447; AMS, XXI 1548, fol. 460^v).

B. His father immigrated from Sélestat 1484 (Wittmer, No. 3639).

C. 1536/37, 44/45, 50/51 (Hatt, p. 447).

D. Ammeister 1553, 59, 65, 71 (Hatt, p. 622).

E. 1548–52 (AMS, XXI 1548, fol. 460^v; AMS, XXI 1552, fols. 277^v–278^r).

F. 1552–72 (AMS, XXI 1552, fols. 277^v–278^r; BNUS, Ms. 626, fol. 161^v; Hatt, p. 659).

H. *Junker* Nicolaus H. of Sélestat; Ursula Ungerer of Strasbourg (AMS, KS 17, fol. 197^r; BNUS, Ms. 1058, fol. 77^r; AMS, VI 591/1d).

J. Genoveva, m. Hermann Baumgarter, "mercator"; Georg, a priest; Agnes, m. MATTHEUS GEIGER; Salome, m. JOHANN ERHARD V. ROTWEIL; Sebastian, "mercator," m. Apollonia Bischoff; Theodor, goldsmith (BNUS, Ms. 1058, fol. 77^r).

K. 1) Dorothea Pfarrer, sister of MATHIS P.; 2) Margarethe Conradj (d. 1579), widow of VEIT BEINHEIM (BNUS, Ms. 1058, fols. 77^r).

L. Hans Heinrich, "tuchmann," m. Rosina Obrecht, daughter of Thoman O. (Büheler, *Chronique,* No. 426; BNUS, Ms. 1058, fols. 77^r, 78^v).

M. Cloth merchant ("venditor pannorum") (AMS, KS 21, fol. 37^v; AMS, KS 25, fol. 235^r; Winckelmann, II, 109, No. 57).

N. 1539–58 in cloth trade with MATHIS PFARRER; active at Frankfurt/M.; active in securing trade privileges in France (AMS, KS 98/I, fols. 70^{r}ff.; Winckelmann, II, 109, No. 57; AMS, XXI 1547, fols. 311^v– 313^r).

P. His father, a civic *Ungelter* (tax collector), deposed 1522 a worth of 3,500 fl.; 1530 member of a credit syndicate with CLAUS BRAUN, Onophrius Brant, and HERBART HETTER (AMS, IX 1/6; AMS, KS 27/I, fol. 18^v; E. Ungerer, II, 115, No. 16; AMS, V 24/4).

R. Gerstheim; Strasbourg (Fuchs, *Documents,* No. 859; Büheler, *Chronique,* No. 340; Seyboth, pp. 37, 145; AMS, VII 1436, fols 19^v, 58^r).

S. 1512 University of Heidelberg (*Matrikel Heidelberg,* II, 485).

U. Brother-in-law of MATTHEUS GEIGER, HANS ERHARD V. ROTWEIL, and MATHIS PFARRER.

XXXVII. *HERLIN, Martin* b. 1471 (WLBS, Ms. Hist. fol. 580, fol. 1^v) d. 2.VIII.1547 (AMS, XXI 1547, fol. 418^{r-v})

A. Zum Spiegel 1501–09; Kürschner 1519–47 (AMS, VI 591/1; ADBR, 3B 779/4, fols. 17^v, 18^r; Hatt, p. 453).

C. 1519/20 (Hatt, p. 453).

D. Ammeister 1522, 28, 34, 40, 46 (Hatt, p. 617).

E. 1521 (Rott, "Magistrat," p. 107, No. 2).

F. 1523–47 (*PCSS,* I, 507; *Ann. Brant,* No. 4030; AMS, XXI 1547, fol. 418^{r-v}).

J. Arbogast (d. by 1506) (AMS, KS 8, fol. 1^r).

K. 1) Jacoba Mergentheim (d. by 1531), 2) Katharina Sebott, daughter of Lamprecht S., Sr., and widow of Friedrich V v. Gottesheim, and 3) Barbara Kniebis (d. ca. 1559), daughter of CLAUS K. and widow of Daniel Knobloch (AMS, KS 31/II, fol. 209^v; AMS, KS 26, fols. 125^r–129^r; Lehr, III, 490; BNUS, Ms. 1058, fol. 75^r; BCGA, No. 31 [1975], p. 80).

L.   Margarethe; Ottilia, m. 1) Friedrich Geiger, 2) Sebastian Jung, and
     3) Leonhard Seitz, notary publ.; Hans, 1546 *Zeugmeister*; Katharina;
     Barbara; Jacob (d. ca. 1601), 1580–87 *Amtmann* at Illkirch, m.
     Johanna Hecker (AMS, KS 21, fols. 185^v–186^r; AMS, XXI 1546,
     fol. 622^r; BNUS, Ms. 1058, fol. 75^r; Kindler, *OG*, I, 513; *BCGA*,
     No. 31 [1975], p. 80; Wunder, *Landgebiet*, pp. 116, 147).
M.   Merchant ("mercator") (*Ann. Brant,* No. 4030).
P.   1524 judgment of 100 fl. at Rottweiler Hofgericht against Jacob v.
     Schauenburg (AMS, KS 16, fols. 189^r, 204^r).
R.   Strasbourg (Seyboth, p. 35; AMS, VII 1436, fol. 19^v).
S.   No Latin education (Sturm, *Classicae epistolae,* ed. Rott, p. 74, No. 12).
T.   Zealous Evangelical since ca. 1522/23 (Sturm, pp. 5–6; "Imlin Chronik,"
     p. 412).
U.   Son-in-law of Claus Kniebis; related to Diebold Sebott; father-in-law
     of Sebastian Jung.
V.   Often confused with Martin H., Jr., his nephew; Martin, Jr., Christmann
     H. (the mathematician), and Margarethe H. (wife of Hans Baldung
     Grien) were the children of Arbogast H. (Brady, "Social Place,"
     p. 304).

XXXVIII. HETTER, Herbart (Herwart)
d. after 1542 (AMS, XXI 1542, *passim*)

A.   Zum Spiegel; armiger (Hatt, p. 454; Frank, II, 198).
C.   1517/18 (Hatt, p. 454).
E.   1514–25 (AGCS, Comptes in Heilewog: "1514"; AMS, VI 495: "1518";
     PCSS, I, 152; Rott, "Artisanat," p. 167n15; Rott, "Magistrat,"
     p. 107, No. 4).
G.   Family migrated from Recklinghausen, where the H. were men of
     substance, one member becoming a notary of Cologne 1429 and
     another a beneficed canon at St. Andreas Cologne and pastor at
     Recklinghausen; the family was armigerous since a grant to Herbart
     Hetter of Recklinghausen, Nuremberg, 11.III.1431 (Pennings,
     Gesch. der Stadt Recklinghausen, II, 20, 22, 39, 414; Frank, II, 198).
H.   Herbart H. "von Reckelinghusen, der kremer," who purchased citizen-
     ship 13.XI.1456 (Wittmer, No. 1278).
J.   Elisabeth, m. Caspar Oberlin of Ulm, X.1499 (Wittmer, No. 4959).
K.   Richardis Sebott, daughter of Diebold S.; they separated in 1541 and
     were divorced, and she remarried Jacob Pfeffinger 1543 (E. Ungerer,
     II, 108; AMS, XXI 1541, fol. 204^v; ADBR, 3B 580).
L.   Erasmus (Fuchs, "Une usine de raffinage," pp. 730–736).
M.   Cloth merchant (*Ann. Brant,* No. 4532; Rott, "Artisanat," p. 167n15).
N.   His son, Erasmus, was engaged in copper mines in the Vosges and
     partner of Erasmus Krug, *fils* (Fuchs, "Une usine de raffinage,"
     pp. 730–736).
P.   As a young man wealthy enough to serve "zu Ross"; bankrupt by 1539
     and being dunned 1539–42 by creditors from Middle Rhenish cities
     (AMS, VI 591/1; AMS, XXI 1539–1542, *passim*).

T. In II.1524 he intervened to protect the O.P. against popular violence; this, plus his apparent resignation from offices ca. 1525, suggest that he remained a Roman Catholic (AST 38, fol. 9^r; AST 192, fol. 12^v).

U. Son-in-law of Diebold Sebott.

XXXIX. *HEUSS, Michael, Sr.* d. 10.VII.1556 (BNUS, Ms. 626, fol. 161^v)

A. Zum Encker to 1550; Schneider 1550–56; armigerous by grant from Charles V on 21.VI.1541 (AST 75, fol. 490; Hatt, pp. 454, 622; BMS, Ms. 936, fol. 5^v).

C. 1544/45, 48 (Hatt, p. 454).

D. Ammeister 1550, 56 died in office (Hatt, p. 622).

E. 1549 (AMS, XXI 1549, fol. 3^r).

F. 1552–56 (AMS, XXI 1552, fols. 380^v–381^r; AMS, XXI 1556, fol. 385$^{r\,-v}$; Meyer, *Chronique*, p. 161).

H. Michael H. (d. by 1525); Ottilia Schuster, who remarried by 1525 Balthasar Bischoff (AMS, KS 16, fols. 280^v–281^r; BNUS, Ms. 1058, fol. 82^r).

K. 1) Barbara Merckel, and 2) Margarethe Stösser, daughter of Hans S. (BNUS, Ms. 1058, fol. 81^v; Lehr, III, 444).

L. Barbara, m. Jacob Bosch (d. 14.IV.1563), XVer 1557–63; Michael, Jr., m. Apollonia Lindenfels, daughter of Hans L.; Carl, j.u.D., *Amtmann* zu Wogelburg, m. Susanna Schütterlin (BNUS, Ms. 1058, fol. 82^r; *BCGA*, No. 23 [1973], p. 77).

M. Soapmaker ("seifensieder") and probably a merchant (AMS, KS 16, fol. 239^v; AMS, KS 26, fols. 55^r–57^v).

R. Dachstein; Königshofen; rented land from the city (Fuchs, *Documents*, No. 785; AMS, XXI 1548, fol. 60$^{r\,-v}$; AMS, VII 1436, fol. 19^v).

S. University of Cologne 1519 (*Matrikel Köln*, II, 814).

U. Son-in-law of Hans Stösser; related to Hans Lindenfels.

V. An alternative death date is 18.VIII.1556 ("Imlin Chronik," p. 430).

XL. *HOFFMEISTER, Caspar*   b. ca. 1466 (AMS, IX 1/6)
                              d. 13.XII.1532 (Winckelmann, I, 158)

A. Zur Blume (Hatt, p. 456).

B. Acquired by marriage 29.X.1495, native of Weil der Stadt in Swabia (Wittmer, No. 4613).

C. 1510/11, 14/15 (Hatt, p. 456).

E. 1518–32 (AMS, VI 495: "1518"; *Ann. Brant*, Nos. 3427, 4419, 4548; Winckelmann, I, 158; Rott, "Magistrat," p. 113).

K. 1) Barbara N., widow of Hans Meyen, butcher, and 2) Margarethe Graff (d. 1525), widow of Bartholome Jörger (Wittmer, No. 4613; AMS, KS 20, fol. 14^r).

M. Cloth merchant ("venditor pannorum"); 1522 he "nun zumal sich keins gewerbs wurt" (AMS, KS 12, fol. 19^r; AMS, IX 1/6).

P. 1508 loaned money to Margrave Christoph of Baden and received a non-heritable fief-rente of 15 fl./yr.; 1522 deposed that "er hab ein zimliche narung, deren er sich wol benugen lasse" (GLAK, 67/43, fol. 630^r; AMS, IX 1/6).

T. Roman Catholic at least until November 1524; 1527 permitted a sectarian preacher at the *Blatterhaus* (Ficker–Winckelmann, II, 48; *TQ Strassburg*, I, 132, No. 109).

U. His second wife was sister-in-law to HANS JÖRGER.

V. Founder and patron of the civic hospital for syphilitics, the *Blatterhaus* (Winckelmann, I, 49–50, 53–55, 63–64, 158–159, 169).

XLI. *v. HOHENBURG, Gottfried*   b. 1468 (AMS, IX 1/6)
                                  d. ca. 1531 (AMS, KS 25, fol. 259ᵛ)

A. Zur Blume; ennobled 1.IX.1509 (Hatt, p. 456; Kindler, *GBS*, p. 464; Riedenauer, p. 70).

B. Renounced 28.IX.1524 (Wittmer, No. 7436).

C. 1504/05, 08, 18/19 (Hatt, p. 456).

D. Ammeister 1509, 15, 21 (Hatt, p. 623).

F. 1510–24 (AGCS, Comptes in Heilewog: "1514"; AMS, VI 495: "1518"; Rott, "Magistrat," p. 113).

G. Family apparently of Hagenau origin; "Götz von Homberg genandt von Hagenaw," father of GOTTFRIED, was civic *Rentmeister* 1450 (AMS, VI 493/6).

H. Götz v. H. (d. 1498), Ammeister 1494; Brigitta Hapmacher, daughter of the Ammeister Andreas H. (Lehr, III, 444; AMS, KS 16, fol. 91ʳ).

K. 1) Ottilia v. Rotweil (d. 1508), daughter of HANS WILHELM v. R. and 2) Adelheid v. Büre (d. 1525) (Lehr, III, 444; AMS, KS 22, fols. 18ᵛ–21ᵛ; Mieg, p. 12).

L. Jacob (d. 1543), episcopal official, m. 1) Anna Ligler, and 2) 1531 Anna Ebel, daughter of Hans E. and sister of FRIEDRICH E.; Anna (ca. 1495–1558), m. CARL MIEG, Sr.; Aurelia (d. 1566), m. CONRAD MEYER (Wittmer, No. 7014; BNUS, Ms. 1058; Mieg, p. 13).

M. Rentier.

P. 1522 deposed that he was worth more than 9,000 fl.; served the commune "zu Ross" (AMS, IX 1/6; AMS, VI 591/1).

R. Lingolsheim 1523 (BNUS, Ms. 1052, No. 7; Sturm, pp. 9–10).

T. Roman Catholic; 1518 had a church built in Lingolsheim; 1524 resigned offices and citizenship over the religious question (*Ann. Brant*, No. 3445; Sturm, pp. 9–10).

U. Father-in-law of CONRAD MEYER and CARL MIEG, Sr.; related by marriage to HANS LUDWIG and HANS ERHARD, Sr., v. ROTWEIL; related to FRIEDRICH EBEL.

XLII. *HUG v. OTTENHEIM (v. Utenheim), Philips*
                                  d. 1532? (AST 40, fol. 114ʳ)

A. Zur Blume to 1513; Schneider 1518–32, *Oberherr* (Hatt, p. 510; BNUS, Ms. 1058, fol. 201ʳ).

C. 1512/13, 18, 23/24 (Hatt, p. 510).

D. Ammeister 1520, 26 (Hatt, p. 624).

E. 1518–19 (AMS, VI 495: "1518").

F. 1521–31 (AST 37, fol. 39ʳ; Rott, "Magistrat," p. 113; Baum, pp. 67, 91n2; *Ann. Brant,* No. 4933).

G. Merchant family of Hagenau? (*BCGA,* No. 9 [1970], p. 112n3).

J. Elisabeth, m. 1) Bastian Pfitzer, and 2) Michael Heer, Dr. med. (Wittmer, No. 8676; AST 40, fol. 114ʳ).

L. Martin, m. Maria Braun, sister of CLAUS B. (BNUS, Ms. 1058, fol. 29ᵛ).

M. "dann er seiner handtwercks ein Metzger war," and perhaps a dealer in livestock; his son was a merchant (HABW, 2. Aug. 2°, fol. 99ʳ; *Fragments,* No. 4028).

R. Utenheim; rented property from the city (AMS, KS 14, fols. 264ᵛ–265ʳ; AMS, VII 1436, fols. 7ᵛ, 13ᵛ).

T. Evangelical from an early date, perhaps 1523 (Sturm, p. 5).

U. His son married a sister of CLAUS BRAUN.

V. Often appears as P. v. Utenheim or Ottenheim (BNUS, Ms. 1058, fols. 85ᵛ, 201ʳ).

XLIII. *INGOLD, Claus* d. VII.1525 (AST 35: "Cartus," fol. 2ᵛ)

A. Zum Freiburg to 1518; Tucher 1521–25; noble (Hatt, p. 462; BMS, Ms. 936, fol. 5ʳ).

C. 1518, 21/22 (Hatt, p. 462).

E. ca. 1519–25 (AST 37, fol. 47ʳ; Rott, "Magistrat," p. 111, No. 82).

G. Merchant-banking family of Hagenau, at Strasbourg since 1470; armigerous since 1466, noble since 21.VII.1473 (Fuchs, "Ingold," pp. 203ff.; Wolff, "Ingold," pp. 112–116; BMS, Ms. 936, fol. 5ʳ; Riedenauer, p. 70; Kageneck, p. 389).

H. Hans I. (d. 1507), merchant-banker; Brigitte Dedinger (d. 1496) (Wolff, "Ingold," p. 114).

J. Mathis, merchant, m. Agnes Breuning; Friedrich, m. Margarethe Arg; Hans (d. 1516), m. Margarethe Dolde; Jacob (d. 1524), m. Veronika Mieg (d. 1541) (Wolff, "Ingold," p. 115).

K. 1505 Ursula v. Truchtersheim, daughter of Johann v. T. and probably mother of WOLF SIGISMUND WURMSER v. VENDENHEIM (Wolff, "Ingold," p. 115; Lehr, III, 233).

L. Hans (d. 1585), merchant, m. Ursula Prechter, daughter of FRIEDRICH II P.; Katharina, illegitimate daughter (Wolff, "Ingold," p. 115; AMS, KS 17, fol. 229ʳ ⁻ᵛ).

M. Merchant-banker (Fuchs, "Ingold," pp. 204–205).

N. He and his brothers formed an Ingold commercial firm; 1524 moneylender to regimes of Basel and Solothurn (Fuchs, "Ingold," pp. 204–205; *UBB,* X, 22–23).

Q. Three fiefs at Neuenstein, Bläsheim, and Kolbsheim, held from margraves of Baden in common with brothers and cousins (GLAK, 67/42, fol. 19ʳ; GLAK, 67/43, fols. 24ʳ ⁻ᵛ, 26ʳ–29ᵛ; GLAK, 67/44, fols. 170ʳ–177ʳ, 245ʳ–247ᵛ; GLAK, 67/46, fols. 168ᵛ–181ᵛ, 218ᵛ–223ʳ).

U. Grand-nephew of HEINRICH I.; related to DANIEL MIEG, whose sister married his brother, to FRIEDRICH II and WILHELM PRECHTER; and probably first husband of the mother of WOLF SIGISMUND WURMSER.

XLIV. *INGOLD, Heinrich*   d. 20.XII.1523 (*Ann. Brant*, No. 4480)

A. Zum Spiegel (Hatt, p. 462).
C. 1491/92, 1501/02, 07/08, 11/12 (Hatt, p. 462).
D. Ammeister 1508, 14 (Hatt, p. 623).
F. 1507–20 (Brant, pp. 263, 280; AGCS, Comptes in Heilewog: "1514"; AMS, VI 495: "1510", "1518"; Wolff, "Ingold," p. 117).
G. See under CLAUS INGOLD; the main Strasbourg line descends from Claus I Ingold (d. 1474), brother of this Heinrich's father.
H. Heinrich, citizen since 1470 (Wittmer, No. 2382; Wolff, "Ingold," pp. 116–117).
J. Hans (d. 1499); Brigitta, m. ca. 1506 Hans Ebel (Wolff, "Ingold," p. 117).
K. Clara Gerbott (d. 1495) (Wolff, "Ingold," p. 117).
M. Merchant (Schulte, III, 347, No. 64; Fuchs, "Ingold," p. 203).
P. Accumulated a large fortune, numerous donations to churches and convents (Fuchs, "Ingold," pp. 203–204); borrowed 3,500 fl. from the Wurmser (Hefele, No. 728).
R. Strasbourg (Fuchs, "Ingold," p. 204).
S. Patron of literature (Sturm, p. 41).

XLV. *JOHAM (v. MUNDOLSHEIM), Conrad*
    d. VIII.1551 (Ficker–Winckelmann, I, 13)

A. Zum Spiegel (father's guild) to 1521; Gerber 1521–48; ennobled by Charles V on 15.XI.1536 (Hatt, p. 463; ADBR, E 1356/1; AMS, IV 110; Reidenauer, p. 70).
B. Renounced 28.VIII.1548 (AMS, KS 63/I, fol. 5^r; AMS, XXI 1548, fols. 434^r–435^r).
C. 1521/22 (Hatt, p. 463).
E. 1522–30 (Ficker–Winckelmann, I, 13, 15; *Ann. Brant*, Nos. 4499, 4504; Rott, "Magistrat," p. 113).
F. 1530–48 (*PCSS*, I, 507; AMS, XXI 1548, fols. 434^r–435^r).
G. The J. were a merchant family of Saverne, at Strasbourg since 1486; Anshelm J. was knighted by Maximilian I in 1506; family ennobled on 15.XI.1536; politically active 1505–1789, since 1556 as Constofler (Kindler, *GBS*, pp. 137–138; *BCGA*, No. 21 [1973], pp. 28–29; Hatt, pp. 463, 601, 660).
H. Anshelm J. (d. 1512), *Ritter*; Katharina v. Molsheim (AMS, KS 43/I, fol. 1, correcting BNUS, Ms. 1058, fol. 93^v; Lehr, II, 255; *BCGA*, No. 21 [1973], pp. 28–29).
J. Hans, m. 1520 Agnes Ingold, daughter of Mathis I. and Agnes Breuning; Margarethe, m. 1507 Paul Mieg; Ursula, m. Bartholome Fuchs of Hagenau; Katharina (BNUS, Ms. 1058, fol. 93^v; Lehr, II, 255; *BCGA*, No. 21 [1973], pp. 28–29).

K. Susanna v. Mülnheim (d. 26.IX.1564), daughter of Diebold v. M. and Martha Merswin (AMS, KS 16, fol. 20^r; AMS, KS 43/I, fol. 1).

L. Diebold (d. 1578), m. 1) Ursula Ingold, daughter of Friedrich I., and 2) Sara Minckel, sister of Israel M.; Philipp, m. Barbara v. Barr, daughter of Nicolaus Ziegler, Lord of Barr; Susanna, m. 1) Hans v. Massmünster, and 2) ULMAN BÖCKLIN v. BÖCKLINSAU; David (d. 1585), m. 1) Sibilla v. Barr, sister of Barbara, and 2) Veronika Ingold; Martha, m. Sebastian Zorn v. Bulach; Christiana, m. Daniel Stallburger of Frankfurt/M. (BNUS, Ms. 1058, fol. 93^v; AMS, KS 43/I, fol. 1; AMS, KS 70/I, fols. 48^r–49^r; Lehr, II, 255–256; Fuchs, "Israël Minckel," p. 117).

M. Merchant-banker, dealer in silk and metals (Dietz, p. 59; Fuchs, "Prechter," p. 170).

N. Prechter firm; Frankfurt/M.; Genoa, Lyons; Venice; Speyer; Ulm; banker to Landgrave Philipp of Hesse and the Smalkaldic League; creditor of counts Nassau–Saarbrücken (Fuchs, "Prechter," p. 170; Dietz, p. 59; *PCSS*, III, 62, 146, 358n2; AMS, KS 13, fols. 131^r–132^r; AMS, KS 17, fol. 243^r; *PCSS*, II, 100, 210, 210n2, and IV, 398, 401–402; ADBR, 25 J 30).

P. Built a mansion in the Judengasse, where princely visitors frequently lodged (*Fragments, No.* 4278).

Q. Mundolsheim and Mittelhausbergen, fiefs of the H.R.E.; 1542 Geispolsheim, fief of Bp. of Strasbourg (Schoepflin, IV, 382, 570).

R. Strasbourg (AMS, KS 16, fols. 20^r–23^r; Seyboth, pp. 27, 28).

S. Spoke and read French (*PCSS*, III, 331n1).

T. 1550–64 he and his son Diebold presented Catholic priests to the Bp. as lay patrons of a chaplaincy at Hohenberg on Mont Ste.-Odile (Barth, in *AEA*, 6 [1955], p. 82, No. 66, and p. 95, No. 180).

U. Father-in-law of ULMAN BÖCKLIN v. B.; related to the MÜLNHEIM and the MIEG.

XLVI. *JÖRGER, Hans, Sr.*   b. 1471 (AMS, IX 1/6)
d. 9.VII.1540 (AMS, XXI 1540, fol. 263^r)

A. Zum Encker; armiger, *Junker* (Hatt, p. 463; AMS, VI 591/1; BMS, Ms. 936, fol. 6^r).

C. 1532/33, 36/37 (Hatt, p. 463).

E. 1531–40 (*Ann. Brant,* No. 4947; Hatt, p. 634; AMS, XXI 1540, fol. 263^r).

G. The J. rose in the episcopal service and as successors to the feudal titles of the Hohenstein; active in Strasbourg regime for two generations 1484–1540 (Kindler, *GBS*, p. 136; Hatt, p. 463).

H. Hans J. (d. ca. 1487), wealthy merchant-banker (ADBR, G 675; Fuchs, "Droit de bourgeoisie," p. 39).

J. Bartholome, m. Margarethe Graff, who remarried CASPAR HOFFMEISTER (AMS, KS 20, fol. 14^{r-v}; ADBR, G 675).

K. 1) Adelheid Kärling (d. before 1522), and 2) Elisabeth Müller (AMS, IX 1/6; AMS, KS 13, fol. 39^v; AMS, KS 18, fol. 168^{r-v}).

L.   Susanna, m. Heinrich Trautwein v. Hofen, armiger; Marx; Jörg, who
     emigrated (AMS, KS 20, fols. 16ʳ–17ʳ; Kindler, *GBS*, p. 374).
M.   Rentier (AMS, IX 1/6).
P.   1522 admitted to property worth only 300–400 fl., but his children
     owned large rentes purchased from the duke of Württemberg; very
     active as a moneylender to peasants (AMS, IX 1/6; AMS, KS 20,
     fols. 15ʳ, 16ʳ–17ʳ; AMS, KS 12, fols. 23ᵛ, 85ʳ–86ᵛ, 223ᵛ–224ᵛ,
     266ʳ–268ʳ, 270ᵛ–271ᵛ).
Q.   Fiefs from the Bp. of Strasbourg at Rufach, Molsheim, Ernolsheim,
     Pfaffenheim, Morschweiler, Berscheim, Schwersheim, and Stras-
     bourg (ADBR, G 675).
R.   1/2 each of Flexburg and Orschweiler, and extensive rural properties
     elsewhere (AMS, KS 12, fols. 266ʳ–268ʳ, 270ᵛ–271ᵛ; AMS, KS 20,
     fols. 8ʳ–10ᵛ).
V.   Not to be confused with Hans J., Jr., who was the son of Bartholome J.
     (AMS, KS 20, fol. 14ʳ).

XLVII.   *JUNG, Sebastian (Bastian)*
                              d. 24.VIII.1554 (BNUS, Ms. 626, fol. 162ᵛ)

A.   Schmiede, *Zunftmeister* 1525; armiger by grant from Duke Heinrich the
     Younger of Braunschweig 18.IX.1541 (Hatt, p. 464; AMS, KS 18,
     fol. 230ʳ; BMS, Ms. 936, fol. 3ᵛ).
B.   Purchased 25.I.1492, a native of Baden–Baden (Wittmer, No. 4230).
C.   1526/27, 36/37, 42/43, 46/47 (Hatt, p. 464).
E.   1548–54 (AMS, XXI 1548, fol. 460ᵛ; BNUS, Ms. 626, fol. 162ᵛ).
K.   1) by 1532 Gertrud Storck (d. by 1537), 2) before 1541 Barbara Hurtzbeck
     (d. ca. 1542), 3) Martha Stösser, sister of HANS S., and 4) Ottilia
     Herlin, daughter of MARTIN H. (Winckelmann, II, 254, 256; BNUS,
     Ms. 1058, fols. 75ʳ, 176ᵛ; AMS, KS 46/I, fol. 54).
L.   Barbara, m. 1554 Heinrich Engelmann (1521–97), son of Christoph E.
     (1494–1541) and Margarete Surgant (1498–1540); Agnes (*BCGA*,
     No. 31 [1975], pp. 65–66, Nos. 106, 212–213; Winckelmann, II,
     259).
M.   Tinsmith ("Kannengiesser," "cantrifusor") (AMS, KS 25, fol. 192ᵛ).
P.   1552 bought a large rente from the city (BNUS, Ms. 4757/5).
R.   Strasbourg; 1533 leased farms at Oetigheim from Kloster Frauenalb
     (AMS, KS 18, fol. 230ʳ; *KDBadens*, XII/1, p. 302).
U.   Brother-in-law of HANS STÖSSER; son-in-law of MARTIN HERLIN; related
     by marriage to VELTIN STORCK.

XLVIII.   *v. KAGENECK, Philips*
                              d. 15.XI.1545 (AMS, XXI 1545, fol. 509ᵛ)

A.   Constofel zum Hohensteg (AMS, I 20a/3).
B.   Acquired by marriage 17.VII.1529 (Wittmer, No. 8825).
C.   1534/35, 38/39 (Hatt, p. 463).
D.   Stettmeister 1541/42, 44/45 (Hatt, p. 602).
E.   1539–42 (AMS, VII 1438, fol. 40a; AMS, XXI 1542, fol. 424ᵛ).

F.   1542–45 (AMS, XXI 1542, fol. 414^v; AMS, VI 496; AMS, XXI 1545, fol. 509^v; Hatt, p. 644).

G.   One of Strasbourg's oldest noble families, active in the Senate 1212–1734 (Kindler, *GBS*, pp. 140–143).

H.   Moritz v. K. (d. 1492/93), *Ritter* (knighted at Murten 1475); Margarethe v. Utweiler, daughter of Georg v. U. and Susanna v. Mittelhausen (*GHDA, GH*, A IV [1962], p. 229; Kindler, *OG*, II, 224–225; Lehr, II, 262).

J.   Reimbolt (d. 1512), m. 1) Ursula Hüffel, daughter of Goso H. and Catharina Merswin, and 2) Agnes Rebstock (d. after 1525), daughter of Hans Diebold R. and Euphrosyna v. Deislingen; Stephan, priest at Strasbourg 1518, rector at Illkirch 1534; Ludwig; Margarethe (d. by 1532), m. 1) Erhard Berer, 2) Daniel Wurmser, and 3) REIM-BOLD SPENDER; Ottilia, m. 1532 Simon Seckrowe v. Oberehnheim (*GHDA, GH*, A IV [1962], p. 229; Kindler, *OG*, II 224–225, 228; AMS, KS 20, fols. 156^r–157^r).

K.   1529 Katharina Wurmser v. Vendenheim, daughter of BERNHARD W. v. V. (Kindler, *OG*, II, 226; *GHDA, FH*, A IV [1962], p. 123).

L.   Christina, m. Wolf Dietrich Ritter v. Urendorf; Bernhard (1532–1606), Stettmeister 1586–93, m. Symburgis Böcklin v. Böcklinsau, daughter of Jacob B. v. B. and Catharina v. Brandeck; Maria Magdalena, m. 1583 Georg Jakob Bock v. Erlenburg; Susanna, m. 1571 Nicolaus v. Bietenheim, son of SIFRIDT v. B. (Kindler, *OG*, II, 226; *GHDA, FH*, A IV [1962], p. 123).

M.   Rentier; seigneur.

N.   He and Friedrich V v. Gottesheim bought 1521 a seigneury from Badouin, bastard of Burgundy, for 17,000 livres; he owned several perpetual rentes at Strasbourg (AMS, I 24b/23; AMS, VIII 134/10).

Q.   Fief of H.R.E. at Schwindratzheim; fief of Bp. of Strasbourg; Austrian fief at Oberhausbergen; fief of Wild- and Rhinegraves at Hipsheim (*GHDA, GH*, A IV [1962], p. 229; ADBR, G 503; Fritz, p. 105n10).

R.   Strasbourg; Romansweiler (AMS, KS 12, fols. 35^v, 112^v; AMS, KS 23/II, fol. 143^v; AMS, VII 63/3; AMS, V 1/88).

T.   Roman Catholic at least until 1528 (*Ann. Brant,* No. 4729).

U.   Son-in-law of BERNHARD WURMSER v. VENDENHEIM; brother-in-law of REIMBOLD SPENDER; his daughter married a son of SIFRIDT v. BIETENHEIM.

XLIX.   *KIPS, Valentin (Veltin)*
                              d. ca. 5.VIII. 1551 (AMS, XXI 1551, fol. 260^r)

A.   Zum Freiburg 1516–33; Brotbecker 1542–51 (Wittmer, No. 6590; AST 75, fol. 492^r; Hatt, p. 470).

B.   Purchased 27.IX.1516 (Wittmer, No. 6590).

C.   1537/38, 42/43 (Hatt, pp. 469, 470).

D.   Ammeister 1543, refused as a fiefholder (Hertzog, VIII, 97).

E.   1541–51 (AMS, XXI 1541, fol. 480^r; AMS, XXI 1551, fol. 260^r; Hatt, p. 634).

H.   Hans K. of Buchsweiler (d. by 1520); Barbara Messinger, sister of Lux M. (Wittmer, Nos. 3979, 6590; Lehr, III, 445; BNUS, Ms. 1058, fol. 134^r; ADBR, E 5948/5).

J.   Anna?, m. Jacob v. Duntzenheim (AMS, KS 14, fol. 152^r; AMS, KS 23/I, fols. 12^r–13^v).

K.   Margarethe v. Gottesheim, sister of Friedrich VI v. Gottesheim (BNUS, Ms. 1058, fol. 97^v).

L.   Jacob, Ammeister 1594, 1600, 06, m. 1) Martha Ingold, daughter of Georg I. and Susanna Ebel, and 2) Martha v. Molsheim; Hans, m. Susanna Ingold (BNUS, Ms. 1058, fol. 97^v; ADBR, E 5948/10; Lehr, III, 445–446).

M.   Connections with Duntzenheim, Ingold, and Gottesheim families make it highly probable that he was a merchant.

P.   Probably wealthy; family of Hagenau origin and intermarried with other wealthy families from Hagenau (Fuchs, "Ingold," p. 203; Fuchs, "Prechter," p. 147).

Q.   1520–51 fief at Kintzweiler and Geisweiler from counts of Zweibrücken–Bitsch–Lichtenberg and Hanau–Lichtenberg (ADBR, E 5948/5–9).

R.   Strasbourg (Seyboth, p. 21; Specklin, *Collectanées*, No. 297).

U.   Nephew of Lux Messinger; brother-in-law? of Jacob v. Duntzenheim; related to Heinrich Ingold and Friedrich Ebel; brother-in-law of Friedrich VI v. Gottesheim.

L.   *KNIEBIS, Claus*   b. 1479 (Rott, "Un recueil," p. 756)
                                     d. 4./5.X.1552 (Ficker–Winckelmann, I, 4)

A.   Schmiede, *Oberherr* 1525–52 (Hatt, p. 473; AMS, KS 18, fol. 42^r).

C.   1512/13, 16/17 (Hatt, p. 473).

D.   Ammeister 1519, 25, 31, 37, refused 1543 (Hatt, p. 623; Hertzog, VIII, 97).

E.   1514–18 (AGCS, Comptes in Heilewog: "1514"; Winckelmann, II, 24; AMS, VI 495: "1518").

F.   1520–52 (AMS, VI 495; AMS, VI 589/6, fols. 51^r–58^r; Rott, "Magistrat," p. 113).

G.   The family name and the maternal inheritance at Rastatt suggest an origin in Middle Baden; active in the regime of Strasbourg 1464–1679 (Hatt, pp. 473, 662).

H.   Claus K., senator 1464; and N. Meyger (AMS, KS 19, fol. 279^v; Kindler, *OG*, II, 314, who gives his mother as Katharina Rot).

J.   Elisabeth (d. 1526), m. 1) Bartholome Barpfennig (d. 1518), armiger, and 2) Daniel Knobloch (AMS, KS 18, fol. 13^r; AMS, KS 19, fols. 273^v–274^r; Kindler, *OG*, II, 314).

K.   Ottilia Rot, sister of Michael R., Dr. med. (AMS, KS 31/I, fol. 145^v).

L.   Sebastian, m. Katharina Münch, daughter of Claus M.; Nicolaus Hugo (d. 1588), m. Barbara Pfarrer, daughter of Mathis P.; Anna, m. Johann Baptist Fuchs, Dr. med. (d. by 1546); Barbara, m. 1) Daniel Knobloch (d. by 1537), and 2) Martin Herlin; Margarethe, novice at St. Margarethe Strasbourg 1522, m. 1525 Caspar Engelmann;

Aurelia, m. Jakob Wolff (AMS, KS 18, fol. 94^v; AMS, KS 19, fol. 115^{r-v}; AMS, KS 55/II, fol. 62^r; BNUS, Ms. 1058, fol. 98^r; Kindler, *OG*, II, 313–314).

M. Rentier.

R. Extensive maternal inheritance near Rastatt; properties at Offenheim, Königshofen; properties at Mommenheim bought from St. Clara auf dem Wörth Strasbourg 1524 (AMS, KS 19, fols. 279^v–280^r; AMS, KS 15, fols. 176^r–177^r; AMS, KS 63/I, fol. 195^{r-v}; AMS, KS 63/II, fols. 107^{r-v}, 126^r–127^r; AMS, KS 17, fols. 270^r–275^r).

S. University of Freiburg i. Br. 1494, bacc. art. 1495; lic. utr. iur.; Scholarch 1526–51 (*Matrikel Freiburg*, I, 113, No. 36; AST 16/51; Ficker–Winckelmann, I, 4).

T. Zealous Evangelical by 1522; leader of Evangelical faction in regime in 1520s (Rott, "Un recueil," pp. 746–754; "Imlin Chronik," p. 412).

U. Father-in-law of CASPAR ENGELMANN, SEBASTIAN MÜNCH, and MARTIN HERLIN; related through childrens' marriages to CLAUS MÜNCH and MATHIS PFARRER.

LI. *v. LAMPERTHEIM, Hans* d. 14.XI.1562 (BNUS, Ms. 626, fol. 162^r)

A. Schmiede (Hatt, p. 480).

C. 1550/51, 54/55 (Hatt, p. 480).

E. 1554–62 (BNUS, Ms. 626, fol. 162^r; Hatt, pp. 217, 663).

K. 1) Margarethe Wigker of Barr (d. by 1537), widow of Andres Offinger, 2) ? Alithea, daughter of Johannes Oecolampadius and Wibrandis Rosenblatt (AMS, KS 35/I, fol. 100^r; AMS, KS 58/I, fol. 61^v).

L. Anton; Hans; Cleophe; Margarethe (AMS, KS 35/I, fol. 100^r).

M. 1540 Merchant ("Krämer"), or more probably tinsmith ("kannen-giesser") 1547 (AMS, KS 40/I; AMS, KS 58/I, fol. 61^v).

LII. *LEIMER (Lymer), Georg*
        b. 1506 (Lehr, III, 447)
        d. 7.VIII.1572 (BNUS, Ms. 626, fol. 161^v; Hertzog, VIII, 101)

A. Zum Spiegel 1530/31; Brotbecker 1552–72; armiger (ADBR, E 1356/1; Hatt, p. 487).

C. 1552/53 (Hatt, p. 487).

D. Ammeister 1556, 62, 68 resigned due to ill health (Hatt, p. 623; Städel, "Chronik," III, 471).

E. 1551–55 (AMS, XXI 1551, fol. 260^r).

F. 1558–68 (AMS, XXI 1558, fol. 261^r; BNUS, Ms. 626, fol. 161^v; "Imlin Chronik," p. 438).

G. His son Carl was the last male L.; the family was said to have had a common origin with the wealthy Barpfennig family (Kindler, *OG*, II, 478–479).

H. Carl L. (d. 1506), armiger; Magdalena Zettler (BNUS, Ms. 1058, fol. 112^v).

K. Einbethe Schott, whose sister m. HANS LINDENFELS (BNUS, Ms. 1058, fol. 112^v).

L. *Junker* Carl (d. 1571), unmarried; Barbara, m. 1) Jakob Theobald, and
2) Philipp Messinger; Magdalena, m. Jakob Ringler; Anna, m. Paul
Graseck; Ursula, m. Daniel Koleffel (Kindler, *OG*, II, 479; BNUS,
Ms. 1058, fol. 112^v).

M. Probably a merchant; 1548 *Schaffner* of WOLF SIGISMUND WURMSER v.
VENDENHEIM (AMS, KS 63/I, fols. 24^r–27^v).

R. His wife inherited one-third interest in her father's properties at Lampertheim (AMS, IV 105a).

S. University of Tübingen 5.V.1523 (*Matrikel Tübingen*, I, 245, No. 81, 1).

T. Reputed to have been exceptionally pious; supporter of conservative
Lutheranism (Lehr, III, 447; Horning, p. 188).

U. Distantly related to HANS LINDENFELS and LUX MESSINGER.

LIII.   *LINDENFELS, Hans*   d. 30.IV.1548 (AMS, XXI 1548, fol. 228^r)

A. Zur Möhrin (Hatt, p. 484).

C. 1518/19, 23, 26/27 (Hatt, p. 484).

D. Ammeister 1532, 38, 44 (Hatt, p. 623).

E. 1521–31 (Rott, "Magistrat," p. 113; AMS, III 11/2; AMS, KS 16, fol.
65^v; AMS, VI 495).

F. 1534–48 (AMS, VI 589/6, fols. 51^r–56^v; AMS, XXI 1547, fol. 423^r;
PCSS, IV, 324, No. 306n1).

G. No other L. ever served in the regime of Strasbourg.

J. Lienhart?, "der altgewender," m. 1514 Margred, daughter of Hans v.
Wasselnheim, a mason (Wittmer, No. 6425).

K. 1) Barbara v. Odratzheim (d. 1519), and 2) 1539 Brigitte Schott, sister of
the wife of GEORG LEIMER (Lehr, III, 449; AMS, KS 35/IV, fol. 81).

L. Barbara?, m. Lux Vogler, the apothecary (Seyboth, p. 111).

M. Retail merchant ("institor"), probably of cloth and clothing (AMS, KS 9,
fol. 187^r; Schmoller, p. 157, No. 77).

P. Moneylender to peasants and artisans (AMS, KS 23/II, fols. 265^v–266^r,
267^{r-v}; AMS, KS 25, fols. 139^v, 140^r).

R. Strasbourg; rented properties from several convents 1531 and from the
city (Seyboth, pp. 95, 97; ADBR, H 27/(6); AMS, KS 18, fols. 201,
221; AMS, VII 1436, fol. 9^r).

T. Evangelical by 1.IX. 1524; he and "sein anhang" conducted an iconoclastic riot at Old St. Peter Strasbourg 20.II.1529 (*Ann. Brant*, No.
4537; *Fragments*, No. 4011).

U. Related to HANS v. ODRATZHEIM and GEORG LEIMER.

LIV.   *MARX v. ECKWERSHEIM, Jerg*
                    b. ca. 1454 (AMS, IX 1/4)
                    d. 1535 (Fuchs, *Documents*, No. 1115)

A. Constofel zum Hohensteg (Wittmer, No. 7798).

B. Renounced 26.VIII.1522; purchased 9.V.1525 (Wittmer, Nos. 7205,
7798).

C. 1512, 16/17, 20, 22 (Hatt, p. 490).

D. Stettmeister 1519 (Hatt, p. 604).

E. 1518–22 (AMS, VI 495: "1518"; Rott, "Magistrat," p. 113).
G. Old family of episcopal ministeriales; Jerg M. v. E. was the only Marx in regime of Strasbourg after 1382; family extinct in male line 1596 (Kindler, *GBS*, pp. 186–187; Hatt, p. 490).
H. Jacob M. v. E. (d. by 1503); Margareth Burggraff (Kindler, *OG*, III, 36–37).
K. Ursula Böcklin v. Böcklinsau, daughter of Wirich B. v. B. and Zona Gürtler (Kindler, *OG*, III, 36–37).
L. Veronica (d. 1587), m. Adam v. Berstett (d. 1572); Ursula, m. Adolf Baumann (Kindler, *OG*, III, 38).
M. Rentier; seigneur.
Q. Chateau and village of Stotzheim, fief of Rappoltstein; Berstett and Olwisheim, fief of Bp. and H.R.E.; Schnersheim, fief of Metz (ADBR, E 600/5–7; ADBR, G 403; Adam, *EKET*, pp. 525–526).
R. Eckwersheim, Kolbsheim, Schnersheim, Berstett (Fritz, p. 107n17; Wunder, "Verzeichnis," p. 63).
T. The M. v. E. were lay patrons of St. Andreas Strasbourg as vassals of the Bp. 1483–1525, where they refused to accept an Evangelical pastor 1525; Evangelical religion introduced at Olwisheim 1565 and Schnersheim 1559 (AST 134; Adam, *EKSS*, p. 70; Adam, *EKET*, pp. 525–526).
V. Jerg M. v. E., *Ritter,* was the uncle of this man.

LV. *MESSINGER (Mesner), Lux*
b. 15.X.1491 (*BCGA*, No. 31 [1975], p. 67, No. 250)
d. 9.X.1555 (BNUS, Ms. 626, fol. 162^r)

A. Zum Spiegel 1530–31; Zum Freiburg to 1548; Zur Möhrin 1548–55 (ADBR, E 1356/1; Hatt, p. 494; AMS, XXI 1548, fol. 482^r).
C. 1527/28, 35/36, 41/42, 45/46 (Hatt, p. 494).
D. Ammeister 1552 (Hatt, p. 624).
E. 1548–51 (AMS, XXI 1548, fol. 482^r; AMS, XXI 1551, fol. 417^v).
G. The name appears variously as "Messinger," "Mössinger," and "Mesner"; family active in regime from 14th century until 1588 (AMS, KS 16, fol. 149^v; AMS, KS 22, fol. 53^{r-v}; BNUS, Ms. 1058, fol. 134^r; Hatt, p. 494).
H. Adam M. (ca. 1440–ca. 1494), XIIIer and merchant; 1) ca. 1460 Adelheid Cun of Westhoffen, and 2) ca. 1485? Anna Dedinger (ca. 1470–ca. 1514) (BNUS, Ms. 1058, fol. 134^r; *BCGA*, No. 31 [1975], p. 68, Nos. 500–501).
J. Barbara, m. Hans Kips, father of VELTIN K.; Daniel, canon of St. Thomas Strasbourg; Agnes, m. Dr. Johann Fuchs; Elisabeth, m. Johann Wilhelm zum Rust; Susanna, m. JACOB MEYER; Ottilia, m. Onophrius Brant; and ca. 21 others (BNUS, Ms. 1058, fol. 134^r; *BCGA*, No. 31 [1975], p. 68, No. 500).
K. 1) ca. 1515 Aurelia Hess, and 2) ca. 1528 Catharina Wolff called Schönecker (ca. 1510/25–56) (Mieg, p. 13; *BCGA*, No. 31 [1975], p. 67, Nos. 250–251).

L. Martha, m. Johann Waldeck; Adam, m. Anna Mieg, daughter of CARL MIEG; Jacob, m. Dorothea Ingold; Eva, m. Philipp Wörlin; Felicitas (1543–1624), m. 1) 1568 Philipp Ingold d. Jüng. (1543/49–1610), 2) 1583 Heinrich or Sigismund Roth, Dr. med. and 3) Didymus Obrecht, Dr. med. (BNUS, Ms. 1058, fol. 134^r; BCGA, No. 31 [1975], p. 66, Nos. 124–125).

M. Cloth merchant ("venditor pannorum," "tuchman") (AMS, KS 12, fol. 28^v; AMS, KS 20, fol. 263^r; AMS, XXI 1546, fol. 361^v).

N. Active 1520ff. as moneylender to peasants and as cloth merchant (AMS, KS 12, fols. 28^v, 54^v, 94^v, 133^r, 160^v–161^r, 190^v, 153^v).

P. The M. were a wealthy merchant family ruined in collapse of the 1570s; Adam M. served the commune "zu Ross" (Fuchs, "Ingold," pp. 203, 215; AMS, R 28, fol. 102^r).

R. 1517 rents at Wolfisheim, Ergersheim, Dambach, Eckwersheim, Wingersheim, and Epfig; Strasbourg (Hefele, No. 854; Seyboth, pp. 52, 180; AMS, VII 1438, fol. 65^r).

U. Uncle of VELTIN KIPS; brother-in-law of JACOB MEYER; related through the Brant to MATHIS PFARRER; a son married a daughter of CARL MIEG, Sr.; a daughter married a nephew of CLAUS INGOLD.

V. The death date 19.X.1555 ("Imlin Chronik," p. 430) is wrong.

LVI. *MEYER (Meyger), Conrad*   d. 6.III.1555 (AMS, II 76b–77/7)

A. Zum Encker (father's guild); Zum Spiegel 1530–40; Schuhmacher 1540–48 (AMS, VI 591/1; ADBR, E 1356/1; Hatt, pp. 495–496; AST 75, fol. 506).

B. Renounced 28.VIII.1548 (AMS, KS 63/I, fol. 3^v).

C. 1535/36, 42/43 (Hatt, pp. 495–496).

D. Ammeister 1543, refused as a fiefholder (Hertzog, VIII, 97).

E. 1540–48 (AMS, XXI 1540, fol. 352^r; AMS, KS 63/I, fol. 3^v).

G. Related to the family Meyer v. Sasbach in Baden; this man may be identical with a "Conrad Meyger olim hospitus in Keule [=Kehl]" 1524 (Kindler, OG, III, 83; AMS, KS 17, fols. 27^r, 28^r).

H. Conrad M. (d. by 1514); Ursula N., who remarried 1514 Antonj v. Sigolsheim, a prominent merchant (AMS, KS 20, fols. 211^r–215^r; BNUS, Ms. 1058, fol. 127^v; Wittmer, No. 6394; Fuchs, "Israël Minckel," p. 116).

K. 1) 1525 Elisabeth Büchsner, and 2) Aurelia v. Hohenburg (d. 1566), daughter of GOTTFRIED v. H. (AMS, KS 17, fol. 158^r; Mieg, p. 13).

M. Merchant ("mercator," "der köuffer") (AMS, KS 19, fol. 163^v; AMS, KS 20, fol. 38^v).

N. 1525 engaged in ransoming Alsatians held in Lorraine after the Peasants' War (AMS, KS 20, fols. 37^v–38^v, 51^r).

P. 1497 his father was a principal supplier of paper to the printer Anton Koberger of Nuremberg (Dietz, p. 58).

Q. Fief of fishing rights at Zell am Harmersbach held from abbot of Gengenbach (Kindler, OG, III, 83; AMS, XXI 1542, fol. 535^r).

R. Strasbourg; rented property from the city (Seyboth, p. 32; *Kleine Strassb. Chronik,* p. 7; AMS, KS 35/II, fols. 63^r–64^v; AMS, VII 1436, fol. 35^v).

S. Almost certainly not the Conrad Meyer of Strasbourg who entered the University of Heidelberg 20.X.1529 (*Matrikel Heidelberg,* I, 545).

U. Son-in-law of GOTTFRIED V. HOHENBURG; related to ALEXIUS BÜCHSNER and CARL MIEG, Sr.

LVII. *MEYER, Frantz*   d. 27.II.1565 (BNUS, Ms. 626, fol. 162^r)

A. Maurer (father's guild); Zur Luzern 1553–65 (Hatt, p. 495).

C. 1555/56 (Hatt, p. 495).

E. 1553–63 (BNUS, Ms. 626, fols. 161^v, 162^r).

F. 1563–65 (BNUS, Ms. 626, fols. 161^v).

G. See JACOB MEYER (Maurer).

H. JACOB MEYER (Maurer) (d. 1562); Susanna Messinger, sister of LUX M. (BNUS, Ms. 1058, fol. 128^r).

J. See JACOB MEYER (Maurer).

K. Anna Burckheusser (AMS, KS 66/II, fols. 110^v–112^v; AMS, KS 98/II, fols. 105^r–115^r).

M. 1559 operated a powder mill (Saladin, *Chronik,* p. 379).

U. Son of JACOB MEYER (Maurer); nephew of LUX MESSINGER.

LVIII. *MEYER, Jacob*
         d. 29.I.1562 (AMS, XXI 1562, fol. 23^v; Ficker–Winckelmann, I, 10)

A. Maurer, *Oberherr* (Hatt, p. 496; Büheler, *Chronique,* No. 402).

C. 1519, 22/23, 26/27 (Hatt, p. 496).

E. 1521–24 (Rott, "Magistrat," p. 113; *Ann. Brant,* No. 4413; Winckelmann, I, 88).

F. 1525–62 (AMS, KS 18, fol. 32^v; AMS, VI 589/6, fols. 51^r–59^r; Büheler, *Chronique,* No. 402).

K. 1) Susanna Messinger (d. by 1546), sister of LUX M., and 2) 1546 Magdalena Brant, daughter of Sebastian B. (d. 1521) and widow of Peter Butz (d. 1531) (AMS, KS 16, fol. 149^v; AMS, KS 55/I, fols. 230^v–231^v; AMS, KS 66/II, fols. 94^v–96^v).

L. Jacob, Jr.; Regula; FRANTZ, m. Anna Burckheusser (BNUS, Ms. 1058, fol. 128^r).

P. Moneylender to peasants (AMS, KS 20, fol. 295^r).

R. Rented lands from the city (AMS, VII 1436, fols. 9^r, 19^v, 35^v).

S. Scholarch 1526–62 (*Ann. Brant, No.* 4659; Büheler, *Chronique,* No. 402).

T. Evangelical, probably by 1523; 1558 guardian of Katharina Schütz, widow of Mathis Zell (Ficker–Winckelmann, I, 10; AMS, XXI 1558, fol. 437^r).

U. Brother-in-law of LUX MESSINGER; father of FRANTZ MEYER.

V. Not to be confused with JACOB MEYER "zum Heroldt."

LIX. MEYER, Jacob "zum Heroldt"
d. 4.IV.1567 (BNUS, Ms. 626, fol. 161^v)

A. Zur Blume (Hatt, p. 624).
D. Ammeister 1549, 55, 61, 67 (Hatt, p. 624).
E. 1548 (AMS, XXI 1548, fol. 460^v).
F. 1554–67 (AMS, XXI 1554, fol. 153^r; BNUS, Ms. 626, fol. 161^v).
K. Margarethe Krug (Lehr, III, 451).
L. Bastian; Claus, who resigned from the XV 1578 (BNUS, Ms. 1058, fol. 127^v).
M. Merchant; butcher (AMS, KS 63/II, at 17.V.1548; PCSS, V, 513, No. 409n1).
N. His son Bastian was a Prechter factor at Lyons (BNUS, Ms. 1058, fol. 127^v).
R. Strasbourg (Seyboth, p. 111).
V. Also called Jacob Meyer "im Schmidgasse" or "Altammeister" to distinguish him from JACOB MEYER of the Maurerzunft.

LX. MIEG, Andreas
b. ca. 1488
d. 3.X.1551 (Mieg, p. 19)

A. Zum Spiegel; armiger (Hatt, p. 499; AMS, KS 14, fol. 160^v).
C. 1525/26 (Hatt, p. 499).
D. Ammeister 1543, refused as a fiefholder (Hertzog, VIII, 97).
E. 1532–43 (Mieg, p. 19; AMS, VI 488/10; AMS, XXI 1542, fol. 539^v).
F. 1543–51 (Mieg, p. 19; AMS, XXI 1542, fol. 539^v; AMS, XXI 1551, fol. 318^r).
G. Merchant-banking family, migrants from Mulhouse to Strasbourg in later fifteenth century; numerous marriages with patricians (Mieg, pp. 1–20).
H. Jakob M. (ca. 1452–1513); Anna Gross (d. 1494) (Mieg, p. 8).
J. Katharina (ca. 1485–ca. 1535), m. 1505 Jacob Wetzel v. Marsilien (d. 1525); Jacobe (ca. 1490–1546), m. 1508 Lux Ritter (d. 1512) (Mieg, pp. 8–9).
K. Barbe Ingold, daughter of Mathias I. and Agnes Breuning (Mieg, p. 19).
L. None (Mieg, p. 19).
M. Rentier (Mieg, p. 19).
P. Extremely wealthy, sole heir of his father and of his uncle, Ludwig M. (Mieg, p. 19).
Q. Fief of the counts of Eberstein (AMS, XXI 1542, fol. 533^r).
R. Strasbourg, Witternheim (Mieg, p. 19).
S. Wrote and read French (PCSS, III, 351n4).
T. Roman Catholic and opponent of reform; Evangelical by 1532 (Mieg, p. 20).
U. Nephew of CARL M., Sr., and first-cousin of CARL M., Jr.; cousin of DANIEL M.; related to HEINRICH INGOLD, and to JACOB and MARTIN WETZEL V. MARSILIEN.

LXI. *MIEG, Carl, Sr.* b. 1473
d. 9.XI.1541 (Mieg, p. 12)

A. Zum Spiegel 1517–31; Tucher 1532–41; armiger (AMS, VI 591/1; ADBR, E 1356/1; Hatt, p. 499; AMS, KS 17, fol. 37^r).
C. 1521/22, 35/36, 41 (Hatt, p. 499).
E. 1532–41 (AMS, VI 488/10; Hatt, p. 634; Mieg, p. 12; Schmoller, pp. 155, 157; AMS, XXI 1541, fol. 480^r); he was not a member of the XIII (Hatt, p. 644).
G. See under ANDREAS MIEG.
H. Jacob M. (ca. 1420–98); and Columba Betscholt (ca. 1450–1526).
J. Philipp (ca. 1472–1503), m. 1503 Apollonia v. Mülnheim; Susanna (ca. 1477–1524), m. ca. 1500 BERNHARD WURMSER V. VENDENHEIM; Elisabeth (ca. 1480–1541), m. 1) 1503 Albrecht v. Kippenheim, and 2) Wolfgang Zorn v. Plobsheim; Hieronymus (ca. 1482–after 1557), m. 1) 1515 Anna van de Mortel, 2) ca. 1520 Maria Holtzapfel, and 3) Margarethe van der Baar (Mieg, p. 3).
K. Anna v. Hohenburg (ca. 1495–1558), daughter of GOTTFRIED v. H. (Mieg, p. 12).
L. Sebastian (1520–1609), m. Veronika Prechter, daughter of FRIEDRICH II P.; CARL, Jr.; Agnes (b. 1523), m. 1) Johann Jakob Becherer, and 2) Conrad Roesch; Dorothea (1525–64), m. 1558 Nicolaus Fuchs; Anna (1526–94), m. 1562 Adam Messinger, son of LUX M.; Jacob (1528–60), m. 1552 Jacobe Knobloch; Anastasia (1532–96), m. 1566 Lux Vogler, son of Lux V. (Mieg, p. 12).
M. Merchant (Mieg, p. 12).
N. He and his brother, Hieronymus, formed a firm to trade with Antwerp, where the latter lived (Mieg, p. 12).
P. After the death of his half-brother, Ludwig, in 1523, he headed the family firm; served the city "zu Ross"; creditor of the Counts of Mörs–Saarwerden 1519–20 (Mieg, p. 12; Brant, p. 282; AMS, VI 591/1; Herrmann, I, Nos. 1780, 1782).
R. Strasbourg; Illkirch (Mieg, p. 12).
U. Uncle of ANDREAS M.; first-cousin of DANIEL M.; father of CARL M., Jr.; son-in-law of GOTTFRIED v. HOHENBURG; related to LUX MESSINGER, FRIEDRICH II PRECHTER, and WILHELM PRECHTER; brother-in-law of BERNHARD WURMSER v. VENDENHEIM.

LXII. *MIEG, Carl, Jr.* b. 1521
d. 14.III.1572 (Mieg, p. 22)

A. Tucher, *Oberherr* 1551–72 (Mieg, pp. 22–23).
B. Renounced 28.VIII.1548; purchased VI.1549 (AMS, KS 63/I, fol. 2^v; AMS, XXI 1549, fols. 245^v–246^r).
C. 1553/54 (Hatt, p. 499).
D. Ammeister 1558, 64, 70 (Hatt, p. 624).
E. 1552–57 (AMS, XXI 1552, fols. 277^v–278^r; Hatt, p. 665).
F. 1558–72 (Hatt, p. 665).
G. See under ANDREAS MIEG.

H. CARL M. (1473–1541); and Anna v. Hohenburg, daughter of GOTTFRIED
    v. H. (Mieg, p. 12).
J. See under CARL M., Sr.
K. 1551 Apollonia Ferber, daughter of Colin F. and Anna Bosch (Mieg,
    p. 22).
L. Susanna (1553–96), m. 1) 1573 Jacob Vogler, son of Lux V., and 2) 1589
    Johann Friedrich Lumbart; Sebastian (1555–96), ennobled 1577, m.
    1557 Apollonia Nierlin; Carl (1558–87); Apollonia (1563–1624), m.
    Johann Friedrich v. Botzheim (Mieg, p. 22; Riedenauer, p. 70).
M. Rentier.
R. See under CARL M., Sr.
S. University of Wittenberg, law, 1541; Scholarch 1562–72 (Mieg, pp.
    22–23).
T. Orthodox Lutheran (Sturm, *Classicae epistolae,* pp. xxvii, 13n1; Horning,
    p. 188).
U. Son of CARL M., Sr.; grandson of GOTTFRIED V. HOHENBURG; cousin
    of DANIEL and ANDREAS M.; nephew of CONRAD MEYER.
V. The death date 24.III.1572 ("Imlin Chronik," p. 450) is wrong.

LXIII. *MIEG, Daniel*   b. ca. 1484 (AMS, IX 1/6)
                                                d. 27.X.1541 (Mieg, p. 17)

A. Zum Spiegel 1517–31; Brotbecker 1520–41, *Oberherr* 1527; armiger
    (AMS, VI 591/1; ADBR, E 1356/1; Hatt, p. 499; Winckelmann, II,
    114, No. 67).
C. 1520/21, 26/27 (Hatt, p. 499).
D. Ammeister 1524, 30, 36 (Hatt, p. 624).
E. 1519–22 (Mieg, p. 17; Rott, "Magistrat," p. 113).
F. 1522–41 (AMS, IX 1/6; AMS, VI 589/6, fols. 51^r–56^r; Mieg, p. 17;
    Hatt, p. 665).
G. See under ANDREAS MIEG.
H. Florenz M. (ca. 1435–1511); and Maria (ca. 1450–1524), daughter of
    Peter I Schott (1427–1504) and Margarethe v. Köllen (d. 1498)
    (Mieg, p. 7).
J. Peter (b. ca. 1472), m. Margarethe Dedinger; Veronika (ca. 1480–1541),
    m. Jacob Ingold (Mieg, p. 7).
K. 1) ca. 1506 Clara Prechter (d. before 1523), sister of FRIEDRICH II P., and
    2) 1525 Margarethe (d. 1541), daughter of Bläsi Dolde and Maria
    Hügels (Mieg, p. 17).
L. Anna (ca. 1508–41), m. ca. 1532 Sebastian Bock v. Gerstheim (Mieg,
    p. 17; Winckelmann, II, 257, No. 128).
M. Rentier; as a youth destined for the church, held a prebend at St. Thomas
    Strasbourg 1504–06 (Mieg, p. 17).
P. Served the city "zu Ross"; popularly believed to be as wealthy as the
    Prechter; son of a wealthy merchant; major creditor of the counts of
    Mörs–Saarwerden 1523–41 (Brant, p. 282; *TQ Strassburg,* I, 274,
    No. 224; Mieg, p. 8; Herrmann, I, No. 1838, 1873; ADBR, 25 J 23).

R. Strasbourg; Molsheim (Mieg, p. 19; Fuchs, "Ingold," p. 204; *PCSS*, I, 173).

S. Educated at homes of his parents and his grandfather, Peter I Schott (Mieg, p. 17).

T. Zealous Evangelical by 1523, his election as Ammeister in 1524 is considered a turning point in the reform movement (Mieg, p. 17; "Imlin Chronik," p. 412; Ficker–Winckelmann, I, 1; Schelp, pp. 180–181).

U. First-cousin of CARL M., Sr.; related to CARL M., Jr., ANDREAS M., MARTIN, FRIEDRICH, JACOB, and PETER STURM; brother-in-law of FRIEDRICH II PRECHTER: uncle of WILHELM PRECHTER.

LXIV. *v. MITTELHAUSEN, Adolf*
               b. 1479 (ADBR, 3B 1357)
               d. 9.III.1565 (BNUS, Ms. 626, fol. 161^v)

A. Constofel zum Mühlstein (AMS, VI 496: "1557").

C. 1547/48, 51/52, 54/55 (Hatt, p. 496).

D. Stettmeister 1557/58, 60, 63/64 (Hatt, p. 604).

E. 1552–60 (BNUS, Ms. 626, fol. 163^r; AMS, XXI 1560, fol. 159^v; Hatt, p. 635).

F. 1560–65 (AMS, XXI 1560, fol. 159^v; BNUS, Ms. 626, fol. 161^v).

G. From a large and widespread Lower Alsatian noble family; the Adolf v. M. who was senator at Strasbourg 1521–27 was Adolf, Sr. (d. after 1537), first-cousin to this man (Kindler, *OG*, III, 94; *TQ Strassburg*, I, 52, No. 45n1).

H. Adolf v. M., Jr. (d. 1522/23); Agnes Erlin v. Rorburg (Kindler, *OG*, III, 94).

J. Sebastian, m. N. v. Ratsamhausen (Kindler, *OG*, III, 94; AMS, KS 23/II, fol. 36^v; Habich, I/1, No. 579, p. 86, and table LXXIV, 1).

M. Rentier; seigneur.

Q. Fief at Reichstett from Bp. and Cathedral Chapter of Strasbourg; fief from counts of Mörs–Saarwerden (ADBR, G 503; ADBR, G 2942/12–14; Herrmann, I, Nos. 1104, 1411, 1488, 1532, 1673, 1858).

R. 3/24 of Allmannsweier and Wittenweier; Oberbergheim (Wunder, *Landgebiet,* pp. 112–113; BNUS, Ms. 3775).

LXV. *v. MÖRSSMÜNSTER, Ludwig* d. 13.II.1560 (BNUS, Ms. 626, fol. 162^r)

A. Zur Steltz (Hatt, p. 498).

C. 1549/50, 55/56 (Hatt, p. 498).

E. 1552–60 (AMS, XXI 1552, fol. 151^r; AMS, XXI 1560, fol. 64^v).

H. Hans v. M., *Glasmaler,* active 1475–1501; and Agnes N. (Rott, *Oberrhein,* I, 210, 282, and Textband, pp. 68, 109).

K. 1539 Katharina Spatzinger, widow of Hans Hug, *Kaufhausschreiber* (AMS, KS 35/V, fols. 34^r–35^v).

M. Glazier (*Glasmaler*) (Rott, *Oberrhein*, I, 215, 282).

V. The only privy councillor of the guild Zur Steltz 1520–55 who was not a goldsmith.

LXVI.   *v. MÜLNHEIM gen. HILDERBRAND, Heinrich*
         b. 17.IV.1507
         d. 22.IV.1578 (Ficker–Winckelmann, I, 12; AST 70/1, fol. 52^r)

A. Constofel zum Mühlstein (AMS, I 20a/2).
B. Renounced 15.VII.1548; purchased by 1553 (AMS, XXI 1548, fol. 353^v).
C. 1537/38, 43/44, 46 (Hatt, p. 401).
D. Stettmeister 1554/55, 58/59, 61/62, 64/65, 67/68, 70/71, 73/74, 76/77 (Hatt, p. 605).
E. 1546–48, 1553–59 (AMS, XXI 1546, fol. 46^r; AMS, XXI 1548, fol. 353^v; AMS, XXI 1559, fol. 253^r).
F. 1559–78 (AMS, XXI 1559, fol. 253^r; BNUS, Ms. 626, fol. 161^v; Hatt, p. 666).
G. One of Strasbourg's great noble clans, active in the regime from the late 13th century until the French Revolution (Hatt, pp. 500–506; Kindler, *OG*, III, 129–147).
H. Caspar v. M., *Ritter*; Gertrud Böcklin v. Böcklinsau (Kindler, *OG*, III, 132).
J. Elisabeth, m. 1) Sigelin Völtsch (d. by 1501), and 2) 1501 Melchior Zuckmantel v. Brumath; Salome (d. 1531), m. 1) Georg Zorn v. Bulach, and 2) EGENOLF RÖDER v. DIERSBURG (Wittmer, No. 5096; Kindler, *OG*, III, 132–133).
K. Martha Wurmser v. Schäffolsheim, widow of BERNHARD OTTFRIEDRICH (Kindler, *OG*, III, 132–133).
M. Rentier; seigneur.
Q. Fief of the Bp. of Strasbourg (ADBR, G 503).
R. Strasbourg; Entzheim, Mutzig, Ruda, Wasselnheim, Offenburg; rented land from the city (Seyboth, p. 175; Müllenheim, *Bethaus*, pp. 45, 48, 50; AMS, VI 173/5; AMS, V 11/36; AMS, VII 1438, fol. 57^v).
S. University of Basel 1524 (Ficker–Winckelmann, I, 12).
T. Conservative Lutheran during the 1560s and 1570s (Ficker–Winckelmann, I, 12; Horning, p. 188).
U. Brother-in-law of EGENOLF RÖDER v. DIERSBURG; cousin of FRIEDRICH, JACOB, and PETER STURM; related to HILTEBRANT v. M.; married the widow of BERNHARD OTTFRIEDRICH.

LXVII.   *v. MÜLNHEIM v. ROSENBURG, Hiltebrant*
          d. 4.VI.1559 (AMS, XXI 1559, fol. 246^r)

A. Constofel zum Mühlstein (AMS, I 20a/2).
C. 1532/33 (Hatt, p. 501).
D. Stettmeister 1537/38, 40/41, 43/44, 46/47, 49/50, 52/53, 55/56 (Hatt, p. 590).
E. 1540–44 (AMS, XXI 1540, fol. 251^v; AMS, VI 496).
F. 1544–1559 (*PCSS*, IV, 324; AMS, XXI 1559, fol. 246^r; Hatt, p. 666).
G. See under HEINRICH v. M.
H. LUDWIG v. M.; and Katharina zum Trübel (d. 1498) (Kindler, *OG*, III, 147).
J. See under LUDWIG v. M.

K. 1) Clara Bock zu Hagenau (d. by 1535), and 2) Clara Bock v. Erlenburg (Kindler, *OG*, III, 147).
L. Ursula, m. Conrad Joham v. Mundolsheim; Ludwig, canon of Aller-heiligen Strasbourg, m. Ursula v. Bärenfels; Johanna, m. Eberhard v. Keppenbach (Kindler, *OG*, III, 147).
M. Rentier.
Q. Fief of Bp. of Strasbourg (ADBR, G 503).
R. Strasbourg; Kogenheim, Romansweiler; 1541 Truchtersheim (Seyboth, pp. 115, 117; Müllenheim, *Bethaus,* pp. 51, 55; Hefele, No. 963).
U. Son of LUDWIG v. M.; related distantly to EGENOLF RÖDER v. DIERS-BURG; related to HEINRICH v. M.

LXVIII. *v. MÜLNHEIM, Ludwig*

d. after 4.I.1526 (AMS, Fonds Mullenheim)

A. Constofel zum Mühlstein (AMS, VI 495: "1520").
B. Purchased 22.VIII.1481 (Wittmer, No. 3343).
C. 1483/84, 86/87, 90/91, 96/97, 1500/01, 03/04, 06/07, 09/10, 16/17, 25/26 (Hatt, p. 501).
D. Stettmeister 1512/13, 20/21 (Hatt, p. 605).
E. 1507-17 (Brant, p. 287; AGCS, Comptes in Heilewog: "1514").
F. 1518-26 (AMS, VI 495: "1518"; AMS, KS 18, fol. 22ᵛ).
G. See under HEINRICH v. M.
H. Diebold v. M. v. Rosenburg (d. 1496); Katharina Schenck *gen.* Missbach (d. 1506) (Kindler, *OG*, III, 146-147).
J. Sigelin (d. ca. 1503); Diebold; Magdalena, m. Wendelin zum Trübel (d. 1515) (Kindler, *OG*, III, 146-147).
K. 1) Salome v. Wangen, and 2) Katharina zum Trübel (d. 1498) (Kindler, *OG*, III, 147).
L. Cleopha, m. Jakob v. Brumbach; Reimbold; HILTEBRANT; Agnes Elisabeth, m. Christoph Zuckmantel v. Brumath; Martha Lut-gardis, m. Andreas Röder v. Diersburg; Margarethe Magdalena, m. Schweickhard v. Schauenburg (d. 1518) (Kindler, *OG*, III, 147).
M. Rentier; seigneur.
Q. Fief of Bp. of Strasbourg (ADBR, G 503).
R. Strasbourg (AMS, KS 18, fol. 22ᵛ).
U. Father of HILTEBRANT v. M.; related to HEINRICH v. M. and to EGENOLF RÖDER v. DIERSBURG.

LXIX. *MÜNCH, Nicolaus (Claus)*

d. 1522 (AMS, KS 15, fols. 100ᵛ, 143ʳ)

A. Gerber (Hatt, p. 503).
C. 1509/10, 15/16 (Hatt, p. 503).
E. 1514-19 (AGCS, Comptes in Heilewog: "1514"; AMS, VI 495: "1518").
F. 1519-22 (Rott, "Artisanat," p. 161n14; AMS, KS 15, fols. 100ᵛ, 143ʳ; BNUS, Ms. 1058, fol. 125ʳ).
H. Hans M. (d. 1507), *Ratschreiber* of Strasbourg (BMS, Ms. 936, fol. 2ᵛ).

J.   Hans, m. Maria, daughter of CONRAD V. DUNTZENHEIM (BMS, Ms. 936, fol. 2^r; AMS, V 137/23).
K.   Margarethe Rülin of Truchtersheim (AMS, KS 15, fol. 229^v; BMS, Ms. 936, fol. 2^r).
L.   SEBASTIAN; Georg (d. 1583), m. Margarethe Gerbott; Claus; Anna, m. HANS V. ODRATZHEIM; Kunigunde, m. Christmann Herlin; Susanna, m. Georg Robenhaupt; Katharina, m. 1) Sebastian Kneibis, 2) PETER ARG, 3) Sebastian Gerbott, and 4) Georg Messinger; Ursula, m. Ulrich Geiger (Chelius), Dr. med. (AMS, KS 18, fol. 94^v; BNUS, Ms. 1058, fols. 64^v, 125^r; BMS, Ms. 936, fol. 2^v).
M.   Merchant or rentier.
P.   Wealthy enough to serve the commune "zu Ross"; moneylender, who left numerous interest-bearing rents to his children (Brant, p. 282; AMS, KS 17, fols. 15^v, 53^r; AMS, KS 18, fols. 9^{r-v}, 94^v; AMS, KS 21, fols. 32^v, 34^r).
U.   Father of SEBASTIAN MÜNCH; father-in-law of HANS V. ODRATZHEIM; related to CONRAD, BATT, and JACOB V. DUNTZENHEIM, to HANS LINDENFELS, to CLAUS KNIEBIS, to LUX MESSINGER, and to PETER ARG.

LXX.   *MÜNCH, Sebastian (Bastian)*
d. 10.XI.1578 (BMS, Ms. 936, fol. 2^r)

A.   Gerber to 1548; Maurer 1556–57; Zur Möhrin 1558–78, *Oberherr* (AMS, XXI 1546, fol. 624^r; Hatt, p. 503; AMS, VI 493/4, fol. 10^v; BMS, Ms. 936, fol. 2^r).
B.   Renounced 6.IX.1548; repurchased 1549 (AMS, KS 63/I, fol. 4^v; AMS, R 29, fols. 70^r–71^v).
C.   1556/57 (Hatt, p. 503).
D.   Ammeister 1558, refused as a fiefholder (AMS, VI 496: "1558").
E.   1546–48, 1555–56 (AMS, XXI 1546, fol. 591^v; AMS, KS 63/I, fol. 4^v; AMS, XXI 1555, fol. 494^{r-v}; Hatt, p. 666).
F.   1558–78 (AMS, XXI 1558, fol. 412^v; BNUS, Ms. 626, fol. 161^v; Hatt, p. 666).
H.   CLAUS M.; Margarethe Rülin of Truchtersheim.
J.   See under CLAUS MÜNCH.
K.   1) 1539 Katharina Thedinger, 2) Ursula Arg, and 3) Barbara, daughter of HANS LINDENFELS and widow of Lux Vogler (BNUS, Ms. 1058, fol. 125^r; AMS, KS 35/IV, fols. 103^r–106^r).
M.   Merchant; rentier.
P.   Inherited rents and lands from his father; moneylender to counts of Nassau–Saarbrücken 1533–47 (AMS, KS 17, fol. 15^v; AMS, KS 21, fols. 32^v, 34^r; ADBR, 25 J 43).
R.   Strasbourg; Truchtersheim (Seyboth, p. 111; Hefele, No. 1046).
U.   See under CLAUS MÜNCH.

LXXI.   *v. ODRATZHEIM, Hans, Jr.*
d. 16.VIII.1558 (AMS, XXI 1558, fol. 406^v)

A.   Weinsticher (Hatt, p. 508).

C.   1542/43, 48/49, 54/55, 58 (Hatt, p. 508).

E.   1548–53 (BNUS, Ms. 1058, fol. 140^v; AMS, XXI 1552, fol. 501^r; Hatt, p. 667).

F.   1553–58 (BNUS, Ms. 1058, fol. 140^v; AMS, XXI 1552, fol. 501^r; AMS, XXI 1558, fol. 406^v; Hatt, p. 667).

H.   Hans v. O., Sr. (1472–1530+); Kunigunde Ryff (d. by 1522); he remarried 1526 Salome Hess (BNUS, Ms. 1058, fol. 140^v; AMS, IX 1/6; AMS, KS 17, fol. 294^r).

J.   Ursula, m. Diebold Becherer; Susanna, m. Hans Storck, brother of Veltin S. (BNUS, Ms. 1058, fols. 140^v, 181^v).

K.   Anna, daughter of Claus Münch and sister of Sebastian M. (AMS, KS 17, fol. 225^v).

L.   Salome, m. Johann Caspar Eberhard; Kunigunde (BNUS, Ms. 1058, fol. 140^v).

M.   Wine merchant ("weinsticher") 1524; his father was a moneylender and dealer in grain and wine, who in 1522 deposed that he lived from investments and "trübt kheim gewerb" (AMS, VIII 132/90; AMS, KS 17, fols. 7^v–8^r, 21, 28, 47, 76^r, 79^{r-v}, 90^{r-v}, 109^v, 110^v, 110^v; AMS, IX, 1/6).

P.   Hans, Sr., deposed 1522 a worth of ca. 3,000 fl. (AMS, IX 1/6).

R.   Strasbourg; a château at Schiltigheim (AMS, KS 21, fol. 6^r; AMS, KS 27/II, fols. 16^r–17^r; PCSS, V, 400, No. 298).

U.   Son-in-law of Claus Münch; brother-in-law of Sebastian Münch and of Veltin Storck; related to Hans Lindenfels.

LXXII.   OTTFRIEDRICH, Bernhard   d. 1539 (Kindler, OG, III, 295)

A.   Constofel zum Mühlstein (Wittmer, No. 6293).

B.   Purchased 28.V.1513 (Wittmer, No. 6293).

C.   1519/20, 22/23, 26/27, 29/30, 35/36 (Hatt, p. 510).

D.   Stettmeister 1532 (Hatt, p. 590).

E.   1521–33 (AMS, R 26/1, fol. 2^v; Ann. Brant, No. 4491; Winckelmann, I, 88; Rott, "Magistrat," p. 113).

F.   1533–39 (AMS, VI 495).

G.   Noble family active in regime since late 13th century; this Bernhard was the last male Ottfriedrich (Hatt, p. 510; Kindler, OG, III, 295).

H.   Bernhard O. (d. 1472); Veronika, daughter of Friedrich Sturm and sister of Martin S. (Kindler, OG, III, 295; Wittmer, Nos. 2008, 3340).

J.   Christoph, canon of Allerheiligen Strasbourg; Heinrich (d. 1521), m. 1) Susanna Mans v. Husenburg, and 2) Christina Zorn; and 7 other siblings (Kindler, OG, III, 295; Kindler, GBS, pp. 241–242; ADBR, G 817/2, 4; Wittmer, No. 7545).

K.   1) Stephania Böcklin, and 2) Martha Wurmser v. Schäffolsheim, who remarried Heinrich v. Mülnheim (Kindler, OG, III, 295).

L.   Anna (d. 1536), m. Johann v. Mittelhausen (d. 1537); Susanna, m. 1) Petermann Truchsess v. Rheinfelden, and 2) Hans Jacob Widergrien v. Staufenberg (AMS, KS 15, fol. 132^r; Wittmer, No. 8746; Kindler, OG, III, 295).

M. Rentier.
Q. Fief at Virdenheim, Molsheim, and Quatzenheim of the Bp. of Strasbourg (ADBR, G 817/2, 4; ADBR, G 503).
R. Eckbrechtsweiler, Hoselnhurst (AMS, KS 20, fol. 238^v).
T. Zealous Evangelical (Sturm, p. 4; *ZW*, X, Nos. 946, 955, 986, 1031, 1042, and XI, Nos. 1159, 1166, 1168, 1235; "Imlin Chronik," p. 412).
U. Nephew of MARTIN STURM and first-cousin of FRIEDRICH, JACOB, and PETER STURM; father-in-law of HANS JACOB WIDERGRIEN v. STAUFENBERG; related by marriage to ADOLF v. MITTELHAUSEN.

LXXIII.   *PFARRER, Mathis*
                b. 24.II.1489 (BNUS, Ms. 1058, fol. 143^r; ADBR, 3B 1357)
                d. 19.I.1568 (Ficker–Winckelmann, I, 5)

A. Zum Freiburg to 1523; Weinsticher, *Oberherr* 1523–68 (AMS, VI 591/1; Hatt, p. 512; AMS, KS 18, fol. 173^v; AMS, III 12/3).
C. 1519/20, 24/25 (Hatt, p. 512).
D. Ammeister 1527, 33, 39, 45, 51, 57, 63 (Hatt, p. 624).
E. 1523–25 (Winckelmann, I, 88; Rott, "Magistrat," p. 113).
F. 1525–68 (AMS, KS 18, fol. 34^v; AMS, VI 589/6, fols. 51^r–59^r).
G. Family of unknown origin, active in regime only in this and preceding generations (Hatt, p. 512).
H. Heinrich (d. 1495), senator 1483/84; Dorothea Spirer (d. 1516) (BMS, Ms. 1024, fol. 98; BNUS, Ms. 1058, fol. 143^v; *Fragments*, No. 3973).
J. Dorothea, m. HANS HAMMERER; Veronika (d. 1499); Heinrich, "venditor pannorum," m. Margarethe N. (Lehr, III, 440; BNUS, Ms. 1058, fol. 143^v; AMS, KS 12, fol. 39^{r-v}; AMS, KS 11, fol. 163^r).
K. 1508 Euphrosine (d. 1561), daughter of Sebastian Brant (Winckelmann, II, 261; *Fragments*, No. 3964).
L. Six children, none of whom survived him, including Barbara, m. Nicolaus Hugo, son of CLAUS KNIEBIS (Lehr, III, 458).
M. Cloth merchant ("venditor pannorum") (AMS, KS 11, fol. 163^r).
N. 1539–58 in cloth trade with HANS HAMMERER (AMS, XXI 1539, fols. 325^v–326^v; AMS, KS 98/I, fol. 70^r).
P. He and his brother served "zu Ross"; his brother-in-law Onophrius Brant was a partner in the second Prechter firm (AMS, R 28, fol. 103^v; AMS, VI 591/1; Fuchs, "Prechter," p. 158).
R. Strasbourg; rented property from the city (ADBR, G 3652; Seyboth, p. 5; AMS, KS 16, fols. 230^r–232^r; AMS, KS 23/I, fol. 96^{r-v}; AMS, VII 1436, fols. 19^v, 68^r).
T. Evangelical by III.1523 (AST 176, fol. 404^{r-v}, communicated by Jean Rott).
U. Brother-in-law of HANS HAMMERER; father-in-law to son of CLAUS KNIEBIS; the sister of his wife was married successively to Peter Butz (d. 1531) and JACOB MEYER (Maurer).
V. MATHIS P. served more times (7) as ruling Ammeister than any other person in the history of the city.

LXXIV. *PRECHTER, Friedrich II* d. 5.X.1528 ("Imlin Chronik," p. 410)

A. Zum Spiegel; *kaiserlicher Rat* (Hatt, p. 514; AMS, I 5/15).

C. 1509/10 (Hatt, p. 514).

F. 1528 (Fuchs, "Prechter," p. 148).

G. The P. were a wealthy merchant-banking family of Hagenau, at Strasbourg since 1475; son WILHELM P. ennobled 26.VIII.1556, confirmed 31.V.1566; grandson Friedrich III P. entered Constofel zum
Hohensteg 1584 (Burg, p. 359; Riedenauer, p. 70; Kageneck,
pp. 389–390; Kindler, *OG*, I, 152–153).

H. Friedrich I P.; Susanna Pfeffinger (d. 1538) (Fuchs, "Prechter," p. 148;
BCGA, 1974, p. 85).

J. Susanna (d. 1551), m. Hans Ebel (d. 1543), parents of FRIEDRICH EBEL;
Clara (d. by 1525), m. ca. 1506 DANIEL MIEG; Christoph (d. 1562),
professor of law at U. of Marburg (Mieg, p. 17; Fuchs, "Prechter,"
pp. 147–149; Burg, "Les Brechter," p. 186).

K. Ursula, daughter of CONRAD v. DUNTZENHEIM, Jr. (Fuchs, "Prechter,"
p. 148).

L. Susanna, m. Heinrich Joham, first-cousin of CONRAD J.; Margarethe, m.
Friedrich V v. Gottesheim, uncle of FRIEDRICH VI v. G.; WILHELM
(d. 1563), m. Ursula König; Felicitas, m. 1) Ulrich Varnbühler, and
2) Daniel Wurmser v. Schäffolsheim; Ursula, m. Johann Ingold;
Veronika, m. Sebastian Mieg, son of CARL M., Sr.; Dorothea, m.
WOLF SIGISMUND WURMSER v. VENDENHEIM (Fuchs, "Prechter,"
pp. 147–149).

M. Merchant-banker.

N. Agent of the Fugger in Alsace; partner of Hans Ebel and other merchants;
agents in major centers of European trade (Fuchs, "Prechter,"
pp. 156–189).

Q. Hochfelden, a fief of the H.R.E. held in pledge with the Ebel since 1521
against a loan of 10,283 fl.; Breuscheck, since before 1528 a fief of
the counts of Eberstein (Fuchs, "Prechter," p. 190; *PCSS*, III,
256n1; Kindler, *OG*, I, 153).

R. Strasbourg; Renchen; Oberachern and Niederachern (Fuchs, "Prechter,"
pp. 189–192).

T. Roman Catholic, he and his wife were buried in the O.P. convent at
Frankfurt/M. (Kindler, *OG*, I, 153).

U. Brother-in-law of DANIEL MIEG and BATT and JACOB v. DUNTZENHEIM;
son-in-law of CONRAD v. DUNTZENHEIM, Jr.; uncle of FRIEDRICH
EBEL; father of WILHELM PRECHTER; related to CONRAD JOHAM,
FRIEDRICH VI v. GOTTESHEIM, and CARL MIEG, Sr.; father-in-law of
WOLF SIGISMUND WURMSER v. VENDENHEIM.

LXXV. *PRECHTER, Wilhelm* d. 26.I.1563 (Fuchs, "Prechter," p. 147)

A. Zum Spiegel; ennobled 26.VIII.1556, confirmed 31.V.1566 (Hatt, p. 514;
Riedenauer, p. 70).

B. Renounced 28.VIII.1548; purchased 1549 (Fuchs, "Prechter," pp. 152–
153).

C. 1555/56 (Hatt, p. 514).
E. 1548 (Fuchs, "Prechter," pp. 152–153).
G. See under FRIEDRICH II P.
H. FRIEDRICH II P. (d. 1528); Ursula v. Duntzenheim (d. ca. 1580).
J. See under FRIEDRICH II P.
K. Ursula König (d. ca. 1563) (Fuchs, "Prechter," pp. 147–149).
L. Friedrich III, m. 1572 Johanna v. Botzheim; Heinrich, m. Juliana v.
    Botzheim; Balthasar, m. Ursula Böcklin; Wilhelm, m. Ursula v.
    Rechberg; Margarethe, m. 1563 Johann Bernhard v. Botzheim
    (Fuchs, "Prechter," pp. 147–149).
M. Merchant-banker.
N. Partner of FRIEDRICH VI v. GOTTESHEIM and Balthasar and Sebastian
    Mieg; engaged in mines at Sainte-Marie-aux-Mines (Fuchs,
    "Prechter," pp. 158–159, 163–176).
R. See under FRIEDRICH II P.
U. Son of FRIEDRICH II P.; grandson of CONRAD and nephew of BATT
    and JACOB v. DUNTZENHEIM; nephew of DANIEL MIEG; first-
    cousin of FRIEDRICH EBEL.

LXXVI.   RÖDER v. DIERSBURG, Egenolf
                    b. 1475 (Becke–Klüchtzner, p. 370)
                    d. 13.VIII.1550 (AMS, XXI 1550, fol. 352^v)
A. Constofel zum Hohensteg (AMS, I 20a/2).
B. Acquired by marriage 26.VIII.1507; renounced 15.IX.1519; purchased
    26.V.1520 (Wittmer, Nos. 5700, 6900, 6911).
C. 1515/16, 19 (Hatt, p. 523).
D. Stettmeister 1518, 23/24, 26/27, 29/30, 32/33, 35/36, 38/39, 49/50 (Hatt,
    p. 607).
E. 1525–29 (AMS, R 29/224; Rott, "Magistrat," p. 113).
F. 1530–50 (Rott, "Un recueil," p. 796; PCSS, I, 507; Hatt, p. 607).
G. Principal vassals of the margraves of Baden since the High Middle Ages;
    no other Röder served in the regime of Strasbourg between 1360
    and 1638 (Theil, Lehnbuch, pp. 84–89; Hatt, p. 523).
H. Hans R. v. D. (1452–1516); Anna Schnewelin (d. 1517) or Anna v. Weier
    (d. 1514) (Kindler, OG, III, 570; Becke–Klüchtzner, p. 369).
J. Brigitte (d. by 1535), m. Jacob Wurmser v. Vendenheim, Jr. (d. by 1531),
    brother of BERNHARD W. v. V.; Magdalena (d. 1531), abbess of St.
    Stephan Strasbourg; Margarethe, m. 1) Heinrich v. Falkenstein,
    and 2) Wolf Erlin v. Rorburg; Martin (d. by 1520); Walburga and
    Anna, nuns at St. Marx Strasbourg; Anna m. after 1529 Hans v.
    Botzheim; Verena (d. by 1516), nun at Andlau (Kindler, OG, III,
    572).
K. 1) by 1507 Salome v. Mülnheim (d. 1531), daughter of Caspar v. M. and
    Gertrud Böcklin, sister of HEINRICH v. M. and widow of Georg
    Zorn v. Bulach, and 2) 1531 Clara v. Neuneck (1506–54), daughter of
    Heinrich v. N. and Magdalena Hüffel (AMS, KS 12, fol. 228^r;

AMS, KS 25, fols. 398ᵛ–400ʳ; Kindler, *OG*, III, 572; Becke-Klüchtzner, p. 554).

L. Magdalena (d. by 1536), m. 1523 Hans Caspar Knobloch; Ursula, m. 1) 1527 Melchior v. Schauenburg, and 2) 1534 Christoph Zuckmantel v. Brumath; Franz (ca. 1533–ca. 1575), m. ca. 1555 Martha Agathe Bettscholt; Katharina (d. 1584) m. ca. 1556 Georg Veit v. Wickersheim zu Pfaffenhofen (d. 1573); Amalia (d. by 1554); Claus (1541–1611), m. 1) 1569 Juliana v. Sulz, widow of Hans Jakob Remchingen, and 2) 1591 Anna Franziska v. Stein zum Reichenstein, widow of Johann Mattheus Mussler (Kindler, *OG*, III, 573).

M. Rentier; seigneur; soldier (Sturm, p. 4; Kindler, *OG*, III, 572).

P. A large rente purchased 1523 from Count Wilhelm v. Fürstenberg (AMS, KS 16, fols. 135ᵛ–136ʳ).

Q. Diersburg and other fiefs of margraves of Baden; fief of Bp. and Cathedral Chapter of Strasbourg (GLAK, 67/43–44, 46–47; ADBR, G 503).

R. Various properties in Baden; Strasbourg (Kähni, pp. 63–64; Baum, p. 169).

T. Son of an excommunicant; Evangelical from 1523–24, though most of his siblings remained Catholics, and some of his children became Catholics; reputed to have cast decisive vote in the abolition of the Mass II.1529; ca. 1534 introduced Evangelical clergy into his seigneuries (Kindler, *OG*, III, 572–573; Sturm, p. 4; "Imlin Chronik," p. 412; "Les éphémérides de Jacques de Gottesheim," p. 273; Büheler, *Chronique,* No. 239; F. Röder v. Diersburg, in *FDA*, 15 [1882], 227–228; *Ann. Brant*, No. 4779).

U. Brother-in-law of HEINRICH v. MÜLNHEIM; related to BERNHARD WURMSER v. VENDENHEIM.

LXXVII. *ROETTEL, Hans Ulrich (ULRICH, Hans)*
d. III.1522 (AMS, VI 488/3)

A. Fischer (Hatt, p. 560).

C. 1507/08, 15/16, 19/20 (Hatt, p. 560).

E. 1518–22 (AMS, VI 488/3; AMS, KS 13, fol. 134ᵛ).

G. Judging by the number of privy councillors, the Roettel or Ulrich were, after the Baldner, the most influential family in the guild.

H. ?Claus Ulrich "der fischer," XVer 1488–1504 (AMS, VI 488/3).

K. Margarethe Gimbrecht, daughter of Martin G., a cooper (BNUS, Ms. 1058, fol. 156ʳ; AMS, KS 13, fols. 47ᵛ–48ʳ).

L. Hans Ulrich, 1539 *Schaffner zu den Guten Leuten,* m. Agnes Tost; Agnes (d. 1531), m. 1523 Dr. Wolfgang Capito; Balthasar (AMS, XXI 1539, fol. 11ʳ; BNUS, Ms. 1058, fol. 156ʳ; AMS, KS 13, fol. 134ᵛ).

M. Fisherman ("piscator") (ADBR, H 27 [6]).

LXXVIII. *v. ROTWEIL, Hans Erhard, Sr.*
d. after 23.III.1531 (Winckelmann, II, 140)

A. Zum Encker; armiger (Hatt, p. 526; AMS, KS 10, fol. 255ᵛ).

C.   1524/25, 28/29 (Hatt, p. 526).
E.   1527–31 (AST 37, fols. 66ᵛ–67ʳ, 69ᵛ, 90ʳ⁻ᵛ).
G.   A family of armigerous rentiers in the guild Zum Encker; the male line
      extinct in 1559 (Kindler, *GBS*, p. 292).
H.   Hans Ludwig v. R.; Ottilia Brucher (BNUS, Ms. 1058, fol. 157ʳ).
K.   1) Salome Hammerer, sister of Hans H., and 2) Helene Geiger (d. ca.
      1525), sister of Mattheus G. and widow of Steffan Thoman (BNUS,
      Ms. 1058, fol. 157ʳ; AMS, KS 17, fol. 155ʳ).
L.   Hans Erhard, Jr. (d. 1559), m. Anna Geiger, daughter of Mattheus G.;
      Hans; Anna (BNUS, Ms. 1058, fol. 157ʳ; AMS, KS 17, fol. 155ʳ).
M.   Rentier.
P.   1525 his son's marriage agreement includes 800 fl.; Hans Erhard, Jr.,
      left most of the family property encumbered and an income of only
      100 fl./yr. (AMS, KS 17, fol. 155ʳ; AMS, V 138/25).
Q.   The *Botenlehen* from the Bp. of Strasbourg and the hereditary office of
      Pedell of the episcopal *Manngericht* (ADBR, G 503).
R.   Marlenheim (AMS, V 138/25).
U.   Son of Hans Wilhelm v. R.; brother-in-law of Hans Hammerer and
      Mattheus Geiger; his son married a daughter of Mattheus
      Geiger.

LXXIX.   *v. ROTWEIL, Hans Ludwig*
                              b. ca. 1458 (AMS, IX 1/6)
                              d. by II.1531 (AMS, KS 25, fol. 209ʳ⁻ᵛ)

A.   Zum Encker; armiger (Hatt, p. 526; AMS, KS 12, fol. 129ᵛ).
C.   1510/11, 14/15, 18/19 (Hatt, p. 526).
F.   1514–26 (AGCS, Comptes in Heilewog: "1514"; AMS, IX 1/6; Winckel-
      mann, II, 64, No. 27; AST 98/6; Rott, "Magistrat," p. 113).
G.   See under Hans Erhard v. R., Sr.
J.   Hans Wilhelm v. R., m. Merga Ingold, daughter of Claus I. (BNUS, Ms.
      1058, fol. 92ᵛ; Wolff, "Ingold," p. 114).
K.   1) Ottilia Brucher, and 2) 1528 Anna Rot (BNUS, Ms. 1058, fol. 157ʳ;
      AMS, KS 21, fols. 152ᵛ–153ʳ).
L.   Hans Erhard, Sr. (d. ca. 1531), m. 1) Salome Hammerer, sister of
      Hans H., and 2) Helene Geiger, sister of Mattheus G. (BNUS, Ms.
      1058, fol. 157ʳ).
M.   Rentier; from 1485 held various posts in civic territorial administration
      (Kindler, *GBS*, pp. 291–292).
P.   1522 deposed a worth of ca. 6,000 fl. (AMS, IX 1/6).
Q.   See under Hans Erhard v. R., Sr.
T.   1524 complained of poor health and seems to have resigned offices ca.
      1526, possibly because of the religious question (AST 35: "S.
      Margarethen").
U.   Uncle of the wife of Gottfried v. Hohenburg; father of Hans Erhard
      v. R., Sr.; father-in-law of sisters of Hans Hammerer and Mattheus
      Geiger; his brother married an aunt of Claus Ingold.

LXXX. RUMLER, *Caspar*
  d. 11./12.III.1563 (BNUS, Ms. 626, fol. 161^v; BNUS, Ms. 1058, fol. 158^v)

A. Zur Luzern (father's guild) to 1522; Zimmerleute 1527–63; armiger (Hatt, pp. 524, 528; AMS, KS 11, fol. 27^v).
C. 1517/18, 21/22, 27/28, 37/38 (Hatt, pp. 524, 528).
D. Ammeister 1543, refused as a fiefholder (Hertzog, VIII, 97).
E. 1525–48 (*Ann. Brant,* No. 4584; AMS, VI 495–496; Rott, "Magistrat," p. 113; Winckelmann, I, 88).
F. 1548–63 (AMS, XXI 1547, fol. 700^v; AMS, VI 589/6, fols. 57^r–59^r; AMS, VII 1438, fol. 110^v; *PCSS*, IV, 116, No. 851).
G. An armigerous family of rentiers in the guild Zur Luzern; politically active 1489–1563 (Hatt, p. 528).
H. Florentz R.; Ursula v. Bietenheim (AMS, KS 17, fol. 150^r; BNUS, Ms. 1058, fol. 21^r; Lehr, III, 461).
K. Agnes Meyer (AMS, KS 13, fol. 179^r).
M. Rentier.
P. He and his father active as moneylenders to peasants (AMS, KS 10, fols. 136, 256; AMS, KS 8, fols. 23^v, 102^r, 109^r, 113^r; AMS, KS 19, fols. 1–150).
Q. Unknown (Hertzog, VIII, 97).
R. Strasbourg and environs (AMS, KS 13, fol. 39^r; AMS, H 590, fol. 29^r; Seyboth, p. 73; AMS, KS 15, fols. 67^r–68^v, 144^v–145^r).
U. Son of Florentz R.; nephew of Sifridt v. Bietenheim.

LXXXI. RUMLER, *Florentz* d. 5./6.II.1525 (*Ann. Brant,* No. 4658)

A. Zur Luzern; armiger (Hatt, p. 528).
C. 1489/90, 93/94, 99/1500, 11/12 (Hatt, p. 528).
D. Ammeister 1501, 07, 13 (Hatt, p. 625).
F. 1502–20, resigned 1520 (AGCS, Comptes in Heilewog: "1514"; AMS, VI 495: "1518"; AMS, VI 492/1; *Ann. Brant,* Nos. 4517, 4658).
G. See under Caspar R.
K. Ursula v. Bietenheim, sister of Sifridt v. B. (Lehr, III, 461; BNUS, Ms. 1058, fol. 21^r).
L. Caspar, m. Agnes Meyer.
M. Merchant and/or rentier.
P. See under Caspar R.
Q. See under Caspar R.
R. See under Caspar R.
U. Father of Caspar Rumler; brother-in-law of Sifridt v. Bietenheim.

LXXXII. SCHETZEL, *Nicolaus (Claus),* called *Bocks Claus*
         d. ca. 1453 (AMS, IX 1/4)
         d. IV.1530 (E. Ungerer, II, 79)

A. Weinsticher? (Hatt, p. 533).
B. Acquired by marriage 4.IX.1488; native of Würzburg (Wittmer, No. 3969).
E. 1518–23 (AMS, VI 495: "1518"; Rott, "Magistrat," p. 113).

G. Immigrant from Würzburg.
H. Bock Schetzel (AMS, IX 1/4).
J. Hans, citizen 1491, senator 1524/25, m. Katharina Kipkorn (Wittmer, Nos. 2842, 4225; Hatt, p. 533).
K. 1488 Bärbel N., widow of Anthonj Spielmann (E. Ungerer, II, 79; Wittmer, No. 3969).
L. Salome, m. 1513 Hans Spiegelberg of Winterthur, a surgeon ("der scherer") (Wittmer, No. 6253).
P. Inventory of his estate 1530 includes livestock worth more than 5 lb., plus 11 fl. and 4 *kronen* in gold; moneylender to peasants (E. Ungerer, II, 79–80; AMS, KS 18, fols. 168^r–170^r); his step-daughter, Jacobe Spielmann, married 1506 the wealthy Nuremberg immigrant goldsmith, Erasmus Krug (Wittmer, No. 5629; Fuchs, "Nuremberg et Strasbourg," p. 87).
R. No real property in his estate (E. Ungerer, II, 79–80).

LXXXIII.   *SCHORP v. FREUDENBERG, Hans Jacob*
d. 8.XII.1558 (BNUS, Ms. 626, fol. 163^r)

A. Constofel zum Hohensteg (AMS, VI 496: "1557").
C. 1546/47, 49/50, 52/53, 56/57 (Hatt, p. 537).
E. 1552–58 (AMS, XXI 1558, fol. 645^v; BNUS, Ms. 626, fol. 163^r).
G. Kindler's account (*GBS*, p. 329), according to which the Schorp migrated to Strasbourg in 1495 from Freudenberg near Ragaz in the Grisons, is false; the Schorp were vassals of Baden by 1476 at the latest and appear in the region by 1453 (GLAK, 67/42, fol. 102^{r-v}; GLAK, 67/43, fols. 12^r–13^r, 153^{r-v}; *FUB*, VII, 448, No. 334).
H. Jacob S. v. F.; Ursula v. Dürnheim, who remarried Ludwig Völtsch (Kindler, *GBS*, p. 329; AMS, Livre de bourgeoisie III, col. 9).
K. N.N. (d. 1558) (AMS, XXI 1558, fol. 510^v).
L. Jerg; Melchior (AMS, Livre de bourgeoisie III, col. 9).
M. Rentier.
Q. Fief of a share of Schloss Staufenberg, from margraves of Baden (GLAK, 67/44, fols. 259^r–263^r).

LXXXIV.   *SCHÜTZ, Hans, Sr.*   d. 1533 (AMS, VI 495: "1533")

A. Schuhmacher (Hatt, p. 540).
C. 1520/21, 24/25, 28/29, 30/31 (Hatt, p. 540).
E. 1524–33 (AMS, KS 18, fols. 4^r, 31^r; AST 75, fol. 504; Rott, "Magistrat," p. 113).
J. Jacob (d. by 1525), m. Elisabeth Gerster; two of their daughters m. the preacher Mathis Zell and MICHAEL SCHWENCKER; Anna, m. Albert Haberer, a tailor; N., m. Barbara Keller, daughter of Hans Keller, *gen.* Volmar, a butcher (AMS, KS 18, fols. 16^v–17^v; AMS, KS 12, fol. 251^r; AMS, KS 22, fol. 80^v).
K. Margarethe Selig (or: Sloge) (AMS, KS 15, fol. 62^r; AMS, KS 17, fol. 242^r).
L. N. m. Jacob Breuscher; Hans, Jr. (AMS, KS 27/I, fols. 141^v–142^r).

M. Leather dyer ("lederferber"), tailor ("sutor") (AMS, KS 12, fol. 241^r; AMS, KS 17, fol. 242^r).
P. His son, Hans, Jr., belonged to the guild Zum Spiegel (ADBR, E 1356/1).
R. Strasbourg (AMS, KS 8, fol. 1^r; AMS, KS 15, fol. 62^r).
U. Uncle of the wife of MICHAEL SCHWENCKER.

LXXXV. *SCHWENCKER, Michael, Sr.*
d. 1.V.1556 (AMS, XXI 1556, fol. 183^v)

A. Zur Luzern (Hatt, p. 540).
B. Purchased 27.IV.1523; native of Gernsbach (Wittmer, No. 7263; AMS, KS 20, fol. 214^v).
C. 1543/44, 51/52 (Hatt, p. 540).
E. 1548–56 (AMS, XXI 1547, fol. 700^v; AMS, XXI 1556, fol. 183^v).
K. Elisabeth Schütz, daughter of Jacob S. and niece of HANS S., Sr. (AMS, KS 18, fols. 16^v–17^v).
L. Michael, Jr. (AMS, XXI 1554, fol. 275^r).
M. Notary, active at Strasbourg since 1518; employed in episcopal administration 1518–23; *Schaffner* of St. Clara auf dem Rossmarkt 1525 (AMS, KS 20, fol. 214^v; ADBR, G 2961; AMS, II 71/22; Wittmer, No. 7263; AMS, KS 18, fol. 16^v).
R. Dambach (AMS, VI 393/1; Vogt, "Propriété," p. 51).
S. University of Heidelberg 1505, bacc. art. 1506 (*Matrikel Heidelberg*, I, 455).
T. Closely connected with the reformer Wolfgang Capito; his wife was sister of Katharina Schütz, wife of the reformer Mathis Zell.
U. His wife was a niece of HANS SCHÜTZ, Sr.

LXXXVI. *SEBOTT, Diebold*   d. 1534 (AMS, VI 495)

A. Zur Steltz, *Oberherr* 1520–34 (Hatt, p. 541; BMS, Ms. 1024, fol. 74).
C. 1509/10, 15/16, 25/26 (Hatt, p. 541).
E. 1519–34 (BMS, Ms. 1024, fol. 74; AMS, VI 591/3, 2; AMS, VI 495).
G. The S. were, at least until the death of DIEBOLD S., for several generations the leading political family in the guild Zur Steltz (Hatt, p. 541; Brady, "Privy Councils," p. 75).
H. Ulrich S., goldsmith (AMS, KS 7, fol. 29^v; Rott, *Oberrhein*, I, 286; Hatt, p. 541).
J. Lamprecht, Sr., goldsmith and XVer (d. 1519), whose daughters m. Friedrich V v. Gottesheim, Bastian Joham of Saverne, Hans Krossweiler, "institor," and Balthasar König, a wealthy merchant (AMS, KS 13, fol. 2^r; ADBR, 3B 580).
L. Richardis, m. HERBART HETTER; Bastian (ADBR, H 1622, fols. 255^v–257^r).
M. Goldsmith (AMS, KS 15, fol. 38^v; Rott, *Oberrhein*, I, 223, 286).
P. In 1517 the only member of his guild to serve "zu Ross"; member of a prominent goldsmith family (AMS, VI 591/1; Rott, *Oberrhein*, I, 286).
R. Molsheim, Mutzig (AMS, KS 17, fols. 19^v–20^r, 88^r, 99^v).

U. Father-in-law of HERBART HETTER; a niece married the uncle of FRIED-
    RICH VI v. GOTTESHEIM, and another a cousin of CONRAD JOHAM.

LXXXVII. *SPENDER, Reimbolt*   d. 1534 (Schoepflin, V, 715)
A. Constofel zum Mühlstein; *Ritter* (AMS, I, 17–19/1).
B. Renounced 24.XII.1491 and 27.VI.1495; purchased 25.II.1493 and
    14.IV.1496 (Wittmer, Nos. 4227, 4315, 4635, 4661).
C. 1508, 14/15, 20/21 (Hatt, p. 546).
D. Stettmeister 1523/24, 26/27 (Hatt, p. 590).
F. 1521–30, resigned by 1533 (*Ann. Brant,* Nos. 4411, 4508; AST 35: "St.
    Claire en Woerth"; AMS, VI 495; Rott, "Magistrat," p. 113).
G. One of Strasbourg's oldest patrician families, politically active since
    1231; extinct in the male line 1534 (Hatt, p. 546; Schoepflin, V, 715).
H. Claus S., armiger (AMS, KS 7, fol. 11^r).
J. Hans (d. by 1526), *Ritter*; Claus; Walther (AMS, KS 20, fol. 125^{r-v};
    AMS, I, 17–19/1, fol. 1^r).
K. Margarethe v. Kageneck, sister of PHILIPS v. K. (AMS, KS 20, fols.
    156^r–157^v).
L. Anna, m. Ludwig Wolf v. Renchen (AMS, KS 22, fol. 208^{r-v}).
M. Rentier.
Q. Fief of the Bp. of Strasbourg (ADBR, G 503).
R. Bischheim (AMS, KS 16, fol. 186^v).
U. Brother-in-law of PHILIPS v. KAGENECK; his niece married PETER
    ELLENHART.

LXXXVIII. *STÄDEL, Christoph II*
                            b. 1504 (BNUS, Ms. 1058, fol. 186^r)
                            d. 12./13.V.1554 (AMS, XXI 1554, fol. 151^r)
A. Zur Steltz (Hatt, p. 547).
C. 1543/44, 51/52 (Hatt, p. 547).
E. 1541–54 (AMS, XXI 1541, fol. 390^v; AMS, XXI 1554, fol. 151^r; Hatt,
    p. 671).
G. A famous Strasbourg goldsmith family, politically active from 1529 into
    the 18th century (Hatt, "Staedel," pp. 225–231; Hatt, pp. 547–548).
H. Christoph I S.; 1497 Anna Bertsch, sister of Frantz B., an apothecary
    (BNUS, Ms. 1058, fol. 186^r; AMS, KS 27/II, fol. 30^r).
J. Affra, m. HANS STÖSSER; and 14 others (BNUS, Ms. 1058, fol. 186^r).
K. Margarethe Schott, daughter of Lorentz Schott, tanner, and Elisabeth
    Storck (Hatt, "Staedel," p. 226).
L. Christoph III (d. 1585), m. 1) Barbara Krossweiler, 2) Katharina Schertz-
    heimer; David, who on 17.XII.1569 murdered his brother, Jacob
    (Hatt, "Staedel," pp. 226–227; Lehr, III, 464; BNUS, Ms. 1058,
    fol. 186^r; *Fragments,* No. 4053).
M. Goldsmith (AMS, KS 27/II, fols. 30^r–33^v; Rott, *Oberrhein,* I, 286).
N. The male Städel of this era were all goldsmiths, and their children tended
    to marry children of other goldsmiths (Hatt, "Staedel," pp. 226–
    227).

P. Commodity rentes in the region of Kochersberg (Vogt, "Städel," p. 58).
R. Strasbourg (Seyboth, p. 36; Hatt, "Staedel," p. 226).
U. Brother-in-law of HANS STÖSSER; related by marriage to VELTIN STORCK.

LXXXIX. *STORCK, Valentin (Veltin)* d. 1561 (BNUS, Ms. 626, fol. 162^r)

A. Gerber (Hatt, p. 550).
C. 1533/34, 39/40, 45/46 (Hatt, p. 550).
E. 1543–59, resigned offices 1559 (AMS, XXI 1559, fol. 2^r; Hatt, p. 634).
G. Family at Strasbourg since 1452, politically active 1533–1678, mainly from *Gerberzunft*; armigerous by grant from emperor Rudolph II on 12.VII.1579 (*DGB*, LXXX, 519–520; BMS, Ms. 936, fol. 4^r; Hatt, pp. 550, 672).
H. Conrad, senator 1485 (*DGB*, LXXX, 520; Lehr, III, 467).
J. Hans, m. Susanna, sister of HANS V. ODRATZHEIM; Elisabeth, m. Lorentz Schott, parents of wife of GEORG LEIMER; and three others (BNUS, Ms. 1058, fol. 181^v; *DGB*, LXXX, 520).
K. Anna Christmann of Dangolsheim (d. 1578) (AMS, KS 147, fol. 262; BNUS, Ms. 1058, fol. 181^v; Winckelmann, II, 64, No. 28; *DGB*, LXXX, 520).
L. Valentin, Jr., m. 10.I.1552 Agnes, daughter of AUGUSTIN DRENSS; Peter (1554–1627), XVer, XIIIer, Ammeister, m. 28.II.1581 Genoveva Baumgartner (b. 1558), daughter of Hermann B., merchant, and Genoveva, sister of HANS HAMMERER (BNUS, Ms. 1058, fol. 181^v; *DGB*, LXXX, 520).
M. Saddler ("sellator") (AMS, KS 8, fol. 196^r).
P. Moneylender to peasants (AMS, KS 8, fol. 183^r; AMS, KS 12, fols. 70^r, 74^r, 141^r, 179^v, 212^v, 249^v; AMS, KS 63/II, at 1.IX.1549).
R. Bergbietenheim (AMS, XXI 1560, fol. 61^r).
U. Related to HANS V. ODRATZHEIM, AUGUSTIN DRENSS, GEORG LEIMER, CHRISTOPH II STÄDEL, and HANS HAMMERER.

XC. *STÖSSER, Hans* d. 15.II.1558 (BNUS, Ms. 626, fol. 162^r)

A. Zum Spiegel (Hatt, p. 550; ADBR, E 1356/1).
C. 1549/50 (Hatt, p. 550).
E. 1551–58 (AMS, XXI 1551, fol. 324^r; BNUS, Ms. 626, fol. 162^r; Hatt, p. 672).
G. Merchant family active politically 1494–1626; the surviving sons of HANS S., Hans, Balthasar, Jacob, Friedrich, and Caspar, ennobled Prague 20.VIII.1584, although they did not move from the guild Zum Spiegel to a Constofel (Frank, IV, 61; Hatt, p. 550).
H. Veltin S., cooper, of Bernsweiler; Clara Wullmann (BNUS, Ms. 1058, fol. 176^v; Wittmer, No. 3003).
J. Moritz? (d. by 1532), m. Agnes N. (Winckelmann, II, 264).
K. 1) Aurelia Kirchhofer, daughter of Conrad K., merchant, and 2) Affra Städel, sister of CHRISTOPH S. (BNUS, Ms. 1058, fol. 176^v).

L. 1) Margarethe, m. 1) Daniel Vogel, 2) MICHAEL HEUSS, and 3) Sebastian
    Wurmser v. Schäffolsheim; Aurelia, m. Mattheus Weicker, Am-
    meister 1576, 82, 88; Martha, m. SEBASTIAN JUNG; Anna, m. 1553
    Werner Ferber (d. 1599); Johann Jacob, m. Susanna v. Molsheim;
    Friedrich, m. Salome Mürsel; and 3 others;
    2) Ursula, m. Jacob Meyer of Hagenau; Walpurgis, m. Nicolaus Braun;
    Salome, m. Gottfried v. Hohenburg, grandson of GOTTFRIED v. H.;
    Barbara, m. 1) Daniel Obrecht, and 2) Caspar Kniebis, grandson of
    CLAUS K.; Caspar David, m. Emilia Gerbel, daughter of Dr. Nico-
    laus G.; Apollonia, m. Mattheus Stöffler; and 3 others (BNUS, Ms.
    1058, fol. 176^v).
M. Cloth merchant ("Tuchmann") (Winckelmann, II, 256; Vogt, "Les
    rentes," p. 670).
N. Lorraine (AMS, III 135/1).
P. Important supplier of grain; 1555–57 moneylender to peasants; borrowed
    from the city (Fuchs, "L'espace économique," p. 312; Vogt, "Les
    rentes," pp. 670–671; AMS, VII 10/28).
R. Neuhof; the Gantzau; extensive woodlands (Wunder, Landgebiet,
    pp. 33–34, 36–37; AMS, V 2/18–20; PCSS, V, 400).
S. Spoke and read French (AMS, II 84b/6 and 9).
U. Brother-in-law of CHRISTOPH STÄDEL; father-in-law of MICHAEL HEUSS
    and SEBASTIAN JUNG; his children married grandchildren of
    GOTTFRIED v. HOHENBURG and CLAUS KNIEBIS.
V. His son, Hans, was Württemberg Amtmann und Vogt at Blamont 1550
    (HStAS, A 149/2).

XCI. STURM, Friedrich   d. 10.XI.1562 (BNUS, Ms. 626, fol. 161^v)

A. Constofel zum Mühlstein (AMS, VI 495: "1520").
C. 1520/21, 38/39, 42, 50/51 (Hatt, p. 552).
D. Stettmeister 1553/54, 56/57, 60, 62 (Hatt, p. 609).
E. 1550–53 (AMS, XXI 1550, fol. 503^v; AMS, XXI 1553, fol. 387^v).
F. 1553–62 (AMS, XXI 1553, fol. 387^v; BNUS, Ms. 626, fol. 161^v).
G. See under MARTIN STURM.
H. MARTIN S.; Ottilia v. Köllen.
J. See under MARTIN STURM.
K. Unmarried (Büheler, Chronique, No. 533).
M. Rentier; seigneur.
P. See under MARTIN STURM.
Q. See under MARTIN STURM; family Lehenträger 1521–62.
R. Strasbourg; Molsheim (Ann. Brant, No. 3535; AMS, KS 18, fol. 250^v).
U. Son of MARTIN S.; brother of JACOB and PETER S.; cousin of STEPHAN
    and HANS S.; cousin of HEINRICH v. MÜLNHEIM and ULMAN and
    WOLFGANG BÖCKLIN v. BÖCKLINSAU, and of DANIEL MIEG.

XCII. STURM, Hans   d. 1536 (Winckelmann, II, 255, No. 77)

A. Constofel zum Mühlstein; armiger (Wittmer, No. 7291; AMS, KS 23/II,
    fol. 45^v).

B. Renounced 15.I.1520; purchased 18.VIII.1523 (Wittmer, Nos. 7115, 7118, 7291).
C. 1528/29, 31/32 (Hatt, p. 552).
D. Stettmeister 1534/35 (Hatt, p. 609).
E. 1531–36 (AMS, VI 488/10; Winckelmann, II, 255, No. 77).
G. See under MARTIN S.; descended from a collateral line and not closely related to the other Sturm.
H. Hans S. v. Sturmeck (d. by 1505), Stettmeister 1482–86; Sophia Kress v. Kogenheim (*FUB*, IV, 360–361, No. 395; AMS, KS 8, fol. 80^r; AMS, KS 15, fol. 154^v; Lehr, III, 419).
M. Rentier.
U. See under MARTIN S., his second cousin.
V. In Palatine service 1518 (Krebs, "Die kurpfälzischen Dienerbücher," No. 2756).

XCIII. *STURM, Jacob*   b. 10.VIII.1489
                            d. 30.X.1553 (Ficker–Winckelmann, I, 6)

A. Constofel zum Mühlstein (AMS, I 20a/2).
C. 1524/25 (Hatt, p. 552).
D. Stettmeister 1527/28, 30/31, 33/34, 36/37, 49/50 (Hatt, p. 610).
E. 1525–26 (*Ann. Brant*, No. 4702).
F. 1526–53 (*Ann. Brant*, No. 4702; Specklin, *Collectanées*, No. 2401).
G. See under MARTIN S.
H. MARTIN S.; Ottilia v. Köllen.
J. See under MARTIN S.
K. N. Bock v. Gersteim (d. ca. 1529), daughter of HANS B. v. G. (*BSCMHA*, N.S. 9, p. 86; AMS, AA 407a/8).
L. None.
M. Rentier; seigneur.
P. Owned various small rentes and probably inherited, with his brothers, his mother's rentes (AMS, KS 14, fol. 23^r; AMS, KS 16, fols. 57^v–61^v; AMS, KS 23/I, fols. 77^r–79^r).
Q. See under MARTIN S. and FRIEDRICH S.
R. See under MARTIN S. and FRIEDRICH S.
S. University of Heidelberg 1501, bacc. art., via ant. 1503; University of Freiburg i.Br. 1504, mag. art. 1505, theology 1504–ca. 1509; spoke neither French nor English (*Matrikel Heidelberg*, I, 442; *Matrikel Freiburg*, I, 157, No. 26; PCSS, IV, 312, No. 291).
T. Evangelical since ca. XI.1523 (Ficker–Winckelmann, II, 48).
U. Son-in-law of HANS BOCK v. GERSTHEIM; see under MARTIN S. and FRIEDRICH S., his father and his brother.

XCIV. *STURM, Martin*   d. X.1521 (Rott, "Magistrat," p. 109, No. 35)

A. Constofel zum Mühlstein; armiger (AMS, I 20a/2).
C. 1502/03, 08/09, 12/13, 15/16 (Hatt, p. 553).
E. 1506–21 (Brant, p. 246; AGCS, Comptes in Heilewog: "1514"; Rott, "Magistrat," p. 109, No. 35).

G. A prominent patrician family of Strasbourg since the late 13th c.; this branch became extinct in the male line with the deaths of Martin's sons; the entire family became extinct in the male line in 1640 (Kindler, *GBS*, pp. 72–73; Hatt, pp. 552–553).

H. Friedrich S. (d. 1476), armiger, senator 1447–55 (Lehr, III, 419; Schoep-flin, II, 671; Hatt, p. 552).

J. Ludwig (d. 1516), m. Anna v. Endingen (d. 1516); Ottman (d. 1521), *Ritter* (knighted on the field of Nancy 1476), m. 1) Apollonia Völtsch, and 2) Margarethe Pfeffinger (d. after 1528); Veronika, m. Bernhard Ottfriedrich (d. 1472) (Lehr, III, 419–420; Kindler, *GBS*, pp. 72–73; Grandidier, V, 366–367; Kraus, p. 516).

K. Ottilia v. Köllen, daughter of Peter v. K. and Ottilia Schott, and grand-daughter of Peter I Schott (d. 1504) (AMS, KS 16, fol. 57^v).

L. FRIEDRICH (d. 1562), unmarried; JACOB (d. 1553), m. N. Bock v. Gerst-heim, daughter of HANS B. v. G.; PETER (d. 1563), unmarried; Veronika (d. 1581), unmarried; Clara, nun at St. Margarethe Stras-bourg 1508–24; Anna, m. 1) Hans Jakob Zorn v. Plobsheim, and 2) Caspar v. Hanau; Stephan (d. by 1526) (Büheler, *Chronique*, No. 533; Lehr, I, 93; AMS, AA 407a/8; Wittmer, No. 6457; Rapp, *Réformes et Réformation*, p. 520; Baum, p. 124n4; ADBR, 12J 2022/15; ADBR, E 2764/[1]).

M. Rentier; seigneur.

P. Creditor of counts of Mörs–Saarwerden 1505–13; owned numerous rentes (Herrmann, I, No. 1590; AMS, KS 9, fols. 108^v–109^r; AMS, KS 10, fols. 283^v, 289^v–290^r; AMS, KS 16, fols. 57^v–61^v; *RUB*, V, 518–519).

Q. Fief of the H.R.E.; fief of Bp. of Strasbourg at Düppigheim; fief of the Palatine Elector at Nordheim; fief of lords of Rappoltstein at Kitzelsheim (GLAK, 44/818; GLAK 67/1011, 1013, 1016, 1023, 1057–1058; ADBR, G 503; AMS, AA 1552; ADBR, G 802–804; ADBR, 3B 1484; ADBR, 12J 2006; ADBR, 16J 154).

R. Seigneury, chateau, and village of Breuschwickersheim; Achenheim; Düttelnheim (Wolff, p. 34; Wunder, "Verzeichnis," p. 63; AMS, KS 12, fols. 101^r–103^r; AMS, KS 20, fols. 53^r–54^r).

S. Patron of Jacob Wimpheling and of Strasbourg literary sodality (Rapp, *Réformes et Réformation,* p. 447).

U. Father of FRIEDRICH, JACOB, and PETER S.; uncle of STEPHAN S.; cousin of HANS S.; uncle of BERNHARD OTTFRIEDRICH; related to DANIEL MIEG, HANS BOCK v. GERSTHEIM, and HEINRICH v. MÜLNHEIM.

XCV. *STURM, Peter*
  d. 5./6.VII.1563 (Ficker–Winckelmann, I, 8; "Imlin Chronik," p. 433)

A. Constofel zum Mühlstein (AMS, I, 20a/2).

C. 1524/25, 27/28, 30/31, 33/34, 36 (Hatt, p. 553).

D. Stettmeister 1539/40, 42/43, 45/46, 48/49, 51/52, 53, 56/57 (Hatt, p. 610).

E. 1533–63 (AMS, VI 495: "1533"; AMS, XXI 1559, fol. 266^v).

G. See under MARTIN S.

H.   MARTIN S.; Ottilia v. Köllen.

J.   See under MARTIN S.

K.   Unmarried (Büheler, *Chronique*, p. 533).

M.   Rentier; seigneur.

P.   See under MARTIN S. and JACOB S.

Q.   See under MARTIN S. and FRIEDRICH S.

R.   See under MARTIN S. and FRIEDRICH S.

S.   University of Freiburg i. Br. 1506; University of Heidelberg 1509, law; Scholarch 1533–63 (*Matrikel Freiburg*, I, 172; *Matrikel Heidelberg*, I, 472; AMS, XXI 1553, fol. 387ᵛ).

T.   Evangelical; defended Girolamo Zanchi against the conservative Lutherans (*Zurich Letters*, 2nd series, p. 99, No. 43).

U.   See under MARTIN S. and FRIEDRICH S.

XCVI.   *STURM, Stephan*   d. 31.V.1578 (AMS, VIII 186, fol. 23ʳ)

A.   Constofel zum Mühlstein (AMS, I, 20a/2).

B.   Renounced 28.VIII.1548; purchased IX.1550 (AMS, KS 63/I, fol. 3ᵛ; AMS, XXI 1550, fol. 387ʳ).

C.   1536/37, 39/40, 42/43, 45/46, 48, 51 (Hatt, p. 553).

D.   Stettmeister 1554/55, 57/58, 60/61, 63/64, 66/67, 69/70, 72/73, 75/76, 78 (Hatt, p. 590).

E.   1546–48 (AMS, XXI 1546, fol. 4ᵛ; AMS, KS 63/I, fol. 3ᵛ; the year 1542 by Hatt, p. 634, is an error).

F.   1562–77 (BNUS, Ms. 626, fol. 161ᵛ; Hatt, p. 673).

G.   See under MARTIN S.

H.   Ottman S. (d. 1521), *Ritter*, brother of MARTIN S., Stettmeister 1484–1512; Margarethe Pfeffinger (Lehr, III, 420; AMS, KS 17, fol. 111ᵛ).

J.   Hans; Ludwig; Ott, m. Veronika Wurmser v. Schäffolsheim (d. 1565); Veronika, m. Jerg Fessler v. Arnsberg (d. by 1524) (AMS, Livre de Bourgeoisie III, col. 52; AMS, KS 16, fol. 187ʳ⁻ᵛ; Lehr, III, 229, 419–420).

K.   Veronika Völtsch, daughter of Reimbolt V. v. Stützheim and Salome v. Mülnheim (Lehr, III, 420–421).

L.   Hugo (d. 1616), Stettmeister 1587–1615, m. 1) Katharina v. Brumbach, and 2) Anna Margarethe v. Eltz; Veronika, m. Conrad Joham v. Mundolsheim, grandson of CONRAD J.; Friedrich (d. ca. 1604); Wernher (d. 1593) (GLAK, 44/818; Lehr, III, 421).

M.   Rentier; seigneur.

Q.   Succeeded FRIEDRICH S. as family *Lehenträger* and inherited the properties of the sons of MARTIN S. (Hertzog, VI, 278–280; Schoepflin, IV, 582).

R.   See under MARTIN S. and FRIEDRICH S.

U.   First cousin of FRIEDRICH, JACOB, and PETER S.; nephew of MARTIN S.; cousin of HANS S.; related to SIFRIDT v. BIETENHEIM and DANIEL MIEG.

XCVII.   *WETZEL v. MARSILIEN, Jacob*   d. after 1555 (ADBR, G 503)

A.   Constofel zum Hohensteg (AMS, I, 20a/3).

B. Purchased 23.XII.1528; renounced 28.VIII.1543 (Wittmer, No. 8740; AMS, VI 495; AMS, XXI 1543, fol. 385^{r-v}).

C. 1533/34, 36/37, 40/41 (Hatt, p. 568).

E. 1536–43 (*Ann. Brant,* No. 5129; AMS, VI 496; Hatt, p. 634).

G. See under MARTIN W. v. M.

H. Heinrich W. v. M.; Margarethe v. Andlau (ADBR, 12J 2022/4; Lehr, III, 205).

J. Reimbold; Philipp (d. before 1539), m. Brigitte v. Bergheim; Johann (d. ca. 1539), canon at Old St. Peter Strasbourg; Salome, unmarried (Lehr, III, 205; AMS, XXI 1539, fol. 354^{r-v}; AMS, KS 63/I, fol. 3^{r}; ADBR, 12J 2022/4; ADBR, E 6033/1–4).

K. 1) Salome v. Mülnheim, and 2) Clara v. Hatstatt (Lehr, III, 205).

L. Nicolaus, m. Apollonia v. Wattweil; Kunigunde (d. 1566), abbess of St. Stephan Strasbourg (ADBR, E 6033/5; Lehr, III, 205).

M. Rentier.

P. 1545 loaned 1,000 fl. to the Elector Palatine (GLAK, 67/1013, fols. 457^{r}–458^{v}).

Q. Fief from Bp. of Strasbourg; fiefs at Eckbolsheim, Wolfisheim, and Bischofsheim from counts of Hanau–Lichtenberg; a chateau at Quatzenheim (ADBR, G 503; ADBR, E 6033/1–4; AMS, XXI 1539, fol. 354^{r-v}).

T. A pronounced interest in theology led him to consult Melchior Hoffman; he was an enemy of Bucer's and may have been a Roman Catholic; for not entirely apparent reasons connected with his views, he was placed under a loose house arrest and later resigned his offices and renounced his citizenship (*TQ Strassburg,* I, 288, and II, 357, 368; AMS, XXI 1541, fols. 126^{v}, 173^{r-v}; AMS, XXI 1542, fol. 158^{v}; AMS, XXI 1543, fol. 385^{r-v}).

U. Cousin of MARTIN W. v. M., whose grandfather was the brother of his father.

XCVIII. *WETZEL v. MARSILIEN, Martin*
d. 24.I.1554 (AMS, Livre de Bourgeoisie I, fol. 248)

A. Constofel zum Hohensteg (AMS, I, 20a/3).

B. Renounced 28.VIII.1548 (AMS, KS 63/1, fol. 3^{r}).

C. 1540/41, 44/45, 53/54 (Hatt, p. 568).

E. 1548 (AMS, XXI 1548, fol. 365^{v}; AMS, KS 63/I, fol. 3^{r}).

G. A noble family whose original seat was at Appenweier in the county of Horburg; very active in regime of Strasbourg during the 14th c. but rarely during the 15th century; MARTIN's grandfather and the father of JACOB, W. v. M. were brothers; the genealogy by Lehr, II, 205, is incorrect (Schoepflin, IV, 180; Hatt, p. 568; ADBR, 12J 2022/4).

H. Jacob W. v. M., armiger (d. 1524/25); Katharina Mieg, daughter of Jacob M. (Lehr, III, 205; BNUS, Ms. 1058, fol. 121; AMS, KS 17, fols. 159^{r}, 166^{v}; Wittmer, No. 5431).

J. Juliana, m. Christoph Schnewelin; Beatrix, m. Johann Theobald Rebstock; Maxima, m. 1) Ptolemy v. Brumbach, and 2) Jacob v.

Brumbach; Jenapha (AMS, KS 23/II, fol. 79^r; BNUS, Ms. 1058, fol. 121^v).

K. Ursula Zorn zum Riet, daughter of JACOB Z. z. R. and Elisabeth Mussler (ADBR, E 2775/23; BNUS, Ms. 1058, fol. 121^v; Lehr, III, 205).

L. Maria, m. 1557 Gladi Böcklin v. Böcklinsau (AMS, Livre de Bourgeoisie II, col. 124; BNUS, Ms. 1058, fol. 121^v).

M. Rentier: seigneur.

Q. Fief of Bp. of Strasbourg; fief of counts of Hanau–Lichtenberg (ADBR, G 503; ADBR, E 6033/2–4).

R. Neuweiler (ADBR, E 2024).

T. 1544–47 there was a Catholic priest beneficed in the chapel of his *Hof* at Strasbourg (Barth, in *AEA*, 6 [1955], p. 79, No. 30, and p. 81, No. 51).

U. Cousin of JACOB W. v. M.; nephew of ANDREAS MIEG; son-in-law of JACOB ZORN ZUM RIET.

XCIX. *WIDERGRIEN v. STAUFENBERG, Hans Jacob*
d. 6.XI.1551 (AMS, XXI 1551, fol. 352^r)

A. Constofel zum Mühlstein (AMS, I 20a/2).

C. 1541/42 (Hatt, p. 569).

D. Stettmeister 1544/45, 47/48, 50/51 (Hatt, p. 611).

E. 1542–50 (AMS, XXI 1542, fol. 424^v; AMS, XXI 1550, fol. 503^v).

F. 1550–51 (AMS, XXI 1550, fol. 503^v; AMS, XXI 1551, fol. 352^r).

G. Family perhaps of Strasbourg origin, principal vassals of the margraves of Baden since at least the 14th century; this man was the only member of his family who ever held high office at Strasbourg (Theil, *Lehnbuch,* pp. 101–103; Hatt, p. 569).

H. Johann Friedrich W. v. S.; Beatrix v. Berckheim (Lehr, III, 423; Fuchs, *Documents,* No. 1298).

J. Gervasius (d. by 1545) (AMS, KS 55/II, fols. 1^r–3^r).

K. 1) Susanna Ottfriedrich, daughter of BERNHARD O., and 2) Margarethe Gretter (Kindler, *GBS,* pp. 421–422; Lehr, III, 423; AMS, XXI 1558, fols. 135^v–136^v).

L. Susanna, m. Heinrich v. Mülnheim v. Rosenburg; Bersabe, m. Ludwig Fessler v. Arnsberg; Hester (d. 1585), m. Blasius v. Mülnheim–Rechberg; Maria (d. 1613), m. 1) Dietrich v. Ratsamhausen, and 2) Hans Caspar v. Ratsamhausen–Ehenweier; Judith, m. 1561 Mathias Mönch v. Löwenburg; and 2 others (Fuchs, *Documents,* No. 1116; Kindler, *GBS,* p. 422).

M. Rentier; seigneur.

Q. Fief of the Bp. of Strasbourg; fief at Staufenberg of margraves of Baden; fief at Meissenheim from counts of Mörs–Saarwerden (ADBR, G 503; GLAK, 67/46, fols. 229^r–236^r; Herrmann, I, No. 1493).

R. Strasbourg; leased chateau of Fürsteneck from city of Strasbourg (Seyboth, p. 115; Wunder, *Landgebiet,* p. 47).

U. Son-in-law of BERNHARD OTTFRIEDRICH; related through the Fessler v. Arnsberg to STEPHAN STURM; related to HILTEBRANT v. MÜLNHEIM.

C. *WINICH, Johann (Hans)*   b. 21.X.1488
                                 d. 22.IX.1541 (BNUS, Ms. 847, fol. 10ᵛ)
A. Zum Freiburg 1533; Schuhmacher 1534–41 (AST 75, fol. 492; Hatt, p. 570).
C. 1534/35 (Hatt, p. 570).
E. 1533–40 (BNUS, Ms. 847, fol. 10ᵛ; AMS, VI 495: "1533"; AMS, XXI 1540, fol. 352ʳ; Hatt, p. 634).
L. Apollonia (1517–78), m. 1538 Jakob Wencker (d. 1567) (BNUS, Ms. 847; L. Dacheux, "Notice sur la famille Wencker," *BSCMHA*, N.S., 15, cvi–cvii).
M. 1506 official of Cathedral Chapter of Strasbourg; *Schaffner* of the Great Hospital of Strasbourg 1520–41 (*BCGA*, 1 [1968], p. 1; Winckelmann, I, 136, 136n6).

CI. *WOLFF, Claus*   d. ca. 1520
A. Gartner (Hatt, p. 573).
C. 1494/95, 1502/03, 10/11, 18/19 (Hatt, p. 573).
E. 1514–20 (AGCS, Comptes in Heilewog: "1514"; AMS, VI 495: "1518," "1520").
L. Jacobe, m. 1520 Stephan Gassener of "Gretz," a furrier (Wittmer, No. 7033).
M. Gardener, tanner ("gartner vnd geruer") (Wittmer, No. 7033).

CII. *WURMSER v. VENDENHEIM, Bernhard*
                                 d. 27.VI.1540 (Ficker–Winckelmann, I, 3)
A. Constofel zum Hohensteg; *Ritter* (AMS, XXI 1540, unnumbered folio before fol. 1).
B. Renounced 28.XII.1504; purchased 12.VIII.1508; renounced 14.X.1525; purchased 7.V.1528 (Wittmer, Nos. 5402, 5820, 8041, 8598).
D. Stettmeister 1520/21, 24/25, 30/31, 33/34, 36/37, 39/40 (Hatt, p. 590).
E. 1524–25, 1528–31 (*Ann. Brant,* Nos. 4548, 4574; Rott, "Magistrat," p. 113; AMS, VI 488/10).
F. 1532–40 (AMS, VI 495; *PCSS*, II, 158).
G. Strasbourg merchant family ennobled Rome 6.IV.1452; divided by 1500 into Vendenheim and Schäffolsheim lines; extremely active politically from the mid-15th century until the French Revolution (Riedenauer, p. 70; Kindler, *GBS*, pp. 437–438; Hatt, pp. 574–576, 612, 675–676; Frank, IV, 248).
H. Jacob W., Stettmeister 1509–16; Agnes Erlin v. Rorburg (Lehr, III, 230; Hatt, p. 590).
J. Nicolaus (1473–1536), *Dr. iur. et theol.,* Dean of St. Thomas Strasbourg; Magdalena, a nun; Erhard, m. Barbe v. Schauenburg; Jacob, m. Brigitte Röder v. Diersburg, sister of EGENOLF R. v. D.; Ursula, m. Claus Böcklin v. Böcklinsau, father of ULMAN and WOLFGANG B. v. B.; Caspar, m. Susanna Joham, daughter of CONRAD J.; Ottilia; Wolfgang (d. 1529), mercenary captain and father of WOLF SIGIS-

MUND W. v. V., m. Ursula v. Truchtersheim (Lehr, III, 230; AMS, KS 18, fol. 47^r; *QBLG*, II, 142).

K. 1) N. Büchsner, 2) Susanna Mieg, sister of CARL M., Sr., and 3) Agnes Berer, daughter of Claus B. and sister of the wife of ALEXIUS BÜCHSNER (AMS, KS 16, fol. 97^{r-v}; AMS, KS 27/I, fols. 170^r–172^r; Lehr, III, 230).

L. Maria, m. Heinrich v. Mülnheim; Agnes, m. Johann Albrecht v. Kippenheim; Elisabeth, m. Conrad v. Kippenheim; Balthasar, m. 1) Maria Zorn, and 2) Ursula v. Lichtenfels; Katharina, m. PHILIPS v. KAGENECK; Columba, m. Ludwig v. Wittersheim; Magdalena; Wolf Jacob (Lehr, III, 230; Hefele, No. 1028).

M. Rentier; seigneur; soldier.

P. Creditor of counts of Mörs–Saarwerden 1505–18 (Herrmann, I, No. 1591).

Q. Fief of the H.R.E. at Vendenheim; fief of the Bp. of Strasbourg (ADBR, G 503; Fritz, p. 108).

R. The Schutterwald, sold to Strasbourg 1501; Oberschäffolsheim; Bossendorf (AMS, VII 84/20; Wunder, "Verzeichnis," pp. 63, 64; AMS, XXI 1539, fol. 57^r).

T. Probably Evangelical by 1524, although known to have been a moderate, and his departure from the city 1525–28 is suspicious (Rott, "Nuremberg et Strasbourg," p. 100).

U. Uncle of WOLF SIGISMUND W. v. V., of ULMAN and WOLFGANG BÖCKLIN v. BÖCKLINSAU, and of CARL MIEG, Jr.; brother-in-law of CARL MIEG, Sr.; father-in-law of PHILIPS v. KAGENECK; related to EGENOLF RÖDER v. DIERSBURG, CONRAD JOHAM, ALEXIUS BÜCHSNER.

V. He played a major role in diplomacy during the Peasants' War 1525, when the peasants called him "the red-bearded knight of Strasbourg" (Rott, "La Guerre des Paysans," p. 27 and note 77).

CIII. *WURMSER v. VENDENHEIM, Wolf Sigismund*
         d. 14./15.II.1574 (AMS, VIII 186, fol. 23^r; AST 70/1, fol. 52^r)

A. Constofel zum Mühlstein (AMS, VI 496: "1557").

B. Renounced VIII.1548 and repurchased 1549 or 1550 (Pastorius, p. 171).

C. 1552/53 (Hatt, p. 576).

D. Stettmeister 1555/56, 58, 61/62, 64/65, 67/68, 70/71, 73/74 (Hatt, p. 612).

E. 1554–56 (AMS, XXI 1554, fol. 231^r; AMS, XXI 1555, fols. 508^r–509^r).

F. 1556–74 (AMS, XXI 1555, fols. 508^r–509^r; BNUS, Ms. 626, fol. 161^v; Hatt, p. 675).

G. See under BERNHARD W. v. V.

H. Wolfgang W. (d. 1529), mercenary soldier and brother of BERNHARD W. v. V.; Ursula v. Truchtersheim (Lehr, III, 233).

K. Dorothea Prechter, daughter of FRIEDRICH II PRECHTER (Fuchs, "Prechter," pp. 147–149; Lehr, III, 233).

L. Hans Jacob (d. 1610), m. Susanna Joham v. Mundolsheim, grand-

daughter of CONRAD J.; Ursula, m. 1) Bernhard Friedrich Widergrien v. Staufenberg, and 2) Georg Baumann (Lehr, III, 233).

M. Rentier; seigneur.

Q. Fiefs at Vendenheim and Meienheim from Bp. of Strasbourg; family
    Stammgut at Vendenheim (ADBR, G 503; ADBR, E 1251/1).

T. Anti-Calvinist; received Roman Catholic sacrament on his deathbed
    (Horning, p. 189; Büheler, *Chronique*, No. 501).

U. Nephew of BERNHARD W. v. V.; son-in-law of FRIEDRICH and brother-
    in-law of WILHELM PRECHTER; related to HANS JACOB WIDER-
    GRIEN V. STAUFENBERG.

CIV. *ZORN ZUM RIET, Jacob*   d. 13.XI.1531 (*Ann. Brant,* No. 4951)

A. Constofel zum Hohensteg (AMS, IX 1/4).

B. Acquired by marriage 14.X.1499 (Wittmer, No. 4958).

C. 1507/08, 13/14, 19 (Hatt, p. 581).

D. Stettmeister 1525/26, 28/29, 31 (Hatt, p. 614).

E. 1525?–31 (*Ann. Brant,* Nos. 4625, 4633, 4634, 4951; Rott, "Magistrat,"
    p. 113).

G. A cadet line of the enormous Zorn clan, active politically at Strasbourg
    1439–1548 (Hatt, pp. 581, 614; Kindler, *GBS,* p. 448).

H. Bechtold Z. z. R. (d. 1479), Stettmeister 1463–68 (Kindler, *GBS,* p. 448).

J. Bernhard; LUDWIG (d. ca. 1529) (Kindler, *GBS,* p. 448).

K. 1499 Elisabeth Mussler, widow of Caspar Knobloch (Wittmer, No.
    4958; AMS, KS 13, fol. 152^r).

L. Claus (d. 1551), Stettmeister 1542–48; Ursula, m. MARTIN WETZEL V.
    MARSILIEN (d. 1554); Kunigunde, m. Jerg Zorn (Kindler, *GBS,*
    p. 448; ADBR, E 2775/23).

M. Rentier; seigneur.

N. Partner of Conrad Kirchhofer, merchant, 1524 (AMS, KS 17, fol. 31^{r-v}).

P. Moneylender to peasants; guarantor of a debt of 500 lb. 1527 (AMS, KS
    12, fol. 151^r; AMS, KS 15, fol. 96^r; AMS, KS 21, fol. 35^r).

Q. Fief of the Bp. of Strasbourg (ADBR, G 503).

R. Wolfisheim, held in pledge from count of Hanau–Lichtenberg 1522–
    31; Ernolsheim; Breuschwickersheim; Matzenheim; Strasbourg
    (ADBR, E 2775/18–19; AMS, KS 14, fol. 45^v; ADBR, 3B 1484;
    Fuchs, *Documents,* No. 511; AMS, KS 16, fols. 227^v–230^r; Seyboth,
    p. 17).

T. Evangelical by 11.VII.1525 ("Les éphémérides de Jacques de Gottes-
    heim," pp. 269–270).

U. Brother of LUDWIG Z. z. R.; father-in-law of MARTIN WETZEL V.
    MARSILIEN.

CV. *ZORN ZUM RIET, Ludwig*   d. ca. 1529 (AMS, KS 23/II, fol. 184^v)

A. Constofel zum Hohensteg (AMS, VI 495: "1520").

C. 1501/02, 05/06, 09/10, 17/18 (Hatt, p. 581).

E. 1507–24 (Brant, p. 287; AGCS, Comptes in Heilewog: "1514"; AMS,
    VI 495: "1518," "1520"; AST 35: "Augustiner").

G. See under JACOB Z. z. R.
H. Bechtold Z. z. R. (d. 1479), Stettmeister 1463–68 (Kindler, *GBS*, p. 448).
J. Bernhard; JACOB (d. 1531) (Kindler, *GBS*, p. 448).
M. Rentier; seigneur.
Q. See under JACOB Z. z. R.
R. See under JACOB Z. z. R.
T. Apparently resigned offices ca. 1524/25, possibly because of the religious
        struggle (AST 35: "Augustiner").
U. Brother of JACOB Z. z. R.

APPENDIX B

Ranking of ten politically most active patrician families at Strasbourg,
1449–1600, at 38-year intervals, based on their shares (in %) of all
patrician offices (A) and of the office of Stettmeister only (B)

In the following lists, the 152-year period 1449–1600 is divided into four
equal periods. The first division point (1486/87) coincides roughly with the
final revision of the constitution (1482), the second (1524/25) with the chief
crisis of the Reformation, and the third (1562/63) with the ultimate longevity
of the Reformation generation. "Family" is taken here in the broad sense of
those sharing a common family name, so that the various lines of the Zorn
(Zorn zum Riet, Jung Zorn, Lapp Zorn, Zorn von Bulach, etc.) are grouped
under "Zorn," the Wurmser von Schäffolsheim and von Vendenheim under
"Wurmser," and the Bock von Bläsheim and von Gerstheim under "Bock."
    In each period, the Column A shows the shares of the leading ten families in
the offices of patrician senator and Stettmeister together; and the Column B
shows the shares in the office of Stettmeister alone. The figures are all percent-
ages, which seemed necessary as the total number of office-terms varies among
the periods. Thus, a figure of 9.7 under Column A means that the family in
question furnished the incumbent in 9.7% of all the annual terms of senators
and Stettmeister in the designated period. Each year is considered separately,
although in fact the senators and Stettmeisters *normally* served two-year terms.

I. 1449–86.

	A.				B.		
	1.	v. Mülnheim	12.1		1.	v. Mülnheim	28.4
	2.	Ellenhart	9.7		2.	Bock	13.5
	3.	Bock	8.5		3.	Böcklin	12.8
	4.	Sturm	6.7		4.	Zorn	10.1
	5.	Zorn	6.0		5.	Hüffel	8.1
	6.	Hüffel	6.0		6.	Burggraff	6.3
	7.	Böcklin	5.8		7.	v. Endingen	5.4
	8.	Lentzel	3.7		8.	Sturm	4.0
	9.	Burggraff	3.5		9.	Zum Rust	3.4
	10.	Völtsch	3.1		10.	v. Kageneck	2.7
			———				———
			54.3%				94.9%

II. 1487–1524.

A.			B.		
1.	Böcklin	13.1	1.	Böcklin	19.1
2.	Sturm	8.4	2.	Bock	15.8
3.	v. Mülnheim	7.4	3.	Sturm	11.8
	Wurmser	7.4	4.	Berer	9.7
5.	Bock	6.8	5.	v. Endingen	9.2
6.	Zorn	6.6	6.	Wurmser	7.2
7.	Völtsch	5.8		Völtsch	7.2
8.	Spender	5.5	8.	Spender	5.3
9.	Berer	5.3		Zorn	5.3
10.	Ellenhart	5.0	10.	Ellenhart	4.6
		71.3%			95.4%

III. 1525–62.

A.			B.		
1.	Sturm	17.4	1.	Sturm	25.5
2.	v. Mülnheim	9.8	2.	v. Mülnheim	13.8
	Wurmser	9.8	3.	Wurmser	12.4
4.	Böcklin	7.1	4.	Böcklin	9.0
5.	v. Mittelhausen	6.3	5.	Bock	8.3
6.	Zorn	5.3		Zorn z. Riet	8.3
7.	Bock	4.8		Röder v. Diersburg	8.3
8.	Röder v. Diersburg	3.2	8.	Widergrien v. Staufenberg	4.1
	Wetzel v. Marsilien	3.2	9.	v. Kageneck	4.0
10.	Büchsner	2.9	10.	Ellenhart	2.8
		69.6%			96.4%

IV. 1563–1600.

A.			B.		
1.	Joham v. Mundolsheim	12.9	1.	Joham v. Mundolsheim	20.4
2.	Sturm	11.1	2.	Sturm	13.8
3.	Wurmser	10.8	3.	Bock v. Erlenburg	9.9
4.	Böcklin	6.1		v. Kettenheim	9.9
5.	v. Kettenheim	5.0	5.	Wurmser	8.6
6.	Bock v. Erlenburg	4.8	6.	v. Mülnheim	6.6
7.	Prechter	4.2		Mieg v. Boofzheim	6.6
8.	Mieg v. Boofzheim	4.0	8.	Böcklin	4.6
9.	Büchsner	3.7		v. Mittelhausen	4.6
	Rechburger	3.7		Zum Trübel	4.6
		66.2%			89.5%

APPENDIX C

Vassals of the Bishop of Strasbourg, 1511–57. Based on the Lists of Vassals called to Meetings of the Bishop's Manngericht *at Molsheim*

The following alphabetical list includes names and dates of all persons mentioned in the extant lists of vassals called to the episcopal feudal court between 1511 and 1557, plus a few entries not in the lists but noted in accompanying documents. These documents are now in ADBR, G 501–503. The following notations in the documents are reproduced here:

(+)= a cross next to the name for that year; probably means that the vassal was reported to have died;

(−)= the name is stricken for that year.

Four other commonly appearing remarks are reproduced: "nit beschryben," "kranck," "obijt" or "todt," and "zu empfahen." The latter expression means that the person named was yet to be invested with the fief.

Where a (+) appears for one year but the same name appears in the next list, I have not divided the entries into two persons—except where I know them to be two persons with the same Christian name(s). Where the name is missing in one or more lists after that in which a (+) appears, but the same name appears again in later lists, I have assumed that two persons are involved and have divided the entries accordingly. Also noted are entries for persons who acted as feudal proxies ("lehenträger") for others.

The utility of the lists is limited by several things. First, the irregular holding of the *Manngericht* means that there are numerous gaps in the lists, including several extensive ones. The most serious is the nine years from 1523 until 1532, although other major gaps appear between 1532 and 1537 and between 1544 and 1551. Secondly, the vassals listed here are only the family *Lehenträger* of the episcopal vassal families, presumably the eldest males in each generation. Orthographically, I have standardized various forms of Christian names but have reproduced the families names as they appear in the sources.

Two other remarks about the use of the sources seem in order. First, for 1511 and 1548, I have used correspondence concerning the *Manngericht*, as the rolls are not extant. Secondly, the list here cited as (1516) is undated and is assigned that date by the hand of a modern archivist. The list certainly belongs after 1511 and is more likely to fall in the years 1512–16 than in the years after 1516; a comparison of death dates suggests that the most likely year may be 1513, but I have nonetheless retained the conventional dating and placed it in parentheses to indicate its uncertainty.

A

v. Adeltzheim, Martin, 1522, 23, 32, 37, 40, 51, 54, 55, 57(+).
Zeisolf, 1511, (16), 22(+).

ALTORFF *gen.* WOLLSCHLEGER, Jacob, 1554 (obijt).
                    Jörg, 1548, 51.
                    Philips, (1516), 20, 22, 23, 32(+).
                    Philips, 1537, 40, 44.

v. ANDLAU, Alexander, 1544, 54, 55, 57.
                Arbogast, 1520, 22, 23, 32, 37, 40.
                Batt Morandt, 1555, 57.
                Bernhard, *Ritter,* (1516), 20, 22.
                Eberhard d. Ält., 1520, 22(—).
                Eberhard d. Jüng., 1520, 22, 23.
                Friedrich, 1520, 22, 23.
                Hans, *Ritter,* 1520.
                Hans, *Ritter*, 1551, 54 (obijt).
                Hertwig, *Ritter,* 1511.
                Jerg, 1520, 22, 23.
                Rudolff Meinolff, 1520, 22, 23, 32, 37, 40, 44.
                Rulannd, 1520, 22, 23.
                Sigmund, 1520, 22, 23.
                Wolff, (1516).

B

v. BACH, Jerg, (1516), 20, 22, 23, 32, 37.
BAPST v. BOLSENHEIM, Hans Jacob, 1551, 54, 55, 57.
                        Jacob, (1516), 20, 22, 23, 32(+).
                        Lutelman, 1537, 40, 44.
BARPFENNIG, Caspar, for the Matzenheim fief, 1532, 37.
BAUMANN, Mattheus, (1516).
BEGER, Mathis, 1532(+).
BEGER v. GEISPOLSHEIM, Jacob, *Ritter,* (1516), 20(+), 22(+).
v. BERCKHEIM, Hans Jacob, *Ritter,* (1516), 20, 22, 23.
              Jacob, 1540, 44, 51, 55, 57.
v. BERN, Jacob, 1555, 57.
        Jörg, (1516), 20, 22, 23, 32, 37, 40, 44, 51, 54(obijt).
v. BERSTETT, Adam, 1523, 32, 37, 40, 44, 54, 55, 57.
             Hug, (1516), 20, 22(+).
v. BIETENHEIM, Sifridt, 1523, 44.
BOCK, Friedrich, 1544, 54(obijt).
        Hans, *Ritter,* (1516), 20, 22, 23, 32, 37, 40.
        Ludwig, 1551, 54, 55, 57.
BOCK v. ERLENBURG, Eucharius, 1520, 22, 23, 32(+).
                Eucharius, 1537, 40, 44, 51.
                Jörg Wirich, 1555, 57.
BOCK zu HAGENAU, Jacob, (1516).
BÖCKLIN, Claudius, (1516).
          Haman, 1520, 22(+).
          Ludwig, *Ritter,* 1523.

Philips, 1532, 37, 40, 44.
Ulman, 1554, 55, 57.
Wirich, *Ritter,* (1516).
v. BOLLWEILER, Hans, 1544, 48.
v. BOLSENHEIM, Conrad Dietrich, 1520, 22, 23, 32(+).
Jacob, (1516).
BONNER IM ZOLLKELLER, Andreas, (1516).
BOTZHEIM, Dr. Bernhard, 1540, 44, 51, 54, 55, 57.
Conrad, 1532, 37, 40, 44, 51, 54, 55, 57.
Conrad Wolff, 1520(−), 22, 23.
Conrad Wolff, 1544(+).
Michel, 1511, (16).
Michel, 1544, 48, 51(kranck), 54, 55, 57.
Wilhelm, 1522, 23.
BRACK v. KLINGEN, Anthonj, 1544, 54, 55, 57.
Erpf, 1540.
Hans, (1516), 20, 22, 23, 32(+), 40.
v. BRANDECK, Balthasar, (1516).
BRAUN, Adolf, zu Strassburg, 1557.

C/K

v. KAGENECK, Fridolin, 1551, 54, 55, 57.
Hilarius, 1532(−).
Philips, (1516), 20, 22, 23, 32, 40, 44.
Reimbolt, 1511(todt), (16).
Reimbolt, 1554(−).
KALLENRETTER, Martin, 1544.
CHRISTOFF, Reyn, 1544.
KLETT v. UTTENHEIM, Hans Jacob, 1540, 44, 51, 54, 55, 57.
KNOBLOCH, Hans Jacob, for sons of Wolff Füll, 1537, 40.
KÖNIGSBACH *gen.* NAGEL, Hans, (1516), 20, 23.
Hans Jacob, 1540, 44, 51, 54, 55, 57.
KORNER, Jacob, 1555, 57.
Jerg, 1544(nit beschryben).
CRANTZ v. GEISPOLSHEIM, Alexander, 1540, 44(+).
Hertwig, 1544(zu empfahen).
Wilhelm, 1554, 55, 57.
Wolff, (1516), 20, 22, 23, 32.
CREMER, Dietrich, 1540.
v. CRONBERG, Hartmut, 1544, 48, 55.
Philips, 1551.
KYL, Paulus, for Philips v. Waltenheim, 1537.

D

DAUN v. LEININGEN, Eberhart, 1523, 32(+).

Friedrich, 1554, 55, 57(+).
Philips, 1520, 22, 23.
Reinhart, 1511, (16).
Reinhart, 1537, 40.

E

ECKBRECHT V. DÜRCKHEIM, Chun, 1537, 40, 44, 51, 54, 55, 57.
　　　　　　　　　　Hertwig, (1516), 20, 22, 23, 32(+), 37, 40.
　　　　　　　　　　Wolff, (1516), 20, 22, 23.
v. ENDINGEN, Hans Balthasar, 1511, (16), 20(+).
　　　　　　Hans Rudolf, 1554, 55, 57.
　　　　　　Thoman, 1520, 22, 23, 32, 37, 40, 44.
v. ENNINGEN, Bernhard, 1532, 40.
v. ENTZBERG, Jerg, (1516), 22, 23.
ERSTHEIM *gen.* ARMBRUSTER, Felix, 1522, 23, 32, 37, 40, 44, 51, 57.
　　　　　　　　　　Lorentz, 1520.
　　　　　　　　　　Ulrich, (1516).
v. ETTENDORF, Eraclius, (1516), 20(+), 22(+), 23(+), 32(+).
　　　　　　Hans, 1554, 55, 57.

F

FEIG V. EYSTETT, Jacob, 1511, (16), 20, 22, 23, 32(−).
v. FLECKENSTEIN, Friedrich, 1532(+).
　　　　　　　　Friedrich, Jr., 1537, 40, 44, 48, 51, 54, 55, 57.
　　　　　　　　Heinrich, (1516).
　　　　　　　　Jacob, 1520, 22, 23.
　　　　　　　　Ludwig, 1511, 32(+).
　　　　　　　　Nicolaus, (1516), 22(+).
FÜLL, Wolfgang, (1516), 20, 22, 23, 32.
FÜLL V. GEISPOLSHEIM, Heinrich, 1554, 55, 57.

G

GOSS V. OBEREHNHEIM, Bernhard, 1532, 40, 44, 51, 54, 55, 57.
　　　　　　　　Landolff, 1520, 22, 23.

H

HAFFNER, Wolfgang, (1516), 20(+), 22(+).
HAFFNER V. WASSELNHEIM, Wolff, 1532, 37, 40, 44, 51, 54, 55, 57.
v. HAMMERSTEIN, Adolff, 1532(+).
HASS V. LAUFEN, Heinrich (der Pfaltzen Cantzler), 1554, 55, 57.
v. HATSTATT, Claus, 1544, 51, 54, 55, 57.
　　　　　　Friedrich, 1544, 51.
HELD, Abraham, for the Bietenheim, 1554(nit beschryben).

v. Helmstatt, Wyprecht, 1511, (16)(+).
Henner, Bastian, (1516).
Hoffwart v. Kirchheim, Adam, 1532, 37, 40.
        Adam, 1554, 55, 57.
        Hans, *Ritter*, (1516), 20.
v. Hohenstein, Jörg, (1516), 20(+), 22(+), 23(+), 32(+).
v. Holtz, Hans Jerg, 1537, 40, 44, 48, 51(todt).
        Hans Sifridt, 1532(+).
v. Hundsbach, Reynard, (1516).
v. Hündtingen, Carlin, 1544, 48.
        Hans, 1548.
        Heinrich, (1516).
        Heinrich, 1532, 37, 40, 44.

I/J

v. Ingenheim, Florentz, 1555, 57.
        Hans, (1516).
        Wolff, (1516), 20, 22, 23, 32(+), 37, 40, 44, 51.
Joham, Conrad (zu Strassburg), 1544, 51 (kranck).
        Diebold, 1554, 55, 57.
Jörger, Maximilian, 1544, 54(nit beschryben), 57.

L

v. Lampertheim, Hans, 1554, 55, 57.
v. Landenberg, Rudolff, 1544, 48, 54, 55, 57.
v. Landsberg, Hans Jerg, 1532, 37, 40, 44.
        Jerg, 1532, 37, 40.
        Jacob, (1516), 20, 22, 23.
        Dr. Jacob, 1532(+), 37.
        Sebastian, 1544(+).
        Wolff, (1516), 20, 22, 23.
        Wolff Dietrich, 1554, 55, 57.
v. Landsberg zum Schramberg, Hans, 1537, 40(+).
Laubgass, Gilg, 1523(−), 54, 55, 57.
v. Lützelburg, Bernhard, 1555, 57.
        Friedrich, (1516), 20, 22, 23, 32, 37, 40, 44, 51(+).

M

Marx v. Eckwersheim, Adolf, 1554, 55, 57.
        Hans Jacob, 1551.
        Jacob, 1537, 40, 44, 48(kranck).
        Jerg, *Ritter,* (1516), 20, 22, 23.
        Jerg, (1516), 20, 22, 23, 32.
        Mathis, 1537, 40.

v. Matzenheim, Hans, 1520, 22, 23.
        Hans Jacob, 1544, 48(todtlich krank), 51, 54.
        Jacob, (1516).
        Jörg, (1516).
Mey, Reinhart, 1520, 22, 23.
Meyer v. Sasbach, Claus, (1516), 20, 22, 23, 32, 37, 40(+).
v. Mittelhausen, Adolf, (1516), 20, 23, 32(+).
        Adolf, 1537, 40.
        Adolf, for the Ramstein, 1554, 55, 57.
        Adrian, 1557.
        Hans, 1522, 23, 32(+).
        Jeronimus, 1544(todt).
        Simon Wecker, 1548, 54(obijt).
v. Mülnheim, Assmuss, 1532, 37, 40, 44.
        Blasius, (1516), 20, 22, 23.
        Caspar, 1554, 55, 57.
        Christoph, 1540, 44, 51, 54, 55, 57.
        Daniel, 1511, (16), 20, 22, 23, 32.
        Heinrich, 1544, 51, 54(jst nit mer trager).
        Hilteprant, 1532, 37, 40, 44, 51, 54, 55, 57.
        Jerg, 1523, 32, 37, 40.
        Ludwig, (1516), 20, 22, 23.
        Wendling, (1516), 20, 22, 23.
        Wolff, (1516), 20, 22, 23, 32(+), 37, 40.
Münch v. Wilsberg, Anthonj, (1516).
        Christoff, 1544(+).
        Conrad, (1516), 20, 22, 23, 32(+).
        Conrad, Jr., 1523, 32, 37, 40, 44, 51(+).
        Jacob, 1537, 40.
Mussler, Elisabeth, Heinrich M.'s widow, (1516).
        Reimbolt, (1516), 20, 22, 23.
        Hans Mattheus, 1532, 37, 40, 48, 51, 54, 55, 57.

N

v. Neuenstein, Gebhart, 1544.
        Hans Jerg, 1557.
v. Nippenburg, Hans, 1520, 23, 32(+).
        Hans Jacob, for his mother, 1537, 40, 44, 48, 51, 54, 55, 57.

O

v. Oberkirch, Jacob, (1516), 20, 22, 23, 32(+).
        Sifrid, 1537, 40, 44, 48, 51, 54, 55, 57.
Offweiler, Friedrich, (1516).
Ottfriedrich, Bernhard, 1522, 23, 32.
        Heinrich, (1516), 22(+).

P

PFAFFENLAPP, Appollinaris, 1554, 55, 57(+).
          Conrad, (1516), 20, 22, 23.
          Diebold, 1532, 37, 40.
          Michel, 1544(todt).
PFAU v. RÜPPUR, Arnold, (1516), 20, 22, 23.
v. PRIFT, Hans, 1544, 51, 54, 55, 57(+).
PLERFELL, Conrad (lehentrager der Schindtenbubel), 1544.

Q

QUINTNER v. SAARBURG, Jacob, (1516), 20, 22, 23.
          Ludwig, 1532, 37, 40, 44, 51, 54, 55, 57.

R

v. RAMSTEIN, Hans Jacob, 1544, 48, 51.
          Philips, (1516), 20, 22, 23, 32(+), 37, 40(kranck).
v. RATHSAMHAUSEN, Albrecht, 1532(+).
          Egenolff, (1516).
          Hans Heinrich, (1516), 20, 22, 23.
          Hans Jerg, 1540, 44, 48, 51, 54, 55, 57.
          Samson, 1532, 37(−).
          Wolff, 1520, 22, 23, 32.
v. RATHSAMHAUSEN ZUM STEIN, Jacob, 1540, 44, 51, 54.
          Jörg, (1516), 20, 22, 23.
          Ulrich, 1520, 22, 23, 32, 37, 40.
REBSTOCK, Gabriel, (1516), 20, 22, 23, 32(+), 37, 40, 44, 51, 54(obijt).
          Hans Diebold, 1511(+), 32(−).
RECHBERG v. HOHENRECHBERG, Hans, 1511, (16), 20(+), 22(+).
          Hans, 1523, 32(+).
RECHBURGER, Leupold, 1544, 51, 54, 55, 57.
v. REINACH, Ludwig, 1544, 48, 51, 54, 55, 57.
v. RENDTINGEN, Melchior, 1522, 32, 37, 40, 44, 51, 54, 55, 57.
v. REUTTELHAUSEN, Hans, (1516), 20.
RITTER, Philips, (1516), 22(+).
RITTER v. HAGENAU, Anthonj, 1532, 40, 44.
          Anthonj, 1554, 55, 57.
          Jacob, 1520, 22, 23.
RITTER v. URENDORF, Cosmas, (1516), 20, 23, 32.
          Damian, 1537 (jst nit beschryben).
          Hans Caspar, 1544, 51, 54, 55, 57.
v. RIXINGEN, Blicker, 1520, 22, 23.
          Jerg, 1511, 32(+).
ROHART v. NEUENSTEIN, Gebhart, (1516), 20, 22, 23, 32(+), 37, 40, 44.
          Jacob, 1551(kranck).

Romeler v. Bliensweiler, Anthonj, (1516).
              Bernhard, 1544, 54(nit beschryben).
v. Rosenburg, Balthasar, 1523, 44, 54(obijt).
v. Rosenfeld, Jörg, 1511.
v. Rotenburg, Reimbold, 1554(obijt).
             Reinhart, 1551.
v. Rottberg, Jacob, 1544, 48(kranck), 51, 54, 55, 57.
v. Rottenburg, Bliecker, 1555, 57 (obijt).
              Heinrich Pliecker, (1516), 20, 22, 23, 32, 37, 40.
              Jacob Pliecker, (1516), 20, 22, 23.
v. Rotweil, Hans Erhart (*Pedell*), (1516), 20, 22, 23.
            Hans Erhart, Jr., 1532, 37, 40, 44, 51, 54, 55, 57.
Ryster zu Dambach, Jacob (1516).

S

v. Schauenburg, Bernhard, Jr., 1554, 55, 57.
             Claus, Sr., 1523, 32, 44.
             Claus, 1551.
             Hans Friedrich, 1544.
Schenck, Ludwig, 1554, 55, 57.
Schindtenbub, Dietrich, (1516).
             Heinrich, 1555, 57.
             Valerius, 1523.
Schlempf, Eucharius, (1516), 20, 22, 23, 32(+), 37.
Schnewelin *gen.* Bernlap v. Bolsweiler, Hans Christoffel, 1532, 44, 51, 54, 55, 57.
v. Schonau, Hans Othmar, 1551, 54(obijt).
          Jerg, 1532(+).
          Melchior, 1555, 57.
Schonmans [Mans], Wilhelm, (1516), 20(+), 22(+), 23(+), 32(+).
v. Sebach, Jost, 1532, 37, 40, 44, 51, 54, 55.
Sebe(?), Friedrich, 1522(−).
v. Sickingen, Franciscus, 1511, (16), 20, 22(−).
            Frantz Conrad, 1544, 48, 51, 54, 55, 57.
Sigelman, Gregorius, 1537(lehentrager Vrbans von Bolsenheym).
Sigrist, Hans Heinrich, (1516).
Sonnenbuhel, Steffan, (1516).
Spender, Reimbolt, *Ritter,* (1516), 20(+), 22(+), 23(+).
Stand (Sand), Gebhart, (1516).
              Gebhart, 1544.
Stanng, Sebastian, 1544, 54(nit beschryben).
v. Stoll *gen.* Spantzinger, Claus, (1516).
Stoll v. Stauffenberg, Caspar, 1551, 54, 55, 57.
               Wolf, 1520, 22, 23, 37, 40.

STÖRE, Diebold, 1551, 54.
      Hans Jacob, 1551, 54(obijt).
      Humprecht, 1555, 57.
STURM, Friedrich, 1522, 23, 32, 37, 40, 44, 51, 54, 55, 57.
      Ludwig, (1516).
      Martin, (1516), 22.
SULGER v. VILLINGEN, Friedrich, (1516), 22.
                      Hans Jacob, 1544, 51, 54(obijt).
v. SULTZ, Jacob, 1555, 57.
         Wolff, (1516), 20, 22, 23, 32(+).
         Wolff, 1537, 40, 44.

T

THEDINGER v. OFFENBURG, Hans Rulman (lehentrager Eva Mönnerin),
    1544, 54, 55, 57.
TRAUTWEIN v. HAGENAU, Hans, 1544, 51, 54, 55, 57.
                Heinrich, (1516), 20, 22, 23, 32, 37, 40.

U/V

v. VEGERSHEIM, Batt, 1523, 32, 40, 44.
           Jacob, (1516), 20, 22, 23.
           Sebastian, 1554, 55, 57.
VESSLER v. ARNSBERG, German, (1516), 20, 22, 23.
              Jerg, 1523, 32, 37, 40, 44.
v. VIRDENHEIM, Frantz, 1540, 44, 51, 54, 55.
          Martzolff, 1532.
          Peter, (1516), 20, 22, 23.
          Peter, 1557.
VISCHER, Hans, (1516).
      Jheronimus, 1544, 54(nit beschryben).
      Martin, 1544.
VÖLTSCH, Eucharius, (1516).
      Ludwig, 1537, 40, 51, 54, 55.
      Reimbolt, (1516), 20, 22, 23, 32.
VOLTZ, Wolff, 1532.
      Wolfgang, (1516), 20, 22, 23.
VOLTZ v. ALTENAU, Ludwig, 1544, 51, 54, 55, 57.
VOLTZ zu KOLBSHEIM, Wolff, 1544(+).
VORSTER, Martin, (1516).
VORSTER v. BITSCH, Martin, 1532, 37, 40.
v. UTTENHEIM, Bernhard, *Ritter,* (1516), 20, 22, 23.
           Jacob Christoff, 1548, 51, 54, 55, 57.
           Ludeman, (1516), 20, 22(+).
           Wilhelm, 1523, 32(+), 37, 40, 44.

W

WALDNER, Wolff, 1523.
WALDNER v. FREUDENSTEIN, Hans Diebold, 1544, 54, 55, 57.
v. WALSTEIN, Conrad, (1516), 20, 22, 23, 32(+).
        Egenolff, 1537, 40, 44, 51, 54, 55, 57.
v. WALTENHEIM, Dietrich, (1516), 20, 22, 23, 32(+).
        Philips, 1548, 51, 54(nit beschryben).
v. WANGEN, Hans, (1516), 20, 22, 23.
        Jerg, 1540, 44.
        Steffan, 1522, 23.
v. WANGEN ZU GEROLDSECK AM WASICHIN, Jörg, 1554, 55, 57.
v. WESTHAUSEN, Anstatt, 1544, 48, 54, 55, 57.
WETZEL v. MARSILIEN, Heinrich, 1511, (16), 20(+).
        Jacob, 1522, 23, 32(+).
        Jacob, 1537, 40, 44, 51, 54, 55, 57.
        Philips, 1532, 37.
v. WICKERSHEIM (WEICKERSHEIM), Wolff, 1555, 57.
WIDERGRIEN v. STAUFENBERG, Anthonj, 1511, (16), 20, 22, 23.
        Gervasius, 1537(−), 40, 44(+).
        Hans Friedrich, 1523, 32.
        Melchior, 1554, 55, 57.
v. WILSBERG, Bechtold, 1557.
        Friedrich, (1516).
        Wilhelm, 1544, 54, 55, 57.
v. WINDECK, Jacob, 1544, 51, 54, 55, 57.
        Philips, 1520(+), 22, 23(+), 32(+).
        Wolff, 1511, (16), 20, 22, 23, 32(+), 37, 40.
WIRICH, Andres, (1516).
        Andres, Sr., (1516), 20, 22, 23(+).
WIRICH v. EPFICH, Andres, 1532, 37(+).
v. WITTERSHEIM, Marzolff, (1516), 20, 22, 23.
        Wilhelm, 1537, 40, 44, 51, 54, 55, 57.
v. WITTSTAT *gen.* HAGENBACH, Conrad, 1523, 40.
WURMSER, Balthasar, 1544, 51, 54, 55, 57.
        Jacob, (1516), 20, 22, 23, 32, 37, 40(todt).
WURMSER v. SCHÄFFOLSHEIM, Daniel, 1554, 55, 57.
        Jerg, 1540, 44.
WURMSER v. VENDENHEIM, Bernhard, *Ritter*, (1516), 20, 22, 23, 32, 37, 40(+).
v. WYSTENAU, Bartholomeus, 1544, 54(nit beschryben).

Z

ZORN, Adam, *Ritter*, 1511, (16).
        Hans Jacob, 1523.
ZORN v. BULACH, Ludwig, 1520, 22, 23, 32, 37, 40, 44, 51(todt).

Corporate and Individual Owners of Public Debt (?) at Strasbourg, 1533–34

The following lists analyze the register of debt now in AMS, IV 98/1, and described in pp. 158–162 above. Lists A and B contain the names of corporate and individual lenders respectively; and within each list the entries are numbered consecutively, beginning with the biggest lenders. Information in brackets has been added. The names have been handled according to the principles explained in the Preface. All sums are in Rhenish florins.

A. CORPORATE LENDERS

1. Jung St. Peter	366 fl.	
2. Die Carthäuser	292	
3. St. Thomas	292	
4. St. Johann im grünen Wörth	284	
5. Die Barfüsser	172	
6. Die Reuerer [St. Magdalena]	170	
7. Alt St. Peter	156	
8. Unserer Frauen Haus	152	
9. St. Clara auf dem Wörth	144	
10. St. Catharina	116	
11. St. Nicolaus ("den Caplenen in s. Niclaus pfarren")	112 fl. 10s. 6d.	
12. Spital ("vormals den predigern")	112	
13. Augustiner	100	
14. St. Margarethe	100	
15. Die Sammlung zu Innenheim*	83	
16. Die Presentz des Hohen Stiftes	70	
17. St. Stephan	66	
18. St. Wilhelm ("S. Wilhelms orden")	62	
19. Allerheiligen	60	
20. Das Hohe Stift	60	
21. Das Blatterhaus	56	
22. Das Stift zu Haslach ("Haslo")	56	
23. St. Nicolaus in Undis	42	
24. Das Waisenhaus ("etwan den predigern")	38	
25. Die Gesellschaft zum Grossen Spiegel	32	
26. St. Marx	32	
27. Zu der Roten Kirche	24	
28. Die Elenden–Herberge	20	

* Beguinages at Strasbourg.

29. Die Sammlung zu Offenburg* 20 fl.
30. Die Vicarien des Hohen Stiftes 20
31. St. Martins Werck 18
32. St. Agnes Altar im Münster ("entpfoht h. Michel Hanen") 14 fl. 7s.
33. Die Beginen im Giessen* 13.5
34. St. Clara auf dem Rossmarkt 12
35. "der statt Strassburg" 12
36. Das Stift zu Surburg 12
37. Die Bruderschaft der Brotbecker Knechte 11 fl. 4s. 6d.
38. Der Caplan zu Widderichen 5
39. Die Fabrica zu Illkirch 4

B. Individuals and Groups of Individuals

Numbers after the name: 1 = noble and/or patrician of Strasbourg
2 = member of the XV or the XIII of Strasbourg

1. Bock [v. Gerstheim], Herr Hans (1, 2) 348 fl.
2. Beger, Junker Mattheus, erben (1) 200
3. Wurmser [v. Vendenheim], Herr Bernhard (1, 2) 188
4. Ottfriedrich, Junker Bernhard (1, 2) 176
5. Pfau [v. Rüppur], Diebold, witwe (1) 168
6. v. Utenheim, Hans (1) 160
7. Mieg, Herr Daniel (2) 140
8. Ritter, Lux, witwe (= Frau Jacobe) (1) 140
9. Zuckmantel, Junker Christoffel, kinder (1) 140
10. Wurmser, Erhart, erben (1) 130
11. v. Wilsberg, Herr Pangrat, tochter (1) 125
12. Ellenhart, Junker Peter (1, 2) 123 fl. 0s. 6d.
13. Sturm, Herr Jacob (1, 2) 116.25
14. v. Baden, Osswaldt (1) 112
15. v. Andlau, Rudolf Meinolf (1) 100
16. Joham, Herr Conrad (2) 100
17. Röder v. Diersburg, Egenolf (1, 2) 95
18. König, Wernher 84
19. v. Andlau, Meinolf (1) 83 fl. 3.5s.
20. Mieg, Andreas (2) 83 fl. 3.5s.
21. Mieg, Carl, Sr. (2) 83 fl. 3.5s.
22. Sturm, Junker Hans (1, 2) 82 fl. 3s.
23. Böcklin, Junker Philips (1) 81
24. Böcklin, Junker Ulman (1, 2) 80
25. v. Landsberg, Dietrich (1) 80
26. v. Rathsamhausen, Junker Ulrich (1) 80
27. v. Schauenburg, Frau Ursula (1) 80
28. v. Utenheim, Herr Bernhard, erben (1) 80
29. Wurmser, Wolf, witwe (1) 80
30. v. Zeissgen, Rudolf (1) 80

31. Fyrtägin, Margred, "zu lypgeding"   78 fl.
32. v. Andlau, Arnoldt (1)   74
33. Gerbott, Jacob, *kinder* (2)   74
34. v. Mülnheim, *Junker* Heinrich (1)   74
35. Böcklin, Wirich, *witwe* (1)   69
36. Christion, Gangloff and Hans   68
37. Thedinger, Hans (1)   68
38. v. Landsberg, Dr. Jacob (1)   62 fl. 7s.
39. Bock [v. Bläsheim], Friedrich (1)   60
40. Münch v. Wilsberg, Jacob (1)   60
41. Sturm, Peter (1, 2)   56
42. Wurmser, Jacob, Sr. (1)   52 fl. 2s.
43. Bock v. Erlenburg, Eucharius (1)   52
44. Mieg, Jerg   52
45. Böcklin, Dr. Wolfgang (1)   50
46. Vogel, Daniel, "dem goldtschmit"   50
47. v. Blumenau, *Junker* Hans (1, 2)   49.5
48. v. Landsberg, Christoffel, *hausfrau* (1)   48
49. Wurmser, *Herr* Sebastian (1)   48
50. v. Brumbach, *Junker* Jacob (1)   45
51. v. Duntzenheim, Wolf   45
52. Münch, Hans, *witwe* [Maria v. Duntzenheim]   44
53. Beger, *Herr* Jacob, *witwe* (1)   40
54. Bock, Sebastian (1)   40
55. Boumgarter, Blesi   40
56. Daun v. Leiningen, Reinhard (1)   40
57. Mergentheimer, Hans, *erben*   40
58. v. Mülnheim, Diebold, *erben* (1)   40
59. v. Neuneck, *Junker* Jörg (1)   40
60. Ritter, Jacob, *witwe* (1)   40
61. Schonmans, Wilhelm & Lentzel, Gabriel (1)   40
62. v. Utenheim, Martin (1)   40
63. Werlin, Claus, *kinder* (1)   40
64. Wurmser, Wolf, *erben* (1)   40
65. Bohem, Claus [son-in-law of Conrad v. Duntzenheim]   36
66. Büchsner, Alexius (1, 2)   36
67. Harter, Conrad "von wissenburg"   36
68. v. Virdenheim, Peter, *witwe* (1)   34 fl. 3s.
69. v. Andlau, Friedrich (1)   34
70. Sturm, Veronica, widow of Jerg Vessler [v.
     Arnsberg] (1)   34
71. v. Brumbach, *Junker* Bartholomes (1)   32
72. Pfarrer, Heinrich [brother of Mathis Pfarrer]   32
73. v. Utenheim, Wilhelm (1)   32
74. Vogler, Hans, *erben*   32
75. Wurmser [v. Vendenheim], Jacob (1)   32
76. v. Utenheim, Wolf (1)   31.5

77. BERCKHEIM, Balthasar, *witwe* (1)	30 fl.
78. DEGENBECK, Andres "des goldtschmidts hussfrouwen zu lypgeding"	30
79. ECKART, Clara "zu lypgeding" [3 entries]	30
80. KRESS, *Frau* Sophie [mother of Hans Sturm] (1)	30
81. ZORN [v. DUNTZENHEIM], Wolff (1)	28
82. TRUCHSESS [v. RHEINFELDEN], Peterman (1)	26.5 fl. 0s. 5d.
83. BEINHEIM, Hans	24
84. BOPP, *Herr* Jacob	24
85. STUSSINGER, Arbogast	24
86. BADERUS, Johann	20 fl. 4s. 6d.
87. v. DUNTZENHEIM, Jacob (2)	20
88. EBEL, Hans [father of Friedrich Ebel]	20
89. INGOLD, Friedrich	20
90. JÖRGER, Hans (2)	20
91. KÖNIG, Balthasar	20
92. LEYMER, Lienhart, *witwe*	20
93. MIEG, Paulus, *erben*	20
94. v. MÜLNHEIM, Bläsy, *kinder* (1)	20
95. v. MÜLNHEIM, Wolff (1)	20
96. v. RATHSAMHAUSEN, Heinrich, *witwe* (1)	20
97. v. UTENHEIM, Ludwig, *witwe* (1)	20
98. STURM, *Herr* Ott, *witwe* (1)	18
99. v. BERSS, Hans (2)	16
100. v. HOHENBURG, Jacob	16
101. v. SCHAUENBURG, Bernhard (1)	16
102. STURM, Friedrich (1, 2)	16
103. WURMSER [v. SCHÄFFOLSHEIM], Dr. Bernhard, *kinder* (1)	16
104. KNIEBIS, Claus (2)	15 fl. 6s. 6d.
105. v. BRUMBACH, Arbogast (1)	14
106. v. BERSTETT, Adam (1)	12
107. v. DALNHEIM, Antheng	12
108. MARX, *Herr* Jörg, *witwe* (1, 2)	12
109. RYFF, Diebold	12
110. SPIRER, Martin	12
111. VRINGER, Jörg & HUNDT, Sebastian	10
112. WISSBACH, Jacob, *witwe* (2)	10
113. MELICH [= MENNLICH?], Hans	9
114. DOBFUSSEN, Anna "entphacht her hans lindenfels" (2)	8
115. MERSWIN, Wolff (1)	8
116. NOL, Erhard	8
117. WETZEL v. MARSILIEN, *Herr* Johann (1)	8
118. DRACHE, *Herr* Peter, Caplan zu s. Thoman	7 fl. 6s. 6d.
119. v. DACHSTEIN, Heinrich	4

APPENDIX E

Renunciations of Citizenship at Strasbourg, July 15–September 10, 1548

The following list collates in alphabetical order the various lists of persons who renounced citizenship, or had citizenship renounced on their behalf by guardians, at Strasbourg between July 15 and September 10, 1548. Since the average number of renunciations per month was between three and four, the number of persons included who actually renounced for reasons not related to the crisis of the summer of 1548 is bound to be negligible. The data is given in this order: family name, Christian name(s); relationships; office(s); date of renunciation (sources).

Sources: A = AMM, I, 4447 (31.IX.1548).*
           KS = AMS, KS 63/I, fols. 1^r–5^r.
           M = J. M. Pastorius, *Kurze Abhandlung von den Ammeistern der Stadt Strassburg* (Strasbourg, 1761), pp. 169–172.
           P = *PCSS*, IV, 1070, No. 819n5.
           S = Daniel Specklin, "Collectanea," II, 292, excerpt in BNUS, Ms. 1223, fols. 48^v–49^r.
           Z = Jacob Bernays, "Zur Biographie Johann Winthers von Andernach," *ZGO*, 55 (1901), 36n1.

Notation: GR = Senator; xGR = former Senator; XV = member of the XV; XIII = member of the XIII; XXI = "lediger" XXIer; T = Stettmeister.
           [1] designated as contemplating renunciation.
           [2] future senator or privy councillor.

ARG, Ursula, Barbara, Katharina, Rosina, Agnes, Jakob; children of Diebold
     A. (dec.), renounced by Georg Ingold; 30.VIII. (KS, M).
BAER, Caspar (S).
BARPFENNIG, *Herr* Caspar; xGR (M).
BECHERER, *Herr* Hans Jakob; son-in-law of Carl Mieg, Sr.; 28.VIII. (KS, M).
BECK v. ZABERN, *Junker* Jakob; 31.VII. (KS, M).
v. BERWANGEN, *Frau* Apollonia, *wittwe*; 1.IX. (KS, M).

---

*I use the Mulhouse copy of the list appended to the anonymous letter from Strasbourg of 31 August 1548, printed by Gerber in *PCSS*, IV, No. 819; but the letter was not, as Gerber thought, addressed to Mulhouse. The original was sent from Strasbourg to Basel, where copies were made and sent to Bern (Bern Staatsarchiv, UP 67, Nos. 265–266), Schaffhausen (Schaffhausen Staatsarchiv, Korrespondenzen 1548, No. 8), Mulhouse, and, as indicated in the letter of transmittal from Basel to Bern (Bern Staatsarchiv, UP 67, No. 267, dated 4 September 1548), to Zürich. The names in the Mulhouse and Bern copies are the same. Jean Rott generously told me about the documents in Bern and Schaffhausen and allowed me to use his photocopies and notes.

Bock, *Junker* Jakob, Jr.; son of Jakob B. (M).

——, *Junker* Ludwig; son of Hans B. v. Gerstheim; GR (A, M, S).

——, *Junker* Stephan; son of Friedrich B. (A, M).

Böcklin [v. Böcklinsau], *Junker* Assmuss; son-in-law of Conrad Joham; GR; 23.VIII. (A, KS, M, S).

——, *Junker* Georg; xGR; 6.IX. (KS, M, S).

——, *Jungfrau* Maria; daughter of Nicolaus B. v. B.; 24.VIII. (KS, M).

——, *Junker* Ulman; XIII, T; 28.VIII. (A, KS, M, S).

——, *Junker* Wolfgang; XV, T; 28.VIII. (A, KS, S).

——, children of *Junker* Wolff B. and *Frau* Jacobe Ritter; 28.VIII. (KS, M).

Bosch, *Frau* Anna; widow of Kolin Ferber of Saarburg (M).

Brant, Anna, Margarethe, Onophrius; children of *Herr* Onophrius B., renounced by their *Vogt*, Conrad Meyer; 28.VIII. (KS, M).

Braun, Maria (or: Marius) (S).

Braun v. Reichenberg, *Herr* Matthias; GR; 28.VIII. (A, KS, M, S).

v. Duntzenheim, Jacob "in Dorngasse"; husband of a Joham of Saverne; GR; by 31.VIII. (A, P, S).

Drach, Ottmarius (S).

Ebel, *Frau* Dorothea; widow of Reinhard Widt; by 31.VIII. (A, M).

——, Friedrich; son of Hans E.; by 31.VIII. (A, P).[2]

——, *Herr* Hans; son of Hans E.; 30.VIII. (A, KS, M, S).

——, Heinrich; son of Hans E.; by 31.VIII. (A, P).

Eberbach, *Herr* Conrad (M).

Engelmann, *Herr* Caspar; 21.VII. (KS, M, S).

Ferber, *Herr* Werner; son of Kolin F., by his *Vogt*, Hans Christian; 30.VIII. (KS, M, S).

v. Gottesheim, *Herr* Friedrich; XV; 30.VIII. (KS, M, S).[2]

Graff, Ciriakus; 15.XII. (KS, M).

Hans, Martin, of Rosheim (M).

Hillis, Richard, of England; 8.VIII. (M, Z).

v. Hohenburg, *Frau* Anna; daughter of Gottfried v. H., widow of Carl Mieg, Sr.; 13.VIII. (A, KS, M).

——, *Herr* Jakob; son of Gottfried v. H.; 30.VIII. (A, KS, M, S).

Hug v. Ottenheim, Martin; son of Philips H. v. O.; 31.VIII. (A, P).[1]

Ingold, Florentz; son of Jacob I. (S).

——, Georg; son of Friedrich I.; 30.VIII. (A, KS).

——, *Herr* Hans, Sr.; son of Claus I.; 30.VIII. (A, KS, M, S).

——, *Herr* Hans; son of Jacob I.; 28.VIII. (A, KS, M, S).

——, *Herr* Jacob; son of Jacob I.; 30.VIII (M, KS, S).

——, *Herr* Philips; son of Jacob I.; XXI; 28.VIII. (A, KS, M, S).

Joham, *Herr* Conrad; XIII; 28.VIII. (A, KS, M, S).

——, *Junker* Diebold; son of Conrad J.; 25.VIII. (A, KS, M, S).[2]

——, *Junker* Heinrich; 6.IX. (A, KS, M, S).[2]

——, *Frau* Margarethe; daughter of Conrad J., widow of Sebastian Zorn von Bulach (A, M).

——, *Junker* Philips; son of Conrad J. (A, M, S).

JUNGVÖGLIN, *Frau* Magdalena; widow of Jeremias Hirsskorn; 31.VII. (KS, M).

KLEBERGER, Wolff; 30.VIII. (KS, M, S).

KLETT v. UTTENHEIM, *Junker* Hans Jakob; son-in-law of Friedrich Bock (A, M).

KROSSWEILER, *Herr* Martin; GR; 30.VIII. (A, KS, M, S).

MELTINGER, *Frau* Ursula; widow of Veltin Becherer; 1.IX. (KS, M).

MEYER, *Herr* Conrad; XV; 28.VIII. (A, KS, M, S).

MIEG, Jakob, Dorothea, Anna, Anastasia; children of Carl M., Sr., renounced by their brother, Carl Mieg, Jr., by power of their guardian, Andreas M.; 28.VIII. (KS, M).

——, *Junker* Sebastian; 30.VIII. (A, KS, M).[2]

MINCKEL, Isaac; son of Israel M.; 31.VIII. (A, P).[1]

v. MITTELHAUSEN, *Junker* Adolf; son-in-law of Jakob Spender; GR (A, M, S).[2]

——, *Jungfrau* Agnes; later wife of Harthart v. Schauenburg (M).

v. MOLSHEIM, Jakob (S).

MORAND, Konrad, *Maler*; 1.IX. (KS, M, S).

v. MÜLNHEIM, *Junker* Christoph; son of Daniel v. M.; 1.IX. (KS, M).

——, *Junker* Heinrich; XV; 11.VII. (A, M, S, Z).[2]

——, *Junker* Hiltprant; XIII (S).[2]

MÜNCH, *Herr* Sebastian; XV; 6.IX. (A, KS, P, S).[1,2]

NIEDENFELS (Neidenfels), Hans, *Weber*; 10.IX. (KS, M).

NUMER (?), Balzar (S).

OTTER, *Herr* Theobald (M).

PRECHTER, Ursula (von Duntzenheim); daughter of Conrad v. Duntzenheim, Jr., widow of Friedrich II Prechter; by 31.VIII. (A, P).

——, *Frau* Susanna; widow of Hans Ebel (A, M).

——, Wilhelm; XV; 28.VIII. (A, KS).[2]

QUINTNER v. SAARBURG, *Junker* Ludwig (M, S).

REHLINGER, *Junker* Wolff, of Augsburg (A, M, S).

SCHORP v. FREUDENBERG, *Junker* Hans Jakob; xGR (A, P, S).[2]

SCHULTHEISS v. HALL, Johann; 1.IX. (KS, M).

SELMER (Söllmer), Balthasar, *Maurer* of Oberkirch; 16.VIII. (KS, M).

SELMER, David, *Maurer* of Oberkirch; 12.IX. (KS).

STENGEL, Engelhard, of Geispolsheim; 1.IX. (KS, M).

STEUDLIN, *Frau* Margarethe; widow of Andreas Sauren; 18.VIII. (KS, M).

STÖFFELIN, Matthias; 31.VIII. (A, P).[1]

STURM, *Junker* Stephan; son of Ott S.; 25.VIII. (A, KS, M, S).[2]

TOXITES, Michael; 24.IX. (KS, M, Z).

v. TÜRCKHEIM (Dürnheim), *Frau* Ursula; divorced from Ludwig Völtsch, mother of Hans Jacob Schorp v. Freudenberg; 22.IX. (KS, M).

VARNBÜHLER, *Herr* Ulrich; son-in-law of Friedrich II Prechter; 1.IX. (KS, M, S).

VETTERLE, Hans, of "Oberbürn"; 13.VIII. (KS).

VÖLTSCH, Hans (S).

VOLTZ, *Frau* Elisabethe; widow of Georg Armbruster (M).

WENCKER, *Herr* Jacob; 14.VII. (KS, M).

WETZEL V. MARSILIEN, *Junker* Martin; XV; 28.VIII. (A, KS, M, S).

——, *Jungfrau* Salome; sister of Martin W. v. M.; 28.VIII. (KS, M).

WIDT, Friedrich, Heinrich, Reinhardt, Dorothea; children of Reinhard W. and Dorothea Ebel, renounced by their *Vogt*, Philips Ingold; 28.VIII. (KS, M).

WOLFF V. RENCHEN, *Junker* Ludwig; xGR (A, M, S).[2]

WURM, Wolff (S).

WURMSER, *Jungfrau* Agnes; daughter of Erhard W.; 21.VIII. (KS, M).

——, *Frau* Katharina; widow of Philips v. Kageneck (M).

——, *Jungfrau* Merg; daughter of Erhard W.; 21.VIII. (KS, M).

——, *Junker* Wolff Sigismund (A, M, S).[1,2]

ZELLER, Caspar (S).

ZENZEL (Zengler), Matthias; 1.IX. (KS, M).

ZORN, *Junker* Georg (M, S).

ZORN V. BULACH, Sebastian (S).

ZORN ZUM RIET, Nicolaus; T; 28.VIII. (A, KS, M, S).

APPENDIX F

The Privy Councillors of Strasbourg, 1433–1570/75

The *geheime Räte* were true *arcanae regiminis* at Strasbourg, and nominative lists of them are very rare among the extant records of the civic regime.[1] The following lists are derived from a wide variety of sources. The first comprises separate chronological (by known beginning year of service) lists of the Simple XXIers, the XVers, and the XIIIers from 1433 to 1575 (for the XVers until 1570). The more significant sources for the lists are:

1. the protocols of the Senate & XXI (AMS, XXI 1539–75);
2. the notarial registers (AMS, KS 1–73);
3. annual *Ratsbücher* (AMS, VI 494–496);
4. lists of the XIII for 1534–50 (AMS, VI 589/6);
5. a unique running list of XVers from the *Fischerzunft*, 1488–1635 (AMS, VI 488/3);
6. notes on the privy councillors by Jerg Ingold (BNUS, Ms. 626, fols. 158ᵛ–165ᵛ);
7. lists for 1514 (AMS, Archives du Grand-Chapitre de Strasbourg, Documenta particularia. Colligends de différends bénéfices, "Comptes in Heilewog 1514"), 1518, 1520, and 1533–34 (AMS, VI 495); and
8. scattered notices, especially for the fifteenth century, in AMS, series R, and in several printed collections.[2]

In addition to direct sources, valuable indirect indications of tenures as privy councillors can be derived from notices of committee assignments ("verordnete Herren"): if a man was not a senator in the year of a given assignment, then he was a XXIer, XVer, or XIIIer.

These lists incorporate, extend, and correct those published by Jacques Hatt in 1963.[3] That of the XXIers is extremely fragmentary. As for the XVers and XIIIers, there are likely to be few or no missing names after 1518 and almost certainly none after 1539; the terms of office are complete after 1539 and nearly so from 1518 to 1539; all terms before 1518 are fragmentary, and a number of names are missing. A rough idea of the number of missing names

---

[1] These lists expand on those that appeared as "The Privy Councils of Strasbourg (XV and XIII): A Supplement to Jacques Hatt, *Liste des membres du grand sénat de Strasbourg*," *BCGA*, No. 27 (1974), 73–79.

[2] A good many notices are scattered through Eheberg's enormous collection of documents, and, for the first half of the 1520s, see Rott, "Magistrat et Réforme à Strasbourg: les dirigéants municipaux de 1521 à 1525," *RHPR*, 54 (1974), 103–114.

[3] Despite Hatt's claim of completeness (Hatt, p. 5), he made no systematic search for names of privy councillors for the period before the beginnings of the extant series of protocols of the Senate & XXI, XV, and XIII.

in the list of XVers may be gained from the fact that, between 1510 and 1570, about twenty-one new XVers appear per decade. Projecting this figure into the fifteenth century yields the theoretical number of 147 new XVers between 1433 and 1499, or sixty-seven more names than the list of XVers in fact contains for those years. Add to these the numbers—perhaps two or three per decade—who entered the XIII directly, and the estimate of 100 missing names before 1500 will not be far wrong.

The lists below nonetheless improve on those published by Hatt in two ways. First, where Hatt names 15 XXIers, 76 XVers, and 48 XIIIers for these years, the lists below provide 31, 221, and 106 names respectively; and where Hatt names 117 individuals, these lists name 270. Secondly, the dates of tenures in the privy councils have been expanded or fixed more accurately. As a general rule, no entry, either name or date of tenure, has been accepted into these lists unless supported by a contemporary source.

In the alphabetical list (II.) all patricians are entered as "Constofler," and no attempt has been made to divide them between the two Constofeln. As for changes in guild names around 1500 (discussed in Chapter III above), the significant changes were: Schiffleute = Zum Encker; Krämer = Zum Spiegel; Metzger = Zur Blume; Würte = Zum Freiburg; Kornleute = Zur Luzern; Salzmütter = Zur Möhrin; and Goldschmiede = Zur Steltz. The guild designated is in each case the one represented by the privy councillor.

I. PRIVY COUNCILLORS OF STRASBOURG, 1433–1570/75: *Chronological Lists*

A.   Simple XXIers (*ledige XXIer*), 1460–1575

1460	BETSCHOLT, Wilhelm	1565–69	v. RECHBERG, Arbogast
1460	MÜRSEL, Bernhard	1567–68	OETTEL, Hans
1463	RYFF, Conrad	1569	ERLIN V. RORBURG,
1496–1506	MIEG, Jacob		Eucharius
1506	v. HOHENBURG, Gottfried	1569	JOHAM V. MUNDOLSHEIM,
1522–24	SPENDER, Jacob		Georg
1540–42	BÜCHSNER, Alexius	1571–72	FUCHS, Nicolaus
1541–49	PFITZER, Gregorius	1572	GEIGER, David
1542–?	v. DUNTZENHEIM, Hans	1572–75	v. MOLSHEIM, Jacob
1542	ERB, Sebastian	1572–77	v. GOTTESHEIM, Mathis
1542–48	v. ODRATZHEIM, Hans, Jr.	1575–78	STÄDEL, Christoph III
1544–48	FRANCK, Simon		
1547–48	HAGEN, Marx	B. XVers, 1433–1570	
1548	INGOLD, Philips		
1548–49	HEUSS, Michael, Sr.	1433	ARMBRUSTER VOR DEM
1554–62	STURM, Stephan		PFENNIGTHURM, Conrad
1556	v. ETTLINGEN, Jacob	1433	BÜCHSNER, Claus Friedrich
1557–58	GERFALCK, Diebold	1433	SPIEGEL, Walther
1557–65	RÖMER, Christoph	1433	SPORER, Stephan
1562–63	JOHAM V. MUNDOLSHEIM,	1433	STURM V. STURMECK, Hans
	Heinrich	1433	VOLTZ, Peter
1562–68	v. KIPPENHEIM, Gregorius	1433	ZORN V. ECKERICH, Hans
1564	v. BADEN, Hans Caspar	1433–37	DRACHENFELS, Lienhardt
1565–66	MARX V. ECKWERSHEIM,	1433–37	ELLENHARDT, Hans, Sr.
	Hans Jacob	1433–39	WURMSER, Claus

1433–41	BLEYWEGER, Diebold	1467	SPIRER, Hans
1433–43	AMELUNG, Hans	1467–73	STURM, Hans
1433–43	SPETE, Hans	1468–69	VOGT, Walther
1433–50	v. BERSS, Hans	1469–70	REBSTOCK, Peter
1433–52	ARMBRUSTER, Conrad	1470–71	KERLING, Marx
1439–52	MISSEBACH, Peter	1470–88	RENNER, Claus
1441	SPENDER, Reimbold	1471	v. ENDINGEN, Hans
1441–50	RENNER, Hans, Jr.		Rudolph
1443–45	MEYER, Heinrich	1471	MUSSLER, Reimbold
1444–55	NOPE, Cuno	1471–73	RENNER, Claus
1447–55	RYFF, Peter	1472	v. NORTHAUSEN, Hans
1448	DRACHENFELS, Hans	1474–75	OFFENBURG, Bechtold
1449–55	v. MÜLNHEIM, Burckhardt	1475–78	VÖLTSCH, Hans
1450–59	v. ROSHEIM, Ludwig	1476–77	v. ROTWEIL, Hans Erhard
1451	BARPFENNIG, Rudolph	1477	WURMSER, Bernhard
1451	v. BERSS, Claus	1483	DRENSS, Daniel
1451	MELBRÜ, Hans	1488?–94	VENDENHEIM, Hans
1451–53	HÜFFEL, Hans Heinrich	1488–1504	ULRICH, Claus
1451–59	ELLENHARDT, Hans, Jr.	1492	ROTSCHILT, Stephan
1451–72	BOCK, Hans Conrad	1492	WURMSER, Jacob, Sr.
1452	SPIRER, Hans	1494–96	VENDENHEIM, Lorentz
1452–55	v. DUNTZENHEIM, Claus	1500–03	ARG, Peter
1454	BETSCHOLT, Wilhelm	1503–18	v. BRUMATH, Hans
1455	BISINGER, Heinrich	1504–11	SCHWENDT, Hans
1455	LINSER, Claus	1505	v. DUNTZENHEIM, Claus
1455	MÜRSEL, Bernhard	1505	MIEG, Ludwig
1455–56	RENNER, Claus	1506–13	BARPFENNIG, Bartholome
1455–70	BRANDT, Diebold	1506–13	MIEG, Jacob
1456–72	BURGGRAFF, Dietrich	1506–19	SEBOTT, Lamprecht, Sr.
1457	BETSCHOLT, Friedrich	1506–21	STURM, Martin
1457–64	ZERINGER, Cuntz	1507–17	v. MÜLNHEIM, Ludwig
1458	ARMBRUSTER, Hans	1507–24	ZORN zum RIET, Ludwig
1458	HÜFFEL, Hans	1507–28	v. DÜRNINGEN, Veltin
1458	v. KAGENECK, Arbogast	1507–33	ELLENHARDT, Peter
1458	RYFF, Hans	1510–15	BOCK v. GERSTHEIM, Hans
1459	BETSCHOLT, Hans	1511–18	LAMP, Friedrich
1459	Zum RUST, Friedrich	1514	RUMLER, Hans
1459–70	LEISTMANN, Dietrich	1514–15	BRAUN, Adolph
1460	BERER, Hans	1514–18	KNIEBIS, Claus
1460–66	ELLENHARDT, Thoman	1514–19	MÜNCH, Claus
1461–65	v. MÜLNHEIM, Ludwig	1514–20	ARBOGAST, Hans Claus
1461–67	STANGE, Erhard	1514–20	WOLFF, Claus
1463	v. DINGSHEIM, Hans	1514–25	HETTER, Herbart
1463–64	ARG, Heinrich	1518	GERBOTT, Jacob
1464	v. LEUTRESHEIM, Hans	1518–19	HUG v. OTTENHEIM, Philips
1464–72	WINGERSHEIM, Stephan	1518–22	MARX v. ECKWERSHEIM,
1464–77	ZORN v. BULACH, Claus		Jerg
1465	MOSUNG, Claus	1518–22	ROETTEL, Hans Ulrich
1466–67	MESSINGER, Adam		(ULRICH, Hans)
1467	AMELUNG, Jacob	1518–23	SCHETZEL, Nicolaus (Bocks
1467	v. ROHR, Walther		Claus)
1467	SPIELMANN, Hans	1518–32	HOFFMEISTER, Caspar

1519–22	Mieg, Daniel	1542–50	Widergrien v. Staufen-
1519?–25	Ingold, Claus		berg, Hans Jacob
1519–34	Sebott, Diebold	1542–52	Drenss, Augustin
1521	Herlin, Martin	1543	Büchsner, Alexius
1521–24	Meyer, Jacob	1543–59	Storck, Veltin
	(Maurerzunft)	1545–48	Böcklin v. Böcklinsau,
1521–31	Lindenfels, Hans		Wolfgang
1521–33	Ottfriedrich, Bernhard	1546–48	Sturm, Stephan
1522–26	Baldner, Heinrich	1546–48, 53–59	v. Mülnheim, Heinrich
1522–30	Joham (v. Mundolsheim),	1546–48, 55–56	Münch, Sebastian
	Conrad	1548	Erstein gen. Armbruster,
1523–25	Pfarrer, Mathis		Felix
1523–32	Betscholt, Martin	1548	Meyer, Jacob, "zum
1523–36	v. Blumenau, Hans		Heroldt"
1524–25, 28–31	Wurmser v. Venden-	1548	Prechter, Wilhelm
	heim, Bernhard	1548	Wetzel v. Marsilien,
1524–33	Schütz, Hans, Sr.		Martin
1524–42	Graff, Lorentz	1548, 51	v. Gottesheim, Friedrich
1525–26	Sturm, Jacob	1548–51	Messinger, Lux
1525–29	Röder v. Diersburg,	1548–52	Hammerer, Hans
	Egenolph	1548–53	v. Odratzheim, Hans, Jr.
1525?–31	Zorn zum Riet, Jacob	1548–54	Jung, Sebastian
1525–41	Braun, Nicolaus	1548–56	Schwencker, Michael, Sr.
1525–48	Rumler, Caspar	1549	Heuss, Michael, Sr.
1526–35	Baldner, Paulus	1550–53	Sturm, Friedrich
1527–31	v. Rotweil, Hans Erhard,	1551–54	v. Berss, Hans
	Sr.	1551–55	Leimer, Georg
1531–36	Sturm, Hans	1551–58	Stösser, Hans
1531–40	Jörger, Hans, Sr.	1551–80	Goss v. Oberehnheim
1532–33	Geiger, Mattheus		(Goss v. Dürckelstein),
1532–39	Böcklin v. Böcklinsau,		Bernhard
	Ulman	1552–57	Drenss, Jacob
1532–41	Mieg, Carl, Sr.	1552–57	Mieg, Carl, Jr.
1532–43	Mieg, Andreas	1552–58	Schorp v. Freundenberg,
1533–38	v. Duntzenheim, Batt		Hans Jacob
1533–40	Winich, Johann	1552–60	v. Mittelhausen, Adolph
1533–42	Franck, Simon	1552–60	v. Mörssmünster, Ludwig
1533–63	Sturm, Peter	1553–63	Meyer, Frantz
1535–63	Baldner, Anshelm	1554–55	Ebel, Friedrich
1536–43	Wetzel v. Marsilien,	1554–56	Wurmser v. Vendenheim,
	Jacob		Wolff Sigismund
1537?–39	Engelmann, Caspar	1554–62	v. Lampertheim, Hans
1539–42	v. Kageneck, Philips	1556–57	v. Ettlingen, Jacob
1539–?, 58–64	Gerfalk, Diebold	1556–63	Bosch, Jacob
1539–44	v. Bietenheim, Sifridt II	1557–65	Graff, Andres
1539–46	v. Duntzenheim, Jacob	1558–63	Mieg v. Boofzheim,
1540?–41	Beinheim, Veit		Sebastian, Sr.
1540–44	v. Mülnheim, Hiltebrant	1559–63	Wurmser, Wolff
1540–48	Meyer, Conrad	1559–72	Joham v. Mundolsheim,
1541–51	Kips, Veltin		Diebold
1541–54	Städel, Christoph II	1559–72	Vollmar, Hans Heinrich
1542–48	Erb, Sebastian	1560, 68–69	v. Kippenheim, Gregorius

1562–65	MEYER, Claus	1448	DRACHENFELS, Lienhardt
1562–84	KNIEBIS, Nicolaus Hugo	1448	MEYER, Heinrich
1563–64	MIEG, Mathis	1448	v. MÜLNHEIM, Heinz
1563–64	WURMSER, Sebastian	1448	OBRECHT, Hans?
1563–65	JUNG, Sebastian	1448–55	v. MÜLNHEIM, Burckhardt
1563–65	LORCHER, Johann Carl	1448–55	NOPE, Cuno
1563–69	FUCHS, Blasius	1448–60	MELBRÜ, Hans
1563–73	JOHAM v. MUNDOLSHEIM, Heinrich	1448–63	WURMSER, Jacob
		1448–66?	BETSCHOLT, Wilhelm
1564	v. SCHAUENBURG, Wilhelm	1455	BOCK, Hans Conrad
1564–65	BÖCKLIN v. BÖCKLINSAU, Gladi	1460	Zum RUST, Friedrich
		1463–90?	BAUMGARTER, Claus
1565–83	BALDNER, Sixt	1466?–77?	ARG, Heinrich
1564–65	LICHTENSTEIGER, Michael	1466	BRANT gen. SPIRER, Hans
1564–68	HELDT, Abraham	1470?–95	AMELUNG, Jacob
1564–72	FÜLL v. GEISPOLSHEIM, Heinrich	1471	MESSINGER, Philips
		1471?–1504	SCHOTT, Peter
1564–75	SCHENCKBECHER, Johann	1484?–91	DRACHENFELS, Mattern
1564–67	RÖMER, Christoph	1492?–1503?	HAPMACHER, Andres
1565–69	SCHORP v. FREUDENBERG, Hans Jörg	1498?–1508	WISSBACH, Jacob
		1501–24	DRACHENFELS, Andres
1565–83	MÜNCH, Georg	1502–20	RUMLER, Florentz
1566	MARX v. ECKWERSHEIM, Hans Jacob	1505–21	ARG, Peter
		1506–14	WURMSER, Jacob, Sr.
1567–68	SCHOTT, Hans	1506–19	MUSSLER, Peter
1568–69	MIEG, Jörg	1506–30	v. DUNTZENHEIM, Conrad
1568–72	SCHÜTTERLIN, Wolfgang	1507–20	INGOLD, Heinrich
1568–75	SCHONHERR, Jörg	1507–24	v. ENDINGEN, Hans Ludwig
1568–85	OETTEL, Hans	1510–24	v. HOHENBURG, Gottfried
1569–78	v. RECHBERG, Arbogast	1514–16	MÖRDEL, Gabriel
1569–84	JOHAM v. MUNDOLSHEIM, Georg	1514–18	BARPFENNIG, Bartholome
		1514–26	v. ROTWEIL, Hans Ludwig
		1514–29	BÖCKLIN v. BÖCKLINSAU, Ludwig
C. XIIIers, 1433–1575		1517–26	v. MÜLNHEIM, Ludwig
		1518–42	BOCK v. GERSTHEIM, Hans
1433	v. BERSS, Lixius	1519–22	MÜNCH, Claus
1433	v. ENDINGEN, Hans Balthasar	1520–52	KNIEBIS, Claus
		1521–30	SPENDER, Reimbold
1433	GERBOTT, Hans	1521–31	HUG v. OTTENHEIM, Philips
1433	LENTZEL, Claus	1522–41	MIEG, Daniel
1433	MÜRSEL, Hans	1523–47	HERLIN, Martin
1433	RYFF, Peter	1525–62	MEYER, Jacob (Maurerzunft)
1433	SPENDER, Reimbold	1525–68	PFARRER, Mathis
1433	STEFFAN, Heinrich	1526–53	STURM, Jacob
1433	Zum TRÜBEL, Cune	1528	PRECHTER, Friedrich II
1433	WANNER, Hans	1530–48	JOHAM (v. MUNDOLSHEIM), Conrad
1433–48	ARMBRUSTER IN DER BRANDGASSE, Conrad		
1433–55	LINSER, Claus	1530–50	RÖDER v. DIERSBURG, Egenolph
1436	BOCK, Wölflin/Wolffhelm		
1437	v. KAGENECK, Thoman	1532–40	WURMSER v. VENDENHEIM, Bernhard
1448	BOCK, Ulrich, Sr.		

1532–46	BETSCHOLT, Martin	1556–74	WURMSER V. VENDENHEIM,
1533–39	OTTFRIEDRICH, Bernhard		Wolff Sigismund
1533–49	GEIGER, Mattheus	1557–69	V. BERSS, Hans
1534–48	LINDENFELS, Hans	1557–69	V. ETTLINGEN, Jacob
1538–43	V. DUNTZENHEIM, Batt	1558–68	LEIMER, Georg
1539–48	BÖCKLIN V. BÖCKLINSAU,	1558–72	MIEG, Carl, Jr.
	Ulman	1558–78	MÜNCH, Sebastian
1542–45	V. KAGENECK, Philips	1559–78	V. MÜLNHEIM, Heinrich
1543–51	MIEG, Andreas	1560–65	V. MITTELHAUSEN, Adolph
1544–59	V. MÜLNHEIM, Hiltebrant	1562–78	STURM, Stephan
1546–48, 49–54	V. DUNTZENHEIM,	1563–65	MEYER, Frantz
	Jacob	1563–85	MIEG V. BOOFZHEIM,
1548–52	ERSTEIN *gen.* ARMBRUSTER,		Sebastian, Sr.
	Felix	1565	BÖCKLIN V. BÖCKLINSAU,
1548–56	FRANCK, Simon		Gladi
1548–63	RUMLER, Caspar	1565–78	MEYER, Claus
1550–51	WIDERGRIEN V. STAUFEN-	1565–89	LICHTENSTEIGER, Michael
	BERG, Hans Jacob	1565–88	LORCHER, Johann Carl
1551–81	V. GOTTESHEIM, Friedrich	1568–94	HELDT, Abraham
	VI	1569–75	FUCHS, Blasius
1552–56	HEUSS, Michael, Sr.	1569–78	V. RECHBERG, Arbogast
1552–72	HAMMERER, Hans	1569–93	TRAUSCH, Heinrich
1553–58	V. ODRATZHEIM, Hans, Jr.	1572–78	JOHAM V. MUNDOLSHEIM,
1553–62	STURM, Friedrich		Diebold
1554–67	MEYER, Jacob, "zum	1572–1612	SCHÜTTERLIN, Wolfgang
	Heroldt"	1574–1602	V. KETTENHEIM, Hans
			Philips
		1575–90	SCHENCKBECHER, Johann

II.   PRIVY COUNCILLORS OF STRASBOURG, 1433–1570/75: *Alphabetical List*

1. AMELUNG, Hans. Schiffleute. XV: 1433–43.
2. AMELUNG, Jacob (†1495). Küfer. XV: 1467. XIII: 1470?–95.
3. ARBOGAST, Hans Claus († ca. 1520). Zimmerleute/Wagner. XV: 1514–20.
4. ARG, Heinrich. Goldschmeide. XV: 1463–64. XIII: 1466?–77?
5. ARG, Peter (†1521). Zum Encker. XV: 1500–03. XIII: 1505–21.
6. ARMBRUSTER, Conrad. Schiffleute? XV: 1433–52.
7. ARMBRUSTER, Hans. Goldschmiede? XV: 1458. XIII: 1448.
8. ARMBRUSTER IN DER BRANDGASSE, Conrad. Schiffleute. XIII: 1443–48.
9. ARMBRUSTER VOR DEM PFENNIG-THURM, Conrad. Tucher. XV: 1433.
10. V. BADEN, Hans Caspar († ca. 1575). Constofler. XXI: 1564.
11. BALDNER, Anshelm († 2.IX.1563). Fischer. XV: 1535–63.
12. BALDNER, Heinrich († I.1526). Fischer. XV: 1522–26.
13. BALDNER, Paulus († by 21.XII.1535). Fischer. XV: 1526–35.
14. BALDNER, Sixt (†1583). Fischer. XV: 1565–83.
15. BARPFENNIG, Bartholome (†1518). Schuhmacher. XV: 1506–13. XIII: 1514–18.
16. BARPFENNIG, Rudolph. Krämer. XV: 1451.
17. BAUMGARTER, Claus. Würte. XIII: 1463–90?
18. BEINHEIM, Veit († 3./4.IX.1541). Zur Steltz. XV: 1540?–41.
19. BERER, Hans. Constofler. XV: 1460.
20. V. BERSS, Claus. Metzger. XV: 1451.

21. v. Berss, Hans (†after 1474).
    Metzger. XV: 1433–50.
22. Berss, Hans (†27.I.1569). Zum
    Encker. XV: 1551–54. XIII:
    1557–69.
23. v. Berss, Lixius. Metzger. XIII:
    1433.
24. Betscholt, Friedrich (†1467).
    Metzger. XV: 1457.
25. Betscholt, Hans. Metzger. XV:
    1459.
26. Betscholt, Martin (†27.XI.1546).
    Zur Blume. XV: 1523–32. XIII:
    1532–46.
27. Betscholt, Wilhelm (†1466).
    Metzger. XXI: 1460. XV: 1454.
    XIII: 1448–66?
28. v. Bietenheim, Sifridt II (†ca.
    1553). Zur Luzern. XV: 1539–44.

29. Bisinger, Heinrich. Würte. XV:
    1455.
30. Bleyweger, Diebold. Kürschner.
    XV: 1433–41.
31. v. Blumenau, Hans (†VIII.1536).
    Constofler. XV: 1523–36.
32. Bock, Hans Conrad. Constofler.
    XV: 1451–72. XIII: 1455.
33. Bock, Ulrich, Sr. Constofler. XIII:
    1448.
34. Bock, Wölflin/Wolffhelm (†by
    1443). Constofler. XIII: 1436.
35. Bock v. Gerstheim, Hans
    (†12.X.1542). Constofler. XV:
    1510–15. XIII: 1518–42.
36. Böcklin v. Böcklinsau, Gladi
    (†9.VII.1565). Constofler. XV:
    1564–65. XIII: 1565.
37. Böcklin v. Böcklinsau, Ludwig
    (†II.1529). Constofler. XIII:
    1514–29.
38. Böcklin v. Böcklinsau, Ulman
    (†ca. 1565). Constofler. XV:
    1532–39. XIII: 1539–48.
39. Böcklin v. Böcklinsau, Wolf-
    gang. Constofler. XV: 1545–48.
40. Bosch, Jacob (†14.IV.1563).
    Schneider. XV: 1556–63.
41. Brandt, Diebold (†1471).
    Weinsticher. XV: 1455–70.
42. Brant gen. Spirer, Hans. Würte.
    XIII: 1466.

43. Braun, Adolph. Zur Luzern. XV:
    1514–15.
44. Braun, Nicolaus (†1541). Zur
    Luzern. XV: 1525–41.
45. v. Brumath, Hans (†1518/19).
    Tucher. XV: 1503–18.
46. Büchsner, Alexius
    (†19./20.V.1547). Constofler.
    XXI: 1540–42. XV: 1543.
47. Büchsner, Claus Friedrich.
    Constofler. XV: 1433.
48. Burggraff, Dietrich (†1476).
    Constofler. XV: 1456–72.
49. v. Dingsheim, Hans. Küfer. XV:
    1463.
50. Drachenfels, Andres (+ ca.
    1530). Zur Möhrin. XIII:
    1501–24.
51. Drachenfels, Hans. Salzmütter.
    XV: 1448.
52. Drachenfels, Lienhardt. Salz-
    mütter. XV: 1433–37. XIII: 1448.
53. Drachenfels, Mattern (†1491).
    Salzmütter. XIII: 1484?–91.
54. Drenss, Augustin †3.V.1552).
    Gartner. XV: 1542–52.
55. Drenss, Daniel. Gartner. XV:
    1483.
56. Drenss, Jacob (†1571). Gartner.
    XV: 1552–57.
57. v. Duntzenheim, Batt (†1543).
    Schneider. XV: 1533–38. XIII:
    1538–43.
58. v. Duntzenheim, Claus. Gerber.
    XV: 1452–55.
59. v. Duntzenheim, Claus. Gerber.
    XV: 1505.
60. v. Duntzenheim, Conrad, Jr.
    (†1532). Zum Freiburg. XIII:
    1506–30.
61. v. Duntzenheim, Hans. Zum
    Freiburg. XXI: 1542–?
62. v. Duntzenheim, Jacob
    (†16.IV.1554). Zum Encker.
    XV: 1539–46. XIII: 1546–48,
    1549–54.
63. v. Dürningen, Veltin (†1530/31).
    Küfer. XV: 1507–28.
64. Ebel, Friedrich (†1564). Zum
    Spiegel. XV: 1554–55.
65. Ellenhardt, Hans, Sr. Constofler.
    XV: 1433–37.

66. ELLENHARDT, Hans, Jr. Constofler.
    XV: 1451–59.
67. ELLENHARDT, Peter (†17.IX.1533).
    Constofler. XV: 1507–33.
68. ELLENHARDT, Thoman. Constofler.
    XV: 1460–66.
69. v. ENDINGEN, Hans Balthasar
    (†after 1459). Constofler. XIII:
    1433.
70. v. ENDINGEN, Hans Ludwig
    (*1474 †1548). Constofler.
    XIII: 1507–24.
71. ENDINGEN, Hans Rudolph
    (†1493). Constofler. XV: 1471.
72. ENGELMANN, Caspar
    (†11./12.XII.1539). Zum
    Spiegel? XV: 1537?–39.
73. ERB, Sebastian (*1478
    †22.II.1548). Tucher. XXI:
    1542. XV: 1542–48.
74. ERLIN v. RORBURG, Eucharius
    (†11.I.1575). Constofler. XXI:
    1569.
75. ERSTEIN *gen.* ARMBRUSTER, Felix
    (†24.XI.1559). Tucher XV:
    1548. XIII: 1548–52.
76. v. ETTLINGEN, Jacob (†1569).
    Kürschner. XXI: 1556. XV:
    1556–57. XIII: 1557–69.
77. FRANCK, Simon (†26./27.IX.1557).
    Küfer. XXI: 1544–48. XV:
    1533–42. XIII: 1548–56.
78. FUCHS, Blasius. Zum Spiegel. XV:
    1563–69. XIII: 1569–75.
79. FUCHS, Nicolaus (†1598). Tucher.
    XXI: 1571–72.
80. FÜLL v. GEISPOLSHEIM, Heinrich
    (†20./28.VIII.1572). Constofler.
    XV: 1564–72.
81. GEIGER, David (*1530 †1589).
    Zum Spiegel. XXI: 1572. XV:
    1572–89.
82. GEIGER, Mattheus (*1485
    †27.XII.1549). Zum Freiburg.
    XV: 1532–33. XIII: 1533–49.
83. GERBOTT, Hans. Gerber. XIII:
    1433.
84. GERBOTT, Jacob (†1519). Zum
    Freiburg. XV: 1518.
85. GERFALCK, Diebold (†7.IX.1564).
    Weinsticher. XXI: 1557–58. XV:
    1539–?, 1558–64.

86. GOSS v. OBEREHNHEIM (G. v.
    DÜRCKELSTEIN), Bernhard
    (†4.V.1580). Constofler. XV:
    1551–80.
87. v. GOTTESHEIM, Friedrich VI
    (*1506 †3./4.II.1581). Zur
    Blume. XV: 1548, 1551. XIII:
    1551–81.
88. v. GOTTESHEIM, Mathis (†1610).
    Zum Freiburg. XXI: 1572–77.
    XV: 1577–81. XIII: 1581–
    1610.
89. GRAFF, Andres (†1565). Gartner.
    XV: 1557–65.
90. GRAFF, Lorentz (†8./9.VII.1553).
    Gartner. XV: 1524–42.
91. HAGEN, Marx (* ca. 1510 †1551).
    Constofler. XXI: 1547–48.
92. HAMMERER, Hans (†26.X.1572).
    Schuhmacher. XV: 1548–52.
    XIII: 1552–72.
93. HAPMACHER, Andres. Krämer.
    XIII: 1492?–1503?
94. HELDT, Abraham (†25.IX.1594).
    Schneider. XV: 1564–68. XIII:
    1568–94.
95. HERLIN, Martin (†2.VIII.1547).
    Kürschner. XV: 1521. XIII:
    1523–47.
96. HETTER, Herbart (†after 1542).
    Zum Spiegel. XV: 1514–25.
97. HEUSS, Michael, Sr.
    (†10.VII.1556). Schneider.
    XXI: 1548–49. XV: 1549. XIII:
    1552–56.
98. HOFFMEISTER, Caspar (* ca. 1466
    †13.XII.1532). Zur Blume. XV:
    1518–32.
99. v. HOHENBURG, Gottfried (* 1468
    †ca. 1531). Zur Blume. XXI:
    1506. XIII: 1510–24.
100. HÜFFEL, Hans (†after 1478).
    Constofler. XV: 1458.
101. HÜFFEL, Hans Heinrich. Constofler.
    XV: 1451–53.
102. HUG v. OTTENHEIM, Philips
    (†1532?). Schneider. XV:
    1518–19. XIII: 1521–31.
103. INGOLD, Claus (†VII.1525).
    Tucher. XV: 1519?–25.
104. INGOLD, Heinrich (†20.XII.1523).
    Zum Spiegel. XIII: 1507–20.

105. INGOLD, Philips (†ca. 1575). Zum Spiegel. XXI: 1548.

106. JOHAM (v. MUNDOLSHEIM), Conrad (†VIII.1551). Gerber. XV: 1522–30. XIII: 1530–48.

107. JOHAM v. MUNDOLSHEIM, Diebold (†1578). Constofler. XV: 1559–72. XIII: 1572–78.

108. JOHAM v. MUNDOLSHEIM, Georg (†1584). Constofler. XXI: 1569. XV: 1569–84.

109. JOHAM v. MUNDOLSHEIM, Heinrich (†26.V.1573). Constofler. XXI: 1562–63. XV: 1563–73.

110. JÖRGER, Hans, Sr. (*1471 †9.VII.1540). Zum Encker. XV: 1531–40.

111. JUNG, Sebastian (†24.VIII.1554). Schmiede. XV: 1548–54.

112. JUNG, Sebastian (†5.II.1565). Fischer. XV: 1563–65.

113. v. KAGENECK, Arbogast (†17.IV.1471). Constofler. XV: 1458.

114. v. KAGENECK, Philips (†15.XI.1545). Constofler. XV: 1539–42. XIII: 1542–45.

115. v. KAGENECK, Thoman (†after 1453). Constofler. XIII: 1437.

116. KERLING, Marx. Metzger. XV: 1470–71.

117. v. KETTENHEIM, Hans Philips (†1602). Constofler. XIII: 1574–1602.

118. v. KIPPENHEIM, Gregorius (†1569). Constofler. XXI: 1562–68. XV: 1560, 1568–69.

119. KIPS, Veltin (†VIII.1551). Brotbecker. XV: 1541–51.

120. KNIEBIS, Claus (*1479 †4./5.X.1552). Schmiede. XV: 1514–18. XIII: 1520–52.

121. KNIEBIS, Nicolaus Hugo (†1588). Schmiede. XV: 1562–84. XIII: 1584–88.

122. LAMP, Friedrich (†1518). Fischer. XV: 1511–18.

123. v. LAMPERTHEIM, Hans (†14.XI.1562). Schmiede. XV: 1554–62.

124. LEIMER (LYMER), Georg (*1506 †7.VIII.1572). Brotbecker. XV: 1551–55. XIII: 1558–68.

125. LEISTMANN, Dietrich. Schneider. XV: 1459–70.

126. LENTZEL, Claus († by 1435). Constofler. XIII: 1433.

127. v. LEUTRESHEIM, Hans. Schiffleute. XV: 1464.

128. LICHTENSTEIGER, Michael (†18.XII.1589). Maurer. XV: 1564–65. XIII: 1565–89.

129. LINDENFELS, Hans (†30.IX.1548). Zur Möhrin. XV: 1521–31. XIII: 1534–48.

130. LINSER, Claus. Brotbecker. XV: 1455. XIII: 1433–55.

131. LORCHER, Johann Carl (†1588). Zimmerleute. XV: 1563–65. XIII: 1565–88.

132. MARX v. ECKWERSHEIM, Hans Jacob (†21.V.1592). Constofler. XXI: 1565–66. XV: 1566.

133. MARX v. ECKWERSHEIM, Jerg (* ca. 1454 †1535). Constofler. XV: 1518–22.

134. MELBRÜ, Hans. Kornleute. XV: 1451. XIII: 1448–60.

135. MESSINGER, Adam (*ca. 1440 †1494). Würte. XV: 1466–67.

136. MESSINGER, Lux (*15.X.1491 †9.X.1555). Zur Möhrin. XV: 1548–51.

137. MESSINGER, Philips. Würte? XIII: 1471.

138. MEYER, Claus. Zur Steltz. XV: 1562–65. XIII: 1565–78.

139. MEYER, Conrad (†6.III.1555). Schuhmacher. XV: 1540–48.

140. MEYER, Frantz (†27.II.1565). Zur Luzern. XV: 1553–63. XIII: 1563–65.

141. MEYER, Heinrich. Schmiede. XV: 1443–45. XIII: 1448.

142. MEYER, Jacob (†29.I.1562). Maurer. XV: 1521–24. XIII: 1525–62.

143. MEYER, Jacob, "zum Heroldt" (†4.IV.1567). Zur Blume. XV: 1548. XIII: 1554–67.

144. MIEG, Andreas (* ca. 1488 †3.X.1551). Zum Spiegel. XV: 1532–43. XIII: 1543–51.
145. MIEG, Carl, Sr. (* 1473 †9.XI.1541). Tucher. XV: 1532–41.
146. MIEG, Carl, Jr. (* 1521 †14.III.1572). Tucher. XV: 1552–57. XIII: 1558–72.
147. MIEG, Daniel (* ca. 1484 †27.X.1541). Brotbecker. XV: 1519–22. XIII: 1522–41.
148. MIEG, Jacob (* ca. 1452 †29.IV.1513). Zum Spiegel. XXI: 1496–1506. XV: 1506–13.
149. MIEG, Jörg (* 18.XI.1519 †21.IV.1569). Zum Encker. XV: 1568–69.
150. MIEG, Ludwig (* ca. 1455 †25.V.1523). Tucher. XV: 1505.
151. MIEG, Mathis (* 24.VII.1514 †18.VII.1581). Zum Encker. XV: 1563–64.
152. MIEG v. BOOFZHEIM, Sebastian, Sr. (* 19.I.1520 †4.III.1609). Constofler. XV: 1558–63. XIII: 1563–85.
153. MISSEBACH, Peter. Goldschmiede. XV: 1433–52.
154. v. MITTELHAUSEN, Adolph (* 1479 †1.III.1565). Constofler. XV: 1552–60. XIII: 1560–65.
155. v. MOLSHEIM, Jacob (†1582). Zur Luzern. XXI: 1569–75. XV: 1575–82.
156. MÖRDEL, Gabriel (†ca. 1516). Zum Freiburg. XIII: 1514–16.
157. v. MÖRSSMÜNSTER, Ludwig (†13.II.1560). Zur Steltz. XV: 1552–60.
158. MOSUNG, Claus (†by 1478). Krämer? XV: 1465.
159. v. MÜLNHEIM, Burckhardt (†18.XII.1457). Constofler. XV: 1449–55. XIII: 1448–55.
160. v. MÜLNHEIM, Heinrich (* 17.IV.1507 †22.IV.1578). Constofler. XV: 1546–48, 1553–59. XIII: 1559–78.
161. v. MÜLNHEIM, Heinz (†by 1480). Constofler. XIII: 1448.

162. v. MÜLNHEIM, Hiltebrant (†4.VI.1559). Constofler. XV: 1540–44. XIII: 1544–59.
163. v. MÜLNHEIM, Ludwig. Constofler. XV: 1461–65.
164. v. MÜLNHEIM, Ludwig (†ca. 4.I.1526). Constofler. XV: 1507–17. XIII: 1517–26.
165. MÜNCH, Claus (†1522). Gerber. XV: 1514–19. XIII: 1519–22.
166. MÜNCH, Georg (†ca. 1583). Zur Luzern. XV: 1565–83.
167. MÜNCH, Sebastian (†10.XI.1578). Maurer/Zur Möhrin. XV: 1546–48, 1555–56. XIII: 1558–78.
168. MÜRSEL, Bernhard (†by 1478). Constofler. XXI: 1460. XV: 1455.
169. MÜRSEL, Hans. Constofler. XIII: 1433.
170. MUSSLER, Peter (†1519). Zum Encker. XIII: 1506–19.
171. MUSSLER, Reimbold (†by 1503). Schiffleute. XV: 1471.
172. NOPE, Cuno (†12.V.1465). Constofler. XV: 1444–55. XIII: 1448–55.
173. v. NORTHAUSEN, Hans. Weinsticher. XV: 1472.
174. OBRECHT, Hans? XIII: 1448.
175. v. ODRATZHEIM, Hans, Jr. (†16.VIII.1558). Weinsticher. XXI: 1542–48. XV: 1548–53. XIII: 1553–58.
176. OFFENBURG, Bechtold (†ca. 1505). Metzger. XV: 1474–75.
177. OETTEL, Hans (†1585). Kürschner. XXI: 1567–68. XV: 1568–85.
178. OTTFRIEDRICH, Bernhard (†1539). Constofler. XV: 1521–33. XIII: 1533–39.
179. PFARRER, Mathis (* 24.II.1489 †19.I.1568). Weinsticher. XV: 1523–25. XIII: 1525–68.
180. PFITZER, Gregorius (†1549). Kürschner. XXI: 1541–49.
181. PRECHTER, Friedrich II (†5.X.1528). Zum Spiegel. XIII: 1528.
182. PRECHTER, Wilhelm (†26.I.1563). Zum Spiegel. XV: 1548.

183. REBSTOCK, Peter (†by 1495).
Constofler. XV: 1469–70.

184. v. RECHBERG (RECHBURGER),
Arbogast (†12.IV.1580).
Constofler. XXI: 1565–69. XV:
1569–78. XIII: 1578–80.

185. RENNER, Claus. Tucher. XV:
1455–56.

186. RENNER, Claus (†after 1488).
Krämer? XV: 1470–88.

187. RENNER, Claus. Salzmütter. XV:
1471–73.

188. RENNER, Hans, Jr. Tucher. XV:
1441–50.

189. RÖDER v. DIERSBURG, Egenolph
(*1475 †13.VIII.1550).
Constofler. XV: 1525–29. XIII:
1530–50.

190. RÖMER, Christoph (†14.XI.1567).
Kürschner. XXI: 1557–65. XV:
1565–67.

191. ROETTEL, Hans Ulrich (ULRICH,
Hans) (†III.1522). Fischer. XV:
1518–22.

192. v. ROHR, Walther. Würte. XV:
1467.

193. v. ROSHEIM, Ludwig. Constofler.
XV: 1450–59.

194. ROTSCHILT, Stephan. Goldschmiede. XV: 1492.

195. v. ROTWEIL, Hans Erhard. Krämer.
XV: 1476–77.

196. ROTWEIL, Hans Erhard, Sr.
(†after 23.III.1531). Zum
Encker. XV: 1527–31.

197. v. ROTWEIL, Hans Ludwig (* ca.
1458 †II.1531). Zum Encker.
XIII: 1514–26.

198. RUMLER, Caspar (†11./12.III.1563).
Zimmerleute/Wagner. XV:
1525–48. XIII: 1548–63.

199. RUMLER, Florentz (†5./6.II.1525).
Zur Luzern. XIII: 1502–20.

200. RUMLER, Hans. Brotbecker. XV:
1514.

201. Zum RUST, Friedrich (†1473).
Constofler. XV: 1459. XIII:
1460.

202. RYFF, Conrad. Krämer. XXI: 1463.

203. RYFF, Hans. Constofler. XV: 1458.

204. RYFF, Peter († by 1445). Krämer.
XIII:1433.

205. RYFF, Peter († by 1461).
Constofler. XV: 1447–55.

206. v. SCHAUENBURG, Wilhelm
(†1.X.1564). Constofler. XV:
1564.

207. SCHENCKBECHER, Johann
(1529–90). Weinsticher. XV:
1564–75. XIII: 1575–90.

208. SCHETZEL, Nicolaus (Bocks Claus)
(* ca. 1453 †IV.1530).
Weinsticher? XV: 1518–23.

209. SCHONHERR, Jörg. Brotbecker?
XV: 1568–75.

210. SCHORP v. FREUDENBERG, Hans
Jacob (†8.XII.1558). Constofler.
XV: 1552–58.

211. SCHORP v. FREUDENBERG, Hans
Jörg (†1569). Constofler. XV:
1565–69.

212. SCHOTT, Hans (†1568). Gerber.
XV: 1567–68.

213. SCHOTT, Peter (*1427
†8.VIII.1504). Kornleute. XIII:
1471?–1504.

214. SCHÜTTERLIN, Wolfgang
(†10.XI.1612). Zum Encker.
XV: 1568–72. XIII: 1572–1612.

215. SCHÜTZ, Hans, Sr. (†1533).
Schuhmacher, XV: 1524–33.

216. SCHWENCKER, Michael, Sr.
(†1.V.1556). Zur Luzern. XV:
1548–56.

217. SCHWENDT, Hans (†1511). Fischer.
XV: 1504–11.

218. SEBOTT, Diebold (†1534). Zur
Steltz. XV: 1519–34.

219. SEBOTT, Lamprecht, Sr.(*1468†1519).
Zur Steltz. XV: 1506–19.

220. SPENDER, Jacob († ca. 1525).
Constofler. XXI: 1522–24.

221. SPENDER, Reimbold. Constofler.
XV: 1441. XIII: 1433.

222. SPENDER, Reimbold (†1534).
Constofler. XIII: 1521–30.

223. SPETE, Hans. Gartner. XV:
1433–43.

224. SPIEGEL, Walter. Constofler. XV:
1433.

225. SPIELMANN, Hans. Wagner. XV:
1467.

226. SPIRER, Hans. Kürschner. XV:1452.

227. SPIRER, Hans. Würte. XV: 1467.

228. SPORER, Stephan. Schmiede. XV: 1433.
229. STÄDEL, Christoph II (* 1504 †12./13.V.1554). Zur Steltz. XV: 1541–54.
230. STÄDEL, Christoph III (†1585). Zur Steltz. XXI: 1575–78. XIII: 1578–85.
231. STANGE, Erhard. Krämer/ Schiffleute. XV: 1461–67.
232. STEFFAN, Heinrich. Goldschmiede. XIII: 1433.
233. STORCK, Veltin (†1561). Gerber. XV: 1543–59.
234. STÖSSER, Hans (†15.II.1558). Zum Spiegel. XV: 1551–58.
235. STURM, Friedrich (†10.XI.1562). Constofler. XV: 1550–53. XIII: 1553–62.
236. STURM, Hans. Constofler. XV: 1467–73.
237. STURM, Hans (†1536). Constofler. XV: 1531–36.
238. STURM, Jacob (* 10.VII.1489 †30.X.1553). Constofler. XV: 1525–26. XIII: 1526–53.
239. STURM, Martin († X.1521). Constofler. XV: 1506–21.
240. STURM, Peter († 5./6.VII.1563). Constofler. XV: 1533–63.
241. STURM, Stephen (†31.V.1578). Constofler. XXI: 1554–62. XV: 1546–48. XIII: 1562–78.
242. STURM v. STURMECK, Hans. Constofler. XV: 1433.
243. TRAUSCH, Heinrich (†1593). Gerber. XIII: 1569–93.
244. Zum TRÜBEL, Cune. Constofler. XIII: 1433.
245. ULRICH, Claus (†1504). Fischer. XV: 1488–1504.
     ULRICH, Hans. See: ROETTEL, Hans Ulrich.
246. VENDENHEIM, Hans. Gerber. XV: 1488?–94.
247. VENDENHEIM, Lorentz. Gerber. XV: 1494–96.
248. VOGT, Walther. Kürschner. XV: 1468–69.
249. VOLLMAR, Hans Heinrich (†1572). Zur Blume. XV: 1559–72.
250. VÖLTSCH, Hans († after 1478). Constofler. XV: 1475–78.

251. VOLTZ, Peter († after 1436). Krämer. XV: 1433.
252. WANNER, Hans. XIII: 1433.
253. WETZEL v. MARSILIEN, Jacob († after 1555). Constofler. XV: 1536–43.
254. WETZEL v. MARSILIEN, Martin († 24.I.1554). Constofler. XV: 1548.
255. WIDERGRIEN v. STAUFENBERG, Hans Jacob († 6.XI.1551). Constofler. XV: 1542–50. XIII: 1550–51.
256. WINGERSHEIM, Stephan. Tucher. XV: 1464–72.
257. WINICH, Johann (* 21.X.1488 †22.IX.1541). Schuhmacher. XV: 1533–40.
258. WISSBACH, Jacob († 24.I.1508). Zur Blume. XIII: 1498?–1508.
259. WOLFF, Claus († ca. 1520). Gartner. XV: 1514–20.
260. WURMSER, Bernhard. Constofler. XV: 1477.
261. WURMSER, Claus. Weinleute. XV: 1433–39.
262. WURMSER, Jacob. Krämer. XIII: 1448–63.
263. WURMSER, Jacob, Sr. Constofler. XV: 1492. XIII: 1506–14.
264. WURMSER, Sebastian († 3.IX.1564). Constofler. XV: 1563–64.
265. WURMSER, Wolff (†1563). Constofler. XV: 1559–63.
266. WURMSER v. VENDENHEIM, Bernhard († 27.VI.1540). Constofler. XV: 1524–25, 1528–31. XIII: 1532–40.
267. WURMSER v. VENDENHEIM, Wolff Sigismund (†14./15.II.1574). Constofler. XV: 1554–56. XIII: 1556–74.
268. ZERINGER, Cuntz. Ölleute. XV: 1457–64
269. ZORN v. BULACH, Claus. Constofler. XV: 1464–77.
270. ZORN v. ECKERICH, Hans. Constofler. XV: 1433.
271. ZORN zum RIET, Jacob (†13.XI.1531). Constofler. XV: 1525?–31.
272. ZORN zum RIET, Ludwig († ca. 1529). Constofler. XV: 1507–24.

BIBLIOGRAPHY

The bibliography is divided into three sections: manuscript sources (A), printed sources (B), and literature (C). The manuscripts and groups of manuscripts in section A are listed alphabetically by the city in which the archive or library is located. In section B, the sources and groups of printed sources are listed alphabetically according to author, editor, or title, in every case following the manner in which the item is cited in the notes. In section C, the order is entirely alphabetical according to the same principle, usually following the name of the author. Collective volumes are not listed separately where only one item from the volume is cited, in which case the bibliographical information on the volume itself is entered under the item cited. Where two or more items from the same volume are cited, however, there are both separate entries under the authors of the items and an entry, normally by title, for the volume; in this case, only short titles are used in the entries for separate items from the volume. This principle, plus the decision to list all literature alphabetically rather than to classify it by subject, was dictated by the extensive use of short titles and abbreviations in the notes and appendices. The sigla used in the bibliography are identical to those used in the notes and appendices. Severely abbreviated forms for printed sources and for literature are entered in parentheses at the end of the relevant entries. Finally, every collection, article, and book employed in the preparation of this study is listed in the bibliography, which seemed desirable because of the frequent use of short titles and abbreviations. The entire bibliography is designed to enable the reader to find easily information on individual items without unnecessary searching and to eliminate as much as possible the repetition of information.

A. MANUSCRIPT SOURCES

BERN, Staatsarchiv
    Unnutze Papiere 67, Nos. 265–267
CHICAGO, The Newberry Library
    Ms. 63: "Oraciones varies"
DARMSTADT, Hessisches Staatsarchiv (HStAD)
    B 2 (Hanau–Lichtenberg Akten) 60, 5
GÖTTINGEN, Niedersächsische Staats- und Universitätsbibliothek (NSUG)
    Ms. Hist. 154: "Chronik von Strassburg bis gegen Ende des 16. Jh."
KARLSRUHE, Badische Landesbibliothek (BLBK)
    Ms. Ettenheim–Münster 17
    Ms. Ortenau 1
KARLSRUHE, Badisches Generallandesarchiv (GLAK)
    44/818: Adelsarchiv (Sturm)
    67/42–46, 48–49: Baden feudal registers, 1471–1565
    67/1006–1008, 1010–1016, 1022–1023, 1057–1058: Palatine feudal
        registers, 1449–1565

MARBURG, Hessisches Staatsarchiv (HStAM)
  PA (Politisches Archiv des Landgrafen Philipp), 326, 330, 359, 2915, 2917
MULHOUSE (Haut–Rhin), Archives Municipales (AMM)
  Series I, No. 4447: Anonymous letter from Strasbourg, 31.VIII.1548
OSTHOUSE (Bas–Rhin), Fonds Zorn de Bulach
  Laden I, Nos. 86–86bis
  Laden IVbis, Nos. 2–4
SCHAFFHAUSEN, Staatsarchiv
  Korrespondenzen 1548, No. 8: Anonymous letter from Strasbourg, 31.VIII.1548
STRASBOURG, Archives Départementales du Bas–Rhin (ADBR)

Series E	27	2024	5589/(2)
	600	2764	5948
	1251/1	2775	6033
	1356/1		

Series G	501–503	802–804	911
	526	817	1375/1
	634	821	2691
	675	841–842	2942
	704	853/6	

Series H	27/(6)	1622	3325
	1408	1630	

Series 3B	62	580	1357
	92	711	1484
	122	779	

Series 12J	2006		
	2022/1–4, 15		

Series 25J	23	290a	
	28–28b	344k–n	
	30	388	
	33	388b	
	36–36a	667	
	43	795	

  Fonds Landsberg
    "Censier des Bock de Blaesheim"
  Fonds Saverne
    1 G 158/34

STRASBOURG, Archives Municipales (AMS)
  Series XXI   1539–1562:   "Procès-verbaux du Sénat et des Vingt-et-Un"

Series AA	294	1552	
	407a/8	1555a/43–44, 66	
	564–565	1808/11, 15	
Series I	17–19/1–2, 4		
	20a/2–3		
	24b/23		
Series II	7/20	76b–77/7	
	16/39	84a/27	
	71/22	84/6, 9	
	76a/1	93/2–4	
Series III	2/9	71/3	
	11/25	85/1	
	12/3	135/1	
	20		
Series IV	22, 1	102/4	
	48	102/9	
	86	105a	
	98/1	110	
	101/5		
Series V	1/14	21/1	138/12–13
	1/52	24/4	138/25
	1/82	55/4	139/2
	1/88	79/20	139/4
	2/18–20	132/27	139/14
	11/36	137/14	139/20–21
	14/112	137/23–26	152/5
Series VI	145/3	488/3	495
	146/2	488/10	496
	173/5	491/3	589/6
	210/6	492/1	591/1
	279/1	493/4–6	591/3
	393/1		
Series VII	10/4	12/5	84/1–6
	10/25	57/1	84/20
	10/27–40	63/3	1436
	11/1	80	1438
	11/3		
Series VIII	132/90	186	
	134/10	197/83	
Series IX	1/4		
	1/6		
Series H	590	4688	

Series R	26/1	29/107
	26/29	29/110
	28, fol. 102^r	29/253
	29/92a	

Series KS	7–23	55
	25–27	58
	31	63
	35	66
	40	70
	43	98
	46	

Ms. 852: Johannes Wencker, "Argentoratensia historico–politico," I, No. 105

Livre de Bourgeoisie　I (1440–1530)
　　　　　　　　　　 II (1543–1618)
　　　　　　　　　　 III (1559–1713)

Archives des Tribus
　Pelletiers, No. 6

Archives du Grand-Chapitre de Strasbourg (AGCS)
　"Comptes in Heilewog" in "Documenta particularia. Colligends de différents bénéfices"

Fonds Mullenheim

Archives du Chapitre de Saint-Thomas (AST)
　Ms.　16/51
　　　　35–36: "Sécularisation des couvents"
　　　　37: "Réforme des chapitres et des couvents"
　　　　38/1: "Diarium N. Gerbellii"
　　　　40: "Buceriana," etc.
　　　　45: "Rapports sur les inspections des églises"
　　　69/2–6: "Augustin Trenss contra Dr. Hedio"
　　　　70/1: Oseas Schad, "Kirchengeschichte"
　　　　75: "1533. Actes du synode"
　　　　80: "1525–1529. Ecrits contre la messe"
　　　　98/6: "Lettres de plusieurs communes rurales"
　　　　134: "Pièce concernant l'église de St.-André"
　　　　166: Wencker, "Varia ecclesiastica," Ia
　　　　176: Wencker, "Varia ecclesiastica," IX
　　　　192: "Protocolla Wurmseriana, 1513–1524"
　　　1655: Johannes Schenckbecher, "Biographia autographa"

STRASBOURG, Bibliothèque Municipale (BMS)
　Ms.　936: Papers of Ludwig Schneegans
　　　1024: Papers of Léon Dacheux

STRASBOURG, Bibliothèque Nationale et Universitaire (BNUS)
Ms.   626, fols. 158ᵛ–165ᵛ: Notes on the regime 1539–74
     660–683: "Thesaurus epistolarum reformatorum alsaticorum"
          (Baum)
     741:     "Der Steinmetzen Bruoderschafft," 1515–16
     752:     "Necrologium der Johanniter zu Strassburg"
     847:     Christoph Koleffel, "Memorial oder Gedenckbuechlein"
     1018:   Strasbourg Chronicle to 1625
     1053/7: Land purchase at Lingolsheim by G. v. Hohenburg 1523
     1058:   "Collectanea genealogica"
     1223:   Jean Pfeffinger, "Noblesse alsacienne"
     1266:   Imlin Chronicle
     3775:   Mittelhausen *censier* for Oberbergheim 1557–69

STRASBOURG, Musée Historique
     Johannes Städel, "Chronica Aller Denckwürdigsten Historien, Ge-
     schichten vnd Thaten," vols. II (1332–1449) and III (1500–99)

STUTTGART, Hauptstaatsarchiv (HStAS)
     A 26
     A 149/1
     A 104/2

STUTTGART, Württembergische Landesbibliothek (WLBS)
     Ms.   580 fol.: Strasbourg *Ammeisterbuch* of Martin Herlin and Jacob
          Braun

WOLFENBÜTTEL, Herzog August Bibliothek (HABW)
     Ms.   2 Aug. 2°: Strasbourg chronicle to 1563.

B. PRINTED SOURCES

Die ältesten Schriften Geilers von Kaysersberg. Ed. Léon Dacheux. Freiburg/Br.,
     1882. (*Schriften Geilers*).
"Les annales des frères mineurs de Strasbourg, redigées par le frère Martin
     Stauffenberger, économe du couvent (1507–1510)," ed. Rodolphe Reuss,
     BSCMHA, N.S. 18 (1897), pp. 295–314.
Annales de Sébastien Brant, ed. Léon Dacheux, *BSCMHA*, N.S. 15 (1892),
     pp. 211–279, Nos. 3238–3645bis; N.S. 19 (1899), pp. 33–260, Nos.
     4391–5132. (*Ann. Brant*).
Barth, Medard, ed., "Der Liber investiturarum sub Erasmo episcopo argenti-
     nensi datarum (1541–1568)," *AEA*, 6 (1955), 69–102.
Berler, Matern, "Chronik," in *Code historique et diplomatique de la Ville de
     Strasbourg,* II, 1–130.
de Bèze, Théodore. *Icones.* Geneva, 1580.
Bodin, Jean. *Six Books of the Commonwealth.* Trans./ed. M. J. Tooley. Oxford,
     n.d.
Botero, Giovanni. *The Reason of State.* Trans. P. J. Waley and D. P. Waley.
     New Haven–London, 1956.

Brant, Sebastian, "Bischoff Wilhelms von Hoensteins waal und einritt. Anno 1506 et 1507," in *Code historique et diplomatique de la Ville de Strasbourg*, II, 239–299. (Brant).

Briefwechsel der Brüder Ambrosius und Thomas Blaurer 1509–1548/67. Edited for the Badische Historische Kommission by Traugott Schiess. 3 vols. Freiburg/Br., 1908–12.

Bucer, Martin. *Deutsche Schriften*. Eds. Robert Stupperich, *et al*. Gütersloh–Paris, 1960-

Büheler, Sebald, *La chronique strasbourgeoise*, ed. Léon Dacheux, *BSCMHA*, N.S. 13 (1888), pp. 23–149, Nos. 85–599. (Büheler, *Chronique*).

Calvin, Jean. *Ioannis Calvini opera quae supersunt omnia*. Eds. Johann Wilhelm Baum, *et al*. 59 vols. *Corpus Reformatorum*, vols. 29–87. Braunschweig, 1863–1900.

Die Chroniken der deutschen Städte vom 14. bis ins 16. Jahrhundert. Ed. Carl Hegel. Vols. VIII–IX: *Strassburg*. Leipzig, 1870–71.

Corpus Reformatorum. *See*: Melanchthon, Philipp, Calvin, Jean, and Zwingli, Huldrych.

Cowie, Murray A., and Cowie, Marian L., eds. *The Works of Peter Schott (1460–1490)*. 2 vols. North Carolina University Studies in the Germanic Languages and Literatures, 41, 71. Chapel Hill, N.C., 1963, 1972.

Deutsche Reichstagsakten, Jüngere Reihe. Edition sponsored by the Historische Kommission bei der Bayerischen Akademie der Wissenschaften. Vols. 1–4, 7–8. Gotha, 1893–1938; Göttingen, 1970–71.

Eheberg, Karl Theodor, ed. *Verfassungs-, Verwaltungs- und Wirtschaftsgeschichte der Stadt Strassburg bis 1681*. Vol. I: *Urkunden und Akten*. Strasbourg, 1899. (Eheberg).

"Les éphémérides de Jacques de Gottesheim, docteur en droit, prébendier du Grand-Choeur de la Cathédrale (1524–1543)," ed. Rodolphe Reuss, *BSCMHA*, N.S. 19 (1898), pp. 261–281.

Farmer, John S., ed. *The Spider and the Fly*. London, 1908.

Farner, Oskar, ed., "Ein unveröffentlichter Zwinglibrief," *Zwingliana*, 9 (1950), 247–249.

Ficker, Johannes, ed., "Jakob Sturms Entwurf zur Strassburger reformatorischen Verantwortung für den Augsburger Reichstag 1530," *ELJb*, 19 (1941), 149–158.

Ficker, Johannes, and Winckelmann, Otto, eds. *Handschriftenproben des 16. Jahrhunderts nach Strassburger Originalen*. 2 vols. Strasbourg, 1902–05. (Ficker–Winckelmann).

Fragments de diverses vieilles chroniques, ed. Léon Dacheux, *BSCMHA*, N.S. 18 (1900). (*Fragments*).

Fuchs, François-Joseph, ed. *Documents alsaciens des chartriers nobles du pays de Bade d'après les inventaires publiés*. Publications de la Fédération des Sociétés d'histoire et d'archéologie d'Alsace, 2. Strasbourg, 1961.

Fürstenbergisches Urkundenbuch. Ed. Sigmund Riezler. 7 vols. Tübingen, 1877–91. (*FUB*).

Gebwiler, Hieronymus. *Die Strassburger Chronik des elsässischen Humanisten Hieronymus Gebwiler*. Ed. Karl Stenzel. SWIELR. Berlin–Leipzig, 1926.

Hefele, Friedrich, ed., "Freiherrlich von Gaylingisches Archiv im Schlosse zu Ebnet bei Freiburg," *MBHK*, 38 (1916), pp. m74–m120; 39 (1917), pp. m11–m112; 40 (1921), pp. m5–m30; 41 (1940), pp. m2–m64; 42 (1941), pp. m1–m64; 43 (1941), pp. *m1–*m53. (Hefele).

Herberger, Theodor, ed. *Sebastian Schertlin von Burtenbach und seine an die Stadt Augsburg geschriebenen Briefe.* Augsburg, 1852.

Herrmann, Hans Walter. *Geschichte der Grafschaft Saarwerden bis zum Jahre 1527.* 2 vols. Veröffentlichungen der Kommission für saarländische Landesgeschichte und Volksforschung, 1. Saarbrücken, 1957–59. (Herrmann).

Hertzog, Bernhard. *Chronicon Alsatiae. Edelsässer Chronik vnnd aussfürliche Beschreibung des untern Elsasses am Rheinstrom.* Strasbourg, 1592. (Hertzog).

Horning, Wilhelm, ed./trans. *Briefe von Strassburger Reformatoren, ihren Mitarbeitern und Freunden über die Einführung des "Interims" in Strassburg (1548–1554).* Strasbourg, 1887.

"Imlin Chronik" = "Strassburg im sechszehnten Jahrhundert, 1500–1591. Auszug aus der Imlin'schen Familienchronik," ed. Rodolphe Reuss, *Alsatia,* 10 (1873/74), 363–476.

Irschlinger, Robert, ed., "Die Aufzeichnungen des Hans Ulrich Landschad von Steinach über sein Geschlecht," *ZGO*, 86 (1934), 205–258.

Isenbart, Hugo, ed., "Verzeichnis der in dem Familienarchiv der Freiherrn Roeder von Diersburg in Baden enthaltenen Archivalien," *MBHK*, 16 (1894), pp. m57–m118.

Kentzinger, Antoine, ed. *Documents historiques rélatifs à l'histoire de France, tirés des archives de la ville de Strasbourg.* 2 vols. Strasbourg, 1818–19.

Kleine Strassburger Chronik. Denckwürdige Sachen alhier in Strassburg vorgeloffen und begeben 1424–1615. Ed. Rodolphe Reuss. Strasbourg, 1889.

Kohls, Ernst-Wilhelm, ed. *Die evangelischen Katechismen von Ravensburg 1546/1733 und Reichenweier 1547/1559.* VKLBW, A 10. Stuttgart, 1963.

Krebs, Manfred. *Quellensammlung zur oberrheinischen Geschlechterkunde.* Vol. I, part 1. Karlsruhe, 1943.

Krebs, Manfred, and Rott, Hans Georg, eds. *Quellen zur Geschichte der Täufer.* Vols. VII–VIII: *Elsass. Stadt Strassburg 1522–1535.* 2 vols. QFRG, 26–27. Gütersloh, 1959–60. (*TQ Strassburg*).

Lenz, Max, ed. *Briefwechsel des Landgrafen Philipp des Grossmüthigen von Hessen mit Bucer.* 3 vols. Publikationen aus den königlich preussischen Staatsarchiven, 5, 28, 42. Leipzig, 1880–97.

Letters and Papers, Foreign and Domestic, of the Reign of Henry VIII, 1509–47. Eds. J. S. Brewer, *et al.* 21 vols. London, 1862–1929.

von Liliencron, Rochus, ed. *Die historischen Volkslieder der Deutschen.* 4 vols. Leipzig, 1865–96.

Luther, Martin. *Werke. Kritische Gesamtausgabe. Briefwechsel.* 14 vols. Weimar, 1930–70.

Machiavelli, Niccolò. *Arte della guerra et scritti politici minori.* Ed. Sergio Bertelli. Milan, 1961.

Die Matrikel der Universität Basel. Ed. Hans Georg Wackernagel. 3 vols. Basel, 1951–62. (*Matrikel Basel*).

Die Matrikel der Universität Freiburg im Breisgau von 1460–1656. Ed. Hermann Mayer. 2 vols. Freiburg/Br., 1907–10. (*Matrikel Freiburg*).

Die Matrikel der Universität Heidelberg 1386–1662. Ed. Gustav Toepke. 3 vols. Heidelberg, 1884–93. (*Matrikel Heidelberg*).

Die Matrikel der Universität Köln. Ed. Hermann Keussen. Publikationen der Gesellschaft für Rheinische Geschichtskunde, 8. 3 vols. Bonn, 1919–31. Vol. I in 2nd ed. (*Matrikel Köln*).

Die Matrikeln der Universität Tübingen. Ed. Heinrich Hermelink. Vol. I: *Die Matrikeln von 1477–1600*. Stuttgart, 1906, plus index volume (Stuttgart, 1931). (*Matrikel Tübingen*).

Melanchthon, Philipp. *Opera quae supersunt omnia*. Eds. Carl Gottlieb Bretschneider, *et al*. 28 vols. *Corpus Reformatorum*, vols. 1–28. Halle, 1834–60.

Meyer, Johann Jacob, *La Chronique strasbourgeoise*, ed. Rodolphe Reuss, *BSCMHA*, N.S. 8 (1872), pp. 121–287. (Meyer, *Chronique*).

de Montaigne, Michel. *Oeuvres complètes*. Eds. Robert Barral and Pierre Michel. Paris, 1967.

Neu, Heinrich, ed., "Freiherrlich von Türckheimisches Archiv in Altdorf, Bezirksamt Ettenheim," *MBHK*, 29 (1907), pp. m49–m82.

——, ed., "Freiherrlich von Türckheimisches Archiv auf Schloss Mahlberg, Bezirksamt Ettenheim," *MBHK*, 29 (1907), pp. m40–m48.

Opus epistolarum Des. Erasmi Roterodami denuo recognitum et auctum. Eds. P. S. Allen and H. S. Allen. 12 vols. Oxford, 1906–46.

Pantaleon, Heinrich. *Prosopographiae heroum*. Basel, 1566.

Pasquier, Etienne. *Lettres historiques pour les années 1556–1594*. Ed. Dorothy Thickett. Textes littéraires français, 123. Geneva, 1966.

Politische Correspondenz der Stadt Strassburg im Zeitalter der Reformation. Eds. Hans Virck, *et al*. 5 vols. in 6. Urkunden und Akten der Stadt Strassburg, part II. Strasbourg, 1882–99; Heidelberg, 1928–33. (*PCSS*).

Quellen zur Geschichte des Bauernkriegs in Oberschwaben. Ed. Franz Ludwig Baumann. Bibliothek des Litterarischen Vereins in Stuttgart, CXXIX. Tübingen, 1876.

Quellensammlung der badischen Landesgeschichte. Ed. Franz Joseph Mone. 4 vols. Karlsruhe, 1845–63. (*QBLG*).

Queller, Donald E., ed. *Early Venetian Legislation on Ambassadors*. Travaux d'Humanisme et Renaissance, 88. Geneva, 1966.

Rappoltsteinisches Urkundenbuch 759–1500. Ed. Karl Albrecht. 5 vols. Colmar, 1891–98. (*RUB*).

Riegger, J. A. *Amoenitates litterariae friburgenses*. 3 parts. Ulm, 1775–76.

Rosenkranz, Albert. *Der Bundschuh. Die Erhebung des südwestdeutschen Bauernstandes in den Jahren 1493–1517*. 2 vols. SWIELR. Heidelberg, 1927.

Röder von Diersburg, Felix, ed., "Mittheilungen aus dem Freiherrlich von Röder'schen Archive," *FDA*, 14 (1881), 93–100; 15 (1882), 225–236.

Rott, Hans. *Quellen und Forschungen zur südwestdeutschen und schweizerischen Kunstgeschichte im XV. und XVI. Jahrhundert*. Part III: *Der Oberrhein*. 3 vols. Stuttgart, 1936–38. (Rott, *Oberrhein*).

Saladin, Johann Georg, *Strassburg Chronik*, eds. Aloys Meister and Aloys

Ruppel, *BSCMHA*, N.S. 22 (1908), pp. 127–206; N.S. 23 (1911), pp. 182–281, 283–435. (Saladin, *Chronik*).

Schadeus, Oseas. *Summum argentoratensium templum.* Strasbourg, 1617. (Schadeus).

Schmoller, Gustav. *Die Strassburger Tucher- und Weberzunft. Ein Beitrag zur Geschichte der deutschen Weberei und des deutschen Gewerberechts vom 13.–17. Jahrhundert.* Strasbourg, 1879. (Schmoller).

Schneegans, Ludwig. *Strassburgische Geschichten.* Strasbourg, 1855.

Schulte, Aloys. *Geschichte der Grossen Ravensburger Handelsgesellschaft 1380–1530.* 3 vols. DHMN, I–III. Stuttgart, 1923. (Schulte).

de Seyssel, Claude. *La monarchie de France.* Ed. J. Poujol. Paris, 1961.

Simonsfeld, Henry. *Der Fondaco dei Tedeschi in Venedig und die deutsch–venezianischen Handelsbeziehungen.* 2 vols. Stuttgart, 1887.

Specklin, Daniel, *Les Collectanées*, ed. Rodolphe Reuss, *BSCMHA*, N.S. 13 (1888), pp. 157–360, Nos. 600–1299; N.S. 14 (1889), pp. 1–178, 201–404, Nos. 1300–2561. (Specklin, *Collectanées*).

"Strassburgische Archiv-Chronik," in *Code historique et diplomatique de la Ville de Strasbourg,* II, 131–220.

Strieder, Jakob, ed. *Aus Antwerpener Notariatsarchiven. Quellen zur deutschen Wirtschaftsgeschichte des 16. Jahrhunderts.* DHMN, IV. Stuttgart–Berlin–Leipzig, 1930.

Sturm, Jean. *Classicae epistolae, sive scholae Argentinenses restitutae.* Ed. Jean Rott. Paris–Strasbourg, 1938.

——, *Quarti Antipappi tres partes priores.* Neustadt an der Hardt, 1580. (Sturm).

Summenhart, Conrad. *Tractatulus bipartitus de decimis defensivus opinionis theologorum adversus communiter canonistas de quotta decimarium, si debita sit iure divino vel humano.* Hagenau, 1500.

Theil, Bernhard, ed. *Das älteste Lehnbuch der Markgrafen von Baden (1381).* VKLBW, A 25. Stuttgart, 1974.

Trausch, Jacob, and Wencker, Johann, *Les chroniques strasbourgeoises,* ed. Léon Dacheux, *BSCMHA*, N.S. 15 (1892), pp. 3–207, Nos. 2562–3237h.

Ungerer, Edmund, ed. *Elsässische Altertümer in Burg und Haus, in Kloster und Kirche. Inventare vom Ausgang des Mittelalters bis zum dreissigjährigen Kriege aus Stadt und Bistum Strassburg.* 2 vols. Quellen und Forschungen zur Kirchen- und Kulturgeschichte von Elsass und Lothringen, II. Strasbourg, 1913–17.

Urkundenbuch der Stadt Basel. Ed. Rudolf Wackernagel. 11 vols. Basel, 1890–1910. (*UBB*).

Wimpheling, Jacob, "Germania," in *Wimpfeling und Murner im Kampf um die ältere Geschichte des Elsasses. Ein Beitrag zur Charakteristik des deutschen Frühhumanismus,* ed. Emil von Borries, SWIELR (Heidelberg, 1926).

——. *Opera selecta.* Vol. I: *Jakob Wimpfelings "Adolescentia."* Ed. Otto Herding. Munich, 1965.

Winckelmann, Otto. *Das Fürsorgewesen der Stadt Strassburg vor und nach der Reformation. Ein Beitrag zur deutschen Kultur- und Wirtschaftsgeschichte.* 2 vols. QFRG, 5. Leipzig, 1922. (Winckelmann).

Wittmer, Charles, ed., "L'obituaire de l'Eglise Rouge de Strasbourg," *AEA*, 1 (1946), 87–131.

Wittmer, Charles, and Meyer, J. Charles, eds. *Le Livre de Bourgeoisie de la Ville de Strasbourg 1440–1530*. 3 vols. Strasbourg, 1948–55. (Wittmer).

Wunder, Gerhard, ed., "Ein Verzeichnis des Strassburger Landgebiets aus dem Jahr 1516," *ZGO*, 114 (1966), 61–65. (Wunder, "Verzeichnis").

Wunder, Gerhard, and Leckner, G., eds. *Die Bürgerschaft der Reichsstadt Hall von 1395–1600*. Württembergische Geschichtsquellen, 25. Stuttgart, 1956.

Zimmerische Chronik. Ed. K. A. von Barack. 4 vols. Bibliothek des Litterarischen Vereins in Stuttgart, XCI–XCIV. Tübingen, 1869. (*ZC*).

The Zurich Letters. Ed./trans. Hastings Robinson. 2 vols. Parker Society. Cambridge, 1842, 1845.

Zwingli, Huldrych. *Sämtliche Werke*. Eds. Emil Egli, *et al.* 14 vols. *Corpus Reformatorum*, vols. 88–101. Berlin–Leipzig-Zürich, 1905–59. (*ZW*).

C. LITERATURE

Abel, Wilhelm. *Agrarkrisen und Agrarkonjunktur; eine Geschichte der Land- und Ernährungswirtschaft Mitteleuropas seit dem hohen Mittelalter*. 2nd ed. Berlin–Hamburg, 1966.

Adam, Johann. *Evangelische Kirchengeschichte der elsässischen Territorien bis zur französischen Revolution*. Strasbourg, 1928. (Adam, *EKET*).

——. *Evangelische Kirchengeschichte der Stadt Strassburg bis zur französischen Revolution*. Strasbourg, 1922. (Adam, *EKSS*).

Adam, Paul. *Histoire religieuse de Sélestat*. Vol. I: *Des origines à 1615*. Sélestat, 1967.

——. *L'humanisme à Sélestat. L'école, les humanistes, la bibliothèque*. 2nd ed. Sélestat, 1967.

Alter, Jean V. *Les origines de la satire anti-bourgeoise en France. Moyen âge-XVIe siècle*. Travaux d'Humanisme et Renaissance, 83. Geneva, 1966.

Ammann, Hektor. *Von der Wirtschaftsgeltung des Elsass im Mittelalter*. Lahr/Schwarzwald, 1955. Also in *AJb*, 1955, pp. 95–202.

Artisans et ouvriers d'Alsace. PSSARE, 9. Strasbourg, 1965.

Baillet, Lina, "Deux villes de la Moyenne Alsace: Sélestat et Colmar, face aux conflits religieux et sociaux," *La Guerre des Paysans 1525*, ed. A. Wollbrett, pp. 93–102.

Bainton, Roland H., "Katherine Zell," *Medievalia et Humanistica,* N.S. 1 (1970), 3–28. Also in *Women of the Reformation in Germany and Italy* (Minneapolis, 1971).

Baron, Hans. *Calvins Staatsanschauung und das konfessionelle Zeitalter*. Beiheft 1 der *Historischen Zeitschrift*. Berlin–Munich, 1924.

——. *The Crisis of the Early Italian Renaissance*. 1st ed., Princeton, 1955; 2nd ed., 1966.

——, "Religion and Politics in the German Imperial Cities during the Reformation," *The English Historical Review,* 52 (1937), 405–427, 614–633.

Barth, Medard. *Der Rebbau des Elsass und die Absatzgebiet seiner Weine. Ein geschichtlicher Durchblick*. 2 vols. Strasbourg–Paris, 1958.

Barton, Peter F., "Das Jahr 1525 und die Abschaffung der Messe in Strassburg," *Reformation und Humanismus. Robert Stupperich zum 65. Geburtstag*, eds. Martin Greschat and J. F. G. Goeters (Witten, 1969), pp. 141–157.

Bátori, Ingrid, "Besitzstrukturen in der Stadt Kitzingen zur Zeit der Reformation," *Festgabe für Ernst-Walter Zeeden*, pp. 128–141.

——, "Das Patriziat der deutschen Stadt. Zur Klärung einer historischen Frage," *ZSSD*, 2 (1975), 1–30.

Batt, Franz. *Das Eigenthum zu Hagenau im Elsass.* 2 vols. Colmar, 1876–81. (Batt).

Bauer, Clemens, "Probleme der mittelalterlichen Agrargeschichte im Elsass," *AJb*, 1953, pp. 238–250.

Bauernkriegs-Studien. Ed. Bernd Moeller. SVRG, No. 189. Gütersloh, 1975.

Bauernschaft und Bauernstand 1500–1970. Ed. Günther Franz. DFN, 8. Limburg/Lahn, 1975.

Baum, Adolf. *Magistrat und Reformation in Strassburg bis 1529.* Strasbourg, 1887. (Baum).

Baum, Johann Wilhelm. *Capito und Butzer, Strassburgs Reformatoren.* Leben und Ausgewählte Schriften der Väter und Begründer der Reformierten Kirche. Elberfeld, 1860.

Baumgarten, Friedrich, "Hans Baldungs Stellung zur Reformation," *ZGO*, 58 (1904), 245–264. (Baumgarten).

von der Becke-Klüchtzner, E. *Stamm-Tafeln des Adels des Grossherzogthums Baden.* Baden-Baden, 1886–88. (Becke-Klüchtzner).

Becker, Marvin B., "Aspects of Lay Piety in Early Renaissance Florence," *The Pursuit of Holiness*, pp. 177–199.

——, "Some Common Features of Italian Urban Experience (c. 1200–1500)," *Medievalia et Humanistica*, N.S. 1 (1970), 175–201.

Becker, Winfried. *Reformation and Revolution.* Katholisches Leben und Kirchenreform im Zeitalter der Glaubensspaltung, 34. Münster/W., 1974.

Beiträge zur Wirtschaftsgeschichte Nürnbergs. 2 vols. Beiträge zur Geschichte und Kultur der Stadt Nürnberg, 11. Nuremberg, 1967.

Bellardi, Werner, "Anton Engelbrecht (1485–1558), Helfer, Mitarbeiter und Gegner Buchers," *ARG*, 64 (1973), 183–205.

——, "Bucers 'Summarischer Vergriff' und das Interim in Strassburg," *ZKiG*, 85 (1974), 64–76.

——. *Die Geschichte der "christlichen Gemeinschaft" in Strassburg (1546/1550). Der Versuch einer "zweiten Reformation."* QFRG, 18. Leipzig, 1934.

Benecke, G., "Ennoblement and Privilege in Early Modern Germany," *History*, N.S. 56 (1971), 360–370.

Berdahl, Robert M., "The *Stände* and the Origins of Conservatism in Prussia," *Eighteenth Century Studies*, 6 (1972/73), 298–321.

Bergier, Jean-François. *Genève et l'économie européene de la renaissance.* Ecole Pratique des Hautes Etudes, VIe section, série "Affaires et gens d'affaires," 29. Paris, 1963.

Berkner, Lutz K., "The Stem Family and the Developmental Cycle of the Peasant Household: An Eighteenth-Century Austrian Example," *AHR*, 77 (1972), 398–418.

Bernays, Jacob, "Zur Biographie Johann Winthers von Andernach," *ZGO*, 55 (1901), 47–52.

Bernhardt, Walter. *Die Zentralbehörden des Herzogtums Württemberg und ihre Beamten 1520–1629.* 2 vols. VKLBW, B 70–71. Stuttgart, 1973.

Berthold, Brigitte, Engel, Evamaria, and Laube, Adolf, "Die Stellung des Bürgertums in der deutschen Feudalgesellschaft bis zur Mitte des 16. Jahrhunderts," *ZfG*, 21 (1973), 196–217.

Birnbaum, Norman, "The Zwinglian Reformation in Zurich," *Toward a Critical Sociology* (New York, 1971), pp. 133–161.

Bitton, Davis. *The French Nobility in Crisis, 1560–1640.* Stanford, 1969.

Blaich, Fritz. *Die Reichsmonopolgesetzgebung im Zeitalter Karls V. Ihre ordnungs-politische Problematik.* Schriften zum Vergleich von Wirtschaftsordnungen, 8. Stuttgart, 1967.

Blaschke, Karlheinz, "Qualität, Quantität und Raumfunktion als Wesens-merkmale der Stadt vom Mittelalter bis zur Gegenwart," *JRG*, 3 (1968), 34–50.

Bleeck, Ludwig. *Das Augsburger Interim in Strassburg.* Dissertation, Berlin. Berlin, 1893.

Blendinger, Friedrich, "Die wirtschaftlichen Führungsschichten in Augsburg 1430–1740," *Führungskräfte der Wirtschaft in Mittelalter und Neuzeit 1350–1850. Teil I,* pp. 51–86.

——, "Versuch einer Bestimmung der Mittelschicht in der Reichsstadt Augsburg vom Ende des 14. bis zum Anfang des 18. Jahrhunderts," *Städtische Mittelschichten,* pp. 32–78.

Bloch, Marc. *French Rural History. An Essay on its Basic Characteristics.* Trans. Janet Sondheimer. Berkeley–Los Angeles, 1966.

Boehler, Jean–Michel, "Clément Ziegler, un prédicateur populaire au pied du Mont Sainte-Odile," *La Guerre des Paysans 1525,* ed. A. Wollbrett, pp. 15–19.

Bonadeo, Alfredo, "The Role of the 'Grandi' in the Political World of Machiavelli," *Studies in the Renaissance,* 16 (1969), 9–30.

——, "The Role of the People in the Works and Times of Machiavelli," *Bibliothèque d'Humanisme et Renaissance,* 32 (1970), 351–378.

Bopp, Marie-Joseph, "Evangelische Geistliche und Theologen aus Deutsch-land und der Schweiz im Elsass. Ein Beitrag zur oberrheinischen Geistes-und Familiengeschichte," *AJb*, 1961, pp. 175–234.

——. *Die Evangelischen Geistlichen und Theologen im Elsass und Lothringen.* 3 vols. Neustadt/Aisch, 1959. (Bopp).

Bosl, Karl, "Kasten, Stände, Klassen im mittelalterlichen Deutschland," *Die Gesellschaft in der Geschichte des Mittelalters,* 2nd ed. rev., Kleine Vandenhoeck–Reihe, 231/231a. Göttingen, 1966; also in *ZBLG*, 52 (1969). French version in *Problemes de stratification sociale,* ed. Roland Mousnier, pp. 13–29.

Bourdieu, Pierre, "Reproduction culturelle et reproduction sociale," *Informa-tions en sciences sociales,* 10, No. 2 (1972), 45–79. German version in Bour-dieu, Pierre, and Passeron, Jean-Claude, *Grundlagen einer Theorie der symbolischen Gewalt,* trans. Eva Moldenhauer (Frankfurt/M., 1973), pp. 88–139.

La bourgeoisie alsacienne. Études d'histoire sociale. PSSARE, 5. Strasbourg, 1954.

Boutruche, Robert, ed. *Bordeaux de 1453 à 1715.* Bordeaux, 1966.

Bouwsma, William J., "Renaissance and Reformation: An Essay in their Affinities and Connections," *Luther and the Dawn of the Modern Era,* pp. 127–149.

Bowsky, William J., "The Anatomy of Rebellion in Fourteenth Century Siena: from Commune to Signory?" *Violence and Civil Disorder in Italian Cities,* pp. 229–273.

Brackert, Helmut. *Bauernkrieg und Literatur.* Frankfurt/M., 1975.

Brady, Thomas A., Jr., "The Privy Councils of Strasbourg (XV and XIII): A Supplement to Jacques Hatt, *Liste des membres du grand sénat de Strasbourg,*" *BCGA,* No. 27 (1974), 73–79.

——, "Jacob Sturm of Strasbourg and the Lutherans at the Diet of Augsburg, 1530," *CH,* 42 (1973), 183–202.

——, "Jacob Sturm of Strasbourg (1489–1553) and the Political Security of German Protestantism, 1526–1532," Unpublished Ph.D. Dissertation, University of Chicago, 1968.

——, "'Sind also zu beyden theylen Christen, des Gott erbarm.' Jacob Sturm's Memorial on Public Worship at Strasbourg (August, 1525," in *L'Alsace, la Réforme et l'Europe au XVIe siècle. Mélanges offerts à Jean Rott,* eds. Marc Lienhard and Marijn de Kroon (Leiden, 1978).

——, "The Social Place of a German Renaissance Artist: Hans Baldung Grien (1484/85–1545) at Strasbourg," *Central European History,* 8 (1975), 295–315.

——, "The Themes of Social Structure, Social Conflict, and Civic Harmony in Jakob Wimpheling's *Germania,*" *Sixteenth Century Journal,* 3 (1972), 65–76.

Braudel, Fernand. *La méditerranée et le monde méditerranéen à l'epoque de Philippe II,* 2nd ed., 2 vols. Paris, 1966.

Brauer-Gramm, Hildburg. *Der Landvogt Peter von Hagenbach. Die burgundische Herrschaft am Oberrhein 1469–1474.* Göttinger Bausteine zur Geschichtswissenschaft, 27. Göttingen, 1957.

Brecht, Martin, "Die Bedeutung des Bauernkrieges in Südwestdeutschland," *Schwäbische Heimat. Zeitschrift zur Pflege von Landschaft, Volkstum, Kultur,* 26 (1975), 297–301.

Brendler, Gerhard. *Das Täuferreich zu Münster 1534/35.* Leipziger Übersetzungen und Abhandlungen zum Mittelalter, B 2. Berlin, 1966.

Bresard, Marcel. *Les foires de Lyon aux XVe et XVIe siècles.* Paris, 1914.

Brown, Elizabeth A. R., "The Tyranny of a Concept: Feudalism and Historians of Medieval Europe," *AHR,* 79 (1974), 1063–1088.

Brucker, Gene A., Jr. *Florentine Politics and Society, 1343–1382.* Princeton Studies in History, 12. Princeton, 1962.

Brunner, Otto, "Europäisches Bauerntum," *Neue Wege der Verfassungs- und Sozialgeschichte,* 2nd ed. (Göttingen, 1968), pp. 199–212.

Brunner, Otto, *Land und Herrschaft. Grundfragen der territorialen Verfassungs-geschichte Österreichs im Mittelalter*. 4th ed. rev. Vienna–Wiesbaden, 1959.

———, "Souveränitätsproblem und Sozialstruktur in den deutschen Reichs-städen der frühen Neuzeit," *Neue Wege der Verfassungs- und Sozial-geschichte*, 2nd ed., pp. 294–321; reprinted from *VSWG*, 50 (1963), 329–360.

Bücking, Jürgen, "Das Geschlecht Stürtzel von Buchheim (1491–1790). Ein Versuch zur Sozial- und Wirtschaftsgeschichte des Breisgauer Adels in der frühen Neuzeit," *Blätter für deutsche Landesgeschichte*, 118 (1970), 238–278.

Bumke, Joachim. *Studien zum Ritterbegriff im 12. und 13. Jahrhundert. Euphorion*, Beiheft 1. Heidelberg, 1964.

Burg, André-Marcel, "La famille de Gottesheim, remarques sur sa généalogie publiée par Hertzog," *BCGA*, No. 18 (1972), 47–48.

———, "Grandeur et décadence de la bourgeoisie haguenauienne. Deux familles, les Brechter et les Hoffmann," *La bourgeoisie alsacienne*, pp. 181–196.

———, "Patrizier und andere städtische Führungsschichten in Hagenau," *Deutsches Patriziat 1430–1740*, pp. 353–376. (Burg).

Buszello, Horst. *Der deutsche Bauernkrieg von 1525 als politische Bewegung, mit besonderer Berücksichtigung der anonymen Flugschrift "An die versamlung gemayner pawyerschafft."* Studien zur europäischen Geschichte, 8. Berlin, 1969.

von Campenhausen, Hans, "Die Bilderfrage in der Reformation," *ZKiG*, 68 (1957), 96–128.

Chrisman, Miriam Usher. *Strasbourg and the Reform; a Study in the Process of Change*. Yale Historical Publications, Miscellany, 87. New Haven–London, 1967. (Chrisman, *Strasbourg*).

Clauss, Joseph M. B., "Das Münster als Begräbnisstätte und seine Grabin-schriften," *Strassburger Münster-Blätt*, 2 (1905), 9–26; 3 (1906), 11–31.

Cohn, Henry J. *The Government of the Rhine Palatinate in the Fifteenth Century*. Oxford, 1965.

Cohn, Norman. *The Pursuit of the Millennium*. 2nd ed. New York, 1961.

Coornaert, Emile. *Les français et le commerce international à Anvers, fin du XVe–XVIe siècle*. 2 vols. Paris, 1961.

Cox, Oliver Cromwell. *Class, Caste and Race; a Study in Social Dynamics*. New York, 1959.

Crämer, Ulrich, "Die Wehrmacht Strassburgs von der Reformationszeit bis zum Fall der Reichsstadt," *ZGO*, 84 (1932), 45–95.

———. *Die Verfassung und Verwaltung Strassburgs von der Reformationszeit bis zum Fall der Reichsstadt (1521–1681)*. SWIELR, N.S. 3. Frankfurt/M., 1931.

Czok, Karl, "Die Bürgerkämpfe in Süd- und Westdeutschland im 14. Jahr-hundert," *JGOR*, 12/13 (1966/67), 40–72.

———, "Zur Stellung der Stadt in der deutschen Geschichte," *JRG*, 3 (1968), 9–33.

———, "Zunftkämpfe, Zunftrevolution oder Bürgerkämpfe?" *Wissenschaftliche Zeitschrift der Karl-Marx-Universität Leipzig*, 8 (1958/59), 129–143.

Davis, Natalie Zemon, "Poor Relief, Humanism, and Heresy," *Society and Culture in Early Modern France,* pp. 17–64; reprinted from *Studies in Medieval and Renaissance History,* 5 (1968).

——, "The Rites of Violence," *Society and Culture in Early Modern France,* pp. 152–187; reprinted from *Past & Present,* No. 59 (May 1973).

——. *Society and Culture in Early Modern France.* Stanford, 1975.

——, "Some Tasks and Themes in the Study of Popular Religion," *The Pursuit of Holiness,* pp. 307–336.

De Boor, Helmut, and Newald, Richard, eds. *Geschichte der deutschen Literatur von den Anfängen bis zur Gegenwart,* IV, 2: *Das Zeitalter der Reformation 1520–1570,* by Hans Rupprich. Munich, 1973.

Den Boer, W., "Die prosopographische Methode in der modernen Geschichtsschreibung der Hohen Römischen Kaiserzeit," *Mnemosyne,* 22 (1969), 268–280.

Deppermann, Klaus, "Melchior Hoffmans Weg von Luther zu den Täufern," *Umstrittenes Täufertum 1525–1975,* ed. Hans-Jürgen Goertz (Göttingen, 1975), pp. 173–205.

Deutscher Adel 1430–1555. Ed. Helmuth Rössler. DFN, 1. Darmstadt, 1965.

Deutsches Geschlechterbuch. 172 vols. Berlin, 1889–1904; Görlitz, 1906–43; Glücksburg/Ostsee, 1955–58; Limburg/Lahn, 1959–75. (*DGB*).

Deutsches Patriziat 1430–1740. Ed. Helmuth Rössler. DFN, 3. Limburg/Lahn, 1968.

Dictionnaire des communes administratif et militaire, France et départements français d'outre-mer. Edition of January 1964. Paris, 1964.

Dietz, Alexander. *Frankfurter Handelsgeschichte.* 4 vols. in 5. Frankfurt/M., 1910–25.

——, "Strassburg und Frankfurt a. M. Eine Städtefreundschaft," *ELJb,* 1 (1922), 49–67. (Dietz).

Doehaerd, Renée. *Etudes anversoises. Documents sur le commerce international à Anvers 1488–1514.* 3 vols. Paris, 1962–63.

Dollinger, Philippe, "Commerce et marchands strasbourgeois à Fribourg en Suisse au moyen âge," *Beiträge zur Wirtschafts- und Stadtgeschichte. Festschrift für Hektor Ammann,* eds. Hermann Aubin, *et al.* (Wiesbaden, 1965), pp. 124–143.

——, "La évolution politique des corporations strasbourgeoises à la fin du moyen âge," *Artisans et ouvriers d'Alsace,* pp. 127–135.

——. *The German Hansa.* Trans. D. S. Ault and S. H. Steinberg. Stanford, 1970.

——, "Marchands strasbourgeois à Fribourg en Suisse au XIVe siècle," *L'Alsace et la Suisse à travers les siècles.* PSSARE, 4 (Strasbourg, 1952), pp. 75–84.

——, "Notes sur les échevins de Strasbourg au moyen âge," *CAAAH,* N.S. 11 (1967), 65–72.

——, "Patriciat noble et patriciat bourgeois à Strasbourg au XIVe siècle," *RA,* 90 (1950/51), 52–82.

——, "La tolérance à Strasbourg au XVIe siècle," *Hommage à Lucien Febvre,* 2 vols. (Paris, 1953), II, 241–249.

Dollinger, Philippe, "Les villes allemandes au moyen âge: les groupements sociaux," *La ville*, vol. 2, pp. 371–401.

——, "Les villes allemandes au moyen âge: leurs statuts juridiques, politiques, administratifs," *La ville,* vol. 1, pp. 445–466.

Douglass, E. Jane Dempsey. *Justification in Late Medieval Preaching. A Study of John Geiler of Keisersberg.* SMRT, 1. Leiden, 1966.

Dreher, Alfons. *Das Patriziat der Reichsstadt Ravensburg. Von den Anfängen bis zum Beginn des 19. Jahrhunderts.* Stuttgart, 1966. Also in *ZWLG*, 19 (1960), 51–88, 215–313; 21 (1962), 237–386; 23 (1964), 1–140; 24 (1965), 1–131.

Dubled, Henri, "L'administration de la seigneurie rurale en Alsace du XIIIe au XVe siècle," *VSWG*, 52 (1965), 433–484.

——, "Aspects de la vie économique de Strasbourg aux XIIIe et XIVe siécles: baux et rentes," *AEA*, 6 (1955), 23–56.

——, "L'écuyer en Alsace au moyen âge," *RA*, 92 (1953), 47–56.

——, "Les grandes tendances de l'exploitation au sein de la seigneurie rurale en Alsace du XIIIe au XVe siècle," *VSWG*, 49 (1962), 41–121.

——, "Grundherrschaft und Dorfgerichtsbarkeit im Elsass vom 13.–15. Jahrhundert und ihr Verhältnis zueinander," *Deutsches Archiv für Erforschung des Mittelalters,* 17 (1961), 518–526.

——, "Grundherrschaft und Landgemeinde im mittelalterlichen Elsass," *Saarbrücker Hefte,* 18 (1963), 16–28.

——, "Der Herrschaftsbegriff am Oberrhein, hauptsächlich im Elsass," *AJb*, 1959, pp. 77–91.

——, "La justice de la seigneurie foncière en Alsace aux XIVe et XVe siècles," *Revue d'histoire suisse,* 10 (1960), 337–375.

——, "Servitude et liberté en Alsace au moyen âge. La condition des personnes au sein de la seigneurie rurale du XIIIe au XVe siècle," *VSWG*, 50 (1963), 164–203, 289–328.

Duby, Georges, "La grand domaine de la fin du moyen âge en France," *First International Conference for Economic History, Stockholm 1960. Contributions, Communications,* Ecole Pratique des Hautes Etudes, VIe section, série "Congrès et Colloques," I (Paris–The Hague, 1960), 333–342.

——, "Lignage, noblesse et chevalerie au la région maconnaise," *AESC*, 27 (1972), 803–823.

——. *Rural Economy and Country Life in the Medieval West.* Trans. Cynthia Postan. Columbia, S. C., 1968.

Ebeling, Gerhard, "Luther and the Beginning of the Modern Age," *Luther and the Dawn of the Modern Era,* pp. 11–37.

Ehrenberg, Richard. *Das Zeitalter der Fugger. Geldkapital und Creditverkehr im 16. Jahrhundert.* 3rd ed. 2 vols. Jena, 1922.

Eichler, Helga, "Die geschichtliche Rolle des deutschen Bürgertums im Feudalismus," *ZfG*, 21 (1973), 1505–1508.

Eirich, Raimund. *Memmingens Wirtschaft und Patriziat von 1347 bis 1551. Eine wirtschafts- und sozialgeschichtliche Untersuchung über das Memminger Patriziat während der Zunftverfassung.* Weissenhorn, 1971.

Eitel, Peter. *Die oberschwäbischen Reichsstädte im Zeitalter der Zunftherrschaft.*

Untersuchungen zu ihrer politischen und sozialen Struktur unter besonderer Berücksichtigung der Städte Lindau, Memmingen, Ravensburg und Überlingen. Schriften zur südwestdeutschen Landeskunde, 8. Stuttgart, 1970.

Eitel, Peter, "Die politische, soziale und wirtschaftliche Stellung des Zunftbürgertums in den oberschwäbischen Reichsstädten am Ausgang des Mittelalters," *Städtische Mittelschichten,* pp. 78–93.

Elben, Ruth. *Das Patriziat der Reichsstadt Rottweil. Von den Anfängen bis zum Jahre 1550.* VKLBW, B 30. Stuttgart, 1964.

Elert, Werner. *Morphologie des Luthertums.* Rev. ed. 2 vols. Munich, 1953; 1st ed., 1931–32.

Elliott, J. H., "Revolution and Continuity in Early Modern Europe," *Past & Present,* No. 42 (February 1969), 35–56.

Engels, Friedrich, *Der deutsche Bauernkrieg,* in *Marx-Engels Werke,* ed. by the Institut für Marxismus–Leninismus beim ZK der SED, VII (Berlin, 1960).

Ennen, Edith, "Die Stadt zwischen Mittelalter und Gegenwart," *Rheinische Vierteljahrsblätter,* 30 (1965), 118–131; reprinted in *Die Stadt des Mittelalters,* ed. Carl Haase, I (Darmstadt, 1969), pp. 416–435.

Ennen, Reinald. *Zünfte und Wettbewerb. Möglichkeiten und Grenzen zünftlerischer Wettbewerbsbeschränkungen im städtischen Handel und Gewerbe des Spätmittelalters.* Neue Wirtschaftsgeschichte, 3. Cologne–Vienna, 1971.

Fabian, Ekkehart. *Die Entstehung des Schmalkaldischen Bundes und seiner Verfassung 1529–1531/33. Brück, Landgraf Philipp von Hessen und Jakob Sturm.* 2nd ed. SKRG, 1. Tübingen, 1956.

Festgabe für Ernst-Walter Zeeden. Eds. Horst Rabe, *et al.* Reformationsgeschichtliche Studien und Texte, Supplementary vol. 2. Münster/W., 1976.

Festschrift für Hermann Heimpel zum 70. Geburtstag zum 19. September 1971. Ed. by members of the Max-Planck-Institut für Geschichte. 3 vols. Göttingen, 1971–72.

Ficker, Johannes. *Das Bekenntnis zur Reformation im Strassburger Münster.* Theologische Studien und Kritiken, 109/1. Leipzig, 1941.

Fiume, Enrico, "Sui rapporti tra città e contado nell'eta communale," *Archivio storico italiano,* 114 (1956), 18–68.

Les fluctuations du produit de la dîme. Conjoncture décimale et domaniale de la fin du moyen âge au XVIIIe siècle. Eds. Joseph Goy and Emannuel Le Roy Ladurie. Cahiers des études rurales, 3. Paris–The Hague, 1972.

The Fontana Economic History of Europe. Ed. Carlo M. Cipolla. Vol. I: *The Middle Ages.* London–New York, 1972.

Fourquin, Guy. *Les campagnes de la région parisienne à la fin du moyen âge (du début du XIIIe siècle au début de XVIe siècle).* Paris, 1964.

von Frank, Karl Friedrich. *Standeserhebungen und Gnadenakte für das Deutsche Reich und die Österreichischen Erblande bis 1806.* 4 vols. Schloss Senftenegg, Lower Austria, 1967–74. (Frank).

Friedensburg, Walter. *Der Reichstag zu Speyer 1526 im Zusammenhang der politischen und kirchlichen Entwicklung Deutschlands im Reformationszeitalter.* Historische Untersuchungen, 5. Berlin, 1887.

Friedrichs, Christopher R., "Capitalism, Mobility and Class Formation in the

Early Modern German City," *Past & Present,* No. 69 (November 1975), 24–49.

Friesen, Abraham. *Reformation and Utopia. The Marxist Interpretation of the Reformation and Its Antecedents.* VIEGM, 71. Wiesbaden, 1974.

[Fritz, Johannes]. *Die alten Territorien des Elsass nach dem Stande vom 1. Januar 1648.* Statistische Mittheilungen über Elsass–Lothringen, 27. Strasbourg, 1896. (Fritz).

Fritze, Konrad, "Eigentumsstruktur und Charakter des mittelalterlichen Städtebürgertums," *ZfG,* 22 (1974), 331–337.

Frölich, Karl, "Kaufmannsgilden und Stadtverfassung im Mittelalter," *Die Stadt des Mittelalters,* II, 11–54; reprinted from *Festschrift Alfred Schultze zum 70. Geburtstag,* ed. Walther Merck (Weimar, 1934), pp. 85–128.

Fuchs, François-Joseph, "Bourgeois de Strasbourg propriétaires ruraux au XVIIe siècle," *Paysans d'Alsace,* pp. 99–120.

——, "Les catholiques strasbourgeois de 1529 à 1681," *AEA,* 22 (1975), 141–169.

——, "Le droit de bourgeoisie à Strasbourg," *RA,* 101 (1962), 19–50.

——, "L'espace économique rhénan et les relations commerciales de Strasbourg avec le sud-ouest de l'Allemagne au XVIe siècle," *Oberrheinische Studien,* III: *Festschrift für Günther Haselier aus Anlass seines 60. Geburtstages am 19. April 1974,* ed. Alfons Schäfer (Karlsruhe, 1975), pp. 289–325.

——, "Une famille de négociants banquiers du XVIe siècle. Les Prechter de Strasbourg," *RA,* 95 (1956), 146–194. (Fuchs, "Prechter").

——, "Heurs et malheurs d'un marchand-banquier strasbourgeois du XVIe siècle, Israël Minckel (vers 1522–1569), bailleur de fonds du Roi de France et des Huguenots," *RHPR,* 54 (1974), 115–127. (Fuchs, "Israël Minckel").

——, "L'immigration artisanale à Strasbourg de 1544 à 1565," *Artisans et ouvriers d'Alsace,* pp. 185–198.

——, "Un orfèvre strasbourgeois du XVIe siècle à la recherche de métaux précieux, Erasme Krug, exploitant de mines à Disentis (Grisons) et à Silenen (Uri)," *CAAAH,* N.S. 11 (1967), 77–88. (Fuchs, "Un orfevre").

——, "Le paiment de la rançon des prisonniers du Duc de Lorraine," *La Guerre des Paysans 1525,* ed. A. Wollbrett, pp. 127–128.

——, "Les relations commerciales entre Nuremberg et Strasbourg aux XVe et XVIe siècles," *Hommage à Dürer,* pp. 77–90.

——, "Richesse et faillité des Ingold, financiers et commerçants strasbourgeois du XVIe siècle," *La bourgeoisie alsacienne,* pp. 203–233. (Fuchs, "Ingold").

——, "Une usine de raffinage de cuivre dans la vallée de la Bruche (Alsace) au XVIe siècle," *Festschrift für Hermann Heimpel,* I, 729–740.

Fuchs, Konrad, "Zur Politik der protestantischen Reichsstände vor der Eröffnung des Augsburger Reichstags von 1530," *ZGO,* 118 (1970), 157–174.

Führungskräfte der Wirtschaft in Mittelalter und Neuzeit 1350–1850, I. Ed. Herbert Helbig. DFN, 6. Limburg/Lahn, 1973.

Galpern, A. N., "Late Medieval Piety in Sixteenth-Century Champagne," *The Pursuit of Holiness*, pp. 141–176.

Gansslen, Gerhard. *Die Ratsadvokaten und Ratskonsulenten der Reichsstadt Ulm, insbesondere ihr Wirken in den Bürgerprozessen am Ende des 18. Jahrhunderts.* Forschungen zur Geschichte der Stadt Ulm, 6. Ulm, 1966.

Gascon, Richard. *Grand commerce et vie urbaine au XVIe siècle. Lyon et ses marchands (environs de 1520-environs de 1580).* 2 vols. École Pratique des Hautes Études, VIe section, série "Civilisations et Sociétés," 22. Paris–The Hague, 1971.

Gasser, Adolf. *Die territoriale Entwicklung der schweizerischen Eidgenossenschaft 1291–1797.* Aarau, 1932.

Geiger, Gottfried. *Die Reichsstadt Ulm vor der Reformation. Städtisches und kirchliches Leben am Ausgang des Mittelalters.* Forschungen zur Geschichte der Stadt Ulm, 11. Ulm, 1971.

Genealogisches Handbuch des in Bayern immatrikulierten Adels. 10 vols. Schellenberg bei Berchtesgaden, 1950–52; Neustadt/Aisch, 1953–70.

Génicot, Léopold, "Naïssance, fonction et richesse dans l'ordonnance de la société médiévale. Le cas de la noblesse du nord-ouest du continent," *Problèmes de stratification sociale,* pp. 83–100.

Gerber, Harry, "Jakob Sturms Anteil an den Religionsverhandlungen des Augsburger 'geharnischten' Reichstags von 1547/48," *ELJb,* 8 (1929), 166–191.

——, "Die Kriegsrechnungen des Schmalkaldischen Bundes über den Krieg im Oberland des Jahres 1546, I–V," *ARG,* 32 (1935), 41–93, 218–247; 33 (1936), 226–255; 34 (1937), 87–122, 272–288.

Gesellschaftliche Unterschichten in den südwestdeutschen Städten. Protokoll über die V. Arbeitstagung des Arbeitskreises für südwestdeutsche Stadtgeschichtsforschung. Eds. Erich Maschke and Jürgen Sydow. VKLBW, B41. Stuttgart, 1967.

Gierke, Otto. *Das deutsche Genossenschaftsrecht.* 4 vols. Berlin, 1868–1913.

Ginzburg, Carlo. *Il nicodemismo. Simulazione e dissimulazione religiosa nell'Europa del '500.* Biblioteca di cultura storica, 107. Turin, 1970.

Gothein, Eberhard. *Wirtschaftsgeschichte des Schwarzwaldes und der angrenzenden Landschaften.* Vol. I: *Städte- und Gewerbegeschichte.* Strasbourg, 1892.

Grandidier, Philippe A. *Nouvelles oeuvres inédites.* Ed. A. M. P. Ingold. 5 vols. Colmar, 1897–1900.

Graus, František. *Das Spätmittelalter als Krisenzeit.* Medievalia Bohemica, I, Supplementum 1. Prague, 1969.

Grimm, Harold J., "The Reformation and the Urban Social Classes in Germany," *Luther, Erasmus and the Reformation. A Catholic–Protestant Reappraisal,* eds. John C. Olin, *et al.* (New York, 1969), pp. 75–86.

——, "Social Forces in the German Reformation," *CH,* 31 (1962), 3–12.

La Guerre des Paysans 1525. Etudes alsatiques. Ed. Alphonse Wollbrett for the Société d'histoire et d'archéologie de Saverne et environs. Saverne, 1975.

Guyer, Paul, "Politische Führungsschichten der Stadt Zürich vom 13. bis zum 18. Jahrhundert," *Deutsches Patriziat 1430–1740,* pp. 395–417.

Gyss, Joseph. *Histoire de la ville de Obernai et ses rapports avec les autres villes ci-*

devant impériales d'Alsace et avec les seigneuries voisines. 2 vols. Strasbourg, 1866. (Gyss).

Habich, Georg. *Die deutschen Schaumünzen des XVI. Jahrhunderts.* Part I: *Die deutschen Schaumünzen des XVI. Jahrhunderts geordnet nach Meistern und Schulen.* 2 vols. in 4. Munich, 1929–34. (Habich).

Hägglund, Bengt, "Renaissance and Reformation," *Luther and the Dawn of the Modern Era,* pp. 150–158.

Hahn, Karl. *Die katholische Kirche in Strassburg unter dem Bischof Erasmus von Limburg 1541–1568.* SWIELR, N.S. 24. Frankfurt/M., 1941.

Hall, Basil, "The Reformation City," *Bulletin of the John Rylands Library,* 54 (1971), 103–148.

Haller von Hallerstein, Hellmut, "Grösse und Quellen der Vermögen von hundert Nürnberger Bürgern um 1500," *Beiträge zur Wirtschaftsgeschichte Nürnbergs,* I, 117–176.

Hanauer, Auguste. *Etudes économiques sur l'Alsace ancienne et moderne.* 2 vols. Paris–Strasbourg, 1876.

Handbuch der deutschen Wirtschafts- und Sozialgeschichte. Vol. I: *Von der Frühzeit bis zum Ende des 18. Jahrhunderts.* Eds. Hermann Aubin and Wolfgang Zorn. Stuttgart, 1971.

Hatt, Jacques, "Une famille d'Ammeistres strasbourgeois, les Staedel," *La bourgeoisie alsacienne,* pp. 225–232.

——. *Liste des membres du grand sénat de Strasbourg, des stettmeistres, des ammeistres, des conseils des XXI, XIII et des XV du XIIIe siècle à 1789.* Strasbourg, 1963. (Hatt).

——. *Une ville du XVe siècle. Strasbourg.* Strasbourg, 1929.

Haug, Hans, "Notes sur Pierre d'Andlau, peintre-verrier à Strasbourg, et son atelier," *AAHA,* 15 (1936), 91–105.

Hauswirth, René. *Landgraf Philipp von Hessen und Zwingli. Voraussetzungen und Geschichte der politischen Beziehungen zwischen Hessen, Strassburg, Konstanz, Ulrich von Württemberg und reformierten Eidgenossen 1526–1531.* SKRG, 35. Tübingen, 1968.

——, "Politische Führungsschicht und Reformation. Zum Buche von Walter Jacob," *Zwingliana,* 13, No. 4 (1970), 255–260.

Heers, Jacques. *L'occident aux XIVe et XVe siècles. Aspects économiques et sociaux.* Nouvelle Clio, 23. Paris, 1970.

Herde, Peter, "Politische Verhaltensweisen der Florentiner Oligarchie 1382–1402," *Geschichte und Verfassungsgefüge. Frankfurter Festschrift für Walter Schlesinger,* Frankfurter Historische Abhandlungen, 5 (Wiesbaden, 1973), pp. 156–249.

Herding, Otto, "Zu einer humanistischen Handschrift, 63 der Newberry Library Chicago," *Geschichte, Wirtschaft, Gesellschaft. Festschrift Clemens Bauer zum 75. Geburtstag,* eds. Erich Hassinger, *et al.* (Berlin, 1974), pp. 153–187.

Herlihy, David, "Mapping Households in Medieval Italy," *The Catholic Historical Review,* 58 (1972), 1–22.

——. *Medieval and Renaissance Pistoia. The Social History of an Italian Town, 1200–1430.* New Haven–London, 1967.

Herlihy, David, "Some Psychological and Social Roots of Violence in the Tuscan Cities," *Violence and Civil Disorder in Italian Cities*, pp. 129–154.

Hermann, Jean-Frédéric. *Notices historiques, statistiques et littéraires sur la ville de Strasbourg*. 2 vols. Strasbourg, 1817–19.

Hertner, Peter. *Stadtwirtschaft zwischen Reich und Frankreich. Wirtschaft und Gesellschaft Strassburgs 1650–1714*. Neue Wirtschaftsgeschichte, 8. Cologne–Vienna, 1973.

Hibbert, A. B., "The Origins of the Medieval Town Patriciate," *Past & Present*, No. 3 (February 1957), 15–27.

Himly, François-Joseph. *Chronologie de la Basse Alsace, Ier–XXe siècle*. Strasbourg, 1972.

Hirsch, Emanuel. *Der Reich–Gottes–Begriff des neueren europäischen Denkens*. Göttingen, 1921.

Hitchcock, William R. *The Background of the Knights' Revolt, 1522–1523*. University of California Publications in History, 61. Berkeley–Los Angeles, 1958.

Hobsbawm, Eric J., "From Social History to the History of Society," *Daedalus*, 100, No. 1 (1971), pp. 20–45.

——, "Labour Traditions," *Labouring Men. Studies in the History of Labour* (London, 1964).

Hoffmann, Hildegard, and Mittenzwei, Ingrid, "Die Stellung des Bürgertums in der deutschen Feudalgesellschaft von der Mitte des 16. Jahrhunderts bis 1789," *ZfG*, 22 (1974), 190–207.

Hofmann, Hans Hubert, "Der Adel in Franken," *Deutscher Adel 1430–1555*, pp. 95–126.

——, "Nobiles Norimbergenses. Beobachtungen zur Struktur der reichsstädtischen Oberschicht," *Untersuchungen zur gesellschaftlichen Struktur*, pp. 53–92.

Hofmann, Wilhelm. *Adel und Landesherren im nördlichen Schwarzwald von der Mitte des 14. Jahrhunderts bis zum Beginn des 16. Jahrhunderts*. Darstellungen aus der württembergischen Geschichte, 40. Stuttgart, 1954.

Hofpfalzgrafen-Register. Ed. by the HEROLD, Verein für Heraldik, Genealogie und verwandte Wissenschaften zu Berlin. Neustadt/Aisch, 1964–

Hollaender, Alcuin. *Strassburg im Schmalkaldischen Krieg*. Strasbourg, 1881.

Hommage à Dürer. Strasbourg et Nuremberg dans la première moitié du XVIe siècle. PSSARE, collection "Recherches et documents," 12. Strasbourg, 1972.

Horning, Wilhelm. *Dr. Johann Marbach, Pfarrer zu St. Nikolai, Münsterprediger 1545–1581*. Strasbourg, 1887. (Horning).

Hotz, Walter. *Handbuch der Kunstdenkmäler im Elsass und Lothringen*. Berlin, 1965.

Hughes, Diane Owen, "Urban Growth and Family Structure in Medieval Genoa," *Past & Present*, No. 66 (February 1975), 3–28.

Imbs, Anne-Marie, "Tableaux des corporations alsaciennes, XIVe–XVIIIe siècles," *Artisans et ouvriers d'Alsace*, pp. 34–45.

Irschlinger, Robert, "Zur Geschichte der Herren von Steinach und der Landschaden von Steinach," *ZGO*, 86 (1934), 421–508.

Irsigler, Franz, "Kölner Wirtschaftsbeziehungen zum Oberrhein vom 14. bis 16. Jahrhundert," *ZGO*, 122 (1974), 1–21.

——, "Soziale Wandlungen in der Kölner Kaufmannschaft im 14. und 15. Jahrhundert," *Hansische Geschichtsblätter*, 92 (1974), 59–78.

Jacob, Walter. *Politische Führungsschicht und Reformation. Untersuchungen zur Reformation in Zürich 1519–1528*. Zürcher Beiträge zur Reformationsgeschichte, 1. Zurich, 1970.

Jaenger, Fernand, "Zur Geschichte des Schlosses Breuschwickersheim," *CAAAH*, 30 (1939), 81–89.

Janssen, Johannes. *Geschichte des deutschen Volkes seit dem Ausgang des Mittelalters*. Vol. I: *Allgemeine Zustände des deutschen Volkes beim Ausgang des Mittelalters*. 7th ed. Freiburg/Br., 1881.

Jeannin, Pierre. *Merchants of the 16th Century*. Trans. Paul Fittinghoff. New York, 1972.

Jouanna, Arlette, "Recherches sur la notion d'honneur au XVIème siècle," *RHMC*, 15 (1968), 597–623.

Juillard, Etienne. *L'europe rhénane. Géographie d'un grand espace*. Paris, 1968.

——, "Indifférence de la bourgeoisie alsacienne à l'égard de la propriété rurale aux XVIIIe et XIXe siècles," *La bourgeoisie alsacienne*, pp. 377–386.

Kageneck, Alfred Graf, "Das Patriziat im Elsass unter Berücksichtigung der Schweizer Verhältnisse," *Deutsches Patriziat 1430–1740*, pp. 377–394. (Kageneck).

Kähni, Otto, "Zur Geschichte Diersburgs," *Die Ortenau*, 29 (1959), 61–68.

Kallen, Gerhard. *Die oberschwäbischen Pfründen des Bistums Konstanz und ihre Besetzung (1275–1508). Ein Beitrag zur Pfründgeschichte vor der Reformation*. Kirchenrechtliche Abhandlungen, 45/46. Stuttgart, 1907.

Kamen, Henry. *The Iron Century. Social Change in Europe 1550–1650*. London–New York, 1972.

Kauss, Dieter. *Die mittelalterliche Pfarrorganisation in der Ortenau*. Veröffentlichungen des Alemannischen Instituts, 30. Bühl/Baden, 1970.

Kellenbenz, Hermann, "Die Finanzen der Stadt Köln 1515–1532," *Wirtschaftliche und soziale Strukturen im saekularen Wandel. Festschrift für Wilhelm Abel zum 70. Geburtstag*, eds. Ingomar Bog, *et al.*, 3 vols. (Hannover, 1974), II, 366–376.

——, "Les foires de Lyon dans la politique de Charles-Quint," *Cahiers d'histoire*, 5 (1960), 17–32.

——, "Isny im Allgäu. Von den wirtschaftlichen Möglichkeiten einer Reichsstadt zwischen Mittelalter und Neuzeit," *JGOR*, 12/13 (1966/67), 100–123.

Kiener, Fritz, "Zur Vorgeschichte des Bauernkriegs am Oberrhein," *ZGO*, 58 (1904), 479–507.

Kindler von Knobloch, Julius. *Das goldene Buch von Strassburg*. Vienna, 1885–86. (Kindler, *GBS*).

——. *Oberbadisches Geschlechterbuch*. 3 vols. Heidelberg, 1898–1919. (Kindler, *OG*).

——, "Die pfalzgräfliche Registratur des Dompropstes Wilhelm Böcklin von Böcklinsau," *ZGO*, 45 (1891), 263–282, 645–672.

Kintz, Jean-Pierre, "Anthroponymie en pays de langue germanique. Le cas de l'Alsace, XVIIe–XVIIIe siècles," *Annales de démographie historique*, 1972, p. 311–317.

——, "La société strasbourgeoise du milieu du XVIe siècle à la fin de la guerre de trente ans 1560–1650." Thèse, Strasbourg, 1977.

Kirchgässner, Bernhard, "Probleme quantitativer Erfassung städtischer Unterschichten im Spätmittelalter, besonders in Reichsstädten Konstanz und Esslingen," *Gesellschaftliche Unterschichten*, pp. 75–81.

Kittelson, James M., "Martin Bucer and the Sacramentarian Controversy: The Origins of his Policy of Concord," *ARG*, 64 (1973), 166–183.

——, "Wolfgang Capito, the Council and Reform Strasbourg," *ARG*, 63 (1972), 126–140.

——. *Wolfgang Capito from Humanist to Reformer*. SMRT, 17. Leiden, 1975.

von Klocke, Friedrich. *Das Patriziatsproblem und die Werler Erbsälzer*. Veröffentlichungen der Historischen Kommission Westfalens, XXIII, 7. Münster/W., 1965.

Knod, Gustav, "Elsässische Studenten in Heidelberg und Bologna," *ZGO*, 46 (1892), 329–355.

——, "Oberrheinische Studenten im 16. und 17. Jahrhundert auf der Universität Padua," *ZGO*, 54 (1900), 197–258, 432–453; 55 (1901), 246–262, 612–637.

——. *Die Stiftsherren von St. Thomas zu Strassburg (1518–1548). Ein Beitrag zur Strassburger Kirchen- und Schulgeschichte*. Strasbourg, 1892. (Knod).

Kofler, Leo. *Zur Geschichte der bürgerlichen Gesellschaft. Versuch einer verstehenden Deutung der Neuzeit*. 5th ed. Soziologische Texte, 38. Darmstadt–Neuwied, 1974.

Kohls, Ernst-Wilhelm, "Evangelische Bewegung und Kirchenordnung in oberdeutschen Reichsstädten," *ZSSR, KA*, 84 (1967), 110–134.

——. *Luther oder Erasmus. Luthers Theologie in der Auseinandersetzung mit Erasmus*. Vol I. *Theologische Zeitschrift*, Beiheft 3. Basel, 1972.

——. *Die Schule bei Martin Bucer in ihrem Verhältnis zu Kirche und Obrigkeit*. Pädagogische Forschungen, 22. Heidelberg, 1963.

——. *Die Theologie des Erasmus*. 2 vols. Basel, 1966.

——. *Die theologische Lebensaufgabe des Erasmus und die oberrheinischen Reformatoren. Zur Durchdringung von Humanismus und Reformation*. Arbeiten zur Theologie, 1st series, 39. Stuttgart, 1969.

Kopf, Hermann, *Ritter Wilhelm Böcklin von Böcklinsau, Hofmarschall–Dompropst–Stifter in Freiburg*. Freiburg/Br., 1974. Also in *Schauinsland*, 1974.

Koser, Otto. *Repertorium der Akten des Reichskammergerichtes, untrennbarer Bestand*. 2 vols. Heppenheim/Bergstrasse, 1933–36.

Krahn, Henry George. "An Analysis of the Conflict between the Clergy of the Reformed Church and the Leaders of the Anabaptist Movement in Strasbourg, 1529–1534." Unpublished Ph.D. Dissertation, University of Washington, 1969.

Kramm, Heinrich, "Besitzschichten und Bildungsschichten der mitteldeutschen Städte im 16. Jahrhundert," *VSWG*, 51 (1964), 454–491.

Kraus, Franz Xaver. *Kunst und Alterthum in Elsass-Lothringen.* Vol. I: *Kunst und Alterthum im Unter-Elsass.* Strasbourg, 1876.

Krebs, Manfred, "Die Dienerbücher des Bistums Speyer 1464–1768," *ZGO,* 94 (1948), 55–195.

——, "Die kurpfälzischen Dienerbücher 1476–1685," *Mitteilungen der Oberrheinischen Historischen Kommission,* 1 (1942).

Kreil, Dieter. *Der Stadthaushalt von Schwäbisch Hall im 15./16. Jahrhundert.* Forschungen aus Württembergisch Franken, 1. Schwäbisch Hall, 1967.

Kressner, Helmut. *Schweizer Ursprünge des anglikanischen Staatskirchentums.* SVRG, 170. Gütersloh, 1953.

Kroeschell, Karl, "Stadtrecht und Stadtgeschichte," *Die Stadt des Mittelalters,* II, 281–299; reprinted from *Studium Generale,* 16 (1963), 481–488.

Kühne, Eckehard. *Historisches Bewusstsein in der deutschen Soziologie. Untersuchungen zur Geschichte der Soziologie von der Zeit der Reichsgründung bis zum Ersten Weltkrieg auf wissenssoziologischer Grundlage.* Marburg/Lahn, 1970.

Kulischer, Josef. *Allgemeine Wirtschaftsgeschichte des Mittelalters und der Neuzeit.* 3rd ed. 2 vols. Munich–Vienna, 1965.

Die Kunstdenkmäler (des Grossherzogtums) Badens. Vol. VII: *Kreis Offenburg,* by Max Wingenroth (1908). Vol. XII, 1: *Landkreis Rastatt,* by Peter Hirschfeld (Karlsruhe, 1963). *(KDBadens).*

Küttler, Wolfgang, "Zum Problem der Anwendung des marxistischen Klassenbegriffs auf das mittelalterliche Stadtbürgertum," *ZfG,* 22 (1974), 605–615.

Lambs, Johann Philipp. *Die Jung St. Peter Kirche zu Strassburg.* Strasbourg, 1854. (Lambs).

Lang, August. *Der Evangelienkommentar Martin Butzers und die Grundzüge seiner Theologie.* Studien zur Geschichte der Theologie und der Kirche, II, 2. Leipzig, 1900.

Laslett, Peter, and Wall, Richard, eds. *Household and Family in Past Time.* Cambridge, 1972.

Lau, Franz, "Der Bauernkrieg und das angebliche Ende der lutherischen Reformation als spontaner Volksbewegung," *Luther–Jahrbuch,* 26 (1959), 109–134; reprinted in *Wirkungen der deutschen Reformation bis 1555,* ed. Walther Hubatsch, Wege der Forschung, 203 (Darmstadt, 1967), pp. 68–100.

Le Goff, Jacques, "The Town as an Agent of Civilisation," *The Fontana Economic History of Europe,* I, 71–107.

Lehr, Paul-Ernest. *L'Alsace noble, suivie de la livre d'or du patriciat de Strasbourg.* 3 vols. Paris–Strasbourg, 1870. (Lehr).

Le Roy Ladurie, Emmanuel. *Les paysans de Languedoc.* 2 vols. Paris, 1964.

Levallet-Haug, Geneviève, "Quelques exemples d'orfèvrerie strasbourgeoise des XVe et XVIe siècles," *ASAVS,* 5 (1975), 41–44.

Levresse, René-Pierre, "Prosopographie du chapitre de l'église cathédrale de Strasbourg de 1092 à 1593," *AEA,* 18 (1970), 1–39.

Lévy-Mertz, Georges, "Le commerce strasbourgeois au XVe siècle," *RA,* 97 (1958), 91–114.

Lewis, P. S. *Later Medieval France. The Polity.* London–New York, 1968.

Lieberich, Heinz, "Rittermässigkeit und bürgerliche Gleichheit. Anmerkungen zur gesellschaftlichen Stellung des Bürgers im Mittelalter," *Festschrift für Hermann Krause,* eds. Sten Gagner, *et al.* (Cologne–Vienna, 1975), pp. 66–93.

Lienhard, Marc, and Rott, Jean, "Die Anfänge der evangelischen Predigt in Strassburg und ihr erstes Manifest: der Aufruf des Karmeliterlesemeisters Tilman von Lyn (Anfang 1522)," *Bucer und seine Zeit. Forschungsbeiträge und Bibliographie,* eds. Marijn de Kroon and Friedhelm Krüger, VIEGM, 80 (Wiesbaden, 1976), pp. 54–73.

Loeper, Carl. *Die Rheinschifffahrt Strassburgs in früherer Zeit und die Strassburger Schiffleut-Zunft.* Strasbourg, 1877. (Loeper).

Loosz, Sigrid, "Butzer und Capito in ihrem Verhältnis zu Bauernkrieg und Täufertum," in *Weltwirkung der Reformation,* eds. Max Steinmetz and Gerhard Brendler, 2 vols. (Berlin, 1969), I, 226–232.

Lütge, Friedrich. *Geschichte der deutschen Agrarverfassung vom frühen Mittelalter bis zum 19. Jahrhundert.* 2nd ed. Stuttgart, 1967.

Luther and the Dawn of the Modern Era. Papers for the Fourth International Congress for Luther Research. Ed. Heiko A. Oberman. SHCT, 8. Leiden, 1974.

Macek, Josef. *Der Tiroler Bauernkrieg und Michael Gaismair.* Trans. from the Czech by R. F. Schmiedt. Berlin, 1965.

Macpherson, C. B. *The Political Theory of Possessive Individualism: from Hobbes to Locke.* Oxford, 1962.

Major, J. Russell, "The Crown and the Aristocracy in Renaissance France," in *Lordship and Community in Medieval Europe,* ed. Frederic Cheyette (New York, 1968), pp. 242–251; reprinted from *AHR,* 69 (1964).

Mandrou, Robert. *Introduction à la France moderne. Essai de psychologie historique, 1500–1640.* L'évolution de l'humanité, 52. Paris, 1961.

Martines, Lauro, "The Historical Approach to Violence," *Violence and Disorder in Italian Cities, 1200–1500,* pp. 3–18.

——. *Lawyers and Statecraft in Renaissance Florence.* Princeton, 1968.

——. *The Social World of the Florentine Humanists, 1390–1460.* Princeton, 1963.

Maschke, Erich, "Das Berufsbewusstsein des mittelalterlichen Fernkaufmanns," *Die Stadt des Mittelalters,* III, 177–216; reprinted from *Miscellanea Medievalia,* 3 (Berlin, 1964), pp. 306–335.

——, "Deutsche Stadtforschung auf der Grundlage des historischen Materialismus," *JGOR,* 12/13 (1966/67), 121–141.

——, "Mittelschichten in den deutschen Städten des Mittelalters," *Städtischen Mittelschichten,* pp. 1–31.

——, "'Obrigkeit' in spätmittelalterlichen Speyer und in anderen Städten," *ARG,* 57 (1966), 7–23.

——, "Verfassung und soziale Kräfte in der deutschen Stadt des späten Mittelalters, vornehmlich in Oberdeutschland," *VSWG,* 41 (1959), 289–349, 433–476.

Mattausch, Rudolf. "Die Reichsstadt Strassburg im Schmalkaldischen Bund am Vorabend des Krieges von 1546/47." Unpublished dissertation, Freiburg/Br., 1954.

Mieg, Philippe, "L'établissement de la Réforme et les premiers pasteurs à Boofzheim," *Bulletin de la Société d'histoire du protestantisme français,* 78 (1929), 84–85.

———, *Histoire généalogique de la famille Mieg.* Mulhouse, 1934. (Mieg).

———, "Note sur les négociants strasbourgeois Muege an XVe siècle," *RA,* 98 (1959), 138–145.

Mitchell, Charles Buell. "Martin Bucer and Sectarian Dissent; a Confrontation of the Magisterial Reformation with Anabaptists and Spiritualists." Unpublished Ph.D. Dissertation, Yale University, 1961.

Moeder, Marcel, "Les ex-libris alsaciens du XVIe siècle," *AAHA,* 1 (1922), 53–64. (Moeder).

Moeller, Bernd, "Die deutschen Humanisten und die Anfänge der Reformation," *ZKiG,* 70 (1959), 46–61.

———, "Frömmigkeit in Deutschland um 1500," *ARG,* 56 (1965), 5–31.

———, "Die Kirche in den evangelischen freien Städten Oberdeutschlands im Zeitalter der Reformation," *ZGO,* 112 (1964), 147–162.

———. *Imperial Cities and the Reformation. Three Essays.* Trans. H. C. Erik Midelfort and Mark U. Edwards, Jr. Philadelphia, 1972.

———, "Kleriker als Bürger," *Festschrift für Hermann Heimpel,* II, 195–224.

———, "Probleme der Reformationsgeschichtsforschung," *ZKiG,* 75 (1965), 246–257; trans. in *Imperial Cities and the Reformation,* pp. 3–16.

———. *Reichsstadt und Reformation.* SVRG, 180. Gütersloh, 1962. Engl. trans. in *Imperial Cities and the Reformation,* pp. 39–115.

———. *Villes d'Empire et réformation.* Trans. Albert Chenou. Travaux d'histoire éthico-politique, 10. Geneva, 1966.

Mohls, Ruth. *The Three Estates in Medieval and Renaissance Literature.* New York, 1933.

Mollat, Michel, and Wolff, Philippe. *Ongles bleus, Jacques et Ciompi. Les révolutions populaires en Europe aux XIVe et XVe siècles.* Paris, 1970. Engl. trans. *The popular revolutions of the late Middle Ages* (London, 1973).

Moore, Barrington, Jr. *Social origins of Dictatorship and Democracy: Lord and Peasant in the Modern World.* London–New York, 1974. 1st ed., 1966.

Morf, Hans, "Obrigkeit und Kirche in Zürich bis zu Beginn der Reformation," *Zwingliana,* 13 (1970), 164–203.

Mosbacher, Helga, "Kammerhandwerk, Ministerialität und Bürgertum in Strassburg. Studien zur Zusammensetzung und Entwicklung des Patriziats im 13. Jahrhundert," *ZGO,* 119 (1972), 33–173.

Mottek, Hans. *Wirtschaftsgeschichte Deutschlands.* Vol. I. 5th ed. Berlin, 1968.

von Müllenheim-Rechberg, Hermann. *Das alte Bethaus Allerheiligen zu Strassburg i. Elsass und Regesten zur Familiengeschichte der Freiherren von Müllenheim.* Strasbourg, 1880. (Müllenheim).

Müller, K. O., ed. *Welthandelsbräuche 1480–1540.* DHMN, V. Wiesbaden, 1962.

von Müller, Achatz Freiherr, "Ständekampf oder Revolution? Die Ciompi–Bewegung in Florenz," *Ansichten einer künftigen Geschichtswissenschaft,* 2: *Revolution—ein historischer Langschnitt,* eds. Immanuel Geiss and Rainer Tamchina (Munich, 1974), pp. 34–75.

Münch, Johann. *Die sozialen Anschauungen des Hans Sachs in seinen Fastnacht-spielen.* Erlangen, 1936.

von Muralt, Leonhard, "Stadtgemeinde und Reformation in der Schweiz," *Zeitschrift für schweizerische Geschichte,* 10 (1930), 349–384.

Naujoks, Eberhard. *Obrigkeitsgedanke, Zunftverfassung und Reformation. Studien zur Verfassungeschichte von Ulm, Esslingen und Schwäb. Gmünd.* VKLBW, B 3. Stuttgart, 1958.

Obenaus, Herbert. *Recht und Verfassung der Gesellschaft mit St. Jörgenschild in Schwaben. Untersuchungen über Adel, Einung, Schiedsgericht und Fehde im fünfzehnten Jahrhundert.* Veröffentlichungen des Max-Planck-Instituts für Geschichte, 7. Göttingen, 1961.

Oberman, Heiko A., ed. *Deutsche Bauernkrieg 1525 = ZKiG,* 85/2 (1975).

——, "The Gospel of Social Unrest: 450 Years after the so-called 'German Peasants' War' of 1525," *Harvard Theological Review,* 69 (1976).

——, "Headwaters of the Reformation: *initia Lutheri—initia reformationis,*" *Luther and the Dawn of the Modern Era,* pp. 40–88.

——, *Vom Wegestreit zum Glaubenskampf. Werden und Wertung der Reformation aus akademischer Sicht.* Tübingen, 1977.

Ossowski, Stanislaw. *Class Structure in the Social Consciousness.* Trans. Sheila Patterson. London–New York, 1963.

Ottmar, Johann. *Die Burg Neuneck und ihr Adel. Ein Beitrag zur Geschichte des niederen Adels am Neckar und Schwarzwald.* Göppinger Akademische Beiträge, 84. Göppingen, 1974.

Overfield, James H., "Nobles and Paupers at German Universities to 1600," *Societas,* 4 (1974), 175–210.

Overmann, Alfred, "Die Reichsritterschaft im Unterelsass bis zum Beginn des dreissigjährigen Krieges," *ZGO,* 50 (1896), 570–637; 52 (1897), 41–82.

Ozment, Steven E. *The Reformation in the Cities: The Appeal of Protestantism to Sixteenth-Century Germany and Switzerland.* New Haven–London, 1975.

Pariset, Jean-Daniel. "Les relations des rois de France et des princes protest-ants allemands 1541–1559." Thèse de l'Ecole des Chartes. 2 vols. Paris, 1972.

Pastorius, Johann Martin. *Kurze Abhandlung von den Ammeistern der Stadt Strassburg.* Strasbourg, 1761. (Pastorius).

Paysans d'Alsace. PSSARE, 7. Strasbourg, 1969.

Pennings, Heinrich. *Geschichte der Stadt Recklinghausen und ihrer Umgebung.* 2 vols. Recklinghausen, 1930–36.

Peter, Rodolphe, "Le maraîcher Clément Ziegler: l'homme et son oeuvre," *RHPR,* 34 (1954), 255–282.

Petri, Franziskus, "Strassburgs Beziehungen zu Frankreich während der Reformationszeit," *ELJb,* 8 (1929), 134–165; 10 (1931), 123–192.

Pfeiffer, Gerhard, "Das Verhältnis von politischer und kirchlicher Gemeinde in den deutschen Reichsstädten," *Staat und Kirche im Wandel der Jahr-hunderte,* ed. Walther Peter Fuchs (Stuttgart–Berlin–Köln–Mainz, 1966), pp. 79–99.

——, "Die Bemühungen der oberdeutschen Kaufleute um die Privilegierung ihres Handels in Lyon," *Beiträge zur Wirtschaftsgeschichte Nürnbergs,* I, 408–423.

Pfleger, Luzian. *Die elsässische Pfarrei, ihre Entstehung und Entwicklung. Ein Beitrag zur kirchlichen Rechts- und Kulturgeschichte.* Forschungen zur Kirchengeschichte des Elsass, 3. Strasbourg, 1936.

———. *Kirchengeschichte der Stadt Strassburg im Mittelalter.* Forschungen zur Kirchengeschichte des Elsass, 6. Colmar, 1943.

———, "Die Stadt- und Ratsgottesdienste im Strassburger Münster," *AEKG,* 12 (1937), 1–55.

Pitz, Ernst, "Wirtschaftliche und soziale Probleme der gewerblichen Entwicklung im 15./16. Jahrhundert nach hansisch-niederdeutschen Quellen," *Jahrbücher für Nationalökonomie und Statistik,* 179 (1966), 200–227.

Planitz, Hans. *Die deutsche Stadt im Mittelalter.* 2nd ed. Weimar, 1965.

———, "Zur Geschichte des städtischen Meliorats," *ZSSR, GA,* 67 (1950), 141–175.

———, "Studien zur Rechtsgeschichte des städtischen Patriziats," *Mitteilungen des Instituts für österreichische Geschichtsforschung,* 58 (1950), 317–335.

Pocock, J. G. A. *The Machiavellian Moment: Florentine Political Thought and the Atlantic Republican Tradition.* Princeton, 1975.

von Pölnitz, Götz Freiherr. *Jakob Fugger. Kaiser, Kirche und Kapital in der oberdeutschen Renaissance.* 2 vols. Tübingen, 1949–51.

Post, Gaines. *Studies in Medieval Legal Thought: Public Law and the State, 1100–1322.* Princeton, 1964.

Poulantzas, Nicos. *Pouvoir politique et classes sociales de l'état capitaliste.* Paris, 1968. German trans. by Günter Seib and Erika Hültenschmidt, *Politische Macht und gesellschaftliche Klassen* (Frankfurt/M., 1974).

Press, Volker. *Calvinismus und Territorialstaat. Regierung und Zentralbehörden der Kurpfalz 1559–1619.* Kieler Historische Studien, 7. Stuttgart, 1970.

———, "Die Ritterschaft im Kraichgau zwischen Reich und Territorium 1500–1623," *ZGO,* 122 (1974), 35–98.

Problèmes de stratification sociale. Actes du colloque international (1966). Ed. Roland Mousnier. Publications de la Faculté des lettres et sciences humaines de Paris–Sorbonne, series "Recherches," 43. Paris, 1968.

Pullan, Brian. *Rich and Poor in Renaissance Venice. The Social Institutions of a Catholic State, to 1620.* Cambridge, Mass., 1971.

The Pursuit of Holiness in Late Medieval and Renaissance Religion. Papers from the University of Michigan Conference. Eds. Charles Trinkaus and Heiko A. Oberman. SMRT, 10. Leiden, 1974.

Queller, Donald E. *The Office of Ambassador in the Middle Ages.* Princeton, 1967.

Rapp, Francis, "Die bäuerliche Aristokratie des Kochersberges im ausgehenden Mittelalter und zu Beginn der Neuzeit," *Bauernschaft und Bauernstand 1500–1970,* pp. 89–102.

———, "Haut et bas clergé dans le diocèse de Strasbourg à la veille de la réforme," *RA,* 103 (1965), 7–20.

———. *Réformes et Réformation à Strasbourg. Eglise et société dans le diocèse de Strasbourg (1450–1525).* Collection de l'Institut des Hautes Etudes Alsaciennes, 23. Paris, 1974.

Rapp, Francis, "Die soziale und wirtschaftliche Vorgeschichte des Bauern-kriegs im Unterelsass," *Bauernkriegs-Studien*, pp. 29–46.

——, "Les Strasbourgeois et les Universités rhénanes à la fin du Moyen Age jusqu'à la Réforme," *ASAVS*, 4 (1974), 11–22.

Raubenheimer, Richard. *Paul Fagius aus Rheinzabern. Sein Leben und Wirken als Reformator und Gelehrter*. Veröffentlichungen des Vereins für pfälzische Kirchengeschichte, 6. Grünstadt/Pfalz, 1957.

Recht, Roland, "Nicolas de Leyde à Strasbourg. L'épitaphe dite 'du chanoine de Busnang,'" *ASAVS*, 4 (1974), 23–39.

Das Reichsland Elsass-Lothringen. Landes- und. Ortsbeschreibung. Ed. by the Statistisches Bureau des Ministeriums für Elsass-Lothringen. 3 vols. Strasbourg, 1898–1903.

Reintges, Theo. *Ursprung und Wesen der spätmittelalterlichen Schützengilden*. Rheinisches Archiv. Veröffentlichungen des Instituts für geschichtliche Landeskunde der Rheinlande an der Universität Bonn. Bonn, 1963.

Rieber, Albrecht, "Das Patriziat von Ulm, Augsburg, Ravensburg, Mem-mingen, Biberach," *Deutsches Patriziat 1430–1740*, pp. 299–351.

Riedenauer, Erwin, "Kaiser und Patriziat. Struktur und Funktion des reichs-städtischen Patriziats im Blickpunkt kaiserlicher Adelspolitik von Karl V. bis Karl VI.," *ZBLG*, 30 (1967), 516–653.

——, "Kaiserliche Standeserhebungen für reichsstädtische Bürger 1519–1740," *Deutsches Patriziat 1430–1740*, pp. 27–98. (Riedenauer).

Riff, Adolphe, "La corporation des maréchaux de la ville de Strasbourg de 1563 à 1789," *Artisans et ouvriers d'Alsace*, pp. 171–184.

Rochefort, Michel. *L'organisation urbaine de l'Alsace*. Thèse, Faculté des Lettres de l'Université de Strasbourg. Strasbourg, 1960.

Rörig, Fritz. *The Medieval Town*. Berkeley–Los Angeles, 1967.

Rosen, Josef, "Prices and Public Finance in Basle," *Economic History Review*, 2nd series, 25 (1972), 1–17.

Roth, August, "Wilhelm Böcklin von Böcklinsau 1555–1585," *Hofpfalz-grafen-Register*, I, 9–23.

Rott, Jean, "Artisanat et mouvements sociaux à Strasbourg autour de 1525," *Artisans et ouvriers d'Alsace*, pp. 137–170. (Rott, "Artisanat").

——, "La Guerre des Paysans et la ville de Strasbourg," *La Guerre des Paysans 1525*, ed. A. Wollbrett, pp. 23–32.

——, "Histoire du Chapitre cathédrale de Strasbourg du XIVe et au XVe siècle." Thèse de l'Ecole des Chartes. 2 vols. Paris, 1933.

——, "Magistrat et Réforme à Strasbourg: les dirigéants municipaux de 1521 à 1525," *RHPR*, 54 (1974), 103–114. (Rott, "Magistrat").

——, "Un recueil de correspondances strasbourgeoises du XVIe siècle à la bibliothèque de Copenhague (ms. Thott 197, 2°)," *Bulletin philologique et historique (jusqu'a 1610) de la Comité des travaux historiques et scientifiques*, année 1968 (1971), pp. 749–818. (Rott, "Un recueil").

——, "La Réforme à Nuremberg et à Strasbourg. Contacts et contrastes (avec des correspondances inédites)," *Hommage à Dürer*, pp. 91–142.

Rublack, Hans-Christoph. *Die Einführung der Reformation in Konstanz von den Anfängen bis zum Abschluss 1531*. QFRG, 40 (= Veröffentlichungen des

Vereins für Kirchengeschichte in der evang. Landeskirche in Baden, 27).
Gütersloh–Karlsruhe, 1971.

Ruppert, A., "Strassburger Adel in der Mortenau, I: Die Erlin von Rorburg,"
*Strassburger Studien. Zeitschrift für Geschichte, Sprache und Litteratur des
Elsasses,* 2 (1884), 68–77.

Sabean, David Warren. *Landbesitz und Gesellschaft am Vorabend des Bauern-
kriegs. Eine Studie der sozialen Verhältnisse im südlichen Oberschwaben in den
Jahren vor 1525.* Quellen und Forschungen zur Agrargeschichte, 26.
Stuttgart, 1972.

Sattler, Hans-Peter, "Die Ritterschaft der Ortenau in der spätmittelalterlichen
Wirtschaftskrise. Eine Untersuchung ritterlicher Vermögensverhältnisse
im 14. Jahrhundert," *Die Ortenau,* 42 (1962), 220–258; 44 (1964), 22–39;
45 (1965), 32–57; 46 (1966), 32–58.

von Schauenburg, R. *Familiengeschichte der Reichsfreiherren von Schauenburg.*
N.p., 1954.

Schelp, Robert. *Die Reformationsprozesse der Stadt Strassburg am Reichskammergericht zur Zeit des schmalkaldischen Bundes (1524)/1531–1541/(1555).*
2nd ed. Kaiserslautern, 1965.

Schimpf, Anselme, "Les tailleurs de pierre strasbourgeois," *Artisans et
ouvriers d'Alsace,* pp. 97–126.

Schindling, Anton. *Humanistische Hochschule und freie Reichsstadt—Gymnasium
und Akademie in Strassburg 1538 bis 1621.* VIEGM, 77. Wiesbaden, 1976.

Schmidt, Charles G. A. *Histoire littéraire d'Alsace à la fin du XVe et au commencement du XVIe siècle.* 2 vols. Paris, 1879.

Schmidt-Sibeth, Friedrich, "Die Völsch im Niederelsass," *Archiv für Sippenforschung,* 35 (1969), 41–45.

Schmoller, Gustav. *Strassburg zur Zeit der Zunftkämpfe und die Reform seiner
Verfassung und Verwaltung.* Quellen und Forschungen zur Sprach- und
Culturgeschichte der germanischen Völker, 11. Strasbourg, 1875.
Reprinted in his *Deutsches Städtewesen in älterer Zeit,* Bonner Staatswissen-
schaftliche Untersuchungen, 5 (Bonn, 1922), pp. 177–230.

Schnapper, Bernard. *Les rentes au XVIe siècle. Histoire d'un instrument de crédit.*
Ecole Pratique des Hautes Etudes, VIe section, série "Affaires et gens
d'affaires," 12. Paris, 1957.

Schnéegans, Louis. *L'église de Saint-Thomas à Strasbourg et ses monuments
historiques.* Strasbourg, 1842.

Schneider, Jean. *La ville de Metz aux XIIIe et XIVe siècles.* Nancy, 1950.

——, "Les villes allemandes au moyen âge: compétence administrative et
judiciaire de leurs magistrats," *La ville,* vol. 1, pp. 467–516.

——, "Les villes allemandes au moyen âge: les institutions économiques,"
La ville, vol. 2, pp. 403–482.

Schoepflin, Johann Daniel. *L'Alsace illustrée, ou recherches sur l'Alsace pendant la
domination des celtes, des romains, des francs, des allemands et des français.*
Trans. L. W. Ravenèz. 5 vols. Mulhouse, 1849–52. (Schoepflin).

von Schubert, Hans. *Bekenntnisbildung und Religionspolitik (1524–1534).
Untersuchungen und Texte.* Gotha, 1910.

Schultz, Selina Gerhard. *Caspar Schwenckfeld von Ossig (1489–1561)*. Norristown, Pa., 1946.

Schultze, Alfred. *Stadtgemeinde und Reformation*. Recht und Staat in Geschichte und Gegenwart, 11. Tübingen, 1918.

Schwer, Wilhelm. *Stand und Ständeordnung im Weltbild des Mittelalters. Die geistes- und gesellschaftsgeschichtlichen Grundlagen der berufsständischen Idee*. Görres–Gesellschaft, Sektion für Wirtschafts- und Sozialwissenschaft, 7. 2nd ed. Paderborn, 1952.

Scribner, R. W., "Civic Unity and the Reformation in Erfurt," *Past & Present*, No. 66 (February 1975), 28–60.

Seyboth, Adolph. *Das alte Strassburg vom 13. Jahrhundert bis zum Jahre 1870*. Strasbourg, 1890. (Seyboth).

Sittler, Lucien, "Les associations artisanales en Alsace au moyen âge et sous l'ancien regime," *RA*, 97 (1958), 36–80.

Smith, R. B. *Land and Politics in the Reign of Henry VIII*. Oxford, 1970.

Sohm, Walter. *Die Schule Johann Sturms und die Kirche Strassburgs in ihren gegenseitigen Verhältnis 1530–1581*. Historische Bibliothek, 27. Munich–Berlin, 1912.

Spach, Louis, "Deux hommes d'armes de Strasbourg à Bamberg (1512–1513)," *BSCMHA*, N.S. 8 (1871), 1–61.

Spitz, Lewis W., "Headwaters of the Reformation: Studia Humanitatis, Luther Senior, et Initia Reformationis," *Luther and the Dawn of the Modern Era*, pp. 89–116.

Sprandel, Rolf, "Sozialgeschichte 1350–1500," *Handbuch der deutschen Wirtschafts- und Sozialgeschichte*, I, 360–382.

Die Stadt des Mittelalters. Ed. Carl Haase. 3 vols. Wege der Forschung, CCXLIII–CCXLV. Darmstadt, 1969–73.

Steinmetz, Max, "Forschungen zur Geschichte der Reformation und des deutschen Bauernkrieges," *Historische Forschungen in der DDR 1960–1970. Analysen und Berichte* (Berlin, 1970), pp. 338–350.

——, "Reformation und Bauernkrieg," *Kritik der bürgerlichen Geschichtsschreibung. Handbuch*, eds. Werner Berthold, *et al.*, 3rd ed. (Cologne, 1970), pp. 140–141.

——, "Reformation und Bauernkrieg in der Historiographie der DDR," *Historische Forschungen in der DDR. Analysen und Berichte* (Berlin, 1960), pp. 142–162.

——, "Probleme der frühbürgerlichen Revolution in Deutschland in der ersten Hälfte des 16. Jahrhunderts," *Die frühbürgerliche Revolution in Deutschland. Referat und Diskussion zum Thema Probleme der frühbürgerlichen Revolution in Deutschland 1476 bis 1535*, ed. Gerhard Brendler (Berlin, 1961), pp. 17–52.

Stephan, Horst. *Geschichte der evangelischen Theologie in Deutschland seit dem Idealismus*. 3rd ed. by Martin Schmidt. Berlin–New York, 1973.

Stephens, W. P. *The Holy Spirit in the Theology of Martin Bucer*. Cambridge, 1970.

Stolze, Alfred Otto. *Der Sünfzen zu Lindau. Das Patriziat einer schwäbischen Reichsstadt*. Ed. Bernhard Zeller. Lindau–Constance, 1956.

Stone, Lawrence, "Prosopography," *Daedalus,* 100, No. 1 (Winter 1971), pp. 46–79.

Stratenwerth, Heide. *Die Reformation in der Stadt Osnabrück.* VIEGM, 61. Wiesbaden, 1971.

Straub, Alexandre, "Notes généalogiques sur une ancienne famille patricienne de Strasbourg [Schott]," *BSCMHA,* N.S. 9 (1872), 80–88.

Strauss, Gerald, "Protestant Dogma and City Government: The Case of Nuremberg," *Past & Present,* No. 36 (1967), 38–58.

Strieder, Jakob. *Studien zur Geschichte kapitalistischer Organisationsformen. Monopole, Kartelle und Aktiengesellschaften im Mittelalter und zu Beginn der Neuzeit.* 2nd ed. Munich–Leipzig, 1925.

——. *Zur Genesis des modernen Kapitalismus. Forschungen zur Entstehung der grossen bürgerlichen Kapitalvermögen am Ausgange des Mittelalters und zu Beginn der Neuzeit, zunächst in Augsburg.* 2nd ed. Munich–Leipzig, 1935.

Strobel, Albrecht. *Agrarverfassung im Übergang. Studien zur Agrargeschichte des badischen Breisgaus vom Beginn des 16. bis zum Ausgang des 18. Jahrhunderts.* Forschungen zur oberrheinischen Landesgeschichte, 23. Freiburg/Br.–Munich, 1972.

von Stromer, Wolfgang. *Oberdeutschen Hochfinanz 1350–1450.* 3 vols. Beihefte der *VSWG,* 55–57. Wiesbaden, 1970.

——, "Reichtum und Ratswürde. Die wirtschaftliche Führungsschicht der Reichsstadt Nürnberg 1348–1648, *Führungskräfte der Wirtschaft in Mittelalter und Neuzeit 1350–1850* I, pp. 1–50.

Stupperich, Robert, "Strassburgs Stellung im Beginn des Sakramentsstreits (1524–1525)," *ARG,* 38 (1941), 249–262.

Swanson, Guy E. *Religion and Regime: A Sociological Account of the Reformation.* Ann Arbor, 1968.

Thiriet, Freddy, "Sur les relations commerciales entre Strasbourg et l'Italie du Nord à la fin du moyen âge," *RA,* 100 (1961), 121–128.

Thomas, Keith, "History and Anthropology," *Past & Present,* No. 24 (April 1963), 3–24.

Thrupp, Sylvia L., "Medieval Industry, 1000–1500," *The Fontana Economic History of Europe,* I, 221–274.

——. *The Merchant Class of Medieval London.* Ann Arbor, 1948.

Trusen, Winfried, "Zum Rentenkauf im Spätmittelalter," *Festschrift für Hermann Heimpel,* II, 140–158.

Ungerer, Jacques. *Le pont du Rhin à Strasbourg du XIVe siècle à la Révolution.* Publications de l'Institut des Hautes Etudes Alsaciennes, 4. Strasbourg–Paris, 1952.

Untersuchungen zur gesellschaftlichen Struktur der mittelalterlichen Städte in Europa. Reichenau-Vorträge 1963–64. Vorträge und Forschungen, 11. Constance–Stuttgart, 1966.

Van der Wee, Herman. *The Growth of the Antwerp Market and the European Economy.* 3 vols. The Hague, 1963.

Van Houtte, Jan A., "Gesellschaftliche Schichten in den Städten der Niederlande," *Untersuchungen zur gesellschaftlichen Struktur,* pp. 259–276.

Van Werveke, Hans, "Les villes belges. Histoire des institutions économiques et sociales," *La ville*, vol. 2, pp. 551–576.

Van Winter, Johanna Maria. *Rittertum. Ideal und Wirklichkeit*. Trans. from the Dutch by Axel Plantiko and Paul Schritt. Munich, 1969.

La ville libre de Strasbourg au carrefour des courants de pensée du XVIe siècle. Humanisme et Réforme à Strasbourg. Exposition du 5 mai au 10 juin 1973. Strasbourg, 1973.

Violence and Disorder in Italian Cities, 1200–1500. Ed. Lauro Martines. Berkeley–Los Angeles, 1972.

Vogler, Günter, "Probleme der Klassenentwicklung in der Feudalgesellschaft. Betrachtungen über die Entwicklung des Bürgertums in Mittel- und Westeuropa vom 11. bis zum 18. Jahrhundert," *ZfG*, 21 (1973), 1182–1208.

——, "Revolutionäre Bewegung und frühbürgerliche Revolution. Betrachtungen zum Verhältnis von sozialen und politischen Bewegungen und deutscher frühbürgerlicher Revolution," *ZfG*, 22 (1974), 394–411.

——, "Zur Dialektik von Klassenentwicklung und sozialen und politischen Bewegungen in der Feudalgesellschaft Mittel- und Westeuropas vom 11. bis 18. Jahrhundert," *ZfG*, 20 (1972), 1234–1240.

——, *et al.*, eds. *Illustrierte Geschichte der deutschen frühbürgerlichen Revolution*. Berlin, 1974.

Vogt, Jean, "Biens et revenus fonciers des Städel, bourgeois de Strasbourg (XVIe au XVIIIe siècle)," *ASAVS*, 2 (1971), 51–69.

——, "A propos de la propriété bourgeoise en Alsace (XVIe–XVIIIe siècles)," *RA*, 100 (1961), 48–66.

——, "Pour une étude sociale de la dîme. Esquisse de la tenure de la dîme en Alsace, XVIe–XVIIIe siècles," *Les fluctuations du produit de la dîme*, pp. 103–133.

——, "Remarques sur les rentes en nature rachetables payées par les campagnards aux prêteurs strasbourgeois (deuxième moitié du XVIe siècle)," *RHMC*, 15 (1968), 662–672.

Wackernagel, Rudolf. *Geschichte der Stadt Basel*. 4 vols. Basel, 1907–24.

Wagner, Johann Volker. *Graf Wilhelm von Fürstenberg und die politisch-geistigen Mächte seiner Zeit*. Pariser Historische Studien, 4. Stuttgart, 1966.

Wallerstein, Immanuel. *The Modern World System. Capitalist Agriculture and the Origins of the European World-Economy in the Sixteenth Century*. New York–London, 1974.

Walton, Robert C. *Zwingli's Theocracy*. Toronto, 1967.

Weinstein, Donald. *Savonarola and Florence: Prophecy and Patriotism in the Renaissance*. Princeton, 1970.

Wendel, François. *L'église de Strasbourg, sa constitution et son organisation, 1532–1535*. Etudes d'histoire et de philosophie religieuses, 38. Paris, 1942.

Werner, Ernst, "Spätmittelalterlicher Strukturwandel im Spiegel neuer Forschungen: Das italienische Beispiel," *Jahrbuch für Wirtschaftsgeschichte*, 1969, pp. 223–240.

Weyrauch, Erdmann, "Zur Auswertung von Steuerbüchern mit quantifizierenden Methoden," *Festgabe für Ernst-Walter Zeeden*, pp. 97–127.

——, "Konfessionelle Krise und soziale Stabilität. Versuch der Beschreibung und systemtheoretischen Analyse des Interims in Strassburg (1548–1562) mit einer methodologischen Einleitung." 2 vols. Dissertation, Berlin, 1976.

——, "Paper on Social Stratification. Zur Konzeptualisierung der Forschung im Unterprojekt Z 2.2." Sonderforschungsbereich 8, Projektbereich Prof. Zeeden, Unterprojekt Z 2.2, Arbeitspapier 17. Tübingen, 1974. Mimeographed.

Wichelhaus, Manfred. *Kirchengeschichtsschreibung und Soziologie im neunzehnten Jahrhundert und bei Ernst Troeltsch.* Heidelberger Forschungen, 9. Heidelberg, 1965.

Winckelmann, Otto, "Jakob Sturm," *Allgemeine Deutsche Biographie*, 37 (1894), 5–20.

——, "Strassburgs Verfassung und Verwaltung im 16. Jahrhundert," *ZGO*, 57 (1903), 493–537, 600–642.

——, "Zur Entstehungsgeschichte der Strassburger Einundzwanzig und Dreizehn," *ZGO*, 75 (1921), 112–114.

Winterberg, Hans. *Die Schüler von Ulrich Zasius.* VKLBW, B 18. Stuttgart, 1961.

Wittmer, Charles, "Das Strassburger Bürgerrecht bis zum Jahre 1530," *AJb*, 1961, 235–249.

Wohlfeil, Rainer, "Adel und neues Heerwesen," *Deutscher Adel 1430–1555*, pp. 203–233.

——, ed. *Der Bauernkrieg 1524–26. Bauernkrieg und Reformation.* nymphenburger texte zur wissenschaft, 21. Munich, 1975.

——, ed. *Reformation oder frühbürgerliche Revolution?* nymphenburger texte zur wissenschaft, 5. Munich, 1972.

Wolff, Christian. *Guide des recherches généalogiques en Alsace.* Strasbourg, 1975.

——, "Les Ingold aux XVIe et XVIIe siècles. Essai de mise au point de leur généalogie," *BCGA*, No. 9 (1970), 112–118.

Wolff, Philippe. *Commerce et marchands de Toulouse (vers 1350–vers 1450).* Paris, 1954.

——, "Les luttes sociales dans les villes du Midi français, XIIIe–XIVe siècles," *AESC*, 2 (1947), 443–454.

Wunder, Gerhard, "Die Sozialstruktur der Reichsstadt Schwäbisch Hall," *Untersuchungen zur gesellschaftlichen Struktur*, pp. 25–52.

——. *Das Strassburger Landgebiet. Territorialgeschichte der einzelnen Teile des städtischen Herrschaftsbereiches vom 13. bis zum 18. Jahrhundert.* Schriften zur Verfassungsgeschichte, 5. Berlin, 1967.

Zeller, Gaston, "Deux capitalistes strasbourgeois du XVIe siècle," *Etudes d'histoire moderne et contemporaine*, 1 (1947), 5–14.

Zimmermann, Jean-Robert. *Les compagnons de métiers à Strasbourg du début du XIVe siècle à la veille de la Réforme.* PSSARE, collection "Recherches et documents," 10. Strasbourg, 1971.

Zorn, Wolfgang, "Sozialgeschichte 1500–1648," *Handbuch der deutschen Wirtschaftsgeschichte*, I, 465–494.

ADDENDA

Code historique et diplomatique de la Ville de Strasbourg. Eds. Adam Walther Strobel and Ludwig Schnéegans. 2 vols. Strasbourg, 1843–48.

Mélanges Jean Rott=Horizons européens de la Reforme en Alsace. Mélanges offerts à Jean Rott. Eds. Marijn de Kroon and Marc Lienhard. Leiden, 1978.

Städtische Mittelschichten. Protokoll der VIII. Arbeitstagung des Arbeitskreises für südwestdeutsche Stadtgeschichtsforschung. Eds. Erich Maschke and Jürgen Sydow. VKLBW, B 69. Stuttgart, 1972.

INDICES

The indices consist of four parts:

The abbreviations used in them will be found on pp. xix–xx above.

I. INDEX OF PERSONAL NAMES

This index includes the names of all persons named in this book, except for modern authors. Orthographically it follows the principles laid down on p. xvii above and the article of Jean-Pierre Kintz cited there. In addition, users of this index should be aware of the relative interchangeability of such letters and combinations as "d" and "t," "b" and "p," "c" and "k," and "f" and "v." The form chosen for indexing may differ slightly from forms found in the text and notes, and this choice sometimes affects the alphabetization. This is especially true with short forms, such as Hans (Johann), Claus (Nicolaus), and Bastian (Sebastian), but sometimes also with old-fashioned South German forms, such as Jörg or Jerg (Georg) and Philips (Philipp). Particles (e.g., "von" and "de") do not affect alphabetization, except that names formed with the particles "zum" and "zur" preceding the surname are alphabetized under "Z." Birth and death years and dates are supplied wherever possible; and those for Strasbourgeois are frequently taken from manuscript sources.

Sporer, Stephan (fl. 1433) 382, 392
Städel, Affra (d. 1619) 348–349
——, Christoph I (d. after 1530) 348
——, Christoph II (1504–12./13.V.1554)
144, 179n, 267, 348–349 (LXXXVIII.),
349–350, 384, 392
——, Christoph III (d. 1585) 348, 382, 392
——, David 348
——, Jacob (d. 17.XII.1569) 348
Stallburger, Agnes 106n
——, Claus, "the Rich" (1469–1524) 106n
——, Daniel (1515–1553) 106n, 323
Stand (Sand), Gebhart 369
Stange, Erhard (fl. 1461–67) 383, 392
——, Sebastian 369
Steffan, Heinrich (fl. 1433) 385, 392
v. Stein zum Reichenstein, Anna Franziska
(d. by 2.IX.1635) 343
Stengel, Engelhard 379
Steudlin, Margarethe 379
Stöffelin. See Stöffler
Stöffler, Caspar . 118
——, Conrad 92n
——, Mattheus (1560–1619) 350, 379
v. Stoll gen. Spantzinger, Claus 369
Stoll v. Stauffenberg, Caspar 369
——, Wolff 369
Stoltz, Martzolff 118
Storck (fam.) 111n
——, Conrad (d. after 1485) 181n, 349
——, Elisabeth (d. 1537) 348–349
——, Gertrud (d. by 1537) 324
——, Hans 181n, 339, 349
——, Peter (4.X.1554–22.V.1627) 181n,
191n, 349
——, Veltin, Sr. (d. 1561) 181, 191n, 260–
261, 265n, 307, 324, 339, 349
(LXXXIX.), 384, 392
——, Veltin, Jr. 181n, 349
Störe, Diebold 370
——, Hans Jacob 370
——, Humprecht 370
Stösser (fam.) 111, 111n, 136, 183
——, Anna 350
——, Apollonia 350
——, Aurelia 135, 350
——, Balthasar 349
——, Barbara 263n, 350
——, Caspar 349
——, Caspar David 350
——, Friedrich 349–350
——, Hans (d. 15.II.1558) 135n, 149n,
263n, 319, 324, 348, 349–350 (XC.), 384,
392
——, Hans, Jr. 349
——, Jacob 349
——, Johann Jacob 350
——, Margarethe 319, 350

——, Martha 324, 350
——, Moritz (d. by 1532) 349
——, Moritz, Agnes N., wife of 349
——, Salome 350
——, Ursula 350
——, Veltin 349
——, Walpurgis 350
Strozzi (fam.) 156n
Sturm (fam.) 78, 82, 85–88, 87n, 93, 126,
128, 131, 140–141, 149, 149n, 152, 182,
182n, 219, 219n, 223, 230–231, 239, 360–
361
——, Agnes 85n
——, Anna 302–303, 352
——, Clara 219, 223, 352
——, Friedrich (d. 1476) 85n, 339, 352
——, Friedrich (d. 10.XI.1562) 82–83,
129, 173n, 186, 287, 304, 335–336, 340,
350 (XCI.), 351–353, 370, 376, 384, 386,
392
——, Friedrich (d. ca. 1604) 353
——, Hans (fl. 1467–73) 383, 392
——, Hans (d. 1536) 84n, 161, 186, 350–
351 (XCII.), 352–353, 374, 376, 384, 392
——, Huglin 88n
——, Hugo (d. 1616) 353
——, Jacob (10.VII.1489–30.X.1553) 67n,
83, 85n, 89–90, 108–109, 126, 139, 154,
161, 164n, 169n, 173n, 186–187, 188n, 189,
189n, 190n, 192–193, 195, 197, 210–211,
213, 216, 216n, 227n, 228, 240–245, 242n,
244n, 247–249, 248n, 251–257, 252n,
255n, 260n, 272, 272n, 273, 274, 276–277,
279, 281, 283–285, 287, 290, 292, 294,
302–304, 335–336, 340, 350, 351
(XCIII.), 352–353, 374, 384–385, 392
——, Ludwig (d. 1516) 311, 352, 370
——, Ludwig (son of Ott S.) 353
——, Martin (d. X.1521) 80, 82, 82n, 85n,
129, 146n, 202n, 219, 226, 304, 311–312,
335, 339–340, 350, 351–352 (XCIV.), 353,
370, 383, 392
——, Ott, Ritter (d. 1518) 88n, 219, 226,
301, 352–353, 376, 379
——, Ott, Jr. 353
——, Peter (d. 5./6.VII.1563) 186, 189,
193, 197, 242, 254, 266–267, 288, 304,
335–336, 340, 352 (XCV.), 375, 384, 392
——, Stephan (d. by 1526) 352
——, Stephan (d. 31.V.1578) 131n, 186,
283, 289, 301, 350, 352, 353 (XCVI.), 355,
379, 382, 384, 386, 392
——, Veronika 339, 352
——, Veronika (d. 1581) 352
——, Veronika 353, 375
——, Veronika 353
——, Wernher 88n
——, Wernher (d. 1593) 353

II. INDEX OF MODERN AUTHORS

Modern authors are indexed only where their works are discussed in the text or the footnotes; and bare citations are not indexed.

III. INDEX OF PLACE NAMES

Included in this index are the places named in the text and notes, including appendices, except for names of countries ("Holy Roman Empire," "Germany," "France," "Italy," etc.) and the names of "Strasbourg," "Alsace," "Upper Rhine," and "Lower Alsace." Place names in the Upper Rhine Valley have been handled according to the principles described on pp. xvi–xvii above: traditional German forms for village names; and either the German or the French forms for town and city names (with the other form cross-referenced). They have been further identified wherever possible as lying in Lower Alsace (BR), Upper Alsace (HR), or approximately the modern state of Baden (B).* The two divisions of Alsace correspond approximately to the modern departments of Bas-Rhin and Haut-Rhin.

* They have been identified through the following publications: *Das Reichsland Elsass-Lothringen* (Strasbourg, 1898–1903), vol. 3. *Ortsbeschreibung; Dictionnaire des communes administratif et militaire, France et départements français d'outre-mer* (Paris, ed. of January, 1964); Albert Krieger, ed., *Topographisches Wörterbuch des Grossherzogtums Baden*, 2 vols. (Heidelberg, 1904–05); and André Humm, *Villages et hameaux disparus en Basse-Alsace. Contribution à l'histoire de l'habitat rural (XIIe–XVIIIe siècles)*, PSSARE, Collection "recherches et documents," 7 (Strasbourg, 1971).

Surburg (BR) 160, 316, 374
Swabia, region 76, 80, 85, 99, 100, 111, 121n, 128n, 189, 225, 244n, 319

Truchtersheim (BR) 337–338
Tübingen (Württ.) 67n, 201n, 256, 256n, 328
Tuscany 39

Ulm 35, 77, 77n, 96, 98, 106, 121, 121n, 156, 189, 221, 256n, 257n, 259, 275, 318, 323
Uri (Switzerland) 107
Utenheim. *See* Uttenheim
Uttenheim (BR) 321

Vaihingen (Württ.) 256n
Vendenheim (BR) 143–145, 306, 357–358
Venice 39, 54, 76, 95, 102, 106, 251n, 309, 323
Virdenheim (BR) 340
Vorderösterreich 38n
Vosges, mountains 101, 107, 291, 318

Wahlenheim (BR) 316
Walburg (BR) 311
Wasselnheim. *See* Wasselonne

Wasselonne (BR) 80n, 146n, 288, 302, 336
Weil der Stadt 111, 134, 319
Werd (BR) 315
Westphalia, region 253n
Weyersheim (BR) 220n
Wilstätt (B) 69, 69n, 304, 309
Wingersheim (BR) 330
Winterthur 346
Wissembourg/Weissenburg im Elsass (BR) 375
Wittenberg 13, 334
Wittenweier (B) 135, 335
Witternheim (BR) 332
Wogelburg 319
Wolfisheim (BR) 88n, 330, 354, 358
Worms (B) 85, 209, 255, 257n
Württemberg 89, 89n, 155, 278, 324
Würzburg 271n, 345–346

Zabern. *See* Saverne
Zell am Harmersbach (B) 330
Zürich 13, 37, 103n, 121, 178, 238–240, 377n
Zutzendorf (BR) 303
Zweibrücken-Bitsch-Lichtenberg, county 87, 89n, 131, 154–155, 157, 190n, 255n, 306, 311, 326

IV. SUBJECT INDEX

DATE DUE

OCT 10 1995			